Social Cognition

Social Cognition

from brains to culture   2nd edition

Susan T. Fiske and Shelley E. Taylor

Los Angeles | London | New Delhi
Singapore | Washington DC

Los Angeles | London | New Delhi
Singapore | Washington DC

SAGE Publications Ltd
1 Oliver's Yard
55 City Road
London EC1Y 1SP

SAGE Publications Inc.
2455 Teller Road
Thousand Oaks, California 91320

SAGE Publications India Pvt Ltd
B 1/I 1 Mohan Cooperative Industrial Area
Mathura Road
New Delhi 110 044

SAGE Publications Asia-Pacific Pte Ltd
3 Church Street
#10-04 Samsung Hub
Singapore 049483

Editor: Michael Carmichael
Editorial assistant: Alana Clogan
Production editor: Imogen Roome
Copyeditor: Sarah Bury
Proofreader: Neil Dowden
Indexer: David Rudeforth
Marketing manager: Alison Borg
Cover design: Jennifer Crisp
Typeset by: C&M Digitals (P) Ltd, Chennai, India
Printed by: MPG Books Group, Bodmin, Cornwall

To Doug, Lydia, Vanessa, Geoff, Meredith, Sam, and Max
and
To Mervyn, Charlie, Sara, Karl, and Sebastian

Contents

Acknowledgements   ix
Preface   x

1   Introduction   1

PART ONE: BASIC CONCEPTS IN SOCIAL COGNITION   29

2   Dual Modes in Social Cognition   31

3   Attention and Encoding   59

4   Representation in Memory   87

PART TWO: TOPICS IN SOCIAL COGNITION:
            FROM SELF TO SOCIETY   117

5   Self in Social Cognition   119

6   Attribution Processes   149

7   Heuristics and Shortcuts: Efficiency in Inference and Decision Making   177

8   Accuracy and Efficiency in Social Inference   205

9   Cognitive Structures of Attitudes   232

10   Cognitive Processing of Attitudes   257

11   Stereotyping: Cognition and Bias   281

12   Prejudice: Interplay of Cognitive and Affective Biases   311

PART THREE: BEYOND COGNITION   339

13   From Social Cognition to Affect   341

14   From Affect to Social Cognition   370

15   Behavior and Cognition   394

Glossary   423
References   463
Index   568

Acknowledgements

This book has benefited from the help of many colleagues, who read one or more chapter drafts: Courtney Bearns, Cydney Dupree, Jill Swencionis. Thanks to all of them.

Our Sage Editor, Michael Carmichael, believed in the timeliness of this new edition and firmly insisted on making it fully 21st century: realigned, streamlined, and on-lined. We appreciate Sage's support.

Finally, we thank our families, both immediate and far-flung, for their more personal support.

STF, Princeton
SET, Los Angeles
June 2012

Preface

Since the publication of our first text on Social Cognition, a lot has changed for us personally (children come and gone, grandchildren have arrived, new jobs, new houses) and professionally (both of us are doing a lot more neuroscience and culture than we would have predicted). For our first text, we were dictating or writing long-hand on lined pads, with secretaries who typed our day's writing and chided us on our less productive days. We used physical mail to send drafts. And we chose the color of the first edition's cover based on airline ticket carbons, its design enlivened by some decidedly 1980s woodcut portraits of hipsters.

That text had its day, defining the birth of social cognition in its modern form. Social psychology was emerging from a crisis, which was partly resolved in the excitement of the fresh ideas and methods newly available from cognitive psychology. Skeptics predicted social cognition to be a short-lived fad. Social psychologists faulted it for not being social enough, and cognitive psychologists faulted it for not being cognitive enough. But the intrepid investigators remained enthused about the cutting-edge insights into social attention, memory, inference, and schemas, as applied to topics from self to health to prejudice to primaries. At first, we debated the inclusion of classic areas such as attribution, self, and attitudes in a book on current social cognition. We ultimately aimed for inclusion, showing the relevance of social cognitive approaches to both classic and newer issues. This joint relevance remains true today.

The second edition demonstrated the robust health of social cognition, which proved not to be a mere fad, an interlude, or an era. Social cognition is here to stay, and indeed has permeated all corners of social psychology. The second cover took a longer view, featuring a more subdued, classic green and reaching back to Renoir. The painting is crowded with people, and so was our bibliography; the book was encyclopedic in its coverage, reflecting the explosion of research in the intervening seven years.

The newly subtitled edition (From Brains to Culture) – nearly 18 years after our first – took an even longer view, still starting with the founding ideas but fast-forwarding to the present. That text reflected the latest in social neuroscience, which for some skeptics is not social enough and for others is not neuroscientific enough. (Sound familiar?) But we cheerfully predicted the thriving of this new field, social cognitive affective neuroscience, building substantially on the social cognition that was controversial in its own early days.

What's more, the current title began to reflect much more research on culture, an increasingly salient topic in social cognition, as globalization takes hold in our field as well as in our lives.

This newly revised Sage edition stays close to its original purpose: describing how people make sense of other people and themselves, a source of enduring commonsense and scholarly fascination. Completely updated, the new edition includes even more material on the latest social neuroscience and cultural social psychology. We have also tried to make it even more reader friendly. Each fully revised chapter is streamlined to more uniform lengths across chapters. Keywords are bolded, defined both in the text and in a separate Glossary. Chapters each include an online Summary and Abstracts with keywords. Each chapter includes about ten downloadable figures and tables. Each chapter includes suggested further readings. Using a trifecta synergy, this text coordinates with the just-finished Fiske & Macrae *Sage Handbook of Social Cognition* (2012), which picks up-to-date topics and mostly next-generation authors, based on independent expert editorial advisor feedback. The text also coordinates with the Fiske 2013 five-dozen selections for *Sage Major Works in Social Cognition*, being completed simultaneously.

Thirty years ago, social cognition originally helped pull social psychology out of its doldrums, but the other factor has always been a lively concern for the human condition – health, intergroup relations, politics, education, inequality, and more. We hope this book makes clear the contributions of this exciting field.

Introduction

1

- Approaches to Studying the Social Thinker
- The Ebb and Flow of Cognition in Psychology
- What is Social Cognition?
- People are Not Things
- Brains Matter
- Cultures Matter

Most of us care about what other people think of us. All of us care about understanding other people. Social cognition explains both processes. This is not a self-help book, but it will aid you as you navigate your social world. This is not a do-good book, but it will help you make a difference in the world. This is not fiction, but it tells some good stories. Social cognition captures a remarkable range of phenomena useful to individuals and to the human condition.

Consider a common experience of mistaken social cognition. Try telling someone at a party that you are a psychologist or even that you are simply studying psychology. It does no good to say you do research and do not read minds. The inevitable reaction is either that the person draws back in horror of being analyzed on the spot or that the person leans over to disclose all sorts of intimate secrets. One psychologist we know avoids these situations by claiming to be a computer programmer. We have hit upon a different strategy, which is to say calmly, "I study how people make first impressions on strangers." This comment promptly stops that conversation.

Suppose, however, that the conversation did not end right there. Suppose the person began to talk about what makes people tick, about impressions of various friends, relatives, and strangers at the party. That is the kind of raw data with which this book is concerned. **Social cognition** is the study of how people make sense of other people and themselves. It focuses on how ordinary people think and feel about people – and on how they think they think and feel about people.

People's understanding of the social world can be studied by *asking* them how they make sense of others (Heider, 1958). This is the route of **phenomenology**: to describe systematically how ordinary people say they experience their world. If people are right, researchers can use these insights to build formal theories by pulling together patterns across many people's intuitions. Even if people are wrong, researchers can study people's commonsense theories in and of themselves to learn how people think. Social cognition researchers are also concerned with this commonsense theory, **naive psychology,** for its own sake. That is, people's everyday theories about each other are themselves interesting to study. Thus, if the person at the party has some ideas about how people form impressions of each other, the person's informal ideas are interesting in their own right.

Social cognition also goes beyond naive psychology. Studying social cognition entails a fine-grained analysis of how people think about themselves and others, and it leans heavily on the theory and methods of cognitive psychology. One of the hallmarks of social cognition is the influence of detailed models from cognitive psychology. These models are important because they precisely describe mechanisms of learning and thinking that apply in a wide variety of areas, including social perception. Because these models are general and because cognitive processes presumably influence social behavior heavily, it makes sense to adapt cognitive theory to social settings.

Both the naive psychology viewpoint and the cognitive viewpoint are important themes in social cognition research. These two viewpoints characterize the double appeal of social cognition. The entertaining part of studying how people think about others is its appeal to your intuitions; it resembles what is fun and absorbing about sitting around with a friend after midnight, speculating about human nature. The fine-grained part forces you to be accurate and precise; its appeal resembles that of a favorite intricate puzzle. Whether your taste runs to crosswords, math games, jigsaw puzzles, or mystery novels, there is considerable pleasure in getting all the pieces to fit.

APPROACHES TO STUDYING THE SOCIAL THINKER

Knowing something of social cognition's intellectual history gives perspective to researchers' current efforts. This section contrasts two primary approaches that have proved useful.

Asch's Competing Models

Suppose you read a letter of reference describing someone as "intelligent, skillful, industrious, cold, determined, practical, and cautious." Would you be inclined to recommend hiring the person? Would you enjoy working together? How did you form these impressions so quickly? In his pioneering work, Solomon Asch (1946) examined how people make sense of other people, combining their personality components and coming up with an integrated overall impression. In this, he set the stage for person perception research (E. E. Jones, 1990; D. J. Schneider, Hastorf, & Ellsworth, 1979). Asch theorized that we experience another person as a psychological unit, that we fit the person's various qualities (traits) into a single unifying theme (impression).

Asch (1946) originally made this point in 12 brilliant studies. Participants had to form an impression of someone described by one or another list of personality traits. One group, for example, learned about someone described by the list that opened this paragraph. Another group instead learned about someone who was "intelligent, skillful, industrious, warm, determined, practical, and cautious." The experimental manipulation was simple: switching the traits warm and cold created completely different descriptions of the target person. For example, the cold, intelligent person seems calculating, and the warm, intelligent person seems wise.

Asch proposed two models to account for these results: The configural model and the algebraic model (see Figure 1.1). The **configural model** hypothesizes that people form a unified overall impression of other people; the unifying forces shape individual elements to bring them in line with the overall impression. The pressure toward unity changes the meaning of the individual elements to fit better in context. An intelligent con artist is sly; an intelligent child is clever; an intelligent grandmother is wise. In addition to meaning change, people use a variety of strategies to organize and unify the components of an impression; they not only change the meaning of ambiguous terms, but they also resolve apparently discrepant terms with considerable ingenuity. All of this mental activity results, according to the configural model, in an impression made up of traits and their relationships, just as a **schema** later would be defined as consisting of attributes and their relationships.

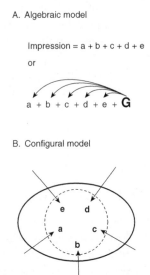

Figure 1.1 Solomon Asch's (1946, p. 257) contrasting models for person perception: A. The algebraic model has one version using simple evaluative summation and another with summation after the halo (overall positivity or negativity of the impression) that adjusts the evaluation of each individual trait all equally up or down; B. The configural model shows the traits being integrated to form a unified impression of the person, in which the meaning of individual traits changes in the context of all other traits

The alternative, the algebraic model, directly contrasts with the configural model and, by extension, with the subsequent schema models. The **algebraic model** takes each individual trait, evaluates it in isolation, and combines the evaluations into a summary evaluation. It is as if, upon meeting someone new, you were simply to combine together all the person's pros (e.g., intelligence) and cons (e.g., coldness) to form your impression. The algebraic model of information averaging boasts an impressive program of research (N. H. Anderson, 1981), as does a related algebraic model of combining beliefs to form an overall attitude (Fishbein & Ajzen, 1975).

The configural and algebraic models represent, respectively, the holistic and elemental approaches to social cognition described next. As such, they represent two fundamentally different ideas about how people form impressions of others. These two competing approaches originally proposed by Asch were thoroughly researched and, as you might imagine, hotly debated for a number of years (North & Fiske, 2012). However, from a theoretical perspective, the contest was essentially a draw because both models were flexible enough to account for each other's data. Neither was stated in a strictly falsifiable form. This led to a consensus on the "futility of the adversarial approach" (Ostrom, 1977) and pleas for more theory development. Neither approach any longer tries to "disprove" the other side. Indeed, many of the dual-process theories described in Chapter 2 in effect resolve this old debate by noting that both models are right but that people follow each under different informational and motivational circumstances that, not surprisingly, mimic the respective research paradigms of the two approaches.

Because these two models form the core of much research we will encounter, some historical context is in order. Two broad intellectual approaches to the study of social cognition – elemental and holistic – go back to psychology's origins in philosophy. The **elemental approach** breaks scientific problems down into pieces and analyzes the pieces in separate detail before combining them. The **holistic approach** analyzes the pieces in the context of other pieces and focuses on the entire configuration of relationships among them. This distinction will become clearer in describing the two approaches.

Elemental Origins of Social Cognition Research

Until the beginning of the 20th century, psychology was a branch of philosophy, and philosophers provided some basic principles of mind that still carry weight today (Boring, 1950). The British philosophers' elemental tradition likened the mind to chemistry, with ideas as the elements. Any concept, whether concrete, such as "sneeze," or abstract, such as "shame," is a basic element, and any element can be associated with any other element. The bonds between concepts create mental chemistry (Locke, 1690/1979).

In the elemental view, ideas first come from our sensations and perceptions. Then they become associated by contiguity in space and time (Hume, 1739/1978). That is, if sneezes use tissues, the two can become a unit through contiguity. Repetition is the key to moving from simple contiguity to a mental compound (Hartley, 1749/1966). If sneezes and tissues go together throughout your life, when you think of sneezes you will automatically think of tissues. Sneeze-and-tissue becomes a mental compound. Similarly, if the concept "shame" often comes up at the same time as the concept "dancing," they are likely to be associated simply as a function of repeated pairings. People consciously use the principles of repetition and contiguity in daily life too; think of the last time you attempted to remember the digits of a phone number by repeating them until they became a unit. Frequency of repetition is a major factor that determines the strength of an association (Mill, 1869, 1843/1974).[1]

Psychology emerged as a discipline separate from philosophy in the early 20th century, and finally the notions of mental chemistry were tested empirically. The first laboratory psychologists, such as Germans Wilhelm Wundt and Hermann Ebbinghaus, trained themselves and their graduate students to observe their own thought processes: to introspect on how they committed ideas to memory and on how they retrieved ideas from memory (Ebbinghaus, 1885/1964; Wundt, 1897). Their method analyzed experience into its elements to determine how they connect, and to determine the laws that govern those associations. These themes, which began with the British philosophers, continue to form one basis of modern experimental psychology. We saw one elemental model in Asch's algebraic model. Later in this chapter and in Chapter 4, we will see how the elemental approach is currently represented within the study of social cognition.

Holistic Origins of Social Cognition Research

Reacting against the elemental approach, German philosopher Immanuel Kant (1781/1969) argued for tackling the whole mind at once. In his view, mental phenomena are inherently subjective. That is, the mind actively constructs a reality that goes beyond the original thing in and of itself. A bunch of grapes seems like a unit, but that perception is the mind's construction. Perceiving a "bowl of grapes" differs from perceiving each individual grape separately. Similarly, if someone cuts off some grapes and the remaining ones topple out of the bowl, the two movements are perceived as linked in a cause–effect relationship. Again, the mind furnishes that perception; it is not inherent in the stimulus. The intellect organizes the world, creating perceptual order from the properties of the surrounding field.

German-American Gestalt psychology drew on these initial holistic insights (Koffka, 1935; Kohler, 1938/1976). In contrast to analysis into elements, psychologists who use Gestalt methods first describe the phenomenon of interest, the immediate experience of perception, without analysis. This method, already introduced as phenomenology, focuses on systematically describing people's experience of perceiving and thinking. It later became one of the major foundations of social cognition research: the reliance on asking people how they make sense of the world.

Although both the elemental and holistic groups drew on introspections, Gestalt psychologists focused on people's experience of dynamic wholes, and elementalists focused on the expert's ability to break the whole into pieces. As an illustration of the difference between Gestalt and

---

[1] Other principles of association were proposed at various times and then dropped in favor of repeated contiguity. These included similarity and causality as creating associations, and vividness as strengthening associations (Boring, 1950).

elemental approaches, think of a song in your mind. A song can be perceived as a series of individual notes (elemental) or as a melody that emerges from the relationships among the notes (Gestalt). The emergent structure is lost by analyzing it into its sensory elements, in the Gestalt view. Gestalt psychologists saw the mental chemistry metaphor of the elementalists as misguided because a chemical compound has properties not predictable from its isolated elements. Similarly, the perceptual whole has properties not discernible from the isolated parts. For example, the note middle C can seem high in the context of many lower notes or low in the context of many higher notes, but it would not stand out at all in the context of other notes close to it. Similarly, an average-height basketball player stands out in the subway but not on the team. Many arriving college students who had topped their high-school classes discover that they no longer stand out as intellectual stars in college. Again, the individual acquires meaning in the immediate context, and those contexts change. Psychological meaning goes beyond raw sensory parts to include the organization people impose on the whole. The importance of Gestalt stimulus configurations guided two researchers whose work directly informs social cognition research and theory. We have already met Solomon Asch; now meet Kurt Lewin.

Lewin's Person-Situation Field Theory

German-American Kurt Lewin (1951) imported Gestalt ideas to social psychology and ultimately to social cognition research (Boring, 1950; Bronfenbrenner, 1977; Deutsch, 1968). Like other Gestalt psychologists, Lewin focused on the person's subjective perceptions, not on "objective" analysis. He emphasized the influence of the social environment, *as perceived by the individual*, which he called the **psychological field**. A full understanding of a person's psychological field cannot result from an "objective" description by others of what surrounds the person because what matters is the person's own interpretation. This is not to say that the person can necessarily verbalize his or her perceived environment, but that the person's own reports typically provide better clues than do the researcher's intuitions. For instance, a researcher may objectively report that Barb complimented Ann on her appearance. The researcher may even have strong hunches about why Barb did it. But Ann's reaction will depend on her own perception of Barb's intent: ingratiation, envy, reassurance, or friendliness. A prime way to find that out is to ask Ann to describe what happened in her own terms. Just as in Gestalt psychology generally, Lewin emphasized the individual's phenomenology, the individual's construction of the situation.

Another theme imported from Gestalt psychology to social psychology was Lewin's insistence on describing the total situation, not its isolated elements. A person exists within a psychological field that is a configuration of forces. One must understand all the psychological forces operating on the person in any given situation in order to predict anything. For example (see Figure 1.2), some forces might motivate an individual to study (e.g., an upcoming exam, the sight of one's roommate studying), but other forces might motivate the individual to spend the evening another way (a group of friends suggesting a movie), and still other forces (loud music next door) might prevent acting on the motivation to study. No one force predicts action, but the dynamic equilibrium among them, the ever-changing balance of forces, does predict action.

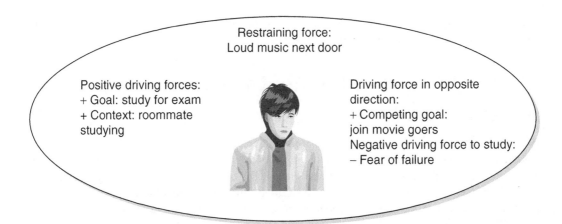

Figure 1.2 Kurt Lewin's (1951) psychological field theory representing an individual's pressures to study or not, based on subjectively perceived driving forces and restraining forces that together motivate behavior

The total psychological field (and hence behavior) is determined by two pairs of factors. The first pair consists of the *person in the situation*. Neither alone is sufficient to predict behavior. The person contributes needs, beliefs, perceptual abilities, and more. These act on the environment to constitute the psychological field. Thus, to know that a particular person is motivated to study does not predict whether or how much he or she will study. But a motivated person in a library is extremely likely to study a lot. Ever since Lewin, social psychologists have seen both the person and the situation as essential to predicting behavior. The study of social cognition focuses on perceiving, thinking, and remembering as a function of who and where a person is.

The second pair of psychological field factors that determines behavior is *cognition* and *motivation*. Both are joint functions of person and situation and jointly predict behavior. Cognition provides the perceiver's interpretation of the world; without clear cognitions, behavior is not predictable. If a person has incomplete or confused cognitions about a new setting, behavior will be unstable. For example, if you do not have the foggiest idea about what an upcoming exam in music composition will be like, you may behave erratically and unpredictably; you may try several study strategies, none of them very systematically. Cognitions help determine *what* a person will do, which direction behavior will take. If a musician friend explains what composition exams typically contain, your cognitions and your studying will settle down along the lines laid out. But this assumes that you actually do study. The second feature of the psychological field is motivation; its strength predicts *whether* the behavior will occur at all and, if it does, how much of it will occur. Knowing what to do does not mean you will do it; cognition alone is not enough. Motivation provides the motor for behavior.

To summarize, Lewin focuses his analysis on psychological reality as perceived by the individual; on confronting a whole configuration of forces, not single elements; on the person and the situation; and on cognition and motivation. These major themes, which date back through

Gestalt psychology to Kant, are theoretical points that still survive in modern approaches to social cognition as well as in psychology as a whole.

Conclusion about Elemental and Holistic Views

We have characterized the historical origins of social cognition by contrasting the elemental and holistic viewpoints. The elemental approach aims to build up from the bottom, combining smaller pieces into larger ones to assemble the whole puzzle. The piecemeal nature of this approach contrasts sharply with the holistic nature of the Gestalt alternative. To describe a person's active construction of reality, the holistic view aims to tackle the entire configuration as the perceiver sees it. The tension between the elemental and configural or holistic approaches will surface again, in a different form, in Chapter 2. We will see that they can be integrated as two complementary processes.

THE EBB AND FLOW OF COGNITION IN PSYCHOLOGY

Psychologists have not always agreed on the importance getting inside the mind. The study of cognition has received both good and bad reviews over time. To prevent an overly myopic view of the importance of cognition, let's take a brief look at its place in experimental and social psychology. Early psychologists, whether elemental or holistic, relied heavily on introspection as a central tool for understanding human thought. As you will see, however, introspection developed a bad reputation, and with it, cognition fell into disrepute. Experimental psychology rejected cognition for many years, but social psychology did not. The next two sections contrast the fate of cognition in the two subfields, experimental and social psychology.

Cognition in Experimental Psychology

Wundt's work at the dawn of empirical psychology relied heavily on trained **introspection**.[2] Using introspection linked to Wundt's emphatically cognitive goal: People's experience was his

---

[2] Wundt also took measures that did not rely on people's own reports of their internal processes; for example, he also emphasized the measurements of reaction time, which is the time between stimulus and response. If you ask us how old we are, we can respond instantly. If you ask either of us how old the other author is, we have to calculate it, and that takes longer. Thus from reaction time one could infer more or less intervening thought. Such measures supplemented introspective data.

topic. Wundt and others gathered data about mental events and constructed theories to account for those data. However, experimental psychology ultimately abandoned introspection as a method because it did not conform to scientific standards, namely: One's data should be publicly reproducible. Other scientists ought to be able to examine the data, replicate them following the same procedures, and analyze the data to see if they confirm the theory. In early experimental psychology, theories had to account for introspections (i.e., self-observations), and therein lay the problem. If the criteria for a theory's success depended on private experience, the evidence could not be produced in public. The research could not be checked by others. The most absurd version of the problem would be this: If my theory accounts for my introspections and your theory accounts for yours, how do we decide who is right?

When introspection was abandoned because of such problems, the study of cognition also languished. Psychologists shifted away from studying internal (cognitive) processes and toward external, publicly observable events. The ultimate development of this approach was American **behaviorist** psychology in the early decades of the 20th century. Behaviorists held that only overt, measurable acts were sufficiently valid objects for empirical scrutiny. One founder was Edward L. Thorndike; B. F. Skinner and others further developed his work. For example, Thorndike's (1940) theory of instrumental learning held no place for cognition. According to the theory, behavior has certain rewarding and punishing effects, which cause the organism to repeat or avoid the behavior later. In short, "the effect becomes a cause." Both effect and cause are observable, and cognition seems irrelevant (Skinner, 1963). One behaviorist even called the idea of cognition a superstition (Watson, 1930).

Behaviorists argued that specifying an observable stimulus (S) and response (R) for every part of one's theory is the strict scientific discipline necessary to the advancement of psychology, including social psychology (Berger & Lambert, 1968). For example, a behaviorist might approach the topic of racial and ethnic discrimination by noting that some children are punished for playing with children of certain other ethnic groups and rewarded for playing with children of the family's own ethnic group. A simplified model of this would include "the other ethnic group" as the stimulus and "not playing together" as the response. A behaviorist would not consider the possible role of stereotyping (cognition). In experimental psychology generally, one net effect of behaviorism was that ideas about cognition fell into disrepute for about half a century, while behaviorist theories dominated.

Several events caused experimental psychologists to take a fresh interest in cognition during the 1960s (Holyoak & Gordon, 1984). First, linguists criticized the failure of the stimulus–response framework's attempts to account for language (cf. Chomsky, 1959, criticizing Skinner, 1957). Clearly, the complex, symbolic, and uniquely human phenomenon of language would not easily yield to behaviorist approaches.

Second, a new approach called information-processing arose out of work on how people acquire knowledge and skills (Broadbent, 1958). **Information processing** refers to the idea that mental operations can be broken down into sequential stages. If you ask one of us when her niece was born, she thinks back to personal circumstances surrounding the event and recalls that it was August 1979. An information processing theory might represent those cognitive operations in Figure 1.3.

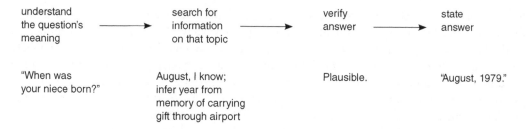

Figure 1.3   Sample steps in an information-processing sequence: Cognitive mechanisms in an oversimplified question–answering model

Information processing theories try to specify the steps intervening *between* stimulus (question) and response (answer). The important feature is the sequential processing of information. Unlike behaviorists, information-processing approaches aim to specify cognitive mechanisms, to get inside the black box of the mind.

As new scientific tools developed, cognitive psychologists had new ways to trace the nonobservable processes presumed to intervene between stimulus and response. The first important tool was the widely available computer, a methodological tool as well as a theoretical metaphor. As a tool, cognitive scientists use computers to simulate human cognitive processes; they write complex programs that play chess, learn geometry, and summarize the news (J. R. Anderson, 1976; Newell & Simon, 1972; Schank & Abelson, 1977). Social cognition researchers have developed computer simulations of how people form impressions, explanations, and memories of each other (Hastie, 1988a; Linville, Fischer, & Salovey, 1989; E. R. Smith, 1988; Van Overwalle, 1998) and change their attitudes (Latané & Bourgeois, 2001; Van Overwalle & Jordens, 2002). As a metaphor, the computer provides a framework and a jargon for characterizing mental processes; cognitive psychologists began to talk about input–output operations, or memory storage and retrieval, with respect to human cognition. Much of that early cognitive theory built on the idea that human cognition resembles computer information processing in important ways.

With the advent of cognitive neuroscience, the metaphors and models are changing. Cognitive psychologists are focusing more on modeling processes that are plausible with regard to increasingly understood brain systems, neural networks, their timing, and even single-cell responses. The current challenges include modeling how clusters of individually dumb neurons generate such exquisite intelligence. Some models draw on insights from individually simple organisms, such as ants, that collectively accomplish optimal choices, such as finding nests safe from predators (Mallon, Pratt, & Franks, 2001). Another example is the coordination of flocks of birds that individually have, well, birdbrains, but collectively move together across thousands of miles, alighting, flying, and taking off in unison, in effect making group decisions (Couzin, Krause, Franks, & Levin, 2005). Simple biological collectives may provide metaphors, models, and methods for understanding neural systems.

To conclude, experimental psychology began with introspection as a legitimate method for gaining insight into thinking and with cognition as a legitimate focus for theory. Behaviorists virtually eliminated such techniques and concerns for decades, and cognition fell into disrepute. During the 1970s, cognitive psychology reemerged as a scientifically legitimate pursuit (Neisser, 1980). More recently, during and after the 1990s Decade of the Brain, cognitive neuroscience has profoundly altered the landscape, for example, highlighting the interplay between human cognition and emotion (Phelps, 2006), the diffuse neural systems involved in language production and comprehension (Gernsbacher & Kaschak, 2003), the neural bases of cognitive control including inconsistency monitoring (Miller & Cohen, 2001), the distinct neural bases for distinct types of **category** learning (Ashby & Maddox, 2005), and the neural evidence for long-standing concepts such as **episodic memory** for past experiences, supported by both the **neuropsychology** of brain damage and neuroimaging studies of memory (Tulving, 2002). Perhaps these neural emphases seem remote from social cognition, threatening to tear psychology apart. Fortunately, human neuroscience has the potential to glue psychology back together, because the brain is not divided up the way psychology departments are. We are simultaneously social, affective, cognitive actors in the world.

Cognition in Social Psychology

In contrast to experimental psychology, social psychology has consistently leaned on cognitive concepts, even when most psychology was behaviorist. Social psychology has always been cognitive in at least three ways (Figure 1.4). First, since Lewin, social psychologists have decided that social behavior is more usefully understood as a function of people's perceptions of their world rather than as a function of objective descriptions of their stimulus environment (Manis, 1977; Zajonc, 1980a). For example, a donation that seems selfishly motivated to make the donor feel

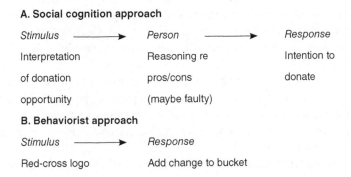

Figure 1.4 Cognitive features of a social decision: Social cognition (and social psychology generally) works from Stimulus through the Organism (person) to Response (S–O–R), in contrast to behaviorism's S–R framework, and each step is viewed as cognitively mediated

good may encourage gifts in the short term but not in the long run (Anik, Aknin, Norton, & Dunn, 2011). People's reaction depends on their perception, not simply by the giver's actions.

Other people can influence a person's actions without even being present, which is the ultimate reliance on perceptions to the exclusion of objective stimuli. Thus someone may react to a donation opportunity by imagining the reactions of others (e.g., "How grateful will the recipients be?", "What would my mother say?", or "What will my friends think?"). Of course, such thoughts are the person's own fantasies, having perhaps tenuous connection to objective reality. Thus the causes of social behavior are doubly cognitive; our perceptions of others actually present and our imagination of their presence both predict behavior (cf. G. W. Allport, 1954).[3]

Social psychologists view not only causes but also the end result of social perception and interaction in heavily cognitive terms, and this is a second way in which social psychology has always been cognitive. Thought often comes before feeling and behaving as the main reaction that social researchers measure. A person may worry about a donation (thought), feel good about the idea (affect), and do it (behavior), but social psychologists often mainly ask: "What do you think about it?" Even when they focus on behavior and affect, their questions are often, "What do you intend to do?" and "How would you label your feeling?" These arguably are not behavior and feelings but cognitions about them. Thus social psychological causes are largely cognitive, and the results are largely cognitive.

A third way in which social psychology has always been cognitive is that the person in between the presumed cause and the result is viewed as a thinking organism; this view contrasts with regarding the person as an emotional organism or a mindless automaton (Manis, 1977). Many social psychological theories paint a portrait of the typical person as reasoning (perhaps badly) before acting. In attempting to deal with complex human problems, as social psychology always has, complex mental processes seem essential. How else can one account for stereotyping and prejudice, propaganda and persuasion, altruism and aggression, and more? It is hard to imagine how a narrowly behaviorist theory would even begin. A strict stimulus–response (S–R) theory does not include the thinking organism that seems essential to account for such problems. In several senses, then, social psychology contrasts with stringent S–R theories in its reliance on S–O–R theories that include stimulus, organism, and response. Consequently, the thinker, who comes in between stimulus and response, has always been paramount in social psychology.

The social thinker has taken many guises in recent decades of research (S.E. Taylor, 1998). These guises describe the various roles of cognition in social psychology. Besides the varied roles of cognition, motivation has played different roles in the view of the social thinker. Keeping in mind these two components, cognition and motivation, we can identify five general views of the thinker in social psychology: consistency seeker, naive scientist, cognitive miser, motivated tactician, and activated actor (Table 1.1).

The first view emerged from the massive quantities of work on attitude change after World War II. The late 1950s produced several theories, all sharing some crucial basic assumptions. The consistency theories, as they were called, viewed people as **consistency seekers** motivated by

---

[3] One might well ask, what is the logical alternative to this approach? Who does research on reactions to the objective as opposed to the cognized world? The answer is behaviorists, as described, and some perceptual theorists (Gibson, 1966; see Chapter 3).

Table 1.1   Models of the social thinker in social cognition research

Model of the social thinker	Era	Main role of motivation	Main role for cognition	Theoretical example (relevant chapter)
Consistency seeker	1950–1960s	Drive to reduce discomfort from cognitive discrepancy	Cognitions about behavior, beliefs	Dissonance theory of attitudes (Ch. 9)
Naive scientist	1970s	Prediction and control, qualified rationality	Primary, rational analysis	Covariation model of attribution (Ch. 6)
Cognitive miser	1980s	Rapid, adequate understanding	Shortcuts conserve limited capacity	Heuristic decision making (Ch. 7)
Motivated tactician	1990s	Thinking is for doing in social context	Interaction goals organize cognitive strategies	Dual-process models (Ch. 2), especially stereotyping (Ch. 11)
Activated actor	2000s	Social surviving and thriving	Automatic affect and behavior	Implicit associations (Ch. 3–4, Ch. 12–15)

perceived discrepancies among their cognitions (e.g., Festinger, 1957; Heider, 1958; see Abelson et al., 1968, for an overview). Dissonance theory is the best-known example: If David has publicly announced he is on a diet and knows that he has just eaten a hot fudge sundae, he must do some thinking to bring those two cognitions into line. (Changing the subjective definition of "diet" would be a start.)

Chapter 9 returns to consistency theories, but for the moment two points are crucial. First, these theories relied on perceived inconsistency, which places cognitive activity in a central role. For example, if would-be dieters can convince themselves that one splurge will not matter, eating a sundae is not inconsistent for them. Objective inconsistency is not important. Subjective inconsistency among various cognitions or among feelings and cognitions is central to these theories. Actual inconsistency that is not perceived as such does not yield psychological inconsistency.

Second, upon perceiving inconsistency, the person is presumed to feel uncomfortable (a negative drive state) and to be motivated to reduce the inconsistency. Reducing the aversive drive state is a pleasant relief, rewarding in itself. This sort of motivational model is called a drive reduction model. Less formally, the sundae-consuming dieter will not be free from anxiety until he manufactures some excuse. Hence, consistency theories posit that people change their attitudes and beliefs for motivational reasons because of unmet needs for consistency. In sum, motivation and cognition both are central to the consistency theories.

Ironically, as they proliferated, consistency theories ceased to dominate the field, partly because the variants on a theme became indistinguishable. Moreover, it was difficult to predict what a person would perceive as inconsistent and to what degree, and which route to resolving inconsistency a person would take. Finally, people do, in fact, tolerate a fair amount of inconsistency, so the motivation to avoid it as an overriding principle was called into doubt (cf. Kiesler, Collins, & Miller, 1969).

Research in social cognition began in the early 1970s, and with it new models of the thinker emerged. Cognition and motivation play rather different roles in these new models compared with the roles they played in the consistency seeker model. In the new models, motivation is secondary to cognition. These views are central to social cognition research, and they will appear in more detail throughout the book. At present, however, a brief look is useful.

The first view within the social cognition framework is the **naive scientist,** a model of how people uncover the causes of behavior. Attribution theories concern how people explain their own and other people's behavior; they came to the forefront of early 1970s research (see Chapter 6). **Attribution theories** describe people's causal analyses of (attributions about) the social world. For example, an attribution can address whether someone's behavior seems due to the external situation or the person's internal disposition. If you want to know why your acquaintance Bruce snapped at you one morning, perhaps there were mitigating circumstances (e.g., his girlfriend left him; his dog ran away; you just backed into his truck) or whether he has an irritable disposition (he always behaves this way to everyone).

Attribution theorists initially assumed that people are fairly rational – like scientists – distinguishing among various potential causes. In part, this was a purposeful theoretical strategy designed to push a rational view of people as far as possible to discover its shortcomings. The theories started with the working hypothesis that, given enough time, people will gather all the relevant data and arrive at the most logical conclusion. In this view, you would think about your friend's behavior in a variety of settings and carefully weigh the evidence for a situational or a dispositional cause of his behavior. Thus the role of cognition in the naive scientist model is as an outcome of fairly rational analysis.

If you are wrong about why Bruce was irritable, the early theories would have viewed your error as an emotion-based departure from the normal process or as a simple error in available information. For example, if you attribute Bruce's unpleasant behavior to his irritable disposition, it may be because you are motivated to avoid the idea that he is angry at you. Viewed from this perspective, errors arise mainly as interference from nonrational motivations. In the early attribution theories, motivation enters mainly as a potential qualification on the usual process.

Recall that for consistency theories, in contrast, motivation drives the whole system. The role of motivation in consistency theories is central; the aversive drive state persists until inconsistencies resolve. Attribution theorists traditionally have not viewed unresolved attributions as causing an aversive drive state. Motivations for predicting and controlling one's social world presumably set attributions in motion; hence, motivation does help to catalyze the attribution process, just as it catalyzes the entire consistency-seeking process. Nevertheless, motivation is far more explicit in consistency theories than in attribution theories.

Unfortunately, people are not always such careful naive scientists. The cognitive system is limited in capacity, so people take **shortcuts.** The limitations of the cognitive system can be illustrated by such trivial problems as trying to keep a credit card number, an area code, and a telephone number in your head as you dial, or by more serious problems such as working poorly when you are distracted. The impact of cognitive limitations shows up in social inferences too.

To illustrate, in deciding why Bruce was irritable, you may seize on the easiest explanation rather than the most accurate one. Rather than asking Bruce what is disturbing him, you may simply label him as unpleasant, without giving it much thought. Quite often, people are simply not very thorough.

Hence, the third general view of the thinker is the **cognitive miser** model (S. E. Taylor, 1981b). The idea is that people are limited in their capacity to process information, so they take shortcuts whenever they can (see Chapters 7–8). People adopt strategies that simplify complex problems; the strategies may not be correct or produce correct answers, but they emphasize efficiency. The capacity-limited thinker searches for rapid, adequate solutions rather than for slow, accurate solutions. Consequently, in this view, errors and biases stem from inherent features of the cognitive system, not necessarily from motivations. Indeed, the cognitive miser model is silent on the issue of motivations or feelings of any sort except gaining a rapid, adequate understanding (which is cognitive rather than motivational in flavor). Cognition's role was central to the cognitive miser view, and motivation's role vanished almost entirely, with isolated exceptions.

As the cognitive miser viewpoint matured, the importance of motivations and emotions again became evident. Having developed considerable sophistication about people's cognitive processes, researchers began to appreciate anew the interesting and important influences of motivation on cognition (see Chapter 2). In addition, affect has been a continued source of fascination, as Chapters 13–14 indicate. With growing emphasis on motivated social cognition (Showers & Cantor, 1985; Tetlock, 1990), researchers returned to old problems with new perspectives gained from studying social cognition. Social interaction became more important. People's thinking is for doing, to paraphrase William James (1890/1983), and their social thinking is for their social doing (S. T. Fiske, 1992, 1993). The 1990s view of the social perceiver might best be termed the **motivated tactician**, a fully engaged thinker with multiple cognitive strategies available, who (consciously or unconsciously) chooses among them based on goals, motives, and needs. Sometimes the motivated tactician chooses wisely, in the interests of adaptability and accuracy, and sometimes the motivated tactician chooses defensively, in the interests of speed or self-esteem. Thus views of the social thinker came full cycle back to appreciating the importance of motivation, but with increased sophistication about cognitive structure and process.

As the 21st century gets well under way, views of the social perceiver are shifting slightly yet again, building on all that came before. The motivated tactician is nowhere near as deliberate as the goals viewpoint seemed to imply. Currently, with a heavy emphasis on unconscious associations, cued in the barest fraction of a second, people are viewed as **activated actors**. That is, social environments rapidly cue perceivers' social concepts, without awareness, and almost inevitably cue associated cognitions, evaluations, affect, motivation, and behavior (e.g., Dijksterhuis & Bargh, 2001; Fazio & Olson, 2003; Greenwald et al., 2002; Macrae & Bodenhausen, 2000; Nosek, Hawkins, & Frazier, 2012; Payne, 2012). This latest look emphasizes fast reactions, variously viewed as implicit, spontaneous, or automatic indicators of responses unconstrained by perceiver volition (see Chapters 3–4 and 10–13). These interpretations remain provocative, but one thing is clear: People's motives affect surprisingly unconscious responses. Using ever-faster and more precise methods for presenting stimuli at speeds outside awareness, as well as neuroscience measures of neural responses from the earliest moments of perception, we are rapidly learning just how much occurs in the first moments of social perception. At the same time, social cognition is not simply returning to the cognitive miser view (i.e., fast but not very good). The current view combines the cognitive economy view with a view that incorporates motivation and affect at every stage, even the preconscious ones. The farther upstream we go, the more we realize that cognition, affect, and behavioral readiness are inseparable.

In summary, social psychology has always been cognitive in the broad sense of positing important steps that intervene between observable stimulus and observable response. One early, major set of theories viewed people as consistency seekers, and motivation played a central role in driving the whole system. With the rise of social cognition research, new views emerged. In one major wave of research, psychologists view people as naive scientists. These psychologists regard motivation mainly as a source of error. In another recent view, psychologists see people as cognitive misers and locate errors in the inherent limitations of the cognitive system, saying almost nothing about motivation. More recently, motivational influences on cognition have reemerged in a revitalized view of the social thinker as a motivated tactician. Finally, researchers are currently realizing the limited degree of conscious choice in engaging automatic and controlled processes. With an emphasis on the functioning social thinker-feeler-actor, current work views people as activated actors, influenced by their social environments at even earlier stages than previously understood.

WHAT IS SOCIAL COGNITION?

The study of social cognition does not rely on any one theory. The field concerns how people make sense of other people and themselves in order to coordinate with their social world. Most social cognition research shares some basic features: unabashed mentalism, orientation toward process, cross-fertilization between cognitive and social psychologies, and at least some concern with real-world social issues (Augustinos & Walker, 1995; Bless, Fiedler, & Strack, 2004; Fiske, 2012; Kunda, 1999; Macrae & Bodenhausen, 2000; Macrae & Miles, 2012; Moskowitz, 2005; Ostrom, 1984; S. E. Taylor, 1981b).

Mentalism

The first of these assumptions, an unabashed commitment to mentalism (cognition), has just been discussed at some length. **Mentalism** is the belief in the importance of cognitive representations (Table 1.2). The cognitive elements people naturally use to make sense of other people constitute the "what" of social cognition. Mental representations are cognitive structures that both represent one's general knowledge about a given concept or stimulus domain and one's memory for specific experiences. For example, your general knowledge about a new friend may be organized into a view of him as independent but not a loner, friendly but not intrusive, and athletic but not a star. A concept (e.g., this person) includes both relevant attributes (e.g., independent, friendly, athletic) and the relationships among the attributes (e.g., what his independence has to do with

Table 1.2   Identifying features of social cognition approaches

Mentalism	Process	Cross-fertilization	Real-world issues
What: Cognitive representation (e.g., general knowledge & instances)	How: Cognitive mechanisms (e.g., attention, memory, inference)	Whence: Adapting cognitive science methods (e.g., response time, neuroimaging)	Why: Social problems (e.g., mental & physical health, law, prejudice, persuasion, prosociality)

his friendliness). General knowledge about ourselves and others provides us with the expectations that enable us to function in the world; as noted, thinking is (mostly) for doing. People also have specific memories for unique events. Both the general and specific types appear in Chapter 4 on mental representation. People also have mental representations of self (Chapter 5), attitude objects (Chapter 9), and outgroups (Chapter 10), among other significant social cognitions. That being said, some new approaches focus on embodied and enacted knowledge that may not be mediated by mental processes, as we will see.

Cognitive Processes in Social Settings

The second basic assumption in research on social cognition concerns **cognitive process**; that is, how cognitive elements form, operate, and change over time. A process orientation follows from the fundamental commitment to cognition: Concern with cognitive elements that intervene between observable stimulus and observable response requires an explanation of *how* one gets from S to R. Recall that behaviorists explicitly avoided discussion of internal processes because they were concerned with predicting a publicly observable response from a publicly observable stimulus. In that sense, they were response or outcome oriented rather than process oriented.

But outcome orientations arose elsewhere too. The early methodology of research on consistency theories, for example, was more outcome oriented than process oriented. Although the researchers originally theorized and made assumptions about process, they focused empirically on predicting outcomes from stimuli. For example, inconsistency was manipulated (stimulus) and the resulting attitude change measured (outcome). Later psychologists conducting consistency research did attempt to measure the intervening processes, but the initial thrust of the research methods was outcome oriented. One of the recent shifts in attitude research and in social psychology generally has been away from outcome-oriented approaches and toward examinations of process.

In social cognition research, theories are now available to describe – and the tools are available to measure – various implicit but hitherto unexamined assumptions about process. Social cognition research often attempts to measure the stages of social information processing or at least the mechanism by which social perception translates to social response. That is, when a person confronts a social stimulus, several steps may occur before he or she reacts, or the reaction may be more automatic, habitual, or unthinking. Social cognition, and now social neuroscience, analyzes all these processes from the earliest moments.

Cross-Fertilization

So far we have described two themes in social cognition research and in this book: a commitment to representation or mentalism and a commitment to process analysis. The third theme, cross-fertilization between cognitive and social psychology (and both with human neuroscience), addresses another feature of social cognition research. Although social psychology has always been cognitive, it has not always had purely cognitive neighbors from whom it can borrow new approaches. Adopting relatively fine-grained cognitive and cognitive neuroscience theory and methods has proved fruitful for social psychological research. Not only do researchers specify the steps in a presumed process model, but researchers attempt to measure the steps in some detail. For example, the first new-wave social cognition research relied heavily on measuring milliseconds of reaction time. The most recent social cognitive neuroscience relies on detailed brain imaging techniques. Borrowing measures from other areas of psychology enriches social psychology's home-grown methods, as we will see. Various traditional and newer experimental methods enable researchers to support differing aspects of process models: for example, attention, memory, and inference.

Real-World Social Issues

The fourth theme of social cognition research is application to the real world. Social psychologists have a long tradition of addressing important contemporary issues. Early research provided insights into crowd behavior, propaganda, anti-Semitism, military morale, and other social issues. In keeping with this tradition, research in social cognition informs us about important issues. It applies the often heavily cognitive theory and method to real-world social problems. Throughout this book, we illustrate the ways social cognition can guide work in areas such as psychotherapy, health care, the legal system, stereotyping, advertising, political campaigns, strangers helping strangers, and romantic involvements. All these applications illustrate the flexibility of social cognition research and demonstrate how some otherwise highly technical or abstract ideas generalize outside the laboratory.

Social cognition applications to real-world issues define some boundary conditions for cognitive processes. That is, the research reveals phenomena that do not lend themselves to a purely cognitive analysis; other factors must be considered in many interpersonal settings of consequence. For example, how does cognition trade off accuracy and efficiency? How does social information processing operate in situations of intense personal involvement? How do social cognitions translate into voting behavior? How does the neuroscience of social cognition relate to the social problems of people with autism? Stay tuned.

This book addresses the four major themes of social cognition research: unabashed mentalism in the study of cognitive representations of people, a commitment to fine-grained analyses of cognitive process, cross-fertilization between cognitive and social theory and methods, and a commitment to real-world social issues.

PEOPLE ARE NOT THINGS

As we review research on social cognition, the analogy between the perception of things and the perception of people becomes increasingly clear. The argument is made repeatedly: Principles that describe how people think in general also describe how people think about people. Many theories of social cognition have developed in ways that undeniably build on fundamental cognitive principles. Nevertheless, in borrowing such principles we discover fundamental differences when applying them to cognition about people. After all, cognitive psychology is relatively more concerned with processing information about inanimate objects and abstract concepts, whereas social psychology is more concerned with processing information about people and social experience.

At this point you already may be saying, "Wait, you can't tell me that the way I think about mental arithmetic or about my coffee cup has anything to do with the way I think about my friends." The wisdom or folly of applying the principles of object perception to the perception of people has been debated for some time (Heider, 1958; Higgins, Kuiper, & Olson, 1981; Macrae & Miles, 2012; Ostrom, 1984; Schneider, Hastorf, & Ellsworth, 1979; Tagiuri & Petrullo, 1958). Some of the important differences between people and things as targets of perception include the following (Table 1.3):

- People intentionally influence the environment; they attempt to control it for their own purposes. Objects, of course, are not intentional causal agents.
- People perceive back; as you are busy forming impressions of them, they are doing the same to you. Social cognition is mutual cognition.
- Social cognition implicates the self because the target is judging you, because the target may provide you with information about yourself, and because the target is more similar to you than any object could be.
- A social stimulus may change upon being the target of cognition. People worry about how they come across and may adjust their appearance or behavior accordingly; coffee cups obviously do not.
- People's traits are nonobservable attributes that are vital to thinking about them. An object's nonobservable attributes are somewhat less crucial. Both a person and a cup can be fragile, but that inferred characteristic is both less important and more directly seen in the cup.
- People change over time and circumstance more than objects typically do. This can make cognitions rapidly obsolete or unreliable.
- The accuracy of one's cognitions about people is harder to check than the accuracy of one's cognitions about objects. Even psychologists have a hard time agreeing on whether a given person is extraverted, sensitive, or honest, but most ordinary people easily could test whether a given cup is heat resistant, fragile, or leaky.

- People are unavoidably complex. One cannot study cognitions about people without making numerous choices to simplify. The researcher has to simplify in object cognition too, but fewer distortions may result. One cannot simplify a social stimulus without eliminating much of the inherent richness of the target.
- Because people are so complex, and because they have traits and intents hidden from view, and because they affect us in ways objects do not, social cognition automatically involves social explanation. It is more important for an ordinary person to explain why a person is fragile than to explain why a cup is.

For these reasons, social cognitive psychology will never be a literal translation of cognitive psychology. It profits from theories and methods adapted to new uses, but the social world provides perspectives and challenges that are dramatic, if not unique, features of thinking about other people and oneself.

Table 1.3   Why and how people differ from inanimate objects as stimuli

People are (and objects are not, so much):
Intentional causal agents
Perceiving back
Similar to self
Self-conscious targets
Holders of crucial but nonobservable traits
Changeable
Known with indeterminant accuracy
Intrinsic complex
Requiring explanation

BRAINS MATTER

The Decade of the Brain in the 1990s acknowledged the exciting and crucial roles of neural systems in a variety of human processes, including social ones (Klein & Kihlstrom, 1998; Ochsner & Lieberman, 2001; Todorov, Fiske, & Prentice, 2011). Social psychophysiology was not new, of course (e.g., Cacioppo & Berntson, 1992; Table 1.4). The current palpable excitement among researchers and the public stems partly from the invention and popularity of **functional magnetic resonance imaging** (fMRI) techniques, which yield images of the brain at work. These techniques allow researchers to place a person into an MRI magnet, provide some stimuli, and observe blood flow to distinct areas of the brain, revealing clues as to their possible functions in different tasks. The fMRI techniques are developing increasingly precise indicators of spatial location in the brain (Lieberman, 2010). These are complemented by older techniques, such as **electroencephalography** (EEG) and facial **electromyography** (EMG), as well as new techniques being developed as we write, such as **transcranial magnetic stimulation** (TMS). EEG provides only approximate spatial locations (noninvasive electrodes are distributed over the surface of the skull) but extremely precise temporal information. The facial EMG (electrodes

Table 1.4   Sampling of neuroscience techniques in use for social cognition

Neuropsychology	Considers personal and social lives of patients with brain impairments
Functional magnetic resonance imaging	fMRI records re-oxygenizing blood flow to just-activated brain areas
Electroencephalography	EEG records voltage fluctuation on the scalp, detecting neural activity
Electromyography (mostly facial)	EMG records voltage changes on skin over muscles, so their activity
Transcranial magnetic stimulation	TMS's electromagnetic induction stimulates or inhibits brain regions
Electrodermal responses	EDR (also GSR, galvanic skin response) measures skin moisture
Cardiovascular activity	CV indexes cardiac output, ventricle activity, total peripheral resistance
Hormone levels	Hormones (e.g., cortisol, testosterone, oxytocin) link to sociality
Immune functioning	Assays track specific immune cells and system operation
Genetic analyses	Combined with environment, detect interactive links to social cognition

at crucial locations on the face) can detect micromovements of facial muscles not yet visible to observers but potentially indicative of facial expressions. TMS "freezes" selected brain areas, to detect their causal role in mental processes.

Added to these techniques are measures of **cardiovascular activity** and **electrodermal** responses (e.g., palmer sweat), which measure various forms of arousal in the sympathetic adrenal medullary system (Blascovich & Mendes, 2010). Assessments of cardiovascular activity provide information about relatively short-term physiological arousal. Some social neuroscientists, those who are especially interested in stress processes, also often assess longer-term hypothalamic pituitary adrenal (HPA) functioning, especially changes in **hormone levels,** such as cortisol in response to threat or stressful tasks. Elevations in **cortisol** or disruptions in its diurnal rhythm have been tied to stressful events and to psychosocial states. For example, social threat predicts elevated cortisol responses to stressful tasks (Dickerson & Kemeny, 2004), and psychosocial resources such as a strong sense of self have been tied to lower cortisol responses to stress (Creswell et al., 2005). Social neuroscientists make use of a broad array of immunological measures as well, which include assessing frequencies of different types of immune cells and overall **immune functioning**. The immune system is responsive to stress and other threats (Dickerson, Kemeny, Aziz, Kim, & Fahey, 2004); assessing immunologic functioning in conjunction with resources, such as optimism or a sense of personal control, can help identify those aspects of social cognition that protect against stress and psychological distress (Reed, Kemeny, Taylor, & Visscher, 1999; Segerstrom, Taylor, Kemeny, & Fahey, 1998). **Genetic analyses** also shed light on the interplay of populations, evolution, and culture (Ackerman, Huang, & Bargh, 2012; Chiao, Cheon, Bebko, Livingston, & Hong, 2012. Taken together, these measures open new doors into the life of the social mind.

For social cognition researchers, the possibilities also allow dissociating distinct social cognitive processes on the basis of distinct neuroscientific responses. Relevant to our assertion that "people are not things," recent studies demonstrate distinct neural systems activating in social perception compared to object perception. In one early study (Castelli, Happé, Frith, & Frith, 2000), people watched a large red triangle and a small blue triangle under one of three labels for the animation: interaction with feelings and thoughts, random movement, or simple interaction. Independently, the animated movements (on different trials) resembled scripts involving either mental inferences (e.g., persuading, bluffing), simple goals (e.g., chasing, dancing), or straightforward physical movement (e.g., floating, bouncing off walls). When the movements involved attributing a (quasi-human) mental state to the triangles, distinct activation patterns emerged, among them, **medial prefrontal cortex** (mPFC), superior temporal sulcus (STS or TPJ, **temporoparietal junction**), and **fusiform face area** (FFA) (see Figures 1.5 and 1.6).[4] This study is exciting because it was one

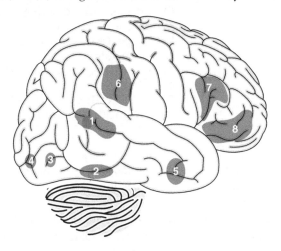

1 posterior superior temporal sulcus
2 fusiform "face" area
3 extrastriate "body" area
4 occipital "face" area
5 amygdala
6 inferior parietal lobule
7 ventrolateral PFC
8 ventrolateral PFC

Figure 1.5   Some lateral brain regions involved in social cognition

Note: The brain regions involved in social perception (face and body perception [2–4], biological motion perception [1], action observation [6, 7], and emotion recognition [5, 8]). Numbers in brackets correspond to the regions in the figure reliably associated with a particular aspect of social perception. The amygdala is displayed on the surface for convenience but is far more interior.

---

[4] The Castelli et al. study also showed activation to temporal poles and the extrastriate cortex (occipital gyrus). The Mitchell et al. study described next activated the intraparietal sulcus. We focus on the other areas for simplicity here.

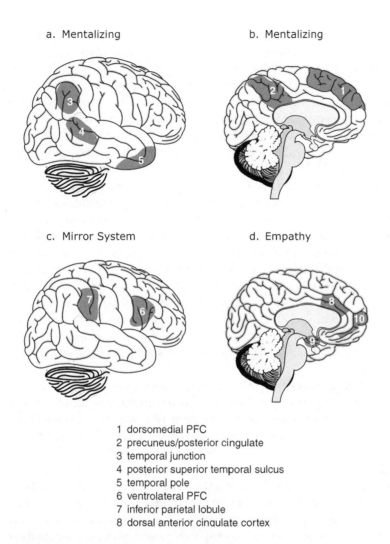

a. Mentalizing

b. Mentalizing

c. Mirror System

d. Empathy

1 dorsomedial PFC
2 precuneus/posterior cingulate
3 temporal junction
4 posterior superior temporal sulcus
5 temporal pole
6 ventrolateral PFC
7 inferior parietal lobule
8 dorsal anterior cingulate cortex

Figure 1.6   Some medial brain regions involved in social cognition

The brain regions involved in social inference. The top row of images displays the regions commonly activated in mentalizing and theory of mind tasks. The bottom-left image displays the mirror system. The bottom-right image displays brain regions identified in studies of empathy.

Note: Anterior insula is displayed on the medial wall for presentation purposes, but is actually between the medial and lateral walls of the cortex.

of the first to show something special about perceiving an entity as having intentions and personality, dubbed a **theory of mind** effect. Note how this study fits our earlier distinctions between people and things.

A related study (Mitchell, Heatherton, & Macrae, 2002) supports this distinction, also at the neural systems level. Undergraduates saw a series of adjective–noun pairs and had to decide if the adjective "could ever be true of" the noun. The nouns named people (e.g., David, Emily) or objects (e.g., shirt, mango), and the adjectives included typical person descriptors (e.g., assertive, nervous) and relevant object descriptors (e.g., patched, seedless). Neural activity differed when people made these semantic judgments about people and objects. Brain activity associated with people included some of the same areas previously seen by Castelli et al. (2000) and others for social cognitive responses: medial prefrontal cortex (mPFC), superior temporal sulcus (STS), and fusiform gyrus (FFA).

These areas of the brain (mPFC and STS) appear frequently throughout this book when people are generally engaged in social cognition (mPFC) or judgments of intent and trajectory (STS). The mPFC in particular appears to have a unique role in social cognition across many studies (Amodio & Frith, 2006). What's more, the FFA particularly responds to faces or other objects in one's domains of **expertise**, such as birds for a birdwatcher and cars for a car expert (Farah, 1994; Gauthier, Skudlarski, Gore, & Anderson, 2000). The main point, made by the Mitchell et al. (2002) study, as in the prior one, is the dissociation (separation) between the social and the nonsocial neural activation patterns. Moreover, in these two studies and others (e.g., Mitchell, Macrae, & Banaji, 2005), some of the same areas are implicated in social cognition. One exciting possibility is that these areas link to reward systems in the brain, accounting for the attraction people have to social interaction and belonging (S. T. Fiske, 2010; Baumeister & Leary, 1995).

What is also exciting about these findings is the provocative possibility that social cognition could be the default, resting state (Iacoboni, et al., 2004). In many social neuroscience studies, the characteristically social "activations" often emerge as relatively little change from a supposedly neutral baseline (e.g., staring at the fixation point between trials). In contrast, object judgments often create *de*activations from the baseline. This study suggested that the neutral condition may not be neutral at all, but instead people spontaneously engaging in social cognition (What's that experimenter doing now? I hope she knows what she's doing. Will my friends wait for me for lunch? Why didn't my roommate wake me up as promised?). Suppose for the moment that much of people's random thinking concerns other people, engaging relatively active social systems in the brain. When the experimenter makes people do mental arithmetic or other nonsocial tasks, the social cognition processes shut down, so these socially implicated areas shut down. In contrast, when people look at social stimuli, their activation in these areas does not change much from baseline because they were already thinking about other people. This is essentially Iacoboni et al.'s (2004) argument. They compared people watching film clips of two people interacting with a single person engaged in everyday activities or a resting baseline. They found activations even relative to baseline in the **dorsal** (upper) part of the mPFC, as well as in the STS and FFA. And similarly, in the Mitchell et al. study, for example, the socially relevant regions were generally marked by relatively little change from baseline brain activity for person judgments along with significant deactivations for object judgments. Other studies that intensify social thinking at levels above social daydreaming do find activations above baseline (Harris, Todorov, & Fiske, 2005).

As the evidence accumulates for the unique neural status of thinking about other people's dispositions and states, researchers are learning much about what makes social cognition special. Some of the more intriguing recent findings using these neural criteria suggest that people can think about dogs as people (Mitchell, Banaji, & Macrae, 2005a) more easily than they can think about drug addicts and the homeless as people (Harris & Fiske, 2006). That is, people's default response to an outgroup that elicits disgust (as evidenced by typical ratings of homeless people and drug-addicted people) activates neural patterns typical of disgust (e.g., insula) but not neural patterns typical of social cognition to ingroups and even other outgroups (e.g., mPFC). On the other hand, people readily attribute psychological states (anthropomorphize) to dogs (Mitchell, Banaji, & Macrae, 2005a), at least as indexed by mPFC and "yes" responses to trait terms ("curious") as potentially applicable to a dog. While interpreting the activation of the vast mPFC is rapidly developing, it clearly is implicated in cognition that is emphatically social.

In discussing the importance of the social brain, we should clarify its context. People sometimes mistakenly pit biological explanations against cultural explanations, rehashing the nature–nurture debate. Although individual researchers tend to be drawn to distinct levels of analysis, brains and cultures are not competing explanations for the same phenomena.

First, our brains are predisposed to pick up our cultures as they socialize us. For example, as just hinted, social thinking activates particular neural configurations. Moreover, social exclusion recruits neural systems linked to the experience of physical pain (Eisenberger, Lieberman, & Williams, 2003). That is, people who are ostracized – even from a simple video game with strangers – activate the **anterior cingulate cortex** (ACC), and this activation is dampened by activation of the right **ventral prefrontal cortex** (rvPFC). These patterns also occur for physical pain. Adding to the evidence for this parallel, people's baseline sensitivity to physical pain predicts their sensitivity to social pain, and experiencing social pain sensitizes people to physical pain (Eisenberger, Jarcho, Lieberman, & Naliboff, 2006). As we increasingly understand the neural correlates of social life, we will see how sensitive our brains are to social cues.

Second, cultural information is stored in our brains. As Chapter 4 indicates, mental representations of social information are complex and distinctly characterized by features that differ from nonsocial representations. People's neocortex varies with the size of their social networks, and this holds for more socially bonded primates as well (Dunbar, 2003, 2012).

Third, people's brains change physically depending on their cultural experience. For example, taxi drivers have larger **posterior** (rear) hippocampus areas (associated with spatial memory storage) the longer they drive, as a function of their learning street locations (Maguire et al., 2000). As these examples indicate, our brains dwell in particular cultural experiences, and both matter to social cognition.

CULTURES MATTER

Exciting new cultural comparisons have been forcing social cognition researchers to reexamine the entire basis of our field. Many of the basic assumptions about how people think about other people turn out to be culturally bounded, which challenges long-held assumptions. At first, social cognition researchers focused on frankly **WEIRD** (Western, Educated, Industrialized, Rich, Democratic) undergraduates (Henrich, Heine, & Norenzayan, 2010), but now more comparative work reveals alternative social worlds. Many of these comparisons to date contrast American or Canadian with Japanese, Chinese, or Korean undergraduates. Even with these limited comparisons, some provocative findings are emerging (Morling & Masuda, 2012). For example, cultures vary in thinking about causality more analytically (Westerners) or holistically (East Asians), as Chapter 6 will show (Nisbett, Peng, Choi, & Norenzayan, 2001). This affects, for example, how people decide whether people or social circumstances are responsible for actions taken, which has implications for law, morality, social roles, and more.

As another example, configurations of beliefs differ across cultures (Leung & Bond, 2004). Cultures with general beliefs in social cynicism assume that power displays elicit compliance, and accordingly, people endorse such influence strategies (Fu et al., 2004). The same goes for variations in beliefs about religiosity, reward for effort, and fate control; that is, people endorse influence strategies that fit their culture's expectations about what makes people tick. Given globalization of business, education, and politics, these social cognitive insights into cultural variation are crucial for people to understand each other's assumptions about interaction.

One of the most striking social cognitive differences in cultures compares the self as more **independent** and autonomous (Westerners) or more **interdependent** and harmonious (East Asians) (e.g., Markus & Kitayama, 1991; see Chapter 5). The implications of this distinction range from self-definition to self-esteem to life tasks to the roles of others – all critical to social cognition.

All of these cultural patterns relate to each other, as we will see. While the contrasts are real, so are the similarities and so are the places between the extremes. At their best, cultural comparisons create interesting complexity, not stereotypes or caricatures. As social cognition research outgrows its original Western (North American and European) boundaries to explore other settings and simultaneously reaches into the brain (Chiao et al., 2012), it extends its cultural reach as well.

Cultural social cognition reflects the importance of humans as adaptive social beings, evolved to focus on other people, to imitate behavior, discern intent, cooperate together, and learn symbol systems (Ackerman, Huang, & Bargh, 2012; Morling & Masuda, 2012). People are culturally diverse precisely because of our inherited flexibility and responsiveness to social context.

Summary

The study of social cognition concerns how people make sense of other people and themselves. It focuses on people's everyday understanding both as the phenomenon of interest and as a basis for theory about people's everyday understanding. Thus it concerns both how people think about the social world and how they think they think about the social world. It also draws heavily on fine-grained analyses provided by cognitive theory and method.

Solomon Asch first proposed two competing models for social perception, one more algebraic and the other more configural. These two contrasting approaches to social cognition date back to early modern philosophy. The elemental approach begins with ideas as elements that become linked into increasingly complex compounds. People form associations between ideas by the ideas' repeated contiguity in space or time. Early psychologists used introspective analysis as a method to break down their memory processes into those basic elements.

Gestalt psychologists adopted a holistic approach. They focused on the mind's active construction of reality rather than on objective descriptions of the stimulus field. They also focused on the person's experience of dynamic wholes rather than elements. Lewin and Asch imported such ideas to social psychology. As noted, Asch focused on Gestalt impressions. Lewin emphasized that the perceived environment – that is, the psychological field – predicts behavior and that one must consider the entire dynamic equilibrium of forces acting on an individual. The psychological field is the joint product of person and situation, and of motivation and cognition.

Cognition has not always been prominent in experimental psychology. When introspection proved to be a weak basis for an empirical science, cognition fell into disfavor with psychologists. Behaviorists dominated psychology for decades, insisting on an observable stimulus, an observable response, and no intervening cognitions. Later, behaviorist approaches seemed inadequate to explain language; at the same time, information-processing theories and computer-aided theory and technology paved the way for the reemergence of cognition in experimental psychology.

In social psychology, however, cognition has always been a respectable idea. The causes of social interaction predominantly lie in the perceived world, and the results of social interaction are thoughts as well as feelings and behavior. In addition, social psychologists have always been cognitive in their view of the thinker who reacts to the perceived stimulus and generates a substantially cognitive response. They have viewed the social thinker at some times as a consistency seeker, motivated to reduce perceived discrepancies; at other times, they have seen the social thinker as a naive scientist who makes every effort to ferret out the truth, with motivation contributing mainly error. Subsequently, social psychologists regarded the social thinker as a cognitive miser who attempts to increase or maintain the efficiency of a capacity-limited cognitive apparatus, and they had little to say about motivation. This viewpoint was followed by a view of the social perceiver as a motivated tactician, which gained acceptance as researchers documented the flexibility of the social perceiver. Currently, with emphasis shifting to ever-faster, more immediate responses, as well as their effects on overt behavior, researchers tend to emphasize social perceivers as activated actors, heavily influenced by social environments.

Social cognition, as an area of study, emphasizes unabashed mentalism, social settings, cross-fertilization, and real-world social issues. Social cognition departs from the general principles of cognition in some ways: Compared to objects, people are more likely to be causal agents, to perceive as well as being perceived, and to involve intimately the observer's self. People are difficult targets of cognition; because they adjust themselves upon being perceived, many of their important attributes (e.g., traits) must be inferred, and the accuracy of observations is difficult to determine. People frequently change and are unavoidably complex as targets of cognition. Hence those who study social cognition must adapt the ideas of cognitive psychology to suit the specific features of cognitions about people.

Some of the most exciting recent developments include work on social cognitive affective neuroscience, adding to insights about the special status of emphatically social cognition at the neural level, with particular systems implicated in uniquely social cognitive processes. Complementing that work are insights from cultural psychology, examining variations in the way humans solve the challenge of making sense of each other in a variety of settings.

FURTHER READING

Ackerman, J. M., Huang, J. Y., & Bargh, J. A. (2012). Evolutionary perspectives on social cognition. In S. T. Fiske & C. N. Macrae (Eds.), *Sage handbook of social cognition* (pp. 451–473). Thousand Oaks, CA: Sage.

Asch, S. E. (1946). Forming impressions of personality. *Journal of Abnormal and Social Psychology, 41(3)*, 258–290.

Chiao, J. Y., Cheon, B. K., Bebko, G. M., Livingston, R. L., & Hong, Y-y. (2012). Gene x environment interaction in social cognition. In S. T. Fiske & C. N. Macrae (Eds.), *Sage handbook of social cognition* (pp. 516–534). Thousand Oaks, CA: Sage.

Fiske, S. T. (2012). "One word: Plasticity" – Social cognition's futures. In S. T. Fiske & C. N. Macrae (Eds.), *Sage handbook of social cognition* (pp. 535–541). Thousand Oaks, CA: Sage.

Henrich, J., Heine, S. J., & Norenzayan, A. (2010). The weirdest people in the world? *Behavioral and Brain Sciences, 33(2–3)*, 61–83.

Lieberman, M. D. (2010). Social cognitive neuroscience. In S. T. Fiske, D. T. Gilbert, & G. Lindzey (Eds.), *Handbook of social psychology* (5th edn, Vol. 1, pp. 143–193). Hoboken, NJ: Wiley.

Macrae, C. N., & Miles, L. K. (2012). Revisiting the sovereignty of social cognition: Finally some action. In S. T. Fiske & C. N. Macrae (Eds.), *Sage handbook of social cognition* (pp. 1–11). Thousand Oaks, CA: Sage.

Morling, B., & Masuda, T. (2012). Social cognition in real worlds: Cultural psychology and social cognition. In S. T. Fiske & C. N. Macrae (Eds.), *Sage handbook of social cognition* (pp. 429–450). Thousand Oaks, CA: Sage.

North, M. S., & Fiske, S. T. (2012). Social cognition. In A. W. Kruglanski & W. Stroebe (Eds.), *Handbook of the history of social psychology* (pp. 81–100). New York: Psychology Press.

Ostrom, T. M. (1984). The sovereignty of social cognition. In R. S. Wyer, Jr., & T. K. Srull (Eds.), *Handbook of social cognition* (Vol. 1, pp. 1–38). Mahwah, NJ: Erlbaum.

Todorov, A., Fiske, S. T., & Prentice, D. (Eds.) (2011). *Social neuroscience: Toward understanding the underpinnings of the social mind*. New York: Oxford University Press.

PART ONE

Basic Concepts in Social Cognition

Dual Modes in Social Cognition 2

- Automatic Processes
- Controlled Processes
- Motivations Influence which Modes Operate
- Models of both Automatic and Controlled Processes

First impressions really do count. People judge each other within a fraction of a second, for better or worse. Luckily, under some circumstances people are capable of going beyond those split-second impressions. The relatively automatic first impressions nevertheless anchor subsequent thinking, so they are difficult to undo. Conventional wisdom is correct in this instance – that first impressions matter – but common sense doesn't know the half of just how automatic impressions can be, nor does common sense reveal much about exactly how the deliberate processes operate when they do kick in.

This chapter addresses these two modes of social cognition, a theme that appears and reappears throughout the book. The dual-mode approach has become so established that one edited volume collected thirty-some chapters on this framework (Chaiken & Trope, 1999) and one social psychology handbook devoted a full chapter to it (Wegner & Bargh, 1998). The mind contains a multitude of processes, so these models aim to explain the diversity of people's thoughts, feelings, and behaviors toward each other, most models assuming more than one core process (Aarts, 2012; Gilbert, 1999; Nosek, Hawkins, & Frazier, 2012; Payne, 2012; Winkielman & Schooler, 2012).

The **motivated tactician**, described in Chapter 1, refers to people's tendency to rely on relatively automatic processes or alternatively on more effortful ones, depending on the situational and motivational demands. The term *tactician* implies that people choose modes in the thick of the action, in the midst of dealing with other people, thinking harder or less hard as their motivation deems necessary. However, people typically do not consciously choose between automatic and controlled processes. Automatic processes influence the motivations that trigger social cognition, as well as behavior that results.

This chapter begins by explaining automatic processes, then describes controlled ones. Next, we examine the motivations that move people between modes. We then illustrate two-mode models, anticipating their appearance in subsequent chapters. Finally, we close with some counterpoints to the prevailing two-mode view.

AUTOMATIC PROCESSES

Automatic processes come in all varieties. Everyday examples include times when people seem not to be thinking; early research dubbed this **mindlessness** (Langer, Blank, & Chanowitz, 1978). Table 2.1 shows the progression from most automatic toward controlled processes. We begin our discussion with the purest form of **automaticity**, which is unintentional, uncontrollable, efficient, autonomous, and outside awareness (Bargh, 1997).

Table 2.1   Varieties of automatic and controlled processes

Mode	Definition
Full Automaticity	*Unintentional, uncontrollable, efficient, autonomous responses outside awareness*
Subliminal priming, or preconscious	Prime registers on senses, but no awareness of it or its effect on responses; depends on context
Conscious priming, or postconscious	Conscious perception of prime, but no awareness of its effects on responses; depends on context
Individual differences in chronic accessibility	Can be preconscious or postconscious, habitual processing by particular categories or concepts, as if chronically primed; depends on person (role, personality, culture, practice – a process called proceduralization)
Goal-dependent automaticity	Intentional control starts process, but without subsequent awareness, need to monitor completion, or intending all specific outcomes
	Unintended effects of goal-dependent automaticity include failures of thought suppression and unwanted rumination (Table 2.2)
Intent	Requires having options, especially obvious when making the hard choice, and paying attention to the intended response (Table 2.3)
Conscious will	Experienced when a thought precedes, fits, and explains a subsequent action
Consciousness	Defined variously (Table 2.4)
Full Control	*Intentional responses with conscious awareness*

Subliminal Priming

Consider the following study (Bargh, Chen, & Burrows, 1996): Undergraduate participants in a psychology experiment saw four to 20 circles on a series of screens for three seconds each time and had to judge whether they were odd or even in number. After 130 tiresome trials, the computer suddenly beeped and displayed an error message indicating that none of the data had been saved and that the experiment would have to restart. Needless to say, participants reacted. Without their prior knowledge (although with their subsequent consent), their faces were videotaped as the computer and experimenter conveyed the bad news. Also unknown to the participants, just prior to each set of circles, they had seen a black-and-white photo of an African American or European American man, displayed at subliminal speeds (13–26 milliseconds). Participants were non-African American, and their facial expressions were reliably more hostile when they had been exposed to a series of Black faces than when they had been exposed to White faces. Hostile emotions were primed, especially ready to appear under provocation.

Subliminal priming occurs when a concept is activated by the environment, but at exposure times below conscious awareness. Subliminal priming of emotion appears reliable. Besides Bargh et al. (1996), rapidly presented smiling and frowning faces influence later liking for Chinese ideographs, which were otherwise neutral and without meaning to the research participants (e.g., Murphy, Monahan, & Zajonc, 1995). A host of other studies similarly show how affect can be conveyed by verbal concepts that are primed by being flashed below awareness (Bargh & Williams, 2006). For example, priming hostility-related words affects impressions of others (one of the earliest demonstrations being Bargh & Pietromonaco, 1982).

The neural mechanisms of immediate emotional priming likely include the **amygdala**, an interior almond-shaped pair of brain regions implicated in detecting emotionally significant stimuli (Figure 2.1; Phelps, 2005). Faces with fearful expressions elicit amygdala responses even when presented subliminally, below conscious thresholds (Whalen et al., 1998). Emotionally arousing words presented rapidly are easier to detect than more neutral words, and the amygdala again is key because patients with amygdala lesions show a diminished ability to detect these same words (A. K. Anderson & Phelps, 2001). The amygdala orients to automatically detecting cues that are negative (Lieberman, Gaunt, Gilbert, & Trope, 2002) or extreme (Cunningham, Raye, & Johnson, 2004; Todorov, Said, Engel, & Oosterhof, 2008). A variety of other regions may be more implicated in automatic processes related to social rewards or positive **valence** (**orbitofrontal cortex** or **ventral** (lower) **medial** (midline) prefrontal cortex, vmPFC: Harris, McClure, van den Bos, Cohen, & Fiske, 2007; van den Bos, McClure, Harris, Fiske, & Cohen, 2007; right **insula**: Cunningham, Raye, & Johnson, 2004; **basal ganglia**: Lieberman, Gaunt, Gilbert, & Trope, 2002; and ventral **striatum**: Cikara, Botvinick, & Fiske, 2011; O'Doherty, 2004; O'Doherty, Kringelbach, Rolls, Hornak, & Andrews, 2001); evidence understanding these valence linkages develops as we write.

Besides the amygdala and reward areas, the more reflex-like, relative automatic forms of social cognition apparently implicate (a) the **lateral** temporal cortex (posterior **superior temporal sulcus**, pSTS, and **temporal pole**), (b) the ventral medial prefrontal cortex (vmPFC), and (c) the **dorsal** anterior cingulate cortex (dACC). Figure 2.1 shows the locations of these areas, for those

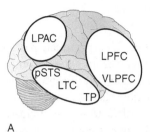

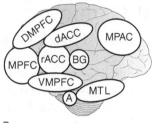

A

B

X-System (Automaticity)

Ventromedial PFC (VPFC) [BA11]
Basal Ganglia (BG)
Amygdala (A)
Lateral Temporal Cortex (LTC)
Posterior Superior Temporal Sulcus (pSTS)
Temporal Pole (TP)
Dorsal Anterior Cingulate (dACC)

C-System (Control)

Lateral PFC (LPFC)
Medial Temporal Lobe (MTL)
Medial Parietal Cortex (MPAC)
Lateral Parietal Cortex (LPAC)
Rostral ACC (rACC)
Medial PFC (MPFC) [BA10]
Dorsomedial PFC (DMPFC) [BA8/9]

Figures 2.1 and 2.2   Hypothesized neural correlates of the C-system supporting reflective social cognition (analogous to controlled processing) and the X-system supporting reflexive social cognition (analogous to automatic processing) displayed on a canonical brain rendering from (a) lateral (side) and (b) medial (center) views

Source: Adapted from "Social cognitive neuroscience: A review of core processes" by M. D. Lieberman, p. 262. Reprinted, with permission, from the *Annual Review of Psychology*, Volume 58. Copyright 2007, by Annual Reviews, www.annualreviews.org

inclined toward brain imaging. For those not so inclined, the point is that relatively automatic social cognitive-affective processes dissociate from relatively controlled ones in the neural areas typically activated (Lieberman, 2007).

Subliminal priming is not limited to emotionally significant cues; emotionally neutral concepts also can be primed below awareness (Dijksterhuis, 2004; Nosek, Hawkins, & Frazier, 2012; Payne, 2012). Conceptual priming that is not primarily affective is likely to invoke brain systems particularly involved in pattern-matching, categorizing, and identifying processes that implicate the inferior **temporal cortex** (Lieberman et al., 2002). A prime's perceptual pattern and cognitive category influence perceptions and interpretations of related subsequent stimuli, especially ambiguous ones; the neural accounts fit the cognitive activation data.

In addition to priming emotions and neutral cognitions, subliminal priming can affect behavior (Aarts, 2012; Ferguson & Bargh, 2004a). In the Bargh et al. (1996) study that opened this section, after participants' subliminal exposure to different race faces and subsequent provocation, the experimenter privately rated the participant's behavior on irritability, hostility, anger, and unco-operativeness, based on their interaction. Non-Black participants primed with Black faces behaved in reliably more hostile ways when provoked.

Subliminal priming studies are not easy to run; they require that the prime be displayed precisely and reliably for exceedingly brief times, and often that the prime be masked immediately afterward by perceptually related but conceptually neutral stimuli. For example, a subliminally primed word might be immediately followed by a scrambled letter-string of the same length; a subliminally primed face might be immediately masked by a random pattern of color-matched clusters covering the same visual area. A **subliminal prime** has to pass the objective standard of registering on the senses but not exceed the subjective standard of registering on awareness. The delicate threshold between perceptual-but-not-conscious impact depends on the prime, participant, current goal, context, and technical features of the presentation screen (Dijksterhuis et al., 2005). Each factor can change a prime's tendency to be activated above or below perception, and, if so, above or below consciousness. All this means that advertisers, for example, cannot easily convey subliminal messages, although in theory they could (Cooper & Cooper, 2002).

So far, the illustrative experiments all exemplify the most subliminal, **preconscious** form of automatic processing, in which people are not aware of the priming cue, nor of its effects on their reaction to a relevant stimulus. Although the most dramatic automatic response, fully automatic processes are likely to be rare. This kind of empirical demonstration most usefully makes the theoretical point that even unconsciously activated concepts prime related concepts, which then shape the interpretation of subsequent stimuli, all outside awareness. This fits the most stringent definition of pure **automaticity**, which, as noted earlier, is unintentional, uncontrollable, efficient, autonomous, and outside awareness (Bargh, 1997).

Conscious Priming

Less dramatic but probably more impactful on a daily basis, **postconscious automaticity** entails conscious perception of the prime but no awareness of its effects on subsequent reactions (see Table 2.1). In one study, participants first imagined a day in the life of a typical professor, listing activities and lifestyle. Then they played Trivial Pursuit, the knowledge quiz game. Primed participants actually outscored other participants who had skipped the professor-priming task (Dijksterhuis & van Knippenberg, 1998). Although the mechanism remains unclear, they may have been prompted to try harder, use better strategies, or trust their hunches. Priming a soccer hooligan or the trait of stupidity was not helpful to the knowledge test, but priming the trait of intelligence was. As another example, students unscrambled word lists to make sentences that primed the category "elderly" (and thus, slowness); they walked to the elevator more slowly after the experiment (Bargh et al., 1996). In still another study in that series, students covertly but consciously primed with the trait "rudeness" were faster to interrupt another person.

Many priming studies replicate with either postconscious or preconscious priming, as in the Bargh et al. (1996) series. As another example, students primed either consciously or preconsciously with words related to the elderly then expressed more conservative attitudes; others primed with the skinhead category expressed more prejudiced attitudes (Kawakami, Dovidio, & Dijksterhuis, 2003). Both pre- and postconscious effects operate similarly, in part because people are unacquainted with priming effects, so even conscious primes – if subtle and covert – do not typically prompt efforts to counteract them.

Chronic Accessibility

Somewhere around preconscious and postconscious automaticity are individual differences in **chronically accessible concepts**. People may or may not be aware that they habitually code other people in terms of, say, their friendliness, intelligence, or independence (Higgins, King, & Maven, 1982). Nevertheless, particular trait dimensions tend to capture different people's attention and repeatedly surface in their impressions of others. One can simply count the frequency of traits used to describe a series of familiar others. The chronically used traits ease people's impression formation processes along familiar, well-established grooves, for better or worse, but certainly more efficiently than would be the case without these habitual sources of influence.

How do people develop certain favorite trait dimensions? Certain traits might be family favorites ("this is my smart one; this is my nice one") or cultural favorites (Americans tend to focus on honesty and friendliness) or reflect survival skills (in certain neighborhoods, for example, aggressiveness) or job requirements (probation officers judging trustworthiness). If a person (e.g., a probation officer) over time judges hundreds of instances of behavior as honest or dishonest, some of those repeated inferences (e.g., shoplifting is dishonest) will show specific practice effects, becoming faster and easier to invoke over time. The development of automaticity occurs through practice, a process termed **proceduralization**. Becoming a procedure can happen relatively quickly, within a few dozen trials, and can last over at least a day's delay (E. R. Smith & Branscombe, 1987, 1988; E. R. Smith, Branscombe, & Bormann, 1988).

Procedural processes constitute one theoretical account of some priming effects. People may start with the effortful use of general rules that are independent of the particular setting (behavior reflects a trait), but with practice they can make automatic inferences about certain frequently encountered stimuli (E. R. Smith, 1984). Proceduralization involves two kinds of practice effects. With practice, any judgment of honesty, regardless of the particular behavior, will speed up, showing a trait-specific practice effect. A second kind of practice effect speeds judgments of traits even in general (E. R. Smith, 1990; E. R. Smith et al., 1988). That is, proceduralization requires repeated execution of the same process, for example, making trait inferences; it can entail judging identical content such as judging only honesty (E. R. Smith & Lerner, 1986). But it can also entail more general processes, such as rapidly judging any trait. With consistent practice, both kinds of judgments (specific and general) become proceduralized so that exposure to an appropriate stimulus (e.g., either honesty or any trait) automatically speeds the inference. Chapter 4 discusses different memory systems that may account for these two effects (E. R. Smith, 1984), but the point here is that practice can automate the judgment process.

Does it matter socially that procedural (automatic) judgments speed up people's responses? Yes: well-practiced judgments preempt equally reasonable but less-practiced judgments (E. R. Smith, 1990). For example, if a teacher is used to judging intelligence, a person who is intelligent but unsociable would be viewed positively, primarily in terms of the intelligence; in contrast, a sales supervisor might emphasize the unsociability over the intelligence and make a negative judgment. The speed-up of proceduralized judgments may also have implications for stereotyping: People are members of several social categories; observers' well-practiced reliance on, say, race might cause them to emphasize that dimension over others, such as age, gender, social class, or individual traits (Zárate & Smith, 1990). Proceduralization of judgment also may matter in accounting for the speed and unconscious quality of some affective responses (Branscombe, 1988).

Conclusion about Automaticity

As we have seen so far, automated responses differ in degree. Some encoding occurs automatically, below consciousness, in subliminal or preconscious perception. Postconscious processes are cued by a conscious prime and can proceed rapidly, without effort, intent, or awareness. Practice seems to be the crucial element in developing automatic responses, as research on proceduralized processes suggests.

Certain types of judgments seem especially likely to be automated: Trait inferences seem to be necessary first steps in encoding information about others (see Chapter 6). This makes sense in that trait inferences allow people to predict what others will do in future encounters. Moreover, much of the time, people's behavior probably does reflect what they will do again later, at least in the situations in which we habitually encounter them. We can also explain people's behavior rapidly via their roles in situations; later chapters discuss the cultural variation in what comes to mind easily.

Other types of encoding are likely to be automatic as well, although there is less accumulated evidence on these points: Self-relevant knowledge is likely to be encoded automatically (see Chapter 5). Certain people (e.g., depressed ones) automatically encode certain content (e.g., negative traits) about themselves (Bargh & Tota, 1988). For people in general, stimuli related to threat would be likely candidates for automatic encoding; for example, even slightly angry-looking faces trigger rapid judgments of untrustworthiness and immediate amygdala responses (Todorov et al., 2008), and an angry face in a crowd of happy faces stands out (more than vice versa), suggesting a preattentive search for threatening cues (Hansen & Hansen, 1988a); negative cues may carry particular weight preconsciously (Erdley & D'Agostino, 1988). Stimuli relevant to our current needs and goals may be encoded automatically (Aarts, 2012; Bruner, 1957), so people especially notice others their own age, and men especially notice attractive women (Rodin, 1987), a process that may represent automatic encoding. Research on all kinds of automaticity, especially automatic behavior, led us to coin the term **activated actors** in Chapter 1. Much social reaction is relatively automatic.

Why might so many of people's social cognitive responses be automatic? The main reason, of course, is sheer efficiency. To the extent that people are much of the time **cognitive misers**, they simply take well-worn shortcuts because they cannot always deal with other people in all their complexity. Apart from sheer processing capacity, people can recruit similar previous decisions that worked well enough in the past, in order to predict adequate outcomes of similar decisions in the future. Finally, unconscious thought can manage more complex information more rapidly, leading to more coherent and clear choices (Dijksterhuis, 2004).

Automatic activation of mental representations subliminally (preconsciously) and supraliminally (consciously) have similar effects. Both can influence evaluations and emotions, associated cognitions and strategies, and behavior. The main difference is that activation above awareness can invoke controlled strategies, if one is aware that the prime might affect responses. That takes us to our next topic.

CONTROLLED PROCESSES

Just as automaticity comes in degrees, so does control. A **controlled process** is any process in which the perceiver's conscious intent substantially determines how the process operates. Midway along the range between relatively automatic processes of the last section and relatively controlled processes of this section lie goal-driven automatic processes. They could have appeared at the end of the previous section because they occupy the boundary between the two extremes (see Table 2.1).

Goal-Driven Automatic Processes

As befits its location at the boundary, **goal-dependent automaticity** is automatic according to some of the criteria, such as lack of awareness of the process itself, not needing to monitor the process to completion, and lack of intending all the specific outcomes. For example, on a bleary Saturday morning, more than one distracted parent operating on autopilot has been known to feed the cereal to the dog and the kibbles to the kids (A. P. Fiske, Haslam, & Fiske, 1991). In this example, two goal-dependent automatic processes interfere with each other. A simpler example would be someone at a party asking about your research, whereupon you launch into a standardized automatic account more suited to your thesis committee than to a prospective romantic interest.

However, by definition, goal-dependent automaticity also varies by the perceiver's goals, so it is partially responsive to intentional control. Goal-dependent automaticity thus is not entirely automatic in that it requires intentional processing and depends on the task undertaken. Conscious intent can launch preconscious automaticity.

Nevertheless, even goals can also be preconscious, if a **goal** is defined as a mental representation of desired outcomes (Aarts, 2012). One example is **habits**, behaviors that one repeats frequently. Activating relevant goals cues thoughts about habitual behaviors. along with the relevant behavior itself. When bike riders think about getting to the other side of town, bike-related thoughts are accessible (Aarts & Dijksterhuis, 2000). This is not the case for people who do not habitually ride their bikes. The goal–habit linkage likely drives more of our actions than we like to admit, as one example of goal-driven automaticity.

Other examples of goal-dependent automaticity are illustrated by what happens at a party when one approaches some people and avoids others. Attending the party presupposes the goal to socialize, and various relatively automatic processes support this goal: spontaneous trait inferences based on other people's behavior (see Chapter 6) or face (see Chapter 3). People form first impressions at a party, deciding rapidly and superficially who looks entertaining and who looks boring. This process has both automatic and controlled components. Because **spontaneous trait inferences** (elaborated soon) occur more under certain goals (socializing) than others (as a distraction while memorizing a phone number), spontaneous trait inference is goal dependent and therefore not fully automatic. However, once launched, such trait inferences (who looks entertaining or boring) do seem to occur unintentionally and without much awareness, so they are automatic once the appropriate goal triggers the process.

Many social cognitive processes qualify as goal-driven automaticity. Forming impressions depends on one's goals, as a later section details, but the process itself otherwise can occur without much awareness or effort. Remembering someone's attributes likewise depends on one's goals, but otherwise occurs automatically (Chapter 4). Noticing covariation between linked social events (Chapter 7) may be another example. A variety of other goal-directed processes with substantial automatic components – such as typing, driving, or perhaps rehashing the same old issues in a relationship – also illustrate this category.

Goal-Inconsistent Automaticity

Sometimes people's goals trigger automatic thoughts consistent with their conscious preferences, but people can't always think what they want, even if they try (Wenzlaff & Wegner, 2000). Here's an example of **goal-inconsistent automaticity**: Try to spend the next 60 seconds *not* thinking about a white bear but noting the instances when you fail. (If you try it, you'll find it's harder than you think.) A pair of studies (Wegner, Schneider, Carter, & White, 1987) asked participants to think aloud for five minutes while suppressing thoughts of a white bear; however, they were asked to ring a bell whenever they did think about a white bear. They were unable to suppress white-bear thoughts. Moreover, when asked afterward to think about white bears, they showed a rebound effect, thinking about white bears quite a lot; most important, they thought about white bears even more than did people who had been explicitly thinking about them all along. Both parts of this phenomenon are familiar to dieters, unrequited lovers, and procrastinators. (The dieter in particular knows all too well the potential for a postdiet binge of food thoughts and compensatory eating.) The only way out, as successful dieters and practiced meditators know, is to find a substitute thought. Participants who thought about a red Volkswagen as a distracter were no more successful in suppressing white-bear thoughts, but they showed no rebound afterward, suggesting that the suppression had not created the same kind of mental logjam as it had without the distracting thought.

The process is ironic (Wegner, 1994): Because one has the goal to suppress a specific thought, one sets up an automatic detection-monitoring system, which keeps the forbidden thought active, making it come to mind more easily. **Thought suppression** involves the failure to prevent unwanted cognitions, through the ironic process of monitoring their occurrence. This kind of goal-dependent automaticity shows how goals can prime automatic processes that defeat the very goals they were intended to serve. For example, people who care about suppressing their stereotypes can do so when they are self-focused (attending to their internal standards), but this spontaneous suppression of stereotypes nevertheless produces a **rebound** effect: Stereotypic associations return with a vengeance (Macrae, Bodenhausen, & Milne, 1998).

Future neuroscience may identify the neural correlates of this goal-driven automatic inconsistency. The anterior cingulate cortex, which monitors a variety of disruptions (Botvinick, Cohen, & Carter, 2004), also monitors attempts to suppress unwanted thoughts (Wyland, Kelley, Macrae, Gordon, & Heatherton, 2003). This may be one neural indicator of the ironic process, showing how deeply embedded it is in fundamental systems of goal maintenance.

Table 2.2   Rumination

Stage	Unrequited attraction example
(a) Initially intensified repetition of the interrupted behavior	Despite rebuffs, one persists in attempts to contact the loved person
(b) Problem solving at lower and lower levels	One tries to calculate details of the person's schedule and habits to maximize successful contact
(c) End-state thinking	One fantasizes about the desired outcome of being together
(d) Trying to abandon the goal	One attempts to give up on the person
(e) Channelized thinking	Even after resolving to give up, one may persist in thinking along well-worn associative pathways that all lead to thoughts of the other
(f) Depression from continued powerlessness	If one cannot escape from the preoccupation, one must mourn the lost ideal

The difficulty of thought suppression is implicated in the inability of depressed people to avoid negative thoughts, although they can suppress positive thoughts just as well as control subjects can (Wenzlaff, Wegner, & Roper, 1988). As Chapter 5 shows, depression makes negative thoughts more accessible. For example, depressed people perseverate on (i.e., persist in ruminating about) failures longer than do nondepressed people (Carver, La Voie, Kuhl, & Ganellen, 1988). Providing depressed people with positive distracter thoughts seems to be helpful in the suppression of negative material (Wenzlaff et al., 1988).

When not successfully repressed, a single intrusive thought may lead the way to brooding and rumination; that is, unwanted thinking about a particular object for a long time. **Rumination** – repetitive, counterproductive thinking – may stem both from cognitive associations cued by goal-directed thinking, as already noted, and from the motivation to remember uncompleted tasks (Zeigarnik, 1927). Rumination apparently entails several stages, illustrated by the difficulty of not dwelling on an unrequited attraction (Table 2.2). After trying in vain to reconnect, one calculates, fantasizes, agonizes, persists, and generally perseverates (Martin & Tesser, 1989). One study asked newly arrived college women how much they thought about a close person they had left behind; ruminations were positively related to the number of overlapping goals (shared activities) that were interrupted by being apart (Millar, Tesser, & Millar, 1988).

Although some of the most entertaining research on goal-directed automaticity has emphasized people's failures, much of the time goals can aid the performance of habitual behavior. As creatures of habit, this result may be less surprising but still important because adaptive forms of automaticity run our days.

Intent

Having moved through preconscious, postconscious, chronic, and goal-dependent automaticity, as well as unintended consequences of automaticity, we land on intent, a crucial feature of control.

Table 2.3 Characteristics of intent

Example: Partner says "I hate you!"		
Having options:	Unintended default:	Intentional alternative:
How to interpret	Take at face value	Excuse as person having a bad day
↓	↓	↓
Making the hard choice	Reciprocate hostility	Not to reciprocate hostility
↓	↓	↓
Paying attention	React thoughtlessly	Focus on other person's situation
↓	↓	↓
Result	Process is less intentional	Process is more intentional

When is it fair to say that we fully intend a particular train of thought? This matters because people are often held legally and morally responsible for intended consequences. Attributed intent informs a range of social problems, such as prejudice, aggression, biased judgments, and the like. For example, consider prejudice (detailed in Chapters 11–12). If people's prejudice is not strictly intentional, then perhaps they are not responsible for its consequences. Similarly, aggression in self-defense or the heat of jealous passion is viewed as less bad than premeditated aggression, which is defined by intent.

How do laypeople, psychologists, and the law define intent (Table 2.3)? People are said to intend their train of thought and resulting interpretation if they perceive themselves as *having options* to think in other ways (S. T. Fiske, 1989). Hence, if on reflection one understood that another interpretation were possible, then the way one does think seems more intentional. For example, if one interprets a family member's "I hate you!" as a murder threat, reasonable people might claim one had options to think in other ways. Similarly, if one categorizes an African American man in a three-piece suit as a potential mugger, reasonable people might note that one had options to make other interpretations.

When one does have options, a particular choice is likely to be easier, and others are likely to be harder. That is, if one's accustomed way of thinking is the easy way, then *making the hard choice* is likely to be seen as especially intentional, by ordinary observers, psychologists, and even legal experts. Thus a disagreeable person who resists interpreting family hostility as a threat will be viewed as overcoming a predisposition to respond in the easier way, and this harder response will be viewed as especially controlled and intended. Similarly, if one overcomes a societal stereotype of a young street tough as necessarily a mugger, observers will judge this as an act of will more so than if one goes along with the prevailing stereotypes. Rejecting the default, making the harder choice, is seen as especially intentional. However, if one has the capability of thinking either way, then both the hard and easy choice are intentional by the first criterion.

Finally, people implement their intended way of thinking by *paying attention*. Hence if a person wanted to interpret an intimate's hostility as a provocation to violence and attended to details of revenge, observers would interpret this as intentional. Similarly, to overcome a habitual stereotype applied to another person, paying attention to nonstereotypic attributes is the most effective route (S. T. Fiske & Neuberg, 1990). **Intentional though**t is characterized by having options, most obviously by making the hard choice, and enacted by paying attention to implementing the intent.

From intent, society takes a short step to responsibility. For example, completely unintentional discrimination is not illegal, and accidentally killing someone (manslaughter) is viewed less negatively than killing someone on purpose (murder). Regardless, one is not held socially responsible for one's thoughts, only for one's actions. The intent problem matters especially when analyzing the thoughts that provoked a particular action, but this analysis presumes, as society often does, that people have free will.

Conscious Will

Some social psychologists question the extent of free will. Is the automaticity of social cognition the "cognitive monster" that cannot be stopped (Bargh, 1999)? Perhaps situations automatically cue certain motives, which Bargh (1997) calls **auto-motives**. In this view, situations determine behavior fairly directly. Situations trigger goals, and goals trigger actions – all automatically and outside consciousness. Bargh provocatively aligns himself with Skinnerian stimulus-response behaviorism, which was overthrown by the cognitive revolution in the middle of the 20th century. Back to the future: Social cognition comes full circle in the activated actor metaphor of the social (non)thinker.

In a related vein, Wegner argues that **conscious will** is an illusion created by people thinking about an action before performing it (Wegner, 2003; Wegner & Wheately, 1999). If the thought precedes the action, fits the action, and explains the action, people infer that the thought caused it. People often think about an action before performing it, so they infer that the thought caused the action. But what if something else (e.g., the situation) cued the thought, and the action was independent?

To test this, experimenters first had to create the thought that allegedly caused the result. They subliminally primed the desired endpoint for a square moving through a grid displayed on a computer screen (Aarts, Custers, & Wegner, 2005). Both the participant and the computer controlled squares moving in opposite directions through the grid. When the participant pressed a key, both squares started moving, and when the participant stopped, the endpoint of one square was revealed, without making it clear whether it was the computer's square or the participant's own square. Participants rated whether they felt they had caused that outcome (i.e., whether it was their square or the computer's). Prior subliminal priming of the endpoint biased participants' beliefs that they had caused it, though it did not actually affect how they performed the action (i.e., the timing of their key-press). The participants were more likely to experience **agency** (personal authorship of the outcome) when subliminally primed beforehand to think of the outcome. People can think erroneously that their actions caused outcomes that they demonstrably did not control.

In the extreme, people think they can control even other people's outcomes and behavior. In one experiment (Pronin, Wegner, McCarthy, & Rodriguez, 2006), people developed the illusion that they had magically caused someone else's outcomes. Some participants were first induced to harbor evil thoughts about a confederate who was obnoxious (compared to neutral), and then participants role-played a "witch doctor" by sticking pins into a "voodoo doll" allegedly representing the other person. When the victim indeed reported feeling a slight headache, participants indicated that they felt causally responsible. Similar effects occurred for spectators who silently rooted for a peer shooting basketballs into a hoop when the shooter subsequently succeeded. They felt that their silent wishes had helped the person to succeed.

These demonstrations make the crucial point that, besides not controlling our thoughts, we do not control our own (or other people's) actions as much as we think we do. Is this a reversion to behaviorism? Do situations entirely control behavior, and people's intentions merely correlate as irrelevant epiphenomena? Social cognitive work draws on mental concepts that were forbidden to behaviorists, but social psychology need not pit the conscious person against the deterministic situation (Mischel, 1997). Both are important, and the automaticity of everyday life and the illusion of conscious control remind us that many processes do not operate through conscious intent.

Consciousness

If our conscious control does not influence our actions as much as we might believe, what does occupy our minds? What is in consciousness and why? Consciousness has traditionally been the topic of philosophers, psychoanalysts, and (recently) cognitive scientists. We will not attempt a comprehensive review but merely note some points that potentially inform social cognition research and that increasingly matter as more social cognition researchers tackle these issues (Winkielman & Schooler, 2012).

William James (1890/1983) described **consciousness** eloquently as the stream of thought (Table 2.4):

> Consciousness, then, does not appear to itself chopped up in bits. Such words as "chain" or "train" do not describe it as fitly as it presents itself in the first instance. It is nothing jointed; it flows. A "river" or a "stream" are the metaphors by which it is most naturally described. (p. 233)

Consciousness was not only a stream to James, it was a stream "teeming with objects and relations" (p. 219) private and perpetually separate from the nearby streams belonging to other people.

Consciousness subsequently received a bad name from introspectionist experiments (recall from Chapter 1). Moreover, given the inherent inability to reproduce such introspective data publicly, and given the rise of anti-mentalistic behaviorism, consciousness went into hiding. With early work in cognitive psychology, consciousness crept back in as "attention," then interpreted as what was being held in current awareness (see Chapter 3). Subsequently, some cognitive psychologists narrowly defined consciousness as either (a) simply being aware of (able to talk about) something or, alternatively, (b) being aware of something only in the sense that it reflects one's

Table 2.4   Perspectives on consciousness

Who:	What:
William James	Stream of thought
Behaviorists	Irrelevant epiphenomenon
Introspectionists	Reportable thoughts, or
	Thoughts consistent with behavior
Early cognitivists	Executive directing mental processes
Attributionists	Necessary condition for intent
Later cognitivists	Constructed from accessible concepts
Learning cognitivists	Involved in troubleshooting
Social cognitionists	Being awake and mindful, or
	Subjectively experiencing cognitions available for report and intentional use
Descriptivists	Stimulus field composed of thoughts, emotional experiences, and body sensations that can compete successfully with the external world

behavior even though one might not be able to report on it (Bower, 1990). In the first case, one might report feeling hungry and thinking about food; in the second case, one might find oneself snacking without conscious awareness of feeling hungry or intending to eat.

Consciousness has been viewed more broadly by various cognitive psychologists (Mandler & Nakamura, 1987). However, these views are not well integrated with each other because they usually represent particular attempts to solve other theoretical problems using the concept of consciousness. One view represents consciousness as an epiphenomenon irrelevant to ongoing mental processes, reminiscent of behaviorist views, although distinct because of drawing heavily on cognitive mechanisms.

Another idea is that consciousness is an executive that directs mental structures. When memory contents activate sufficiently above a threshold, they are conscious, coming into short-term or working memory (see Chapters 3 and 4; D. A. Norman & Shallice, 1986; Shallice, 1972, 1978). At that point, the mental representations can be utilized under conscious control. As an **executive**, consciousness can inhibit and therefore control automatic associations, so it makes them responsive to one's current intents (Posner & Rothbart, 2007). A parallel social cognition account similarly labels consciousness simply as an "executor" (Wyer & Srull, 1986).

Another perspective views consciousness as necessary for human understanding and intent. As noted, consciousness determines how people assign blame (K. G. Shaver, 1985) and intent (S. T. Fiske, 1989; Uleman, 1989). That is, one cannot discuss what people intend to do unless one assumes that they are conscious of at least some aspects of their intent.

One novel, provocative viewpoint represents consciousness as a constructed device. In this view, consciousness makes sense of currently activated unconscious contents using a number of applicable concepts. Consciousness is constructed from the accessible concepts. It operates within the constraints of a limited-capacity system, to further the goals of the moment (Mandler & Nakamura, 1987; Marcel, 1983a, 1983b).

Consciousness is involved in learning that proceeds from conscious to automatic and unconscious (as in learning to drive a car). In learning, consciousness helps form new associations, as previously separate items come together into awareness. Should an otherwise over-learned, automatic sequence later fail, consciousness reappears in troubleshooting. And consciousness is necessary for choice, which compares two alternatives held in awareness at the same time. In this view, constructive consciousness serves various functions in ongoing goal-directed behavior. Cognitive psychologists generally have been concerned with such functions of consciousness.

Finally, faced with this range of interpretations, social cognition researchers Winkielman and Schooler (2012) define first-order consciousness as being awake and mindful, subjectively experiencing cognitions available for report and intentional use. But second-order **meta-cognition** is people's beliefs about their own thinking processes, important in daydreaming, as we see next.

Contents of Consciousness

Social-personality psychologists have focused on the contents of consciousness just for its own sake. They describe ongoing consciousness as the stimulus field composed of thoughts, emotional experiences, and body sensations (i.e., daydreaming) that can compete successfully with the external world (Singer, 1978, 1984). Such internal landscapes (Csikszentmihalyi, 1978; Csikszentmihalyi & Larson, 1984) often include unfinished business or current concerns (Klinger, 1978; Klinger, Barta, & Maxeiner, 1980): unmet goals, whether trivial low-level projects (getting to the gym), problems in significant relationships (Will my true love marry me?), or value dilemmas (Should I cooperate in my friend's tax evasion?). College students' thoughts are mostly specific, detailed, visual, unfanciful, controllable, and related to the immediate situation (Klinger, 1978).

Kinds of Thought

Ongoing thought may be **stimulus dependent** (focused on the current environment) or **stimulus independent** (mind-wandering) (Antrobus, Singer, Goldstein, & Fortgang, 1970; Klinger, 1978; Singer, 1966). Even when highly motivated to attend to the environment, we constantly experience stimulus-independent thoughts (Antrobus et al., 1970; Smallwood & Schooler, 2006). **Mind-wandering** activates the brain's default network (Mason, Norton, Van, Wegner, Grafton, & Macrae, 2007), which overlaps considerably with the social-cognition network, consistent with people daydreaming about themselves, others, and their relationships.

Dependency on the outside world is not the only way to carve up the contents of consciousness. A separate set of dimensions differentiates between **operant thought** (instrumental and problem solving) and **respondent thought** processes (ordinary distractions, unbidden images) (Klinger, 1977). Most daily thought is operant, with respondent components (Klinger, 1978). That is, while you are reading this book, your thought is operant; when you stop to think about how you will choose a term paper topic, that thought also is operant. But when you daydream about the party last night, that is respondent thought. People's tasks and their stage of implementation influence the proportion of operant thoughts (e.g., Heckhausen & Gollwitzer, 1987), as do individual differences in task (operant) focus (e.g., Jolly & Reardon, 1985).

Although these two dimensions of thought – stimulus dependent versus stimulus independent, operant versus respondent – may seem completely redundant, they are not. A person may have operant (goal-directed) thoughts that depend on external stimuli or thoughts that are stimulus independent and wholly internal (as when one concentrates on making a decision). Similarly, one may have respondent (spontaneous) thoughts that do or do not depend on external stimuli (funny how the computer keyboard can suddenly demand cleaning just when one is trying write the first sentence of a paper).

Sampling People's Thoughts

Strangers often think newly introduced psychologists or psychology students can read their minds. Fortunately or unfortunately, psychologists have only indirect access to people's inner worlds (see Table 2.5). Some thought-sampling studies examine people's thoughts while they attempt to concentrate on a perceptual task (Antrobus et al., 1970; Smallwood & Schooler, 2006); others attach people to electronic pagers that beep randomly during the day, prompting participants to write down their just-preceding thoughts (Klinger, 1978). **Experience-sampling** methods that allow researchers to query participants about their current states at random moments have explored conscious experiences regarding cooperative learning, loneliness, parenthood, mood, well-being, and everyday psychotic perceptions (respectively: Delle Fave & Massimini, 2004; Hawkley, Burleson, Berntson, & Cacioppo, 2003; Peterson & Miller, 2004; Oishi, Diener, Napa Scollon, & Biswas-Diener, 2004; Updegraff, Gable, & Taylor, 2004; Verdoux, Husky, Tournier, Sorbara, & Swendsen, 2003).

In the laboratory, random **probes** ask people to report their mind-wandering, stimulus-independent thought, zoning out while doing a primary task; together with their spontaneous reports of mind-wandering, these estimates reveal extensive stimulus-independent thought (Smallwood & Schooler, 2006).

Experimenters also thought-sample by asking participants to **think aloud** as they read information about another person (Erber & Fiske, 1984; S. T. Fiske, Neuberg, Beattie, & Milberg, 1987; Ruscher & Fiske, 1990). The taped recordings provide spontaneous and relatively unfiltered reactions, which enables researchers to observe the impression-formation process in detail (S. T. Fiske & Ruscher, 1989; S. E. Taylor & Fiske, 1981). For example, one can trace the gradual development of suspicion about another person's ulterior motives and the evolving negative impressions (Marchand & Vonk, 2005).

Related studies undertake examining people's thoughts during ongoing social interaction. In these studies of **naturalistic social cognition** (Ickes, Robertson, Tooke, & Teng, 1986; Ickes, Tooke, Stinson, Baker, & Bissonnette, 1988), two strangers are unobtrusively videotaped as they pass the time awaiting the experimenter's return. After being informed that they have been recorded on a candid camera and giving permission for use of the tapes, participants separately replay the tape, stopping it each time they recall having a particular thought or feeling. This research examines such dimensions of the interaction partners' thoughts and feelings as their object (self, partner, others, environment), their valence (positive or negative), and their perspective (own or other's).

For example, people's positive thoughts about their partners are related to their involvement in the interaction (as measured by both their verbal and nonverbal behavior). Moreover, in same-sex

Table 2.5 Methods for accessing the content of thought

Method	Technique
Experience sampling	Beeper cues reports of current thought during daily life
Random probes	Cued reports of current mind-wandering and awareness of it during lab
Cognitive response	Report thoughts immediately after processing a communication
Think aloud protocols	Verbalize own reactions as process online
Naturalistic social cognition	Report thoughts during interaction when viewing video afterwards
Role-play participation	Imagine self in and report reactions to partial or overheard interaction

dyads, male strangers show greater convergence in their thought/feeling content than do female strangers, perhaps because they operate within a more narrow range of interactional involvement and thus have to monitor their interaction more closely. That is, in Anglo-American culture, male strangers carefully regulate the degree of intimacy they display, and this results in their thinking and feeling similarly because their options are relatively limited. In contrast, the interactional involvement of female strangers is less constrained, but their thought/feeling content shows more convergence in taking each other's perspective and in focusing on third parties (Ickes et al., 1988). This paradigm explores empathic accuracy by comparing what people think their partners are experiencing and what the partners actually experience. In married couples, empathic accuracy helps emotional intimacy except when one person's thoughts are relationship threatening, in which case empathic accuracy naturally reduces the perceiver's felt closeness (Simpson, Oriña, & Ickes, 2003).

Finally, one can sample people's thoughts within relatively realistic but controlled social settings. Participants **role-play participation** in one part of an audiotaped interpersonal encounter; that is, the tape portrays half the interaction and the participant mentally supplies the remainder. Alternatively, the tape depicts an overheard conversation in which two people discuss a third party, and the participant then role-plays the third party as the self. At predetermined points the tape stops, and participants articulate their thoughts. People report more irrational thoughts (i.e., rigid absolute demands) in stressful, evaluative social situations, and this is especially true for people who are socially anxious (Davison, Robins, & Johnson, 1983; Davison & Zighelboim, 1987; Kashima & Davison, 1989). The inventiveness of these various paradigms illustrates the challenge of obtaining people's thoughts online, during social interactions.

Conclusions about Consciousness

Studies that attempt to access people's thoughts must do so with their cooperation and, more importantly, within their ability to comply. Chapter 8 will describe controversies about people's ability to access their own thought processes. People often cannot report accurately on what affects their behavior (Nisbett & Wilson, 1977b), suggesting that they have imperfect access to at least some of their own thought processes. Nevertheless, within certain limits, people can report usefully on the content of their thoughts under certain conditions: if they do so simultaneously with their thoughts, if the relevant thoughts are already in verbal form, and if they are asked to report content and not process (Ericsson & Simon, 1980; S. T. Fiske & Ruscher, 1989; S. E. Taylor & Fiske, 1981).

Cognition and social cognition researchers think about consciousness in ways that go beyond William James's teeming stream. Consciousness may be an executive, a necessary condition for intent, or a construction inferred from material activated unconsciously. It tends to be occupied by unfinished business, but it may be more or less instrumental and more or less dependent on external stimuli. Studies sampling thought during interaction are currently inventing a number of techniques to cope with this particular challenge. However, all studies of consciousness must be wary of the introspective-access problem.

MOTIVATIONS INFLUENCE WHICH MODES OPERATE

If the primary modes of social cognition are automatic, unconscious thoughts versus controlled, conscious thoughts, with gradations between them, how do people move between modes? As the motivated tactician metaphor implies, people's tactics (the modes they use) depend on their motives. In social cognition, a variety of motives have mattered over the past decades. They go by various names, but five terms capture the most frequent motives: belonging, understanding, controlling, enhancing self, and trusting ingroup (S. T. Fiske, 2010). As a mnemonic device, consider them a buc(k)et of motives (Table 2.6).

Belonging

Social cognition is importantly *social*, as noted in Chapter 1. Social cognition preoccupies people because our social survival depends on it. People do not do well unless they are motivated to get

Table 2.6　Motivations that influence modes of social cognition

Motive	Goal
Belonging	Being accepted by other people, one's group
Understanding	Socially shared cognition; belief that one's views correspond to those of one's group
Controlling	Influencing one's own outcomes that depend on other people
Enhancing self	Viewing self positively or at least sympathetically
Trusting ingroup	Viewing people, at least in one's own group, positively

along with at least a few other people. The age-adjusted mortality risk of social isolation is comparable to cigarette smoking; both cardiovascular and immune responses are damaged by isolation (House, Landis, & Umberson, 1988). People respond poorly to being ostracized: feeling bad, reporting less control, and losing a sense of belonging (Williams, Cheung, & Choi, 2000). The neural signature of social pain mimics the neural signature of physical pain in that both activate the anterior cingulate cortex (Eisenberger et al., 2003), which more generally responds to disruptions and inconsistencies (Botvinick et al., 2004). Clearly, the need to belong is central to people's health and well-being (Baumeister & Leary, 1995; Leary, 1990).

Not surprisingly, then, people's social cognition is shaped by their **belonging** motives to be accepted by other people. This is most evident in the belonging-related motives of socially shared understanding and social control (covered next), but belonging by itself also changes how and what people think. First, the focus of people's thoughts is importantly social. As just noted, people spend a lot of time thinking about current concerns in relationships, and as Chapter 1 noted, people's resting state may be social thought.

People's need to belong can motivate relatively automatic modes of impression formation designed to ease social interaction; people automatically categorize stimuli as related to "us" and "them," for instance (Perdue, Dovidio, Gurtman, & Tyler, 1990). More generally, people readily categorize themselves as part of a group (e.g., Tajfel, 1981; Turner, 1985), automatically attuned to its beliefs, norms, and roles. This feeling of belonging affects people's interpretation of social stimuli. In a classic study, students from Princeton and Dartmouth watched a football game between their schools and rated the number of infractions; school membership biased how many infractions students saw for their own versus the other team (Hastorf & Cantril, 1954). Belonging probably operated fairly automatically in this case. Belonging is also illustrated by the fact that people conform to the majority in relatively automatic ways (Wood, 2000).

The overall need to belong provides an orienting framework for studying social cognition, in that belonging underlies more specific cognitive motives, including social understanding and social control.

Understanding

The social motive that most obviously drives social cognition is **understanding**, the need for socially shared cognition. Socially shared understanding is the need to believe that one's views correspond to those of one's group (Turner, 1991, ch. 10). People think about other people in order to interact with them; one founder of American psychology, William James, noted "my thinking is first and last and always for my doing" (1890/1983, p. 960); much thinking and doing is social (S. T. Fiske, 1992, 1993). Understanding is the dominant motive driving most social cognition. Affiliative motivations make people share others' viewpoints (Sinclair, Lowery, Hardin, & Colangelo, 2005).

Automaticity often serves socially shared understanding well enough. However, people are sometimes socially motivated to be especially accurate or accountable to others (e.g., respectively, S. T. Fiske & Neuberg, 1990; Tetlock, 1992). Sometimes, also, people's level of information falls below acceptable levels (Kelley, 1972a), and this leads them to gather information. Sometimes, too, people arrive in a new place (e.g., the first week of college) or a new culture (e.g., traveling or immigrating), and they cannot assume their perceptions fit the general outlook (Guinote, 2001). When the necessity of socially shared understanding is uppermost, people switch to relatively deliberate processes, seeking and using a lot of information until their judgments become automated again. Socially shared understanding seeks to make the world more predictable, and when this need falls short, people deliberately engage in information seeking and analysis until understanding is restored.

Controlling

Social relationships make people interdependent; that is, their outcomes depend on each other (Thibaut & Kelley, 1959). When another person has **power** over desired resources, people's need for **controlling** tries to influence the contingencies between actions (what they do) and outcomes (what they get) (S. T. Fiske & Neuberg, 1990). Being outcome dependent often shifts people to more controlled, deliberate processes in an effort to feel in control. Control needs also appear in nonsocial circumstances, such as when one receives arbitrary feedback on one's performance, even from a computer, and this impaired sense of control carries over to social circumstances, making people seek additional information about other people (Pittman, 1998). In general, higher control needs make people deliberately seek additional information to avoid error and feel effective. Threatened control increases the apparent costs of being wrong, so people switch to deliberate modes as flexible motivated tacticians.

Control threats do sometimes occur under scarce resources (time pressure, mental fatigue), so pressures for a relatively automatic decision, any decision, increase. Pressures for **urgency** (quick decisions) and **permanence** (lasting decisions) come from various situational factors (Kruglanski & Webster, 1996) and individual differences (Neuberg & Newsom, 1993).

Motives for controlling and for understanding overlap somewhat, but they do differ: People want to predict (understand) even when they cannot influence (control) because understanding aids adjustment even if they can only anticipate but not change an outcome. Both understanding and controlling motives appear relatively cognitive and information-oriented. The next two motives are more affective and feelings-oriented but also trace to the core social motive of belonging.

Enhancing Self

Self-enhancement, people's tendency to see themselves in a positive light, is well documented, particularly in American and European settings (Chapter 5). Both automatic and controlled processes operate here, but Americans' immediate, automatic first reactions favor positive self-esteem. For example, people's relatively automatic reactions favor positive feedback (Swann, Hixon, Stein-Seroussi, & Gilbert, 1990). On subsequent reflection (more controlled), however, people prefer feedback that fits their self-view, even if it is negative.

More generally, much social cognition automatically orients toward viewing the self positively: overly optimistic for the future, exaggerated sense of personal control, and more positive self-concept than is perhaps realistic. Nevertheless, these illusions are adaptive, benefiting both mental and physical health (Taylor, Kemeny, Reed, Bower, & Gruenewald, 2000; Taylor, Lerner, Sherman, Sage, & McDowell, 2003a, 2003b). Positive self-views encourage people to participate in social life, so (within reasonable bounds) self-enhancement helps people to adapt to their groups. Thus the self-enhancement motive shapes social cognition (see Chapter 5).

Trusting Ingroup

Social cognition generally operates with **trust**, a persistent positivity bias for most social stimuli, all else being equal (Matlin & Stang, 1978; Rothbart & Park, 1986; Sears, 1983). People essentially expect good things from other people (not just themselves). For example, people routinely use only the top half of rating scales, only rarely rating another person below the numerical midpoint. Thus, the psychological midpoint is positive, and negativity stands out (S. T. Fiske, 1980). When negative events do occur, people mobilize rapidly (and automatically), seeking to minimize the damage (often a more controlled response) before returning to a positive baseline (S. E. Taylor, 1991). Negativity jumps out incredibly early, within milliseconds (Ito, Larsen, Smith, & Cacioppo, 1998), precisely because it stands out against a relatively positive baseline (Skowronski & Carlston, 1989).

Trust shows individual and cultural differences, as do all social motives. People's intention to trust others and people's receipt of trusting behavior both correlate with the neuroactive hormone **oxytocin** (Zak, Kurzban, & Matzner, 2005). Oxytocin, particularly active in women, is implicated in caretaking and befriending, especially under threat (S. E. Taylor, 2006b). Trusting ingroup others links to the pervasive positivity bias observed throughout social cognition; in this sense, people trust ingroup others to do and be good.

Conclusion about Motives

Social cognition is animated by social motives traceable to belonging, including understanding, controlling, enhancing self, and trusting others. This framework fits the history of motivations in psychology (S. T. Fiske, 2008) as well as current work in social psychology generally (S. T. Fiske, 2010) and social cognition in particular (S. T. Fiske, 2002). Although other frameworks are possible, this highlights some motives that determine when and how people operate in more automatic or more controlled modes.

The distinction between relatively automatic and controlled processes is well established as a social cognitive principle. The motivated tactician metaphor captures the flexible use of different modes. What are the directions for future research? Social neuroscience, at one end of the spectrum, surely will matter increasingly. The social neuroscience of automaticity and control is in its infancy (Lieberman, 2007). Earlier, we noted areas implicated in automatic processing (see Figure 2.1): Controlled processing of the kinds just described involve large portions of the prefrontal cortex toward the front (lateral PFC, medial PFC) and upper back (lateral and medial parietal cortex). The neural patterns are just now emerging; we note this social neuroscience in later chapters where specifically relevant. At the other end of the spectrum, cultural variations in the core motives regarding social cognition also will matter increasingly, as we will note.

MODELS OF BOTH AUTOMATIC AND CONTROLLED PROCESSES

Throughout social cognition, people make sense of themselves and each other in more and less thoughtful ways, depending on the circumstances. *When* they do *what* – that is, the circumstances that guide more automatic or more controlled processing – concerns dozens of theories in social cognition (Chaiken & Trope, 1999). We sample some here, from person perception to attribution, to attitudes, and more (Table 2.7).

Table 2.7   Dual-mode models

Name (Primary author)	Automatic processes	Controlled processes	Domain
Dual-process model of impression formation (Brewer)	Initial identification or categorization using images	Personalized concepts or individuated subtypes and exemplars	Impressions
Continuum model of impression formation (Fiske & Neuberg)	Immediate categorization based on sex, race, age, etc.	Intermediate processing by subtypes; full individuation by attributes	Impressions
Dual-process model of overconfident attributions (Trope)	Identification of behavior	Explanations	Attributions
Cognitive busyness model (Gilbert)	Categorization of behavior characterization by dispositions	Correction for situation	Attributions
Spontaneous trait (Uleman)	Associate accessible traits to behavior	Associate trait with person	Attribution

Name (Primary author)	Automatic processes	Controlled processes	Domain
Elaboration likelihood model (Petty & Cacioppo)	Using peripheral cues	Using central cues	Persuasion
Heuristic-systematic Model (Chaiken)	Heuristic shortcuts	Systematic processes	Persuasion
MODE model (Fazio)	Low motivation and opportunity	High motivation and opportunity	Attitude–behavior

Examples in Person Perception

Several models focus on people perceiving other people in more and less automatic ways. One conceptualizes people's use of automatic expectancies versus deliberation about individuals by viewing the two modes as branching off into different strategies as the situation demands. According to this **dual-process model of impression formation** (M. B. Brewer, 1988; M. M. Brewer & Harasty Feinstein, 1999), people initially identify a person automatically, then they stop there if the person is not relevant to their goals. Identifying the gas-station attendant as a man in the right uniform illustrates this relatively automatic process.

If the person is relevant, and the perceiver is sufficiently involved, people personalize the other using individually tailored concepts in a memory network. If not sufficiently involved, perceivers first categorize using images (holistic, nonverbal patterns), unless the category fit is poor. In that case, they individuate, using subtypes (more specific categories such as local versus highway attendant) or exemplars (familiar examples such as the guy at one's neighborhood station). Chapter 4 details these distinct forms of mental representation, but the point here is that one way to view dual-mode models is as a series of choice points and branching processes that channel people into various relatively automatic and controlled forms of thinking about others.

An alternative viewpoint views impression formation not as a series of branches into distinct types of processing but as an evolving continuum. In this view, people engage in a continuum of processes ranging from the most automatic, category-based processes (relying, for example, on age, gender, race, class) to the most deliberate, piecemeal impression formation processes (relying on the available data about each individual). In this **continuum model of impression formation**, one can specify both information configurations and motivations that move people from one end of the continuum to another (e.g., S. T. Fiske et al., 1987; for reviews, see S. T. Fiske & Neuberg, 1990; S. T. Fiske, Lin, & Neuberg, 1999).

People start at the automatic end and may (or may not) proceed in stages along the continuum. In this view, they initially categorize each other automatically on the basis of noticeable physical cues and verbal labels. For example, the person approaching on the sidewalk is a White, college-aged woman. People automatically use these initial categories, especially when that is all they have. If sufficiently motivated to attend to the other person, people attempt to confirm these initial categories in a slightly more deliberate fashion. On closer inspection, her face confirms her apparent age. Category confirmation is generally successful if the data fit well enough.

If category confirmation fails (e.g., the data contradict the category, as when the woman has a moustache), people recategorize. They generate new, better-fitting categories ("she" is a feminine "he"), subcategories (she is wearing stage makeup and a tie), exemplars (like your cousin, she has facial hair that shows in daylight), or self-reference (well, maybe you yourself are androgynous). Finally, when it is not easy to recategorize, people proceed piecemeal, attribute by attribute, through the data. As you sit across from her on the subway, you try to figure her out by covert but closer inspection. As the continuum model indicates, people are not fools. We often rely on automatic processes when they are good enough, making **category-based responses**, but we also know when to quit and move to more controlled processes, making **attribute-based responses**.

Some important differences distinguish the dual-process and continuum model approaches (Bodenhausen, Macrae, & Sherman, 1999; M. B. Brewer, 1988; S. T. Fiske, 1988). For example, the dual-process model proposes distinct types of cognitive representations (images, categories, exemplars) in distinct branches of impression formation. In contrast, the continuum model posits stable kinds of information across its evolving stages, with the prior stage carrying over to the subsequent one. In addition, the dual-process model posits specific rules for passing along each processing branch, whereas the continuum model proposes constant rules; namely, that ease of categorization depends on information and motivation. Both approaches do integrate relatively automatic and controlled processes within unified frameworks.

Given current knowledge, moving between automatic and controlled impression formation could be cued by relatively automatic neural systems that respond to external features, cuing emotional vigilance (e.g., amygdala, basal ganglia), familiar others (the lateral temporal cortex's temporal pole, TP), and biological movement (the lateral temporal cortex's superior temporal sulcus, STS). Discrepancies register on the anterior cingulate cortex (ACC), thereby engaging more controlled processing about the other as a human being with mental states (medial prefrontal cortex, mPFC) and intentions (Amodio & Frith, 2006; Botvinick et al., 2004; Lieberman, 2007). As social neuroscience research develops, these patterns will doubtless clarify with new data.

Examples in Attribution

People engage more and less automatic forms of causal reasoning (see Chapter 6). For example, suppose you observe a person chewing her fingernails, speaking hesitantly, and avoiding eye contact; you might decide this is a nervous person, or that she is describing on national television the most embarrassing moment of her life. In a **dual-process model of overconfident attribution**

(Trope, 1986; Trope & Gaunt, 1999), people first automatically and effortlessly identify behavior, aided by context (nail-biting could indicate nerves or frustration, but on national TV it's probably nerves). Because much behavior is ambiguous, the **identification stage** is a necessary first step. Next, people more deliberately explain the nervous behavior, now subtracting the situation (everyone's nervous on national television) to infer the person's disposition (maybe not such an anxious type).

A related **cognitive busyness** model splits the first process into stages for **categorization** of behavior and its **characterization** in dispositional terms, both automatic, followed by controlled **correction** for situational factors if the perceiver has both capacity and motivation (i.e., not too cognitively busy; Gilbert, 1991; Gilbert, Pelham, & Krull, 1988). The relative automaticity and control appears when participants have to remember a phone number for the experimenter (a subtle imposition of cognitive load) while simultaneously making a causal attribution about another person. Cognitive load does not interfere with the initial, relatively automatic dispositional inference (categorization and characterization), but it does interfere with the subsequent controlled correction for situational pressures.

A third model contrasts **spontaneous trait inferences,** guided by concepts that come easily to mind, linked to the person, whether appropriate or not, with more intentional, goal-driven processes (Uleman, 1999; Winter & Uleman, 1984). Again, these models do differ (Gilbert, 1998), but all three contrast relatively automatic and controlled causal attributions for behavior. We will return to them in Chapter 6.

Examples in Attitudes

Some of the best-known two-mode models occur in the realm of attitudes – people's evaluations of objects in their world. The **elaboration likelihood model** (Petty & Cacioppo, 1981; Petty & Wegener, 1999) describes two routes to persuasion: **peripheral** (more automatic, superficial) and **central** (more deliberate, controlled). Low-effort processes use peripheral cues, such as noting that the message has many arguments or an ingroup source (it must be right), so people read this message only superficially. In high-effort processes, people carefully scrutinize all the arguments and elaborate them: They add some kind of personal reaction, pro or con. Most variables can serve either as peripheral cues or information for central processing, depending on circumstances.

In a related vein, the **heuristic-systematic model** (Chaiken, 1980; Chen & Chaiken, 1999) contrasts **systematic processing** (relatively analytic, comprehensive) with **heuristic processing** (previously stored rules of thumb). The two modes can operate in parallel, adding to each other's impact, although the heuristic one is usually faster. Perceivers stop when their confidence is sufficient for present purposes, so the balance of the two modes' influence depends on when people make a decision.

Not only persuasion processes but also processes linking attitudes to behavior come in a more spontaneous, rapid form, depending on motivation and opportunity (**MODE model**; Fazio, Powell, & Herr, 1983; Fazio & Towles-Schwen, 1999) or in more deliberate, cost-benefit form (**theory of reasoned action**; **theory of planned behavior**; Ajzen & Fishbein, 1977;

Ajzen & Sexton, 1999). Detailed in Chapters 10 and 15, for now these models integrate relatively automatic and controlled modes in processing persuasive communications.

Automaticity-Control in Other Areas: Self, Prejudice, Inference

In thinking about self (Chapter 5), people sometimes react rapidly, on the basis of self-schemas (automatic self-concepts), and at other times review self-relevant evidence more carefully (Markus, 1977). As we saw earlier, people immediately embrace positive feedback but may deliberate about its consistency (Swann et al., 1990).

In thinking about outsiders, too, people swing between two extremes: relatively automatic, culturally conditioned prejudices and more controlled, personally endorsed viewpoints (Chapters 11–12; Devine, 1989; Devine & Monteith, 1999; Dovidio & Gaertner, 1986; Greenwald et al., 2002).

Indeed, in every kind of inference a kind of **System 1 versus System 2** contrasts intuition versus reasoning (Epstein, 1990a; Gladwell, 2005; Kahneman, 2003, 2011; Smith & DeCoster, 2000). The intuitive side is holistic, rapid, effortless, parallel, affective, associative, crude, and slow-learning. The rational reasoning side is analytic, slow, effortful, serial, neutral, logical, differentiated, and flexible. The intuitive, associative mode relies on the slow-learning but then rapidly responding form of memory, which concentrates on consistencies, whereas the rational, fast-binding, rule-based system acquires detailed new memories quickly, focusing on novel and inconsistent cues for subsequent consideration in deliberate processes. The two-system contrast suggests that each is suited to distinct forms of learning and reacting (see Table 2.8 for a summary). This powerful theme drives much social cognition work as psychological scientists of every stripe document distinct ways people make sense of their social worlds.

Table 2.8   Characteristics of automatic versus controlled processing

Automatic, System 1	Controlled, System 2
Intuitive	Rational
Categorical	Individuated
Holistic	Analytic
Rapid	Slow
Effortless	Effortful
Parallel	Serial
Affective	Neutral
Associative	Logical
Crude	Differentiated
Reflexive	Reflective
Slow-learning	Fast-learning
Rigid	Flexible
Consistency	Novelty

The Dissent: Single-Mode Alternatives

Lest you think this understanding of social cognition represents an uncontested dual-mode supremacy, some alternatives do appear. The **unimode model** builds on a lay **epistemic** theory of ordinary knowledge (Kruglanski, 1980; Kruglanski, Thompson, & Spiegel, 1999). This proposes that people's subjective understanding essentially tests their everyday hypotheses. Because all types of lay hypothesis-testing processes draw on evidence, capability, and motivation, in this view various processes are more similar than different. All these processes theoretically follow "if–then" rules of relevance according to the unimode approach. Regardless of whether relevant evidence under the "if" condition is simple or complex, certain reactions follow. That is, the overarching if–then structure is similar regardless of domain (if fatigued, drink coffee; if in love, get married). Capability and motivation operate in a similar manner, in this view, regardless of mode.

Another single-mode alternative argues that impression formation operates via **parallel processes**, blending attributes all simultaneously activated (Kunda, 1999; Kunda & Thagard, 1996). It treats all types of information as equivalent, not privileging certain kinds (e.g., race, gender) over others (e.g., personality traits). In this view, a person's race, gender, and age are weighted equivalently to the person's personality, abilities, and preferences. This blending operates by combining and resolving every cue simultaneously, in parallel. Impressions develop from all sources of information at once, combining them into a coherent impression immediately and continuously constrained to be internally consistent. This model differs from dual-process models primarily in cases of unmotivated processing in which most dual-process models assume superficial reliance on only a few cues. In motivated processing, both this model and the dual-process models assume people will use more information.

Single-mode models provide a useful counterpoint, but as often occurs in debates, they tend to caricature the opposition. Indeed, all dual-mode theorists take pains to point out that their processes represent theoretical contrasts with most processes taking place somewhere between them.

Summary

This chapter previews one of social cognition's main themes over the past 25 years, but anticipated even earlier: People's thought processes can operate on automatic or in control, or somewhere between the two. The most automatic processes occur without effort, awareness, control, intent, or capacity use. Subliminal, preconscious processing of social cues (faces, concepts) affects cognitive associations, affective reactions, and behavior. Conscious priming of (exposure to) concepts can trigger unconscious, automatic processes. Some cues are chronically accessible to some people, but situations also prime particular concepts and even motives.

People control some types of automatic processing by deliberately instigating a goal, which then triggers automatic processes. Habits illustrate. People also consciously attend to certain actions, plan for them, and execute them. However, people do tend to overestimate the extent to which their thoughts control their actions, or even the extent to which they can control their thoughts. Consciousness serves multiple functions, both internal and external, often occupied by unfinished business and social concerns.

Various motivations determine whether people engage relatively automatic or controlled processes. Each motive can push toward either automaticity or control, depending on circumstances. Belonging with other people powerfully motivates people to get along with others. Socially shared understanding motivates much social cognition, using both consensus and information-seeking. Control emphasizes social contingencies between what one does and what happens, important to well-being. Regarding affect, people enhance the self and optimistically trust ingroup others. The interplay of these motives and available information determines when people rely on well-worn, relatively automatic processes and when on more deliberate, controlled processes.

Dual-mode models appear in person perception, attribution, attitudes, self, inference, and prejudice, to name a few. Single-mode alternatives argue for similar processes, regardless of information and motivation. Social cognition researchers continue to debate, as the next chapters show.

FURTHER READING

Aarts, H. (2012). Goals, motivated social cognition and behavior. In S. T. Fiske & C. N. Macrae (Eds.), *Sage handbook of social cognition* (pp. 75–95). Thousand Oaks, CA: Sage.

Bargh, J. A., Chen, M., & Burrows, L. (1996). Automaticity of social behavior: Direct effects of trait construct and stereotype activation on action. *Journal of Personality and Social Psychology, 71(2)*, 230–244.

Chaiken, S., & Trope, Y. (Eds.), (1999). *Dual-process theories in social psychology.* New York: Guilford Press.

Gilbert, D. T. (1999). What the mind's not. In S. Chaiken & Y. Trope (Eds.), *Dual-process theories in social psychology* (pp. 3–11). New York: Guilford Press.

Nosek, B. A., Hawkins, C. B., & Frazier, R. S. (2012). Implicit social cognition. In S. T. Fiske & C. N. Macrae (Eds.), *Sage handbook of social cognition* (pp. 31–53). Thousand Oaks, CA: Sage.

Payne, B. K. (2012). Control, awareness, and other things we might learn to live without. In S. T. Fiske & C. N. Macrae (Eds.), *Sage handbook of social cognition* (pp. 12–30). Thousand Oaks, CA: Sage.

Wegner, D. M., Schneider, D. J., Carter, S. R., & White, T. L. (1987). Paradoxical effects of thought suppression. *Journal of Personality and Social Psychology, 53*, 5–13.

Winkielman, P., & Schooler, J. W. (2012). Consciousness, metacognition and the unconscious. In S. T. Fiske & C. N. Macrae (Eds.), *Sage handbook of social cognition* (pp. 54–74). Thousand Oaks, CA: Sage.

Attention and Encoding

3

- Faces: The Focus of Social Attention
- Salience: A Property of Stimuli in Context
- Vividness: An Inherent Property of Stimuli
- Accessibility: A Property of Categories in Our Heads
- Direct Perception: Not Just in Our Heads

A friend of ours was sitting on a bench in a crowded shopping mall when he heard running footsteps behind him. Turning, he saw two Black men being pursued by a White security guard. The first runner was past him in a flash, but he leapt up in time to tackle the second runner, overpowering him. From the ground, the panting Black man angrily announced that he was the store owner. Meanwhile, the thief had escaped. Our friend, who is White and devotes his life to helping the oppressed, was mortified.

For our purposes, this case of mistaken identity illustrates the sometimes tragic consequences of instantaneous social encoding based on interpretations. People rapidly take in other people as stimuli and react to them, so encoding determines much of social interaction as people react immediately in the course of their daily encounters. But what do we notice in the first place?

As artist Frank Stella put it, "what you see is what you see." Attention and encoding are the first steps in mental representation. Before any internal information management can occur, the stimuli outside the person have to be represented in the mind. The name for this general process is encoding. **Encoding** transforms a perceived external stimulus into an internal representation. The encoding process involves considerable cognitive work, which nevertheless can be accomplished with relatively little effort. The instant a stimulus registers on the senses, the process of interpretation begins. Immediately, some details are lost, others altered, and still others may be misperceived. Inferences are stored in memory along with the raw data and may become indistinguishable from them.

Attention is an integral part of encoding because attention often focuses on what is currently being encoded. Thinking about something external at least temporarily represents it in mind.

However, attention is not limited to the encoding of external stimuli; it can also be internal (Chun, Golomb, & Turk-Browne, 2011): Whatever occupies consciousness is defined as the focus of attention, as noted in Chapter 2.

Internal attention can also be occupied by information retrieved from memory. If you are thinking about something you remember, that memory is the focus of your attention. Attention is also occupied by the current contents of the mind (see Chapter 4 discussion of active, working, and short-term memory). People attend to the internal or external stimuli that are in conscious focal awareness.

Whether attention is directed outward toward encoding external objects or inward toward memory, attention is usually seen as having two components: direction (selectivity) and intensity (effort). When you read this book, you are presumably focusing on it rather than on the music, the conversation in the hall, the itch on your leg, or your love life. Even given your selective focus on this book, you can allocate more or less intense mental effort to it. Attention is the amount of selective cognitive work you do (Desimone & Duncan, 1995). Some aspects of attention contribute to voluntary control: working memory, top-down sensitivity control, and competitive selection (Knudsen, 2007). In contrast, bottom-up filtering for salient stimuli is automatic.

When people encode external stimuli, they do not attend evenly to all aspects of their environment. They watch some things closely and ignore others altogether. Attention affects what enters thought and memory, but conscious attention is not necessary for encoding into memory. Cognitive psychologists distinguish between early and late selective attention (Hübner, Steinhauser, & Lehle, 2010); that is, the amount of rudimentary perceptual processing that occurs outside of focused attention. Cognitive neuroscience indicates that even unattended stimuli register on the brain (Kanwisher & Wojciulik, 2000), suggesting that selection for conscious attention occurs later. Moreover, with regard to social cognition, the brain is exquisitely attuned to emphatically social stimuli – namely, faces, which we encode obligatorily (Tsao & Livingstone, 2008). This chapter first examines how that most social of stimuli, the face, affects attention.

This chapter next examines what else captures attention in social settings because that affects everything that follows in social interactions. We examine **salience**, the extent to which people stand out relative to others in their environment, and **vividness**, which constitutes the inherent attention-getting features of a person (or other stimulus) regardless of environment. In Chapter 2, we introduced **accessibility**, which describes how people's attention is primed for categories (or particular interpretations of stimuli) that fit what they have thought about recently or frequently. Finally, we close by examining **direct perception** of people, unmediated by cognitive processing, which will set the stage for embodied representations in the next chapter. But before whole persons and their bodies, faces.

FACES: THE FOCUS OF SOCIAL ATTENTION

A dramatically social driver of attention is another person's face. Faces are intrinsically the focus of attention in any social interaction. We examine how faces not only capture attention but direct it elsewhere, then we describe some neuroscience of face perception, and the rapid inference of traits from faces (Todorov, 2012).

Gaze: An Attentional Cue from Other People

People are acutely attuned to other people's gaze direction. Consider how quickly you notice someone staring at you, even out of your peripheral vision. This makes sense, of course: The other person's gaze communicates attention and perhaps intention, so survival dictates being alert to other people's gaze.

Directed-gaze faces (looking at you), as opposed to averted-gaze faces, compel attention: People more rapidly categorize them by gender and link them to stereotypic information (Macrae, Hood, Milne, Rowe, & Mason, 2002). Both adults and children more easily recall them (Hood, Macrae, Cole-Davies, & Dias, 2003; Mason, Hood, & Macrae, 2004). Gaze appears primarily as an encoding phenomenon (Hood et al., 2003). All else being equal, people find direct gaze both likable and attractive (Mason, Tatkow, & Macrae, 2005). "Here's looking at you, kid" can be a compliment, as early film actor Humphrey Bogart knew, but "Whaddaya lookin' at?" can be a response to unwanted and especially provocative attention.

People not only notice people looking at them, but people also use another person's averted gaze to guide their own attention. Try standing on a street corner gazing at the top of a building and see how many people follow your gaze. When someone looks at something besides you, most people find it hard to resist following the other person's gaze to see what is so interesting. We not only look where other people are looking but also where animals are looking (Figure 3.1) and even where arrows point. However, this reflexive shift in our attention is most efficient (rapid) when we take our cues from human eyes (Quadflieg, Mason, & Macrae, 2004), consistent with the idea that the eyes are the window, if not to the soul, to intent. Gaze detection implicates neural systems, including the superior temporal sulcus (Hoffman & Haxby, 2000), often related to tracking biological movement.

Face Perception

Cognitive neuroscience argues that face perception, a highly developed visual skill, implicates a number of neural systems, some for identifying fixed features of faces, and some for changeable facial expressions (Haxby, Hoffman, & Gobbini, 2000; Figure 3.2). A face-responsive region, sometimes called the fusiform face area (FFA), recognizes invariant features of faces (Grill-Spector & Kanwisher, 2005; Kanwisher & Wojciuluk, 2000; Yip & Sinha, 2002). People are so good at faces that they can recognize someone familiar as much as 50 years later (Bahrick, Bahrick, & Wittlinger, 1975). A different face-responsive region in the superior temporal sulcus (STS) responds to changeable aspects of faces (gaze, noted earlier; expression; and movement). And knowledge about the person constitutes a third set of processes (Bruce & Young, 1986). Face perception is distributed both over the brain and over the time course of perception (Haxby, Gobbini, & Montgomery, 2004). Although some argue that people's responsivity to faces merely reflects practice effects or expertise, much

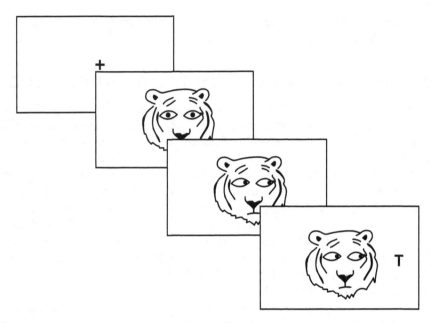

Figure 3.1   Stimulus presentation sequence illustrating a congruent trial (i.e., target appears at the cued location)

Source: From Quadflieg, Mason, & Macrae, 2004. Copyright 2004 Psychonomic Society, Inc.; reprinted by permission

evidence supports the face as a domain of unique neural sensitivity (McKone, Kanwisher, & Duchaine, 2007).

Facial recognition appears to be a **global**, configural, holistic process that perceptually integrates across the whole rather than a local, feature-oriented, piecemeal process. Indeed, the **feature-oriented processing** of a face (separate focus on eyes, nose, mouth, chin, etc.) undermines recognition. Verbally describing a bank robber ironically interferes with recognizing him on a later line-up (Schooler & Engstler-Schooler, 1990), apparently because this **verbal overshadowing** invokes a local, feature-by-feature processing orientation (Tanaka & Farah, 1993). A direct manipulation of global versus local (feature) processing orientation respectively enhances or impairs subsequent recognition of the individual (Macrae & Lewis, 2002).

Faces are processed globally when people distinguish among unique individuals. When people are merely categorizing, treating individuals as more interchangeable, they use single salient cues (e.g., hair) to determine, for example, gender, race, age, and the like. Right hemispheric specialization in global, configural processing facilitates identification and individuation; left hemispheric feature-based processing facilitates categorization (Mason & Macrae, 2004). Similarly, the right hemisphere specializes in individual, person-based learning, whereas the left focuses on group-based learning (Sanders, McClure, & Zárate, 2004). In general, the right hemisphere often participates in basic perceptual, episodic encoding, and the left in conceptual, abstract processes (Zárate, Sanders, & Garza, 2000) such as categorizing.

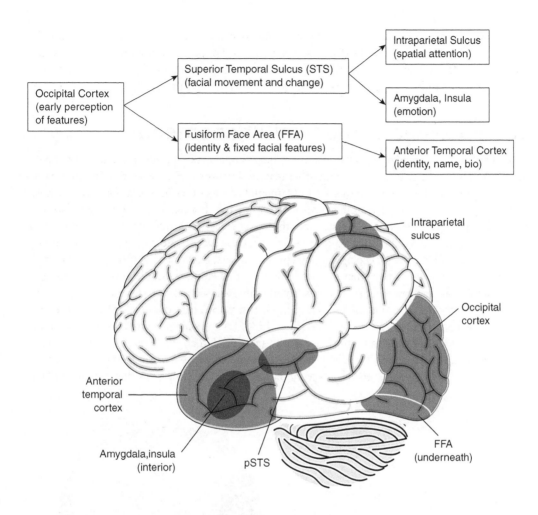

Figure 3.2   Some brain regions key to face perception

Source: After Haxby Hoffman, & Gobbini (2000)

According to face-selective neural activations, people identify a face as a face in 100–200 msec (one or two tenths of a second) and recognize familiar faces almost as rapidly (Ito, Thompson, & Cacioppo, 2004; Liu, Harris, & Kanwisher, 2002). Racial and gender differentiation can also occur within the same timeframe (Ito, Thompson, & Cacioppo, 2004; Ito & Urland, 2003, 2005). In general, categorical information is easier to extract from faces than is individual identity information. When faces are blurry, inverted, or merely glimpsed, people can still readily extract categorical knowledge (Cloutier, Mason, & Macrae, 2005; Martin & Macrae, 2007), and they do this unintentionally (Macrae, Quinn, Mason, & Quadflieg, 2005).

People infer other information besides group category and individual identity, for example, attractiveness (Locher, Unger, Sociedade, & Wahl, 1993; Olson & Marshuetz, 2005). When people examine faces, they also sometimes extract trait information and link it directly to the face. The face-traits links appear in work from two distinct viewpoints, as we shall see now.

Baby Faces as Ecological Phenomena

Research from an **ecological perspective** examines how people make specific inferences about personality on the basis of physical features and other features intrinsic to the social stimulus configuration. Such appearance-based perceptions are fundamental factors in social perception. For example, old-time gangster movies often featured a ruthless criminal with a name like "Babyface" Norton. What made such figures especially sinister was the contrast between their cherubic features and their villainous behavior. Why do we expect people with baby-faced features to have equally innocent personalities? As studies in ecological perception indicate, baby-faced adults are perceived to have more childlike qualities than mature-faced adults; across cultures, people with large eyes, big foreheads, and short features (e.g., snub noses, small chins) are seen as less strong, dominant, and intellectually astute, and as more naive, honest, kind, and warm, regardless of perceived age and attractiveness (Figure 3.3; see Berry & McArthur, 1986, for a review). Some of the same brain regions (FFA and amygdala) respond similarly to baby-faced adult men and to real babies (Zebrowitz, Luevano, Bronstad, & Aharon, 2009). Baby-faced adults are less likely to be judged guilty of intentional criminal behavior (hence, the baby-faced gangster is disconcerting), but they are more likely

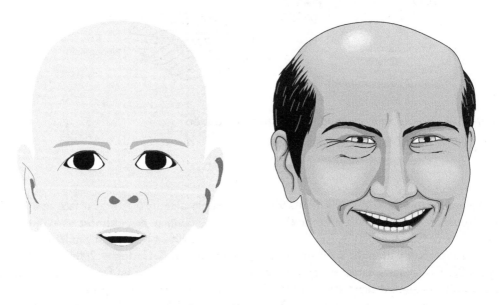

Figure 3.3 Typical baby face and mature male face

to be judged guilty of crimes involving negligence (Berry & Zebrowitz-McArthur, 1988). Cross-culturally, people with babyfaces seem similar (Zebrowitz, Wang, Bronstad, Eisenberg, Undurraga, Reyes-García, & Godoy, 2012), and people with childlike voices are also perceived as weaker, less competent, and warmer (Montepare & Zebrowitz-McArthur, 1987).

The ecological approach argues that these perceptions result from the normal covariation between babylike features and actual age, such that most babyish humans *are* more weak, submissive, intellectually undeveloped, naive, and innocent precisely because they are very likely to be actual babies. Such perceptions based on babylike features are normally adaptive for species' survival because adults must nurture and protect the young. Adults are therefore likely to perceive childlike features as needing or affording the behavioral opportunity of caretaking, which fits with perceiving a babylike person as weak. To a properly attuned organism, such perceptions are biologically and socially useful. Consequently, even children as young as 2½ can use baby-face cues to judge age (Montepare & Zebrowitz-McArthur, 1986).

Spontaneous Inferences from Faces

The attention-grabbing power of faces appears in an early study showing that angry faces "pop-out" of an array of faces, no matter how many other faces are in the crowd, and more so than other incongruent faces (Chapter 2; Hansen & Hansen, 1988a). Angry outgroup faces are especially well encoded (Ackerman et al., 2006). Of course, angry faces are particularly salient given the impact of negative information (described later; S. T. Fiske, 1980; Pratto & John, 1991). Even subliminally presented angry or fearful faces activate the brain's early-warning system of the amygdala (Morris, Ohman, & Dolan, 1998; Whalen et al., 1998).

But people go beyond immediately reading expressions to immediate inferences of personality traits, perhaps building on the same systems that read facial expression (from an angry expression to a hostile personality).

For example, faces otherwise judged as untrustworthy also activate the amygdala, even when people's alleged task is judging the age of the faces (Winston, Strange, O'Doherty, & Dolan, 2002). Faces that structurally happen to resemble emotions – surprise (female faces), anger (White faces), happiness (Black faces) – also elicit the corresponding trait inferences as a form of emotion overgeneralization (Zebrowitz, Kikuchi, & Fellous, 2010).

Although people spontaneously infer various traits from faces (Bar, Neta, & Linz, 2006; Rudoy & Paller, 2009; Rule & Ambady, 2008; Rule, Ambady, & Adams, 2009; Todorov, Pakrashi, & Oosterhof, 2009; Willis & Todorov, 2006), the most central are trustworthiness and competence. They are agreed-upon, but not necessarily accurate (Olivola & Todorov, 2010). In a form of emotional overgeneralization, the first dimension anchors on happiness (trustworthy) versus anger (untrustworthy), while the second anchors on a generalization of strength/age/gender power/dominance/maturity/masculinity (competence) and submission/immaturity/femininity (Todorov, Said, Engell, & Oosterhof, 2008).

When people make **spontaneous trait inferences** from people's behavior, without instruction to do so, they bind (link) them directly to the person's face in memory (Carlston & Skowronksi, 1994; Carlston, Skowronksi, & Sparks, 1995; Todorov & Uleman, 2002, 2004), even under rapid presentation and high cognitive load (Todorov & Uleman, 2003). Trait inferences from merely a minimal interaction also bind to the person's face (Todorov, Gobbini, Evans, & Haxby, 2007), even when people are not focused on inferring personality. Just 100-msec exposures are enough time for people to make trait inferences from faces (Willis & Todorov, 2006) that agree with the judgments of people who have no time constraints.

People's immediate trait inferences from faces can have important consequences: Seeing political candidates for even a second enabled people to make competence judgments that predicted nearly 70% of the actual elections (Todorov, Mandisodza, Goren, & Hall, 2005). At the other extreme, Black faces that are stereotypically Black are more likely to activate associations of criminality in people's immediate inferences (Eberhardt, Goff, Purdie, & Davies, 2004). Blacks and even Whites with Afro-typic features receive longer criminal sentences (Blair, Judd, & Chapleau, 2004; Eberhardt, Davies, Purdie-Vanghns, & Johnson, 2006). Faces can be a matter of life and death.

SALIENCE: A PROPERTY OF STIMULI IN CONTEXT

Moving beyond the face to the whole person, who captures our attention? **Salience**, the seemingly trivial factor of attracting attention, although logically irrelevant to most social judgment, can have important effects. Think back to the last time you were the only one of your "kind" in a room full of other people. The striking experience of being a salient social stimulus is the same. One *feels* conspicuous, that all eyes have a single target, and that one's every move is overinterpreted. As a result, one may feel anxious and concerned about how the interaction is going (Ickes, 1984). Moreover, the mere belief that one is a solo can impair one's ability to take in and remember what people say (Lord & Saenz, 1985; Lord, Saenz, & Godfrey, 1987; Saenz & Lord, 1989) and impair one's performance (Sekaquaptewa & Thompson, 2003). Being a solo more generally depletes a person's ability to self-regulate effectively; symptoms include talking too much, disclosing too much or too little, or being arrogant (Vohs, Baumeister, & Ciarocco, 2005). Solos also worry about how their prominence magnifies their otherwise risky low-status group identity (Duguid, 2011). Research on salience supports the uncomfortable experience of the solo as being a center of attention, as looming larger than life, and as the recipient of extreme reactions (S. E. Taylor, 1981a).

Antecedents of Social Salience

Social salience depends on the immediate or larger context (Table 3.1; McArthur, 1981; S. E. Taylor & Fiske, 1978). For example, solo status results from immediate perceptual and social novelty: having a novel gender, race, or any other visual distinction, such as the only red shirt in a room full of blue ones (e.g., Crocker & McGraw, 1984; Heilman, 1980; Higgins & King, 1981, Study 1; McArthur & Post, 1977; Nesdale, Dharmalingam, & Kerr, 1987; Spangler, Gordon, & Pipkin, 1978).

Table 3.1   The causes and consequences of social salience

Causes: A person can be salient relative to the perceiver's

Immediate context

   By being novel (solo person of that race, sex, hair color, shirt color)

   By being figural (bright, complex, moving)

Prior knowledge or expectations

   By being unusual for that person (e.g., behaving in unexpected ways)

   By being unusual for that person's social category (e.g., behaving in out-of-role ways)

   By being unusual for people in general (e.g., behaving negatively or extremely)

Other attentional tasks

   By being goal relevant (e.g., being a boss, a date)

   By dominating the visual field (e.g., sitting at the head of the table, being on camera more than others)

   By the perceiver being instructed to observe the person

Consequences: Visually salient people seem more

Causally significant

Evaluatively extreme

Organized in impression coherence

The perceptual features of the stimulus make it figural in the immediate context. Gestalt psychology predicts that stimuli will be salient if they are bright, complex, changing, moving, or otherwise stand out from their drab background (McArthur & Post, 1977), and they do attract longer gazes (McArthur & Ginsberg, 1981). People also notice the addition of a person to a group more than the removal of the person; addition is more salient than subtraction. Most of us fail to recognize that our absence from the gathering will not be as salient as our presence (Savitsky, Gilovich, Berger, & Medvec, 2003). (Maybe social excuses are better left aside?)

In the larger social context, people attend to expectancy-inconsistent information. People are salient if they contradict prior knowledge about them as individuals, as social category members, or as people in general (E. E. Jones & McGillis, 1976). Physically disabled people attract attention in part because they are novel compared to people in general (Langer, Taylor, Fiske, & Chanowitz, 1976).

Expectations about people in general also guide salience (S. T. Fiske, 1980). First, extreme social stimuli – being unusual – are more salient than moderate stimuli. For example, people stare at extremely positive social stimuli, such as movie stars, and at extremely negative stimuli, such as traffic accidents. Second, most people expect mildly positive events: Western people at least are optimistic about life outcomes (Parducci, 1968) and rate other individuals positively (Nilsson & Ekehammar, 1987; Sears, 1983; Sears & Whitney, 1973). Hence, negative social stimuli are more salient than positive ones because they are relatively unexpected.[1] Negative events capture preattentive processing (Pratto & John, 1991). What's more, negative events demand immediate coping in order for the individual to return to normal (S. E. Taylor, 1991).

Salience also depends partly on perceiver goals. People attend to significant others, those on whom their outcomes depend. If two people are talking and one is your new boss, a prospective date, or a new teammate, you will watch that person more closely (Berscheid, Graziano, Monson, & Dermer, 1976; Erber & Fiske, 1984; Neuberg & Fiske, 1987; Ruscher & Fiske, 1990; S. E. Taylor, 1975).

Salience can hinge on mere physical position, such as seating position in a group; the person directly opposite you should be especially salient because that person dominates your visual field (S. E. Taylor & Fiske, 1975). People expect that those who sit in the professor's line of sight – in the middle of many people – will be leaders (Raghubir & Valenzuela, 2006). Thus, to have maximum impact, sit in the middle front of a class, or sit at the head or foot of a meeting table; to fade into the background, sit on the sidelines.

Sheer visual exposure is the cause: In a videotape, increasing or decreasing a person's time on camera has similar effects (Eisen & McArthur, 1979; Storms & Nisbett, 1970). Even as consequential a setting as a videotaped confession shows effects of camera perspective on the confession's seeming voluntariness and guilt, even for complexity-minded viewers (Lassiter, 2002; Lassiter, Munhall, Berger, Weiland, Handley, & Geers, 2005). Giving interrogator and suspect equal exposure on camera (i.e., both displayed in profile) makes observers more aware of the interrogator's impact on inducing the suspect's confession (Snyder, Lassiter, Lindberg, & Pinegar, 2009). Visual perspective on merely imagined interactions of self with an outgroup stranger makes people attribute more positive attitudes to themselves, just as an observer would (Crisp & Husnu, 2011). Sheer visual exposure holds even for political issues: The amount of time an issue is aired on the evening news affects how much weight people give it in subsequent decisions (Iyengar & Kinder, 1987).

In summary (Table 3.1), note that the key common to all the ways of creating salience is *relative*: Stimulus novelty occurs relative to an immediate or broader context, a stimulus is figural relative to other stimuli present, and perceiver perspective is created relative to context. The salient stimulus is distinctive in relation to other factors in the perceiver's context.

Consequences of Social Salience

Regardless of its sources, salience effects are robust and wide ranging (McArthur, 1981; S. E. Taylor & Fiske, 1978). As suggested by the experience of the solo, salience makes a stimulus larger than life in various judgments.

Prominence shows up most in perceptions of *causality*. Salient people stand out as especially influential in a given group. This salience–causality principle extends to causal analyses of the person's own behavior. An individual's perceptually salient behavior seems particularly indicative

---

[1] For some exceptions as well as other explanations for the typically higher weight of negative information in impressions of likability, see Skowronski and Carlston, 1989, for a review.

of the person's underlying disposition and as less under the control of the situation. In both cases, causal attributions follow the focus of attention. As just noted, videotaped confessions focused on the suspect make the behavior seem more voluntary and, consequently, the person seems more guilty (Lassiter, 2002).[2]

Salience also exaggerates *evaluations* in whichever direction they initially tend. If a person is unpleasant, being a solo will cause disproportionate condemnation; similarly, a pleasant solo is exaggeratedly praised (S. E. Taylor, Fiske, Close, Anderson, & Ruderman, 1977). Evaluations can be nudged in one direction or another by prior expectations as well. For example, if a defendant in criminal proceedings is viewed negatively, salience should cause the person to be evaluated especially negatively. On the other hand, if the same person is viewed as a person (a more positive expectation), salience causes an especially positive evaluation (Eisen & McArthur, 1979; cf. McArthur & Solomon, 1978). Salience cuts both ways in evaluations.

If salient stimuli elicit attention, perceived prominence, and extreme evaluations, it would stand to reason that they also should enhance memory. Unfortunately, the data are strikingly uneven. Within social cognition research on salience, the main measure of memory has been people's free recall: Sometimes recall improves and sometimes not (McArthur, 1981; S. E. Taylor & Fiske, 1978).

Although salience does not reliably enhance the quantity of recall, it does *organize impressions* in several ways. The more attention one pays to another person, the more coherent the impression becomes. Attention structures impressions, emphasizing features that fit and adjusting those that do not. For example, the solo student at a faculty meeting is likely to be seen as typical of the student category and as presenting the "students' perspective," whether or not the person truly represents most peers (S. E. Taylor, 1981a). The effects of salience on stereotyping mean that salience combines with prior knowledge to produce polarized evaluations (cf. Nesdale et al., 1987). Consequently, a solo man is perceived to be prominent and therefore a good leader, but a solo woman in an all-male group is perceived to be an intruder and is caused to feel like one (Crocker & McGraw, 1984). Attention (mere thought) brings into line the evaluative components of an impression, which then becomes more extreme, at least under certain conditions (Chaiken & Yates, 1985; Millar & Tesser, 1986b; Tesser, 1978).

How robust are all these effects of temporary salience on social judgments? Efforts to increase importance and to enrich stimulus materials, in fact, enhance salience effects (Eisen & McArthur, 1979; McArthur, 1981; McArthur & Solomon, 1978; Strack, Erber, & Wicklund, 1982; S. E. Taylor, Crocker, Fiske, Sprinzen, & Winkler, 1979), and comparable salience effects occur in real-world organizations (Kanter, 1977; Wolman & Frank, 1975) and even television shows (Raghubir & Valenzuela, 2006).

If mere salience affects such significant decisions, just how controllable are they? Despite early speculations that salience effects might be automatic (S. E. Taylor & Fiske, 1978), they

---

[2] Because people generally see other people as causal agents (Heider, 1958; E. E. Jones & Nisbett, 1972; L. D. Ross, 1977), attention normally exaggerates this tendency (S. T. Fiske, Kenny, & Taylor, 1982). However, if a person's passivity is emphasized, attention can exaggerate perceptions of susceptibility to influence as well (Strack, Erber, & Wicklund, 1982). Cultures also vary in attributing causality to individuals versus groups (see Chapter 6). Salience exaggerates causal judgments in the direction implied by prior knowledge.

apparently do not qualify as fully automatic because people sometimes can control them. That is, salience effects can be qualified by some forms of involvement, such as self-interest (Borgida & Howard-Pitney, 1983), although not simply by making the task more important (S. E. Taylor et al., 1979). And salience effects may be qualified by some instructions, such as expecting to "describe each member of the stimulus group" (Oakes & Turner, 1986), which would enhance a person-by-person accuracy goal.

To take a closer look at salience: What mediates its effects? Why should attention have such pervasive effects on social judgment? Several processes might connect differential attention and differential judgments; some candidates for **mediation** (i.e., connection) have been debunked and some supported. Sheer quantity of recall and channel-specific recall do not seem to account for the effects of salience on attributions (quantity: S. T. Fiske, Kenny, & Taylor, 1982, S. E. Taylor & Fiske, 1975; but see Harvey, Yarkin, Lightner, & Town, 1980; E. R. Smith & Miller, 1979; channel-specific: S. T. Fiske et al., 1982; McArthur & Ginsberg, 1981; Robinson & McArthur, 1982; S. E. Taylor et al., 1979, Study 1). The ease or accessibility of recall is one plausible mediator (Pryor & Kriss, 1977; Rholes & Pryor, 1982; see also Higgins & King, 1981). In addition, causally relevant recall, especially memory for dominant behavior and appearance, seems to be enhanced by attention and in turn exaggerates attributions. Accordingly, the judgment is in effect being made at encoding, on the basis of information that is doubly salient – salient because the person is salient and salient because the dominant behavior itself is salient (S. T. Fiske et al., 1982).

Conclusion about Salience

Salience makes a stimulus stand out relative to other stimuli in that context. Salient stimuli may be novel, figural, expectancy-consistent, extreme, negative, rare, physically prominent, or long in duration. Salience exaggerates attention, perceived prominence, evaluations, and the coherence, but not the sheer amount of memory. Salience effects show goal-dependent automaticity in that they typically occur outside awareness but can moderate according to perceiver goals. Salience effects may be mediated by causally relevant recall or its accessibility.

VIVIDNESS: AN INHERENT PROPERTY OF STIMULI

Salience has well-established effects, so its cousin, vividness, would seem obvious. However, whereas salience is determined by the relation of an object to its context, vividness is inherent in a stimulus itself. For example, a plane crash is more salient during peacetime than in the context of wartime carnage. By this logic, a plane crash would be inherently more vivid than a normal flight; a detailed description of a particular accident would be more vivid than the statistics about it; and an accident in your local airport would be more vivid than an accident elsewhere. A stimulus is defined as **vivid** to the extent that it is "(a) emotionally interesting,

(b) concrete and imagery-provoking, and (c) proximate in a sensory, temporal or spatial way" (Nisbett & Ross, 1980, p. 45). Do vivid stimuli have effects similar to those of salient stimuli? Although theory and common sense would suggest that vivid stimuli are especially impactful, research suggests that they are not.

The Case for Vividness Effects

Vividness effects seem commonplace in daily life. Consider two versions of the same sponsor-a-child advertisement, one with a poignant photo and case study, the other with dry statistics. In both cases your conscience gives the same counsel, but the first ad seems more likely to attract your attention initially, to change your attitudes, and to elicit the desired behavior. All this is obvious, and as the idea person in an ad agency, you could have thought up the vivid ad yourself.

Psychological theorists postulated precisely such vividness effects on several conceptual grounds. Vivid information was predicted to be more persuasive than pallid information of equal or greater validity, first, because vivid information should come to mind more easily (Nisbett & Ross, 1980; Tversky & Kahneman, 1973). Second, vivid information by definition easily provokes internal visual representations, which are especially memorable. Third, vivid information seems to have more emotional impact on the perceiver, which would enhance its impact on judgments. In short, the impact of vivid information on human judgment, especially persuasion, would seem to be self-evident.

Unfortunately, scant empirical evidence supports vividness effects (S. E. Taylor & Thompson, 1982). According to the research, messages that are written in concrete and colorful language are no more likely to change attitudes than are abstract and dry messages. Research shows that messages accompanied by photographs usually have no greater appeal. Similarly, videotaped messages only sometimes have enhanced impact. And finally, direct experience, which would seem the ultimate in vividness, does not necessarily change attitudes more effectively than does secondhand contact.[3] In sum, vividness does not work well empirically, although intuitively it seems as if it should.

The major exception to this pattern of negative results is that individual case histories persuade more effectively than do group statistics. The heartrending story carries more impact than worldwide hunger statistics. For example, an individually identified wrongdoer elicits more anger and therefore more punishment than an otherwise similar but unidentifiable wrongdoer (Small & Lowenstein, 2005). However, this result may not speak to the vividness effect, in part because it concerns identifiability, not vividness *per se*.

What's more, other vividness research – which manipulates concrete (versus dull) language, photographs (versus none), and videotapes (versus transcripts) – holds most other information constant. However, holding information constant is more problematic when contrasting case history and statistical information. They differ in far too many ways to assume that it is only

---

[3] Saying that direct experience may not change attitudes is not the same as denying that direct experience may affect the *acquisition* of attitudes or the impact of attitudes on *behavior*; it clearly does both (see Chapters 10 and 15).

differences in vividness that cause any differences in their persuasive impact. For example, a case history communicates one particular scenario by which the existing facts could occur: A starving child might survive by selling firewood. Statistics communicate a different sort of information, such as life expectancy averaged over many instances. Hence, information nonequivalency is confounded with (not separable from) vividness (Table 3.2). Together with the failure to find effects from other types of vividness, this problem suggests that the information difference and not vividness itself accounts for the fact that case histories are persuasive (S. E. Taylor & Thompson, 1982).

Table 3.2   Lack of evidence in vividness research

Operationalizations	Holds constant	Overall effect for
Classic		
Classic Concrete (versus dull) language	Most other information	None
Photographs (versus none)	Most other information	None
Videotapes (versus transcripts)	Most other information	None
Case history (versus statistics)	Confounds information provided, identifiability	Case
Newer		
Vivid message versus context	Message itself (varies examples)	Message only
Capturing attention for message	Message itself	The uninvolved
Individual differences in susceptibility	Message itself	The susceptible

Why Does the Vividness Effect Seem So Plausible?

Apparently, little evidence supports the vividness effect. So what would lead people to the intuitive conclusion that there is a vividness effect? Vividness may have some effects on us that are mistaken for persuasion. For example, we believe that interesting, attention-getting messages are persuasive for other people in general, but we do not rate vivid messages as more personally convincing (R. L. Collins, Taylor, Wood, & Thompson, 1988). People also recall vivid information more easily than pallid information (Lynn, Shavitt, & Ostrom, 1985), but memorability does not explain the persuasion occasionally obtained in vividness studies (Shedler & Manis, 1986; Sherer & Rogers, 1984). Moreover, concrete language makes statements seem more true (Hansen & Wänke, 2010), but vivid information may make us more confident in our opinions without changing the actual judgment (N. K. Clark & Rutter, 1985).

Finally, vivid information is entertaining, arousing, and emotional, as in the visual embellishments of rock-music videos (Zillmann & Mundorf, 1987). The independence of persuasiveness and entertainment was put well by one of Carl Sagan's colleagues in describing Sagan's "gift for vividness": "Carl is very often right and always interesting. That is in contrast to most academics, who are always right and not very interesting" ("A Gift for Vividness," *Time*, 1980, p. 68). Vivid communications are frequently perceived as more graphic, more vivid, or more interesting than nonvivid communication in precisely those studies that go on to find no effect on judgments. Thus the entertainment value of vividness does seem to be functionally distinct from its persuasive impact (S. E. Taylor & Wood, 1983). People can mistakenly infer that their attitudes have changed when they have only been entertained or emotionally aroused (R. L. Collins et al., 1988).

Future Directions for Vividness Research

Assuming for a moment that our real-world intuitions are correct and that a vividness effect does exist, then attempts to examine it experimentally must have been flawed in some important way, or perhaps it does occur, but only under special circumstances that most experiments have so far failed to duplicate. Several principles define the boundaries of the vividness effect (S. E. Taylor & Thompson, 1982). First, many attempts to operationalize vividness confuse vivid messages with vivid presentations. If the message context is too vivid, the gimmicks may draw people's attention away from the message itself (Eagly & Himmelfarb, 1978; Isen & Noonberg, 1979). Vividness that fits the message – as opposed to being incongruent – does enhance cognitive elaboration and persuasion, but incongruent, gimmicky vividness undermines them (Guadagno, Rhoads, & Sagarin, 2011; S. M. Smith & Shaffer, 2000).

Second, some empirical evidence shows that pallid written material conveys more information but that vivid video or live material helps to catch people's attention if they are relatively uninvolved (Chaiken & Eagly, 1976). Video ads do capture people's attention, but they also prompt people to deal mostly with superficial information, such as whether the speaker is good-looking (Chaiken & Eagly, 1983). Vivid information may work on the attentional stage, especially for uninvolved recipients. If recipients of a message are already highly involved, vividness is not needed to capture attention. Their attention is already captured. What they need are cogent arguments and time to think about them. Written materials allow involved recipients the time to consider the message arguments in detail, which is crucial to persuading such individuals (Petty & Cacioppo, 1979; see also Chapter 10). In this view, vivid ads serve mainly to alert people who are uninvolved, if the vivid material is relevant, but written information persuades people who are involved.

Finally, people differ in their chronic reliance on vivid imagery (Pham, Meyvis, & Zhou, 2001). Vivid imagers can exaggerate or attenuate the persuasive effects of vividness because they creatively immerse themselves on the information in front of them and take off from there to rely more on nonobvious cues.

Conclusion about Vividness

Vividness is an inherent property of a stimulus. Although vividness effects seem plausible according to both theory and common sense, they appear mostly in contrasting case histories and statistics, which typically confound other kinds of information with the sheer vividness of the presentation. People may be emotionally aroused or entertained by vividness, which is one reason the effects seem plausible. But vivid presentations if irrelevant and gimmicky can actually interfere with persuasion. Future research could focus on relevance, processing stages, involvement, and individual differences in imagery vividness.

ACCESSIBILITY: A PROPERTY OF CATEGORIES IN OUR HEADS

Besides gaze direction, contextual salience, and inherently vivid stimuli, a third predictor of attention is accessibility of categories, which depends mainly on priming. As noted in Chapter 2's discussion of automaticity, **priming** describes the effects of prior context on the interpretation of new information. We also saw that priming can influence cognition, affect, and behavior. This chapter focuses on the cognitive mechanism of priming – namely, accessibility – and how it determines attention, encoding, and, ultimately, mental representation. **Accessibility** concerns the fact that recently and frequently activated ideas come to mind more easily than ideas that have not been activated. Many years ago, Jerome Bruner (1957, 1958) pointed out that much social information is inherently ambiguous, so social perception is heavily influenced by the accessibility of relevant categories: those easily activated given the perceiver's current goals, needs, and expectations.[4] Priming occurs when knowledge is activated (becomes accessible) and is applicable to currently attended stimuli.

Situational Accessibility Effects

Every charity has a newsletter, or so it seems. Why? Presumably, those who run the charity want to stay on your mind or at least on your screen. Being constantly reminded of pollution, disease, violence, or the local arts council creates a context for interpreting events. In effect, the newsletter primes the issue, keeping it accessible in your mind and presumably when you prioritize the urgency of various charitable causes.

Accessibility also applies for interpreting people. Exposing people to positive or negative trait terms (e.g., adventurous versus reckless) causes people soon afterward to interpret ambiguous behavior (e.g., shooting rapids in a canoe) as correspondingly positive or negative because of the meaning that had been primed (e.g., Bargh, Bond, Lombardi, & Tota, 1986; Higgins, Rholes, & Jones, 1977; Srull & Wyer, 1979; for a review, see Förster & Liberman, 2007).

---

[4] The terms *accessibility* and *availability* have been used in two contradictory ways. We use *accessibility* to mean ease of recall and *availability* to denote whether the information has been stored at all (Higgins & Bargh, 1987, footnote 1; Tulving & Pearlstone, 1966). Note, however, that this is inconsistent with the Tversky-Kahneman usage of availability to mean ease of bringing information to mind (see Chapter 7). In this chapter, accessibility refers to the readiness with which stored knowledge can be used.

Accessibility effects are strongest, as in this example, when relevant meanings as well as positive or negative valences are primed. That is, the ambiguous behavior is more likely to be seen as reckless when *relevant* negative concepts, compared to irrelevant ones, have been primed. Moreover, experimenters construct the priming and stimulus contexts such that participants do not consciously connect the two. In priming studies, participants must not think that the primed interpretation comes to mind because it was previously provided to them (i.e., accessible due to the primed construct). Instead, participants must think the primed construct comes to mind because of the stimulus itself. When they do not consciously link prime and stimulus, primed participants cannot be merely responding because of what they think the experimenters want them to do (i.e., due to **experimental demand**, whereby expected behavior is inadvertently constrained). The apparent independence of the prime and the stimulus also means that participants have no particularly rational reason to be using the prime in their interpretation of the stimulus. As we saw when first introducing the concept, priming can operate automatically, without one's conscious awareness of the initial prime (Bargh et al., 1986; Bargh & Pietromonaco, 1982).

Accessibility is not limited to trait concepts. Other socially significant concepts can be primed – professors, hooligans, old people, Black people – as Chapter 2 indicated, consistent with classic stereotyping studies suggesting that racial categories can be primed spontaneously (Devine, 1989; Dovidio, Evans, & Tyler, 1986; Gaertner & McLaughlin, 1983). When White participants see words related to African Americans, even presented below the threshold for conscious recognition, they subsequently respond faster to stereotype-related words and evaluate an ambiguous (race unspecified) person as more hostile, supporting the idea that their racial categories have been primed. On a more overt level, overhearing an ethnic slur can exaggerate White people's negative evaluations of a poor performance by a Black person (Greenberg & Pyszczynski, 1985), perhaps through priming. Police officers and probation officers subliminally primed with Black, race-related words then interpret a hypothetical adolescent, race unspecified, as having a worse personality, more culpability, expected recidivism, and harsher punishment (Graham & Lowery, 2004).

Similarly, various gender-role stereotypes are subject to priming. For example, men who had just viewed a pornographic film went on to respond more stereotypically to a woman they encountered in an apparently unrelated context: Their behavior was judged to be more sexually motivated, and later they initially remembered mainly her physical features rather than the interview. But these results held especially for gender-schematic men for whom gender role is likely to be especially accessible (McKenzie-Mohr & Zanna, 1990; Rudman & Borgida, 1995). Relatedly, women primed with family terms remember more accurately and judge more confidently the goals of a wife/mother target person compared to a career-woman target or compared to neutrally primed participants (Trzebinski & Richards, 1986; cf. Trzebinski, 1985). And rock-music videos that are gender-role stereotypic seem to prime stereotypic interpretations of men's and women's interactions (Hansen & Hansen, 1988b).

A stunning array of stimulus interpretations also result from accessibility: Unconscious affect primes person categories (Niedenthal & Cantor, 1986); unconscious threat and violence prime reported anxiety (Robles, Smith, Carver, & Wellens, 1987); self-discrepancies from standards prime arousal and reported mood (Higgins, Bond, Klein, & Strauman, 1986; Strauman & Higgins, 1987); unconscious polarized evaluation primes good–bad judgments of affectively loaded words (Greenwald, Klinger, & Liu, 1989); prior exposure to a missing child poster primes perceptions of whether an ambiguous adult–child interaction is a kidnapping (K. James, 1986); relevant prior questions prime reported life satisfaction (Strack, Martin, & Schwarz, 1988); relevant prior questions also prime judged desirability of national policies (Tourangeau, Rasinski, Bradburn, & D'Andrade, 1989); and heat primes aggressive content in stories (Rule, Taylor, & Dobbs, 1987). All kinds of responses, from temporary states to initial judgments to seemingly well-established opinions, change with accessibility due to situational primes (Förster & Liberman, 2007).

Priming subsequently has long-term as well as short-term consequences. The initial priming of a stimulus can affect its ratings as much as a week later when it is no longer in that context (Higgins & King, 1981; Higgins et al., 1977; Sinclair, Mark, & Shotland, 1987; Srull & Wyer, 1980). This is an important point: A transitory and perhaps arbitrary juxtaposition of prime and stimulus can affect the way that stimulus is encoded permanently. If a stimulus potentially can be encoded as fitting one of several alternative categories, short-term priming may determine which category applies in the long run.

Moreover, accessibility affects significant social behavior. Chapter 2 described studies priming race-hostility and elderly-slowness (Bargh, Chen, & Burrows, 1996), as well as professor-intelligence and transportation-biking (Aarts & Dijksterhuis, 2000). Similarly, participants primed by moderately hostile categories of then-famous people (rock singer Alice Cooper, Indiana coach Bobby Knight) in one context next rated an ambiguous partner as more hostile and behaved in a more hostile, competitive manner toward their partner, in line with the primed categories (Herr, 1986). In another study, participants encountered competition-related words at a level below the threshold for conscious recognition; primed participants then played more competitively if they were relatively competitive people. In effect, the primes activated their competitive personalities (Neuberg, 1988). Moreover, one classic set of research can be further interpreted as consistent with the effects of priming on aggression. When people are angry at someone, the impulse to harm the person is more likely to be carried to action in the presence of aggressive cues. A gun lying on a nearby table provokes aggressive behavior even by other means (Berkowitz, 1974), and priming can explain this. More benign responses, such as generosity, also can result from holding a warm (instead of iced) cup of coffee (Williams & Bargh, 2008).

Accessibility can likewise affect problem solving and creativity. In one study, participants attempted to solve the following problem: Given a candle, a book of matches, and a box of tacks, how can the candle be attached to the wall so it burns properly and does not drip wax on the floor? Some participants, who had been primed to think of containers as separate from their contents (e.g., tray *and* tomatoes versus tray *of* tomatoes), were able to solve the problem quickly. The configuration (container and contents as separable entities) primed related configurations and facilitated problem solving (Higgins & Chaires, 1980). The solution to the problem, incidentally, is to empty the box of tacks, treating it as a box *and* tacks, and to tack up the box as a platform for the candle.[5] In a striking enactment of a metaphor, participants

---

[5] This particular study is now interpreted as an instance of **procedural priming** (Higgins, 1996).

sitting outside the box – a five-foot cardboard cube – tested as more creative than those inside it (Leung et al., 2012).

Assimilation and Contrast

Most of the priming research shows **assimilation** to accessible categories. For example, when participants are primed with positive or negative traits, they often interpret relevant ambiguous behavior to make it match the category, as we have just seen. However, **contrast effects** have sometimes emerged. That is, when people are blatantly primed with a trait (e.g., foolhardiness), they may instead contrast their judgment of the ambiguous target, judging Donald wanting to sail across the Atlantic in a sailboat as not especially foolhardy and even adventurous. If the prime is blatant enough, people may avoid using it, rating the person in the opposite or contrasting direction. Certain conditions seem to undermine the usual assimilation effects and instead encourage contrast (Table 3.3).

Contrast occurs particularly when consciousness of the priming task is likely to be higher than usual (Martin, 1986). *Consciousness of the prime* is potentially important, for conscious priming appears to be more flexible than unconscious priming. When people are aware of a blatant prime and its potential link to a stimulus, they may resist its all-too-obvious influence or simply see it as too extreme compared to the ambiguous stimulus. In at least some circumstances, only unconscious perception of the prime leads to assimilation of the stimulus to the accessible category; conscious perception of the prime instead can either contrast or assimilate the stimulus to the accessible category (Lombardi, Higgins, & Bargh, 1987; L. S. Newman & Uleman, 1990).

Assimilation and contrast also depend on features of the stimuli involved. As implied by the previous example, degree of *overlap* between the prime and the stimulus is clearly important; similar primes, which tend to increase overlap, are most likely to show assimilation in either conscious or unconscious priming. Contrast effects obtain when the stimuli do not overlap much with the primed category, as when extreme primes are used (Herr, 1986; Herr, Sherman, & Fazio, 1983).

Table 3.3   Conditions encouraging assimilation versus contrast

Assimilation	Contrast
Preconscious prime	Conscious prime
Prime-stimulus overlap high	Prime-stimulus overlap low
Ambiguous stimulus	Unambiguous stimulus
Category prime	Exemplar prime
Unmotivated perceiver	Motivated (e.g., vigilant) perceiver
Similarity testing	Difference testing

Stimulus *ambiguity* also matters because an ambiguous stimulus easily assimilates to a prime. Unambiguous stimuli may result in contrast effects (Herr et al., 1983). Presumably, with an unambiguous stimulus, the complete lack of fit between prime and stimulus becomes especially obvious, and perceivers overcompensate, contrasting the two.

Finally, the perceiver's *goal* matters, even with unconscious priming, so for example, self-protective motivations can interact with the prime (Spencer, Fein, Wolfe, Fong, & Dunn, 1998). People also assimilate to socially shared goals, implicitly coordinating with an ingroup member pursuing the same goal at the same time, even if not physically present (Shteynberg & Galinsky, 2011). Both affiliative and epistemic (understanding) goals make people assimilate to socially shared reality (Lun, Sinclair, Whitchurch, & Glenn, 2007; Sinclair, Lowery, Hardin, & Colangelo, 2005). Assimilating to similar others contributes to the development of culture (Shteynberg, 2010).

These and other factors come together in a **selective accessibility model** of assimilation and contrast (Mussweiler, 2003). Because the model addresses conscious comparisons rather than automatic ones, it assumes accessibility is more flexible (controllable) and specific to the judgment at hand (rather than general semantic priming). Nevertheless, the model does hinge on accessibility, and it pulls together several useful principles relevant to when assimilation and contrast most likely occur, perhaps extending to both conscious and unconscious accessibility. If similarity testing is the accessible strategy, then people search for similarity, so assimilation results; if difference testing is accessible, then people search for differences, and contrast results. Similarity testing occurs most often; people tend to focus on similarities because they spontaneously make an overall, holistic comparison of a target to the baseline standard. For example, in comparing pineapples and avocadoes, one first decides whether they belong to the same category (tropical fruit), and then assimilates, but if they seem to belong to different categories (sweet versus savory), one contrasts them. In thinking about someone who is neat and tidy, one assimilates to a person of one's own gender and contrasts to someone of the other gender; the mechanism here is accessibility of the standard (Mussweiler & Bodenhausen, 2002). Thus the principles of overlap, ambiguity, and goals that apply to unconscious priming also apply to conscious comparisons to the extent that both depend on accessibility of similarities versus differences.

Priming at Encoding

Priming operates primarily through accessibility at encoding. Researchers suggest several reasons for this role of encoding. First, priming effects decrease with wider gaps between a prime and a stimulus. The wider gap presumably interferes with encoding the stimulus in terms of the prime (Srull & Wyer, 1979, 1980). When the prime and stimulus do occur in close temporal proximity, the effect depends on the stimulus being encoded together with the prime (Figure 3.4).

A second argument for the importance of encoding in priming comes from research that delays just the rating. Priming effects increase with wider temporal gaps between the already-primed stimulus and rating. As the effect increases with time, details of the original stimulus are lost, and the primed representation becomes relatively more important.

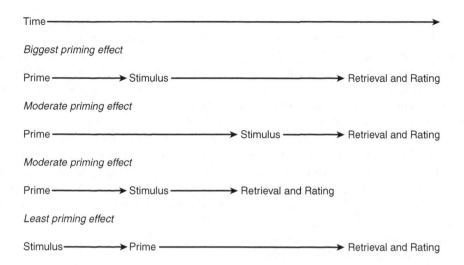

Figure 3.4   Prime–stimulus intervals and priming effect sizes

The third argument for encoding is simpler: Presenting primes *after* the stimulus has little or no effect, whereas presenting primes before the stimulus, which allows it to affect encoding, does show effects. This further supports the conclusion that encoding a stimulus in the context of a prime is more important than retrieving it in the context of the prime (Srull & Wyer, 1980).

Finally, prime-relevant information appears to elicit differential attention (S. J. Sherman, Mackie, & Driscoll, 1988). That is, participants do not rate primed dimensions as more important in decision making, but they do recall them better, suggesting that the primed dimension may elicit attention.

Chronic Accessibility

Accessibility can occur because of categories recently primed or categories frequently primed (e.g., Bargh & Pietromonaco, 1982; Bargh et al., 1986; Förster & Liberman, 2007; Higgins et al., 1977, 1982; Srull & Wyer, 1989; Wyer & Srull, 1986). Various models have been proposed to account for these effects, and experiments clarify the models' differences by setting recency and frequency in competition against each other (Higgins, 1989a), as work on chronically primed concepts shows.

Persistent differences in what is primed by one's typical situation may lead to individual differences in what is chronically accessible for different people. As noted in Chapter 2, well-practiced judgments become automatic through **proceduralization**. We all know people who seem to perceive everyone in terms of how smart they are, how trustworthy, or how good-looking. People for whom a particular personality dimension is an easily and typically accessible construct are more likely to remember and describe others in those terms (Higgins & King, 1981).

For example, Higgins, King, and Mavin (1982) identified people's most typically accessible personality dimensions by recording the first and most frequent dimensions that arose in their descriptions of themselves and their friends (e.g., intelligent, funny, nice). The dimensions that people spontaneously mention are presumably the ones that come to mind most easily when the environment provides cues that can be interpreted in that way. Dimensions that are frequently accessed or permanently primed may become central aspects of one's personality, and one develops **chronicity** on that dimension.

Moreover, given that chronicity theoretically results from a history of frequent exposure to a category, it should operate as does sheer frequency in situational priming, at least in any particular setting. Comparing the principles of frequency and recency, frequently primed constructs have the advantage in the long run, although recently primed constructs predominate in the short term (Higgins, Bargh, & Lombardi, 1985). Parallel results obtain for individual differences in chronicity and for recent priming; that is, recently primed categories predominate in the short term, but like frequently primed categories, chronically primed categories also predominate after a delay (Bargh, Lombardi, & Higgins, 1988).

Chronically accessible categories are used efficiently, allowing one to encode relevant information in less time than would someone who is nonchronic on that dimension (Bargh & Thein, 1985). Moreover, chronically accessible categories seem to be used without one's intention (Bargh et al., 1986; Higgins et al., 1982) and even outside one's control (Bargh & Pratto, 1986). As we saw, these characteristics of chronicity qualify it as truly automatic (Bargh, 1984; Payne, 2012).

The automatic application of chronically accessible constructs to new information has significant social consequences. For example, the automatic, chronic processing of negative social categories regarding oneself – but not others in general – appears to be an important component of depression (Bargh & Tota, 1988). In a meta-analysis related to depression, negative self-focus strongly relates to negative affect across both correlational studies and experimental studies that manipulate self-focus and valence of thoughts; positive self-focus reduces negative affect. These results held for depression, not just temporary bad moods: Depression was especially related to private self-focus (negativity regarding one's own goals, thoughts, and feelings), whereas anxiety was related to public self-focus (negativity in the impression one makes on others) (Mor & Winquist, 2002). The good news is that these effects are not solely a function of individual differences in chronic accessibility. Given that they also differ as a function of context, they potentially can change.

Individual differences in other forms of chronicity also matter interpersonally. For example, gender accessibility exaggerates gender-stereotypic encoding biases (Stangor, 1988). That is, after seeing a series of male- and female-stereotypic behavior performed by men and women equally, gender-accessible participants were especially likely (a) to report stereotype-consistent behaviors (e.g., women doing feminine things) and (b) to mix up the women with each other and the men with each other. Chronic gender-accessibility influences responses even to female politicians' ads, especially when they are positive or uninformative (compared to negative ads) (Chang & Hitchon, 2004). Chronicity may also explain a positive side-effect of stereotyping. People accustomed to being stereotyped (e.g., African Americans) sometimes show more tolerance for another potentially stereotyped person, presumably because they can see the similarity of their shared experiences, at least if their own victimization is also primed (Galanis & Jones, 1986); chronicity for stereotyping may help explain this phenomenon.

Conclusion about Accessibility

This section on accessibility's role in attention and encoding has shown that accessibility is the mechanism by which priming operates. Situational priming affects the accessibility of a wide range of stimuli: traits, social categories, valence (positivity–negativity), procedures, and behaviors. Accessibility usually causes assimilation of the stimulus to the prime, but it can also cause contrast, depending on consciousness of the prime, stimulus and prime overlap, stimulus ambiguity, and perceiver goals. Accessibility is primarily an encoding effect, influencing interpretations of stimuli as they are noticed and stored. Chronic accessibility affects encoding in similar ways to contextual accessibility; both affect important social behaviors.

DIRECT PERCEPTION: NOT JUST IN OUR HEADS

This chapter opened with an example of a social perceiver unfortunately misperceiving who was chasing whom in a series of three runners. One might argue that the example reflects the automatic activation of stereotypic categorization processes (interpreting the trio as a White police officer chasing two Black suspects), and one might marvel at the complexity of the inferential processes that occurred in the split second before the perceiver responded in such a misguided fashion. Alternatively, one might argue that, for that perceiver, the particular stimulus configuration effectively furnished his response. From this perspective, the perception was direct, from seeing and hearing straight to the intrinsic behavioral possibilities.

Inspired by J. J. Gibson's (1966, 1979) work in object perception, several theorists have suggested that much of the important activity in social understanding occurs immediately during perception (Lowe & Kassin, 1980; McArthur & Baron, 1983; Neisser, 1980; Semin, Garrido & Palma, 2012; Weary, Swanson, Harvey, & Yarkin, 1980; Zebrowitz, 1990). This view rejects perception as the result of complex inferential activity, however automated. In particular, the ecological approach emphasizes external stimulus information and the organization inherent in it, rather than the organization constructed or imposed by the perceiver (Zebrowitz, 1990). Organization is "inherent in a stimulus" for a particular perceiver, based on that person's history of perceptual experiences. A particular stimulus **affords** or offers particular behaviors to a perceiver, and the perceiver is reciprocally **attuned** or sensitive to particular stimulus properties. The Gibsonian approach is called **ecological perception** because it emphasizes perceivers interacting with their environments and embedded in their own characteristic niche. Perception is analyzed as adaptive for perceivers; "perceiving is for doing," in this view, so perception will typically be accurate if perceivers are given sufficient information and context.

An Early Example of Ecological Causal Perception

The Gibsonian perspective suggests, for example, that social interpretations result from segmenting the perceptual field, and that inferences and memory are irrelevant (McArthur, 1980). To illustrate, assume you overhear your neighbors quarreling. She screams at him, and he murmurs in reply; this sequence alternates for some minutes. In relating the incident to your roommate, you describe the woman as causing the argument because each segment of the interaction begins with her salient vocal behavior. Each of her loud comments marks a new perceptual unit that finishes with his soft reply. She shouts, he murmurs. Because responsibility requires temporal precedence, starting each unit with her then irresistibly blames her for the argument (Figure 3.5).

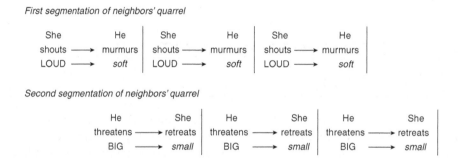

Figure 3.5   Perceptual segmentation of behavioral sequences resulting in different causal judgments

Note: Each vertical rule represents a breakpoint between two perceptual units.

Now replay the fight but assume that you can see what is going on as well as hear it. (Assume further that they both do not turn on you for spying, however scientifically disinterested you might be.) The fight actually commences with him walking into the room and gesturing violently at her. She replies and retreats. He threatens her again, speaking in ominously low tones, and she backs off, arguing defensively. He threatens, and she retreats. The segments now commence each time with his physical gestures and her retreats. His physical gestures are perceptually big relative to her little retreats, in much the same way her shouts were loud compared to his soft murmurs. The units now begin with him: he makes big physical threats, and she makes little movements of retreat. Now the man would be described as causing the argument. Note that this perceptual analysis of responsibility de-emphasizes cognitive activity. The blame judgments are implicit in perception from the outset (McArthur, 1980).

With respect to interpretations, the Gibsonian view would argue that they result from perceptual organization, such as temporal sequence, or the contrast of large to small stimuli, as in our example of the neighbors' fight; the Gibsonian view suggests that inferred blame occurs automatically during the perception of an event, an idea with which others agree (R. C. Sherman & Titus, 1982; E. R. Smith & Miller, 1979).

Early Work on Perceptual Units

The direct perception analysis is all the more interesting because considerable evidence indicates that inherent perceptual units have important effects on social judgments. Measuring perceptual segmentation directly shows this (for a review, see Newtson, Hairfield, Bloomingdale, & Cutino, 1987; for a critique, see Ebbesen, 1980). The technique for measuring perceptual segments or units involves participants watching a film and pushing a button to indicate the end of each given segment and the beginning of a new one; the button push is taken to indicate what is called a breakpoint between segments. Individuals define segments in whatever way seems natural (Newtson & Enquist, 1976; Newtson, Enquist, & Bois, 1977). The unitizing method (as it is called) is reliable, valid, and surprisingly comfortable for participants. People largely agree on the perceptual units in a given scene. For example, if the neighbors' quarrel were shown in a silent film, people would generally agree on the breakpoints.

Unitizing research suggests that the breakpoints between perceptual units have special properties. People break the behavior stream into meaningful units based on the actor's intentions and goals (Baldwin & Baird, 2001). The breakpoint moments of a film, shown as a series of stills in isolation from the rest of the film, nonetheless coherently convey the story. Nonbreakpoints (at equivalent intervals) do not adequately summarize the story. Recognition memory for breakpoints is also superior to recognition for nonbreakpoints. The implication is that behavior is segmented at points of maximal information (Newtson, 1980; but for dissent, see C. E. Cohen & Ebbesen, 1979). Breakpoints occur at peaks of behavioral complexity when many body parts are changing at once (Newtson et al., 1977). That is, one can perceive the core of an action when it is most distinctively changing, so that becomes a breakpoint. If action slows down to a pause or stops, that is not typically a breakpoint. Moreover, the rise and fall of action complexity follow a wave pattern: When two people are interacting, their actions jointly create a coordinated wave pattern (Newtson et al., 1987). This suggests that basic perceptual-motor configurations could function independently of complex cognitive processes.

People can use fine-grained units or grosser units, depending on instructions to do so or other goals. For example, people use finer units when their goal is observing nonverbal behavior (Strenta & Kleck, 1984), remembering task behavior (C. E. Cohen & Ebbesen, 1979), and observing individuals within an aggregate of people (Wilder, 1986). People also use finer units when they encounter an unexpected action (Newtson, 1973; Wilder, 1978a, 1986) or a person about whom they have no prior information (Graziano, Moore, & Collins, 1988). Finer levels of perception are associated with measures indicating more information gained: more confident and differentiated trait inferences, more dispositional attributions (Deaux & Major, 1977; Newtson, 1973; Wilder, 1978a), and better memory for the person observed (Lassiter, 1988; Lassiter, Stone, & Rogers, 1988). Finer unitizing even seems to be associated with greater liking of an otherwise neutral person, perhaps because of an increased sense of familiarity independent of one's improved memory for the finely unitized other (Lassiter, 1988; Lassiter & Stone, 1984).

The unitizing research as a whole addresses basic perceptual processes in ongoing interaction, suggesting how information is gained over time and made immediately useful to action.

A Note on Implications for Social Cognition Research

The direct perception or ecological view argues that it contradicts inferences necessarily depending on complex cognitive processes. According to this view, cognitive constructs (such as observational goals or category-based expectations) enter into the inference process only to the degree that such factors influence the initial perception of an event as it is directly observed (Enquist, Newtson, & LaCross, 1979; Massad, Hubbard, & Newtson, 1979). Although some evidence argues the contrary (Vinokur & Ajzen, 1982), the Gibsonian view is a helpful counterpoint to the standard explanations of complex cognitive processes as the only basis for social judgments. And as Chapter 4 indicates, the Gibsonian perspective influences current work on embodied representation.

The Gibsonian perspective is a useful antidote to some biases in mainstream research on encoding, recognizing the intrinsic richness of stimulus information and insisting that stimuli be *ecologically valid*: namely, that they occur in multiple sensory modes, that they change and not be utterly static, that they be presented in configuration instead of isolation, and that they be extended in time instead of being brief. The Gibsonians' frequent use of naturalistic filmed stimuli illustrates this set of concerns. The ecological approach also emphasizes the *adaptive functions* of perception, in particular the link between perception and action. Hence, it examines why people would develop the perception that baby-faced people need nurturance and protection (namely, that most baby-faced people are in fact babies, whom it is useful for adults to perceive as vulnerable). Moreover, the ecological approach explicitly acknowledges the relationship between the environment and the particular perceiver's goals, capabilities, and history. Although the social cognition literature does this as well, the Gibsonian view emphasizes the environment as full of *action possibilities* (**affordances**). Finally, it points to the relevance of cross-cultural, animal, and developmental research for *comparative* purposes.

In closing, several reasons argue against pitting the ecological and cognitive approach directly against each other. First, each is itself a metatheory, which is not intrinsically falsifiable. At the broadest levels, each can always account for the other's data in perceptual or cognitive terms, respectively. Second, distinguishing between perception and cognition in practice is difficult. On one hand, perception entails taking in stimulus features in order to respond to the environment, and on the other hand, cognition can entail immediate automatic inferential activity. Whether one labels such processes "cognitive," or sometimes "perceptual" and sometimes "cognitive," depending on their rapidity or accessibility to awareness, is a matter of theoretical preference, and the distinction begins to evaporate. Third, the relative impact of perceptual and cognitive activity in any one experiment depends on the relative strengths with which each is manipulated, so any empirical "advantage" of one over the other would be a function of the particular experiment's operationalization of the perceptual process or the cognitive process, not reflecting the intrinsic relative power of the two types of process. Finally, some would argue that stimulus variation (what a particular stimulus intrinsically affords) is the mark of the ecological approach, but perceiver variation (cognitive structures that perceivers bring with them) marks the cognitive approach. If so, one is stuck comparing apples and oranges, phenomena on altogether different scales. That is, one can assess how much the stimulus contributes and how much the perceiver contributes, but they cannot be directly compared because they come from separate populations (the population of all social perceivers or all possible stimuli).

In short, the two approaches are complementary, each with its own strengths (R. M. Baron, 1980). The ecological perception approach focuses on what people learn from particular stimulus configurations. The work on causal perception and unitizing the behavior stream (as well as work, discussed earlier, on trait inferences from physical cues) illustrate important patterns of social stimuli that perceivers use for adaptive functioning. Social cognition focuses more on mental structures and routines that people use to interpret, elaborate, and construct their memory and judgments. This type of ecological perception attunes the perceiver to what actions the context affords.

Summary

We now have some answers to what captures attention. People reflexively orient to people's faces, especially those who are orienting to them. People also look in the direction others gaze. And people immediately infer people's personalities from their faces.

People especially notice what is salient: stimuli that are novel or perceptually figural in context, people or behaviors that are unusual or unexpected, extreme and sometimes negative behavior, and stimuli relevant to our current goals. All such salience subsequently influences reactions to other people. Attention may also be captured by vivid stimuli, often entertaining, but vivid stimuli do not influence reactions much except when they are vivid case histories.

Attention also orients to situationally or personally primed categories. Recently, frequently, and chronically encountered categories are more accessible for use, and they profoundly influence the encoding of stimuli. They are applied to relevant, moderate, ambiguous stimuli, guiding their interpretation and subsequent cognitive representation.

Attention focuses on ecologically relevant features of the social context; that is, features that afford action. In short, we have learned a lot about social attention, which determines what gets encoded into memory, the topic for the next chapter.

FURTHER READING

Bargh, J. A., Bond, R. N., Lombardi, W. J., & Tota, M. E. (1986). The additive nature of chronic and temporary sources of construct accessibility. *Journal of Personality and Social Psychology, 50*, 869–879.

Cloutier, J., Mason, M.F., & Macrae, C.N. (2005). The perceptual determinants of person construal: Reopening the social-cognitive toolbox. *Journal of Personality and Social Psychology, 88*, 885–894.

Fiske, S. T. (1980). Attention and weight in person perception: The impact of negative and extreme behavior. *Journal of Personality and Social Psychology, 38*, 889–906.

Förster, J., & Liberman, N. (2007). Knowledge activation. In A. W. Kruglanski & E. T. Higgins (Eds.), *Social psychology: Handbook of basic principles* (2nd edn, pp. 201–231). New York: Guilford Press.

Guadagno, R. E., Rhoads, K. v. L., & Sagarin, B. J. (2011). Figural vividness and persuasion: Capturing the "elusive" vividness effect. *Personality and Social Psychology Bulletin, 37(5)*, 626–638.

Haxby, J. V., Hoffman, E. A., & Gobbini, M. I. (2000). The distributed human neural system for face perception. *Trends in Cognitive Science, 4*, 223–233.

Higgins, E. T., Rholes, W. S., & Jones, C. R. (1977). Category accessibility and impression formation. *Journal of Experimental Social Psychology, 13*, 141–154.

Lassiter, G. D. (2002). Illusory causation in the courtroom. *Current Directions in Psychological Science, 11*, 204–208.

Mussweiler, T. (2003). Comparison processes in social judgment: Mechanisms and consequences. *Psychological Review, 110*, 472–489.

Semin, G. R., Garrido, M. V., & Palma, T. A. (2012). Socially situated cognition: Recasting social cognition as an emergent phenomenon. In S. T. Fiske & C. N. Macrae (Eds.), *Sage handbook of social cognition* (pp. 138–164). Thousand Oaks, CA: Sage.

Taylor, S. E., & Thompson, S. C. (1982). Stalking the elusive "vividness" effect. *Psychological Review, 89*, 155–181.

Todorov, A. (2012). The social perception of faces. In S. T. Fiske & C. N. Macrae (Eds.), *Sage handbook of social cognition* (pp. 96–114). Thousand Oaks, CA: Sage.

Zebrowitz, L. A., Kikuchi, M., & Fellous, J.-M. (2010). Facial resemblance to emotions: Group differences, impression effects, and race stereotypes. *Journal of Personality and Social Psychology, 98(2)*, 175–189.

Representation in Memory 4

- Associative Networks: Organizing Memory
- Procedural and Declarative Memory: What Memory Does
- Parallel versus Serial Processing: Coordinating Memory Processes
- Embodied Memory: Including Physical Representation
- Social Memory Structures: Why Social Memory Matters

This chapter covers social and nonsocial models of memory and closes with mental representations – the social categories and individual exemplars that we keep in mind. First, we outline each cognitive model, and then we describe the social cognitive models derived from it; social cognition researchers have adapted general cognitive models to develop models specific to social cognition, in particular, memory for people. We discuss associative networks, procedural memory, connectionist (parallel) models, embodied memory, and memory structures such as categories and exemplars.

ASSOCIATIVE NETWORKS: ORGANIZING MEMORY

Suppose you are standing at a busy intersection waiting for the light to change. Across the street, you see a young man knock down an elderly woman, grab her purse, and run away. By the time you can get across the street, he is long gone, so you turn your attention to the woman. Just as you have discovered that she is angry but unhurt, a police officer arrives and takes down your description of what happened. How is this event stored in your memory, and why does its mental representation matter? Several models of memory account for this phenomenon. In this section we detail the classic memory model, the associative network approach. This model underlies most social cognitive studies, especially the earliest ones. Later sections address advances beyond this initial approach.

The Basic Cognitive Model of Associative Networks

The most important general principle of this approach is that the more links or associations from other concepts to any given concept in memory, the easier it is to remember that concept because many alternative routes can locate it in memory. The following sections elaborate this point in detail because social cognition research grew out of this approach, though now social cognition research offers competing alternatives. Table 4.1 summarizes some key features of the classic approach in the first column.

Table 4.1　Key features of cognitive long-term memory (LTM) models

Associative memory (declarative memory for content)	Procedural memory (automatic memory for practiced processes)	Parallel distributed processing (connectionist models)	Embodied memory (perceptual symbol systems)
Storage includes intermediate recent and remote longer-term memory			Includes top-down expectations (frames)
Includes episodic memory for specific events and semantic memory for facts, word meaning, and general encyclopedic knowledge	Includes all kinds of information	Includes all kinds of information	Includes bottom-up, sensory information, introspection, and proprioception
Propositions in node–link structure	If–then (condition–action) productions	Patterns of inhibitory and facilitative connections	Simulators that organize related perceptual symbols
Process: spread activation across alternative retrieval routes	Process: match, select, execute	Process: adjust connection strengths	Process: simulate online in object's presence and offline in object absence
Activation strength determines retrieval	Current goals and stimuli determine selection and use of procedures	Input patterns and connection weights jointly determine retrieval	Focuses on perception for action
Implicates hippocampus immediately, cortical consolidation in longer term	Productions implicate basal ganglia loop; goals implicate dorsolateral prefrontal cortex		

The exact format of the representation is called a memory code. A variety of possible codes are discussed later, but the best known in early cognitive psychology was a **proposition** (J. R. Anderson, 1976; Rumelhart, Lindsay, & Norman, 1972; Wickelgren, 1981). For example, "The woman stands on the corner" is one proposition; others are "The woman is elderly," "The man knocks down the woman," and so forth. Each proposition consists of nodes and links, each node being an idea (noun, verb, adjective) and each link being the relation between ideas.

These models of human memory are **associative**; that is, most refer to connections between nodes (the woman) linked to other nodes (elderly). The associative feature matters for interpersonal events. Suppose you give eyewitness testimony on the mugging case (Figure 4.1). The organization of long-term memory into an associative node–link structure means that you will recall related facts together. That is, if you begin by thinking about the woman herself, it may be easier to recall her attributes (e.g., elderly, standing on the corner) than to recall the man's attributes (e.g., young).

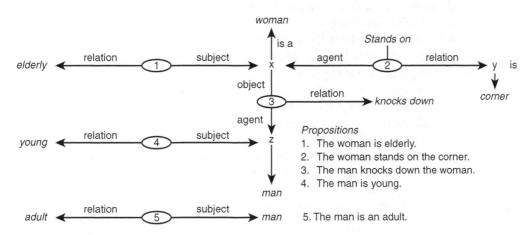

Figure 4.1 Propositional network model for knowledge that "The elderly woman standing on the corner is knocked down by the young man" (after J. R. Anderson, 1980a). Each separate proposition is indicated by an ellipse. For example, the first proposition ("The woman is elderly") is represented by the nodes and links on the upper left of the figure. The numbered ellipses indicate the other propositions. Starting at ellipse 1, anything connected by arrows moving away from the ellipse is part of that particular proposition. For example, "elderly" and "woman" both are connected to the ellipse by arrows from it and to them. But "stands on" is not part of the first proposition; accordingly, the link from the ellipse labeled "1" to "stands on" is interrupted by an arrow pointing the wrong way. The other notation that needs explaining is the use of x, y, and z. They indicate that x is one particular woman, who is also elderly. If the proposition were "Woman are elderly" (i.e., the entire category of women is elderly), the x would be replaced by the word "woman" in the figure. For example, the proposition "The man is an adult" (true of all men) would be denoted differently than "This particular man is young" (see propositions 4 and 5 in the figure). For present purposes, the notation illustrates the precision with which details of meaning can be represented in a propositional network.

In associative memory models, activation spreads: Recall starts at one point (e.g., the woman) and moves out along links between the nodes (Collins & Loftus, 1975). Recalling that the woman was elderly, for example, activates both nodes in memory ("elderly" and "woman"), strengthening their link. Pragmatically, joint activation – frequent rehearsal (repetition) – of your testimony makes it more memorable than unrehearsed facts. The lawyer preparing you to be a witness may know that frequent reviews of the testimony ahead of time will strengthen its coherence and avoid awkward surprises, such as your remembering new events on the witness stand.

In addition to strengthening links among ideas by activating them together, the more separate linkages to any given idea, the more likely it is to be recalled. More links create more alternative **retrieval routes** and enhanced memory. Thus, a smart lawyer will help you to form many ways to access any given fact to minimize last-minute forgetfulness.

Long-Term versus Short-Term Memory

Many network memory models distinguish between long-term memory and short-term (or working) memory. In this view, **long-term memory** consists of the vast store of information one can potentially bring to mind. **Short-term memory** refers to the information that one is considering at any given moment, which is why it is also called **working memory** (Baddeley, 2012). In many memory models, the activated portion of long-term memory represents short-term memory or consciousness, as Chapter 3 noted (Table 4.2). That is, the long-term memory nodes that are currently most active make up the contents of focal attention. The contents of short-term memory can consolidate for storage in long-term memory.

In associative models, memory retrieval consists of activating the appropriate nodes in long-term memory, which brings them to consciousness if activation is above a certain threshold. Because the most active nodes can change rapidly, the conscious part of long-term memory (that is, what you are thinking about right now) is considered short-term. Things move in and out of consciousness, or short-term memory, as they become activated and fade from being activated.

Table 4.2 Key features of cognitive short-term or working memory models

Associative memory models	Procedural memory models
Most activated portion of LTM but also attended stimuli, may be consolidated for storage in LTM	
Fast, easy learning requires STM capacity	Slow learning, requires practice
Automatic or controlled execution	Fast, automatic execution
Widely available use	Specific, focused use
Flexible	Durable
Implicates ventrolateral prefrontal cortex in STM buffer	Implicates basal ganglia in procedural learning

The limited capacity for activation means that short-term memory is small in scope. In other words, few things can be held in mind simultaneously.

The consequences of the severe limits on short-term memory can be illustrated by a lawyer's questioning of a witness on the stand. A witness will be unable to keep lots of details in mind at once, so the person may contradict earlier testimony that is out of current consciousness. Short-term memory is normally assumed to hold about seven items of information (classically, 7 ±2; G. A. Miller, 1956). An "item" of information could be as small as a single letter or digit, or it could be a "chunk" of letters (i.e., a word on the mugger's sweatshirt) or a chunk of digits (i.e., the time on your watch).

In contrast to the limits of short-term memory, the capacity of the overall network of long-term memory storage seems, practically speaking, to be limitless. A lawyer who urges a witness to struggle to remember crucial details may be banking on this: The information all might be there; it is only a question of finding it. For long-term memory, the issue is not capacity (or how much one knows) but retrieval (whether one can find it). Skilled performance depends in part on having efficient cues to relevant material in long-term memory (Ericsson & Kintsch, 1995). Many models of social memory concern primarily the long-term memory organization, the links among items, and accessibility.

The neat distinction between long- and short-term memory may be breaking down. Neuroscience distinguishes among three general time periods of memory. Material may be actively attended in consciousness, in effect in extremely short-term memory, as just described. But two forms of what used to be considered long-term memory appear in distinctions between memory for recent and more remote events, sometimes called **intermediate** and long-term memory. These complementary intermediate and long-term memory systems allow both (a) rapid learning and recall of specific events, implicating the hippocampus, and (b) slow learning but rapid recognition of patterns, implicating the neocortex (medial **temporal lobe**) (e.g., McClelland, McNaughton, & O'Reilly, 1995; Norman & O'Reilly, 2003). These complementary learning systems reflect the hippocampus's role in recall of recent events and the higher brain's role in detecting regularities in the environment, slow to acquire and accept, but also slow to undo.

Associative Network Models of Social Memory

PM-1 Model

What do these cognitive models of memory say about social cognition? Consider one associative network model of social memory, **PM-1** (for Person Memory; Hastie, 1988b). This model works as a computer simulation, which is an important test of its sufficiency (Ostrom, 1988). In a nutshell, PM-1 predicts extra attention to impression-*inconsistent* material (because it is surprising), resulting in extra associative linkages for those items, increasing their alternative retrieval paths and probability of recall. This is called the **inconsistency advantage**.

According to this model, the encoding process invokes a limited-capacity working memory, which allows one to form links among items; the length of time items stay in working memory depends on their relevance to the current impression judgment. A longer stay in working memory forges more links. Links form between items that are unexpected given the current impression because they stay in mind longer as people try to figure them out. (The model also posits that some links are formed stochastically; that is, randomly.) Subsequent retrieval from long-term memory initiates at a random point and randomly spreads along pathways formed by interitem links. It terminates with repeated failures to retrieve an item not already retrieved.

Finally, the model also proposes a mechanism for impression formation, simultaneous with memory encoding and storage. The **anchoring and adjustment** process (Chapter 7) essentially provides for an impression that is updated with each new piece of information, based on an equally weighted average of (a) the cumulative evaluations of the items so far and (b) the items currently staying in working memory, including the new item (N. H. Anderson, 1981; Lopes, 1982).

One of this model's strong points is its simultaneous modeling of the online impression-formation process, plus memory storage and retrieval processes. For example, when people form **online impressions** – that is, as they receive information – their impressions result from this gradual process. However, when people do not form impressions online, they have to retrieve information to create an impression from memory. In this *post hoc* case, their memory for the information will correlate with their impression precisely because they construct a **memory-based impression**. In the online, simultaneous-impression case, memory is irrelevant to the spontaneous impression formed because different factors determine whether each piece of information is important to the impression versus memorable. People can remember trivia but discount them in the impression, for example.

Person Memory Model

Another approach, the **person memory model** (Srull & Wyer, 1989), makes fundamentally similar assumptions. Basic processes create an impression from a target's behavior: interpreting behavior in trait terms, evaluating overall likeability, reviewing behaviors that seem inconsistent with the evaluation, and making memory-based judgments according to either inferred traits or a review of remembered behaviors.

The model provides a detailed analysis of known social cognitive processes. For example, early information most influences the evaluation, a phenomenon called the **primacy effect** (cf. Asch, 1946; E. E. Jones & Goethals, 1972). In other words, first impressions count: Learning first about more positive attributes predisposes one toward a positive impression. In the Srull–Wyer model, an initial evaluation forms as soon as the information is clearly and consistently positive or negative, and subsequent behavior is interpreted in light of this initial information.

Like the Hastie model previously described, the Srull–Wyer model assumes that evaluatively inconsistent behaviors are considered thoughtfully in comparison to other behaviors. This consideration strengthens links between each inconsistent behavior and the remaining behaviors (compared to the links between each evaluatively consistent or neutral behavior and the remaining behaviors). The inconsistency advantage presumably occurs as people think about the inconsistencies, relating them to each other and to the consistent behaviors, creating associative links among them.

One can infer the point at which participants have formed their overall evaluative impression by observing impressions as they form. That is, over blocks (clusters of stimulus behaviors), one can observe the start-up and increase of the inconsistency advantage in memory. (Essentially, one would plot the degree of inconsistency advantage in each successive block; see Figure 4.2.) One study required at least five blocks of five behaviors each to show the inconsistency advantage (Srull, Lichtenstein, & Rothbart, 1985); that is, it took 25 behaviors to develop an evaluative impression strong enough to make people notice new information being inconsistent with an overall evaluative impression. This suggests that evaluatively mixed information does not quickly generate a strong evaluative impression, so it would not easily show an inconsistency advantage in memory. The inconsistency advantage may be limited to impressions with very few pieces of inconsistent information against an extraordinarily consistent information baseline.

Similarly, interfering with the formation of interitem links should eliminate the inconsistency advantage in memory. Studies in which participants perform a competing online task (even rehearsing the stimulus items!) do not show the same inconsistency advantage (Srull, 1981; Srull et al., 1985). The same is true of participants without the capacity and time to form online links

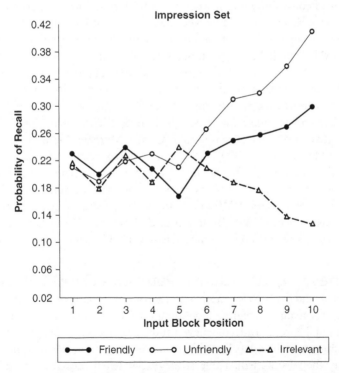

Figure 4.2 Mean proportion of friendly, unfriendly, and irrelevant episodes recalled with friendly expectancy (majority friendly behaviors in each block), under an impression-formation goalset, as a function of input block position

Source: Srull, Lichtenstein, & Rothbart, 1985, Experiment 6. Copyright American Psychological Association; reproduced by permission

(Bargh & Thein, 1985; Barrett, Tugade, & Engle, 2004; Macrae, Bodenhausen, Schloerscheidt, & Milne, 1999). Finally, although participants show an inconsistency advantage within the main person memory paradigm, they may instead preferentially recall consistent items when they have time to think over their impression afterward, perhaps due to bolstering the overall evaluative direction of the impression (Wyer & Martin, 1986). In other words, over the long term, consistent material enjoys a memorial advantage.

This model usefully summarizes vast quantities of research by Srull, Wyer, and their colleagues. One disadvantage of the Srull–Wyer model was its assumption of multiple representations all pertaining to a single person. This cumbersome idea was not endorsed by other models of person memory, and it tends to make this model both counterintuitive (not as much a technical flaw as an aesthetic one) and also perhaps overly flexible, able to account for virtually any result or its opposite.

One prominent feature of person memory models (both the Hastie and Srull–Wyer versions) is their predicting a recall advantage for impression-inconsistent behaviors, based on increased attention, linkages, and retrieval routes for inconsistent material. The inconsistency advantage was a robust effect within the standard laboratory paradigm of instilling a trait impression, then presenting a series of consistent and inconsistent behaviors and asking participants to recall the behaviors (see Srull & Wyer, 1989). However, the inconsistency advantage is *not* obtained when the research paradigm departs from the standard one in any of several ways that complicate the perceiver's task: well-established expectancies (S. T. Fiske & Neuberg, 1990; Higgins & Bargh, 1987; Ruble & Stangor, 1986), multiple trait expectancies (D. L. Hamilton, Driscoll, & Worth, 1989), behaviors that are descriptively but not evaluatively inconsistent (Wyer & Gordon, 1982), time to think about one's impression afterwards (Wyer & Martin, 1986), having to make a complex judgment (Bodenhausen & Lichtenstein, 1987; Bodenhausen & Wyer, 1985), cognitive load or selective memory (Garcia-Marques, Hamilton, & Maddox, 2002), and multitasking (Macrae et al., 1999). Also, when it does occur, the inconsistency advantage occurs for impressions of individuals who are expected to have coherent personalities and not so much for groups, which are viewed as containing less coherent "personalities" (Rothbart, Evans, & Fulero, 1979; Srull et al., 1985). What's more, social processes such as traits and behaviors overheard in a conversation (Wyer, Budesheim, & Lambert, 1990) favor consistency, as do socially-shared retrievals of collective events such as 9/11 (Coman, Maner, & Hirst, 2009).

Twofold Retrieval by Associative Pathways (TRAP) Model

Although the Hastie and Srull–Wyer models can account for many of these results, people probably use multiple processing strategies, depending on the circumstances, as in the dual-process models described in Chapter 2. Indeed, a newer model suggests that people use distinct retrieval processes, depending on their task (Garcia-Marques & Hamilton, 1996). When they attempt to recall information, they use an exhaustive strategy, but when they want to remember specific instances to make a frequency judgment, for example, they use a heuristic retrieval strategy. The exhaustive strategy favors memory for inconsistency, whereas the heuristic strategy favors memory for consistency. This **twofold retrieval by associative pathways (TRAP) model** is consistent with other dual-process models.

Table 4.3   Key person memory models

Person memory models	Social procedural models	Social connectionist models	Embodied social cognition
Hastie: person memory-1	E. R. Smith: proceduralization	Kunda & Thagard: parallel constraint satisfaction model	Niedenthal et al.: embodied social cognition and emotion
Srull & Wyer: person memory and judgment	Lewicki: implicit recognition	Van Overwalle: connectionist models	Feldman Barrett: embodied experience of emotion
Marques & Hamilton: twofold retrieval and associative processing model		Kashima: tensor-product model	E. R. Smith & Semin: socially situated cognition
Carlston: associated systems theory		Read: Gestalt connectionism	
		Vallacher & Nowak: dynamical systems	
		E. R. Smith & DeCoster: social connectionism	

Associated Systems Theory

According to **associated systems theory (AST)**, representations of other people develop through the use of four primary mental systems: (a) the visual system, (b) the verbal/semantic system, (c) the affective system, and (d) the action system (Carlston, 1994). These four modalities are relatively independent at lower levels related to immediate encoding but intertwine as representations become more abstract. Many of the mechanisms otherwise fit prior associative memory models. This view explicitly adds other modalities to the associative memory models' primary focus on cognitive modalities, most notably affect and action.

Conclusion about Associative Memory Models

The most influential model of memory in social cognition has been the node–link structure proposed by associative memory models. In this view, each concept (trait, behavior, person's name) is represented as a node, with links formed by relating two items to each other. Memory retrieval proceeds along the pathways provided by the network. The recall advantage for expectancy-inconsistent versus expectancy-consistent information, under some circumstances, is one of the major empirical legacies of these models. Newer approaches that build on procedural memory, parallel processes, and social neuroscience go beyond these early controversies (Tables 4.1–4.3).

PROCEDURAL AND DECLARATIVE MEMORY: WHAT MEMORY DOES

The Basic Cognitive Model of Procedural and Declarative Memory

As just described, many models assume that memory includes an associative network of concepts, a long-term store of content knowledge. This **declarative memory** is sometimes contrasted with one form of automaticity described earlier, **procedural knowledge** (Squire, 1987). In Chapter 2 we explained one form of automatic processing as **proceduralization** – that is, the speed-up of judgments with practice. However, we did not locate procedural processes within a larger model of memory. With some additional background on memory, we can do so, building on more recent memory models (e.g., J. R. Anderson et al., 2004). Respectively, they roughly cover the "what" (declarative) and the "how" (procedural) forms of memory (Table 4.1).

Newer associative network models posit that declarative memory is activated as a joint function of its general usefulness in the past and its current relevance; together they control both probability and speed of retrieval (Anderson et al., 2004). Retrieval from declarative memory implicates the hippocampus and the temporal lobes. (Recall the taxi drivers with enlarged hippocampi for street location memory in Chapter 1.) Declarative long-term memory includes both **episodic memory** for specific events (Tulving, 1983) and **semantic memory** for facts, word meaning, and encyclopedic knowledge (Squire, 1992). Consistent with earlier ideas about short-term memory, retrieved material occupies a space-limited buffer associated with the ventrolateral prefrontal cortex (Buckner, Kelley, & Petersen, 1999; Wagner, Paré-Blagoev, Clark, & Poldrack, 2001). Related chunks of knowledge activate together, akin to short-term or working memory.

Procedural knowledge concerns skills – namely, how to do things – and is hypothesized to be represented differently. Procedural knowledge is represented as condition–action pairs, or if–then statements, called **productions**. When an input pattern matches the "if," or condition, part of the production, the "then," or action, part immediately operates. For example, a condition might include "if the email subject line advertises a large cash prize." The action part of the production, for some of us, includes "then delete without opening," while for others it must include "then open, read, and respond immediately." Various common cognitive productions (such as matching, selection, and execution) make up **procedural memory**, which globally implicates a loop involving the basal ganglia (J. R. Anderson et al., 2004). People's current goals determine which procedures fire; the goals may be associated with the dorsolateral prefrontal cortex. The current goal may occupy a buffer that tracks progress toward achieving an outcome.

Procedural Models of Social Memory

As described previously, content knowledge is initially represented in the declarative associative networks long familiar to social cognition researchers. The advantages of declarative representation include *easy learning*, for one simply links ideas; *wide applicability of use*, namely, in any situation that cues part of the structure; and *flexibility*, that is, enabling one to work in various directions among associations, depending on need (E. R. Smith, 1998). Thus declarative knowledge is general and independent of domain and is probably accessible to consciousness and verbal expression. Hence it has been amenable to the methods most commonly used by social cognition researchers.

The disadvantage of declarative knowledge is that it tends to be slower and to use up one's limited-capacity working (short-term) memory. Accordingly, as certain processes are used repeatedly, they eventually may be proceduralized to be more efficient, as noted earlier (Table 4.3).

Proceduralization

Social processes are nothing if not frequent, so it makes sense that some would be proceduralized, as in earlier examples of automaticity. Chapter 2 described the work of E. R. Smith and his colleagues, who applied the principles of procedural memory in particular to the speed-up of social inferences with practice (E. R. Smith, 1990; E. R. Smith & DeCoster, 1998); as noted, these practice effects provide one explanation for automaticity.

Procedural memory provides an alternative explanation for priming effects. Recall that priming demonstrates how a recently or frequently activated category influences the processing of new category-relevant information, usually interpreted as category accessibility: Using declarative memory, activation spreads from a prime to relevant concepts along the associative network's pathways. Any linked concept can prime another, whether the priming is based on words, faces, or symbols, as the process itself is general.

However, some priming can instead be process specific, as a procedural account would suggest (E. R. Smith, 1990); E. R. Smith & Branscombe, 1987, 1988; cf. Higgins & Chaires, 1980). Priming a personality trait by reading the word differs from priming a trait by inferring it from behavior. Each process primes faster responses a second time on the exact same task (procedural priming), and each process primes the trait itself (category accessibility). Procedural priming does not replace accessibility but essentially shows that processes can be primed as well as contents.

Implicit Memory

Other applications of procedural memory may explain the accessibility of certain attitudes (see Chapter 10), the selection of one inference or category from among many possible ones (cf. Chapter 11), and the learning of complex patterns that cannot be articulated (Lewicki, Czyzewska, & Hoffman, 1987; Musen & Squire, 1993; for a review, see Seger, 1994). The more a particular procedure is practiced, the more likely it is to be used again instead of other equally applicable procedures. In this view, such procedural effects are a form of **implicit memory**, which is a term for the influence of past judgmental processes on current judgments and reactions (E. R. Smith & Branscombe, 1988; see Jacoby & Kelley, 1987, for another discussion of unconscious memory). Procedural memory ideas have not overtaken social cognition, but their considerable influence appears in work on implicit associations (see Chapters 11–12).

Conclusion about Procedural Memory

Procedural memory introduces the idea of if–then automatic procedures built up through practice to become automatic processes. Social cognition applications of procedural memory focus mainly on priming specific operations and other instances of implicit memory (see Table 4.3).

PARALLEL VERSUS SERIAL PROCESSING: COORDINATING MEMORY PROCESSES

Cutting across issues of declarative (associative) and procedural memory is the issue of parallel versus serial processing. The traditional associative network models viewed spreading activation as a **parallel process** of activating many related pathways at once, but overall processes of encoding, memory retrieval, and response are generally viewed as a **serial process**, sequence of steps. Social categories are often seen as activating before the activation of individuating information (as described in Chapter 2). This could occur via either serial or parallel processing. That is, serially, first one is activated, then the other. Or if both are activated in parallel, perhaps the category information is processed faster and beats out the individuating information. The serial-processing idea is more prevalent in earlier information-processing models, so the newer models focus more on parallel processes, as this section explains.

The Basic Cognitive Model of Parallel Processing

Parallel distributed processing (PDP) is an approach to the structure of cognition that developed as an alternative to more traditional, mostly serial models of mental structure. For reasons that remain obscure, one of us found herself describing PDP to her 80-year-old great aunt, always an astute and intellectually challenging conversationalist, who demanded a sample of "the wave of the future" in cognition research. PDP seemed a safe bet in that the great aunt could be guaranteed to know even less about it than the author did. Precariously launched on an explanation, the metaphor for PDP that came to mind was an old-fashioned time and temperature sign board composed of lightbulbs. Such signs were made of a grid of bulbs, different combinations lighting up depending on the numerals that needed to be displayed. Each lightbulb contributes to all the times and temperatures displayed by being on or off within the overall pattern. In this oversimplified and admittedly flawed PDP metaphor, born of desperation, individual memory units are lightbulbs, each unit participating in many different memory patterns, as simply one feature of the whole. The same bulb could be part of the numeral "1" or "2." Moreover, the numeral "2" could appear in different positions on the board, depending on whether the time were 2:00 or 7:32. For a 21st century audience, pixels would also illustrate.

Consider how this approach differs from associative network models of memory. In such models, each node uniquely represents a concept, and when it is sufficiently activated, the concept is retrieved. In a **parallel distributed processing (PDP) model**, each unit helps to represent many different concepts, which are retrieved when the appropriate pattern of activation occurs across all the basic units. Thus, to return to the time and temperature sign, the specific numeral "3" could occur on the right, left, or middle of the sign, as needed, depending only on the correct configuration of lightbulbs being on. Thus no single lightbulb represents "3," but instead the pattern does, and which set of bulbs do the job is arbitrary. This differs considerably from a neon sign, for example, that has one structure dedicated to lighting up for one particular number whenever it is needed. Traditional memory models would roughly resemble a series of neon letters linked to each other. (The great aunt was skeptical.)

PDP models essentially deal with the subatomic particles of perception and cognition. PDP models assume that memory consists of elementary units (the bulbs in our metaphor, nerve cells in their metaphor) that are connected with facilitative and inhibitory links to each other. The connections represent **constraints** about what units are associated, and the **connection strengths** represent the type and magnitude of association. **Connectionist models** store only the strengths of connections, so they recreate the pattern by activating parts of it and waiting for the connections to reverberate throughout the system until the entire pattern is activated.

The full theory of PDP is beyond the scope of this book (McClelland, Rumelhart, & Hinton, 1986; Rissman & Wagner, 2012). Initially, PDP applied to issues of motor control (typing, reaching) and perception at the level of individual letters in a word, aiming at a lower level than the network models of memory described earlier. That is, a node in the network metaphor would be not a single neuron but a pattern of activation over neurons. If one considered PDP only as a lower-level elaboration of network models – that is, operating at the level of neurons – its implications for social cognition's more macro level of analysis would be limited.

Nevertheless, PDP does have potential utility for a social level of analysis. In the more traditional associative models, knowledge is represented statically, not changing its form between long-term and working memory because it is essentially just more or less activated. In PDP models, however, the patterns themselves are not stored, but the strengths of connections among basic units are stored, enabling the patterns to be re-created. From a practical perspective, this allows knowledge to be implicit in the system rather than being an explicit set of stored rules.

PDP also allows imperfect stimulus patterns to be recognized because approximations can activate part of the pattern of connections, which subsequently generate the remaining aspects of the pattern. PDP models are good at considering several sources of information simultaneously. They are parallel processors, in contrast to the more traditional serial processing models.

Recent models of memory combine serial and parallel processes (e.g., J. R. Anderson et al., 2004). For example, declarative memory retrieval might simultaneously search many related memories in parallel, but the content that comes to mind might form a serial bottleneck because one can attend to only one retrieved memory at a time. Similarly, several potential productions might be activated in parallel in procedural memory, but only a single production could fire at a time, serially.

Parallel Constraint Satisfaction in Social Cognition

Can you imagine an Amish Montessori teacher? One possible domain of PDP application in social cognition is to stereotypes, and in particular to how they simultaneously interact with each other. Combining one's knowledge about traditional Amish farmers and progressive Montessori teachers, one can imagine someone who occupies both roles by considering their shared "back to basics" perspective and shared emphasis on patience. Moreover, one can imagine the person's likely response to novel issues (e.g., cell phones in the classroom). PDP models allow for such emergent properties of previous knowledge.

Parallel Constraint Satisfaction Model

A pertinent example in social cognition is a **parallel constraint satisfaction theory** (Kunda & Thagard, 1996). Introduced briefly in Chapter 2 as a single-mode alternative to the dual-mode models, it views impression formation as similar to text comprehension. The perceiver needs to interpret and integrate a variety of incoming information simultaneously with accessing the relevant knowledge base, which includes representations of stereotypes and traits. The model emphasizes the simultaneity of these processes, balancing the mutual and immediate influence of inputs ranging from the more concrete (e.g., interpretation of specific behaviors) to the more abstract (e.g., application of expectations or stereotypes). All information considered at once constrains the other currently accessed information. For example, a shove coming from a friend may come across as playful, whereas a shove coming from a stranger may come across as violent. The model posits that expectancies and new information constrain each other's interpretation, especially when information is ambiguous. Chapter 11 on stereotyping revisits these issues, but now the point is that processing can occur in parallel, with a variety of information mutually influencing each other's interpretations. The model works as a computer simulation of impression-formation processes.

Connectionist Models

The **connectionist model of impression formation** also applies PDP principles to social cognition (Van Overwalle & Labiouse, 2004). This model goes beyond the Kunda–Thagard parallel constraint satisfaction model because it includes a learning component as well as the perception component. This model also has an initial activation phase in which external inputs (e.g., stimuli) are balanced against internal ones (e.g., expectations). After this activation phase, the connectionist model adds **consolidation** in long-term memory. Consolidation occurs when the external inputs do not precisely match the internal linkages. The model then adjusts the long-term links based on its discrepancy from the short-term input. It's a reality check, in effect. In this model, mismatched expectations should change to fit the most typical input from the environment over time.

Two principles emerge from this computer simulation model. First, acquisition reflects the sheer effects of obtaining more confirming information over less of it, in what is often termed the **set size effect**. People are more certain the more support they have for their perceptions. The other principle is **competition** among the links, whereby the successful (accurate) ones are strengthened at the expense of the less successful (inaccurate) ones. Thus, if the system initially believes that all cats have stubs for tails because its first cat was a Manx, subsequent encounters with fully tailed cats will strengthen the tail belief at the expense of the stub belief.

The computer simulation re-creates standard impression formation effects, such as assimilation and contrast priming effects, the inconsistency advantage in certain kinds of recall, and particular patterns of **primacy** and **recency** (greater weighting of earlier and later information under specific circumstances). The same connectionist model also applies to a range of social cognition topics: causal attributions (Van Overwalle, 1998), dual-process models of attitudes (Van Overwalle & Siebler, 2005), cognitive dissonance (Van Overwalle & Jordens, 2002), group biases (Van Rooy, Van Overwalle, Vanhoomissen, Labiouse, & French, 2003), and communication (Van Overwalle & Heylighen, 2006).

Tensor-Product Model

A related model is the **tensor-product model** (Kashima, Woolcock, & Kashima, 2000), which uses a Hebbian approach instead of the competition approach used in the Van Overwalle connectionist model. A **Hebbian learning approach** describes some kinds of associative learning by changes in the strength of links between nerve cells; simultaneous activation strengthens the links, but there is no provision for inhibition of unactivated links. Also, it is not viewed as a literal representation of neural networks. Nevertheless, this model nicely describes several phenomena in forming impressions of groups.

Conclusion about PDP Models

PDP connectionist models have proved popular for computer simulation models of social cognition in various forms. Another connectionist model addresses basic Gestalt principles of causal reasoning, cognitive consistency, and goal-directed behavior (see Chapters 1, 6, 9, and 15; Read, Vanman, & Miller, 1997). Still others address the self-concept (Nowak, Vallacher, Tesser, & Borkowski, 2000), attitude learning (Eiser, Fazio, Stafford, & Prescott, 2003), and perceptions of outgroups (Read & Urada, 2003). This approach also goes by the name **dynamical perspective** (Vallacher, Read, & Nowak, 2002).

EMBODIED MEMORY: INCLUDING PHYSICAL REPRESENTATION

A Basic Cognitive Model of Perceptual Symbol Systems

PDP approaches originally developed ways to understand perceptual recognition of familiar patterns, for example, a blurred, chipped, or degraded letter. Perceptual approaches in general were not typically viewed as tenable conceptual systems, just as recording systems. However, a newer perceptual theory of knowledge aims to fill that gap (Barsalou, 1999).

Perceptual symbols encode experience, both external and internal. This form of memory representation incorporates bottom-up perceptual processes, that is, processes that work from direct perceptual experiences and resulting associations in the brain that activate sensory motor areas. Perceptual experiences can include all the senses, plus introspection and **proprioception** (sense of one's own bodily position from internal feedback). Selective attention picks out features of the environment, for example, not every available stimulus but specific components. This perceptual side captures useful information about edges, colors, movement, temperature, and the like. It is **embodied** in the sense that the information includes both external stimuli (e.g., heat) and bodily experiences (pain). It is also embodied in the sense that it prepares the perceiver for appropriate action (avoidance). In this way, it is a more sophisticated 21st century version of Gibsonian ecological perception described in Chapter 3, as in "perceiving is for doing."

In addition to the perceptual side, this form of memory representation also captures top-down expectations, after perceptual experiences. The perceptual symbol systems (PSS) record the neural activation during stimulus input, but they also reactivate later for conceptual processing. PSS can represent objects in their presence (perception) or in their absence (imagery or conception). **Imagery** differs from conception in being more conscious and specific about the sensory motor representation, as when you close your eyes and visualize your childhood home. **Conception** entails knowing about it without consciously retrieving visual (or other sensory motor) details.

The key components of PSS include the **simulator** that first registers and later re-creates a perceptual experience. Essentially, it is the pattern of brain activation created by selective attention at the perceptual stage. Related perceptual symbols organize into simulators that allow the system to represent specific entities (e.g., what you see the first time arriving at a new home). The representation is dynamic, changing as you experience more information (walking in, living there over time). The simulator contains two kinds of structures: The underlying **frame** integrates across experience with that category (that home, homes in general), and then **simulations** can be created from the frame; simulations create the experience of a particular example on a particular occasion.

In this view, at one extreme, cognitive processes involve **bottom-up** sensory motor perceptions. At the other extreme are **top-down** sensory motor representations that include conception and imagery. Intermediate are processes such as priming, filling gaps where information is missing, anticipating future events, and interpreting ambiguous information. These all entail complementary processes that are part perceptual and part top-down. The PSS view differs from the associative network models in a particularly important way: The perceptual symbols represent sensory modality, whereas the earlier models were *amodal* in the sense that memory represented abstract structures regardless of original type of sensory or internal input. PSS represent abstract concepts by the integrative frames across specific experiences, selecting the core features, and by incorporating both physical and introspective experiences. From the PSS perspective, working memory runs the perceptual simulations (e.g., as a buffer containing information just experienced). Long-term memory records the experience and relevant simulations. We have described this model at some length because it just now begins to prove useful to social cognition researchers (Hostetter, Alibali, & Niedenthal, 2012; Semin, Garrido, & Palma, 2012).

Social Cognitive Models of Embodiment

The PSS view appeals to social cognition settings because of its focus not just on archiving information but on preparation for **situated action** (Barsalou, 1999). Social interaction is nothing if not situated action, that is, embedded in context. The main intellectual message of social psychology is that social situations greatly influence thoughts, feelings, and behaviors. Social psychologists thus are adopting the embodied cognition viewpoint, as anticipated by Zajonc and Markus's (1984) description of the **hard interface**.

Embodied cognition places the actor squarely in interpersonal context, in socially situated cognition (E. R. Smith & Semin, 2004). Embodiment plausibly underlies social information processing both in direct perception – **online cognition** during interaction – and in the absence of the considered social object – **offline cognition** (Niedenthal, Baraslou, Winkielman, Krauth-Gruber, & Ric, 2005). PSS applies to several recent findings involving effects of facial or bodily positions on social cognition. For example, when people are induced to nod their head vertically or shake their head horizontally while receiving a persuasive communication, they are, respectively, more or less likely to agree with it (Wells & Petty, 1980). When people hold a pencil horizontally in their teeth – making them contract their zygomaticus smile muscles – they find cartoons funnier than when they hold the pencil with their lips (Strack, Martin, & Stepper, 1988). People like unfamiliar Chinese ideographs better when they flex their arms, mimicking an approach motion, than when they extend their arm, making an avoidance motion (Cacioppo, Priester, & Berntson, 1993). When people adopt different postures characteristic of emotions such as sadness, they report feeling those emotions more (Duclos et al., 1989). Making a fist relates to people's conceptions of power (Schubert, 2004), as does standing in a dominant posture, which lowers cortisol and raises testosterone and risk-taking. (Carney, Cuddy, & Yap, 2010). When physically or verbally closer, people express and feel literally warmer (IJzerman & Semin, 2010; Williams & Bargh, 2008). All these examples suggest an effect of embodiment on emotions and evaluations (Hostetter et al., 2012).

Chapter 3 described the reverse: Conceptual priming through words or visual priming through faces makes people enact relevant stereotypic behaviors (Bargh, Chen, & Burrows, 1996). But the effects of bottom-up sensory motor representation and top-down generalized concepts and images are reciprocal between embodiment and affective experience: People feel particularly understood when they imitate each other's nonverbal behavior during interaction (Chartrand & Bargh, 1999). Empathy operates partly through bodily channels (Decéty & Chaminade, 2003). The representation of an emotional experience is especially likely to occur through embodied knowledge about the emotion (Barrett, 2006).

Conclusion about Memory Models

Memory models often build on the idea that associative networks organize concepts in long-term memory and that the currently most activated associations represent short-term or working memory. This framework underlies most work on social memory. When researchers turn to memory in action – what it does – they distinguish declarative memory (the associative networks of what is recalled) and procedural memory (the if–then pairs that determine how recall triggers other operations). Memory models increasingly focus on simultaneous parallel procedures to coordinate memory processes, not just serially sequenced processes. And models of embodied cognition rely on sensory motor perceptual systems for both bottom-up perception and top-down conceptual representation.

SOCIAL MEMORY STRUCTURES: WHY SOCIAL MEMORY MATTERS

"I love you, Jane ... I mean, Sally." What happens when you call someone by another person's name? People typically are annoyed at being treated as equivalent to the other person (not to mention, less cognitively accessible than the other person). And well they should be annoyed, although we know of worse cases in which people confuse their children with the dog (A. P. Fiske et al., 1991). What happens when you forget someone's name or confuse their confidences? Feelings are hurt, and personal tragedies can ensue. People use broad categories to organize their memory for other people. This is often functional, but it has its drawbacks. Social cognition research has long focused on this tension between the general and the particular. This final section discusses mental representations of social categories and specific social exemplars because these structures cut across different memory theories, and all are crucial to social life.

Social Categories

Categories describe our expectations about, for example, people, entities, or social groups. Like it or not, we all make assumptions about other people, ourselves, and the situations we encounter. Sometimes we are dramatically misled by our expectations. However, much of the time our expectations are functional, and indeed, we would be unable to operate without them. Such expectations, assumptions, and generic prior knowledge allow us some sense of prediction and control, which is essential to our well-being (Chapter 2).

Could we do without categories? Consider the seemingly objective alternative of operating within situations and with people about whom we have virtually no expectations or prior knowledge. Arriving on a new campus the first day, coming into an unfamiliar culture for the first time, or meeting a stranger whose gender, age, and role are mysterious – all these are disorienting encounters that challenge our ability to function without the normal level of prediction and control provided by expectations. Prior knowledge about the campus (a map, for instance), guides to the culture (from travel books), or an introduction to the stranger (by a mutual friend) would facilitate each encounter. Of course, our inevitable reliance on such prior knowledge is not perfectly adaptive. We may rely on the wrong assumptions, or our assumptions may be overly rigid. But on the whole, such expectations are useful.

Category-Driven versus Data-Driven Processes

Categories represent knowledge about a concept; sometimes termed a **schema**, such an abstract representation includes the concept's attributes and the relations among them (S. T. Fiske & Linville, 1980; Macrae & Bodenhausen, 2001; Rumelhart & Ortony, 1977; S. E. Taylor & Crocker, 1981). Categorical person perception facilitates what is variously termed **top-down**, conceptually driven, or theory-driven processes, which simply means processes heavily influenced by one's organized prior knowledge as opposed to processes that are more **bottom-up**, stimulus driven, or data driven (Abelson, 1981; Bobrow & Norman, 1975; Rumelhart & Ortony, 1977).

As people's theories and concepts about the world, categorical perceptions are concerned with the general case, abstract generic knowledge that holds across many particular instances. The basic message of this research has been that people simplify reality by storing knowledge at a molar, inclusive level rather than squirreling away, one-by-one, all the original individual experiences in their raw forms, which would be pure data-driven processing.

Recently, however, social and cognitive psychologists have taken a closer look at data-driven processes by focusing on their interplay with category-driven processes. Data-driven processes demonstrate ordinary people's sensitivity to the specific qualities of another individual or situation. Purely categorical theories have, in the extreme case, portrayed people as blithely glossing over important details, as stubbornly refusing to see the information in front of them, and as maintaining their schemas at any cost. In contrast, data-driven approaches show that people do indeed care about the information given (Higgins & Bargh, 1987). We consider both types of phenomenon in this section, beginning with categorical processes.

Our perceptions of the world reflect an interplay between what's out there and what we bring to it. We are, paradoxically, more aware of the contributions of the world out there than of our own contributions to our cognitive processes. That is, we know we are encoding information, but we underestimate the roles of selective attention, interpretation, and gap-filling. Expectations are structured knowledge that we bring to everyday perceptions, so expectations emphasize our active construction of reality. This is not to say that we are unconstrained by the stimuli themselves; contrary to Gertrude Stein, "there is a there there."

Categorical expectations emphasize the part of the perceptual interplay – our own contribution – that is mostly preconscious. We experience the world as if we have added nothing to it, so common sense tells us that we perceive an unchanged or literal copy of the environment. We experience perception as instantaneous and direct, as if our brains were simply videotaping the surroundings. Both ordinary people and some philosophers have held this commonsense view that perceptions are unfiltered and veridical (Aristotle, 1931; J. S. Mill, 1869). An emphasis on the importance of less-filtered experience continues in the present-day study of exemplars (covered later in this section).

In contrast, Gestalt psychology encouraged a different view of perception (Brunswik, 1956; Koffka, 1935). As Chapter 1 noted, Gestalt psychologists argued that perception is constructive and that perceptions are mediated through an interpretive lens (Figure 4.3). What we "see" in any given stimulus depends on context; for example, the "l"s in "1952" and in "life" objectively are similar, but we interpret them differently because of their respective contexts. Context provides a different **Gestalt**, or configuration, that alters the meaning of the individual elements. Hence, the whole is more than the simple combination of its parts. The Gestalt emphasis on people's perception of configurations in context anticipates social categories and expectations as configurations-in-context actively contributed by the perceiver. This organized prior knowledge shapes what is perceived and remembered in much the same way that context-based Gestalt configurations do, but generally as more complex types of configuration involving people and situations. Gestalt stimulus configurations guided two theoretical developments that directly precede current categorical theories: Solomon Asch's (1946) **configural model** of forming impressions of others (Chapter 1) and Fritz Heider's (1958) theory of social configurations that produce psychological **balance** (Chapter 9).

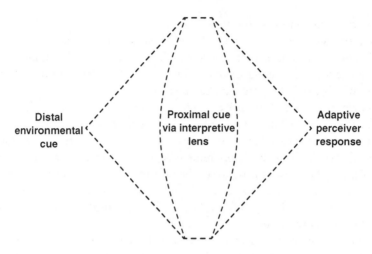

Figure 4.3   Brunswik lens model showing proximal and distal stimuli

Categorical Perception

The commonsense view and the classical view have been that one can precisely define the boundaries of everyday categories (E. E. Smith & Medin, 1981), just as one imagines being able to do in science or mathematics (although even there the classical assumption is questioned). On closer examination, this proves not to be possible. Building on ideas first noted by Wittgenstein (1953), several principles derived in cognitive psychology (Mervis & Rosch, 1981; Rosch, 1978, 1987) and social-personality psychology (Cantor & Mischel, 1979) describe how people categorize things, situations, and other people.

One core notion is that natural categories do not have necessary and sufficient attributes. Instead, the category members fall within **fuzzy sets**, so it is not always clear which instances belong in the category. For example, chess, croquet, and charades are good examples of the category games, but what about playing house, torturing ants, and betting on the Olympics? The perception that some instances are more typical than others led to the idea that instances range from being quite typical to atypical, with a most typical or prototypical instance best representing the category. The **prototype** is the central tendency or average of the category members.

People may never actually encounter their prototypes in real life because they are abstracted from experiences with examples. Even though none of the instances may itself be a perfect proto-type, people abstract out the most typical features (Hayes-Roth & Hayes-Roth, 1977; Posner & Keele, 1968, 1970; Reed, 1972). People then decide if a new instance fits the category by assessing its similarity to the prototype.

In this view, category members are related by the criterion of **family resemblance**. Any given pair of category members will share some features with each other and other features with other category members. For example, Twenty Questions and baseball both include a certain number of turns (the 20 questions or the nine innings), whereas tag and chess do not. On the other hand, Twenty Questions and tag are both played without specific equipment, whereas baseball and chess both require specialized equipment. The more features an instance shares with other category members, the more consistently, consensually, and quickly it is identified as a category member (McCloskey & Glucksberg, 1978; Rosch, 1978; E. E. Smith, Shoben, & Rips, 1974). Thus any given feature is not necessarily present in all category members, only more or less probably so. The point is that the internal structure of categories is more fluid than the classical view would have it, better described as a fuzzy set centering around a prototype.

Moving from within-category to between-category structure, categories are often thought to be organized hierarchically at varying levels of inclusion. That is, under the broad category "entertainment," one might include (at least) games, parties, television, books, and movies (see Table 4.4). Under each of these subcategories, one would have several more subordinate categories, such as car games, board games, outdoor games. Different levels of categorization are useful for different purposes (Rosch, Mervis, Gray, Johnson, & Boyes-Braem, 1976). For example, people propose "let's play a game" or "let's go to a movie" (intermediate level) more often than the generic "let's have some entertainment" and more often than the specific "let's play a car game." In this view, such basic-level or intermediate categories for objects are rich in the attributes people associate with them, are easily distinguished from related categories, and involve well-practiced everyday behaviors.

Both everyday experience and culture determine the contents and organization of our categories, from a young age (Medin & Atran, 2004; Medin, Waxman, Woodring, & Washinawatok, 2010). For example, most undergraduates and urban-dwellers have scant experience of nature, so their categorizations are driven by similarity and typicality. For folk biology, for example, rural-dwelling people, especially indigenous people in the Americas, have richer and more nuanced nature category systems, from a young age, reflecting their lived experience and sensitivity to community beliefs.

Categorical Person Perception

Just as we categorize different kinds of things and activities, so we also categorize different kinds of people, often according to their personalities. Suppose you see a list of another person's prototypically extraverted attributes, such as being energetic, entertaining, and friendly. Later, you may be unsure whether you also saw other prototypical attributes, such as outgoing and

Table 4.4 Hypothetical category prototypes and hierarchy for "Entertainment"

ENTERTAINMENT				
Games (other entertainment categories include parties, television, books and movies)				
Car	Board	Outdoor	Make-Believe	Party
License Plate Poker	Monopoly	Baseball	Playing house	Charades
I Spy	Scrabble	Tag	Fantasy	20 Questions
		Torturing ants		

lively (Cantor & Mischel, 1979; Tsujimoto, 1978). Activating some of the attributes activated related ones, so it is hard to remember which you saw and which you inferred from the prototype. This fits the view that people seem to extract a trait prototype from exposure to category-consistent information. Social categories thus may be viewed as fuzzy sets (without rigid boundaries) centering on a prototype.

One implication of this view is that category-based thinking can generate false memories. People store the general prototype and fit the gist of new information to it. Hence, they may remember category-consistent information that never occurred. In one study (Macrae, Schloerscheidt, Bodenhausen, & Milne, 2002), participants saw 60 first names, half male and half female, paired equally often with the gender-typed occupations of mechanic and hairdresser; that is, half were gender consistent and half gender inconsistent. Later, they had to recognize which names they had previously seen, out of a batch of 120; if they said the name was previously seen, they also had to state its occupation. As is typical with simple materials, and as explained by several person memory models described earlier, people more easily recalled expectancy-inconsistent names (male hairdressers and female mechanics).

More interesting from the categorical perspective were the false memories. **False alarms** mistakenly identify distracter items on the test as being part of the original set. These false alarms were twice as likely to be expectancy consistent as expectancy inconsistent. That is, when they did falsely identify a name as familiar, they most often identified those names as having the gender-consistent occupation. What's more, these false memories were accompanied by a feeling of knowing, so when people falsely recognized a name and attributed a gender-consistent occupation, they were more likely to have a feeling of familiarity for the gender-consistent than gender-inconsistent cases. All this especially occurred when people were either distracted or elderly (cf. von Hippel & Henry, 2012).

This means people can experience a feeling of knowing when a memory is entirely false, and that category-based consistency underlies this phenomenon. Recall the opening example about witnessing a mugging. Do you remember the older woman, the busy intersection, the parked cars, and the traffic light? What about the mugger's sweatshirt, mentioned later? And his cap? What did he steal? Her purse, you answer. Right. What color was his cap? Where were the parked cars? Well, actually, we never mentioned either the cap or the parked cars, but in dozens of controlled experiments, people are led to experience clear and persistent false memories for events that never happened (Loftus, 2004). Lawyers can plant false memories by asking leading questions ("Did you see the parked cars?" when there weren't any). This throws into question, for example, allegedly repressed and recovered memories that may result from other people's suggestions (Loftus & Davis, 2006). Of course, the suggestions have to fit with known categories of experience that are plausible in retrospect. Various forms of categorical processing could account for these effects.

Critiques of Category and Prototype Views

Social categories have well-established effects, but the models are changing as the field progresses (Table 4.5). First, one modification of the basic approach suggests that social categories are more often represented by ideals or extremes (Barsalou, 1985; Chaplin, John, & Goldberg, 1988). That is, the best example of a nun may in fact be the ideal nun rather than an average nun. A more

Table 4.5 Advantages and critiques of category and prototype views, based on evidence about what people do

Prototype advantages	Critiques	Exemplar advantages	Critiques
Abstract over examples	Use ideals, extremes	Remember instances	Use both
Know gist, typical	Collect exemplars	Know variability	Do not do via exemplars
Consult average	Calculate covariance	Correlate features	Do not do via exemplars
Prototype automatically	Use goals, expertise	Generate new inferences	Use both processes
Nest hierarchies	Form fuzzy hierarchies	Need not assume hierarchy	Format by domain
Preserve prototypes	Do change, but how	Accumulate instances	Use both processes

drastic critique of prototypes rejects altogether the idea of a summary representation (ideal *or* typical), arguing that categories are represented as a collection of exemplars previously encountered. Prototypes may not be the only way to store a category.

Second, social categories also had been viewed as activating inevitably and automatically upon perceiving an instance. But category activation may be conditionally automatic, depending on various factors including one's goals (Macrae & Bodenhausen, 2000; also see Chapter 2).

Third, recall that the basic or intermediate levels of nonsocial categories apparently dominate people's everyday usage; the same may not be so true for social categories (Holyoak & Gordon, 1984). In using social categories, people's specific goals and expertise most likely determine which levels they choose to use (Cantor & Kihlstrom, 1987; Hampson, John, & Goldberg, 1986).

Fourth, social categories may not form a clear hierarchy, with more general, broader categories becoming more inclusive (Cantor & Mischel, 1979), as when people can list more instances and attributes that go with broader categories (Goldberg, 1986; Hampson, Goldberg, & John, 1987). This overall approach proved initially useful but provoked several critiques. Many social categories are not so neat, representing a fuzzy hierarchy in which class inclusions do not work strictly (Hampson et al., 1986). For example, the upper levels (male) do not always provide richer associations than do the lower levels (the stereotypic businessman) (Deaux, Winton, Crowley, & Lewis, 1985), contrary to hierarchical predictions. Perhaps people may actually make associations in complex networks that resemble a tangled web rather than a hierarchy (Andersen & Klatzky, 1987; Cantor & Kihlstrom, 1987). Attributes perceived to hold for the top-level category (e.g., extraverts are self-confident) do not always hold for all the intermediate-level categories (politicians are self-confident, but comedians and bullies are not). The overlapping nature of social categories differentiates them from object categories (Lingle, Altom, & Medin, 1984).

To summarize, the prototype approach has introduced several ideas: namely, that social categories do not have rigid boundaries but rather operate as fuzzy sets, organized around a prototypical category member, with category members related by family resemblance rather than by necessary and sufficient rules for inclusion. Some social categories may be organized around ideals or extremes rather than average prototypes. Prototype organization into hierarchies and basic levels has been questioned, suggesting that social categories are related in more flexible and complex ways.

Usage of Social Categories

Current research views social categories as conditionally activated and applied, though everyday life often meets the conditions that activate categories, as Chapter 2 indicated. Categories can be activated, applied, and even inhibited, depending on social conditions (Macrae & Bodenhausen, 2000).

Category activation depends on attentional resources (Gilbert & Hixon, 1991). That is, under some rare circumstances, people may not notice another person's race, gender, or age. Under extreme cognitive overload, perceivers may identify the person's category, but they may not activate the associated stereotypes. If the stereotypes are indeed activated, however, cognitive load increases the odds of applying them.

People belong to multiple categories, and when one is activated, others are inhibited (Bodenhausen & Macrae, 1998; Bodenhausen & Peery, 2009). Category salience, chronic accessibility (Chapter 3), and processing goals (Chapter 2) determine which categories are activated and which are inhibited. People sometimes can inhibit category-congruent information intentionally, although this is costly to attentional resources (Macrae, Bodenhausen, Milne, & Ford, 1997). Relevant information can also be inhibited inadvertently. When people repeatedly retrieve one kind of information, related but not retrieved information is inhibited, a kind of adaptive forgetting that enables the mind to focus on what is currently relevant (MacLeod & Macrae, 2001). Even if activated, categories may be applied in different ways, or not applied at all: Category activation and application depend on a variety of conditions.

Exemplars

Cognitive Models of Exemplars

Just as the prototype view of categories developed in reaction to the shortcomings of the classical view, so the exemplar view originally developed in reaction to the shortcomings of the prototype view (see E. E. Smith & Medin, 1981, for a review), and it may be best understood in that light. As a counterpoint to the prototype perspective, the **exemplar** approach suggests that one remembers separate instances or exemplars one has actually encountered rather than some average prototype one has abstracted from experience. One has several exemplars for a category and, in this view, people categorize a thing by seeing whether it resembles a lot of remembered exemplars from a single category. Although the prototype and exemplar view have subsequently been integrated by many researchers, especially those in social cognition, it is useful first to understand the pure exemplar view.

The exemplar view has several advantages. First, it most directly accounts for people's knowledge of specific examples that guide their understanding of the category. To illustrate, if asked whether restaurants typically contain equal numbers of tables for two or tables for more, one may have to consult several specific mental examples of restaurants to answer the question. Or if someone asserts that all restaurants have cashiers, one may retrieve a specific counterexample to refute the statement. This reliance on concrete instances suggests but, of course, does not require the idea of exemplars. (The prototype view does not dispute that people can remember some specific instances, but the instances are not the focus of the prototype view.)

Moreover, people know a lot about the possible variability between category members; consider the big variety of Chinese restaurants versus the sameness of a particular fast-food chain. A true prototype theory cannot represent information about variability: A pure prototype model would represent only the category average, not its variability. Exemplars provide a simple way to model variability across category members. It is easy to describe people's knowledge of such variation by positing exemplars, although equivalents might be possible within the prototype approach.

Another major advantage of the exemplar view, and probably the best argument for it, is its ability to account for correlations of attributes within a category. For example, people know that within the category restaurant, formica tables tend to go with paying the cashier directly, and tablecloths tend to go with paying through the server. They know this through their theories about inexpensive, convenience-oriented businesses as compared to other kinds (Murphy & Medin, 1985). A single summary prototype does not easily handle this knowledge. The knowledge of which attributes tend to be correlated among category members is especially important in social perception because people have implicit theories about which traits go together (e.g., based on remembering several friends who are both ambitious and hard-working) and which do not (e.g., not being able to retrieve examples of people who are both ambitious and kind; Schneider, 1973).

Finally, the exemplar view makes it easier to modify existing categories with new instances. In the exemplar approach, the new instance may be added as yet another exemplar, which will then contribute to subsequent category judgments (Lingle et al., 1984). In comparison, it is less clear how prototypes are modified.

Social Cognitive Models of Exemplars

The social cognitive evidence for exemplars is convincing. For example, although not interpreted in terms of exemplars, one series of studies (Gilovich, 1981) showed that people's judgments are affected by irrelevant similarities to specific past examples; a new football player from the same hometown as a famous football player may be considered a good bet even though hometown is not especially diagnostic of athletic ability. People's political judgments are also shaped by drawing lessons from history, even when the prior example is similar to the current one only in nondiagnostic ways. As another example, people's judgments about a member of a foreign culture are more heavily influenced by the foreigner's irrelevant similarity to a previously encountered exemplar rather than by general rules they had learned about the culture (Read, 1983, 1984, 1987). If people have causal theories (e.g., that the exemplar somehow influences the new instance), they are even more likely to use the exemplar. And in more everyday settings, people deciding which of two strangers is more approachable will choose the one most superficially similar to another stranger who was recently kind to them (or, conversely, least similar to a recently mean person), without apparently being aware of the reasons for their choice (Lewicki, 1985).

Familiarity, similarity to a previously known individual, whether consciously perceived or not, may create a sense of shared attitudes, attraction, predictability, and safety (S. T. Fiske, 1982, pp. 62–66; Genaro & Cantor, 1987; White & Shapiro, 1987). Familiarity may be a required mechanism for the operation of exemplars. When people encounter unfamiliar compound categories (e.g., male elementary school teachers), they rely on memory for specific instances, whereas when they encounter familiar compound categories (e.g., female elementary school teachers), they rely on abstract stereotypes. It is the familiarity *per se* that changes the judgment strategy (Groom, Sherman, Lu, Conrey, & Keijzer, 2005).

Although some of these studies explicitly relied on exemplar models from cognitive psychology and some did not, they all demonstrate the effect of single, concrete, prior experiences on subsequent judgments and behavior, and as such they provide a counterpoint to the influence of more global, abstract categories.

Some more direct discussion of the evidence for exemplars comes from work on the perceived variability of social categories. For example, people perceive increased variability in groups as their impressions become more differentiated (Linville, Salovey, & Fischer, 1986). As you learn more about a particular group of foreigners through an exchange program, you perceive them to come in more different varieties than you did beforehand (and they view citizens of your country as more variable as well). Linville, Fischer, and Salovey (1989) have explicitly argued that this effect can be best described by exemplar models. Some effects of abstract, category-level information can be explained in terms of pure exemplar models to show that the abstract representations are not necessary, although they certainly may be involved (E. R. Smith, 1988). People do seem to use both abstract and exemplar information when provided; that is, they consider both their generalizations about the other nationality as well as specific citizens they have known. Moreover, when people are first given abstract information, followed by information about specific instances, they perceive less variability and make their judgments based on such prototypes more than when the order is reversed or when they are given no abstract information (Medin, Altom, & Murphy, 1984; Park & Hastie, 1987; E. R. Smith & Zárate, 1992).

Problems with Exemplar Views

Evidence for exemplars is not all clear-cut. That is, people do understand that some groups are more variable than others, and they use this information, first, in deciding whether to generalize from an individual to the group and, second, in classifying new individuals. This might seem to argue for exemplars, but knowledge about variability does not seem to be based on memory for exemplars (Park & Hastie, 1987). Similarly, people often perceive minimal variability in outgroups (i.e., groups of which they are not a member), but differences in exemplar frequencies may (Linville et al., 1986, 1989; Ostrom & Sedikides, 1992) or may not (Judd & Park, 1988) be responsible.

One intriguing possibility is that people may be most likely to use exemplars when they are trying to account for something out of the ordinary. Sometimes we need to know whether something that has just happened is normal or not; that is, we need an immediate check on how surprising it was (assuming we do not already have a relevant schema). For example, after an accident, people think of similar accidents in their past and of the events leading up to the incident to judge how surprising or avoidable it was, and even how upset to be. A model of exemplars developed to describe just this process of people's *post hoc* normality judgments (Kahneman & Miller, 1986). We have seen that category models focus on anticipation and prediction based on what seems typical or probable in the future given one's abstracted prior experience. In contrast, **norm theory** focuses on *post hoc* interpretation based on a past encounter with a particular stimulus in a particular context, with the aim of judging whether the stimulus was normal or surprising. Category and schema theories describe reasoning forward; norm theory describes reasoning backward. According to norm theory, people consider a particular stimulus in light of exemplars it brings to mind. These exemplars allow people to compare the instance to the sum of previous experiences to see the degree to which the instance is normal or surprising. People compute this sum on the fly, so it is *ad hoc* rather than explicit prior knowledge. Chapter 7 returns to this model, but for now, norm theory illustrates the uses of exemplars in active judgment processes.

Prototypes or Exemplars? A Resolution

Exemplar models are not sufficient by themselves any more than prototype models were sufficient by themselves. People rely on a mixture of representations (cf. M. B. Brewer, 1988; Cantor & Kihlstrom, 1987; J. B. Cohen & Basu, 1987; Groom et al., 2005; Lingle et al., 1984; Linville et al., 1989; Messick & Mackie, 1989; E. E. Smith & Medin, 1981). People clearly do recall specific instances and use them to classify new instances, but specific instances also give rise to category generalizations that in turn facilitate classification of new instances, so people are using both (Elio & Anderson, 1981). People can rely on direct experience with exemplars or on previously provided prototypes to classify new instances, depending on the task and the information available (Medin et al., 1984).

Moreover, because using or developing abstract representations depends on the demands of the task, abstracting a prototype is not automatic (Whittlesea, 1987). Indeed, exemplars may be more basic (and therefore more likely to be automatic) because they are used (a) when people's cognitive capacity is strained, (b) for more complex concepts, and (c) especially by younger children (Kossan, 1981; cf. Kemler-Nelson, 1984).

Exemplars may be more basic building blocks for abstract generalizations such as categories, but once the category is established, exceptions require unpacking the category to return to the more concrete individual exemplar level. That is, cognitive generalizations may start with exemplars and return to them for troubleshooting. As we saw earlier, whereas familiar groups encourage abstractions, unfamiliar groups encourage exemplar usage (Groom et al., 2005). A summary-plus-exception model captures this idea in individual impression formation (Babey, Queller, & Klein, 1998). People generalize across individual instances of behavior and retain both the summary and the instances. Trait judgments rely on both the summary and the specific exceptional episodes (Klein, Cosmides, Tooby, & Chance, 2001).

Exemplars might be useful when the summary abstraction is insufficient for reasons besides exceptions to the rule. When people are motivated or simply have more information, exemplars provide elaborated processing. People apparently use both exemplars and prototypes to represent groups to which they belong, but only prototypes to represent groups to which they do not belong and about which they therefore know less (Judd & Park, 1988). People could also use exemplars to represent both their own and other groups, but they have more exemplars available for their own group (Linville et al., 1989).

Clearly, people can use either abstract category-level information, such as prototypes, or instances and memory for exemplars to make categorical judgments. When people do each doubtless depends on task demands and individual differences (cf. M. B. Brewer, 1988; Park & Hastie, 1987; S. J. Sherman & Corty, 1984, pp. 237–245; E. R. Smith & Zárate, 1992). For example, the capacity and the motivation to be accurate or to focus on individuals would probably encourage exemplar-based processes over prototype-based processes (S. T. Fiske & Neuberg, 1990; Kruglanski, 1990; Messick & Mackie, 1989).

When all is said and done, what ultimate use are fuzzy concepts and concrete exemplars in loose hierarchies in tangled webs? Cantor and Kihlstrom (1987) argue that this framework (a) captures the social perceiver's need to represent both the gist of a category and its variability, allowing an economical, functional core representation as well as acknowledging the variability of instances within the category, and (b) describes the multiple paths people use in responding flexibly to the fluidity of social interaction.

Summary

This chapter on mental representation focused on memory; that is, what stays in our heads or is represented by our bodies. We began with associative networks that organize memory in the basic cognitive model, with the basic distinction of long-term versus short-term memory. Associative network models of social memory build on this work. In addition, procedural memory informs some models of social memory. Finally, cognitive models of parallel versus serial processing for coordinating memory processes enlighten ideas about parallel constraint satisfaction in social cognition. Embodied representations rely more on perceptual systems.

Social memory structures matter to social cognition, as in the unique features of categorical person perception and uses of social categories. In response to critiques of classic category and prototype views, the exemplar view, with its own advantages and disadvantages, offers an alternative and a combined resolution.

Chapter 4 has focused on general principles of mental representation that will be useful as we encounter representations of self, causality, attitudes, and stereotypes. Just as in Chapter 2 on dual-mode models, these ideas about mental representation are converging on a consensus useful to the wider field of social cognition.

FURTHER READING

Anderson, J. R., Bothell, D., Byrne, M. D., Douglass, S., Lebiere, C., & Qin, Y. (2004). An integrated theory of the mind. *Psychological Review, 111*, 1036–1060.

Baddeley, A. (2012) Working memory: Theories, models, and controversies. *Annual Review of Psychology, 63*, 1–30.

Hostetter, A. B., Alibali, M. W., & Niedenthal, P. M. (2012). Embodied social thought: Linking social concepts, emotion, and gesture. In S. T. Fiske & C. N. Macrae (Eds.), *Sage handbook of social cognition* (pp. 211–228). Thousand Oaks, CA: Sage.

Loftus, E. F. (2004). Memories of things unseen. *Current Directions in Psychological Science, 13*, 145–147.

Macrae, C. N., & Bodenhausen, G. V. (2000). Social cognition: Thinking categorically about others. *Annual Review of Psychology, 51*, 93–120.

Rissman, J., & Wagner, A. D. (2012). Distributed representations in memory: Insights from functional brain imaging. *Annual Review of Psychology, 63*, 101–128.

Semin, G. R., Garrido, M. V., & Palma, T. A. (2012). Socially situated cognition: Recasting social cognition as an emergent phenomenon. In S. T. Fiske & C. N. Macrae (Eds.), *Sage handbook of social cognition* (pp. 138–164). Thousand Oaks, CA: Sage.

Smith, E. R. (1998). Mental representation and memory. In D. T. Gilbert, S. T. Fiske, & G. Lindzey (Eds.), *The handbook of social psychology* (4th edn, Vol. 1, pp. 391–445). New York: McGraw-Hill.

Srull, T. K., Lichenstein, M., & Rothbart, M. (1985). Associative storage and retrieval processes in person memory. *Journal of Experimental Psychology: Learning, Memory, and Cognition, 11*, 316–345.

Van Overwalle, F., & Labiouse, C. (2004). A recurrent connectionist model of person impression formation. *Personality and Social Psychology Review, 8*, 28–61.

von Hippel, W., & Henry, J. D. (2012). Social cognitive aging. In S. T. Fiske & C. N. Macrae (Eds.), *Sage handbook of social cognition* (pp. 390–410). Thousand Oaks, CA: Sage.

Williams, L. E., & Bargh, J. A. (2008). Experiencing physical warmth promotes interpersonal warmth. *Science, 322(5901)*, 606–607.

PART TWO

Topics in Social Cognition: From Self to Society

Self in Social Cognition

5

- Mental Representations of the Self
- Self-Regulation
- Motivation and Self-Regulation
- The Self as a Reference Point

Understanding the self has been one of the most enthusiastically pursued goals in psychology. William James's (1907) analysis laid the groundwork for many enduring concerns, and sociologists Charles Cooley (1902) and George Herbert Mead (1934) provided frameworks for understanding the self in social interaction. In the past several decades, social cognition researchers have taken up this challenge and added fundamentally to our understanding of the self (Beer, 2012).

This chapter begins with mental representations of the self; namely, what makes up the sense of self that most people experience subjectively. We then explore self-regulation and consider how the self guides the processing of self-relevant information, enabling people both to understand the meaning of situations for themselves and to promote their interests, goals, and values. Overarching motives that guide self-regulation include a desire for accurate knowledge of the self, a consistent sense of self, self-improvement, and **self-enhancement**, which is the tendency to seek and maintain a favorable self-concept. Finally, we consider how self-knowledge affects how we interpret other people, often without our awareness.

MENTAL REPRESENTATIONS OF THE SELF

Self-Concept

People's knowledge about themselves is extensive and complex. During childhood, parents, teachers, and friends treat us in particular ways, and we participate in religious, ethnic, or cultural activities that come to be significant aspects of ourselves. In addition, we develop a sense of our personal characteristics and what others feel we might or should do to fulfill expectations. We know ourselves by our roles, such as student or spouse. We have a private sense of self as well as selves we present to other people. We know ourselves as active participants in the ongoing action of the environment and as people who have already experienced and reflected upon events and relationships. We can say quickly and confidently whether we are outgoing or shy, adventurous or conventional, athletic or clumsy. Our collection of beliefs about ourselves is called the **self-concept**.

Mental representations of the self are complex. Sometimes we are concerned with maintaining self-esteem; at other times we want to maintain a consistent sense of self, and at other times our needs to belong or to be efficacious guide our thoughts, emotions, and behaviors (Vignoles, Regalia, Manzi, Golledge, & Scabini, 2006). In part as a result of this flexibility, much of our self-encoding is done in **person-situation interaction** terms (Mendoza-Denton, Ayduk, Mischel, Shoda, & Testa, 2001). That is, we have diverse senses of ourselves in particular contexts: Each situational **norm** (social rule or pressure) engages different aspects of the self. A person may have one conception of herself in academic situations as bright, attentive, and interested in learning, and a different set of self-beliefs for social situations, which may include being somewhat shy but friendly and generally well-liked. In this viewpoint, self-representation in memory resembles the representation of other constructs. Which aspect of the self influences ongoing thought and behavior depends on which aspect of the self is accessed. This feature of the self is referred to as the working self-concept (Markus & Kunda, 1986). Thus, for example, your **working self-concept** for academic situations will typically differ in content from the one you have for social situations.

Besides situational variability within the self, some self variability depends on activated relations with close others. Self-concepts include knowledge about significant others (Andersen & Chen, 2002). People who influence one's self or with whom one has been emotionally involved – including parents, siblings, close friends, and past and present partners – connect to the self through knowledge that maintains particular aspects of the self linked to these significant others. A person's repertoire of relational selves influences emotions and behavior in social situations (Gardner, Gabriel, & Hochschild, 2002). The activation of mental representations of a significant other evokes the **relational self** with that significant other, a process termed **transference** (Andersen & Chen, 2002). You may, for example, behave like an entirely autonomous mature person until you get home for the holidays, at which point your relational selves as daughter and younger sister may be activated, leading to behavior that conflicts with your usual self-concept.

Typically, we construe ourselves in complementary fashion *vis-à-vis* others (Tiedens & Jimenez, 2003). For example, we reciprocate warm (or quarrelsome) behavior, and thus assimilate on the agreeableness–quarrelsomeness dimension, whereas in terms of control, we contrast our behavior with others, deferring when a relational partner is dominant but taking charge when the partner defers. In both cases, complementary self-construal guides behavior, especially with people we know well (Tiedens & Jimenez, 2003). In extremely tight-knit groups, our personal identities may viscerally fuse with our group identities, motivating extraordinary self-sacrifice (Swann, Jetten, Gómez, Whitehouse, & Bastian, 2012). Relational selves provide both stability in the self-concept (from enduring representations of significant others) and variability (when different situations activate different relational selves).

Self-Schemas

In the array of information about themselves, most people have clear concepts of themselves on some attributes and less clear concepts on others. Those qualities about which people are certain are termed **self-schemas**: cognitive-affective structures that represent the self's qualities in a given domain. People are self-schematic on dimensions that are important to them, on which they think of themselves as extreme, and on which they are certain that the opposite does not hold (Markus, 1977). Self-schemas organize information-processing relevant to that domain. Connie may feel that she is hardworking and full of integrity but may be unsure whether to describe herself as shy. In this case, Connie is schematic for the dimensions hardworking and integrity but not for shy.

Possible and **feared selves** – that is, selves we would like to become or that we fear becoming, respectively – also guide how we think about ourselves and how we select situations and social roles (Markus & Nurius, 1986; Markus & Wurf, 1987). For example, the possible self of becoming a professor might lead one to seek opportunities to supervise student research projects, whereas the feared self of being jobless might lead one to redouble efforts to publish research articles. Possible selves can change in response to environmental input and affect consequent behavior. For example, in one study, low-income eighth-graders participated in a brief intervention that led them to believe that their possible selves might include academic success. This brief intervention increased test scores, grades, and academic initiative and decreased depression, absences, and misbehavior in school over a two-year period; these changes were mediated by changes in the possible selves these students had incorporated into their identity (Oyserman, Bybee, & Terry, 2006; Figure 5.1).

Neural Bases of Self-Views

Clearly, to function effectively in the world, people need to be able to distinguish between things that are "me" and "not me." This function implicates activity in the prefrontal cortex's left hemisphere (Kircher et al., 2002; Turk et al., 2002). The sense of self that most of us experience subjectively appears to emerge from the functions of a left-hemisphere **interpreter** (Gazzaniga, 2000), which integrates diverse self-relevant processing in different parts of the brain (Turk, Heatherton, Macrae, Kelley, & Gazzaniga, 2003). The representations people hold of themselves in long-term memory resemble those held about other concepts, but are more complex, more varied, and more likely to shape interpretation of situations and of other people's actions than are other accessible constructs.

Some patterns of brain activity occur when people reflect on their self-views, compared with others' views of them. In one study (Ochsner et al., 2005), participants' brains were scanned while they rated adjectives as self-descriptive, descriptive of a friend, descriptive of the friend's view of them, or descriptive of a person not close to them; the comparison condition was a perceptual task not related to people. For all of the person-appraisal tasks, the medial prefrontal cortex (mPFC) activated, relative to the comparison perception task. This finding fits manifold studies suggesting the importance of the mPFC in social judgment generally (see Chapter 1). In addition, a larger

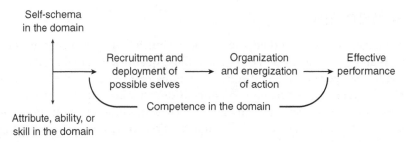

Figure 5.1   How self-schemas, ability, and possible selves interact to regulate performance

network involving the posterior cingulate/precuneus and multiple regions of the temporal lobe was evoked for all self and other evaluations (Figure 5.2). Neural systems involved in direct appraisals of the self resembled those involved in appraisals of close others, and they appear to share many neural pathways, relative to appraisals of people with whom one is less close (Beer, 2012; Ochsner et al., 2005).

Just how much the neural representation of others is incorporated into our self-concept and how much is it distinct? Activation of the lateral PFC distinguishes self-ratings from close-other ratings. Direct appraisals of the self as compared to others activates mPFC and right rostrolateral PFC (Figure 5.2). Apparently, judgments about the self also selectively activate Brodmann's area 10 (Heatherton et al., 2006). Although data are still coming in, distinctive areas within the medial prefrontal cortex activate for self as opposed to intimate others, indicating that self-knowledge is represented at least semi-independently of information about intimate others.

With respect to self-views, neuroimaging investigations distinguish processing **self-schematic** information from non-self-schematic information (Lieberman, Jarcho, & Satpute, 2004). Echoing Chapter 2's distinction between controlled and automatic processing, **non-self-schematic** information (e.g., athletes processing words related to acting) implicates brain regions involved in effortful and intentional processing and the retrieval of episodic memories: lateral prefrontal cortex, hippocampus, and posterior parietal cortex (Figure 5.2). By contrast, processing self-schematic information (e.g., athletes responding to words reflecting sports) activates brain regions involved in automatic, motivational, and affective processing: ventromedial prefrontal cortex, nucleus accumbens, and amygdala. As strong self-schemas develop within a domain, their neural representation apparently moves to regions of the brain that are more affective, motivational, and automatic.

Self-Esteem

Mental representations of the self involve **self-esteem**, the evaluation we make of ourselves. People are concerned not only with what they are like, but also with how they value those qualities. Self-esteem is a resource because it can help people maintain well-being, set appropriate

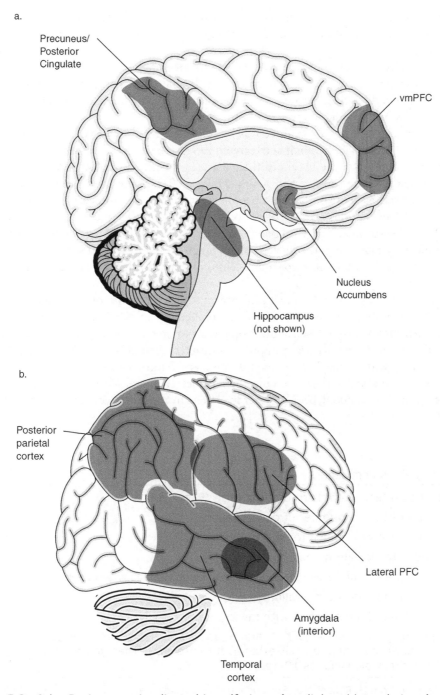

Figure 5.2a & b   Brain areas implicated in self-views (medial and lateral views)

goals, savor positive experiences, and cope successfully with difficult situations (Christensen, Wood, & Barrett, 2003; Creswell et al., 2005; Sommer & Baumeister, 2002; Wood, Heimpel, & Michela, 2003).

Self-esteem has a social component too. People are inherently social, and their desire for self-esteem is driven, in part, by this need to connect with others and gain their approval (Leary & Baumeister, 2000). As such, a person's self-esteem may be considered a **sociometer** – a general indicator of how one is doing in the eyes of others.

Self-esteem can be assessed explicitly, as by (dis)agreeing "I feel that I have a number of good qualities" (Table 5.1). **Implicit self-esteem** can also be assessed, for example, by observing whether people value the letters in their name or quickly link positive adjectives to the self (e.g., Koole, Dijksterhuis, & van Knippenberg, 2001). Sometimes explicit and implicit assessments of self-esteem conflict, and people must devote more processing time to understand their self-conceptions (Briñol, Petty, & Wheeler, 2006). People with high explicit but low implicit self-esteem are prone to behaving defensively (Jordan, Spencer, & Zanna, 2003). For example, they may derogate other people to maintain their own self-esteem because their self-views are fragile and require continual reinforcement (Jordan, Spencer, & Zanna, 2005; Kernis, 2003).

Distinguishing implicit and explicit self-esteem suggests that not only do people explicitly seek to feel good about themselves, but their implicit or unconscious self-evaluations also influence their judgments and behavior. People tend to prefer people, places, and things that resemble the self, a tendency toward implicit egotism (Pelham, Carvallo, & Jones, 2005). For example, women with names like Georgia, Louise, and Virginia are disproportionately likely to have lived in the states that resemble their names (Pelham, Mirenberg, & Jones, 2002; Pelham et al., 2005). As noted, people prefer the letters in their own names (J. T. Jones, Pelham,

---

Table 5.1   Self-esteem scale

Indicate whether each item is true (T) or false (F) for you:

1. I feel that I have a number of good qualities.
2. I feel I do not have much to be proud of.
3. At times I think I am no good at all.
4. I feel I am a person of worth, at least on an equal basis with others.
5. All in all, I feel that I am a failure.
6. On the whole, I am satisfied with myself.

If you answered "true" on items 1, 4, and 6, as well as "false" on items 2, 3, and 5, then you tend to score high on self-esteem. If the reverse, then you tend to score lower. The entire scale includes 10 items.

Source: Adapted from M. Rosenberg, *Society and the adolescent self-image*. Copyright 1965 by Princeton University Press. Copyright renewed. Used by permission of Dr. Florence Rosenberg.

Mirenberg, & Hetts, 2002). Unconscious self-evaluations influence not only mundane but also major life decisions.

Self-esteem reflects what people believe they need to be or do to have worth as a person (Crocker & Knight, 2005). Besides overall self-esteem, people hold domain-specific self-evaluations that influence their global feelings of self-worth. These **contingencies of self-worth** describe people being selective about the domains on which they base their self-esteem. For one person, being a poor student may not matter much and have little bearing on self-esteem, but if one is from a family in which intellectual achievements matter, then being a poor student may reflect back on self-esteem. In the domains of contingent self-worth, people pursue self-esteem by struggling to validate their abilities and qualities, activities that may endanger mental and physical health (Crocker & Knight, 2005). Thus, although thinking well of oneself has benefits, obsessive pursuit of self-esteem can be costly.

Culture and the Self

Conceptions of the self vary depending on one's cultural background (Morling & Masuda, 2012; Rhee, Uleman, Lee, & Roman, 1995; Triandis, McCusker, & Hui, 1990). Markus and Kitayama (1991) contrasted American and Japanese cultures to illustrate the differences in self-conceptions between Western and East Asian cultures. European Americans emphasize individuality and distinguishing oneself from others by using one's unique talents. This **independent self** is "a bounded, unique, more or less integrated motivational and cognitive universe, a dynamic center of awareness, emotion, judgment, action, organized into a distinctive whole and set constrastively both against other such wholes and against a social and natural background" (Geertz, 1975, p. 48). Comparatively, the **interdependent self** of many East Asian, Southern European, and Latin American cultures sees oneself as part of encompassing social relationships and adjusting one's behavior to what one perceives to be the thoughts, feelings, and actions of others in the relationship (Markus & Kitayama, 1991). An interdependent self becomes meaningful and complete largely within the context of social relationships rather than through independent, autonomous action (Table 5.2).

Both independent and interdependent cultures ascribe internal qualities, such as abilities or opinions. However, independent cultures experience such attributes as fixed and relatively stable from situation to situation, whereas interdependent cultures consider these qualities as more situation-specific and unstable, not defining characteristics of the self (Bochner, 1994; Cousins, 1989). The interdependent self is not an autonomous, bounded whole but changes its nature depending on the social context (Kanagawa, Cross, & Markus, 2001). In interdependent cultures, the emphasis on blending in is so fundamental that individually unique attributes do not particularly represent the self. For example, a child from a family in an independent cultural context might experience pressure to develop his talents fully because achieving distinctively on the basis of one's abilities is a valued cultural outcome. By contrast, a child growing up in an interdependent cultural or familial context might experience the pressure to achieve in the form of obligations to family and to the larger social group.

Table 5.2 The measurement of independent and interdependent self-construals

Indicate the extent to which you agree or disagree with each of the items below based on the following scale:

1	2	3	4	5	6	7
Strongly disagree						Strongly agree

1. I have respect for authority figures with whom I interact.
2. I am comfortable with being singled out for praise or rewards.
3. My happiness depends on the happiness of those around me.
4. Speaking up in class is not a problem for me.
5. I should take into consideration my parents' advice when making education and career plans.
6. My personal identity independent of others is very important to me.

If you answered "agree" on items 1, 3, and 5, as well as "disagree" on items 2, 4, and 6, you score tend to score high on interdependence and low on independence; if the reverse, you tend to score high on independence and low on interdependence. The entire scale is longer than the excerpt above.

Source: T. M. Singelis (1994). Copyright 1994 by Sage Publications, Inc. Reprinted by permission of Sage Publications, Inc.

Although being independent is well defined, interdependence assumes different forms, depending on culture and gender. For example, women are more interdependent than men but not in the same way that East Asians may be considered interdependent (Cross, Bacon, & Morris, 2000; Cross & Vick, 2001). Women's interdependence has been referred to as relational interdependence (Cross et al., 2000; Guimond, Chatard, Martinot, Crisp, & Redersdorff, 2006). For example, a European American mother may experience interdependence as an obligation to promote the goals and talents of her children so that they will be successful, and she may make sacrifices with respect to her own personal agenda to achieve these outcomes. This is not the same as the East Asian sense of connectedness, which stems more from a sense of harmonious interdependence with the social group. These two types of interdependence differ from many Latin cultures in which social goals, such as meeting obligations to family and friends, often take priority over personal ones. And we know even less about various African cultures' view of self. We raise this point because in the sections to follow interdependence has been studied largely as a distinction between European American and East Asian cultures. The multiple forms of interdependence have been noted but have received little attention with respect to their implications for cognitive and emotional information processing and for behavioral self-regulation.

Culture, Cognition, and Emotion

Some cultural differences in cognition are fundamental: European Americans tend to extract central or distinctive elements from the context, whereas East Asians are more likely to view the world in a more holistic manner (Masuda & Nisbett, 2001). This distinction carries through in self-perception as well. People who hold an independent sense of self see themselves as distinctive and strive to maximize achievement of their personal goals. In one study, personally choosing a task to perform enhanced motivation for European Americans, whereas it less affected Asian students' intrinsic motivation; the Asian students' motivation was higher when told that someone close to them had chosen the task for them (Iyengar & Lepper, 1999). European Americans select tasks on which they will do well and on which they have done well in the past, whereas East Asians' choices of tasks are based less on such expectations and prior performance (Oishi & Diener, 2003). Motivational differences reliably follow from this distinction as well. Whereas European Americans tend to strive for personal achievement, East Asians strive for the achievement of group goals or see the goals they implement as representing group norms (Table 5.3).

Differences in goals also affect memory (Woike, Gershkovich, Piorkowski, & Polo, 1999). European Americans are likely to reconstruct events in terms of specific actors and their personal qualities, whereas East Asians are more likely to refer to those actors' social groups (Menon,

Table 5.3 Summary of key differences between an independent and an interdependent perception of self

Feature compared	Independent	Interdependent
Definition	Separate from social context	Connected with social context
Structure	Bounded, unitary, stable	Flexible, variable
Important features	Internal, private (abilities, thoughts, feelings)	External, public (statuses, roles, relationships)
Tasks	Be unique Express self Realize internal attributes Promote own goals Be direct: say what's on your mind	Belong, fit in Occupy one's proper place Engage in appropriate action Promote others' goals Be indirect: read other's mind
Role of others	Self-evaluation: others important for social comparison, reflected appraisal	Self-definition: self defined by relationships with others in specific contexts
Basis of self-esteem[a]	Ability to express self; validate internal attributes	Ability to adjust, restrain self: maintain harmony with social context

[a] Esteeming the self may be primarily a Western phenomenon, and the concept of self-esteem should perhaps be replaced by "self-satisfaction," or by a term that reflects the realization that one is fulfilling the culturally mandated task.

Source: Markus & Kitayama (1991). Copyright 1991 by the American Psychological Association. Reprinted with permission.

Morris, Chiu, & Hong, 1999). European Americans are more likely to ignore context in the inferences they draw about the social environment, whereas those with interdependent self-construals process social information by attending to relations of self or others to social context (Kühnen, Hannover, & Schubert, 2001).

These distinctions carry over into the experience of emotion. People with an independent sense of self experience ego-focused emotions frequently, such as pride over doing well or frustration over thwarted personal goals (Mesquita, 2001). In contrast, cultures with interdependent self-conceptions tend to experience other-focused emotions, such as the Japanese experience of **amae**, the sense of being lovingly pampered (Markus & Kitayama, 1991).

The sense of self influences bases for self-esteem. People with an independent sense of self are more likely to endorse items such as "I feel I am a person of worth" on self-esteem scales than people with an interdependent sense of self (Markus & Kitayama, 1991; Yik, Bond, & Paulhus, 1998). In addition, the importance attached to self-esteem and its implication for life satisfaction varies between independent and interdependent cultures. In a study of 31 cultures, Diener and Diener (1995) found that the relation of self-esteem to life satisfaction was lower in interdependent cultures, whereas in independent cultures individuals with high self-esteem reported high life satisfaction as well. In interdependent social contexts, approval from others for subscribing to social norms better predicts life satisfaction.

Individual and collective processes in the construction of the self are abetted by the types of situations that different cultures afford their members. Situations in the United States encourage self-enhancement (that is, regarding and promoting the self in positive terms). By contrast, Japanese situations are relatively conducive to self-criticism. For example, a US student studying in Japan reported that volleyball – a relaxing, fun sport in the United States that gives people the opportunity to demonstrate their prowess or total lack of talent amidst great cheering and booing – is much more competitive and serious in Japan, organized as a win–lose situation and thus conducive to self-criticism or the implicit criticism of others for playing poorly (Kitayama, Markus, Matsumoto, & Norasakkunkit, 1997).

Findings such as these have led many researchers to question the fundamental nature of self-esteem, especially whether it has any transcultural implications. Yet people from interdependent cultures who score high on Western self-esteem scales exhibit behavior consistent with Western people high in self-esteem, such as self-protective responses to negative feedback. Moreover, even in interdependent cultures people show tendencies to self-enhance indirectly, for example, by overvaluing the letters in one's name (Kitayama & Karasawa, 1997).

As may be apparent, much of the research on independent versus interdependent sense of self has contrasted European Americans in the United States with Japanese nationals. In some respects, each culture may represent an outlier on these dimensions, with European Americans being extreme on the independent sense of self, and the Japanese being extreme on the interdependent sense of self. Extreme examples tend to foster strong contrasts. Gaps in our knowledge regarding the interdependent self and its implications suffer both from lack of research in interdependent cultures generally and from examining primarily one type of interdependence.

SELF-REGULATION

Self-regulation describes how people control and direct their own actions, emotions, and thoughts. It focuses especially on how people formulate and pursue goals. Much self-regulation occurs virtually automatically, without awareness or conscious thought. Salient and goal-relevant cues in the environment can automatically guide our behavior (Lieberman et al., 2004). But at other times, we consciously and actively intervene to control our thoughts, emotions, and behaviors (Brandstätter & Frank, 2002).

Sources of Influence on Self-Regulation

Self-regulatory activities spring from several sources. One is the content of self-regulation: namely, what is in the working self-concept. Situational cues, social roles, values, and strongly held self-conceptions influence which aspects of the self predominate in the working self-concept (e.g., Verplanken & Holland, 2002). In a classroom situation, contextual influences on our behavior are likely to be achievement-related, but our behavior will also be influenced by whether our personal goals prioritize achievement. The working self-concept, in turn, depends on the situation. Speaking publicly in class but giving the wrong answer may lead one person with low achievement goals to find the situation to be funny, whereas for someone who values achievement goals, the same incident may cause embarrassment and redoubled efforts to be accurate the next time (Crocker & Knight, 2005; Ehrlinger & Dunning, 2003).

As this example also shows, sometimes the working self-concept is at odds with the stable self-concept (Arndt, Schimel, Greenberg, & Pyszczynski, 2002). After delivering an incorrect answer in class, one may feel stupid and embarrassed, thereby influencing the working self-concept, but assuming that these events do not repeat regularly, the impact may be only short term and not affect the enduring self-concept. If these types of event recur regularly, however, the enduring self-concept may change as well. For example, if staying out late and going to clubs is part of your self-concept as a party person, that aspect of your self-concept is likely to change once you have children. The working self-concept explains how different aspects of self may guide social behavior under different circumstances, and, in turn, be modified by feedback from those situations, ultimately affecting the enduring self-concept.

Behavioral Approach and Avoidance

Self-regulation involves fundamental decisions about what people and situations to approach and which ones to avoid. People have two semi-independent motivational systems that help to regulate behavior in these situations: an appetitive system, referred to as the **behavioral activation system** (BAS), and an aversive system, or **behavioral inhibition system** (BIS). The expression of positive, or approach, motivational concerns is associated with left frontal activation, consistent with the involvement of left frontal activation in goal pursuit (Harmon-Jones, Lueck, Fearn, & Harmon-Jones, 2006).

Table 5.4 Summary of Behavioral Activation System (BAS) and Behavioral Inhibition System (BIS) Self-Reports

Behavioral Activation System	Behavioral Inhibition System
Excited by going after something wanted	Worry about mistakes
Good things affect strongly	Concern with criticism
Go all-out to get things	Frequently nervous
Do fun things for their own sake	Worked up over possibible unpleasantness

Source: Authors' compilation from Carver & White (1996)

When BAS is activated, people tend to approach other people or activities in the environment. When BIS is activated, people are more likely to avoid other people or activities (Carver & White, 1994; see Gray, 1990). Negative or withdrawal motivation is associated with activation of the right frontal region of the cortex (Harmon-Jones et al., 2006).

A number of factors influence whether BAS or BIS is a predominating force, affecting behavior at any given time. Daily experiences, for example, influence the activation of these systems. If good things are happening to you, you are more likely to be in a state of activation (BAS) than in a state of inhibition (BIS) (Gable, Reis, & Elliot, 2000). When things are not going well, behavioral inhibition (BIS) may enable you to regroup.

BAS and BIS also reflect reliable individual differences (Table 5.4). Some people have a stronger behavioral activation system, focused on rewards, whereas others have a stronger behavioral inhibition system, focused on punishments (Carver & White, 1994). BAS-oriented people experience more positive events and positive affect, whereas BIS-dominated people tend to experience more negative affect (Updegraff et al., 2004).

Self-Discrepancy Theory

In a theory related to the activation–inhibition distinction, Higgins (1987, 1989) examined how self-discrepancies guide emotions and coping behavior. Some discrepancies reflect a shortfall between one's current self and ideal self (activating reward-pursuit), and some between one's current self and ought self (inhibiting for fear of punishment).

Higgins distinguished two types of **self-guides**. People differ in whether they are primarily driven by the ideal self or the ought self (Strauman, 1996). The **ideal self** is who one wants to be; the **ought self** is who one thinks one should be, often influenced heavily by one's beliefs about appropriate behavior for self (duties and obligations) and others' expectations. In a key study (Higgins, Klein, & Strauman, 1985), college students reported their self-perceptions, including how they would ideally like to be and how they felt they ought to be. Later, they filled out the same questionnaire from the standpoint of their mother, father, and closest friend and rated how much each of the reported personal attributes was meaningful to them. Discrepancies between actual and ideal self produced dejection-related emotions and lowered self-esteem (see also Higgins, Shah, & Friedman, 1997; Moretti & Higgins, 1990). For example, failing to get into graduate school produced disappointment and sadness. Perceived discrepancies between one's actual self (not good at science) and a friend's or parent's vision of what the self ought to be (doctor) produced anxiety but not sadness (Figure 5.3). The more important the personal attribute was to the respondent, the greater the emotion experienced (Higgins, 1987), and the more one was self-focused, the greater the emotions experienced as well (Higgins et al., 1997; Phillips & Silvia, 2005).

Discrepancies from one's ideal self facilitate efforts to achieve that ideal (a **promotion focus** in service of behavioral activation), whereas efforts to meet the expectation of others represent an inhibitory or **prevention focus** (Förster, Higgins, & Idson, 1998). Perhaps because a prevention focus is fueled by anxiety, people are faster off the mark to meet prevention-related goals than promotion-related goals (Freitas, Liberman, Salovey, & Higgins, 2002; Figure 5.3). This general orientation toward approach (promotion goals) versus avoidance (prevention goals), to a degree, reflects stable personality traits, with extraversion the exemplar of approach and neuroticism the exemplar of avoidance (Carver, Sutton, & Scheier, 2000).

People experience greater well-being given **regulatory fit** between the goals they are pursuing and their regulatory focus (Higgins, 2005). That is, people who are motivated to achieve their ideal selves experience well-being when they feel they are moving closer to those self standards, whereas people who are driven more by desire to avoid negative outcomes and to meet the expectations of others experience greater well-being when they believe they are upholding these social expectations (Higgins, Idson, Freitas, Spiegel, & Molden, 2003).

Socialization and culture influence which of these regulatory foci predominates. Some families endorse the opinions of others as a primary influence on self-concept. Often, this emphasis is accompanied by a parenting style marked by criticism. Other families urge becoming one's ideal self, an orientation more likely in a supportive environment. These differences develop different standards for self and its evaluation. Cultural differences, likewise, influence what aspects of the self govern self-regulatory behavior. People who are raised with a sense of themselves as independent, autonomous individuals are likely to be motivated by discrepancies between themselves and their ideal selves (promotion focus), whereas those who are raised with an interdependent sense of self are more attentive to the concerns of others in the social environment (prevention focus; Lee, Aaker, & Gardner, 2000).

Different patterns of brain activation characterize promotion versus prevention orientation. A promotion regulatory focus tends to be associated with greater left frontal activity, whereas a prevention regulatory focus is associated with greater right frontal activity. This asymmetry fits promotion-focused goals being associated with approaching desired outcomes, whereas prevention-focused goals are more associated with avoiding undesired outcomes (Amodio, Shah, Sigelman, Brazy, & Harmon-Jones, 2004). In one study (M. H. Johnson et al., 2006), when people reflected on hopes and aspirations (promotion), medial prefrontal and anterior cingulate cortex activation predominated (relative to non-self-relevant thought), whereas when people reflected on duties and obligations (prevention), the posterior cingulate cortex and precuneus predominated. Perhaps the medial prefrontal cortex reflects agentic self-reflection and the posterior medial cortex reflects experiential self-reflection. Alternatively, medial prefrontal

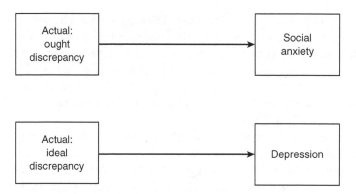

Figure 5.3 Emotional consequences of self-discrepancies

cortex activation may implicate inward focus, whereas posterior cingulate activation implicates outward or social focus (M. H. Johnson et al., 2006).

Self-Efficacy and Personal Control

Other influences on self-regulation include self-efficacy and sense of personal control. **Self-efficacy** beliefs refer to our expectations about our abilities to accomplish specific tasks (Bandura, 2006). Whether individuals undertake an activity or strive to meet a particular goal depends on whether they believe they will be capable in performing these actions. Suppose, for example, that you are offered a prestigious teaching position in the Netherlands but learn that within three years you must be able to lecture in Dutch. Although you may desperately want to accept the position, a low sense of self-efficacy for learning Dutch might lead to a decision not to accept it.

Besides specific control-related perceptions of abilities to perform particular behaviors (self-efficacy beliefs), people have a general sense of **personal control** or mastery that enables them to plan, cope with setbacks, and pursue self-regulatory activities. People with a strong sense of control are more likely to undertake activities in service of their goals, whereas those with a low sense of personal mastery or control may be less likely to do so.

In a study illustrating this point, Pham, Taylor, and Seeman (2001) gave college students who were either high or low in their sense of mastery a manipulation that made salient the unpredictable aspects of college life, its predictable aspects, or neutral features of the college environment. Students in the unpredictable condition were reminded of difficulties getting into one's chosen classes, whereas those in the predictable condition were reminded that exam times and paper dates are always posted at the beginning of the term. After reading this manipulation, the students listed their thoughts and feelings about college, and their heart rate and blood pressure were assessed. Students exposed to the predictable college manipulation made more references to the future and to personal goals in their thoughts listing. They also had lower blood pressure and heart rate compared to those who read about neutral features of the college environment and especially the unpredictable aspects of the college environment. The students who were chronically high in personal mastery were more optimistic and future oriented than those low in personal mastery. Enduring expectations of control, as well as factors that make control or lack of control salient in a particular situation, influence self-regulatory activity at the cognitive, motivational, and physiological levels.

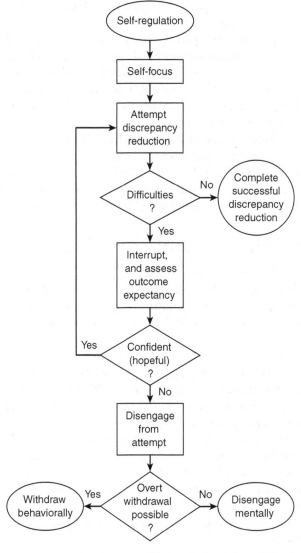

Figure 5.4 Cybernetic theory of self-attention and self-regulation

Source: After Carver (1979)

Self-Focus

Self-regulation is also influenced by the direction of attention, including whether attention is directly inward toward the self or outward toward the environment (Duval & Wicklund, 1972; Silvia & Duval, 2001). When focused on ourselves, a state called **self-awareness** (Wicklund & Frey, 1980), we evaluate our behavior against a standard and subsequently attempt to meet the standard. For example, upon catching your reflection in passing a store window, you may notice your bad posture and straighten up.

Self-attention causes people to compare themselves to various standards: intellectual performance, physical appearance, athletic prowess, and moral integrity (Macrae, Bodenhausen, & Milne, 1998). We try to conform to the standard, evaluate our behavior against it, decide that our behavior either matches the standard or does not, and continue adjusting and comparing until we meet the standard or give up. This feedback process appears in the **cybernetic theory of self-regulation** (Carver & Scheier, 1998; Figure 5.4).

Implicit in these arguments is the idea that self-focus is often experienced as aversive and that people find ways not only to adjust their behavior or personal qualities but also to direct attention away from themselves (Flory, Räikkönen, Matthews, & Owens, 2000). After a bad day, people often need to keep themselves from focusing on personal issues or problems at work and so use drinking or television to reduce self-focus (Moskalenko & Heine, 2003).

Threats to Self-Regulation

Some circumstances reliably compromise the ability to self-regulate. One such condition is social exclusion. When individuals have been rejected by a social group, they have more difficulty performing subsequent tasks. The person quits a frustrating task sooner, attends poorly, and shows less self-control (Baumeister, DeWall, Ciarocco, & Twenge, 2005). In one experiment, participants who were told that no one else in their group wanted to work with them ate more cookies than participants who had not experienced rejection (Baumeister et al., 2005, Study 2). The excluded person adopts a defensive state characterized by lethargy, a poor sense of time, and avoidance of meaningful thought, emotions, and self-awareness (Twenge, Catanese, & Baumeister, 2003). Less extreme self-regulatory threat can also motivate efforts to regain group membership (Williams, Cheung, & Choi, 2000).

More generally, many circumstances involving self-regulation create self-control dilemmas in which one must choose between two preeminent goals or sacrifice short-term costs for long-term benefits. For example, one may have to have an uncomfortable medical procedure to rule out a potentially serious condition. Anticipated short-term costs elicit self-control efforts to minimize those costs (Trope & Fishbach, 2000). One may distract oneself or focus on the long-term benefits of the short-term efforts, to act according to long-term interests, not succumbing to short-term temptations.

Do self-control dilemmas pit reason against emotion, or do some emotions support efforts at control? Although **hedonic emotions** characterize a short-term perspective, **self-conscious emotions** fit a long-term perspective and may help in resolving self-control dilemmas

(Giner-Sorolla, 2001). Patients with orbitofrontal lesions show regulatory deficits with respect to self-control (Beer, Heerey, Keltner, Scabini, & Knight, 2003), and their inappropriate self-conscious emotions (embarrassment or guilt) undermine behavioral self-regulation. Self-regulation apparently depends on both rational responses and self-conscious emotional responses.

Active self-regulation requires effort, especially when one is multi-tasking. Load impairs activities that require active self-regulation but leaves untouched more automatic self-regulation. When self-regulatory resources are depleted, complex thinking is impaired, but performance of simple tasks is not (Schmeichel, Vohs, & Baumeister, 2003; Vohs, Baumeister, & Ciarocco, 2005; Vohs & Schmeichel, 2003).

Neural Bases of Self-Regulation

Exploring some neural bases of self-regulation, the dual-processing distinction helps thinking about these patterns (Chapter 2). Deliberate self-regulation implicates different brain regions than does automatic self-regulation (Banfield, Wyland, Macrae, Münte, & Heatherton, 2004). The prefrontal cortex is involved in conscious self-regulation: higher-order executive control of lower-order processes responsible for planning and enacting. In particular, the dorsolateral prefrontal cortex (dlPFC) has been tied to planning, processing novel information, making choices, controlling memory and working memory, and language functioning (see Banfield et al., 2004, for a review). The dlPFC is also implicated in behavioral self-regulation, specifically selecting and initiating actions (e.g., Spence & Frith, 1999). Converging evidence for this view of the dlPFC appears when damage to this region results in apathy and diminished attention as well as compromised planning, judgment, and insight (Dimitrov, Grafman, Soares, & Clark, 1999), suggesting poor executive functioning.

The ventromedial prefrontal cortex (vmPFC), which is connected to limbic structures that are involved in emotional processing (Pandya & Barnes, 1987), is especially implicated in controlling our behavior, emotional output, and interaction with others (Dolan, 1999). The orbitofrontal cortex (OFC), a portion of the vmPFC, activates under emotional processing, reward, inhibition, decision making, self-awareness, and strategic regulation (Banfield et al., 2004). Damage to this area links to striking behavior changes and a disregard for the potential future consequences of one's behavior (Bechara, Damasio, Damasio, & Anderson, 1994). OFC damage also undermines the ability to adjust behavior to be perceived as acceptable or moral by others (E. Goldberg, 2001).

The anterior cingulate cortex (ACC) interacts with the PFC in monitoring and guiding behavior. It is implicated both in cognitive processing (anterior portion) and in affective-evaluative processing (see Bush, Luu, & Posner, 2000, for a review). ACC function and its connections to the motor and cognitive systems appear to be critical in translating intention into action (Banfield et al., 2004). The ACC also plays a role in processing conflicting information and has been conceptualized as a region that may trigger a shift from automatic to controlled processing (Botvinick et al., 2004). Thus, for example, if one is self-schematic for athletics, a sudden departure from one's usual athletic prowess should trigger ACC activity and initiation of controlled processing in the PFC to comprehend the implications for the self and to regulate subsequent behavior (Lieberman et al., 2002).

MOTIVATION AND SELF-REGULATION

Self-regulation depends on enduring self-relevant concerns. These include the needs for an accurate sense of self, a consistent sense of self, an improving self, and a positive sense of self. In terms of social motives (see Chapters 1 and 2), accuracy and consistency are versions of a social understanding motive, whereas improving and maintaining a positive sense of self are two different ways to self-enhance.

Need for Accuracy

To make our future outcomes predictable and controllable, we need a fairly accurate assessment of our abilities, opinions, beliefs, and emotions (Trope, 1975). Accurate self-assessments enable us to anticipate circumstances and control our future behavior (Trope & Bassok, 1982).

When we need to know our ability, Trope suggests that we pick tasks that will be the most informative (i.e., diagnostic) of our ability. To get accurate feedback about your mathematics ability, a sample Graduate Records Examination (GRE) math section will be more diagnostic than a children's arithmetic test or your performance on a problem frustrating mathematicians for decades.

Feedback from comparisons with others, **social comparisons**, can also meet a need for accurate self-assessment if no objective task is available (Festinger, 1954). For example, if you are invited to a formal dance and you're not sure how good a dancer you are, you are unlikely to go to either a children's dancing class or a ballroom competition. You might, instead, try out your dancing abilities in a setting that offers you opportunities to compare yourself to others, such as a club, to determine if you will need lessons to look good at the ball. Having an accurate sense of self is important when knowledge of our abilities is uncertain (Sorrentino & Roney, 1986).

People especially seek accurate self-relevant information if they anticipate that the news will be good, but they also often desire self-assessment even when they anticipate that the news may be bad (Brown, 1990). If you expect that your dancing ability is nonexistent, your efforts at self-assessment may confirm that belief, and it may be prudent to feign an injury on the day of the ball.

Need for Consistency

Following from the need for an accurate self-concept is the idea that we need a consistent self-concept rather than one that varies from situation to situation. We need to believe that we have intrinsic qualities and goals that will remain relatively stable over time (Swann, 1983). People often seek out situations and interpret their behavior in ways that confirm their preexisting self-concepts; people also resist situations and feedback that are at odds with their self-concepts. This process is called **self-verification**.

For example, suppose you have just started graduate school. During the first social event you are relatively quiet and keep to yourself. If a classmate comes up to you and says "There's no need to be shy; these people won't bite," you may feel offended. Perhaps you didn't talk much because you are learning the lay of the land or perhaps you're just under the weather, but you may think of yourself as someone who is usually fairly outgoing. At the next social event you may be more outgoing than usual as a way of convincing both yourself and others of your enduring quality as an outgoing person (Swann & Read, 1981).

People seek to confirm their positive attributes, but sometimes they seek to confirm their negative ones as well, in order to be realistic. The need to see oneself accurately and consistently affects behavior. We selectively interact with people who see us as we see ourselves (e.g., Swann, Stein-Seroussi, & Giesler, 1992). For example, think of the comfort in relaxing with people who know both your strengths and weaknesses and love you nonetheless. Still, generally speaking, we like the people who see us positively and who value us for the same things we value in ourselves.

Mostly people maintain their self-views without active or conscious effort. Maintaining a consistent sense of self is part of the process of interacting with family, friends, and coworkers in familiar settings performing familiar tasks. Discrepant feedback focuses our attention on the threat to a consistent self-concept, and we either seek to expel the incorrect view or question whether to change our self-concept (Madon et al., 2001), shifting from automatic to controlled processing (Chapter 2).

As for other aspects of social cognition, the desire for a consistent self varies from culture to culture. In independent cultures, people seek to express their distinctive personal qualities. In interdependent contexts – situational influences or social norms guide behavior – people may express inconsistent beliefs about themselves across different contexts (Choi & Choi, 2002). For example, European Americans may see themselves as moderately achievement oriented across many contexts, whereas East Asians may see themselves as quite achievement oriented in some contexts and less so in others. Overall, East Asians view themselves more flexibly across situations, whereas European Americans view themselves more consistently across situations (Suh, 2002).

Need for Improvement

In addition to the needs for an accurate and consistent sense of self, people are motivated by their desire to improve. Many self-regulatory activities serve this need (Kasser & Ryan, 1996). For people to use their self-regulatory activities in service of self-improvement, they need goals. Such goals come from several sources. Markus's concept of possible selves, for example, incorporates the visions that people have of themselves in the future (Markus & Nurius, 1986).

By envisioning a possible self in the future, a person may be able to set appropriate goals, make progress toward achieving those goals, and chart progress.

Self-improvement may also be served by **upward social comparisons** (Taylor & Lobel, 1989; J. V. Wood, 1989). Many people believe this is why having a mentor is so important. People who embody the attributes or skills we wish to possess can motivate us and also provide specific information that is helpful for improvement.

Self-improvement is also motivated by criticism, whether explicit from other people or implicit in the feedback of one's poor performance. The perception that one has fallen short of one's own goal or significant others' aspirations can be esteem-reducing, but it can also contribute to efforts to improve. The desire for self-improvement appears to be an especially important motivation for East Asians (Heine et al., 2001).

Not all efforts toward self-improvement are successful. Making and maintaining changes successfully are difficult processes. Sometimes people perceive that they have improved when they have not (A. E. Wilson & Ross, 2001). For example, if a student goes through a study skills program, she is likely to come out of the experience believing that her skills have improved whether or not they have. This occurs because people have theories about stability and change that may distort their self-assessments, not just of their current standing but of their past standing as well (Conway & Ross, 1984; Ross, 1989). By distorting one's earlier skill level as poorer than it actually was, one may assume that one's current skill level represents improvement (see also Libby, Eibach, & Gilovich, 2005). These insights also point to a large literature on self-enhancement, to which we now turn.

Self-Enhancement

Besides needing accurate and consistent information about self, we need to feel good about ourselves and maintain self-esteem. Western cultures show cognitive and motivational benefits of self-esteem. People with high self-esteem have a clear sense of their personal qualities. They think well of themselves, set appropriate goals, use feedback in a manner that maintains their self-esteem, savor their positive experiences, and cope well with difficult situations (e.g., K. L. Sommer & Baumeister, 2002; Wood et al., 2003).

Collectively, the need for and efforts to maintain or create a positive sense of self is referred to as **self-enhancement**. Self-enhancement needs appear important, perhaps even preeminent, much of the time (Sedikides, 1993), at least in Western cultures. Self-enhancement needs become especially important following threat, failure, or blows to self-esteem (e.g., Beauregard & Dunning, 1998; Krueger, 1998). The desire for a positive sense of self is driven at least in part by the need to connect with others and gain their approval, as noted earlier (the sociometer; Leary & Baumeister, 2000). Social threats become threats to self-esteem, which in turn activate the need to regain approval and acceptance. From this perspective, self-enhancement needs are driven socially by assessing how one is viewed by others.

People can satisfy their self-enhancement needs by holding **positive illusions**: self-perceptions that are falsely positive and somewhat exaggerated with respect to their actual abilities, talents, and social skills (Taylor & Brown, 1988). There are at least three types of positive illusions: People tend to see themselves *more positively* than is true; they believe they have *more control* over the events around them than is actually the case; and they are *unrealistically optimistic* about the future. When students describe whether positive and negative personality adjectives accurately describe them and others, most evaluate themselves more favorably than others (e.g., Suls, Lemos, & Stewart, 2002). We remember positive information about ourselves, but negative information often slips conveniently from mind (Sedikides & Green, 2000). If pressed, most of us have more difficulty reconstructing past failures than successes (Story, 1998). We believe we are more likely than others to engage in selfless, kind, and generous acts (Epley & Dunning, 2000). We often remember our performance as higher than it actually was (Crary, 1966). We believe we are happier than most other people (Klar & Giladi, 1999). We believe that those who flatter us are credible and discerning (Vonk, 2002). We respond to threats by bolstering our self-perceptions in other life domains (Boney-McCoy, Gibbons, & Gerrard, 1999) and by making **downward social comparisons** to less fortunate others (Wills, 1981). And perhaps most poignantly, we see ourselves as less biased than we believe others to be (Ehrlinger, Gilovich, & Ross, 2005; Pronin, Gilovich, & Ross, 2004; Pronin, Lin, & Ross, 2002). In each case, people can self-enhance by seeing themselves as better than other people, or by seeing themselves as better than others see them (Kwan, John, Kenny, Bond, & Robins, 2004).

How do people successfully monitor reality and maintain accurate perceptions about themselves and the world if positive illusions are clouding their vision? Although absolute accuracy may be sacrificed, relative accuracy seems to be high. If one compares a person's self-assessments on a broad array of traits with the same assessments made by a friend, the correlation between the ratings is high, even though people see themselves more positively than their friends see them (Taylor, Lerner, Sherman, Sage, & McDowell, 2003a).

But some circumstances also predict which assessments of the self, the world, and the future become more realistic. When people are about to get feedback from others, they are more realistic, even pessimistic, about the anticipated news (K. M. Taylor & Shepperd, 1998). When people must decide between alternative courses of action or set personal goals, they are more accurate and honest with themselves (S. E. Taylor & Gollwitzer, 1995). People are more modest in their self-appraisals when they believe other people will have accurate information about them, when their self-descriptions can be easily verified, when they expect to receive self-relevant feedback (Armor & Taylor, 1998), or when their self-assessments can potentially be disconfirmed (e.g., Dunning, Meyerowitz, & Holzberg, 1989), such as expecting to perform a task that will test an ability (Armor & Sackett, 2006). Thus, as accountability increases, self-perceptions become more accurate in the absolute sense. Self-enhancement is greater at the beginning of a project, motivating effort, than at the end of a project when shortfalls might be dispiriting (Shepperd, Ouellette, & Fernandez, 1996).

Why are most people so apparently **self-enhancing** in their self-perceptions? Moreover, why do these self-enhancing perceptions persist if they do not conform to reality? Self-enhancing positive illusions may be adaptive for mental health (Taylor & Brown, 1988; S. E. Taylor et al., 2003a; S. E. Taylor, Lerner, Sherman, Sage, & McDowell, 2003b; cf. Ackerman, Huang, & Bargh, 2012). Positive self-perceptions, unrealistic optimism about the future, and a false sense of personal control may help us to feel better about ourselves (Regan, Snyder, & Kassin, 1995), to develop the motivation to pursue goals (S. E. Taylor & Gollwitzer, 1995), and to persist longer in trying to achieve our goals (Armor & Taylor, 2003). Self-enhancing perceptions foster evidence of successful life adjustment: a personal sense of well-being, persistence toward goals, and the ability to engage in creative, productive work (Brown & Dutton, 1995). Reasonably positive self-regard fosters good social relationships as well (Taylor et al., 2003a). However, the upward limit is people who are notably self-enhancing in public settings and can alienate others (e.g., Bonano, Field, Kovacevic, & Kaltman, 2002; Robins & Beer, 2001).

Moreover, under threat to self, people with excessively high self-esteem can become mean, nasty, and self-important (Baumeister, Smart, & Boden, 1996); such people increase stereotyping, disparage others, and compare downward (e.g., Heatherton & Vohs, 2000; Vohs & Heatherton, 2004; see also Baumeister, Campbell, Krueger, & Vohs, 2003). These self-regulation failures appear more common among people who are defensively high in self-esteem, rather than those who are more secure in their high self-esteem (Lambird & Mann, 2006).

Nonetheless, self-enhancement can often yield another unexpected benefit. When people are feeling good about themselves and not threatened by nagging questions about their self-worth, they are often more receptive to negative feedback (e.g., Trope & Neter, 1994). People who are, by nature, more optimistic about the future also process personally relevant risk-related information less defensively than people who are less optimistic (Aspinwall & Brunhart, 1996). When people feel good about themselves, they are more positive about other people as well (Ybarra, 1999). **Social validation** – that is, being accepted for who we are – also reduces defensiveness, and after people have reflected on being liked for intrinsic aspects of themselves, they are more receptive to potentially threatening information (Schimel, Arndt, Pyszczynski, & Greenberg, 2001).

Additional evidence for benefits of a positive sense of self comes from people with chronically low self-esteem. People with low self-esteem suffer a host of disadvantages: They have less clear self-conceptions, think of themselves in more unfavorable terms, often select unrealistic goals or shy away from goals altogether, tend to be pessimistic about the future, remember their past experiences more negatively, wallow in their negative moods rather than self-regulating to restore a positive mood, have more adverse emotional and behavioral reactions to negative feedback, are less able to generate positive feedback for themselves, make upward social comparisons that yield negative self-evaluations, are more concerned about their impact on other people, and are more vulnerable to depression or rumination when they encounter setbacks or stress (Brown & Marshall, 2001; Di Paula & Campbell, 2002; Heatherton & Vohs, 2000; Josephs, Bosson, & Jacobs, 2003; Kernis, Paradise, Whitaker, Wheatman, & Goldman, 2000; Leary, Tambor, Terdal, & Downs, 1995; Setterlund & Niedenthal, 1993; Sommer & Baumeister, 2002; Vohs & Heatherton, 2004)).

Self-enhancement also confers biological benefits during times of stress. Stress produces familiar symptoms: The heart beats faster, blood pressure goes up, and we feel anxious. People who perceive themselves positively, even more positively than others do, have lower cortisol (stress hormone) levels and lower heart rate and blood pressure under laboratory stressful tasks

(Creswell et al., 2005; Taylor et al., 2003b). Self-enhancement can protect against stressful circumstances that might otherwise be personally threatening and adversely affect health. More generally, self-esteem and an internal locus of control in younger people may lower cortisol response to psychological stress and increase hippocampal volume and in older adults decrease age-related cognitive decline, improve cortisol regulation, and decrease global brain volume decline (Pruessner et al., 2005).

Self-Affirmation

Self-affirmation (Steele, 1988) maintains self-enhancement needs and helps people cope with threats to their self-worth by endorsing unrelated aspects of themselves (e.g., Aronson, Blanton, & Cooper, 1995; Blanton, Cooper, Skurnik, & Aronson, 1997; Koole, Smeets, van Knippenberg, & Dijksterhuis, 1999; see Sherman & Cohen, 2006, for a review). When people can affirm valued aspects of the self, they are less likely to respond defensively to threat. In one experiment (Sherman, Nelson, & Steele, 2000), one group of college student participants reflected on a personally important value; the other group reflected on a less important personal value. The participants then saw an AIDS education video. Those who had completed the value-affirmation task recognized themselves as at risk for HIV and engaged in more positive health behaviors (namely, purchasing condoms and taking educational brochures) compared to those who had reflected on a relatively unimportant value. These findings suggest that self-affirming reduces defensive responses to threatening health information. This fits the evidence just reviewed indicating that when people feel good about themselves they are more receptive to potentially negative information. Affirmation of personal values can attenuate perceptions of threat (Sherman & Cohen, 2002), reduce the tendency to ruminate after failure (Koole et al., 1999), and attenuate physiological reactions to stress (Creswell et al., 2005).

One implication of findings from self-affirmation theory is that self-enhancement is a maintenance motive. People do not strive to have the most positive self-assessment possible, but rather they strive to maintain an adequate level of self-regard. Indeed, once reaching a certain level of self-esteem, people may actually avoid activities that might enhance it further (Tesser, Crepaz, Collins, Cornell, & Beach, 2000; Zuckerman & O'Loughlin, 2006).

Self-Evaluation Maintenance

Tesser (1988) suggested another social mechanism whereby people facilitate and maintain their positive self-regard – namely, in dealing with the performance of close others with whom they might compare themselves. For example, John's best friend, Mark, recently won a prestigious prize for writing a short story. Will John be pleased and eager to tell others about his friend's success, or might he instead feel envious of Mark's success and unhappy to be reminded that he is a less talented writer? Tesser's **self-evaluation maintenance theory** deals with questions like these.

Generally, the behavior of close others matters more, psychologically speaking, than the behavior of distant people. Thus, a critical situation arises when a close other person performs well. Whether John will be delighted for Mark or feel envy instead will depend critically on how central writing is to John's self-concept. If John is also a writer who has been trying to get his work published, then Mark's strong performance is likely to be personally threatening and lead to negative emotions and efforts to avoid Mark in the future (the comparison effect). However, if John is an attorney and does not write short stories, he may be delighted with Mark's success and take pride in Mark's award (the reflection effect). Thus the same factors – personal closeness to a target and the target's strong performance – can lead to opposite effects on one's own emotions and behavior, depending on whether another person's performance is relevant or irrelevant to one's self-definition (Figure 5.5).

Terror Management Theory

Threat can stimulate self-enhancement, and there is perhaps no greater threat than death (Gailliot, Schmeichel, & Baumeister, 2006). **Terror management theory** draws on this insight (Greenberg, Pyszczynski, & Solomon, 1986). According to the theory, people are biologically driven for self-preservation, and they manage the threat of death at both the cultural level, by developing worldviews that provide meaning and purpose, and at the individual level, through self-esteem. People form belief systems that endow their lives and their world with enduring meaning. These views help manage the mortality and the anxiety that vulnerability produces (Greenberg, Pyszczynski, & Solomon, 1986). At the individual level,

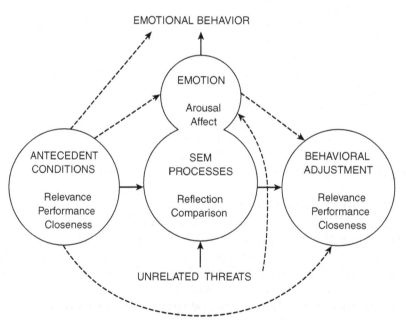

Figure 5.5   Schematic representation of the self-evaluation maintenance model
Source: After Tesser (1988)

people strive to maintain a positive sense of self, which likewise reduces the anxiety associated with mortality.

The theory generates specific predictions as to how cultural worldviews and self-esteem ward off the threat of death. One well-supported prediction is that people suppress death-related thoughts when death is made salient (Greenberg, Arndt, Schimel, Pyszczynski, & Solomon, 2001; Schmeichel & Martens, 2005). The importance of a cultural worldview for coping with the terror of mortality also predicts that when death is salient, people especially subscribe to and attempt to meet culturally approved standards. Such actions protect them from the anxiety that their vulnerability to death might otherwise create (Greenberg, Porteus, Simon, Pyszczynski, & Solomon, 1995; McGregor et al., 1998). Thus norms are, in essence, soothing or reassuring.

But the fear of death and subscribing more fully to social norms also mean that people more harshly evaluate others who violate norms. In one study, following a mortality-salience manipulation, people were more likely to blame severely injured innocent victims – in an apparent effort to restore a sense of order to a frightening environment (Hirschberger, 2006). Likewise, activities that promote self-esteem help people manage the terror of mortality by reaffirming their intrinsic value. The threat of death requires active self-regulation to alleviate disturbing thoughts about mortality (Gailliot et al., 2006).

Culture and Self-Enhancement

Both self-enhancement and related needs represent insights about the self within cultural boundaries. The characterization of self-enhancement just described better characterize Westerners, particularly people in the United States, than people in other countries, especially East Asian countries. East Asians are more self-critical, and self-serving attributions are less common in East Asian cultures (Heine & Renshaw, 2002; Chapter 6). In East Asian cultures, self-effacing biases emerge more commonly than self-enhancing biases. In one study, when Japanese students outperformed another student, they regarded their success as situationally caused, whereas when they were outperformed by another, they were more likely to attribute that person's performance to personal qualities (Takata, 1987). These more modest self-perceptions among East Asians appear consistent (Heine, Takata, & Lehman, 2000; Oishi, Wyre, & Colcombe, 2000).

However, perhaps needs met by self-enhancement in Western cultures are met in different forms in Eastern cultures. For example, enhancing the social group and one's standing with respect to the group may meet enhancement needs in interdependent cultures (Sedikides, Gaertner, & Toguchi, 2003). Comparing participants from collectivistic (Singapore, China) and individualistic (Israeli Jews) cultures, self-enhancement of traits reflecting personal agency was associated with an independent self-construal. Self-enhancement of communal traits was associated with an interdependent self-construal (Kurman, 2001). Maybe enhancement of the self or one's social group has some universality but assumes different forms, depending on cultural values (Sedikides et al., 2003).

Reconciling the Motives that Guide Self-Regulation

Each of the motives just described – need for accuracy, consistency, self-improvement, and self-enhancement – governs behavior under somewhat different circumstances. The search for accurate feedback about the self predominates under instability or ambiguity regarding one's standing (e.g., Sorrentino & Roney, 1986; Trope, 1979). The quest for consistent information is strongest when one is certain of one's standing but feedback or circumstances challenge self-perceptions (Pelham, 1990). A consistent sense of self, about which one is certain, is also more characteristic of people who have a prevention focus in their lives (Leonardelli, Lakin, & Arkin, 2007).

Self-enhancement needs prevail, at least in Western cultures and under conditions of threat. Self-presentational needs may also trigger self-enhancing behavior (Baumeister, Tice, & Hutton, 1989). Cognitions about the self stray in the direction of consistency, whereas affective reactions to the self stray in the direction of enhancement. That is, we like to feel certain of our attributes, whether positive or negative, but we are happiest when we get positive feedback (Swann, Pelham, & Krull, 1989). People motivated primarily by a promotion focus (a concern with growth and nurturance) are more concerned with self-esteem compared to those with a prevention focus (Leonardelli et al., 2007).

Much self-regulatory activity serving self-enhancement (at least in Western cultures), and potentially also self-improvement, may occur automatically without awareness. However, a search for accurate or consistent feedback is more likely to implicate controlled processing because automatic processes are likely to have been interrupted by a challenge to or ambiguity regarding one's self-perceptions. A final way to satisfy these motives simultaneously is the flexibility of the human mind, capable of construing information to fit a variety of motives (Kunda, 1999). People want to believe that they are consistent and may distort the degree to which this is true (Wells & Iyengar, 2005). People want to maintain a positive sense of self and can do so by criticizing their distant past selves, thereby achieving an illusion that they have improved (A. E. Wilson & Ross, 2001).

THE SELF AS A REFERENCE POINT

The self-concept not only explains how people perceive and regulate themselves but also provides a lens for interpreting the qualities and behavior of other people.

Self-Referencing

Information learned with reference to the self has a memory advantage over other kinds of information. Early research supported a **depth of processing** account (Rogers, Kuiper,

& Kirker, 1977): Self-relevant information leaves a richer, more interconnected, and more enduring memory trace. Developments in social cognitive neuroscience help explain the neural basis of such effects (Heatherton, Macrae, & Kelley, 2004). For example (W. M. Kelley et al., 2002), participants judged trait adjectives as either self-descriptive, descriptive of George Bush, or appearing in uppercase letters. Semantic processing tasks typically activate the left prefrontal cortex, and this was true for all three experimental conditions. For self-referencing trials, the medial prefrontal cortex (mPFC) was also implicated. Moreover, the level of activity in the mPFC correlated with how well participants remembered the items, suggesting that mPFC contributes to the formation of self-relevant memories (Macrae, Moran, Heatherton, Banfield, & Kelley, 2004).

Simulation theory describes self-referencing effects: One way that people infer the mental states of others is to imagine their own thoughts, emotions, or behaviors in a similar setting. A region of the ventromedial PFC previously implicated in self-referencing tasks activates in response to ratings of similar others, but not dissimilar others (Mitchell, Banaji, & Macrae, 2005b). Converging evidence comes from studies of people who have damage to areas of the prefrontal cortex (Stuss & Levine, 2002); such damage may impair the ability to reflect on the self and to be introspective. The self-reference effect in memory may depend on the ability to reflect on the self, and neural activity in the mPFC may underlie that self-reflection (Heatherton et al., 2004).

Social Projection

The self actively constructs the social world, to a large degree, in its own image. Our beliefs and personal qualities help construct our assessments of others. **Social projection** refers to people estimating their own preferences, traits, problems, activities, and attitudes to be characteristic of others, or at least more than the evidence warrants (Mullen & Goethals, 1990). We assume that others share our characteristics, emotions, and motives (Holmes, 1978), and we use the same traits to describe acquaintances as we use to describe ourselves (Shrauger & Patterson, 1974). Social projection effects can occur even when people have time to think about their assessments (Krueger & Stanke, 2001), when they receive accuracy feedback (Krueger & Clement, 1994), and when they have relevant information about others (Alicke & Largo, 1995; Kenny & Acitelli, 2001).

Do we project our own attitudes, characteristics, and values onto others because we have a motivation to see our characteristics as good or because the self provides a useful set of cognitive heuristics by which people can draw inferences rapidly and confidently? Both appear to be true. Decades of research pitting cognitive explanations against motivational ones suggest that these two sources of influence are hard to separate. Motivational influences are likely to affect judgments by exerting effects on cognitive processing (Dunning, 1999; Kunda, 1990).

The desire to see the self in positive terms contributes to various social projection processes. We define social concepts that we use for judging others in self-serving ways

(Dunning, Perie, & Story, 1991), use traits central to our own self-concepts for evaluating others (Alicke, 1985), make self-serving social comparisons to others (Dunning & Hayes, 1996), spontaneously judge other people by comparing them with ourselves (Mussweiler & Bodenhausen, 2002), assume that others share our weaknesses but that our strengths are unique (J. D. Campbell, 1986; Mullen & Goethals, 1990; Suls & Wan, 1987), and distance ourselves from others who share our weaknesses (Schimel, Pyszczynski, Greenberg, O'Mahen, & Arndt, 2000).

Nor is the target on whom we project our positive qualities randomly selected. We tend to attribute our own attitudes and qualities to attractive targets (Granberg & Brent, 1980; Marks & Miller, 1982), and we project our undesirable qualities onto unattractive or unfavorable targets (e.g., Bramel, 1963; Sherwood, 1979). Both types of projection increase under threat to self-esteem, such as negative feedback or a poor performance. By contrast, when a person has affirmed the self or has received positive feedback, social projection and defensive social projection are muted (Dunning, 2003; Kunda, 1990). For example (S. J. Sherman, Presson, & Chassin, 1984), participants given false feedback about their task performance then estimated how many other students would perform well or poorly. Those who had apparently failed estimated that more others would also fail, compared to participants who had merely received information that someone else had failed. Depressed people likewise show less social projection, suggesting a compromised ability to repair threats to the self (e.g., Agostinelli, Sherman, Presson, & Chassin, 1992; Tabachnik, Crocker, & Alloy, 1983). People use the self as a standard for inferring qualities in the social world, at least partly guided by self-enhancement needs.

Projection guides judgments in stereotyping processes as well. Threats to self-image reliably increase negative stereotyping. In one study (Fein & Spencer, 1997), participants received positive or negative feedback about their performance on an intelligence test, and in an ostensibly unrelated study, they evaluated an applicant for a job based on her credentials and interview. The applicant was portrayed as either Jewish or not Jewish. Participants who had received negative feedback rated the job candidate less favorably if she was labeled as Jewish, whereas participants who had received positive feedback rated the two job candidates equally regardless of background. Research from terror management theory makes a similar point: Reminding people of their own mortality increases their need to affirm self-worth, which in turn enhances their using stereotypes to characterize others (Greenberg et al., 1990; Schimel et al., 1999).

Stereotypes also help us to invalidate the expertise of those who view us negatively. After being criticized, for example, a person may negatively stereotype to discredit an evaluator and minimize the self-deflating aspects of the criticism. For example, students' evaluations of their professors depend heavily on the grades they expect to receive (Sinclair & Kunda, 2000). When flattered by others whom they might otherwise stereotype, people instead suspend their stereotypes and judge the positive evaluator in a positive manner (Sinclair & Kunda, 1999). Thus stereotyping can serve a self-enhancement purpose.

Summary

People hold complex and varied representations of themselves, including both their current attributes and attributes that may characterize them in the future. The self-concept varies depending on one's situation, temporarily altering the working self-concept; the self-concept also represents significant others. Beliefs about one's current and future qualities act as reference points for setting goals and guiding behavior. Self-esteem is the explicit and implicit valuations of self.

Self-concepts and the cognitions, emotions, and goals that accompany them vary by cultural context. Whereas the independent self, characteristic of Western cultures, reflects a conception of self as autonomous and self-serving, the interdependent self reflects a self-concept interconnected with the social group and influenced substantially by its standards. These differences affect self-regulatory motives and processes.

Self-regulation refers to people controlling their actions, partly influenced by holding a promotion or a prevention focus with respect to personal goals and attention directed inward toward self or outward toward the environment. Generally, self-focus increases the correspondence between behavior and salient standards. Self-regulatory behavior may be either self-consciously activated or automatically pursued.

Self-regulation is guided by underlying motivational processes, overarching goals such as need for accuracy, need for a consistent sense of self, desire to improve, and self-enhancement. Influenced by goals and context, people represent information about themselves in memory, and choose their situations and companions. Each motive affects behavior under different circumstances.

Self-beliefs influence the accessibility of constructs used for judging others. Under neutral circumstances, a person may use personal beliefs and characteristics as a basis for inferring the qualities of others. But conditions of personal threat potentiate social projection processes, ranging from assuming one's weaknesses are widely shared to stereotyping vulnerable social groups.

FURTHER READING

Baumeister, R. F., & Vohs, K. D. (Eds.). (2004). *Handbook of self-regulation: Research, theory, and applications* New York: Guilford Press.

Beer, J. S. (2012). Self-evaluation and self-knowledge. In S. T. Fiske & C. N. Macrae (Eds.), *Sage handbook of social cognition* (pp. 330–349). Thousand Oaks, CA: Sage.

Heatherton, T. F., Macrae, C. N., & Kelley, W. M. (2004). What the social brain sciences can tell us about the self. *Current Directions in Psychological Science, 13*, 190–193.

Higgins, E. T. (2005). Value from regulatory fit. *Current Directions in Psychological Science, 14*, 209–213.

Kunda, Z. (1990). The case for motivated reasoning. *Psychological Bulletin, 108*, 480–498.

Markus, H. R., & Kitayama, S. (1991). Culture and the self: Implications for cognition, emotion, and motivation. *Psychological Review, 98*, 224–253.

Markus, H. R., & Nurius, P. (1986). Possible selves. *American Psychologist, 41*, 954–969.

Morling, B., & Masuda, T. (2012). Social cognition in real worlds: Cultural psychology and social cognition. In S. T. Fiske & C. N. Macrae (Eds.), *Sage handbook of social cognition* (pp. 429–450). Thousand Oaks, CA: Sage.

Sedikides, C., Gaertner, L., & Toguchi, Y. (2003). Pancultural self-enhancement. *Journal of Personality and Social Psychology, 84*, 60–79.

Swann, W. B., Jr., & Bosson, J. K. (2010). Self and identity. In S. T. Fiske, D. T. Gilbert, & G. Lindzey (Eds.), *Handbook of social psychology* (5th edn, Vol. 1, pp. 589–628). Hoboken, NJ: Wiley.

Swann, W. B., Jr., Pelham, B. W., & Krull, D. S. (1989). Agreeable fancy or disagreeable truth? Reconciling self-enhancement and self-verification. *Journal of Personality and Social Psychology, 57*, 782–791.

Taylor, S. E., & Brown, J. (1988). Illusion and well-being: A social psychological perspective on mental health. *Psychological Bulletin, 103*, 193–210.

Attribution Processes

6

- What is Attribution?
- Early Contributions to Attribution Theory
- Processes Underlying Attribution
- Attributional Biases

Why is my friend acting so distant? Why did the teacher ignore my comment in class? Every day we encounter events that require explanation. Attribution – the attempt to identify what social factors give rise to what outcomes – helps explain interpersonal events, and consequently, matters for social cognition more generally.

WHAT IS ATTRIBUTION?

Attribution fundamentally concerns how people infer causal explanations for other people's actions and mental states.

Causal Attributions

Attributional processes aim to infer the causes of social events. Suppose two friends fight over whether celebrate New Year's Day by going to a hockey game or a basketball game. On the surface, such a conflict should be trivial, but such arguments can often mean much more than meets the eye and hurt feelings or even estrange people. How to infer what is going on in this situation? One might consider each friend's known qualities, their respective **dispositions**, such as whether they are routinely quarrelsome or have an enduring need to be in control. One may think about their relationship, and wonder if one or both need to dominate. One may consider the circumstances of the argument, note that both have had several beers, and note that alcohol often fuels contentious behavior. Causal reasoning thus recruits knowledge of other people's qualities and of situational dynamics to infer an event's causes.

In the 1970s, the naïve scientist view identified complex reasoning to underlie causal inference. These analyses created the impression that explicit causal reasoning is time consuming, ubiquitous, and central to other inferential processes and behavior. However, the idea that people use much of their cognitive capacity much of the time for causal reasoning is unlikely to be true. As Chapters 1 and 2 noted, cognitive capacity is costly, and cognitive misers can devote our attention to only a few bits of information at any given time. By contrast, long-term memory is virtually limitless, so probably we solve many causal dilemmas simply by accessing long-term memory for causes relating to specific people, situations, or events. Much of our understanding of causes is embedded in the mental representations we hold about particular life domains. We hear about the breakup of two friends, and we do not need to use laborious causal rules to understand why. We know why couples break up: They tire of each other, they have grown apart, they argue all the time, one betrayed the other, or there is a combination of causes. The causal reasoning here aims to discover which of a limited number of domain-specific causes applies in the particular case.

Decades of research have yielded additional insights about causal reasoning. The dual-processing distinction (Chapter 2) applies to causal reasoning just as it applies to other kinds of social cognition. Much causal reasoning occurs quickly and virtually automatically. People do not necessarily review an array of evidence to reach the best possible causal explanation but rather seize upon a single sufficient explanation.

Under some circumstances we do interrupt our automatic information processing, shift to controlled processing, and focus attention explicitly on answering "Why did that happen?" Explicit causal reasoning often occurs given an unexpected or negative event (Kanazawa, 1992; Wong & Weiner, 1981). If an outcome is positive and expected (enjoying a popular elective course), nothing demands a cause. Instead, we reserve that capacity for circumstances of apparent failure, especially unexpected ones (an **abnormal condition**; Hilton & Slugoski, 1986). We lavish causal attention on the interesting elective we picked that turned out to be a crashing bore because the result was unexpected and negative. That attention may also be social: Another person supplies information that will uniquely close the gap in the listener's knowledge.

Basic Principles of Causation

Research on children's attribution processes highlights some basic principles of causation that people initially learn to understand cause–effect relations (e.g., Kassin & Pryor, 1985). Adults too use these principles when inferring causality, particularly in ambiguous circumstances or uninformative settings (Table 6.1).

One fundamental principle of cause–effect relations is that *causes precede effects* (Kassin & Baron, 1986). This principle appears to be well established by age 3 and virtually never contradicted in spontaneous causal attribution. Second, people perceive as causal those factors that have *temporal contiguity* with the effect. An immediately preceding cause is more plausible than one occurring much earlier. People also use *spatial contiguity* in inferring cause–effect relations. For example, a robbery suspect would be dismissed from consideration if he was elsewhere at the time. *Perceptually salient stimuli* are more likely to be perceived as causal than stimuli that are in the visual background (S. E. Taylor & Fiske, 1975, 1978; Chapter 3). *Causes resemble effects.* For

Table 6.1   Fundamental principles of cause–effect relations in everyday reasoning

Principle	Example: Lay explanations of cancer
Causes precede effects	Causes of cancer precede its outbreak
Causes have temporal contiguity with effect	Recent events seem more plausible than distant ones
Causes have spatial contiguity with effects	Events targeting the site seem more plausible
Perceptually salient stimuli seem more causal	Noticeable causes (a parent's cancer) seem more plausible than a lifetime exposure to sun
Causes resemble effects, e.g., in magnitude	A major stressor might cause a malignancy
Representative causes are attributed to effects	A malignant lump might be attributed to an injury because other kinds of lumps are caused by injuries

example, people generally assume that big effects are produced by big causes, and that little effects are produced by little causes (Kelley & Michela, 1980). Thus, the development of a malignancy might be attributed to a major stressor, such as divorce. *Representative causes* are attributed to effects (Tversky & Kahneman, 1982). Thus, for example, a patient unfamiliar with the causes of cancer may attribute a malignant lump to an injury because other kinds of lumps are caused by injuries.

Under uncertainty or lack of knowledge, adults also employ these basic principles (Einhorn & Hogarth, 1986; S. E. Taylor, 1982). People without knowledge about a particular domain may resort to these basic causal rules; by contrast, people who are sophisticated in the domain may instead consider primarily domain-relevant causal information. In one study (S. E. Taylor, Lichtman, & Wood, 1984), cancer patients generated causal explanations, depending on how knowledgeable they were about cancer. Those unsophisticated about cancer drew spatiotemporal contiguity, for example, inferring that their breast cancer had been caused by being bumped in the breast. By contrast, those sophisticated about cancer attributed their cancers to domain-related causes, such as diet or genetic predisposition.

Dispositional Attributions and Mind Perception

Much causal attributional reasoning focuses on other people, their characteristics, their goals, and why they do what they do. Some of this reasoning builds on **theory of mind**. Children develop abilities early in life to understand the contents of another person's head. As early as age 2, children have developed a system for reasoning about other people minds. By about age 4, a system for representing the contents of people's beliefs develops, most often implicating the superior temporal sulcus (STS) and specifically the temporal parietal junction (TPJ) (Saxe,

Carey, & Kanwisher, 2004). Theory of mind suffers in the atypical social cognitions of children with autism (Pellicano, 2012).

A broader concept, **mind perception,** encompasses everyday mindreading: inferences about another's mental states, including beliefs, but also intentions, desires, and feelings (D. R. Ames & Mason, 2012). People tend to project their own minds onto similar others, overgeneralizing from isolated similarities when behavior is ambiguous to mindread the other (Chapter 5; D. R. Ames, 2004a, 2004b). As Chapter 5 noted, different areas of medial prefrontal cortex activate for thinking about the minds of others who seem similar (more ventral) or dissimilar (more dorsal; Mitchell, Banaji, & Macrae, 2005b).

People are over-enthusiastic mind-perceivers (Epley & Waytz, 2010). We see minds even in objects, animals, and deities, depending on the accessibility of agency (autonomy), motivation to explain (effectance), and motivation to affiliate (sociality) (Epley, Waytz, Cacioppo, 2007; Gilbert, Brown, Pinel, & Wilson, 2000). Consider everyone who talks to their plants, computers, cars, and pets as if they had human dispositions.

In attributing a mind to actual people, the social perceiver sometimes explains an action by the temporary qualities of the person, such as emotions, intentions, and desires, but more commonly by inferring enduring dispositions, such as beliefs, traits, and abilities (Gilbert, 1998). The process of attributing dispositional qualities to other people is remarkably quick and is often based on the faintest of cues. For example, people draw trait inferences from physical attributes such as facial appearance, as Chapter 3 indicated. Indeed, judgments can be made after a 100 millisecond exposure to a person's face (Willis & Todorov, 2006). More astonishing is the fact that these judgments correlate with the same judgments made without time constraints. In short, a tenth of a second is often sufficient for people to make specific trait inferences from faces, reflecting a fast, intuitive, effortless process.

But are these judgments consequential? The answer appears to be yes. In one study, participants saw congressional candidates' photos and rated their competence based solely on their facial appearance. These rapid assessments of competence actually predicted the outcomes of US congressional elections, such that those whose faces were perceived to be especially competent won by a larger margin (Todorov et al., 2005). Thus instead of the rational, deliberate consideration usually assumed to characterize most people's inferences, such as their vote for a congressional representative, rapid effortless trait inferences contribute to voting choices. Dispositional attribution is often a rapid, virtually automatic process.

Neural Bases of Inferences about Others

Several brain regions reliably engage when people draw inferences about others. Theory of mind research implicates a brain network that includes the anterior cingulate cortex (ACC), the posterior superior temporal sulcus (pSTS) at the temporoparietal junction (TPJ), and the temporal pole (Gallagher & Frith, 2003). As for many aspects of social cognition, the medial prefrontal cortex (mPFC) activates both when processing one's own experiences and when inferring the mental states of others. Dorsal mPFC is implicated in a broad array of tasks that require understanding the mental state of others. The right TPJ is recruited selectively for the attribution of mental states but not for other social information about a person (Rilling, Sanfey, Aronson, Nystrom, & Cohen, 2004; Figure 6.1).

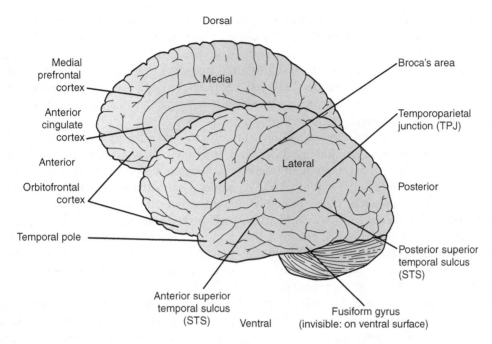

Figure 6.1   Brain regions associated with the attribution of mental states: Beliefs, desires, perceptions, and/or emotions

When people are actually involved in social interaction, theory of mind also implicates anterior paracingulate cortex, alternatively described as the mPFC (Gallagher, Jack, Roepstorff, & Frith, 2002; McCabe, Houser, Ryan, Smith, & Trouard, 2001). Activation in the anterior paracingulate cortex (or pACC) and the posterior STS can appear to be stronger when actual human partners are involved rather than hypothetical interaction partners (Rilling et al., 2004). Some areas apparently involved in reasoning about others' minds may differentially engage during actual social interaction.

EARLY CONTRIBUTIONS TO ATTRIBUTION THEORY

Much attributional reasoning is effortless and virtually automatic. Much attributional reasoning focuses on inferring other people's dispositional qualities. Much causal inference is domain specific, not abstract and generic. Explicit attributional reasoning is reserved for special occasions, most notably when unexpected and negative events occur. And like all social reasoning, attributional reasoning is inherently social: When at a loss to explain an event, we ask someone.

Early attribution theories deal with more effortful processes: how social perceivers gather and combine information to explain events, using generic principles that apply across a wide variety of domains. Why do people make attributions? Attribution theory and research have generally assumed either implicitly or explicitly that attributional analysis is initiated by people's needs to predict and control the future (Heider, 1958; Jones & Davis, 1965; Kelley, 1967). Following from this point is the observation that causal attribution is important for the pursuit of goals. One must know why things happen to make them happen.

Six theoretical traditions form the backbone of early attribution theory. First, Heider's (1958) analysis of **commonsense psychology** (Chapter 1) strongly influenced both E. E. Jones and Davis's (1965) analysis of **correspondent inference**, a theory of how people infer other people's dispositions, and Harold Kelley's (1967) **ANOVA model**, a normative model of causal inference. Other attribution approaches have primarily concerned self-attribution. Schachter's (1964) **emotional lability theory** and Bem's (1967, 1972) **self-perception theory** extended attribution principles to the self-perception of emotions and attitudes, respectively. Bernard Weiner's (1979, 1985) **attributional theory**, pursued largely in the domains of achievement behavior and helping, articulated a dimensional structure for understanding causal inference and extended attributional reasoning to expectations, emotions, and behavior.

As these diverse origins might imply, attribution theory is a set of models that share certain fundamental principles or assumptions. First, as noted, these models are *generic*, in other words, relatively content free, assuming people infer causality in roughly the same way regardless of the particular domain. Thus the rules you might follow in trying to understand why you have gotten sick should be roughly the same as the rules to understand why your houseplant is dying. A second assumption is *minimal determinism*: A relatively simple set of rules can explain how people infer causality. A third assumption made by attribution theorists is a *motivational point of departure*. People have some reason to search for the causes of another person's behavior. Early theories mostly assumed that once motivation initiates it, the search for a causal explanation proceeds in a relatively cold, nonmotivational manner. As such, attribution theories tend to make the **normative** (idealized) assumption that people are essentially rational problem solvers with a few acknowledged biases, processing information as a **naive scientist** (Kelley, 1967).

Heider's Theory of Commonsense Psychology

The historical origin of attribution theory was Heider's 1958 book, *The Psychology of Interpersonal Relations*. Heider maintained that a systematic understanding of how people comprehend the social world can be enlightened by **commonsense psychology**: how people think about and infer meaning from what occurs around them. Early writings on person perception examined whether people accurately perceive another person's qualities. Heider's vision of the social perceiver, by contrast, was heavily influenced by the philosophy of Emmanuel Kant, concerning what the perceiver contributes to perception. This commonsense psychology, or **naive epistemology**, can be inferred from the natural language that people employ for describing their experience. Not that people have insight into their reasoning processes, but their commonsense psychology provides evidence for understanding attribution processes.

Heider especially examined how people extract **dispositional properties** – that is, invariances – from the range of behaviors they observe. According to Heider, fundamental to the question of why individuals behave as they do is whether the locus of causality for that behavior is within the person (personal causation) or outside the person (impersonal causation), or both. Personal factors relevant to attributions consist of the *ability* to accomplish that action and *motivation* (trying). As Figure 6.2 shows, ability combines with environmental factors to influence the capacity for action; thus capacity is a joint function of the person's abilities (for example, talents and strengths) and the environment's facilitating or inhibiting influences (such as task difficulty or chance). Motivation is a joint function of the actor's intentions (goals and plans) and exertion (effort). For example, I may be able to complete my calculus homework and have enough time to do so, but if I decide not to do it or expend no effort, it may remain undone. Action implies that a person has both the capacity and the motivation. Whether one *can* succeed is a joint function of environmental forces and ability; whether one *does* succeed is additionally determined by the motivational factors of intention and effort.

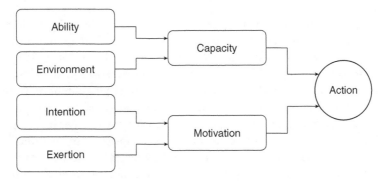

Figure 6.2   Heider's attribution theory

Source: From D. T. Gilbert (1998, p. 97)

Because Heider's goal was broader than providing a theory of attribution, he left his theoretical statements about causality relatively undeveloped. His major contribution to attribution theory was to define basic issues that would later be explored more systematically in other theoretical ventures. In particular, he noted that the social perceiver searches for **invariances** in the environment, factors that reliably account for both stability and change. This assumption helped develop Jones and Davis's correspondent inference theory and Kelley's attribution theory.

Jones and Davis's Correspondent Inference Theory

Jones and Davis's (1965) correspondent inference theory is essentially a theory of person perception: Social perceivers aim to identify intentions underlying behavior with the purpose of inferring dispositions that will be robust across situations. We search for explanations that are both stable and informative. According to the theory, another person's behavior is most informative if judged to be intentional and produced by a consistent underlying intention, not one that changes from situation to situation.

Some cues for inferring others' dispositions can produce rapid causal inferences. For example, the **social desirability** of an outcome is a valuable cue for the social perceiver. Behavior low in social desirability is attributed more to a person's disposition; socially desirable behavior may simply reflect social norms. As such, socially desirable behavior is uninformative about the unique qualities of a particular actor because it describes how most people would behave in the same situation.

Other conditions that help resolve the ambiguity of an action's meaning include whether the person's behavior is part of a **social role** and meets prior expectations. Behavior that is constrained by a social role or that meets expectations is also not particularly informative about an actor's underlying dispositions, although it may be causally informative about why an action occurred. For example, when firefighters put out a fire, we do not assume that they are helpful; it is part of the job.

Jones and Davis hypothesized that the social perceiver uses the unique consequences of a person's behavior to infer dispositions through the analysis of **noncommon** (unique) **effects** (Figure 6.3). The social perceiver asks the question, "What is this action producing that other actions would not have produced?" By comparing the consequences of the chosen action with the consequences of actions not taken, one may infer the underlying intention from the distinctive consequences. For example, if I am offered two jobs that are similar except that one has a gym and I choose that one, then you might infer that a gym is especially important to me. Furthermore, if many relatively negative elements (such as a lower salary or a smaller cubicle) are incorporated into the chosen alternative relative to the unchosen ones, you may infer that the distinctive elements of my choice (the gym) are especially important to me. A disposition will be more confidently inferred given fewer noncommon effects between the chosen and unchosen alternatives.

As Figure 6.3 suggests, analyzing noncommon effects can be time-consuming and complex. Among other complications, a person needs to infer qualities that go well beyond the information given. When and whether people engage in such extensive causal reasoning potentially qualify the analysis of noncommon effects.

Seeing another person's behavior as dispositionally based increases with **hedonic relevance** (that is, whether the action obstructs or promotes the perceiver's own goals and interests) and with the perception of **personalism** (the perceiver's perception that the actor intended to benefit or harm the perceiver). As we will see, implications for the self robustly influence attributional inference.

Another potential basis for inferring an actor's disposition is whether the behavior of the actor is **situationally constrained** or whether it occurs because of the actor's choice. For example, suppose you are asked to take part in a classroom debate, and the teacher assigns you the position of arguing in favor of capital punishment. Knowing that you had been assigned this side of the debate, your audience would be unwise to infer that your statements reflect your true

STUDENT A's CHOICE   STUDENT B's CHOICE

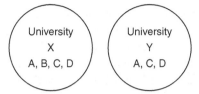
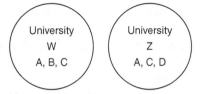

A. Prestigious school   A. Prestigious school
B. Clinical program   B. Clinical program
C. Desirable location   C. Desirable location
D. Lots of requirements   D. Lots of requirements

Result: Student chooses University X.   Result: Student chooses University W.

Conclusion: University X has the noncommon   Conclusion: Either the student wants clinical
effect of a clinical program.   training or he does not want to do
                                                 a lot of work.

Inference: The student wants clinical training.   Inference: Inference unclear due to absence
                                                      of noncommon effects.

Figure 6.3   Analysis of noncommon effects of choosing a graduate school

Source: After E. E. Jones & Davis (1965)

beliefs. If, however, you indeed chose to argue for capital punishment, then the audience might appropriately conclude that your statements do reflect your underlying beliefs.

This prediction from correspondent inference theory – namely, that dispositional attributions are qualified by relevant situational information – was empirically supported to only a degree and ultimately gave rise to one of the most important empirical insights about causal attribution: People often ignore contextual information about circumstances that constrain an actor's behavior and instead infer an actor's disposition from his or her behavior. People pervasively assume that if an actor engages in an activity, such as arguing against capital punishment, the behavior indicates the person's underlying beliefs, even given plausible situational factors that can explain the behavior (Jones & Harris, 1967). A large empirical literature demonstrates that Westerners underappreciate the impact of situational forces on others' behaviors, even when that situational information is salient (e.g., Gilbert & Malone, 1995).

To summarize, Jones and Davis developed an influential theory of why and how people infer others' dispositions, guiding person perception research over decades. Among the insights from its empirical legacy is the finding that people (Westerners at least) not only wish to infer the dispositions of others but are biased to do so and often ignore relevant qualifying information. Second, the theory and its research legacy began to focus the field on when people expend cognitive effort to infer causality and when they seize upon simple cues instead.

Kelley's Attribution Contributions

Kelley's attribution theory concerned when and how people seek to validate their causal attributions. Knowledge about the world, especially the social world, is often elusive or ambiguous. Although people usually have enough information to function effectively on a social level (Thibaut & Kelley, 1959), under some circumstances our information is inadequate. This may occur if one's beliefs receive little support from others, when problems are beyond one's capabilities, when information is poor or ambiguous, when one's views are labeled as untrue or inappropriate, or when one's self-esteem is undermined (Kelley, 1967). Under these circumstances, people seek additional information to validate a tentative impression or to develop an explanation. In short, uncertainty prompts causal analysis. For example, if you did well academically in college and find that you are not doing as well in graduate school, that will prompt efforts to understand the underlying causes.

The Covariation Model

Consider a young man who goes with a young woman to a party only to find himself ignored while she flirts with several other men. He is likely to wonder why she bothered to go out with him in the first place and to be (at least) curious about why this has happened. Because he has inadequate information, he will seek to test his attributions as follows:

> **Distinctiveness**: Does the effect occur when the entity (the young woman) is there and when it is not? (For example, is she the only woman to have behaved this way toward him, or have other women done the same thing in the past?)

> **Consistency over Time/Modality**: Does the effect occur each time the entity is present and regardless of the form of the interactions? (For example, has she done this to him before and at other events as well as at parties?)

> **Consensus**: Do other people experience the same effect with respect to this entity? (For example, has she done this to other people?)

According to Kelley, one makes a confident entity attribution with the combination of high distinctiveness, high consistency, and high consensus information. In this case, one may conclude that this entity, the young woman, is an impossible hussy if she is the only person who treats the wretched young man this way (high distinctiveness); if she has always done this in the past, assuming he has been foolish enough to take her out before (high consistency); and if others have had similar experiences with her (high consensus).

Other combinations of information can also yield meaningful causal inferences. For example, suppose we learn that the young lady has never ignored other dates before (low consensus), she has always ignored this date in the past (high consistency), and most other women have also ignored this young man (low distinctiveness). One might be inclined to infer offensive about the young man, such as rude manners or bad breath. The combination of low distinctiveness, high consistency, and low consensus reliably produces this kind of person attribution (McArthur, 1972).

Covariation principles can also form joint attributions of causality. Suppose we learned that the young man has never been ignored by another date (high distinctiveness), the young lady has never ignored any other date (low consensus), but she has always ignored this fellow every time they have gone out together (high consistency). Under these circumstances, we would be inclined to attribute responsibility to them jointly, concluding that they are a fatal combination as well as gluttons for punishment (McArthur, 1972.) Table 6.2 shows other causal attributions.

Kelley suggested that the social perceiver collects information along one dimension, while holding other dimensions constant, may do this serially for all of the dimensions, and then essentially calculates an F ratio analogous to the statistical analysis of variance in which one seeks high variance in the numerator and low variance in the denominator. That is, one looks for conditions that are highly distinctive with low variance across time, modality, and persons. If my roommate is cold and distant every time I bring home a friend, that is high covariation. If she is cold and distant only sometimes when I bring home a friend, that is lower covariation.

Kelley's model is a **normative model** of inference; that is, it is a formal, idealized set of rules for validating attributions. Kelley did not believe that people routinely calculate F ratios in everyday life. Nonetheless, how well does this normative model describe causal inference? Evidence suggests that social perceivers depart in many ways from the normative model of that Kelley detailed. The particular constellations of consensus, consistency, and distinctiveness information are often unavailable (Hewstone & Jaspers, 1987; Jaspers, Hewstone, & Fincham, 1983). People *can* use information across these dimensions systematically and in roughly the ways Kelley outlined when the information is given to them in this form (e.g., McArthur, 1972), but they do not systematically collect information along these dimensions on their own (Fiedler, Walther, & Nickel, 1999). Often, people draw on whatever covariation information *is* available to identify the necessary and sufficient conditions for the occurrence of an effect (Hewstone & Jaspers, 1987). Echoing an insight from Jones and Davis, research using Kelley's model has found that people exhibit a robust tendency to seek and use information about a target individual; in other words, just as Jones and Davis hypothesized, people tend to make dispositional attributions.

Further, in forming a causal judgment, the social perceiver uses consensus information the least; what other people think tends to be less important to our attributions than what we think other people think, in part because we assume that our personal opinions are widely shared (Olson, Ellis, & Zanna, 1983). This phenomenon is known as the **false consensus effect** (related to Chapter 5's projection of one's own beliefs; Krueger & Clement, 1994). Because we regard our own behavior as typical or expected, we assume that under the same circumstances other people would react in the same way. Therefore, when drawing causal inferences, we may not need to know whether others believe as we do; we already assume that they do (Mullen & Goethals, 1990).

Neuroimaging techniques have enabled attribution researchers to locate the specific neural regions in the brain that are implicated in different types of causal attribution and have also supported Kelley's model. As noted, three neural regions have been consistently implicated in inferences about others' dispositions: Medial prefrontal cortex (mPFC), superior temporal sulcus (STS), and anterior temporal poles (e.g., Frith & Frith, 2001; Leslie, 1994). Using McArthur's (1972) paradigm in the scanner, Harris, Todorov, and Fiske (2005) presented participants with combinations of consensus, distinctiveness, and consistency information about an actor's behavior and examined patterns of brain activation as a function of these different

Table 6.2 Kelley's ANOVA model analysis of why Ralph (person) tripped over Joan's feet (entity)

	High distinctiveness				Low distinctiveness			
Distinctiveness	Ralph trips over almost no other partner's feet.				Ralph trips over lots of partners' feet.			
Consistency	*High consistency*		*Low consistency*		*High consistency*		*Low consistency*	
	In the past, Ralph almost always tripped over Joan's feet.		In the past, Ralph almost never tripped over Joan's feet.		In the past, Ralph almost always tripped over Joan's feet.		In the past, Ralph almost never tripped over Joan's feet.	
	High consensus	*Low consensus*	*High consensus*	*Low consensus*	*High consensus*	*Low consensus*	*High consensus*	*Low consensus*
Consensus	*Almost everyone else who dances with Joan trips over her feet.*	*Hardly anyone else who dances with Joan trips over her feet.*	*Almost everyone else who dances with Joan trips over her feet.*	*Hardly anyone else who dances with Joan trips over her feet.*	*Almost everyone else who dances with Joan trips over her feet.*	*Hardly anyone else who dances with Joan trips over her feet.*	*Almost everyone else who dances with Joan trips over her feet.*	*Hardly anyone else who dances with Joan trips over her feet.*
Attribution	Joan is not coordinated. She is at fault. An *entity* attribution should be made.	Ralph and Joan are jointly responsible. Both are *necessary* to produce the outcome. A *person-entity* attribution is warranted.	Usually Ralph is able to overcome Joan's uncoordination, but not today. A *circumstance* attribution is warranted.	It's a bad day. A *circumstance* attribution is warranted.	Ralph and Joan jointly responsible. Either is *sufficient* to cause the outcome. A *person-entity* attribution is warranted.	Ralph is uncoordinated and is at fault. A *person* attribution should be made.	Ralph and Joan are both uncoordinated. Usually they overcome it. But not today. Attribution is ambiguous.	Ralph is uncoordinated. Joan is usually able to overcome it. But not today. Attribution is ambiguous.

information combinations (see Table 6.2). The combination of low consensus, low distinctiveness, and high consistency led to person attributions as predicated and uniquely elicited activation in the superior temporal sulcus. Low distinctiveness coupled with high consistency (regardless of consensus) evoked mPFC activation relative to the other conditions; this pattern is consistent with evidence that people often neglect consensus information in favor of distinctiveness and consistency. These results converge with results from research on theory of mind but also go beyond that work by identifying the neural activation patterns associated with specific types of attribution.

Causal attribution varies, for example, with the type of event requiring explanation. Kruglanski (1975) distinguished between involuntary **occurrences** and voluntary **actions**. Although occurrences can be caused by either internal (personal) or external (situational) factors, actions are always internally caused. He further maintained that voluntary actions consist of two subtypes: **endogenous acts** (ends in themselves) and **exogenous acts** (in service of other goals). For example, if I read your paper because I am interested in the topic, my action would be endogenously based, whereas if I read it because you are my student, then my action is exogenously based. Kruglanski's theory predicts that exogenously attributed acts seem less freely chosen and yield less pleasure.

Causal Schemas

Kelley's models of causal schemas were also influential on the field. Specifically, he detailed the concepts of **multiple necessary causal schemas**, which entail several causes contributing to produce an effect, and **multiple sufficient causal schemas**, which entail a behavior that may be due to any of several causes. Thus, to succeed on a difficult task (a marathon) requires both effort and ability (multiple necessary causes), whereas to succeed on a simple task (beating a child at checkers) requires only a little ability or a little effort (multiple sufficient causes).

Kelley also contributed to the study of causal attribution by articulating the **discounting principle**, which maintains that people reduce the importance of one cause given another sufficient cause. Its mirror image, the **augmenting principle**, maintains that people increase the value of a cause given no alternative causes. On the whole, research supports the discounting principle (e.g., Van Overwalle & Van Rooy, 2001); the augmenting principle, which requires people to generate information not present, may play a lesser role in attribution.

Kelley's attribution theory generated much research and continues to influence work on causal reasoning. Among its contributions were identifying when people try to validate causal beliefs and articulating dimensions and methods that people use to infer whether their attributions are valid.

We now turn our attention to two theories that concern attributions about the self. Schachter's theory addresses the attribution of one's emotional states, and Bem's theory concerns the processes whereby people infer their attitudes from their behavior.

Schachter's Theory of Emotional Lability

Schachter's theory of emotional lability, an attribution theory about labeling arousal states, initially arose from his work on social comparison processes. Schachter (1959) noticed that under conditions of stress, people sometimes choose to affiliate with others for the apparent purpose of comparing their emotional states. He reasoned that if people do so, then their emotional states must be somewhat labile and potentially subject to multiple interpretations.

To see if the interpretation of arousal is indeed malleable, Schachter and Singer (1962) conducted a now-classic experiment. One group of undergraduate participants was injected with **epinephrine**: Half were told its true side-effects (rapid breathing, flushing, increased heart rate), and half were told to expect effects that are not, in fact, produced by epinephrine (e.g., dizziness, slight headache). A control group was given no drug. Participants were then placed in a room with a confederate and instructed to fill out some papers. After a brief time (during which the epinephrine took effect in those who had received it), the confederate began to act in either a euphoric manner (engaging in silly antics) or in an angry manner (ripping up papers and stomping around the room).

Schachter and Singer reasoned that if physiological experience is indeed subject to multiple interpretations, then those participants who found themselves in a state of arousal with no explanation would seek an explanation for their state. For these participants, the behavior of the confederate could act as a salient cue for explaining their arousal. Participants who had been informed about the side-effects of epinephrine, in contrast, already had an adequate explanation for their arousal state and could remain amused or annoyed by the confederate without acquiring his mood. Participants in the control condition would have no arousal state to explain and also should not catch the mood of the confederate. Generally, Schachter and Singer found this, although the findings are weak. Nonetheless, Schachter and Singer's paper had enormous heuristic value in generating research about the nature of emotional states and the misattribution of arousal.

Schachter's work promotes the idea that attributions for arousal are, to a degree, malleable. This suggests that emotional reactions induced by threat can potentially be reattributed to a neutral or less threatening source, thereby reducing anxiety. Addressing this **misattribution effect** (Valins, 1966), researchers explored the possibility that certain disorders caused or exacerbated by anxiety – such as stuttering, impotence, and insomnia – might ameliorate if people can be induced to reattribute their arousal to a neutral source instead, such as an inert pill.

Although modest empirical support was found for misattribution predictions in laboratory studies (e.g., Ross, Rodin, & Zimbardo, 1969; Storms & Nisbett, 1970), the misattribution effect was neither reliable enough nor powerful enough to produce the kind of significant clinical applications that were originally anticipated. For example, when people are in a state of high anxiety or arousal, they are often motivated to do a thorough search of what is causing this state (Maslach, 1979). Also, people are more likely to attribute arousal to a negative source, such as a feeling of unease or nervousness, than to a positive or neutral source (Marshall & Zimbardo, 1979). For misattribution effects to occur, the alternative source must be plausible, unambiguous, and salient; the actual cause of the arousal must not be obvious; and the person must believe that the misattribution source has more impact on his or her arousal than it actually does (Olson & Ross, 1988). Misattribution effects are limited to a narrow range of emotion-inducing stimuli (Parkinson, 1985), and they are typically short-lived (Nisbett & Valins, 1972). People can reattribute arousal from one stimulus to another, particularly when they underestimate how long the unrelated arousal lasts (Zillmann, 1978) or when the circumstances involving misattribution are short-lived and uninvolving. But when people have strong motives and multiple methods for understanding their emotional experiences, those sources of knowledge overrule misattribution.

Bem's Self-Perception Theory

In 1967 Daryl Bem offered a radical behaviorist view of how people infer the attitudes that underlie their behavior. He maintained that people often infer their own attitudes much as they infer the attitudes of others – that is, by observing their own behavior. He argued that internal cues about people's preferences and beliefs are neither as directly accessible to them nor as unambiguous as one might imagine. Consequently, we observe what we do ("I listen to a lot of jazz") and infer from that our preferences ("I must like jazz").

Self-perception holds primarily when our preexisting attitudes or internal cues are weak but not when we have well-defined, easily accessed beliefs or strong affective preferences (Bem, 1972). Self-perception effects are also stronger for behavior consistent with our preexisting attitudes (Fazio, Zanna, & Cooper, 1977).

One of the most fruitful aspects of Bem's self-perception theory concerned inferences about motivation. Bem's theory predicts that when people are attempting to understand why they perform particular tasks, they consider whether their behavior is under the control of external forces or internal desires. Behavior attributed to external factors ("I'm paid for doing this") produces an external attribution, whereas performing the same task for minimal reward leads to an assumption of intrinsic interest ("I'm not paid very much for doing this. I must really enjoy the work."). Because intrinsic interest can be made more or less salient and because external rewards may also be more or less salient, these findings suggest that **intrinsic** versus **extrinsic motivation** for performing tasks is, to a degree, flexible and depends upon focus of attention and what information happens to be salient (e.g., Lepper, Greene, & Nisbett, 1973; Sansone & Harackiewicz, 2000).

Bem's self-perception theory contributes for several reasons. First, it was one of the first efforts to articulate how people infer the causes of their own behavior. Second, it posited a simple model of self-perception, which, although not the whole picture, is one way that people infer their own beliefs. The simplicity of Bem's model regarding the thought processes of the social perceiver foreshadows the insight that much apparently complex inferential work is, in fact, accomplished quickly with minimal complex cognitive computation. The implied emphasis of the theory on the capacity limitations of the social perceiver and the use of shortcuts to solve problems quickly will be recurring themes.

Weiner's Attributional Model of Motivated Behavior

Weiner's (1985) attribution model derived initially from Heider's theory, but differs from other attribution models. Whereas they attempted to establish generic or content-free rules, Weiner's model developed in the context of specific motivated behaviors, namely, achievement and helping.

When a little-known, predominantly Hispanic high school in East Los Angeles, California, startled the testing world by achieving mathematics scores on standardized tests that greatly exceeded their past performance and that of most other schools in the nation, everyone wanted to know why. Ultimately, the dramatic rise in scores was credited to the teaching of one particularly gifted teacher, but at the time testing officials were so surprised by the outcome that they forced the students to take the exam again, assuming they had cheated. This example illustrates several points about causal attributions in achievement situations. First, unexpected results prompt causal attribution. If the students had achieved the expected scores, no one would have needed to explain the outcome.

Second, the dimensions of locus, stability, and controllability help us to understand the perceived causes of a behavior. Consider first *locus* and the potential internal causes it generates for behavior. *Aptitude* is both stable and uncontrollable, presumably because determined by raw intelligence. *Mood* is also uncontrollable, but unstable: One's mood varies from situation to situation but generally not as a function of one's own attempts to control it. *Effort* is controllable, but it may be either stable or unstable. The typical effort one puts into a task (e.g., studying three hours each night) is stable, but the effort exerted for a particular task (e.g., studying extra hard for a test) is unstable. Among external causes, *objective task difficulty* is stable and uncontrollable: The task cannot be changed. *Luck* is both unstable and uncontrollable. Some external factors are controllable, however. A teacher's belief in your inherent ability, for example, is stable and under personal control. And, finally, unusual help from another person is controllable but unstable. For example, a friend may help you study for a particular test, but she may not do so again.

To summarize, three dimensions underlie the causal attributions that are made for the achievement outcomes of success and failure. The **stability** dimension indicates whether the cause will change and predicts subsequent expectations of success or failure. The **locus** dimension concerns whether an individual attributes performance to internal or external factors and ties to changes in self-esteem-related emotions such as pride and shame. The **controllability** dimension relates to whether a person can influence the outcome at will (Figure 6.4).

The theory also predicts expectations and emotional consequences of attributions. In the typical achievement situation, people first determine whether they succeeded or failed and feel happy or unhappy accordingly. They then make a causal attribution for that outcome, which leads to more specific emotional responses: for example, guilt over an effort attribution for failure or pride over an ability attribution for success. People then generate expectations of the probability of subsequent success, and these expectations are again followed by predictable emotional responses: For example, attributing failure to low ability produces low expectations of subsequent success as well as feelings of hopelessness. Expectations and emotional reactions jointly determine subsequent performance. Weiner's model is thus dynamic, focusing on how attributions regulate expectations, emotions, and behavior over time.

These insights extend to helping behavior (Weiner, 1980). Potential helpers infer the cause of another person's need. Personal control matters here. We are more likely to help someone if we believe the cause of the problem is outside the person's control rather than if it is controllable. For example, students report that they would be more likely to lend their lecture notes to a classmate who needed them because of an uncontrollable misfortune, such as being absent due to a family

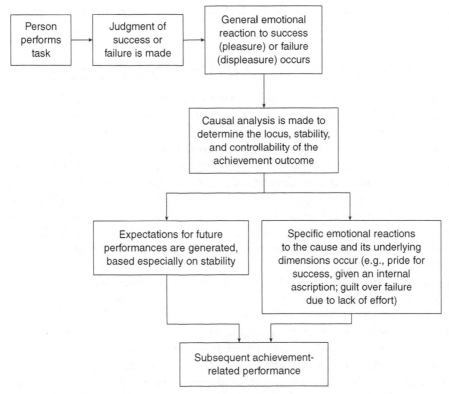

Figure 6.4   A causal analysis of achievement behavior

Source: After Weiner (1979)

death, than because of something controllable, such as being absent due to a hangover (Weiner, 1980). Attributions also affect our emotional responses to another person's need. We feel sympathy and concern for people who suffer through no fault of their own. We feel anger or contempt for those who are responsible for their own problems (Schmidt & Weiner, 1988).

PROCESSES UNDERLYING ATTRIBUTION

Whereas early attribution theories concerned primarily the logical principles that characterize attribution processes, subsequent research has focused primarily on the mental operations by which attributions are made. In other words, what actually happens in a person's head when making a dispositional inference about a new roommate or understanding the origins of an enduring quarrel between friends (Gilbert, 1998)?

The cognitive revolution of the 1970s that so heavily influenced social cognition research in other domains also influenced research on attribution processes. Using an information processing framework, attribution researchers have investigated operational phases of the attribution process.

Stage Models of the Attribution Process

Much of this work began with Trope's (1986) two-stage model of attribution processes: Judgments about others' dispositions result from both a spontaneous identification process and a deliberate inferential process. **Identification** of the action is an automatic, virtually instantaneous process, followed by a more controlled attributional **inference** (see Figure 6.5). The identification stage labels the actor's immediate behavior, the situation, and any prior information about the actor in terms of disposition-relevant categories. For example, perceivers may categorize a behavior as aggressive or nonaggressive, the situation as facilitating or inhibiting aggression, and the actor as being aggressive or nonaggressive in the past. Identification of each informational cue may be influenced by expectancies generated by the others. For example, information indicating that the situation facilitates aggression may bias perceivers toward identifying an ambiguous behavior as aggressive.

Regardless of being biased or unbiased, the identifications supply data for subsequent inferences about the actor's dispositions. At the second stage, situational expectancies *subtract* from the disposition implied by the identified behavior. By the **subtractive rule**, an inhibiting situation augments and a facilitating situation attenuates the diagnostic value of the identified behavior regarding the corresponding disposition. For example, perceivers will see aggressive behavior as less diagnostic of dispositional aggression when the situation facilitates aggression than when it inhibits aggression. The diagnostic value of the immediate behavior, combined with prior information about the actor, yields the actual judgment about the actor's dispositions.

The two-stage model suggests that, depending on how the identification stage utilizes situational, behavioral, and prior information, their effects on dispositional judgment may or may not mirror their role at the inferential stage. Situational information illustrates this logic because it has opposite effects on dispositional judgment at the identification and inferential stages. At identification, situational information may lead perceivers to categorize the behavior into the dispositional category: A situation viewed as facilitating aggression augments identifying the behavior as aggressive. Later, relying on this identification (aggressive behavior) as evidence for the corresponding disposition (aggressive person) also depends on the situation but in the opposite direction; that is, an aggression-provoking situation makes aggressive behavior less dispositionally diagnostic of an aggressive personality.

One determinant of the effect of situational information on behavior identification is the ambiguity of the behavior (Trope, 1986; Trope, Cohen, & Maoz, 1988). In one study, subjects saw ambiguous or unambiguous facial reactions to positive or negative emotional situations and either identified what the face expressed or inferred the target's emotional disposition (Trope, 1986). The identification of unambiguous facial expressions was unaffected by situational provocation, but, as required by the subtractive rule, inferences of dispositional anger from such faces were attenuated by situational provocation. In contrast, situational provocation biased the identification of the ambiguous faces as expressing more anger. Instead of attenuating inferences of dispositional anger,

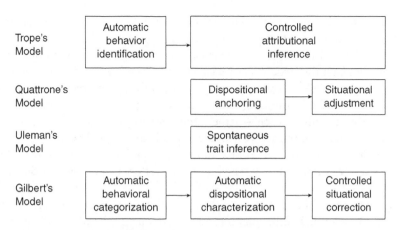

Figure 6.5   Stage models of the attribution process

Source: From D. T. Gilbert (1998, p. 113)

however, provocation only enhanced such inferences. These results suggest that ambiguity allows the situation to bias behavior identification, which, in turn, masks the subtraction of the situation at the inferential stage.

Elements of these insights fit several stage models of attribution processes. For example, Quattrone (1982) maintained that dispositional inferences anchor the attribution process and that situational adjustment may occur only later. Similarly, Uleman and colleagues hypothesized rapid, **spontaneous trait inferences**. In one study (Winter, Uleman, & Cunniff, 1985), participants completed math problems while hearing interposed distracter sentences that implied traits. Although the traits themselves were not explicitly mentioned and subjects believed that the sentences were irrelevant to their task, when the trait terms were later provided to participants, the traits served as retrieval cues for the sentences. Apparently participants had spontaneously generated the trait term without being aware of it. Evidence for automatic behavior identification is plentiful, and clearly dispositional attribution to human action can occur early in perception, at least spontaneously and probably automatically (Todorov & Uleman, 2003).

Dispositional attribution follows several stages integrated into a synthetic model (Gilbert, 1998), supported both psychologically and neurally. In this view, attribution consists of three stages: a **categorization stage**, perceiving the stimulus configuration; a **characterization stage**, attributing dispositional qualities to the action; and a **correction phase**, using situational and other information to discount or augment the initial dispositional attribution (Figure 6.5).

Tests of this integrative model build on the assumption that people's attentional capacities are limited and easily overwhelmed. As such, **cognitive busyness** or load, which may involve multi-tasking or distraction, will diminish attentional resources for inference processes. Although cognitive load should not affect automatic processes, it should interfere with controlled processes and thus impair people's abilities to correct their automatic dispositional characterizations using information about the situation. In one study (Gilbert, Pelham, & Krull, 1988), participants listened to a person read an assigned pro- or anti-abortion speech. Participants in the nonbusy condition simply listened to the speech, whereas those in the busy condition listened to the speech knowing that later they would also be asked to write and read a speech. One can infer that these latter participants were cognitively busy because, as they observed the other reciting his speech, they were presumably thinking about their own speeches. Participants who were not busy used the situational information – namely, the actor had been assigned his essay portion – to discount the importance of the actor's attitude in producing the behavior. In contrast, the busy perceivers were unable to use this situational information and discount appropriately, so instead their dispositional attributions heavily relied on the target's behavior and not on the situational information.

This study and others like it support dispositional attribution as a relatively spontaneous, simple process, whereas using contextual information to qualify the role of dispositional factors is more complex, requiring more cognitive resources. A replication (Gilbert, Krull, & Pelham, 1988) demonstrated that when people are self-regulating (that is, monitoring their own behavior), they act as cognitively busy subjects do. In other words, they are less able to use qualifying situational information to correct their dispositional characterizations of a target. Thus, social interaction, during which people are both forming impressions of others and self-regulating, may usually proceed with people making dispositional attributions unqualified by situational information.

Neural Bases of Dispositional Attributions

Developments in brain science have provided a neural model of the integrative stage theory. Lieberman and colleagues (2002) describe two networks that characterize automatic and controlled processing respectively: (a) the **X system (reflexive)** involves the amygdala, dorsal anterior cingulate, basal ganglia, ventromedial prefrontal cortex, and lateral temporal cortex, all regions implicated in automatic processing, and (b) the **C system (reflective)** implicates the lateral prefrontal cortex, medial prefrontal cortex, rostral anterior cingulate, posterior parietal cortex, and the medial temporal lobe regions, all involved in controlled processing (Figure 6.6). X system processes guide thought and behavior when things are going smoothly, such as the relatively automatic attribution of action to dispositional factors. The X system is biased toward features present in the question or hypothesis the person is trying to answer. Because favored hypothetical causes are dispositional, the result is likely to be dispositional attributions at the initial stage of processing, as the theory predicts.

The reflective system (C system) is engaged by signaling from the anterior cingulate, as may occur when a conflict arises, goals are thwarted, or more controlled processing is required to interpret behavior. Controlled processes govern the more complex, qualified attributions that incorporate situational information. Conditions such as accountability for one's inferences or outcome dependency would produce a switch to C system processing, or if X system processes fail to disambiguate the meaning of behavior, the C system may be brought online. When people lack motivation or attentional resources to do thorough processing, they may instead focus on a simple hypothetical cause, access the consistency of the identified action with that cause, and disregard alternatives.

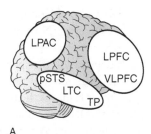 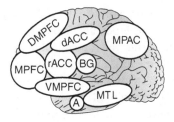

A   B

X-System (Automaticity)   C-System (Control)

Ventromedial PFC (VPFC) [BA11]   Lateral PFC (LPFC)
Basal Ganglia (BG)   Medial Temporal Lobe (MTL)
Amygdala (A)   Medial Parietal Cortex (MPAC)
Lateral Temporal Cortex (LTC)   Lateral Parietal Cortex (LPAC)
Posterior Superior Temporal Sulcus (pSTS) Rostral ACC (rACC)
Temporal Pole (TP)   Medial PFC (MPFC) [BA10]
Dorsal Anterior Cingulate (dACC)   Dorsomedial PFC (DMPFC) [BA8/9]

Figure 6.6 The brain's hypothetical X and C systems

Source: Adapted from "Social cognitive neuroscience: A review of core processes" by M. D. Lieberman, p. 262. Reprinted, with permission, from the Annual Review of Psychology, Volume 58. Copyright 2007, by Annual Reviews, www.annualreviews.org

ATTRIBUTIONAL BIASES

Causal attribution is marked by many errors and biases, and we now turn to the most important ones.

Fundamental Attribution Error

The most commonly documented bias in social perception, accordingly called the **fundamental attribution error** (Heider, 1958; Ross, 1977) or **correspondence bias** (Jones & Davis, 1965), over-attributes another person's behavior to dispositional causes. Instead of realizing that external forces – such as social norms or social pressure – influence behaviors, social perceivers often assume that another's behavior indicates that person's stable qualities.

What leads to the fundamental attribution error? One factor may be that behavior engulfs the field (Heider, 1958). That is, what is dominant when one observes another person is that person's behavior; the person moves, talks, and engages in actions that attract attention. Background factors may be less salient. Consequently, aspects of the person may be overrated as causally important because of a perceptual bias (S. E. Taylor & Fiske, 1975, 1978). Bias toward dispositional attributions cannot solely represent perceptual experience, however. For example, the fundamental attribution error also occurs in written descriptions of other people's behaviors, when behavior does not engulf the perceptual field (e.g., Winter & Uleman, 1984). Other evidence inconsistent with the perceptual explanation includes the increasing tendency to attribute behavior to dispositions as children grow older (Rholes, Jones, & Wade, 1988) and predictions of the distant future behavior being especially marked by the fundamental attribution error (Nussbaum, Trope, & Liberman, 2003). Thus the fundamental attribution error is robust.

Nonetheless, the fundamental attribution error is qualified. It depends on the specific domain; that is, behaviors in different settings map onto dispositions in different ways. For example, whereas friendly behavior may indicate friendly disposition in a linear fashion (the more friendly the person behaves, the more one infers that he is friendly by nature), other behaviors, such as moral actions, do not. Whereas a single dishonest action can clearly indicate a dishonest disposition, an honest behavior is not particularly enlightening: Most people, even dishonest people, behave honestly much of the time (Reeder, 1993; Reeder & Brewer, 1979). Through experience, people learn exactly how behaviors in different domains may map onto underlying dispositions.

The fundamental attribution error also varies. When a social perceiver reflects on the underlying meaning of an actor's behavior, the perceiver adjusts dispositional inferences with reference to qualifying situational information (Weary, Reich, & Tobin, 2001). Cognitive busyness, in contrast, focuses people on the most salient or meaningful aspects of a situation and makes them neglect less salient contextual factors (Chun, Spiegel, & Kruglanski, 2002), leading to stronger dispositional attributions.

Dispositional attributions for another person's behavior increase when people are in a good mood (Forgas, 1998) but reduce when people are accountable to others for their judgments (e.g., Tetlock, 1985), or when they believe the other person may have ulterior motives for an action (Fein, Hilton, & Miller, 1990). For example, when you see a famous actor or actress endorsing a particular product, you assume that person is paid well for the endorsement and do not make a dispositional attribution. Also, when one's outcomes depend on the another person, one is motivated to be accurate and engage in more effortful processing. Thus, under outcome dependency, people seek specific dispositional attributions for the particular person (Erber & Fiske, 1984).

We are more likely to qualify dispositional attributions for the behavior of people we know well. As we become more familiar, we take more information into account, such as the person's personal goals or worldview, and draw less on abstract traits to build an impression of the person (Idson & Mischel, 2001). With increasing information about the person or an insufficient basis for inferring a motive, people begin to look more to the situation as explaining behavior (Reeder, Vonk, Ronk, Ham, & Lawrence, 2004; Wellbourne, 2001).

How significant is the fundamental attribution error? On the face of it, people appear to ignore important qualifying situational information when inferring others' dispositions. Yet the fundamental attribution error can be adaptive. When people draw dispositional attributions, they may not mean exactly the same thing by those attributions as researchers studying trait inferences think they mean. They may not, for example, assume that if behavior is attributed to a certain trait, the person will necessarily evidence behavior consistent with that underlying trait across a broad variety of situations. This is the psychologist's meaning of disposition, not the layperson's. Rather, the layperson seeks **circumscribed accuracy** (Swann, 1984), asking questions such as, "If this person were put in the same situation again, would he or she do the same thing?" A dispositional attribution generates a prediction for the person, whereas a situational attribution does not. If the perceiver's goal is circumscribed predictability, then making a dispositional attribution for the behavior probably results in accurate attributions in the their overlapping situations. If asked to make a statement that opposes abortion at a later date, the person probably would do it again, having done it once. Dispositional attributions, then, may serve circumscribed accuracy rather than global accuracy, enabling confident predictions to similar situations.

Cultural Limitations on the Fundamental Attribution Error

The fundamental attribution error is stronger in Western than in non-Western cultures. In East Asian countries, the roles of situational forces as causes of behavior are more commonly acknowledged (e.g., Miyamoto & Kitayama, 2002; Morris & Peng, 1994). Whereas Westerners correct dispositional attributions by taking account of situational information primarily given extra time, attention, or motive, East Asians automatically correct for situational information (Knowles, Morris, Chiu, & Hong, 2001; Norenzayan, Choi, & Nisbett, 2002). One reason for this difference may be that East Asian cultures are more interdependent, and people adjust their behavior more to situational norms than Westerners so. Consequently, an East Asian social perceiver's consideration of context may reflect the cultural reality of the causes of behavior (e.g., Ishii, Reyes, & Kitayama, 2003; Kitayama, Duffy, Kawamura, & Larsen, 2003; Masuda & Nisbett, 2001). By contrast, Westerners are relatively independent and thus may more commonly demonstrate behavior that indicates their dispositions, feeling less compunction to conform to situational pressures. Thus the Western social perceiver may be more justified in making dispositional attributions.

But the differences between Western and East Asian causal attributions may reflect more fundamental differences in cognition than this characterization suggests. The theories that East Asians hold about the workings of the world are, generally speaking, more holistic and complex than those of Westerners, and so the amount of information that East Asians consider before making an attribution is greater than for Westerners, contributing to the more contextual attributions that East Asians typically draw (Choi, Dalal, Kim-Prieto, & Park, 2003; A. P. Fiske, Kitayama, Markus, & Nisbett, 1998; Morling & Masuda, 2012).

The Actor–Observer Effect

Attribution theory's legacy also revealed robust self-relevant biases: We tend to process information differently when it involves ourselves as compared with others. Recall the last time you encountered a surly store clerk. You may have thought, "what a hostile person." Now think of the last time you snapped at someone. Did you infer that you were a hostile person? Almost certainly not. No doubt you were just in a bad mood.

The **actor–observer effect** maintains that people explain other people's behavior as due to dispositional factors but their own behavior as due to situational factors (Jones & Nisbett, 1972). The actor–observer effect potentially qualifies the fundamental attribution error when the self is involved. However, in a meta-analysis of 172 studies (Malle, 2006), the actor–observer asymmetry holds primarily when the actor seems idiosyncratic or unusual, when measured by free responses rather than ratings, and for hypothetical events. Actors and observers do seek to explain different types of behavior, but not in the way that the model assumes. Actors wonder more about their unintentional and unobservable behaviors, whereas observers more often wonder about intentional and observable behaviors (Malle & Knobe, 1997). Moreover, people sometimes see themselves as if they were observers of their own actions: For example, people make more trait self-descriptions when they consider their past behavior or their likely future behavior than their present behavior. So-called actor–observer effects are reversed when attention is directed inward (Pronin & Ross, 2006).

Moreover, the person–situation distinction is itself problematic. For example, perceivers easily view dispositions and situations as interactive and may infer, for example, that a person is a serious student during the week and a flaming party animal on the weekend (Kammrath, Mendoza-Denton, & Mischel, 2005). Participants have trouble using the simple distinction, and researchers have difficulty coding it. Consider "George acts like a distrustful person because he was so often betrayed by others when he was a child." Such attributions reflect some of the complexity of causal reasoning, but not a clean person–situation distinction (Malle, Knobe, O'Laughlin, Pearce, & Nelson, 2000). People's folk explanations for intentional behavior may work backwards from behavior to intentions, reasons, and the causal history of reasons.

Most important, the actor–observer effect is more likely to hold when an event's valence is negative rather than positive (Malle, 2006). Thus the hostile clerk example would be an instance in which actor–observer differences for explaining behavior would hold because it involves negative behavior. However, when it occurs, the actor–observer effect seems a more self-serving bias than a tendency to over-attribute one's own behavior to situational factors.

Self-Serving Attributional Bias

After soundly beating an opponent at tennis, how often do you hear the gratifying "Gee, you're much better than I am, aren't you?" Usually you hear that it was a bad day, his serve was off, he's still working on his backhand, or the sun was in his eyes. On the other hand, when you have just been badly beaten, the smug look and condescending "bad luck" from the opponent are particularly grating because you know he does not believe it was bad luck. He simply thinks he is better. The tendency to take credit for success and deny responsibility for failure is known as the **self-serving attributional bias** (D. T. Miller & Ross, 1975).

According to meta-analyses, people do indeed take more responsibility for success than for failure (Arkin, Cooper, & Kolditz, 1980). They attribute their success largely to internal factors and their failures to external factors (Mullen & Riordan, 1988), such as task difficulty or bad luck (Whitley & Frieze, 1986). Overall, the evidence that people take credit for success is stronger than evidence that they deny responsibility for failure. People sometimes accept responsibility for failure if they can attribute it to some factor they can control in the future, such as effort. If I blame my bad tennis game on the sun being in my eyes, that will not improve my game, but if I realize that I faulted on nearly every one of my first serves, I have a goal during my next lesson.

Self-serving biases extend beyond explaining one's own behavior to perceiving one's friends and groups. The **group-serving bias** refers to the tendency of ingroup members to attribute positive actions by their own group to ingroup qualities, and negative actions by the ingroup to external causes – and the reverse for outgroup members (Brewer & Brown, 1998; Pettigrew, 1979).

Self-serving attribution biases may be functional, despite their apparent tendencies to play fast and loose with the facts. Attributing success to one's own efforts, particularly one's enduring characteristics, may be motivating. For example (Schaufeli, 1988), a self-serving motivational bias among unemployed workers resulted in more labor-market success because those workers who made self-serving attributions for their circumstances were more optimistic about their chances of becoming reemployed and were more motivated to seek a job. Motivational needs to preserve one's ego and to present oneself favorably explain the self-serving bias as well (e.g., Reiss, Rosenfeld, Melburg, & Tedeschi, 1981).

When people make self-serving attributions, several brain regions activate: The bilateral premotor cortex and cerebellum suggest that general goal-directed action regions are also recruited for self-serving attributions (Blackwood et al., 2003). These areas are involved in imagined action generally. The dorsal premotor cortex tends to activate when simulating one's own intentional actions, and thus may be especially involved in attributing responsibility for actions to the self. The dorsal striatum appears to be distinctively involved in the self-serving bias. This region is implicated in motivational activity more generally. Thus the attribution of one's own positive actions to internal factors and negative actions to external factors links to brain areas implicated in reward. The self-serving bias may itself be experienced as rewarding (Blackwood et al., 2003).

The Self-Centered Bias

If two roommates were asked to estimate how much of the housework each does, each may well believe his or her own share is larger than the other believes it is. The **self-centered attribution bias** consists of taking more than one's share of credit for a jointly produced outcome. Several possibilities explain this bias (Ross & Sicoly, 1979). First, one more easily notices and recalls one's own contributions than those of another person. For example, I know when I'm doing the housework, but I may be unaware when my roommate is doing his share. Second, self-esteem benefits from believing one's own contributions are greater. Each person may think of the self as the kind of person who does more and infer greater responsibility.

Naive Realism

A bias that incorporates some of these self-relevant biases is **naive realism**: the idea that other people in general, especially those who disagree with us, are more susceptible to bias than we are (Pronin et al., 2002). Essentially, naive realism believes that we see the world as it truly is: If others don't see it the same way, they must be biased. By attaching greater credibility to our own introspections than we attach to the introspections of others, we provide ourselves with a false informational base that supports our own beliefs. Among other implications, naive realism suggests that we believe that we know other people better than they know us, resulting in an illusion of asymmetrical insight (Pronin, Kruger, Savitsky, & Ross, 2001).

Naive realism explains the problems that warring groups and nations have in trying to understand each other's vantage points. When one's own position seems so logical, one has difficulty

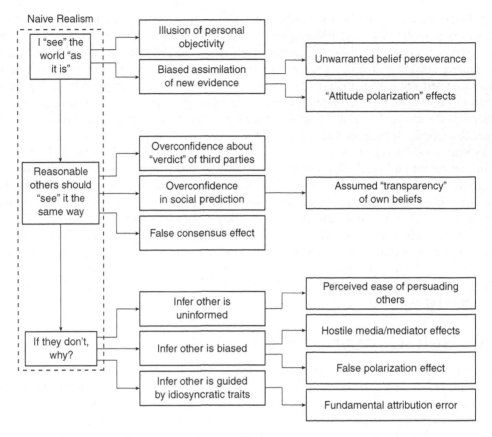

Figure 6.7   Convictions of naive realism and resulting consequences and phenomena relevant to conflict and misunderstanding

construing the world in a way that might have led another group to see it so differently (Robinson, Keltner, Ward, & Ross, 1995). Moreover, opposing parties often overestimate the dissimilarities of their views, seeing their own position as even more liberal and the other's position as even more conservative (Sherman, Nelson, & Ross, 2003). Should a mediator get involved, each side expects that the mediator will see the world as they do. When the mediator is neutral, each side rejects the mediator as biased (Figure 6.7).

Attributions of Responsibility or Blame

Attributions of responsibility concern who or what is accountable for an event, especially if negatively valenced (Shaver, 1975, 1985). Adverse events tend to generate attribution, a belief that someone should have foreseen the situation, that the person's actions were not justified, and that the person operated under free choice. Thus, for example, in the wake of Hurricane Katrina many people faulted President Bush for an inadequate response to the New Orleans flood victims because they felt he was in charge. He and other government officials should have foreseen the situation, which clearly necessitated action, and the right choices could have remedied the situation.

Defensive attribution, a related phenomenon, refers to people attributing more responsibility for actions that produce severe rather than mild consequences. Thus, for example, one might not attribute blame so enthusiastically to the president were the flooding minor, but the fact that the devastation was so widespread and so widely broadcast increased attribution of responsibility.

A meta-analysis confirms the defensive attribution bias (Burger, 1981) and reveals that people make defensive attributions depending on perceived similarity to the person seen as responsible for the adversity. When people see themselves as personally and situationally similar to a perpetrator, they attribute less responsibility to the perpetrator as the severity of the consequences increases. Presumably, the defensive attribution avoids the threatening implications for the self. When people are dissimilar to the perpetrator, however, they attribute more responsibility as the accident severity increases. Because most people see themselves as dissimilar to the president, the severity of the accident may account for the strong attributions of responsibility. However, among public officials who might readily imagine themselves being responsible following a major disaster, attributions of responsibility might be lower for major compared to minor outcomes; after all, they may someday be sitting in the same seat.

Summary

Attribution theory concerns how people infer causal relations and the dispositional characteristics of others. Some attributional inferences form rapidly, often in milliseconds, whereas others engage more thought, as the dual-processing distinction suggests. People often draw on basic causal principles first learned in childhood, such as causes preceding effects and temporally or spatially contiguous factors producing effects.

The foundational theories of causal attribution include Heider's analysis of commonsense psychology, Jones and Davis's theory of correspondent inference, Kelley's attribution contributions, Bem's self-perception theory, Schachter's theory of emotion lability, and Weiner's attributional theories of achievement and helping. These theories, notably those by Jones and Davis and by Kelley, focus on the logical principles that characterize controlled attributional processing and detail the idealized ways to make attributions. Such normative theories outline the appropriate guidelines concerning how a process should proceed.

Later work on attribution processes focused primarily on people's mental operations for inferring another's qualities. Attributions of dispositions appear spontaneously and without awareness, perhaps even automatically, when we learn of someone's behavior. Using situational factors to qualify dispositional inferences seems a second, less spontaneous, and more thoughtful process that corrects the initial dispositional inference. Unless situational information is compelling or salient, the social perceiver may never get to the second stage of correction. In addition, given insufficient processing time or capacity to correct dispositional attributions, situational information influences impressions even less.

The attribution process is also marked by persistent biases, most notably: the tendency to make dispositional attribution for a person's behavior; the tendency to make self-serving and self-centered attributions; naive realism, which stems from the perception that one's own interpretations are correct; and defensive attributions of responsibility or blame to others for serious negative outcomes.

FURTHER READING

Ames, D. R., & Mason, M. F. (2012). Mind perception. In S. T. Fiske & C. N. Macrae (Eds.), *Sage handbook of social cognition* (pp. 115–137). Thousand Oaks, CA: Sage.

Epley, N., & Waytz, A. (2010). Mind perception. In S. T. Fiske, D. T. Gilbert, & G. Lindzey (Eds.), *Handbook of social psychology* (5th edn, Vol. 1, pp. 498–541). Hoboken, NJ: Wiley.

Gilbert, D. T. (1998). Ordinary personology. In D. T. Gilbert, S. T. Fiske, & G. Lindzey (Eds.), *The handbook of social psychology* (4th edn, Vol. 1, pp. 89–150). New York: McGraw-Hill.

Harris, L. T., Todorov, A., & Fiske, S. T. (2005). Attributions on the brain: Neuro-imaging dispositional inferences, beyond theory of mind. *NeuroImage, 28*, 763–769.

Malle, B. F. (2006). The actor–observer asymmetry in attribution: A (surprising) meta-analysis. *Psychological Bulletin, 132*, 895–919.

McArthur, L. Z. (1972). The how and what of why: Some determinants and consequences of causal attribution. *Journal of Personality and Social Psychology, 22*, 171–193.

Morling, B., & Masuda, T. (2012). Social cognition in real worlds: Cultural psychology and social cognition. In S. T. Fiske & C. N. Macrae (Eds.), *Sage handbook of social cognition* (pp. 429–450). Thousand Oaks, CA: Sage.

Pellicano, E. (2012). Atypical social cognition. In S. T. Fiske & C. N. Macrae (Eds.), *Sage handbook of social cognition* (pp. 411–428). Thousand Oaks, CA: Sage.

Schachter, S., & Singer, J. A. (1962). Cognitive, social, and physiological determinants of emotional state. *Psychological Review, 69*, 379–399.

Heuristics and Shortcuts

Efficiency in Inference and Decision Making

7

- What are Heuristics?
- Beyond Heuristics: Other Decision Shortcuts
- Judgments over Time

The social perceiver often makes complex judgments under conditions of uncertainty. A student must guess if a possible course paper topic will lead to a manageable amount of references to review, or if the literature will be either too skimpy or too overwhelming. A person must decide if a safe and reasonably satisfying romantic relationship should be abandoned for a new, exciting fling, the future of which is risky.

The rational person has been assumed by economists to make decisions by weighing pros and cons. The **expected utility (EU) theory** maintains that inferential behavior can be conceptualized as choices among alternatives, each with a designated value and a probability of occurrence. According to the model, people assess the available alternatives for their likelihood and the worth of the outcomes that they promise (i.e., probability and value), calculate the utility of each outcome (the product of each outcome's probability and value), and choose the option that maximizes utility. Thus people make decisions that they think are most likely to provide the benefits they seek.

Seemingly unlimited information could bear on life decisions, but much of it would be useless. Moreover, if thoroughly evaluated, decisions could occupy the better part of the week, and nothing else would get done. For these reasons – time constraints, complexity or volume of the relevant information, and uncertainty about the quality of the evidence – social perceivers cannot realistically use exhaustive strategies for making judgments. Thus the social perceiver is, under many circumstances, a **satisficer** who makes adequate inferences and decisions rather than an **optimizer** who reaches the best ones possible (March & Simon, 1958).

WHAT ARE HEURISTICS?

In field-changing work, Tversky and Kahneman (1974; Kahneman & Tversky, 1973) detailed **heuristics** people use for judgments under uncertainty, shortcuts that reduce complex problem solving to simpler judgmental operations, to meet the pressing demands of the environment. Before turning to that important contribution, some clarifications are in order. The original work described several specific heuristics commonly used to solve inferential problems. Some subsequent writing has implied that these are the primary heuristics that people use. This is an incorrect conclusion. Kahneman and Tversky's profile of selected heuristics was guided not only by these heuristics being commonly employed but by their being good examples of heuristic processes more generally.

People use manifold heuristics, some of which enjoy general use, such as mental simulation, and others that are idiosyncratic, such as a professor's heuristic for writing long and apparently thoughtful letters of recommendation in a brief period of time. People develop heuristics in their daily life for reducing complex operations to simple ones, such as reading the headlines of the newspaper on a busy day and deciding what articles to read based on that limited information. Workers employ heuristics in their jobs to reduce time-consuming activities to relatively less effortful ones. In short, heuristics abound in daily life (e.g., Monin, 2003); some are general, such as those Kahneman and Tversky identified, and many others more idiosyncratic.

A second common misinterpretation of the heuristics research assumes that heuristics are necessarily fallible. They are not. Heuristics are used not because they generally produce incorrect, biased answers but because they typically produce correct ones. By highlighting heuristic processing's flaws, Kahneman and Tversky (1973) were illustrating strategically how heuristics work. Table 7.1 lists some heuristics.

Representativeness Heuristic

One heuristic, termed **representativeness**, generates inferences about probability (Kahneman & Tversky, 1972, 1973; Tversky & Kahneman, 1982). Essentially, the social perceiver matches information about a specific instance against a general category to determine the likelihood of fit. The representativeness heuristic can answer questions such as: How likely is it that person or event A is a member of category B? (e.g., Is George a football player?), or Did event A originate from process B? (e.g., Could the sequence of coin tosses H-H-T-T have occurred randomly?). Consider the following description:

> Steve is very shy and withdrawn, invariably helpful, but with little interest in people, or in the world of reality. A meek and tidy soul, he has a need for order and structure, and a passion for detail. (Tversky & Kahneman, 1974, p. 1124)

Suppose you are now asked to guess Steve's occupation. Is he a farmer, a trapeze artist, a librarian, a salvage diver, or a surgeon?

Table 7.1   Some heuristic strategies for making judgments under uncertainty

Heuristic	Type of judgment	Description	Example
Representativeness	Probability judgment	A judgment of how relevant A is to B; high relevance yields high estimates that A originates from B	Deciding that George (A) must be an engineer because he looks and acts like your stereotype of engineers (B)
Availability	Frequency or probability judgments	The estimate of how frequently or likely is a given instance or occurrence, based on how easily or quickly an association or examples come to mind	Estimating the divorce rate on the basis of how quickly one can think of examples of divorced friends
Simulation	Expectations, causal attributions, impressions, and affective experience	The ease with which a hypothetical scenario can be constructed	Getting angry because of a frustrating event on the basis of how easily one can imagine the situation occurring otherwise
Adjustment and anchoring	Estimates of position on a dimension	The process of estimating some value by starting with some initial value and then adjusting it to the new instance	Judging another person's productivity based on one's own level of productivity

With adequate information about the frequency and personal characteristics of people in these occupations, one could conceivably tally up the probability of a meek surgeon, a shy trapeze artist, and so on, and calculate the odds that Steve is in each occupation. This task would, however, take a long time, and good information to inform the calculations would undoubtedly be lacking. In such cases, the representativeness heuristic provides a quick solution. One estimates how much Steve represents or resembles the average person in each category and judges his occupation accordingly. Hence, one might guess that Steve is a librarian because his description is representative of attributes typically associated with librarians.

The representativeness heuristic is basically a relevancy judgment (How well do these attributes of A fit category B?) that produces a probability estimate (How probable is it that A is an instance of category B?). Using this heuristic usually produces fairly good answers – perhaps as good as those produced by a more exhaustive analysis of the information available for the task – because relevancy is usually a good criterion for making probability judgments. However, when using the representativeness heuristic, a person may be insensitive to other factors independent of judged relevancy that affect actual probability of occurrence (Kahneman & Tversky, 1973).

One such factor is prior probability of outcomes (base rates, to which we will return). If Steve lives in a town with lots of chicken farmers and only a few librarians, one's judgment that he is a librarian should be tempered by this fact; he is simply more likely to be a chicken farmer than a librarian. Nonetheless, people sometimes ignore prior probabilities and instead base their judgment solely on similarity, for example, Steve resembling a librarian.

Another factor that people often ignore in representativeness judgments is sample size. Suppose you are at the state fair running a booth in which you try to guess the occupation of anyone who pays a quarter. Suppose four of your first five clients are librarians, and you discover that the librarians' convention is in town. How confident should you be that the next individual in line is also a librarian? Would you be more or less confident than if 12 of the first 20 individuals you saw had turned out to be librarians? Most people making this judgment feel more confident if four of the first five individuals are librarians than if 12 of the first 20 are. Their confidence is, in fact, misplaced. Sampling theory dictates that estimates derived from a large sample are more reliable than estimates derived from a small one. Thus, even though four out of five looks like better odds than 12 out of 20, the 12 out of 20 is the better indicator because the sample size is larger.

Judgments based on representativeness may also show insensitivity to predictive value: that is, neglecting the relevance or quality of the information as forecasting some outcome. For example, if Steve's portrait description as a meek and tidy soul had been written by Steve's kindergarten teacher after a scant few weeks of class, its relevance to Steve's career choice would be weak indeed; if written by Steve's adviser after four years of college, one might want to give it more weight. Nonetheless, people often behave as though they trust information regardless of its source, and they may make equally strong or confident inferences regardless of the information's predictive value. This illusion of validity occurs especially when information is a particularly good fit to the judgment. For example, if Steve's description also contained, "He is a bookish sort who peers intently over his reading glasses," one's confidence in Steve's status as a librarian might vastly increase. However, upon learning that "he scuba dives in his spare time, and once was a heavy cocaine user," we might retreat from a strong prediction. Whether the information is accurate and reliable or, alternatively, out of date, inaccurate, and based on hearsay may have insufficient bearing on inferences. Apparent fit or lack of fit can assure its acceptance or rejection.

Finally, misconceptions about chance also bias representativeness judgments. People have well-developed ideas of what chance events ought to look like. In flipping a coin several times, for example, one expects to see a sequence like H-T-H-T-T-H, not a seemingly orderly one like T-T-T-H-H-H. When judging which sequence is more likely, many people erroneously pick the first one because it looks random, but the second sequence is, in fact, statistically just as likely.

Table 7.2   Early investigations of availability

Participants' task	Ps' response	Correct answer & reason
"A path in a structure is a line that connects an element in the top row to an element in the bottom row, and passes through one and only one element in each row. In which of the two structures are there more paths?"		
1. Consider structures A and B, displayed below.	85% pick A	Same in both: $8^3 = 2^9 = 512$
(A) (B)		Paths in A are more available:

x x x x x x x x   x x
x x x x x x x x   x x
x x x x x x x x   x x
                x x
                x x
                x x
                x x
                x x
                x x
		(a) A's more columns, easy paths;
		
		(b) A's paths crossing columns are more distinctive, less confusable;
		
		(c) A's paths are shorter, easier to visualize

2. Consider the letter R in English words. Is R more likely to appear in – the first position? – the third position?	69% pick first	Third position more likely. Five consonants (K,L,N,R,V) appear third more than first, but first is easier to bring to mind.
3. A bus has ten stations along a route between Start and Finish. Consider a bus that travels, stopping at exactly r stations along this route. START __ __ __ __ __ __ FINISH What is the number of different patterns of r stops that the bus can make? (r varies from 2–8)	As r increases, the number of estimated different patterns decreases: 2 stops seem to offer more patterns than, say, 5 or 8 stops.	5 stops offer the most patterns, 252; 2 and 8 offer the least

Source: Adapted from Tversky & Kahneman (1973)

The representativeness heuristic is a quick, though occasionally fallible, method of estimating probability via judgments of relevancy (see Table 7.2). It is also perhaps our most basic heuristic. Identifying people as members of categories or assigning meaning to actions is fundamental to all social inference, as Chapters 2 and 3 noted. The question "What is it?" must be answered before any other cognitive task.

Availability Heuristic

The **availability heuristic** evaluates an event's likelihood based on how quickly instances come to mind (Tversky & Kahneman, 1973). When examples or associations are readily accessible, this inflates estimated likelihood. For example, to decide whether people seem to be changing jobs often, one might consider the number of acquaintances who have changed jobs and respond on the basis of the frequency or ease with which examples come to mind. As with the representativeness heuristic, little cognitive work is needed to accomplish this task. If one has no trouble bringing to mind examples of people changing jobs, one will estimate that many people are, whereas if it takes a while to think of anyone changing jobs, one will scale down the estimate.

Often, the availability heuristic produces correct answers. After all, when examples of something come to mind easily, usually there indeed are lots of them. However, biasing factors can alter the accessibility of some classes of phenomena without altering their overall number. For example, if one has recently changed jobs, one may be more likely to notice other people who have done so as well. A category with easily retrieved instances will seem more numerous than will an equally frequent category with less easily retrieved instances (Gabrielcik & Fazio, 1984). Search biases, as well as retrieval biases, can skew one's frequency estimates by biasing the number of available instances. For example, some categories of events help the search for instances more than do other categories. Estimating how many people are changing jobs at a job fair, would, for example, produce a higher estimate than at an office party. The ease of bringing instances to mind varies dramatically between settings.

The ease of imagining particular events is subject to certain biases. For example, when people guess the major causes of death in the US, they assume that more deaths result from dramatic events such as accidents, fires, drownings, or shootings than is actually the case. At the same time, they underestimate death from more common causes such as stroke or heart disease. Newspapers and television programs create colorful, easily imagined instances of attention-grabbing events, so their images or associations come to mind, whereas a death from disease rarely makes it past the obituary page (Slovic, Fischhoff, & Lichtenstein, 1976).

Although most researchers have assumed that ease of recall is the mechanism that explains the impact of availability on judgments, others have suggested that it may be the content of recall. If you can imagine instances easily, you will probably also have more instances in mind, which may actually lead to the errors associated with availability. Untangling these two proposed mechanisms required manipulating volume of recall related to an instance (Schwarz, Bless, Strack, et al., 1991). Some participants had to recall 12 examples of assertive (or unassertive) behaviors, a difficult task, whereas others had to recall six examples of assertive (or unassertive) behaviors, an easy task. Those who did the difficult task (recall 12) rated themselves as less assertive or unassertive, respectively, whereas those who had the easy task (recall six) saw themselves as more assertive or unassertive, respectively. Self-assessments, thus, reflected the implications of recalled content only if recall was easy, and not if it was difficult. Ease or difficulty of recall appears to influence the impact of information on judgments via the availability heuristic and not the overall content of recall. However, when people believe that some arbitrary contextual factor influenced ease of recall, they ignore it as a basis for their inferences (Schwarz, Bless,

Strack, et al., 1991; Wänke, Schwarz, & Bless, 1995). Essentially, the phenomenal experience of recall ease should seem diagnostic for the inference: People not only assess ease of recall but also sometimes take into account factors that might artificially inflate or deflate recall ease when basing their judgments on availability.

Ease of retrieving instances is one way of estimating frequency via the availability heuristic, and strength of association is another. Associative bonds strengthen by repeated examples (as Chapter 4 indicated), so the strength of an association can indeed indicate the frequency of some class of events. As with ease of retrieving instances, however, associative strength may be biased by factors irrelevant to actual numerosity. For example, if one lives in Arizona, a region that attracts retirees, one may overestimate the number of elderly people in the country more than if one lives in a city such as Los Angeles, where widely available plastic surgery easily obscures age.

Memory accessibility facilitates the availability heuristic (MacLeod & Campbell, 1992). When particular types of events have been made accessible in memory, estimates of the future likely occurrence of similar events go up. A dramatic act of terrorism, for example, greatly inflates the perceived likelihood of similar terrorist incidents. Use of the availability heuristic also increases under high memory load, such as a person thinking about several things simultaneously. The social world is often overwhelmingly informative, and as such it usually involves high-memory-load conditions, thus facilitating the likely use of heuristics such as availability (Manis, Shedler, Jonides, & Nelson, 1993; Rothman & Hardin, 1997).

The availability heuristic has been influential within social psychology, and explains a range of social phenomena, including stereotyping (D. L. Hamilton & Rose, 1980) and the perseverance of discredited beliefs (L. Ross, Lepper & Hubbard, 1975; L. Ross, Lepper, Strack, & Steinmetz, 1977; see S. E. Taylor, 1982, for a review). It has also been offered as an explanation for phenomena such as salience (S. E. Taylor & Fiske, 1978), judgments of responsibility (M. Ross & Sicoly, 1979), predictions (Carroll, 1978; Slovic et al., 1976), and causal attributions (Pryor & Kriss, 1977). However, as an explanation, the availability heuristic may well have been overused. Many tasks do not require even the small work engaged by the availability heuristic, and frequency judgments may well occur through other processes (Manis et al., 1993). Information already stored in memory, as in mental representations of well-known types of events or people, means that we already know the answers to many inferences, if we can access the correct mental representation. One implication is that, generally, people will draw on the representativeness heuristic to identify what schema or category is appropriate for retrieving information more than they will draw on the availability heuristic for making judgments.

Simulation Heuristic

To solve problems, people often construct hypothetical scenarios to estimate how something will come out. That is, they run events through in their mind chronologically to assess likely consequences. This inferential technique is known as the **simulation heuristic** (Kahneman & Tversky, 1982). Consider how you would answer the question, "What is your dad going to think when he finds out you have smashed up the car?" You may think of what you know about your father and his reactions to crises, run through these events in your mind, and generate several possibilities.

The ease with which a particular ending comes to mind seems to predict what is likely to happen in real life. Your father could refuse to pay your college tuition next term, or he could ignore the whole thing, but you most easily imagine that he will insist that you find a job so that you can help pay for the car.

The simulation heuristic addresses a variety of tasks, including prediction (Will Joan like Tom?) and causality (Is the dog or the kid to blame for the mess on the floor?). It is particularly relevant to situations of near misses. For example, consider:

> Mr. Crane and Mr. Tees were scheduled to leave the airport on different flights, at the same time. They traveled from town in the same limousine, were caught in a traffic jam, and arrived at the airport thirty minutes after the scheduled departure time of their flights.
>
> Mr. Crane is told his flight left on time.
>
> Mr. Tees is told that his flight was delayed, and just left five minutes ago.
>
> Who is more upset?
>
> Mr. Crane or Mr. Tees? (Kahneman & Tversky, 1982, p. 203)

Virtually everyone says, "Mr. Tees." Why? Presumably, one can imagine no way that Mr. Crane could have made his plane, whereas Mr. Tees would have made it, except for that one long stoplight or the slow baggage man or the illegally parked car or the error in the posted departure gate. Thus the simulation heuristic and its ability to generate "if only" conditions explains the psychology of near misses and the frustration, regret, grief, or indignation they produce (e.g., Kruger, Wirtz, & Miller, 2005; Miller, Visser, & Staub, 2005; Seta, McElroy, & Seta, 2001).

Counterfactual Reasoning

Counterfactual reasoning of this sort – namely, the mental simulation of how events might otherwise have occurred – affects many judgments: assessing causality by trying to identify the unique or unusual specific factor that produced a dramatic outcome (e.g., G. L. Wells & Gavanski, 1989); affective responses to a particular outcome by providing visions of how events might have been otherwise (e.g., Seta et al., 2001), or could be, if one takes the wrong action (Kruger et al., 2005).

In particular, abnormal or exceptional events lead people to simulate alternatives that are normal and consequently dissimilar to the actual outcome (Kahneman & Miller, 1986). According to norm theory (Chapter 4), this contrast between the exceptional circumstance and the normal situation can intensify emotional reactions to unusual situations. In a role-play of compensating victims who experienced an abnormal or normal fate (Miller & McFarland, 1986), rewards were higher for victims in the abnormal circumstances. For example, when a man shopping at a convenience store far from home was shot during a robbery, participants' damage awards were higher than when he had shopped at his usual neighborhood convenience store.

Counterfactual thinking more easily makes a downhill change (replacing an unusual event with an expected one) than an upward change (replacing a normal event with an abnormal one) (Kahneman & Miller, 1986). This predicts generating a counterfactual scenario of inaction will be easier than one of action (Gleicher et al., 1990; Landman, 1988). For example, people more easily imagine that Mr. Tees could have made his plane if the construction had not been blocking his lane, whereas they less easily generate a scenario that Mr. Tees would have reached his plane on time if the city had built an alternate, faster route to the airport.

Imagining an alternative via counterfactual simulation affects expectations, causal attributions, impressions, and emotions. For example, if a person has made a mistake, such as leaving outside a lawnmower that then injured a child, simulation of how things might have been otherwise prompts regret. This is especially likely if one's fatal actions or inactions are inconsistent with one's personal beliefs or orientation (Seta et al., 2001). Thus, the circumstances (the salience and fit of how events might otherwise have been) are predictable and follow rules (incorporating probable and consistent rather than improbable and inconsistent elements into simulations).

Why do people engage in counterfactual reasoning? After all, when something unexpected or negative takes place, imagining how it could have been otherwise is hardly going to change the situation. Counterfactual thoughts serve several motives (Schwarz & Clore, 1996). Sometimes, counterfactual thoughts help people feel better. For example, when people have been through a stressful event, they often imagine how much worse it could have been (S. E. Taylor, Wood, & Lichtman, 1983). An automobile accident victim may focus less on the damage done to her car than on the fact that she could have been killed if the other car had hit her driver's-side door. Counterfactual thinking also provides meaning from pivotal life events via finding benefits and crediting fate (Figure 7.1; Kray, George, Liljenquist, Galinsky, Tetlock, & Roese, 2010).

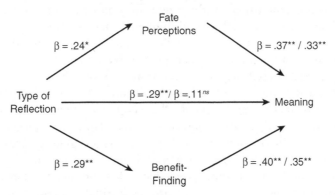

Figure 7.1 Fate perceptions and benefit-finding mediate reflection type's effect on meaningfulness of turning points

Note: Coefficients to the left of backslashes correspond to the direct effect; to the right are mediated effects. Asterisks indicate significant parameter estimates. * p < .05. ** p < .01.

Source: From Kray, George, Lilenquist, Galinsky, Tetlock, & Roese, (2010); reproduced by permission

Anticipating how one will feel after taking a particular action influences behavior as well. For example, many people avoid changing answers on multiple-choice tests even though such changes may improve their scores; they anticipate that a wrong action will generate more self-recrimination than would the inaction of leaving a wrong answer as it is (Kruger et al., 2005). Counterfactual thinking spills over to make people regret-averse in subsequent decisions (Raeva, van Dijk, & Zeelenberg, 2011).

Turning to simulations of the future, imagining hypothetical future events makes those events seem more likely (S. E. Taylor, Pham, Rivkin, & Armor, 1998). Consequently, if the scenario is easy to imagine, it seems more likely than difficult-to-imagine events (C. A. Anderson & Godfrey, 1987; C. A. Anderson, Lepper, & Ross, 1980). Similarly, simply imagining oneself deciding to perform or reject a behavior leads to corresponding changes in self-expectations (C. A. Anderson & Godfrey, 1987), whereas imagining someone else engaging in a behavior does not increase expectations that the self will engage in the behavior (C. A. Anderson, 1983).

Counterfactual thoughts may also serve a preparatory function for the future. If you realize that your car battery wouldn't have died if you hadn't left the inside light on, you probably won't do that again. When imagining how easily you could have avoided the problem produces negative affect, the motivation to improve – an emotional wake-up call – increases (McMullen & Markman, 2000). And when there isn't anything you can do mentally to change the outcome or prepare for the future, you may embrace a counterfactual explanation that puts you in the best light ("I could have *really* bombed the test. At least I studied a little.") (Tetlock, 1998).

Using Mental Simulation

Simulating how events may happen provides a window on the future by helping people envision possibilities and develop plans for producing those possibilities (S. E. Taylor et al., 1998), but people can focus on different aspects of the future. They may envision the future as filled with bountiful possibilities, what some call wishful thinking or **fantasy** (Oettingen & Mayer, 2002). Or they might focus on the steps they need to take to achieve a future that is desired. Which type of mental simulation about the future helps people to achieve their goals?

If you are an avid reader of self-help books, you know that this advice-filled genre urges people to envision actively the state they hope to achieve in the future. Yet research suggests that this idea is misleading. In a study that tested this point (Pham & Taylor, 1999), college students studying for an exam either envisioned their satisfaction and celebration in achieving a good grade (outcome focus) or envisioned themselves studying so as to produce a good grade (process). Those students who had focused on the process improved their grade compared to a control group that practiced neither mental simulation, but those students who focused on the outcome they wanted to achieve had lower scores on the exam than the control group. Clearly, if you want to use mental simulation to reach your goals, better not to engage in wishful thinking and fantasy but to focus your simulations clearly on what you will need to do to get there (Oettingen, Pak, & Schnetter, 2001; S. E. Taylor et al., 1998).

Simulations increase the perceived likelihood of a potential outcome (**mental addition**) more than reducing its perceived likelihood (**mental subtraction**). This asymmetry occurs because people especially weight features of a particular mental simulation that produce rather than inhibit a relevant outcome. So, for example, when assessing the impact of personal actions such as studying for an exam, subjects perceived more impact given an additive framework ("How many more questions will you get right if you study?") as opposed to a subtractive one ("How many fewer will you get right if you do not study?"). This effect is independent of both the valence of the event and personal experience in the simulation domain (Dunning & Parpal, 1989).

Anchoring

When judging under uncertainty, people sometimes reduce ambiguity by starting with a reference point, or **anchor**, and adjusting it to reach a final conclusion. If, for example, you have to guess how many people attended the latest USC–UCLA football game, and you have absolutely no idea, it is helpful to know that the previous week's game in the same stadium drew a crowd of 23,000. You may then guess 30,000, assuming that a USC–UCLA contest would draw a larger crowd.

We have already discussed several phenomena that constitute instances of the anchoring heuristic. Recall projection of the self onto others and false consensus in attribution research (Chapters 4–5). When estimating how many people would perform some activity (e.g., wear a sandwich board around campus), people's estimates are substantially influenced by the decision they themselves would make. Although we know intellectually that not everyone would behave as we do, our estimates of others' behavior are not adjusted sufficiently from the anchor that our own behavior provides. As this example suggests, a prominent anchor from which we estimate or judge others' social behavior is the self and our social environment (e.g., Fong & Markus, 1982. We may judge another person's shyness as an adjusted inference from our own self-rating on this quality or adopt another person's perspective by adjusting from our own (Epley, Keysar, Van Boven, & Gilovich, 2004); children do this too, but adjust less than adults do (Epley, Morewedge, & Keysar, 2004).

Anchors include irrelevant details that, nonetheless, suggest a beginning reference point. For example, judges customarily instruct juries to consider the harshest verdict first, which then may inadvertently function as an anchoring point (Greenberg, Williams, & O'Brien, 1986). When participants in a mock trial were induced to consider the harshest verdict first, they rendered significantly harsher verdicts than participants instructed to consider lenient verdicts first. Similarly, in attributing attitudes to others, you may be aware of constraints on their attitude expression (e.g., a reporter had to write a pro-war article because his editor required it); nonetheless, with the communication itself as an anchor, you may fail to correct sufficiently for the constraints (and thus infer that the writer is indeed in favor of the war). This robust **correspondence bias** – failing to correct for situational constraints in attributing attitudes (Chapter 6) – fits anchoring and insufficient adjustment (Quattrone, Finkel, & Andrus, 1982).

What mechanism underlies the anchoring effect? Research has focused on two possible explanations. First, people anchor on an initial value and then insufficiently adjust away when making an inference (Epley & Gilovich, 2001). Second, anchoring is determined by anchor plausibility and how much people know about both anchor and target. The less people know about a target, the more likely they are to assimilate to an anchor and thus adjust insufficiently (Mussweiler & Strack, 2000). In this view, anchoring depends on the applicability of activated information about the anchor (Mussweiler & Strack, 1999; Strack & Mussweiler, 1997). Essentially, then, an anchor may make knowledge salient that people can use when they need to make new judgments.

Anchoring can be socially useful. Suppose, for example, that you want to sell your idiosyncratic, customized car, and its resale value is uncertain. If you are negotiating with an interested buyer, your opening offer should start high; that will anchor the negotiation and result in a higher price. In contrast, if you offer the car at an auction, such as eBay, your starting offer should be low, to get as many people as possible to enter and compete, driving up the price (Galinsky, Ku, & Mussweiler, 2009).

Examples of anchoring and adjustment are ubiquitous precisely because social behavior is so ambiguous and free of objective yardsticks (Mussweiler, Strack, & Pfeiffer, 2000). When we can, we use ourselves as anchors (e.g., Epley et al., 2004), but when our own reference points are ambiguous, we may use others as anchors, or we may anchor by irrelevant details of a situation. No foolproof method avoids anchoring effects, but substituting the opposite (e.g., "What would someone unlike me do?") is one strategy to reduce them (Mussweiler et al., 2000).

BEYOND HEURISTICS: OTHER DECISION SHORTCUTS

Beyond the Kahneman–Tversky heuristics that estimate odds by what comes easily to mind, people use other efficient shortcuts to decision making.

Decision Framing Effects: Perspectives from Prospect Theory

Judgments are affected by the initial decision **framing,** that is, the description of the background context of the choice (Kahneman & Tversky, 1984; Tversky & Kahneman, 1981). People often fail to recognize that the underlying structure of problems are similar to each other and instead are distracted by surface characteristics concerning how those problems are presented. The presentation of the problem is called the decision **frame.** Seemingly minor alterations in such representations can exert major effects on decisions.

A common frame is whether a decision describes the gains or the losses that might occur (Kahneman & Tversky, 1982). For example, people become cautious when alternatives are phrased in terms of losses, but they are far more likely to take chances when the alternatives are framed in terms of gains (e.g., Roney, Higgins, & Shah, 1995). Consider the following:

Imagine the United States is preparing for the outbreak of an unusual Asian disease, which is expected to kill 600 people. Two alternative programs to combat the disease have been proposed. Assume that the exact scientific estimate of the consequences of the program are as follows: If Program A is adopted, 200 people will be saved. If Program B is adopted, there is a one-third probability that 600 people will be saved, and two-thirds probability that no people would be saved. Which program would you favor?

Now imagine the same situation with these two alternatives: If Program C is adopted, 400 people will die. If Program D is adopted, there is a one-third probability that no one will die, and a two-thirds probability that 600 people will die. (Based on Tversky & Kahneman, 1981)

Tversky and Kahneman presented these problems to college students. Framed in terms of lives saved, 72% of the participants chose Program A, the more certain outcome. However, when the problem was phrased in terms of lives lost, only 22% favored the equivalent Program C; instead they favored the uncertain outcome.

This change in focus represents a robust principle in decision making, namely, **risk aversion** – people tend to avoid risks when they are dealing with possible gains (lives saved) – but **risk seeking** – tending to seek risks when they are dealing with possible losses (lives lost). In the problems phrased as lives gained, people prefer to know that 200 lives would be saved for certain and avoid the option that suggests a risk that no one would be saved. In contrast, when the problem is phrased as lives lost, people prefer the option providing the possibility that no one will die. The important point, of course, is that these two problems are identical, the only difference being whether the options are phrased in terms of lives gained or lives lost.

The influence of framing is pervasive (see Dunning, 2012; Levin, Schneider, & Gaeth, 1998, for reviews) and occurs even for statistical sophisticates as well as for statistical novices. Framing effects emerge across settings, including layoffs (Brockner, Wiesenfeld, & Martin, 1995), product purchases (Levin & Gaeth, 1988), medical treatments (Levin, Schnittjer, & Thee, 1988; Rothman & Salovey, 1997), and condom use (Linville, Fischer, & Fischhoff, 1993).

Framing can interact with personal dispositions to affect choices or decisions. Chapter 5 noted that some people are promotion-focused whereas others are prevention-focused. Promotion-focused individuals are more persuaded by gain than loss frames, whereas prevention-focused people are more persuaded by loss frames (Lee & Aaker, 2004; Sherman, Mann, & Updegraff, 2006). For example, if a person is chronically motivated to avoid harm, an ad for a car that touts its great survival record following car crashes might be more persuasive than an ad touting its contemporary, sleek look, or its powerful engine.

Prospect Theory

Building on these observations, **prospect theory** (Kahneman & Tversky, 1979; Tversky & Kahneman, 1981) describes the decision processes involved when people make comparisons between options. There are two important components in this theory: frame of reference and subjective value function.

Prospect theory posits that selecting a reference point is crucial to evaluating options. A **reference point** is the internal standard that people use to compare the objective value of an option so as to classify the option as positive (i.e., better than the reference point) or as negative (i.e., worse than the reference point). As we have seen, objectively identical options can have positive or negative **frames of reference**, such that an option perceived as a gain in one frame could be perceived as a loss in another frame. A positively framed option decreases one's evoked reference point, whereas the same information framed negatively increases the evoked reference point (Abelson & Levi, 1985; Highhouse & Paese, 1996). In the disease example described earlier, framing the alternatives positively (200 people saved) would evoke a reference point comparison of zero people being saved; however, when the same problem is framed negatively (400 people will die), people adopt a reference point presupposing that no lives are lost – that is, zero people will die. The shift in reference point between the two frames leads to a medical alternative being perceived as more attractive when positively framed than when negatively framed. That is, the positive frame creates a sense of saving 200 lives when compared with losing everyone, whereas the negative frame creates a sense of losing 400 lives compared with the no-lives-lost reference point.

A neutral reference point orients Figure 7.2's typical subjective value function. The **subjective value function** of prospect theory is expressed as positive or negative deviations (i.e., gains or losses) from a neutral point. The value function is S-shaped – concave for gains (reflecting **risk aversion**) and convex for losses (reflecting **risk seeking**). So, as the gain increases in objective value, the increase in the subjective value decreases. For example, the difference in subjective value between $10 and $20 is greater than between gains of $110 and $120. As loss increases objectively, the drop in the subjective value also decreases but it does so faster than for gains. So, for example, the difference in subjective value between losses of $10 and $20 is greater than that between losses of $110 and $120. But also, the curve is steeper for losses than for gains (reflecting **loss aversion**), so that losing $20 looms larger than gaining $20.

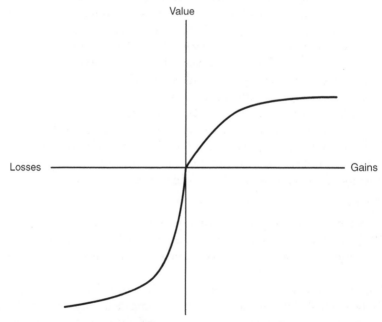

Figure 7.2   The subjective value function of prospect theory

Source: From Kahneman & Tversky (1979). Copyright 1979 by The Econometric Society. Adapted with permission

Exactly why the subjective interpretation of objectively presented information varies with gain or loss is not clear, but the effects are robust. Note that the frame-of-reference effects imply that the same outcome framed positively or negatively produces different subjective values. Thus the same level of objective performance is perceived as better if it is positively framed than if negatively framed. It is more satisfying to know that 70% of the people you invited to a large party showed up than that 30% did not.

Base Rates versus Case Histories

People's objective reference points ought to include overall population frequencies for events. But people often must predict future events with limited background knowledge. You may need to decide, for example, whether or not to get season tickets to your local repertory theater based on the sample of plays you have seen them perform in the past. Or, in trying to match up a friend with a new companion, you may think through the likelihood of whether or not they will be a good match. A normative model, **Bayes' theorem**, dictates how such tasks should proceed (Table 7.3). However, even if people have good estimates of population characteristics (averages, prior probabilities, or proportions), people may not appropriately use them in decision making.

Chapter 6 pointed out that people underutilize consensus information in making causal attributions. This failure is part of a larger problem: namely, the tendency of people to ignore general, broad-based information about population characteristics (**base-rate** information) in favor of easier, more concrete, anecdotal, but less valid, reliable information. Vibrant examples simply outweigh more reliable but abstract base-rate information (Bar-Hillel, 1980; S. E. Taylor & Thompson, 1982; Chapter 3). This reliable bias likely occurs because colorful examples suggest theories to explain what is going on, and as noted, prior theories often bias judgment even without our unawareness.

In one study (Hamill, Wilson, & Nisbett, 1980), participants read a colorful account of a woman who had been living on welfare with her numerous children for many years while maintaining a relatively affluent lifestyle. This stereotypic case of welfare abuse was framed either by base-rate statistics indicating that welfare recipients often take advantage and stay on welfare a long time, or by statistics suggesting that the average welfare recipient is on the rolls only briefly, implying that the case history was atypical. Despite valid base-rate information, subjects responded as if the case history were representative of welfare recipients under both conditions (Hamill et al., 1980; S. E. Taylor & Thompson, 1982).

Why are people so often swayed by colorful examples when they also have better base-rate information? One possibility is that people do not always see the relevance of base-rate information to a particular judgment. One building in Los Angeles has housed four different restaurants in less than three years. Each has failed, and that information should give any prospective restauranteur pause for thought. Nonetheless, as each culinary venture folds, an eager new one steps in to fill the breach, only to fail again. Presumably, each idealistic entrepreneur assumes that his or her own concept is the one that will make the place work (an Irish pub, a pasta place, soup and salad). None seemingly appreciate the base-rate information that virtually screams, "No one comes here!"

Table 7.3 Bayes' theorem, normative model for statistically optimal predictions

Given: Two bags of poker chips, each containing mixtures of red and blue chips.

Reality: Bag A has 10 blue, 20 red; Bag B has 20 blue, 10 red.

Sampling: 80% likely to draw from A, 20% likely to draw from B.

Task: Draw, see color, and replace three chips from one bag, guess which bag it was.

Example: Draw three chips, blue-blue-red.

Common assumption: Bag B, because two-thirds of Bag B chips are blue.

True odds: 2 to 1 that it was Bag A (see calculations).

Calculate exact odds using Bayes' theorem:

1. *Prior odds* of Bag A rather than B are 4 to 1: Bag A appears 80% of the time.
2. *Likelihood*: Ratio of probability that the sample comes from A to the probability that it comes from B.
   a. If Bag A, the probability of drawing a blue is 1 out of 3 and a red is 2 of 3. Consequently, the probability of drawing blue-blue-red is $1/3 \times 1/3 \times 2/3 = 2/27$.
   b. If Bag B, the probability of drawing blue-blue-red is $2/3 \times 2/3 \times 1/3 = 4/27$.
   c. The likelihood ratio is probability that the sample came from A(2/27) divided by the probability that the sample came from B(4/27). This yields the odds of 1 to 2 that the sample is from Bag A rather than from Bag B.
3. *Combining* prior probability (step 1) with the likelihood information (2c): Multiply the prior probability (4 to 1, or 4/1) by the likelihood (1/2), which yields 2 to 1 in favor of guessing that the three chips actually came from Bag A.

Lay response: Most people are surprised that it is more likely that the chips came from Bag A (A. L. Glass & Holyoak, 1986). The reason for their surprise is that they ignore the base-rate information that Bag A will be selected 80% of the time.

People do use base-rate information when its relevance is clear. For example, people use base-rate information if it is the only information available (e.g., Hamill et al., 1980), or if its causal relevance to judgment is salient (Ajzen, 1977; Hewstone, Benn, & Wilson, 1988; Tversky & Kahneman, 1981). In one study, participants were told about a late-night auto accident involving a cab that an eyewitness thought might have been blue. Participants then learned that in that city, 85% of the cabs are green and 15% are blue. Although participants should have concluded that the culprit's cab was probably green, given the base rates, few did. Instead, most drew on the eyewitness report and decided the cab was probably blue. However, a second group learned that 85% of the accidents in the city are caused by blue cabs and 15% by green cabs; these participants did use the base-rate information to qualify their inferences. Presumably, people see accident-rate statistics as causally relevant to judgments about accidents (cf. Ajzen, 1977), whereas they do not perceive information about the prevalence of particular cabs as relevant to the judgment, although it is. Thus, when people perceive base-rate information as relevant to a judgment, they do use it.

Several theories may explain the base-rate fallacy. At least some so-called failures to use base rates implicate experimental procedures. Conversational rules dictate that people communicate primarily information that informs and fills a gap in a recipient's knowledge (Grice, 1975; Turnbull & Slugoski, 1988). Because experiments emphasize individuating case information over base-rate information, subjects may perceive the case history but not the base rates as relevant to the task. Hence, overusing case-history information may simply result from presentation conditions that convey meaningfulness (Schwarz, Strack et al., 1991). People can use base-rate information when it is brief, presented early, or otherwise salient (Chun & Kruglanski, 2006).

Case-history information seems more representative of a category than does base-rate information and thus more likely to invoke theories (Kahneman & Tversky, 1973). When people read a case history, they make immediate associations to larger categories and thus overuse the case for drawing inferences. People more easily see the diagnostic value of case-history than base-rate information, except when the diagnosticity of base-rate information is highlighted (Ginossar & Trope, 1980).

Taking yet another shortcut, then, people often neglect base-rate and other statistical information in inferences. Given less valid, but easier, more engaging, seemingly relevant anecdotes, people ignore relevant base rates (Bar-Hillel & Fischhoff, 1981; Manis, Dovalina, Avis, & Cardoze, 1980). The consequences of ignoring base-rate information can be extreme, as the conjunction error illustrates.

The Conjunction Error

Comedians make their living by sketching recognizable portraits that make us laugh. "Consider the nerd. He's an out-of-shape guy who lives in a cubicle, dresses badly, and has lousy posture, right? He looks like this?" [Comedian imitates the nerd.] With each detail, the audience's laugh of recognition grows. Yet the paradox of the well-drawn portrait is that with each detail, recognizability increases but actual probability decreases. One might well find a nerd in his cubicle, and he might be out of shape, but the likelihood that he would also be round-shouldered and poorly dressed is low. The likelihood that any two or more events will co-occur (i.e., their joint probability) is the product of their probabilities of occurring alone; accordingly, their joint probability cannot exceed the probability of the least probable event. However, people often make more extreme predictions for the joint occurrence of events than for a single event. This error is termed the **conjunction fallacy** (Abelson & Gross, 1987; Tversky & Kahneman, 1983).

In one study (Slovic, Fischhoff, & Lichtenstein, 1977), participants learned that an individual was gregarious and literary. When asked about his likelihood of being an engineering major, they responded, "very unlikely." However, when asked about his likelihood of starting in engineering and switching to journalism, an event with a far lower likelihood of simply majoring in engineering, participants rated this much higher. Presumably, they could readily imagine how a gregarious, literary person would decide journalism was for him and not engineering, but they could not imagine how such a person would remain an engineer.

Preferring easily imagined conjunctive explanations is a robust effect – for both important and trivial actions, whether an individual has a single goal in mind or multiple goals, and whether the information involved is plausible or implausible (Leddo, Abelson, & Gross, 1984). Training people in the more effortful statistical principles underlying the conjunctive fallacy can lower, but not eliminate, it (Crandall & Greenfield, 1986; Morier & Borgida, 1984).

Qualifications to the conjunction effect are several. Conjunctive explanations are more likely when participants explain an event than if they simply interpret the event (Zuckerman, Eghrari, & Lambrecht, 1986). When actors fail to take several particular actions, conjunction effects disappear; that is, people do not systematically prefer explanations that offer multiple explanations for inaction (Leddo et al., 1984; see also Read, 1988).

Several mechanisms may explain conjunction effects. People generally try to understand others' actions in terms of those other persons' personal goals (Leddo et al., 1984). For example, one may visit an art gallery to relax, to get away, to see a particularly exciting artist, to enjoy a friend's companionship, and to collect art, all of which may occur simultaneously. Conjunctive explanations, which provide more detailed information about goals, tend to be appreciated as informative.

Conjunctive explanations seem more likely than single explanations because they co-opt alternative explanations for the behavior (Einhorn & Hogarth, 1986). Thus people are not motivated to consider alternative explanations because the conjunctive explanation apparently rules out those alternatives. Knowing that a friend treated himself to an expensive dinner because he was depressed after he and his girlfriend broke up precludes wondering whether he received a work bonus or a gift certificate.

The representativeness heuristic, which draws on preexisting theories, also explains conjunction effects (Tversky & Kahneman, 1983). As information elaborates a description that rounds out a human portrait and makes the portrait seem more likely, the objective probability that the portrait is true goes down, but its resemblance to a real person goes up: It matches our general theories more closely. In short, when people assess the likelihood that several seemingly related events occur in conjunction, they often ignore the objective probability of their conjunction in favor of a shortcut theory that makes the conjoint probability of the multiple events seem true.

Integrating Information

People take shortcuts too when bringing information together and combining it into a judgment, which is problematic when evaluated against the normative model. We consider two integrative tasks here.

Assessing Covariation

Judgments of **covariation** – that is, how strongly two things are related – are essential to many inference tasks, both formal and informal. Much folk wisdom states correlations, such as, "Blondes have more fun." Mickey Gilley's observation, "Don't the girls all get prettier at closing time?" (Don't the boys too?), assumes a correlation between time and perceived attractiveness (Pennebaker et al., 1979). Covariation also underlies many formal inferences: Kelley's covariation model of attribution (Chapter 6) presupposes social perceivers observing the covariation of an outcome across time, persons, and entities with at least reasonable accuracy, to formulate an attribution.

Given covariation's importance to judgment, how well does the perceiver detect covariation? The answer is not well (Crocker, 1981; Nisbett & Ross, 1980), especially compared with normative statistical models for assessing covariation (Smedslund, 1963; Ward & Jenkins, 1965). The proper model for calculating covariation includes several specific steps, each a source of potentially biasing shortcuts (Figure 7.3).

First, the perceiver must understand what data are relevant to assess covariation. For example, to test the adage, "Blondes have more fun," one needs to know the number of blonde men and women who have fun, the number of blondes who do not, the number of brunettes and redheads who have fun, and the number of brunettes and redheads who do not. Most people do not recognize all four kinds of evidence as relevant; rather, they concentrate primarily on fun-loving blondes, believing that supporting evidence most assesses its truth value. Indeed, this general propensity of the social perceiver echoes other errors: When testing the validity of an idea,

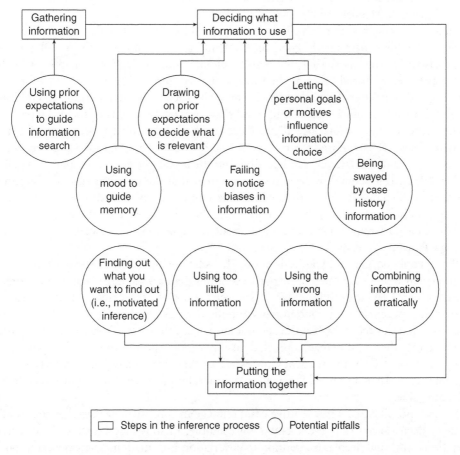

Figure 7.3   The assessment of covariation and its pitfalls: Do blondes have more fun?

people seek confirming instances rather than instances on both sides (e.g., Arkes & Harkness, 1980). Yet, covariation ideas are comparative (All blondes or most? More fun than whom?), so all four types of information are needed.

Second is sampling cases, and as noted, people are poor samplers. The range of contacts they consider is certainly biased, but most people seem to be unaware of this (Crocker, 1981). People also overuse small samples (Tversky & Kahneman, 1974), and when results disagree with their hunches, they may reject the sample results or not even unrecognize the contradiction (Arkes & Harkness, 1980; Crocker, 1981).

Third, covariation process requires classifying instances as to type of evidence. Here again prior expectations allow shortcuts that can get in the way. Negative instances – that is, cases that contradict the proposed relationship – may be mislabeled as positive if they are ambiguous, or if not, dismissed as random or atypical. Positive instances that fit expectations are more quickly or easily identified and incorporated into inferences (e.g., R. J. Harris, Teske, & Ginns, 1975; Owens, Bower, & Black, 1979). Nonoccurrences of the event are especially difficult for people to process (Allison & Messick, 1988).

Fourth, the perceiver must recall the evidence and estimate the frequency of each type. Memory is fallible – particularly good for confirming cases, and sometimes (Chapter 4) for strongly disconfirming cases. Thus, the ecstatic blonde and the deliriously happy raven-haired person may be remembered, whereas the three contented "mousy-browns" may be forgotten.

Finally, and only after the previous four steps, the social perceiver is ready to combine the evidence. How successfully is this task accomplished? In fact, the ability of the social perceiver to estimate degree of covariation once all the data have been assembled appears to be fairly good. Researchers have often confused errors of perceived relevance, sampling, classification, and recall as errors in computation, thereby underestimating the social perceiver's computational abilities (Crocker, 1981). This is not, however, to suggest either that the perceiver successfully computes correlation coefficients or that estimates of covariation, however made, are usually accurate. Perceivers' estimates of covariation generally track, though often underestimate, actual covariation, assuming no strong prior expectation about the relationship between the two variables (Jennings, Amabile, & Ross, 1982).

When people do have a hypothesis about the relationship between variables, they tend to look for evidence that confirms that hypothesis rather than assess the evidence in a more even-handed manner (Klayman & Ha, 1987). The search for positive test cases appears to be a general strategy that cuts across many content areas and many types of inference task; people use it as a problem-solving shortcut (a) when they do not have available a strategy specific to the particular problem or (b) when task demands preclude using a more specific strategy. The positive-cases strategy may result from the tendency to test cases expected to have the property of interest rather than cases that do not, a shortcut that generally produces, but is not equivalent to, a confirmatory bias.

Although people usually test positive cases (engage in confirmatory biases), some conditions increase or decrease covariation detection. For example, a happy mood fosters top-down information processing and decreases attention to covariation information, whereas a sad mood may actually improve covariation detection (Braverman, 2005). Sometimes, people also use information relevant to falsification. People use information about alternative hypotheses when salient (Trope & Mackie, 1987), suggested by context, or recently/frequently activated (Ginossar & Trope, 1987).

Accuracy in assessing covariation depends on whether prior expectations and the specific information converge or diverge, with greater accuracy under convergence. From this standpoint, errors in contingency judgments may stem from a generally successful inferential strategy, which in the long run preserves accuracy by minimally altering contingency estimations from a general principle on the basis of a single and potentially aberrant encounter (Alloy & Tabachnik, 1984).

Illusory Correlation

Expecting a relationship between two variables, people often overestimate the correlation or impose a relationship when none actually exists, a phenomenon termed **illusory correlation**. In an early example (Chapman, 1967), students encountered lists of word pairs, such as lion–tiger, lion–eggs, and bacon–eggs. Participants then reported how often each word was paired with each other word; in fact, all words were paired with each other equally. Nonetheless, subjects reported that words associated in meaning, such as bacon–eggs, had been paired more frequently than those not associated in meaning.

Sometimes illusory correlations result from structural characteristics of the evidence. Within the word list were two items longer than the other words, specifically "blossoms" and "notebook". Participants also inferred that these two words had more frequently been paired, apparently because they shared the distinctive quality of length. Chapman reasoned that at least two factors can produce an illusory correlation: **associative meaning**, in which two items are seen as belonging together because they fit prior expectations (e.g., bacon–eggs), and **paired distinctiveness**, in which two things are thought to go together because they share some unusual feature (e.g. blossoms–notebook). Similarly, people perceive a pseudocontingency if two skewed effects co-occur (Fiedler & Freytag, 2004). If a teacher has a classroom of aggressive children and knows that most watch a lot of television, she may infer that the two phenomena are related when in fact they may or may not relate.

Illusory correlation is one basis of stereotyping (D. L. Hamilton, 1979; D. L. Hamilton & Gifford, 1976; Table 7.4). Paired distinctiveness can explain some negative stereotypes of minority group members. Specifically, majority group members have relatively few contacts with minority group members, and negative behaviors are also relatively infrequent. Majority group members may make an illusory correlation between the two rare events and infer that minority group members more often engage in negative behaviors.

According to meta-analysis, the paired-distinctiveness illusory correlation effect is highly consistent and moderate in size (Mullen & Johnson, 1990), but stronger when the distinctive behaviors are negative and when memory load is high (Mullen & Johnson, 1990). People in a state of arousal show a stronger illusory correlation effect because arousal increases reliance on preexisting theories, and reduces capacity for more elaborate problem solving (Kim & Baron, 1988). Illusory correlations along evaluative dimensions appear to be stronger than for cognitive judgments (Klauer & Meiser, 2000).

Table 7.4   Illusory correlation as a result of associative (stereotypic) meaning (Hamilton & Gifford, 1976). Although each trait type appeared an equal number of times, participants overestimated the stereotype-matching occurrences (in bold, along the table's diagonal)

Type of trait:	Accountant/ librarian	Doctor/ stewardess	Salesman/ waitress	Neutral
Occupation:				
Accountant/librarian	2.67	1.99	2.25	2.34
Doctor/stewardess	2.21	2.66	2.41	2.10
Salesman/waitress	1.94	2.12	2.94	2.31

Illusory correlations formed about individuals differ from those formed about groups (Sanbonmatsu, Shavitt, & Gibson, 1994). Illusory correlations about individuals result from online impression-based judgments, whereas those for groups seem to be memory-based (Sanbonmatsu, Sherman, & Hamilton, 1987). That is, for impressions of individuals, the bias operates at encoding, not at judgment (D. L. Hamilton, Dugan, & Trolier, 1985), whereas group illusory correlations occur when attempting to recall group attributes (Sanbonmatsu et al., 1987).

The twin topics of covariation estimation and illusory correlation are important for several reasons. First, as a complex operation, estimating covariation concatenates many errors and biases in the social perceiver's intuitive strategies, such as detecting relevant information, sampling correctly, and recalling accurately. People take shortcuts past this complexity. Second, because covariation is often an interim inference upon which other more complex inferences rely, the flaws in covariation estimation have repercussions farther down the line for the accuracy with which the social perceiver characterizes and acts on the environment. Third, errors estimating covariation again highlight the inference process's conservative bias toward conclusions that people already expect; people's theories about the social environment predominate in guiding inferences. Finally, covariation estimation and the illusory correlations that may substitute for accurate assessment then make their way into social interaction, shaping erroneous perceptions of reality as through the maintenance of stereotypes.

When Do We Use Heuristics and Other Shortcuts?

Heuristics and other shortcuts are fundamental to inference, making rapid information processing possible. However, sometimes the social perceiver becomes more thoughtful and less reliant on quick-and-easy strategies, and then may reach better inferences. When is the social perceiver most likely to cut corners?

People use heuristics and shortcuts in domains where they have a lot of practice and have developed strategies that have previously served them well. They are more likely to use heuristics when they experience approach emotions (a good mood, versus fear or depression; (e.g., Bodenhausen, Kramer, & Süsser, 1994; Forgas, 1998; Ruder & Bless, 2003), and approach emotions include anger, which encourages heuristics (Tiedens, 2001). People use heuristics to solve unimportant tasks, saving online capacity for more significant judgments. People use heuristics less when the stakes are high, when they distrust the information under consideration (Schul, Mayo, & Burnstein, 2004), when they are accountable for their inferences, or when they have recently made errors or otherwise found the goodness or accuracy of their cognitions to be questionable (e.g., Tiedens & Linton, 2001).

These two sections have seen heuristics that include representativeness, availability, simulation, plus anchoring and adjustment, as well as shortcuts to assessing conjunction, covariation, and correlation. In each case, effort-saving strategies unify under a common mechanism: Faced with difficult questions, people often substitute easier questions and answer those instead (Kahneman & Frederick, 2002). Representativeness makes a probability judgment by fitting the individual case to stereotypic resemblance, and availability does it by ease of recalling instances. Simulation forms expectations and affect based on ease of recall. Anchoring and adjustment estimates a judgment by amending an initial, base value. People simplify conjunction, covariation, and correlation as well. Each strategy suggests how people construct judgments using remembered information (Weber & Johnson, 2006).

JUDGMENTS OVER TIME

As described earlier, expected utility (EU) theory maintains that choices are guided by the probability and value of options. The **discounted utility (DU) model** makes the additional point that the utility of any given choice diminishes as consequences are spread over time (Samuelson, 1937). Originally, this discount rate was thought to be constant over time. Decades of research, however, have clarified that departures from DU are as ubiquitous as those from EU (Frederick, Loewenstein, & O'Donoghue, 2002). Long-term choices are often determined by people's knowledge of their own preferences and how those preferences may change over time. For example, given a choice between $10 today and $11 in a week, most people will choose $10 immediately. But given the choice between $10 in a year and $11 in a week and a year, most people will choose the $11 (Frederick et al., 2002).

DU also predicts that the discount rate is constant across choice types. But the discount rate varies as a function of domain (Frederick et al., 2002) because of mixed attitudes about the future. For example, a person may choose to exercise for health reasons but compromise that same goal by trying to manage on four hours' sleep a night. A person may undermine decades of careful saving with an unwise investment placed with a charlatan.

Small rewards are discounted more steeply than larger rewards. Ten dollars may look better today than $11 in a week, but if the corresponding figures are $1,000 and $1,100, the picture changes. In addition, abstract representative features govern decisions made for the future, whereas consideration of concrete details play a stronger role in judgments about the present. People infer utilities from monetary value, delay, and probability. They discount utility, not intrinsic value, making decisions by combining an outcome's intrinsic utility with the disutility of a delay (Kileen, 2009; Figure 7.4).

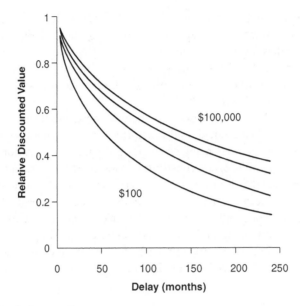

Figure 7.4   Temporal discounting

Source: From Kileen (2009). Copyright APA; reproduced by permission

Affect-based or "hot" outcomes undergo steeper time discounting than cognition-based or "cool" outcomes (Loewenstein, 1996). Put another way, the farther ahead an event may be, the greater the weight of cognitive outcomes and the less the weight of affective outcomes. A "hot" but poorly educated dating partner may seem fantastic in the short term, but cooler reflection on a long-term future might lead one to wonder whether that partner will be an intellectually rewarding companion and be able to pull his or her economic weight in a long-term relationship. People in a cool mindset cannot accurately imagine people, including themselves, acting in a hot mindset; this **empathy gap** misreads the past hot self (how easily hunger sabotages a diet; Nordgren, van der Pligt, & van Harreveld, 2006), the future hot self (the constraint of embarrassment; Van Boven, Loewenstein, Welch, & Dunning, 2012), and other people's hot selves (e.g., sensitivity to pain in what constitutes torture; Nordgren, McDonnell, & Loewenstein, 2011).

Temporal Construal

Every day we think about and plan for future events. Temporal distance in the future not only affects the value of future outcomes, it also affects the way people mentally represent events. Imagine that you are taking a vacation in Spain four months from now. How do you think about it? Then imagine that you leave for Spain tomorrow. How do your perceptions differ? In the first case, you may imagine romantic dinners late at night, the thrill of gazing at exciting art, or the taste of unusual food. If you are leaving tomorrow, no doubt you are more concerned with finding the extra keys for the house sitter, stocking enough dog food, and recalling the Madrid hotel.

This is the core of **temporal construal theory** (Trope & Liberman, 2003, 2010; Shapira, Liberman, Trope, & Rim, 2012): The greater the temporal distance to an event, the more one thinks about that event in abstract terms that convey the essence of the event. Thinking about events in the future prompts high-level construals. One considers future rewards in the abstract: simple, structured, coherent, and goal-relevant. Greater insight and more creative thinking may result (Förster, Friedman, & Liberman, 2004). But as the event approaches, one focuses more on specific, even incidental details. The lower-level construals associated with more immediate outcomes tend to be detailed and complex, often unstructured, incoherent, and heavily dependent on their context. One may be distracted by irrelevant details (Fujita, Eyal, Chaiken, Trope, & Liberman, 2008; Ledgerwood, Trope, & Chaiken, 2010). In the short term, abstract goals seem irrelevant or less pressing than subordinate goals.

As temporal distance to an activity increases, the value of a high-level construal matters more, and low-level construals matter less in determining preferences. For example, deciding to donate blood today is likely to be guided by whether one has extra time and no interfering activities, whereas the decision to donate blood in six months is guided by the higher-level construal of whether donating to help others is a good idea. To put it another way, decisions about distant future activities are more likely to be made on the basis of how desirable they are, whereas decisions about activities in the near future are likely to be made based on how feasible they are.

Events envisioned in the future are regarded more favorably than those generated for the present. For example, the initial impetus for the trip to Spain may have been the superordinate goal of a long, romantic vacation away with one's spouse, whereas the immediate subordinate goal may be simply trying to get everything done to get to the airport on time. Given the chaos, one may wonder why one ever thought this was a good idea.

Spatial distance affects judgments similarly to temporal distance (Henderson & Wakslak, 2010). For example, actions performed at spatially distant locations seem like ends rather than means and tend to be described abstractly rather than concretely (Fujita, Henderson, Eng, Trope, & Liberman, 2006). In one study, when events appeared spatially distant, perceivers were more likely to use broad behavioral units and dispositional attributions than when events were represented as near (Henderson, Fujita, Trope, & Liberman, 2006). Distant events seem more likely if typical, and less likely if atypical (Henderson et al., 2006). In short, people reveal abstract judgmental biases when drawing inferences about distant events (Eyal, Liberman, Trope, & Walther, 2004; Fujita, Eyal, Chaiken, Trope, & Liberman, 2008). Temporal or spatial distance changes judgments and decisions because distant ones reflect high-level rather than low-level construals.

Learning from the Past

The maxim "Those who ignore the past are condemned to relive it" implies that, were we scrupulously to turn our attention backward in time, we would learn important lessons. Although this adage may contain an element of truth, research on hindsight questions how seriously we ought to believe it. Like the present and the future, our interpretation of the past is guided by theory. Everyone is familiar with the Monday-morning quarterback who, with the advantage of retrospection, knows what should have been done to win the weekend's game. He claims that the opposition's moves could have been anticipated, that the home team ought to have foreseen them, and that a particular strategy (his) clearly would have been successful.

Twenty-twenty hindsight (Fischhoff, 1980; Fischhoff, Slovic, & Lichtenstein, 1977; Janoff-Bulman, Timko, & Carli, 1985) indicates the difficulty of ignoring knowledge of an actual outcome to generate unbiased inferences about what could or should have happened. In retrospect, people exaggerate what could have been anticipated. Moreover, comparing people's predictions about future events with postdictions about past events, people misremember their own predictions to conform with what really happened (Fischhoff & Beyth, 1975).

The social perceiver's ubiquitous theory-generating capacity is a major basis for reconstructing the past (cf. M. Ross, 1989; Chapter 5). Even the most random sequence of events can be forced with enough thought into a logical causal chain. Once that causal chain of reasons is in place, events seem inevitable. Further, interventions that would presumably have set some other causal sequence into effect may seem particularly compelling because they seem so logical. Chance or situational factors that may have heavily influenced what actually occurred may be overlooked. For example, in retrospect, an opponent's series of moves in a football game may appear to be part of an overall plan when in fact it capitalizes on chance events such as an injury or a fumble. Nonetheless, once labeled as a plan, it is likely to be seen as predictable ("They did the same thing in the Tennessee game."), and solutions to it may seem obvious ("We should have switched to a running game."). The **hindsight bias** is motivated more by cognitive factors related to the ability to construct causal explanations for events than by motivational factors such as the desire to appear correct in retrospect (Christensen-Szalanski & Willham, 1991).

A meta-analysis of 122 studies (Christensen-Szalanski & Willham, 1991) indicated that hindsight bias is modest but reliable, stronger for events that happened than for events that didn't happen. The hindsight bias reduces when people are experienced in the domain under investigation (Christensen-Szalanski & Willham, 1991). However, people of all ages show the bias, 3–5 year olds because they substitute the correct answer for their own, and elderly people because they forget their own answer and recall one closer to the actual answer (Bernstein, Erdfelder, Meltzoff, Peria, & Loftus, 2011; Figure 7.5).

What ought we to learn from the past? Rarely are the lessons of history clear because inevitably they are tinged with the advantage of hindsight. Participants in events do not know the full import of those events before they happen ("Dear Diary, The Hundred Years' War started today," Fischer, 1970, cited in Fischhoff, 1980, p. 84). Because it is hard to estimate what should have been foreseen and still harder to assess the role of environmental and chance factors in producing outcomes that already occurred, what should actually be learned from history is often unclear.

In short, we are creatures of the present, trapped inferentially by what we already know. As in the case of other inference tasks, our methods of assessment can be driven by a priori or easily constructed theories rather than by objective data. Finally, the answers themselves, what we should be learning from the past, are indeterminate. Perhaps a better maxim than that which opened this section might be one of Fischhoff's own: "While the past entertains, enables, and expands quite readily, it enlightens only with delicate coaxing" (1980, p. 80).

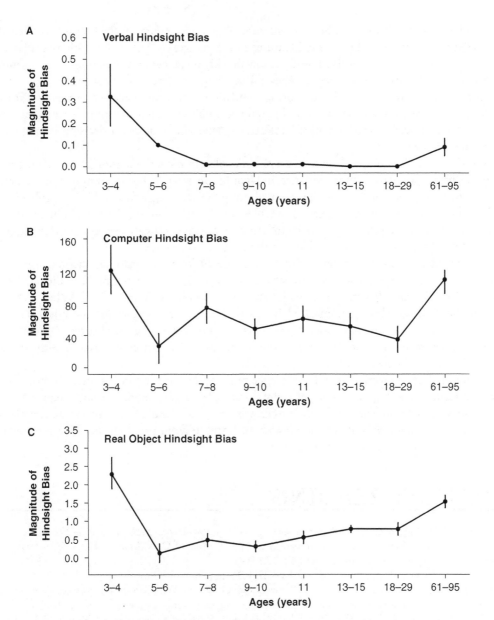

Figure 7.5 Hindsight bias as a function of age

Source: Bernstein, Erdfelder, Meltzoff, Peria, & Loftus (2011)

Summary

Research on judgment under uncertainty has revealed the importance of heuristic strategies that people adopt for making inferences rapidly. One such heuristic is representativeness: The perceiver decides how likely it is that an object is a member of some category on the basis of whether the object's features resemble the essential features of the category. Another heuristic is availability, which estimates frequency or likelihood by how quickly instances or associations come to mind. The simulation heuristic uses mental rehearsal of events to determine what outcome is likely, given a set of circumstances. The anchoring heuristic enables the perceiver to use an already-existing reference point and adjust from that reference point to reach an estimate to answer some new problem. Decision framing affects inferences, especially whether a decision is framed in terms of gains or losses.

Other shortcuts go beyond these heuristics. People often overlook good base-rate information describing population characteristics, in favor of less reliable, but seemingly more relevant, case history or anecdote. People are particularly poor at using and combining probabilistic information, often manifesting great confidence in the truth of unlikely events. When preexisting expectations or theories guide social inference, a positive test case strategy is often adopted that selectively looks for instances that test the expected inference.

Some sources of error affect our ability to combine information into a judgment. Covariation, the estimate of the degree of association between two events, concatenates many of the previously described skills (e.g., detecting relevancy, sampling, combining information). When data are already collected and clearly summarized, instructions are clear, relevance to the statistical model is clear, and no a priori theory about degree of covariation exists, the social perceiver does fairly well at estimating covariation. However, in the absence of these factors, covariation estimates are heavily biased by prior expectations.

Temporal factors clearly guide the inference process, such as the fact that present rewards are typically valued more highly than larger, more distant rewards. In addition, abstract representative features govern decisions made for the future, whereas consideration of concrete details plays a stronger role in judgments about the present. In learning from past behavior or errors, people usually overestimate what could have been foreseen.

FURTHER READING

Crocker, J. (1981). Judgment of covariation by social perceivers. *Psychological Bulletin, 90*, 272–292.
Dunning, D. (2012). Judgment and decision-making. In S. T. Fiske & C. N. Macrae (Eds.), *Sage handbook of social cognition* (pp. 251–272). Thousand Oaks, CA: Sage.
Kahneman, D. (2011). *Thinking, fast and slow.* New York: Farrar, Straus & Giroux.
Nordgren, L. F., McDonnell, M.-H. M., & Loewenstein, G. (2011). What constitutes torture? Psychological impediments to an objective evaluation of enhanced interrogation tactics. *Psychological Science, 22(5)*, 689–694.
Shapira, O., Liberman, N., Trope, Y., & Rim, S. Y. (2012). Levels of mental construal. In S. T. Fiske & C. N. Macrae (Eds.), *Sage handbook of social cognition* (pp. 229–250). Thousand Oaks, CA: Sage.
Tversky, A., & Kahneman, D. (1974). Judgment under uncertainty: Heuristics and biases. *Science, 185*, 1124–1131.

Accuracy and Efficiency in Social Inference

8

- Why is Rationality Assumed?
- When Do Social Inferences Produce Wrong Answers?
- Errors and Biases as Consequential: Improving the Inference Process
- Errors and Biases as Incidental: Perhaps They Don't Matter?
- Are Rapid Judgments Sometimes Better than Thoughtfully Considered Ones?
- Neuroeconomics: Back to the Future?

The idea that human inferential processes are typically conscious, rational, thorough, logical, and accurate was widely held early in social cognition research. This belief continues to a degree in some of the behavioral sciences, despite considerable evidence that this assumption is incorrect. This chapter addresses why the assumption is so resilient, when social inferences are most likely wrong, whether those errors and biases are consequential or not, whether rapid judgments sometimes outperform thoughtful ones, and insights from neuroeconomics.

WHY IS RATIONALITY ASSUMED?

Why was the assumption of rationality such a cornerstone of social cognition research? One reason is that research on inference generally assumes either implicitly or explicitly that inferences are goal directed; that is, they are made to achieve some purpose. A person may need to make a decision, choose among several options, or need to understand a situation before acting on it. If goals dominate the inference process, then clearly some ways of reaching a goal are better than others because they are more thorough and less error-prone. Accordingly, the social perceiver, it would seem, should use them.

Another reason for assuming rationality is more pragmatic. To understand the strategies used by the social perceiver, it is helpful to have a reference point for comparison. Normative models – that is, the optimal ways to use information to reach inferences – provide such reference points.

Even when researchers are well aware that social inference does not correspond to normative models, the comparison of naive inference against normative models can be revealing with regard to the strategies typically used to make social inferences. Normative models for making judgments and choices are known collectively as behavioral decision theory, and it is against the principles of behavioral decision theory that social inferences have typically been compared (e.g., Dunning, 2012; Einhorn & Hogarth, 1981; Hastie & Dawes, 2001).

A primary model against which human inference has been evaluated is expected utility (EU) theory, described in Chapter 7. Other normative models against which social inference is often compared include statistical knowledge, such as the computation of correlation or the law of large numbers (i.e., large samples are more reliable than small ones). We will refer to these in the sections that follow. A larger question, though, is whether normative theories provide descriptive benefit for understanding human inferential processes.

Chapter 7 reviewed social inference as compared against normative models, which revealed that inferential strategies often do not match the criteria dictated by normative theories. One possible conclusion from these comparisons is that our heuristics and shortcuts do not serve us very well. The evidence suggests that, like the proverbial adolescent in his first amorous forays, we may be fast, but we aren't very good. But this conclusion could be misleading.

Some departures from normative models of inference may be understood as meeting alternative goals. Rather than being motivated by accuracy, for example, the social perceiver may draw inferences that are personally motivating or rewarding, as will be seen later in this chapter and as noted in research on the self (Chapter 5). Thus, among other implications, affective considerations clearly guide social inference processes.

Another reason social inference often fails to match normative models is that the social perceiver operates not only under accuracy pressures but also under efficiency pressures, making inferences quickly in a rapidly changing environment with multiple demands. As such, many inferential tasks are solved with reference to prior expectations or theories rather than by means of an exhaustive consideration of the data at hand. Although purchasing the ingredients for a dinner party for one's employer may lead one to devote considerable thought to the purchase of each item, one's typical grocery shopping may be guided by the idea that "cheaper is better" in order to choose quickly from an array of goods. Given the need to process large amounts of information quickly, people's information-processing strategies may lean toward efficiency rather than thoroughness. The criterion of efficiency is not systematically incorporated into normative models of inference, and normative models may not reflect some of the most important pressures that typically operate on the social perceiver.

One reason inference processes often depart from normative models stems from capacity limitations on short-term memory. That is, the ability to process information online is constrained, as Chapter 4 noted. At a minimum, the inference process is often marked by a need to use strategies that move information along quickly though not always thoroughly. The label "cognitive miser" was developed to explain the necessary stinginess with which attention and processing time are often allocated to stimuli in the real world (S. E. Taylor, 1981b). Long-term storage in memory, however, is quite cheap, a point easily illustrated by thinking over all the songs you know or the people you can identify by sight. The advantage of so much storage space is that prior information, beliefs, and inferences can be stored as knowledge structures. They are then accessible when new inferences must be drawn. With limited online capacity and a large amount of stored knowledge, how do these factors affect social inference?

Long-term memory is the source of expectations and theories, and, as seen, social inference is heavily theory driven. Using a priori theories is likely to be an effective strategy for forming judgments and making decisions inasmuch as it represents the impact of past learning on subsequent information processing. It is efficient and effective to use our stored representations for similar situations, events, and people to interpret new and similar situations, events, and people. As such, departures from normative models of inference will tend to stray on the side of supporting already-held expectations or hypotheses and against detecting sources of bias or error in data. A second consequence that follows from this insight is that the inference process is often conservative, avoiding new or counterintuitive beliefs.

Related to the bias in favor of prior theories and conservative inferences is a tendency to look primarily for evidence that supports preexisting expectations rather than to consider the full array of available evidence. As noted earlier, this preference for cases that test the predominant expectation underlies a number of the departures that intuitive inference demonstrates when compared against normative models. All these characteristics predict the contexts in which social perceivers most often go astray.

WHEN DO SOCIAL INFERENCES PRODUCE WRONG ANSWERS?

Because heuristics are rules of thumb rather than normative models of inference, there are predictable circumstances in which the social perceiver's inferences fall short. This section reviews some of those conditions. As suggested, the heuristic processes employed by the social perceiver typically use preexisting theories or hunches to guide considering and interpreting information. In cases without an a priori theory, the social perceiver may use data encountered early in the inference process to suggest a theory and, from then on, use theory-guided inferential strategies. To put it simply, the social perceiver is often biased to see what he or she expects to see (Figure 8.1).

Gathering Information

Even the smallest inference or judgment begins with the process of deciding what information is relevant and sampling the information available. According to normative models, the social perceiver should take in all relevant information, but in fact efficiency pressures often preclude such thoroughness. This leads to a reliable shortcut in the form of gathering information in accordance with preexisting theories.

Selecting data according to preexistent expectations or theories is perfectly appropriate under many circumstances (see Nisbett & Ross, 1980). Only a bad physician would started from scratch

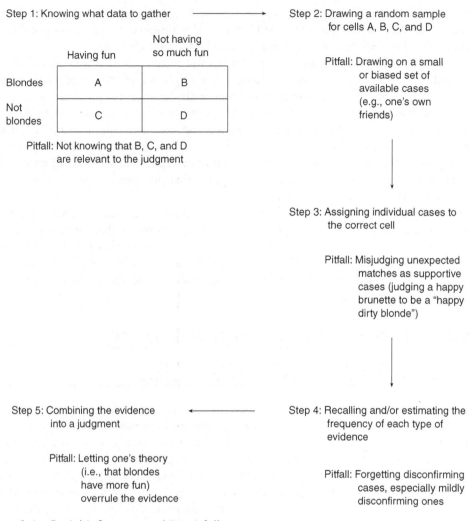

Figure 8.1   Social inference and its pitfalls

with each new medical case; letting the interpretation of symptoms be guided by the frequency of a particular illness, characteristics of the patient, knowledge of what illnesses are going around, and the like is a superior strategy. A pudgy adolescent girl with occasional fainting spells could have a brain tumor, but it is more likely that she is dieting and has not eaten enough.

Nonetheless, in many circumstances, characterizing information on the basis of preexistent theories is unwise. Three such conditions are (Nisbett & Ross, 1980): first, if the theory itself is faulty or suspect. For example, if the physician concludes that the fainting adolescent is possessed by demons, her parents might at least want a second opinion. Second, if an individual character-izes data on the basis of a theory but believes his or her inferences are objectively based on raw data, problems can result. The physician who sends the girl home after a cursory examination with instructions to eat a big dinner may well have ignored other less likely causes of fainting, such as diabetes or epilepsy, but the physician may believe that the examination was thorough. Third, theory-guided inferences create problems when the theory overrules consideration of the data altogether. The doctor who dismisses the adolescent as an overzealous dieter prior to examining her would be guilty of this error, as well as of gross negligence.

Letting theories guide sampling with respect to an inference often leads to considering too little information. If the social perceiver discovers early that the preliminary evidence considered is consistent with the theory guiding the sampling of that data, then further sampling is likely to be aborted. But the perceiver may fail to appreciate the fact that the theory guided consideration of data in the first place, and that these data were then used to justify greater confidence in the theory.

Sampling Information

Once the social perceiver has decided what information is relevant to an inference, a task that can be biased by preexisting theories, the data must be sampled. For example, if you want to know if the students in your class enjoy the course, you must decide whom to ask and how many. When people characterize information from samples provided, their accuracy in estimating frequencies, proportions, or averages is quite good so long as no prior theories or expectations influence such estimates. Thus, if you had students' course evaluations, you could presumably estimate their average evaluation quite easily. However, when prior theories or expectations do exist, describing data can be influenced by a priori theory or by particular characteristics of the sample (Nisbett & Ross, 1980).

When a sample is not already available, the process of sampling and drawing inferences from samples presents potential pitfalls. To begin, sample estimates can be thrown off by extreme examples within the sample. In one study (Rothbart, Fulero, Jensen, Howard, & Birrell, 1978), participants learned about members of two groups, including the fact that some of the members had committed crimes. For one sample, only moderate crimes appeared; in the other sample, a few examples of particularly heinous crimes were included. Although the actual frequency of committing crimes was the same in the two groups, participants appear to have employed an anchoring-and-adjustment heuristic and misremembered that more individuals committed crimes in the second group, presumably because the extreme examples had prompted a strong association between that group and crime. This also fits illusory correlations due to paired distinctiveness.

In drawing inferences from samples, the social perceiver often attends inadequately to sample size. Small samples produce poor estimates of a population's characteristics, whereas larger samples are more reliable. This principle is called the **law of large numbers**. In apparent violation, however, people often overgeneralize from a small unrepresentative sample (Nisbett & Ross, 1980; Tversky & Kahneman, 1974). For example, on witnessing a single instance of another person's behavior, the social perceiver will often make confident predictions about that person's behavior in the future. In this context, a friend of the authors who had spent virtually all of his early years living in Manhattan revealed that, until he was 25 years old, he believed Queens was nothing more than a burial ground for the New York City area. For that entire time, his sole ventures into Queens were to Kennedy or La Guardia airports, trips that afford a view of acres and acres of cemeteries. Presumably, a better sampling of the streets of Queens would have revealed more of its riches.

People do have some intuitive appreciation of the implications of the law of large numbers, but not for all its implications (Kunda & Nisbett, 1986). The social perceiver shows a certain asymmetry in believing that one can use an aggregate to predict a single event with more confidence than one can use a single event to predict the aggregate. Thus, for example, people believe that a score on the full form of an intelligence test better predicts a score on a short form of the test, relative to the short-test score predicting a score on the full test (Kahneman, 2011; Kahneman & Tversky, 1973). These perceptions are mistaken because predicting the aggregate (full test) from a single event (short form) is identical to predicting a single event from the aggregate. This effect seems to occur because people's intuition leads them to believe that increasing the size of the predictor sample of events increases predictability, whereas increasing the size of the predicted sample does not (Kunda & Nisbett, 1988; see also Kunda & Nisbett, 1986).

In addition to sample size, people sometimes attend insufficiently to biases in samples. When gathering one's own sample, an individual may ask a few friends or acquaintances their opinions, forgetting that a sample of one's friends is scarcely random. Usually, one picks friends or acquaintances precisely because they are similar on at least some dimensions, and hence, their opinions are likely to be at least somewhat similar to one's own.

Even given information about a sample's typicality, people sometimes fail to use it. In one study (Hamill, Wilson, & Nisbett, 1980), participants viewed a videotaped interview with a prison guard described as either typical of most guards or atypical of most guards, or no typicality information was provided. In the tape, the guard appeared as a compassionate, concerned individual or as an inhumane, macho, cruel one. Participants later answered questions about the criminal justice system, including questions about prison guards. Even though participants remembered the initial typicality information, those exposed to the interview with the humane guard were more favorable in their attitude toward prison guards than were participants who saw the interview with the inhumane guard.

Rules of sampling and characteristics of samples are not the only kinds of information that people underuse when they attempt to draw inferences. Other characteristics bear on the relevance of data to inferences and likewise elude the social perceiver's cognitive processing. An example is the regression effect.

Regression to the Mean

Regression relates to prediction from probabilistic information, and most people understand it poorly. **Regression to the mean** refers to the fact that extreme events will, on average, be less extreme when reassessed at a different point in time. The message of regression is that when one must make an inference based on limited and unreliable information, one will be most accurate if one ventures a prediction that is less extreme than the initial information. A restaurant that is fabulous one night will probably not be quite as good when you drag your friends there, having raved endlessly about its cuisine. Experience notwithstanding, experimental evidence, as well as common observation, consistently shows that when people encounter extreme values of predictor information, they draw extreme inferences about subsequent behavior (Jennings, Amabile, & Ross, 1982) (Table 8.1).

People can sometimes learn inappropriate rules when they fail to appreciate regression. In one study (Schaffner, 1985), undergraduates used praise and reprimand to improve the promptness of two schoolboys whose arrival times at school were, in fact, randomly determined. Participants "found" a strong "deterioration" in promptness following reward and "improvements" in promptness following reprimand, a pattern that would be expected on the basis of regression. Nonetheless, although the participants believed their praise was effective in modifying the students' behavior, they perceived their reprimands had been more effective because tardiness is farther from the mean and will randomly regress back toward promptness.

Table 8.1 Regression toward the mean: Taking the GREs twice

TIME 1			
Given four students (A, B, C, D) of equal ability, all should score 600 on the Graduate Record Examination:	But random factors enter in, raising or lowering their scores:	Actual scores at Time 1:	Conclusion:
A 600	−10 (slept poorly)	590	B and D look strong;
B 600	+15 (studied examples similar to test items)	615	A and C look weaker
C 600	−17 (gum chewer was a distraction)	583	
D 600	+12 (got a good seat in the test room)	612	
TIME 2			
Given same four students taking test again:	Different random factors are present, raising or lowering scores:	Actual score at Time 2:	Conclusion:
A 600	+12 (had a good breakfast)	612	A and C look stronger and
B 600	−10 (sat near the window)	590	B and D look weaker than at Time 1
C 600	−4 (had a slight cold)	596	
D 600	+5 (was "on" that day)	605	

In rare instances, regression, or at least something like it, is appreciated. For example, the response of literary critics to an author's blockbusting first novel is often to hedge their bets. Praise may be glowing, but often couched in cautionary language that urges readers to wait for the next product; previous experience dictates that second novels are often less stellar than first ones. However, one might well ask if an appreciation of regression underlies these conservative predictions. Although rarely it may, more often some theory, and not random error, is credited with the poor second showing. Authors are said to "burn themselves out" on the first novel or to have "said it all," leaving no material for a second try. Others are thought to be immobilized or blocked by their first success. Although some of these points may, in fact, be true, regression alone is fully capable of accounting for the second-book effect. Yet how often has one read a review of a mediocre second novel in which the critic pointed out that the inferior second product could have been predicted by chance?

People's insufficiently regressive judgments may represent errors or the misapplication of a normally effective judgmental strategy. When the world is stable, people's predictions about events should show an appreciation for regression. But when the world is changing, extreme predictions generated from relevant information may be appropriate. Extreme responses can occur at random, or they can signal that there has been a change in the underlying data. Consider, as an example, a manufacturing company that has posted large losses. If those losses are seen as a random perturbation in an otherwise reasonable record, then one should predict that profits will soon regress to their mean level. However, if the large losses are seen as indicating that manufacturing is moving offshore, even more extreme predictions may be justified. Thus, people may learn from their environment that extreme fluctuations often signal changing conditions, and thus their failure to be regressive may be adaptive in a changing environment. Such sensitivity to change may, however, lead them to be insufficiently regressive when random extreme values occur in stable environments.

The Dilution Effect

Suppose we tell you we have a friend, Judith, who is 35, unmarried, and has lived with the same female roommate for five years, with whom she has just bought a house. You may conclude that she is probably a lesbian. However, if we also tell you that she is a paralegal, takes fiction writing courses in night school, drives a blue Toyota, and is close to her brothers and sisters, you may wonder if she is a lesbian, but not immediately assume that she is. Why? The first four bits of information can be considered diagnostic with respect to Judith being a lesbian or not, because unmarried women with constant female companions are often thought to be so. However, the extra information about her job, car, and leisure activities diluted that diagnostic information with a lot of nondiagnostic information: information that would not lead you to conclude that she is a lesbian or straight, but simply neutral. In short, we reduced her similarity to the stereotype of lesbianism by deepening her characterization and making her a person, so your confidence in drawing an extreme inference about her may thereby lessen. When diagnostic information is weakened by nondiagnostic information, inferences are less extreme, a phenomenon known as the **dilution effect** (Nisbett, Zukier, & Lemley, 1981).

Several circumstances qualify the dilution effect. It does not hold when prior theories about the meaning of the initial information are weak (S. T. Fiske & Neuberg, 1990; Higgins & Bargh, 1987; Ruble & Stangor, 1986). The dilution effect also appears to apply only when new nondiagnostic information is typical and not extreme (G. Zukier & Jennings, 1983–84).

Psychologists have developed training techniques to reduce judgmental errors, and ironically, at least some of these efforts actually increase the dilution effect. For example, one way to induce people to process social information more complexly and reduce the likelihood of theory-guided inferences and overconfident judgments is **accountability**: a need to justify one's judgments to others. In one study (Tetlock & Boettger, 1989), participants who expected to have to justify their predictions in a judgment task diluted their predictions more in response to nondiagnostic information than did subjects who were not accountable for their inferences. Being accountable for their judgments induces people to use a wider range of information in making those judgments, but it does not necessarily make them more discriminating judges of how useful the information is.

ERRORS AND BIASES AS CONSEQUENTIAL: IMPROVING THE INFERENCE PROCESS

Overall, should we regard errors and biases in the social inference process with alarm, bemusement, or respect? At least three perspectives address this puzzle (Table 8.2). The first argues that the errors and biases identified in the social inference process have considerable support and often lead to important errors in judgments and policy, and, consequently, some efforts to improve the inference process must be undertaken. The second perspective maintains that errors and biases in the inference process are more apparent than real, and that in the real world people actually perform inferential tasks quite well. Moreover, although social perceivers are prone to certain systematic errors and biases in their inferences, conditions in the real world safeguard and check on the inference process, so that some of these biases become inconsequential or self-correcting. A third, more recent, perspective argues that in some cases

Table 8.2 Three perspectives on the consequences of inferential error and biases

Perspective	Rationale	Implication
Consequential, real	Quantities of research evidence	Intervene, educate, check
Laboratory byproduct	People's daily functioning	Trust context, social checks-and-balances
Heuristics superior	Evidence for adaptability	Not necessarily over-analyze

rapidly formed judgments based on heuristics may be superior to those based on more careful contemplation. We consider the consequential perspective in this section, and then the other two perspectives each in turn.

Under some circumstances, erroneous inferential strategies do have severe consequences. The contribution of inferential errors to developing and maintaining pejorative stereotypes is one striking example (Chapters 11–12). Group decision making shows marked biases in gathering information and perceiving one's own and another's position, indicating that severe errors can mark naturally occurring conditions of social inference (Janis, 1989). Judgmental errors have unnerving implications for fields as diverse as politics (Jervis, 1976), clinical decision making (Turk & Salovey, 1986), and education (Simon, 1980). In short, biases in inferential processes often matter, and, accordingly, we need methods for detecting and correcting biased inferences.

Were one to undertake to improve the social perceiver's inferential process, the effort would likely begin by alerting perceivers to the problem and instructing them to attend to inferential errors in the future. Such instructions presuppose that people have at least some awareness of the inferential processes they are using and that they can draw on that awareness at will.

In a controversial paper, Nisbett and Wilson (1977b) maintained that people have little or no **introspective access** to their cognitive processes. A substantial amount of anecdotal evidence from psychological studies indicates that many, if not most, experimental participants have no idea of the forces in the experiment influencing their behavior. Taking these observations as their point of departure, Nisbett and Wilson conducted a series of experiments (Nisbett & Wilson, 1977a; T. D. Wilson & Nisbett, 1978; T. D. Wilson, 2011) systematically manipulating factors that influenced participants' behavior and then asking participants to report what factors led them to behave as they did. For example, in one study, billed as an investigation of consumer preferences, participants inspected four nightgowns displayed on a table and indicated which one they would choose. In fact, a strong serial position effect determines these kinds of tasks, such that people typically prefer the right-most item. (Why this position preference exists is not fully known.) Participants in the experiment showed this serial position effect, but when asked why they made their particular choice, they offered explanations that centered on qualities of the chosen garment itself. When told serial position might have influenced their decision, participants expressed considerable skepticism.

Divergences between people's beliefs about the causes of their behavior ("I like pink, and that nightgown was pink") and the actual causes of their behaviors (the pink nightgown was on the right) stem largely from the oft-noted impact of theories on judgment: We believe we do things for reasons that are known to us and are often unaware of or disbelieving about things that have influenced our behavior if they don't fit our theories.

One should not infer from the previous discussion that people are always wrong in their theories of what causes their behavior. Indeed, on many if not most occasions, people are right. If someone asks you why you are crying, and you say, "Because my boyfriend left me," you are probably correct in your analysis. The fact that a theory is correct, however, or that it correctly applies to a particular case, does not imply that its holder has special access to his or her cognitive processes (T. D. Wilson, Hull, & Johnson, 1981). Social cognition research tests the validity of informal theories, fueling effective interventions, for example by editing those personal stories (T. D. Wilson, 2011).

Should We Turn Inference over to Computers?

People's inferential shortcomings are particularly well illustrated when matched against a computer given the same information. The computer always does as well or better (Dawes, Faust, & Meehl, 1989). How can one demonstrate this fact? First, find a judgment task in which roughly the same kinds of information are contained in every case; second, use a decision rule regarding how that information is to be combined to reach a decision for each case. Such judgment tasks are relatively common. A business must replenish stock after considering demand and current inventory. Doctors must diagnose and treat patients given clinical observations, symptoms, and test results. Professors admit or reject students from graduate school on the basis of test scores, grade point average, past work, and letters of recommendation.

A normatively appropriate way of completing such a task is to examine each case (e.g., student), take each of the bits of information relevant to the judgment (e.g., GPA, letters of recommendation, GRE scores), multiply each bit by its weight (e.g., count GREs twice as much as GPA and GPA half again as much as letters of recommendation), add it up for a total case score, and compare the case's score against other case scores to pick the best ones. This process employs a **linear model**, so-called because the total impression is an additive combination of the available information. This task can be efficiently and effectively completed by a properly programmed computer. Various nonlinear combinations can also reliably make decisions: "Weigh GPA twice as heavily as letters of recommendation, unless GPA is lower than 3.0, in which case weigh it evenly with letters." The nonlinear nature of these rules makes them no less readily programmable for a computer, and the computer is more reliable than the human decision maker.

Unfortunately, human decision makers often have an exaggerated view of their ability to accomplish inferential tasks, so much so that the idea of letting it fall to a computer meets with strenuous objections. Clinical intuition, people feel, would be sacrificed to a rigid numerical formula, and unusual instances or special cases would slip through the cracks. Anyone who has ever sat on an admissions or membership committee and seen clinical intuition in operation probably knows that the process is often random and inconsistent, full of blatant stereotyping, unwarranted favoritism, and irrational dislikes.

Dawes (1980) presents a particularly entertaining account of the process at several leading universities. A slang peculiar to the admissions process quickly develops. "Pinocchios" are applicants with high ratings from letter writers on all but one characteristic, such as maturity or independence; hence their profile has a long jag or nose. They are to be avoided because anyone who attracts enough attention to get that low a rating on some attribute must be really bad. "Jock essays" are too short; "geos" are students who would add geographic diversity, such as a Hawaiian applying to an East Coast school. And everyone seems to be looking for the proverbial "neat small-town kid." Often, comparisons are made to apparently similar students with whom one has already had experience. "Aha. Another Smedley. He was smart but a drudge. Not a creative bone in his body" (Abelson, 1981). Frequently, these analogies are drawn on the basis of minimal similarity, such as having a record that excels in everything except physical education.

Despite such problems, this process is loudly defended. Its advocates maintain that, generally, decision makers do use the appropriate algorithm and that departures from the model pick up the late bloomer or the prodigal student returning to the fold. However, collectively made decisions have unique types of errors (e.g., Janis, 1972; Shaw, 1971), and trained statisticians and other experts are sometimes just as vulnerable to inferential errors as laypersons (Kahneman & Tversky, 1973; Tversky & Kahneman, 1974). Table 8.3 presents a hypothetical account of the process employed for two fictitious graduate school admissions cases, given a linear decision rule, a nonlinear decision rule, and an intuitive human decision maker (Burgess, 1941; L. R. Goldberg, 1968, 1970).

Two extensive analyses of studies pitted the clinical judge against the computer or other mechanical aids (Meehl, 1954; J. Sawyer, 1966); both yielded the same conclusion: Computers or other mechanical aids always do as well or better than clinical judges. What does the computer do, and why does it do it so well? The computer merely does more consistently what human judges believe they do. It uses the criteria established by people, but it uses them consistently, weighs them reliably, combines the information accurately, and makes a judgment.

What does the human decision maker do wrong? People usually believe they are using more cues and making more complex judgments than they actually are. One professor, upon reading this research, correlated her own rankings of prospective students with several admissions criteria

Table 8.3   Comparison of the linear model, the nonlinear model, and a human decision maker: Will Stinch and Crabble be admitted to graduate school?

	Case A: Gerald Stinch	Case B: Amanda Crabble
	GRE: 650 Verbal, 710 Math GPA: 3.8 Letters of recommendation: Hard-working, diligent	GRE: 620 Verbal, 590 Math GPA: 2.9 Letters of recommendation A bit of a dreamer, hasn't come into her own
Linear model (as applied by computer)	Score = 2 (GREs) + 1 (GPA) +.5 (Letter of recommendation)	
Decision:	Admit Stinch.	Reject Crabble.
Nonlinear model (as applied by computer)	Score = 2 (GREs) + 1 (GPA) +.5 (Letter of recommendation), unless GRE is less than 3.0, in which case score is 3 (GREs) + .5 (GPA) + 1 (Letter of recommendation)	
Decision:	Admit Stinch.	Reject Crabble.
Human decision maker	Aha. Another Smedley. Not a creative bone in his body.	Aha. Another Woodley? She was a great theoretician – got off to a slow start, though.
Decision:	Reject Stinch.	Admit Crabble.
Probable outcome given reliable and valid admissions criteria	Stinch will do well.	Crabble will do less well.

and found, to her embarrassment and surprise, that GRE scores were virtually the sole basis of her decisions. Not only do people not use as many cues as they think they are using, they also do not weigh those cues the way they believe they do. Although support for clinical judgment lingers, clearly for decisions that use a constant decision rule, the computer outperforms the person. Clinical judges, of course, must pick the variables that go into the decision. However, when integrating the information to reach a decision, the person is often best left out of the process (Dawes et al., 1989).

Teaching Reasoning

Turning problems over to a computer is not always realistic. A second potential way of improving the inference process generally is through education, by teaching reasoning in a formal educational curriculum. Nisbett and his colleagues explored the value of teaching reasoning to see if and when learning rules applicable to specific problems generalizes to a wider array of problems. In one study (Fong, Krantz, & Nisbett, 1986), some participants trained in the law of large numbers, others were shown how to apply the law for several concrete example problems, a third group received both types of training, and a fourth group received no training. People receiving either rule-training or training by examples were more likely to reason statistically than those who received no training; the best statistical reasoning was demonstrated by people who received training in both the abstract rule and the examples. More importantly, using the learning-through-examples approach (**guided induction**) generalized the training effects: Participants improved as much in domains in which they were not explicitly trained as in domains in which they were trained. People clearly possess abstract inferential rules, and they can be trained through guided induction to expand upon and improve their use of these rules in a variety of settings (Cheng, Holyoak, Nisbett, & Oliver, 1986).

Consistent with these conclusions, graduate training also markedly affects reasoning strategies (Lehman, Lempert, & Nisbett, 1988): Graduate students in four disciplines – psychology, medicine, law, and chemistry – both initially upon entrance to graduate school and two years later, were compared to see if graduate training had any impact on a variety of statistical and methodological reasoning tasks (Table 8.4). Consistently, psychology students and, to a lesser extent, students in medicine improved their reasoning, presumably because both specialties involve interpreting probabilistic data. However, for students in chemistry, a science that deals almost exclusively with deterministic causes, no improvement was expected or found. Legal training similarly had minimal impact on changes in statistical and methodological reasoning, with the exception of conditional problems, which the law encounters frequently.

The conclusion, then, is that people are capable of using abstract statistical concepts, and that they do employ them spontaneously but not always entirely correctly in relevant situations. Both formal training and training by example improve the ability to see the applicability of statistical principles to a broad range of situations and make appropriate use of them. In other circumstances, though, a computer might do a better job.

Table 8.4   Statistical, methodological, and conditional reasoning in everyday life

Statistical reasoning – Everyday life

After the first two weeks of the major league baseball season, newspapers begin to print the top ten batting averages. Typically, after two weeks, the leading batter has an average of about .450. Yet no batter in major league history has ever averaged .450 at the end of a season. Why do you think this is?

1. A player's high average at the beginning of the season may be just a lucky fluke.
2. A batter who has such a hot streak at the beginning of the season is under a lot of stress to maintain his performance record. Such stress adversely affects his playing.
3. Pitchers tend to get better over the course of the season, as they get more in shape. As pitchers improve, they are more likely to strike out batters, so batters' averages go down.
4. When a batter is known to be hitting for a high average, pitchers bear down more when they pitch to him.
5. When a batter is known to be hitting for a high average, he stops getting good pitches to hit. Instead, pitchers "play the corners" of the plate because they don't mind walking him.

Methodological reasoning – Everyday life

The city of Middleopolis has had an unpopular police chief for a year and a half. He is a political appointee who is a crony of the mayor, and he had little previous experience in police administration when he was appointed. The mayor has recently defended the chief in public, announcing that in the time since he took office, crime rates decreased by 12%. Which of the following pieces of evidence would most deflate the mayor's claim that his chief is competent?

1. The crime rates of the two cities closest to Middleopolis in location and size have decreased by 18% in the same period.
2. An independent survey of the citizens of Middleopolis shows that 40% more crime is reported by respondents in the survey than is reported in police records.
3. Common sense indicates that there is little a police chief can do to lower crime rates. These are for the most part due to social and economic conditions beyond the control of officials.
4. The police chief has been discovered to have business contacts with people who are known to be involved in organized crime.

Conditional reasoning – Permission schema

You are a public-health official at the international airport in Manila, capital of the Philippines. Part of your duty is to check that every arriving passenger who wishes to enter the country (rather than just change planes at the airport) has had an inoculation against cholera. Every passenger carries a health form. One side of the form indicates whether the passenger is entering or in transit, and the other side of the form lists the inoculations he or she has had in the past six months. Which of the following forms would you need to turn over to check? Indicate only those forms you would have to check to be sure.

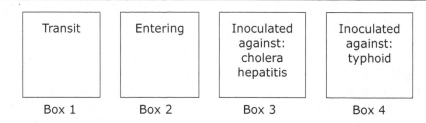

Transit	Entering	Inoculated against: cholera hepatitis	Inoculated against: typhoid
Box 1	Box 2	Box 3	Box 4

(a) Boxes 2 & 3

(b) Box 2 only

(c) Boxes 2, 3, & 4

(d) Boxes 2 & 4

(e) Box 3 only

Correct answers to the problems are (1), (1), and (d).

Source: Lehman, Lempert, & Nisbett (1988)

ERRORS AND BIASES AS INCIDENTAL: PERHAPS THEY DON'T MATTER?

A second perspective on errors and biases in social inference maintains that these errors may be more apparent than real. This perspective (Funder, 1987, 1995; McArthur & Baron, 1983; Swann, 1984) makes two main points. First, experimental research documenting errors and biases does not create the conditions under which people normally make judgments in the real world and, therefore, may make people look worse at inference tasks than they really are. According to this position, social perceivers' naive inference strategies are adapted to the ecological and inter-personal conditions under which inferences must be drawn; experimental studies that create conditions conducive to use of the normative model rarely exist in real-world judgment and decision-making situations.

Second, judgment tasks used in experimental tests are often stacked against intuitive strategies of inference (Fischhoff, 1982; Funder, 1987; Kahneman & Tversky, 1982; McArthur & Baron, 1983). For example, the tasks may be unfamiliar or unfair (e.g., being expected to calculate a cor-relation in one's head), or participants may misconstrued them. Or information may appear in a format conducive to using the normative model and not contain the kind of contextual detail that would facilitate using an effective intuitive strategy. This methodological bias in experimental evidence may portray our inferential abilities more negatively than we deserve.

A parallel point is that normative models, as a result, may be poor standards for evaluating intuitive inferences. Conditions that make it possible to use a normative model are rarely present in the real world. Often, information is neither reliable, unbiased, nor complete. Even if it is, information may not appear in a clear or usable fashion. Sometimes information is not available, and even if it were, using the normative model might be prohibitively time consuming.

Another problem with applying the normative model to most daily inferential situations is that normative models ignore the content and, thus, the context of a decision in favor of its formal structure. For example, deciding which of three brands of eggs to buy and deciding which of three people to marry could be treated as equivalent decisions under the normative model if the information about the three options varied from each other in the same systematic ways. Yet the intuitive processes used for the two decisions would probably vary, and rightfully so. The normative model generates inferential standards given a fixed decision environment (i.e., all else being equal). But decisions are made and inferences are drawn in dynamic environments, so predictions in static environments may be inappropriate for changing conditions.

Also, some circumstances suggest using a different model than a normative one. Take the example of a fledgling job candidate who at lunch spills his water, sends his lamb chop flying into his neighbor's lap, and rests his elbow in the butter (Nisbett, Krantz, Jepson, & Fong, 1982). He is nervous, truly, and his nervousness clearly results from situational factors, not dispositional ones. Furthermore, this is only a modest sample of his behavior, and likely a poor predictor of future behavior. Normatively, one should probably discount these incidents. But consider the alternative practical model of the people who must make the job-hiring decisions. They must select a candidate who can perform well consistently and under pressure. Wouldn't you rather have your sales made by someone who puts his butter on his roll instead of his suit? In short, statistically normative models are only one kind of model applicable to social judgments. Alternative models held by people directly involved in making those judgments may generate useful criteria that inherently conflict with the standards generated by normative models.

Moreover, assessing if and when a person's inferences are accurate is more complex than one might suppose. One can determine whether a judgment corresponds to some criterion (e.g., Hastie & Dawes, 2001); whether it is shared with others (Funder, 1987); or whether it is adaptive, pragmatic, or useful (Swann, 1984). But many social judgments possess no criterion for determining actual correctness because the judgments lack objective referents. Moreover, as we will shortly see, inferences often serve needs other than accuracy, such as protecting or enhancing the self or one's social group.

We do know that such factors as importance of a judgment and personal involvement encourage considering more information, prompt more complex judgmental strategies, and even increase accuracy under some circumstances (e.g., Harkness, DeBono, & Borgida, 1985). As noted, accountability also increases cognitive activity, generating more complex processing strategies than unaccountable ones (Tetlock & Boettger, 1989). Beyond these observations, judging whether the social perceiver is more accurate in the real world than in the experimental laboratory is difficult. Moreover, no stringent criteria define what a "natural" situation is, and many real-world situations themselves may be quite unnatural with respect to the inferential strategies that social perceivers normally use (Kruglanski, 1989).

Are Inferential Errors Inconsequential or Self-Correcting?

Some errors produced by faulty inferential processes will not matter. For example, if one's biased impressions will not affect one's future behavior, as in forming an incorrect impression of a person one meets only once, then the error will be inconsequential. In fact, little is known about the correspondence between inferences and behavior generally; if the correspondence is low, inferential errors may matter little. Biases may also matter little if they are constant over time. For example, if one regards one's boss as gruff, it may not matter that she is gruff only when she is in the boss role, if that is the only circumstance under which one interacts with her (Swann, 1984).

Inferences are not choices that, once made, commit one irrevocably to a cognitive or behavioral course. Rather, inferences may be tentative forays to be modified on the bases of the responses they evoke. Normal conversation reality-tests one's inferences, and often corrects blatantly false conclusions with far-reaching implications. For example, if the assertion that one performs one's share of the housework meets with strenuous objections from one's spouse, that opinion is likely to be modified.

Biases may matter little when decision alternatives are of near equal value. A student choosing between Princeton and Yale may make a final decision based on one friend's experience, but stereotypes and chauvinism aside, the student will receive a trivially better education at one place over the other. Finally, our biases may have little impact on our strategies. Consider the graduate admissions process. It is the rare graduate student who turns out to be a hotshot. If one accepts five students and they have average careers and rejects five students who also have average careers, then one can find little apparent fault with one's decision-making process, even if it was actually made with flawed methods. If one of the five rejected students goes on to excel, then one might identify an error in one case and wish that student had been accepted. Still, one out of ten is not a bad error rate. Obviously, this reasoning is fallacious, but it serves to underscore the fact that many of our processing errors do not yield blatantly bad results, so the processes may appear perfectly adequate.

Some intuitive strategies are relatively robust against certain errors, and in other cases one shortcoming may cancel out another (Nisbett & Ross, 1980). For example, the dilution effect can guard against the failure to appreciate regression toward the mean.

Some sources of error will correct themselves through repeated encounters. For example, if several of one's friends have recently been divorced, one's estimate of the divorce rate may be temporarily exaggerated via the availability heuristic, but assuming that one's friends do not continue to divorce indefinitely, one's estimated divorce rate should eventually come into line with objective data.

In short, although inferential tasks in the laboratory often provide a dramatic portrayal of the human propensity for error and bias, real-world errors and biases may matter less. People's heuristic strategies often approximate statistical and other normative models (Griffiths & Tenenbaum, 2006), and intuitive strategies may not always lead to the dramatic failures that some research highlights. Also, many circumstances in the world require people to be sufficiently smart but not optimally smart. Intuitive models incorporate the content of the problem to be solved. Whereas people may make quick-and-dirty choices and decisions for inconsequential matters, they may be more thorough and circumspect for important decisions. That is, intuitive strategies accommodate pragmatic concerns. Under certain conditions, faulty inferences will be corrected by subsequent evidence through conversation with others (Hirst & Echterhoff, 2012). Thus, one answer to the question "If we're so bad at judgmental tasks, how do we do as well as we do?" is that rapid approximations of normative strategies yield a good-enough way to relate to the world much of the time.

ARE RAPID JUDGMENTS SOMETIMES BETTER THAN THOUGHTFULLY CONSIDERED ONES?

Early social cognition research viewed heuristic inferences as flawed, a position that gave way to observing that, to meet efficiency pressures, sometimes rough approximations to the normative model may suffice for accuracy and be vastly superior for meeting efficiency needs. A more radical view is coming into acceptance at the present time; namely, at least under some circumstances, rapid heuristically based judgments may yield superior inferences compared to deliberative conscious efforts.

The immensely popular book, *Blink*, by Malcolm Gladwell (2005), draws on compelling examples from social psychology to make the case that, for many complex decisions or choices, the brain performs a series of rapid calculations that lead to instant and often correct assessments. For example, very knowledgeable art historians evaluating a kouros reputed to have been carved in 6th-century-BC Greece rapidly concluded that the sculpture was a fake, although none of them could articulate quite why.

Social psychologists have documented many other examples, such as the ability to infer a teacher's teaching ratings from students on the basis of a few seconds of videotaped observations of her teaching (Ambady & Rosenthal, 1993). The inferences from such **thin slices of behavior** show that our minds can integrate or extract information from complex stimuli to reach apparently complex judgments in a matter of seconds (Murphy, 2012; Nosek, Hawkins, & Frazier, 2012; Payne, 2012). In another example, strangers observing college students' rooms judged whether each room's inhabitant was talkative, thorough, reserved, and unselfish; their impressions correlated startlingly well with diagnostic instruments assessing conscientiousness, emotional stability, and openness to experience. All these judgments were made without the evaluators ever meeting the person involved (Gosling, Ko, Mannarelli, & Morris, 2002; Figure 8.2).

Not all instantaneous judgments are correct, of course, nor did *Blink* provide many guidelines for determining which ones might be and which ones are entirely off base. Research suggests a few conditions that may foster rapid and accurate inferences. When people have expertise in a domain and have seen lots of examples of something before, they are more likely to be able to

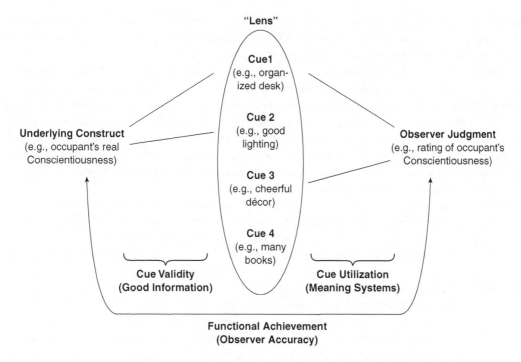

Figure 8.2 Brunswik lens model showing how observers infer conscientiousness from a "Room with a Cue"

Source: Gosling, Ko, Mannarelli, & Morris (2002)

make very rapid accurate judgments; hence, experienced curators could judge the kouros as a fake or experienced students could estimate a teacher's ratings. The abilities to integrate diverse information quickly, to use several diagnostic pieces of information simultaneously, or to pick up a particularly revealing clue may be some sources of this expertise.

Research has also looked at this issue the other way around, showing that when people actively reason about their choices or decisions, they sometimes make worse ones. For example, if one were trying to decide whether to take a particular summer job or choose a particular major, an obvious strategy might be to evaluate each of the various aspects of the decision and analyze one's evidence for the pros and cons of each alternative. Despite its apparent appeal, this strategy actually reduces the relation between inference and choice. Introspecting about the reasons one likes or dislikes some object disrupts one's impressions and reduces the influence of those impressions on subsequent decisions (T. D. Wilson & Hodges, 1992). In essence, analyzing the reasons that underlie one's inferences actually changes the inferences, at least temporarily (T. D. Wilson, Hodges, & LaFleur, 1995; T. D. Wilson & LaFleur, 1995).

The reason this happens may be that people generally don't think a lot about their inferences; when induced to do so, they focus on arbitrary aspects of the inferences, and those aspects become more salient. In doing so, they may fail to discriminate important from unimportant information or properly perceive the relevance of particular information; the result is a poorer decision quality (Tordesillas & Chaiken, 1999). Therefore, reasoning can increase inconsistency in the impact of inferences on other judgments and decisions.

In one set of studies, Dijksterhuis and colleagues (Dijksterhuis, 2004; Dijksterhuis, Bos, Nordgren, & van Baaren, 2006) concluded that engaging in thorough, conscious deliberation before making choices is not always advantageous. Simple choices, such as among oven mitts, produce better results after conscious thought, but more complex tasks, such as choosing among houses, may improve by unconscious thought. In four studies examining consumer choices in both the laboratory and the field, purchases of complex products produced more satisfaction from decisions made in the absence of attentive deliberation; simple decisions, by contrast, appeared to benefit from deliberation.

Why might complex decisions be well served by unconscious, heuristically-driven processing? In a series of studies (Dijksterhuis, 2004), participants with complex decisions had to choose from various alternatives, each with several attributes. Some participants thought about the decision for a few minutes; others were distracted for a few minutes and then made their decisions. Those who made the decision unconsciously (after the distraction) made the best decisions. Dijksterhuis concluded that when unconscious thought takes over, more clear, more polarized, and more integrated representations of choices form in memory, leading to better decisions.

Precisely because these decisions are made unconsciously, determining exactly the shortcuts or heuristic processes undertaken is impossible. Nor is it clear that complex decisions would always be improved by letting the brain unconsciously sift through alternatives with multiple features. Nonetheless, Dijksterhuis's work supports an important conclusion: The idea that rational conscious deliberation always leads to better choices and should only be jettisoned in situations with efficiency pressures is clearly flawed. Under many circumstances, people have evolved heuristics and shortcuts that serve them well in situations involving complex inference choices and decisions.

Motivated Inference

Another reason apparent errors in human inference processes may actually represent benefits, at least under some circumstances, stems from the fact that inferences serve purposes other than accuracy and efficiency. They also meet motivational needs. As we saw in Chapter 5, many of the inferences we form about our personal characteristics, the controllability and orderliness of the world, and the benign future (e.g., S. E. Taylor & Brown, 1988) reduce anxiety, meet needs for self-esteem, or generally serve our theories about how the world works. As such, sometimes we juggle the information in the world so it will come out right.

People actively construct theories concerning why positive and negative events might befall them and enhance the perceived likelihood that positive events will happen to them (Kunda, 1987, 1999). For example, upon learning that the divorce rate for first marriages is 40%, most people predict that they will not be in that 40%, but rather will remain married to their spouse for their lifetime. They convince themselves by highlighting their personal attributes that might be associated with a stable marriage and downplaying the significance of, or actively refuting information that might suggest, a vulnerability to divorce. Thus, for example, one might point to one's parents' 50-year marriage, the close family life of one's early childhood, and the fact that one's high school relationship lasted a full four years, as evidence predicting a stable marriage. The fact that one's husband has already been divorced once, a factor that predicts a second divorce, might be interpreted not only as not leading to divorce in one's own case but as a protective factor ("He does not want this marriage to fail like the last one, so he's working especially hard to keep our relationship strong"). Our ability to draw seemingly rational relationships between our own assets and good events and to argue away associations between our own attributes and negative events helps us to maintain the correlations that we want to see in the world.

Another reason that people hold blatantly false beliefs is that such beliefs may be motivating. Each day many people make a to-do list of the activities they hope and expect to accomplish that day. Such lists are invariably overly optimistic, and the person is left at the end of the day with many tasks undone, which then transfer to the next day. Normatively speaking, people's behavior should change in the direction of listing only the number of tasks they can reasonably expect to complete. Yet the overly optimistic behavior persists daily despite repeated disconfirmation (Buehler, Griffin, & Ross, 1994).

Such robust inferential biases persist probably because they succeed in getting people to accomplish more than if their assessments of their likely accomplishments were more realistic. Such biases as unrealistic optimism and an exaggerated sense of personal control, for example, fuel the desire to reach goals that might otherwise seem out of reach and help people persist when barriers seem formidable (Armor & Taylor, 1998, 2003; S. E. Taylor & Brown, 1988).

Certain robust inferential biases may persist not only because they fuel positive emotions and self-esteem but also because they minimize perceived risk. A friend once consulted with her accountant about what steps she should take to make her financial life more predictable and solid. His response was "Don't do anything, and don't go anywhere." If we recognized objectively the risks to which we are all vulnerable, this recognition might well be incapacitating. Although people often overestimate their vulnerability to low-probability risks, human inference often underestimates common risks (S. E. Taylor & Gollwitzer, 1995), and particularly underestimates cumulative risk (Knäuper, Kornik, Atkinson, Guberman, & Aydin, 2005; Figure 8.3). Some inferential biases may protect against what might otherwise be a paralyzing appreciation of risk. Because many psychologists try to get people to recognize the risks they incur – faulty health behaviors, for example – suggesting, as a potential benefit of inferential strategies, the minimization of risk might seem counterintuitive. Indeed, some risks clearly need to be recognized and dealt with, for example, the necessity of using seatbelts, condoms, and health screening tests. Inferential biases that maintain or restore positive feelings may act primarily on emotions, but to the extent that they affect behavior, they may be problematic. Recall from Chapter 5, however, that when people are feeling good about themselves and their situations (i.e., they are less threatened), they are paradoxically more receptive to the behavioral implications of personal risk-related information.

A more complete consideration of the motives that social inference serves reveals that normatively incorrect inferences may nonetheless be useful for meeting personal goals, maintaining motivation and persistence, and feeling good about oneself and one's future.

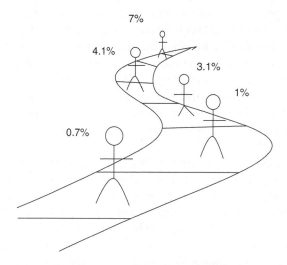

Open-minded	0—1—2—3—4—5—6—7—8—9—⑩
Understanding	0—1—2—3—4—5—6—7—8—⑨—10
Loyal	0—1—2—3—4—5—6—7—8—⑨—10
Caring	0—1—2—3—4—5—6—7—8—9—⑩
Helping partner through rough times	0—1—2—3—4—5—6—7—8—9—⑩

Figure 8.3 Estimating cumulative risk of catching an STD from a prospective sexual partner with personality ratings, a photo, and history of STD risks from past partners: People underestimate cumulative risk from an otherwise appealing partner by over-relying on risk-irrelevant information (trait ratings and a photograph not shown here)

Source: Knäuper, Kornik, Atkinson, Guberman, & Aydin (2005)

NEUROECONOMICS: BACK TO THE FUTURE?

How people make and should make judgments and decisions has not only been central to social cognition research but has also been important in cognitive psychology, economics, and neuroscience. From all these contributions, a recent cross-disciplinary endeavor has emerged that has the potential to integrate these disparate lines of research. **Neuroeconomics** brings together insights from economics, neuroscience, and psychology (Glimcher, 2003; Glimcher & Rustichini, 2004), to clarify the accuracy–efficiency tradeoff and the role of motivation in inference. Roughly, the idea is to use the expected utility (EU) model, which predominates in economics, to undertake the following: generate predictions about how inference *should* proceed and what brain regions may accordingly be implicated; integrate those insights with research on how inference actually *does* proceed to identify other neural subsystems likely to be involved (such as brain regions implicated in affective input or automatic processing); and verify these integrative predictions using insights and methodologies from neuroscience such as fMRI, to see if the expected brain regions do, in fact, activate during inference (Sanfey, Loewenstein, McClure, & Cohen, 2006). Although neuroeconomics adopts expected utility theory as its point of departure, a fact that would seem unwise given all the research just reviewed, it qualifies those predictions with insights from the descriptive theory provided by social cognition research on judgment and decision making.

The usefulness of neuroeconomics for social cognition derives from its potential to provide a unifying theoretical perspective regarding the dynamic processes by which the brain coordinates diverse neural systems to perform the complex tasks involved in inference. From this standpoint, human behavior does not result from a single process (such as the calculation of utility) but instead results from the interaction of a number of subsystems, which may produce different dispositions toward the same information. As we have seen, inferences often serve goals other than maximizing utility. Thus, from the neuroeconomics perspective, human inference is characterized by interactions among different subsystems that may favor alternative processes for a given decision, based on goals other than maximizing utility. These alternative goals might relate to efficiency and thus implicate brain regions involved in automatic processing, or they might implicate motivational concerns, such as the desire to feel good about the self, and thus implicate brain regions involved in reward.

The usefulness of expected utility theory stems from its normative model generating guidelines for predicting and interpreting activity in different brain regions during social inference tasks. EU implicates reward in its value function, and a considerable research has explored regions of the brain implicated in reward and punishment. Single-cell recordings from dopamine neurons and from neurons in the orbitocortex, striatum, and posterior cingulate cortex show relations between neural activity in these regions and reward magnitude (e.g., McClure, Daw, & Montague, 2003; Padoa-Schioppa & Assad, 2006; see Sanfey et al., 2006, for a review; Figure 8.4). The mesencephalic (midbrain) **dopamine system** may be critical to value assessment and involved in signaling errors in reward prediction, generating learning signals, updating goal states, and updating attentional focus in working memory (Sanfey et al., 2006). The **norepinephrine system** is also involved in this regulatory activity, specifically in the balance between maximizing utility from a particular reward and seeking new sources of potential reward.

The EU model also helps identify neural activity involved in negative utility. The anterior cingulate cortex, for example, responds to potential performance costs such as response conflict, errors, and negative feedback (Sanfey et al., 2006). Research from prospect theory (Chapter 7) suggests that these brain regions may be more responsive to relative gains and losses than to absolute levels of reward or punishment.

As for probability estimation (the other component involved in utility calculations), fewer generalizations have been uncovered. Activity in the medial prefrontal cortex appears to be inversely related to the likelihood of obtaining a monetary reward (Knutson, Taylor, Kaufman, Peterson, & Glover, 2005).

Activity in the lateral intraparietal area and in regions of the frontal cortex is implicated in the computation of utility, that is, in integrating the information related to value and probability of different options (Sanfey et al., 2006). The lateral intraparietal findings are significant because

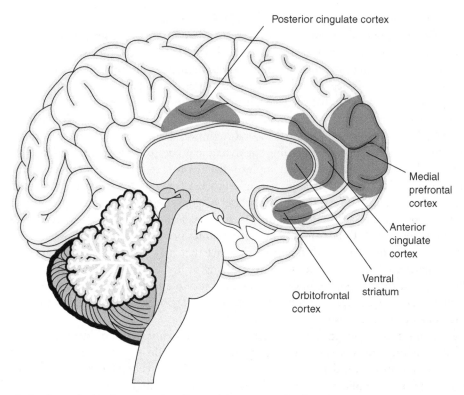

Figure 8.4   Sample brain areas implicated in economic decisions

this region has been implicated in motor preparation, providing a potential link between thought and behavior. Activity in the striatal reward areas also correlates with expected utility.

As noted, many decisions are marked by considerable uncertainty and ambiguity due to missing, incomplete, or otherwise confusing information. When choices are uncertain, the amygdala and orbitocortex activation increase, and the striatal system activation reduces (this system normally correlates positively with expected reward). Thus a neural circuit may respond to degree of uncertainty (Hsu, Bhatt, Adolphs, Tranel, & Camerer, 2005). This is significant because the normative model implies that computations regarding decisional alternatives are not influenced by uncertainty or ambiguity, but this research clearly indicates that they are.

How does neuroeconomics integrate predictions from social cognition research? An example of input from social cognition research comes from the vital distinction between automatic and controlled processing. Whereas automatic processes are fast and efficient, controlled processes are flexible but slow and capacity-limited (Chapter 2). Standard economic theory clearly maps onto controlled processing better than to automatic processing. It thus implicates the lateral prefrontal cortex, medial prefrontal cortex, rostral anterior cingulate, posterior parietal cortex, and the medial temporal lobe. As noted in Chapter 2, automatic processing implicates the amygdala, dorsal anterior cingulate, basal ganglia, ventromedial prefrontal cortex, and lateral temporal cortex, among other brain regions. Predictions that the inferential activities involved in a particular judgment task involve automatic or controlled processing thus provide a basis for predicting in advance the brain regions that might show activity.

Other well-documented departures from the EU model generated by social cognition research involve emotional input. When emotional content is vital to judgmental behavior, one expects to see and does see activity in the brain-stem reward-processing structures of the limbic system (Camerer, 2003): areas of the midbrain and cortex to which they project, including the nucleus accumbens and ventromedial frontal, orbitofrontal, and anterior cingulate cortex; and amygdala and insular cortex (Sanfey, Rilling, Aronson, Nystrom, & Cohen, 2003). Deviations from normative models that include nonlinear probability weighting or loss aversion, for example, may be explicated by exploring input from these regions.

Predictable brain systems are involved in automatic versus controlled evaluative (good–bad) and nonevaluative (e.g., past–present) judgments (Cunningham et al., 2003). Negatively valenced material elicited greater activity in the amygdala than positively valenced material, regardless of whether the judgment was evaluative or nonevaluative. Evaluative judgments were associated with greater medial and ventrolateral PFC activity than were nonevaluative judgments. Judgments engendering ambivalence were related to greater ventrolateral PFC activity. Automatic judgments may be especially sensitive to valence, whereas controlled processing is engaged by complex judgmental tasks. Studies such as these help to specify the predictions for neural activity that can be generated by social cognition research exploring automatic versus controlled processing and evaluation.

Input from the systems involved in emotion regulation may also help to explain departures from the discounted utility (DU) model. People value the present and steeply discount future opportunities (Chapter 7). Consistent with this viewpoint, choices involving immediate reward actively engage the ventral striatum as well as the medial and orbitofrontal areas, which are rich in dopaminergic innervations and are associated with the evaluation of reward. Activity in the frontal parietal region, however, correlates with deferred but superior rewards, suggesting that activity in this region may be less subject to the bias of immediacy in rewards (Sanfey et al., 2006).

Integration across these different levels of analysis adds breadth to the economic models that currently guide the study of judgment and decision making. Although complex decision making and social inference do not conform to optimal strategies, such as EU, simple mechanisms, such as heuristics, may approximate optimal strategies in ways that may make departures from normative models easy to see and interpret with reference to the psychological and neural underpinnings of those inputs (Sanfey et al., 2006). The role of emotional factors in decision making and multiple inputs from both controlled and automatic processing represent two examples of research from social cognition in which the pathways are now sufficiently well mapped as to be distinctly identifiable in the context of exploring the neural pathways known to be involved in value and predictability.

Research in neuroeconomics highlights how decision making involves the interaction of multiple subsystems governed by different parameters and possibly different principles, but it also provides methodologies for understanding what these different subsystems are and what parameters and principles might guide them. It remains to be seen if tracking utility computations using such techniques as neuroimaging will provide insights that will generalize to complex decision tasks. But the effort is worthwhile, given clear predictions from normative and descriptive theory and methodologies for testing them. If evidence is exchanged among all these disciplines, the understanding of social cognition not only is likely to be improved with reference to neuroeconomics but is likely to affect the models that neuroscientists and economists explore as well.

Summary

Social cognition is typically evaluated against normative models, and these evaluations reveal that human inference is marked by several distinctive features: the use of shortcuts or heuristics to make judgments and decisions in a complex and often rapidly changing environment; the role of affective and motivational considerations in inferential processes and outcomes; and the importance of prior theories and expectations for guiding inferential search and outcomes.

Although each of these shortcuts leads to inferences that often approximate those made by normative models, each is susceptible to potential biases. Deciding what data are relevant to a judgment is often marked by prior expectations or theories, sampling is often biased, and biases in already existing samples are often ignored. Strong inferences are frequently drawn from small and unreliable samples. Regression – the fact that extreme events will, on average, be less extreme when observed again – is poorly understood; instead, extreme events are frequently used to predict future extreme events.

How flawed is the social judgment process? Three perspectives on this issue have been voiced. The first position suggests that, at least under certain circumstances, judgmental errors and biases may produce severe distortions, and therefore it is advisable to find ways to correct the inference process. Decision-making methods that can correct for common biases or errors include the use of statistics and computers for aiding judgments. In addition, developing reasoning skills through training improves people's inferential capabilities.

A second perspective suggests that the experimental literature makes people look worse than they really are, and that intuitive inferential strategies are actually quite effective in the real world. According to this viewpoint, intuitive inferential strategies often serve us well because they take into account efficiency pressures, the specific content and context of an inferential problem, and the possibility that the environment is changing. In addition, some errors may be inconsequential for behavior, others will cancel each other out, and others may be detected through communication.

A relatively new position regarding human inference is that, at least under some circumstances, heuristically based judgments are actually better than more thoroughly considered ones. For example, experts may be able to make rapid use of vast stores of nonconscious knowledge to produce judgments that are more accurate than judgments made via conscious deliberation. For many mundane tasks as well, our minds are able to integrate or extract information from a broad array of stimuli to reach complex judgments in a matter of seconds, even milliseconds. Moreover, under at least some circumstances, conscious reflection on the beliefs that go into our inferences may actually harm the inference process.

Where is the study of social inference headed? Increasingly, insights from social cognition are being integrated with insights from economics and neuroscience, and one outcome of these interactions is the field of neuroeconomics. Neuroeconomics draws on the expected utility normative model, descriptive research from social cognition, and insights and methodologies from neuroscience to identify exactly what neurotransmitters and brain regions are implicated in particular types of inference task. The assumptions guiding this endeavor include the fact that, although normative models are not descriptive of human inference, inferential shortcuts may approximate normative models in ways that are useful not only for identifying what neural mechanisms may be involved in normative calculations but also in the automatic, theory-driven, and affectively based shortcuts that people often use. The potential promise of this integrative effort is that research will be able to identify the interaction of multiple subsystems governed by different parameters and different principles by testing hypotheses derived from normative and descriptive research using the methodologies of neuroscience.

FURTHER READING

Dunning, D. (2012). Judgment and decision-making. In S. T. Fiske & C. N. Macrae (Eds.), *Sage handbook of social cognition* (pp. 251–272). Thousand Oaks, CA: Sage.

Funder, D. C. (1995). On the accuracy of personality judgment: A realistic approach. *Psychological Review, 102*, 652–670.

Kunda, Z. (1999). *Social cognition: Making sense of people.* Cambridge, MA: MIT Press.

Murphy, N. A. (2012). Nonverbal perception. In S. T. Fiske & C. N. Macrae (Eds.), *Sage handbook of social cognition* (pp. 191–210). Thousand Oaks, CA: Sage.

Nisbett, R. E., & Ross, L. D. (1980). *Human inference: Strategies and shortcomings of social judgment.* Englewood Cliffs, NJ: Prentice-Hall.

Nosek, B. A., Hawkins, C. B., & Frazier, R. S. (2012). Implicit social cognition. In S. T. Fiske & C. N. Macrae (Eds.), *Sage handbook of social cognition* (pp. 31–53). Thousand Oaks, CA: Sage.

Payne, B. K. (2012). Control, awareness, and other things we might learn to live without. In S. T. Fiske & C. N. Macrae (Eds.) *Sage handbook of social cognition* (pp. 12–30). Thousand Oaks, CA: Sage.

Wilson, T. D. (2011). *Redirect: The surprising new science of psychological change.* New York: Little, Brown.

Cognitive Structures of Attitudes

9

- Early Insights
- Cognitive Representation in Two Consistency Theories
- Discrete versus Distributed Representations
- Lay Theories and Attitude Change
- Functional Dimensions of Attitudes

Suppose a high school classmate is coming to visit for the weekend, and you want to plan a little party. Your classmate happens to be gay. You wonder how your current (mostly straight) friends will react to your guest of honor if they find out. To avoid any potential awkwardness, it might be better to know your friends' attitudes before inviting them. But how best to know? With most of your friends, the topic of homosexuality may never have come up in conversation. You could ask directly, but you might not get an honest answer because some of your friends might try to conceal antigay prejudices.

Your friends' attitudes matter because they can predict behavior, but attitudes cannot be observed directly. Because an attitude must be inferred from an individual's overt response to some stimulus, it is considered a **hypothetical mediating variable**. That is, psychologists assume that an attitude intervenes between an observable stimulus (S) and an observable response (R), providing the necessary link. Even when S–R behaviorism dominated psychology, the attitude concept continued to be indispensable to social psychology, as noted in Chapter 1.

The core definition of this hypothetical variable, **attitude**, is evaluation, though definitions do vary (e.g., Ajzen, 2001; Albarracín, Johnson, & Zanna, 2005; Crano & Prislin, 2006; Eagly & Chaiken, 2005, 2007; Fiske, 2010). Attitudes categorize a stimulus along an evaluative dimension. As such, attitudes broadly dispose people to respond positively or negatively, as inferred from their specific cognitive, affective, and behavioral responses.

EARLY INSIGHTS

Early in the 20th century Gordon Allport (1935) declared attitudes to be "the most distinctive and indispensable concept in contemporary American social psychology" (p. 798). The field sprang from various attitude research motivated by World War II: propaganda and persuasion (Hovland, Janis, & Kelley, 1953; Hovland, Lumsdaine, & Sheffield, 1949); anti-Semitic and antidemocratic prejudice (Adorno, Frenkel-Brunswik, Levinson, & Sanford, 1950); and satisfaction and deprivation in the military (Stouffer, Suchman, DeVinney, Star, & Williams, 1949). These early efforts leaned heavily on attitudes both as measures and as theoretical variables. Most of the first few decades of social psychology concentrated on how to measure and define attitudes. Since then, attitudes have permeated every topic in the field. This book focuses on their cognitive correlates, the current chapter on structure and the next on processes; Chapter 15 considers their links to behavior.

Because attitude research dates to the beginning of social psychology, new-fangled social cognition research at first seemed unnecessary to traditionalists. Social cognition's initial contribution to attitude research was a fine-grained analysis of the mechanisms (e.g., attention, memory) presumably involved in attitude formation and change. Traditional variables, such as features of the communicator or the message, could be examined in new ways, and this helped establish the merits of the cognitive approach. Focusing on this central area illustrated to early skeptics what was unique about social cognition approaches. Now attitudes and social cognition share the first section of the field's flagship *Journal of Personality and Social Psychology*, and attitude research fully complements social cognition perspectives by (a) revealing common processes between cognitions that are less evaluatively laden (e.g., heuristics) and those that are more so (e.g., attitudes), (b) providing theoretical breadth to some central social cognitive topics (e.g., stereotyping, prejudice), and (c) emphasizing affect (or at least evaluation) and behavior.

Although social cognition research enriches current attitude research, cognition was also present in earlier theories. Among the most influential approaches to attitudes have been the **cognitive consistency theories** (Abelson et al., 1968). Dominating social psychology journals in the 1960s, their fundamental assumption held that inconsistencies – among cognitions, among affects, or between cognitions and affects – cause attitude change. Cognitive dissonance theory (Festinger, 1957) and balance theory (Heider, 1958) exemplify this, as we will see. Other major theories of attitudes also reserve an important role for cognition (Fishbein, 1963; Insko & Cialdini, 1969; Kiesler, 1971; Osgood & Tannenbaum, 1955; M. J. Rosenberg, 1956, 1960). Although we can only allude to the vast literature on attitudes, the critical point is this: Cognition plays a major role in practically every attitude theory, except perhaps classically conditioned attitudes (Staats & Staats, 1958) and mere exposure effects (e.g., Zajonc, 1980b; see Chapter 14). However, until the cognitive revolution, attitude theory could not draw on advances in cognitive psychology, social cognition, and, more recently, human neuroscience.

Comparing Older and Newer Cognitive Approaches to Attitudes

The newer cognitive approaches (this chapter, Chapter 10) build on the older attitude theories in several crucial respects. Many of the critical variables are the same. Some of the methodological procedures were established long ago and continue to form the basis of research paradigms. For example, current researchers sometimes reuse old experimental designs, adding mainly a more detailed analysis of intervening cognitive processes. Another carryover from older research is that many of the current theoretical issues are variants on earlier problems. Finally, many of the older approaches were heavily cognitive, as just described.

But the older and newer approaches also differ: First are what might be called **metatheoretical** differences between the two; that is, major conceptual differences separate the overarching framework common to most consistency theories versus the overarching framework behind social cognition's approach to attitude research. Most "cognitive" consistency theories posited a strong motivational basis toward consistency; the usual metatheory behind consistency theories was a drive to reduce internal discrepancies. The consistency theories were not typically designed to be theories about the cognitive system operating on its own nonmotivational principles. A traditional consistency theory might posit that people resolve discrepancies to avoid the uncomfortable feeling of holding two conflicting beliefs. In contrast, cognitive approaches are based on current understandings of the cognitive system. For example, to deal with inconsistencies, a current cognitive approach might posit that people resolve discrepancies mainly for reasons of efficiency in memory storage.

Second, specific theoretical differences distinguish the older and newer approaches. The newer approaches explicitly draw on cognitive theories unavailable earlier. These theories potentially provide precise frameworks that detail the organization and processing of information in persuasion, which permit a more careful analysis of cognitive processes related to attitude change.

Third, many new methods for studying attitude change have evolved in directions borrowed from cognitive psychology. Attitude theories have long posited internal structures (Zajonc, 1968b), but more fine-grained analysis of cognitive organization and dynamics (typical of cognitive psychology) has become possible in attitude research with recent advances in measurement techniques. During the 1970s, information processing research on attitudes expanded in several directions based on metatheoretical, theoretical, and methodological developments.

One framework for persuasion research (described by Lasswell, 1948, elaborated by Hovland, Janis, & Kelley, 1953) is enduring: *Who says what to whom in what channel with what effect.* Thus the research tends to focus on characteristics of the communicator, the message, the audience, the modality, and the lasting effects of attitude change (Table 9.1). As noted, much current cognitive research continues to explain effects originally uncovered by the classic research.

This chapter focuses on cognitive representations of attitudes. For context, we first address some of the more strictly cognitive features of two traditional attitude theories, dissonance theory and balance theory, anticipating modern social cognition. Next, three cognitive approaches rely on people's lay theories of attitudes: audience attributions about the communicator as a person, people's concepts about information exchanged in groups, and people's ideas about their own attitude change. Then we address current theories of attitudes' cognitive representation. In a final section, cognitively oriented attitude research comes full circle to address motivational issues that originally sparked the interest of early attitude theorists.

Table 9.1   Persuasion framework

Concept:	who says	what	to whom	in what channel	with what effect
Variables:	Communicator	Message	Audience	Modality	Change
Examples:	credibility	argument strength	expertise	written/oral	immediate
	attractiveness	superficial appeal	bias	speed	long-term
	similarity	redundancy	involvement	images	implicit

Source: proposed by Lasswell (1948), elaborated by Hovland, Janis, & Kelley (1953)

COGNITIVE REPRESENTATION IN TWO CONSISTENCY THEORIES

The consistency theories of attitudes proposed in the late 1950s predicted the interplay between attitudes and cognitive representation. For each case, we begin by briefly reviewing the most relevant consistency theory as background and then describe current cognitive interpretations. Dissonance theory informs attitude-selective perception and selective learning, while balance theory informs selective recall of information about others (Zajonc, 1968b).

Dissonance Theory Predicts Selective Perception

Dissonance theory (Festinger, 1957) analyzes inconsistency among cognitions to describe how beliefs and behavior change attitudes. In this view, inconsistency causes a motivational state called dissonance. If you believe that smoking causes cancer (a cognition) but you smoke anyway (a conflicting cognition about behavior), you leave yourself open to cognitive dissonance. Dissonance indeed causes an aversive state of arousal (e.g., Elliott & Devine, 1994; Losch & Cacioppo, 1990; see Fazio & Cooper, 1983, for an earlier review). The drive to reduce that arousal (discomfort) consequently makes you rearrange your cognitions to reduce dissonance. Although theoretically one could change one's behavior to reduce the inconsistency, most dissonance research focused on when the inconsistent cognitions are more likely to change, partly an experimental strategy to investigate cognitive processes *per se*. Also, behavior responds more to reality constraints (i.e., it's often public), so it is harder to change than are one's cognitions or attitudes.

Most ways to increase consistency rearrange cognitive representations. Suppose that you smoke and that you have several cognitions relevant to that behavior. You may have a couple of cognitions consonant with your smoking (it tastes good; it is relaxing) and several dissonant with smoking (it causes cancer; it is expensive; it is smelly; other people dislike it). Because the number of dissonant cognitions outweigh the consonant ones, cognitive inconsistency results, and you may experience dissonance. To reduce the dissonance, you can change your cognitions in various ways: Add or subtract cognitions (i.e., change your beliefs) to increase the ratio of consonant to dissonant ones (e.g., add the idea that smoking keeps weight down and subtract the smell and the expense), or reduce the importance of dissonant conditions (e.g., I'll die of something anyway, so why worry about cancer). This by no means exhausts the possibilities (Cooper, Blackman, & Keller, in press; Petty & Wegener, 1998).

Selective Perception

Consistency theorists in general (Abelson et al., 1968) posit that people seek out, notice, and interpret data to reinforce their attitudes. Dissonance theory in particular predicts that people will avoid information that increases dissonance; that is, people favor information consistent with their attitudes and behavior. For present purposes, the work on **selective perception** divides into **selective exposure** (seeking consistent information not already present), **selective attention** (heeding consistent information once it is there), and **selective interpretation** (translating ambiguous information to be consistent) (Table 9.2).

Selective exposure is a principle that deserves to be true (McGuire, 1969), but the initial evidence was unfortunately mixed (Brehm & Cohen, 1962; Freedman & Sears, 1965; J. Mills, 1968; Wicklund & Brehm, 1976). Intellectual honesty and fairness sometimes prompt people to seek information that is inconsistent with their attitudes (Sears, 1965). Information's utility and novelty often override dissonance in determining exposure (Brock, Albert, & Becker, 1970). However, **de facto selective exposure** is clear: Most of us inhabit an environment biased in favor of congenial positions (Sears, 1968; but see E. Katz, 1968). People tend to pick friends, blogs, movies, and television that reinforce their attitudes, which, in turn, are reinforced by those agreeing others (Coman & Hirst, 2012).

Subsequent refinement of the hypothesis suggests that increasing dissonance also increases selective exposure: clear choices or public commitment (Frey, 1986); a personally important attitude

Table 9.2 Consistency theory predictions for attitudinally favorable information processing

Phenomenon	Definition	Evidence strength
Selective perception		
selective exposure	Seeking consistent information	Support only for de facto selective exposure
selective attention	Heeding consistent information	Some people, sometimes
selective interpretation	Judging ambiguity as consistent	Strong support
Selective learning	Retaining consistent information	Under special conditions
Selective recall	Uncued memory for consistency	Balanced triads more easily recalled

(Holbrook, Berent, Krosnick, Visser, & Boninger, 2005); increasing commitment as information arrives sequentially (Jonas, Schulz-Hardt, Frey, & Thelen, 2001); limited search options, presuming supportive information is the best (Fischer, Jonas, Frey, & Schulz-Hardt, 2005); and finally, when reminded that life is short, focusing on relevant and important attitudes (Jonas, Greenberg, & Frey, 2003). Thus, under particular conditions, selective exposure to attitude-consonant information does occur. This aspect of selective perception addresses an important cognitive process – namely, information seeking – and sets up the two other aspects of selective perception: attention and interpretation.

Selective attention clearly responds to consistency pressures. People often look longer at consistent than inconsistent evidence (Brock & Balloun, 1967; A. R. Cohen, Brehm, & Latané, 1959; Jecker, 1964). For example, one study (J. M. Olson & Zanna, 1979) divided participants into repressors (people who typically avoid threatening stimuli) and sensitizers (people who typically investigate threatening stimuli). Both groups reported their attitudes toward some paintings. The experimenter then allowed them to choose a pair to keep. The pairs all included one painting they liked and one they disliked. After the decision, participants looked at the pair they had chosen. Dissonance theory predicts that they would focus on the positive aspects of their choice; that is, the preferred painting within the chosen pair. Only repressors behaved as predicted; their looking times at the choice-consistent painting were high compared to control subjects, and they avoided looking at the painting inconsistent with their expressed choice. Thus consistent information elicited the selective attention of repressors only.

Chronic optimists, like repressors, also avoid threatening stimuli (Isaacowitz, 2005). And stress increases selective attention (Chajut & Algom, 2003), probably because of limited online resources. Selective attention, hence, operates for some of the people some of the time, and also for some stimuli some of the time; for example, people selectively attend to counterarguments that they can easily refute (Kleinhesselink & Edwards, 1975).

People also protect their attitudes by *selective interpretation* (apart from exposure and attention). People's attitudes can change their interpretations of what they see (e.g., Vidmar & Rokeach, 1974). Consider some examples: Attitudes toward presidential candidates influence judged debate performance (Fazio & Williams, 1986; Holbrook et al., 2005), attitudes toward the Palestinian–Israeli conflict influence judged fairness of news coverage (Vallone, Ross, & Lepper, 1985), attitudes toward an outgroup influence attributions about the group's behavior (Pettigrew, 1979), and expectations about the introduction of the Euro influenced Germans' judgments of price increases (Traut-Mattausch, Schulz-Hardt, Greitemeyer, & Frey, 2004). Although not always based precisely on dissonance theory's predictions about selective interpretation, these examples fit, as well as frameworks more explicitly drawn from social cognition.

Culture and Selective Perception

Cognitive dissonance operates differently in different cultural contexts. Consider an example of dissonance reduction involving retrospective perception. Typically, Europeans and European Americans justify their choices by reinterpreting their chosen alternative as clearly superior, emphasizing its virtues and downplaying its flaws while doing the reverse for nonchosen alternatives. This process reduces the dissonance created by the virtues of the nonchosen alternatives and the pitfalls of the chosen alternative. This phenomenon, called **spreading the alternatives**, is well documented in these populations from early on (Brehm, 1956).

However, East Asians do not necessarily justify their decisions (Heine & Lehman, 1997). In keeping with characteristics of relatively interdependent cultures, they do so only when self-relevant others are primed (Kitayama, Snibbe, Markus, & Suzuki, 2004) or when they make a choice for a friend (Hoshino-Browne et al., 2005). Thus postdecisional dissonance reduction and dissonance effects on selective attention and interpretation depend on cultural context (Morling & Masuda, 2012).

Dissonance Theory Predicts Selective Learning

Proponents of dissonance and other consistency theories also predict selective learning and memory for attitude-consistent information. This prediction was not unique to dissonance theorists; selective memory for attitude consistency was one of the first questions in attitude research (J. M. Levine & Murphy, 1943; Watson & Hartmann, 1939). Earlier and some later theories all would predict that if a couple is quarreling over whether to spend winter holidays in Vermont or in the Caribbean, the ski addict will never learn the details of bargain snorkeling tours, and the sun worshipper will never learn the details of the ski packages. Unfortunately, evidence for selective learning was "unambiguously inconclusive" (Greaves, 1972). One reviewer concluded that the published studies yielding evidence for selective learning all must be flukes because so many other studies failed to find such evidence (Greenwald, 1975). Moreover, the evidence often is flawed, and recent research suggests exactly how, based in part on insights from cognitive psychology. For example, many studies have confounded the familiarity and agreeability of arguments (Zanna & Olson, 1982). It is not surprising that the ski enthusiast would recall pro-ski arguments better than pro-sun arguments because the person has thought about the pro-ski arguments more often. Familiar arguments would be easier to recall without having to assume any dissonance-based motivation to forget the disagreeable arguments (see also Schmidt & Sherman, 1984).

Selective learning and retention of attitudinally favorable information do occur under special conditions, defined in part by the contingencies of information processing. Incidental learning, rather than intentional learning, provides clearer support for selective learning effects (Malpass, 1969). That is, people are more likely to be selective when they do not know they will be tested on the material later. A travel agent who frequently has to present the details of cruises and ski packages will remember both kinds of arguments, regardless of how he or she personally feels about them.

Important attitudes specifically encourage attitude-relevant memory (Holbrook et al., 2005). In particular, strong attitudes motivate people to counterargue uncongenial messages, so they remember them (Eagly, Kulesa, Brannon, Shaw-Barnes, & Huston-Comeux, 2000); strong attitudes also motivate people to remember congenial arguments but in this case because they are pleasing. Also, consistency matters more to some people than to others, so they show selective learning (Kruglanski & Sheveland, 2012). Overall, meta-analysis indicates that attitudes do not necessarily encourage attitude-consistent memory because of the effect of actively counterarguing uncongenial messages (Eagly, Chen, Chaiken, & Shaw-Barnes, 1999; Eagly, Kulesa, Chen, & Chaiken, 2001).

When they do occur, consistency processes may operate automatically; even people with impaired memories (amnesiacs) and people operating under cognitive load nonetheless do show dissonance-reducing attitude change (Lieberman, Ochsner, Gilbert, & Schacter, 2001). This suggests that memory's role need not be explicit and conscious.

Balance Theory Predicts Selective Recall

Adolescents fight with their parents, and their perception of these fights is shaped by the nature of their attachment to their parents (e.g., secure, ambivalent). Over time, their memory shifts to reflect their relational style even more (Feeney & Cassidy, 2003). Another consistency theory, balance theory (Heider, 1958), helps explain this. Like dissonance theory, it also inspired research on learning and retention as a function of consistency (Cottrell, Ingraham, & Monfort, 1971; Picek, Sherman, & Shiffrin, 1975; Zajonc & Burnstein, 1965). Balance theory differs from dissonance theory in that it intrinsically concerns relationships between people. According to **balance theory**, structures in the perceiver's mind represent the perceiver (P), another person (O), and the mutual object (X) (Figure 9.1). For example, you (P) may have an attitude toward your roommate (O) and toward his car (X), and you may perceive him as having a certain attitude toward his car. Your perceptions of each relation between you, roommate, and the clunker may be either positive or negative. Liking, owning, or belonging is a positive relationship (+); disliking or not belonging is a negative relationship (-).

In combination, the relationships among you three may be either balanced or imbalanced. Essentially, they are balanced if you are either agreeing friends or disagreeing enemies. Suppose you like your roommate (P–O is +), and he likes his car (O–X is +); then the three of you are a "balanced" trio if you develop affection for the car (P–X is +).

Now consider the possibility that you like your roommate (+), he adores his car (+), and you cannot stand the thing (-). This imbalanced relationship awaits trouble, or at least some pressure to change toward balance, and that is how the theory predicts attitude change. Your perception of any of the three relationships is likely to change in order to create balance. For example, people may interpret people they like (P–O is +) as liking what they like (P–X is +, so O–X is +) and disliking what they dislike (P–X is -, so O–X is -). Most people interpret close friends and favored political candidates as sharing their attitudes more closely than is the case (Ottati, Fishbein, & Middlestadt, 1988), and this may even be adaptive (Levinger & Breedlove, 1966). When people become romantically involved, for example, their attitudes tend to align (Davis & Rusbult, 2001). People are uncomfortable having attitudes that disagree with liked others, and they can experience intense ambivalence as a result (Priester & Petty, 2001). In fact, priming social groups makes people's attitudes fit those groups, as if people are preparing to get along with them (Kawakami, Dovidio, & Dijksterhuis, 2003).

Balance theory shows how cognitive constraints shape learning and memory relevant to attitudes. The prediction that balanced relationships are easier to recall derives from consistency

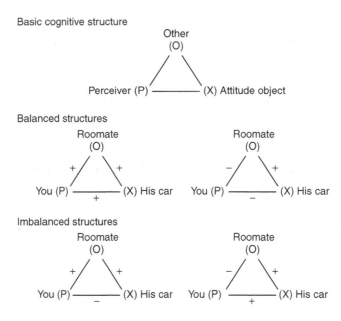

Figure 9.1   Balance theory triads

theories and developed through schema theories. Traditional balance research shows, for example, that people can learn and generate balanced social structures more easily than imbalanced ones (Feather, 1969; Zajonc & Burnstein, 1965).

Social schema research suggests that balanced relationships are stored in memory as a single unit. People more easily remember that two friends agree or that two enemies disagree; either makes a compact chunk of memory. It is harder to recall that one of two roommates likes chocolate and the other hates it and which feels which way (Picek et al., 1975; Sentis & Burnstein, 1979). In this research, people initially learn some imbalanced triads. Subsequently, the time it takes them to retrieve a single relationship depends on the number of relationships (P-O, O-X, X-P) the experimenter uses as a recall cue; the more pieces of the three-way imbalanced relationship that are supplied, the faster the triad of relationships can be retrieved. However, with balanced relationships, the number of pieces supplied by the experimenter does not matter; the time to retrieve the entire balanced triad is the same regardless of the number of recall cues. This implies, then, that a balanced triad is a single cognitive unit that must be retrieved all at once, but an imbalanced triad is not (Sentis & Burnstein, 1979).

Attitudes Organize Memory

A general principle emerges from the research inspired originally by consistency theories: Attitudes often organize memory. In particular, making an attitudinal judgment improves recall of attitude-relevant evidence and creates attitude-consistent inferences. This fits research from person perception as well (Ostrom, Lingle, Pryor, & Geva, 1980). Hence, if you judge a man's suitability as a pilot, you will remember his superior eyesight and infer that he has good spatial ability. If you judge his suitability as a comedian, on the other hand, you will recall his infectious laugh and infer that he has stage presence (Lingle et al., 1979). The effect seems to be mediated by your recalling the attitude itself, once formed, rather than retrieving and resynthesizing all the individual bits of evidence. Once you have formed an attitude about somebody as a pilot instead of a comedian, that attitude organizes subsequent judgments, including recall of the data on which the judgment was based. The attitude is easier to recall than the supporting evidence (Lingle & Ostrom, 1979; Loken, 1984).

Recent research adds a new twist to this organizing role of attitudes. When people's attitudes change, they retain both the old and new attitude in memory, as the old attitude seems to go underground. **Dual attitudes** comprise an older, automatic attitude and the newer, explicitly accessible attitude (T. D. Wilson, Lindsey, & Schooler, 2000). Which one predominates depends on the method of expression; the older attitude may pop out unawares when one responds automatically or under cognitive load. The coexisting attitudes can create subtle forms of ambivalence (Petty, Tormala, Briñol, & Jarvis, 2006), undermining confidence, extending consideration of pros and cons, and creating automatic neutrality under time pressure.

Conclusion about Consistency Theories

Classic consistency theories were among the earliest frameworks to predict how attitudes affect selective perception, learning, and memory. This work both anticipated social cognition approaches and was ultimately developed by them. Dissonance theory views people as motivated to avoid information inconsistent with their attitudes. Although the evidence for selective exposure is uneven, the evidence for selective attention and interpretation is clearer. Dissonance theorists and others also hypothesized the selective learning of attitudinally agreeable arguments, a prediction supported under certain circumstances for certain people for certain attitude objects. In a similar vein, balanced triads (consistent interpersonal pairs with a common attitude object) are easier to learn and remember, apparently because they form a compact unit in memory. Finally, people's attitudes more generally organize memory. All these effects rest on people's lay theories about attitude-relevant cognitions being consistent.

DISCRETE VERSUS DISTRIBUTED REPRESENTATIONS

A prominent consistency theorist once confided to one of the authors that a then-frustrated goal had been to represent the relationships among attitude-relevant cognitions, and now social cognition research was finally opening up new ways to do so. The representation of attitudes continues to offer challenging opportunities. The competing views of attitude structure echo the competing view of social memory more generally: discrete, declarative representations that operate in serial

processes of categorization, reasoning, and deciding, versus distributed, procedural representations that operate in parallel processes of attitude generation and response (Ferguson &
Fukukura, 2012).

Distributed attitude representations are not just representations but also attitude processes,
especially for generating attitudes. Recall Chapter 4's time-and-temperature light bulbs metaphor (or pixels on a computer screen). The patterns of small units (e.g., pixels or even neurons)
activating in concert represent the attitude. This kind of connectionist model views attitudes as
a state of the distributed system, a function of the strength of links among the lower-level units
(Conrey & Smith, 2007; Van Overwalle & Siebler, 2005). Associative processes easily describe
primitive affective processes of attitude activation and possibly indirect, implicit attitudes
(Gawronski & Bodenhausen, 2007; Strack & Deutsch, 2004). Associations and input to that
network determine evaluations.

The more traditional discrete, declarative, propositional approach accounts well for higher-
level thinking about attitudes (Dietrich & Markman, 2003; Strack & Deutsch, 2004). These
representations include propositions, whose truth value matters, unlike the affective-associative,
distributed representations. Cognitive consistency plays a role in propositional representations.
In the end, both kinds or representations appear to play a role, as in the **associative-propositional
evaluation model** of attitudes (Gawronski & Bodenhausen, 2007).

LAY THEORIES AND ATTITUDE CHANGE

Now we turn to people's everyday social theories about why attitudes change (and do not change).
One approach examines people's ideas about the communicator's social context, as it influences
the perceived validity of the message. Another examines arguments that arise when a group
discusses an issue. A third approach examines people contemplating their attitudes alone and
applying their own theories about attitude change to that context. All three approaches acknowledge the importance of people's own beliefs about attitude change, and they fit other cognitive
approaches in emphasizing people's interpretation of the information provided.

Attributional Analyses of Communicators and Their Messages

Producers of television ads are well aware that their messages have maximum impact if delivered
by a gorgeous model, a respected hero, or a well-known millionaire; an alternative way to increase
message impact is to use a communicator blatantly similar to the ordinary person, as is done in
"hidden camera" testimonials. The importance of communicator attractiveness, credibility, power,
and similarity was first demonstrated by Hovland, Janis, and Kelley (1953), and these variables
have generated research ever since (Chapter 10).

One early manifestation of social cognition research influencing attitude research came from
attributional approaches to communicator credibility (Eagly & Chaiken, 1984; Eagly, Chaiken, &

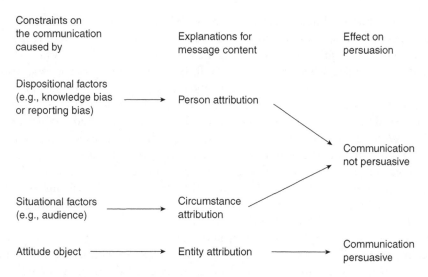

Figure 9.2   An attributional analysis of communicator effects in persuasion

Wood, 1981). For example, persuasion depends in part on the recipient's analysis of why a communicator advocates a particular position. Recipients attempt to determine the validity of a persuasive message, knowing some of the communicator's dispositional and situational constraints (Figure 9.2). When the President of Greenpeace speaks to the local Greenpeace chapter, you know that both his own opinion (a dispositional factor) and that of his audience (a situational factor) predispose him to advocate the environmental advantages of strict auto emission controls. If this is, in fact, the message, it appears less valid and persuasive than if it were completely independent of such dispositional and situational pressures. Messages constrained by the situation or the communicator may or may not validly represent the truth, so they are not impactful. The speaker's harangue obviously reflects an (environmentalist) audience-pleasing bias or his own biases; he can be biased either in what he is willing to say in public (reporting bias) or in what he knows (knowledge bias) (Eagly, Wood, & Chaiken, 1978). In contrast, if the president of a big oil company such as BP makes the same environmentalist point to fellow industry chiefs, he is indeed believable and persuasive.

These predictions about communicator credibility derive from Kelley's (1967, 1972a) analysis of **multiple sufficient causes**: Given several plausible causes, the weaker ones are discounted (Chapter 6). If both disposition (he is a crusader) and circumstances (Greenpeace audience) conspire to produce the speech, the alternative cause, the facts, need not explain the speech. A step-by-step test of this model demonstrates that perceptions of a communicator's background (e.g., he has strong opinions) cause the predicted attributions (e.g., he is biased). Attributions that cast credibility into doubt decrease opinion change (Wood & Eagly, 1981). Thus this approach focuses on the communicator–message interaction.

Communicator attractiveness also profits from an attributional perspective. One study (Eagly & Chaiken, 1975) tested whether attractive communicators are not only more persuasive in general (a well-established finding) but are especially persuasive if they advocate an undesirable position. Because attractive people are expected to advocate attractive positions, an attractive person advocating an undesirable position must be doing so because the position is valid. Participants encountered a communicator who either liked or disliked undergraduates and who made either optimistic or pessimistic statements, for example, about college graduates' employment opportunities or about the future spread of venereal disease. Attractive communicators were considerably more persuasive than unattractive communicators when advocating undesirable (pessimistic) positions (cf. Wachtler & Counselman, 1981). Messages that are unexpected, given the communicator's dispositions and the communication setting, are more persuasive than messages that are wholly predictable on the basis of who is saying them (Eagly, Chaiken, & Wood, 1981; Goethals, 1976). An unexpected position – given the communicator's self-interest – increases perceived trustworthiness and accuracy, so it decreases message processing, resulting in heuristic agreement (Petty, Fleming, Priester, & Feinstein, 2001).

Attribution theory also explains similarity and agreement effects. Those who agree with us seem objective, responding to the facts, while those who disagree with us seem biased by their own values. Both tendencies are exaggerated by other kinds of dissimilarity between self and others (Goethals, 1976). The attributional explanation draws on Kelley's **covariation model of attribution** (Chapter 6) as follows: Consider two people discussing nonsmokers' rights. Their agreement means consensus, and high consensus encourages an entity attribution to the attitude object (i.e., the topic being discussed). In our example, the agreeing pair attribute their shared attitude to the justice of nonsmokers' rights. However, agreement by a dissimilar other is a particularly informative kind of consensus information (Goethals, 1976); the clearer the consensus, the more likely that the opinion is caused by the entity (the topic) in question rather than by peculiar people or situations. Consequently, if one of the pair is a smoker and the other a nonsmoker, and if they could actually agree, each would be especially persuaded that the cause was just, an entity attribution.

In contrast, low consensus, or a disagreement by another, paves the way for person or situation attributions. When the two people disagree, each thinks the other is not an objective judge of the facts but is letting emotional prejudices get in the way. Given that the situation is usually the same for both parties, the remaining cause has to be the other person's dispositions. However, the arguers are even more likely to believe each other biased (i.e., make a dispositional attribution) if one is a beleaguered smoker and the other an angry nonsmoker rather than two similar individuals. Thus a dissimilar other exaggerates the effect of disagreement as well as agreement. Intergroup cultural divides begin this way (D. T. Miller & Prentice, 1999).

People not only believe that an agreeing source is credible; they also misattribute agreeable positions to credible sources (Fragale & Heath, 2004). The heuristic implies that firm beliefs come from good sources. In general, people create a fit among a persuasive message, its source, and its validity: Familiar others are persuasive (Weisbuch, Mackie, & Garcia-Marques, 2003), reasonable messages that fit our motivational focus are persuasive (Cesario, Grant, & Higgins, 2004; Evans & Petty, 2003), and irrelevant emotions spill over to shape source trustworthiness (Dunn & Schweitzer, 2005). All this suggests fit among persuasion's elements, consistent both with attributional analyses and with balance theory.

Again, people have lay theories about which components of attitudes should fit. In sum, attributional analyses clarify various communicator variables interacting with message and context variables.

Group Polarization: Social Cognitive Explanations

Would you rather have a committee discussion or aggregated votes decide your next promotion? Many people think that groups represent the voice of reason and compromise; decisions made by committee are supposed to be safer than decisions made by individuals. A closer look at group decisions reveals that this is not at all the case. Another cognitive analysis of attitudes examines group-level attitude representations. It focuses on how people respond to the information provided by social interaction, based on their theories about where they personally stand compared to other group members.

The background for group-level attitude research comes from work in the early 1960s on group decision making. One research area in particular focused on the comparative riskiness of group and individual decisions (Wallach, Kogan, & Bem, 1962). Graduate students made decisions in and out of groups (see Table 9.3 for sample items). In most cases, students who discussed this case (and others like it) emerged from the group discussion favoring a riskier alternative than when they went into the discussion. Thus the group decision was riskier than the average of the individual decisions, a result termed **risky shift**, or more generally **group polarization**.

Quantities of research were generated by this counterintuitive result (Rajecki, 1982). Some of the explanations relied on traditional variables such as norms and values (**normative influences**), but one relied on a cognitive interpretation of the group interaction (**informational influence**). As an example of the normative explanations, consider the possible influences of group norms. Researchers proposed that people in cohesive groups feel protected from the consequences of their decision; they can hide behind the group, in effect. This "diffusion of responsibility" hypothesis fell into disfavor when it was discovered that group attitudes do not change simply when a group feels cohesive; rather, some relevant discussion appears to be necessary (Pruitt & Teger, 1969).

Another normative explanation was that people value risk more than caution. When people assemble in a group and compare their opinions, most of them discover that at least some others are taking riskier stands than they are. Because risk is valued, so the argument goes, the group gravitates toward the riskier extreme. This explanation in terms of social comparison and "risk as a value" faltered when researchers discovered that many groups shift toward a more cautious extreme after discussion (McCauley, Stitt, Woods, & Lipton, 1973). The shift toward caution also undercut the diffusion of responsibility hypothesis. Why should a group need to diffuse responsibility for more cautious decisions?

These normative theories contrast with some informational explanations, which have support. **Persuasive arguments theory** (Burnstein & Vinokur, 1973; for a review, see Isenberg, 1986) proposed that attitudes in groups polarize toward relatively extreme (cautious or risky) alternatives when people are exposed to new information. Assume a pool of possible arguments for any given

Table 9.3   Sample choice scenarios testing polarization after group discussion

1. An electrical engineer may stick with his present job at a modest but adequate salary, or may take a new job offering considerably more money but no long-term security.
2. A man of moderate means may invest some money he recently inherited in secure "blue chip" low-return securities or in more risky securities that offer the possibility of large gains.
3. A captain of a college football team, in the final seconds of a game with the college's traditional rival, may choose a play that is almost certain to produce a tic score, or a more risky play that would lead to sure victory if successful, sure defeat if not.
4. The president of an American corporation which is about to expand may build a new plant in the United States where returns on the investment would be moderate, or may decide to build in a foreign country with an unstable political history where, however, returns on the investment would be very high.
5. A college senior planning graduate work in chemistry may enter university X where, because of rigorous standards, only a fraction of the graduate students manage to receive the PhD, or may enter university Y which has a poorer reputation but where almost every graduate student receives the PhD.
6. A college senior with considerable musical talent must choose between the secure course of going on to medical school and becoming a physician, or the risky course of embarking on the career of a concert pianist.
7. An American prisoner-of-war in World War II must choose between possible escape with the risk of execution if caught, or remaining in the camp where privations are severe.
8. A research physicist, just beginning a five-year appointment at a university, may spend the time working on a series of short-term problems which he would be sure to solve but which would be of lesser importance, or on a very important but very difficult problem with the risk of nothing to show for his five years of effort.
9. An engaged couple must decide, in the face of recent arguments suggesting some sharp differences of opinion, whether or not to get married. Discussions with a marriage counselor indicate that a happy marriage, while possible, would not be assured.

Source: Wallach, Kogan, & Bem (1962, p. 86)

attitude. When group members argue their positions, they encounter other people's arguments that had not yet occurred to them as individuals. Group attitude change depends on whether everyone already knows similar arguments, in which case the group members are not exposed to much new information. Change also depends on how many arguments potentially could support a given position. An attitude with many good arguments supporting it has a higher probability of those arguments coming to light than does an attitude with fewer supporting arguments.

One critical test of the persuasive arguments theory comes from a study in which students were either (a) exposed to the opinions of others and given time to think about those opinions, (b) exposed to the opinions of others and not given time to think about the opinions, or (c) not exposed to the opinions of others but given time to think about the topic (Burnstein & Vinokur, 1975).

Only some students' attitudes changed: those who knew the opinions of others and who had time to generate supporting arguments for them. In other supportive studies, information is exchanged in an actual discussion (Rajecki, 1982). Both the number and persuasiveness of arguments affect group polarization (Hinsz & Davis, 1984). The effect may be limited to contexts that emphasize reasonableness and considered debate (McLachlan, 1986).

Another informational explanation for group polarization effects relies on **social comparison theory** (Chapter 5). In some cases, choice shift can be produced simply by information about others' positions (e.g., Teger & Pruitt, 1967). People apparently shift their opinions when they learn that, relative to the opinions of others, they themselves were not as risky as they had imagined. Such comparison processes operate most strongly when people know the risk-relevant personality traits of other people because this establishes a basis for the social comparison process (Goethals & Zanna, 1979). (For reviews, see R. Brown, 1986; Isenberg, 1986.)

A variant on the social comparison theory combines informational and normative influences to explain attitude polarization in groups from **social identification** and **self-categorization theories** (Turner, 1987). In Chapter 11 we explain that people categorize themselves and others into distinct social groups. As a result, people stereotype both ingroup and outgroup members and, consequently, themselves. Consistent with this theory, when people categorize others as a group and expect to join them, they perceive the group norm to be more extreme than otherwise (Mackie, 1986). Group members use the group's distinctive and consensual position to signal their identity (Postmes, Spears, Lee, & Novak, 2005). The group develops a prototype of the ideal position, which may be more extreme than the average member (McGarty, Turner, Hogg, Davidson, & Wetherell, 1992; Turner, Wetherell, & Hogg, 1989). Individuals polarize their attitudes when intergroup context is salient (Hogg, Turner, & Davidson, 1990; Turner et al., 1989). Groups polarize in the direction of the group norm especially when members are depersonalized (Turner, 1985) and cannot be individually identified (R. Brown, 1986; Postmes, Haslam, & Swaab, 2005; Spears, Postmes, Lea, & Wolbert, 2002, for reviews). Groups that form around a shared identity gain consensus by top-down deduction from that identity; groups that form around relationships among independent individuals instead gain consensus by bottom-up induction from members' contributions.

Group polarization effects thus depend on categorizing oneself as a member of the group making the arguments. For example, when an overheard discussion is attributed to a group one expects to join, one perceives the group to have more extreme attitudes, and one's attitude shifts in conformity with those stereotypic attitudes (Mackie, 1986; Mackie & Cooper, 1984). Clearly, people use attitudes in the group categorization process (Hymes, 1986).

An emerging approach to attitudes in group processes uses computer simulations to represent the distributions of individuals with various attitudes, knowledge, goals, and other characteristics, all interacting with each other as autonomous agents (E. R. Smith & Conrey, 2007). **Agent-based modeling** applies to a variety of social processes in particular situations, potentially describing networks of social influence (Mason, Conrey, & Smith, 2004).

These cognitive theories of attitude polarization in groups provide informational bases for persuasion, either as a function of exposure to persuasive arguments, social comparison information, or prototypical ingroup opinion. These are only some of the possible explanations and only one type of attitude change in groups. Nevertheless, they illustrate the utility of cognitive approaches to understanding some aspects of groups. People's everyday ideas about the social context of their own attitudes affect their responses to information-based persuasion.

Implicit Theories about Attitude Stability and Change

People's everyday theories related to attitudes take seriously another aspect of social context – oneself. Originally, **self-perception theory** (D. J. Bem, 1972; Chapter 6) posited that, when uncertain, people infer their attitudes from their own behavior. One result is that people may misrecall their own prior attitudes. After successful persuasion, people can conveniently perceive their attitudes as never having changed at all (D. J. Bem & McConnell, 1970). If a person's pre-persuasion attitudes are not salient, the person infers new attitudes from current behavior. Thus people tend to misrecall their attitudes to bring them in line with their behavior (cf. Fazio, Zanna, & Cooper, 1977; Wixon & Laird, 1976). A more recent approach elaborates perceived stability and change in one's attitudes based more explicitly on people's implicit theories of their own attitude change.

What were your attitudes toward religion five years ago? Fairly similar to the ones you have now? Most people assume their attitudes have been fairly stable, and in most instances they are right. However, perhaps you have undergone a conversion experience, in which case you would answer that your attitudes toward religion have changed quite a lot. Often, we stay the same, but sometimes we change. Sometimes we perceive the stability, and sometimes not. Sometimes we perceive the change, and sometimes not.

One theory (M. Ross, 1989) describes people's **implicit theories** that construct their personal histories, arguing that people's perceptions of stability and change depend on their implicit theories of when they do and do not change. The theory posits a two-step process whereby people use their current attitudes as a starting point and then apply their theories to decide whether they would have been different in the past. Consistent with implicit theories of stability, people often do not perceive themselves to have changed when indeed they have. Subtle forms of persuasion have this impact; people perceive their initial attitudes to be similar to their current (changed) attitudes, and they claim not to have changed (D. J. Bem & McConnell, 1970; Goethals & Reckman, 1973; M. Ross & Shulman, 1973). Even when changes spontaneously emerge over time or the course of a relationship, people do not perceive their attitudes to have changed (McFarland & Ross, 1987). Moreover, because people typically assume consistency, they base their recall of past behaviors on current attitudes. The implicit theory seems to run: (a) One behaves consistently with one's attitudes, and (b) one's attitudes are stable; therefore, (c) one's current attitudes are a reliable guide to past behavior. Again, subtle persuasion can alter people's attitudes and bias their recall of prior behavior to fit their current attitude (M. Ross, McFarland, Conway, & Zanna, 1983; M. Ross, McFarland, & Fletcher, 1981). When participants do recall past behaviors just after a changed attitude, they become more committed to the new attitude (Lydon, Zanna, & Ross, 1988; M. Ross et al., 1983). Other things being equal, we expect our attitudes to be stable and make inferences accordingly.

But other things are not always equal: People have conversions, join weight loss programs, enter therapy, get divorced, move to new places, are promoted or fired, survive wars, are victimized, grow older, and so on. People expect some events to change them, so they have implicit theories about events' propensity to change people. Have you ever heard anyone emerge from a significant amount of therapy and perceive no change whatsoever in his or her perceptions, understanding, or feelings? As noted earlier, people in one study skills program expected improvement, so they misperceived themselves as initially worse off than they had been and misremembered their final grades as better than they were. Both processes allowed them to see themselves as having improved, which was consistent with their theories (Conway & Ross, 1984). Such events are expected to promote change (and often do). Similarly, some attributes are expected to change (M. Ross, 1989). For example, attitudes toward social categories in general are expected to be stable across the life span, but attitudes toward one's own age group and its typical activities are expected to change with age (people do not expect attitudes toward skateboards to be stable across the life span).

Considerable evidence suggests that people's reconstruction of their own past is guided by implicit theories of stability and change. Although this evidence primarily regards perceptions of stability and change in attitudes, the theory also applies to people's construction of their own prior traits and feelings (M. Ross, 1989). According to **temporal self-appraisal theory**, people distance themselves from their negative past selves and reduce the distance to their positive past selves, especially when they have high self-esteem (M. Ross & Wilson, 2002; Table 9.4). In general, people disparage their distant past attributes and praise their recent past selves, believing in how much they have improved "from chump to champ" (A. E. Wilson & Ross, 2001). In the attitude domain, people endorse their current attitudes and typically view them as relatively stable, at least in the recent past, enhancing their self-assurance.

Table 9.4   Attitudes toward past self

Rate yourself in your final year of high school, on scales from 1 to 7:
popular/unpopular _____
socially skilled/not socially skilled _____
accepted/rejected _____
cool/uncool _____
a lot of friends/few friends _____
friendly/unfriendly _____
sociable/unsociable _____
lonely/not lonely _____
well-liked/disliked _____

Now rate the subjective distance of your high-school self by placing marks on the two lines

feel very close to my past self	*feel very distant from my past self*
my past self feels very near	*my past self feels very far away*

Source: M. Ross & Wilson (2002)

Conclusion about Lay Theories of Attitudes

We have seen three approaches that rely on people's own ideas about attitude change. The first examines the communicator's motives, in order to infer the credibility of the information given. The second examines people's ideas about the information they receive in groups, both information about other people's positions relative to their own and information about the topic. The third examines people's naive theories about their own attitude change processes. All three involve people using their own social theories to reflect on the social circumstances of their attitudes.

FUNCTIONAL DIMENSIONS OF ATTITUDES

Another approach examines the relationship of attitudes to the self in a different way. Earlier, we discussed cognitive features of two consistency theories of attitudes: dissonance theory and balance theory. These classic cognitive consistency theories have a motivational basis; inconsistency is presumably aversive, prompting people to resolve the inconsistency by various means, including attitude change. As we have seen, subsequent theories of attitudes have tended to focus on their cognitive dynamics such as attributional analyses, persuasive arguments theories in groups, and implicit theories of self.

Some classic theories differentiated motivational functions of attitudes and attitude change, differentiating among **compliance** to gain rewards and avoid punishments, **identification** and conformity to enhance belonging with valued groups, and **internalization** to store attitude-relevant knowledge (Kelman, 1958). Recent approaches again more actively take motivation into account, emphasizing functions that attitudes serve for people. Specifically, some of these functional approaches focus on conviction, strength, and importance, which certainly have motivational components, and others specify particular attitude functions.

Conviction, Strength, and Importance

Some attitudes centrally involve motivation, for they are held with conviction. Such attitudes tend to be stable, and people know they are stable. **Conviction** includes (Abelson, 1988) emotional commitment; attitudes that people hold with conviction are those about which they feel absolutely correct, cannot imagine ever changing their minds, have a moral sense, and they feel committed to work. Conviction also involves ego preoccupation: often thinking about the issue, holding strong views, and being concerned. Finally, conviction implicates cognitive elaboration, which means having held the view for a while, connecting to other issues, seeing its broad implications, knowing a lot about it, and explaining it easily. Most individuals have only one or two such issues. But attitudes held with conviction are stable and central to the self in several respects.

A related concept, attitude **strength,** illustrates some such respects (Eagly & Chaiken, 1998). Attitude strength includes various interrelated components (Bassili & Krosnick, 2000). For example, importance and certainty both predict attempts to persuade others (Visser, Krosnick, & Simmons, 2003). Attitude strength increases until middle age and then declines, meaning that younger and older adults change their minds most easily because their attitudes are less important and certain (Visser & Krosnick, 1998).

By itself, attitude **importance** – a person's interest or concern about an attitude (Krosnick, 1988a) – predicts information seeking (Visser et al., 2003). Attitude importance is most similar to what has been termed **value-relevant involvement**, which generally inhibits persuasion according to a meta-analytic research review (B. T. Johnson & Eagly, 1989). Similarly, important attitudes are stable (Krosnick, 1989), accessible (Krosnick, 1989), and allow one to differentiate among relevant objects. For example, personally important policy attitudes (e.g., toward welfare, abortion, immigration) are accessible when one evaluates political candidates, and one can discern differences among them on that issue better than can someone for whom the attitude is not important. Consequently, important attitudes better predict preferences among presidential candidates than do unimportant attitudes (Krosnick, 1988b). Other people also appreciate the impact of attitude importance. When someone says an issue is important, observers infer that the person holds extreme attitudes (Mackie & Gastardo-Conaco, 1988).

Important attitudes also show greater consistency with each other. Thus, if one holds two important attitudes, they are unlikely to contradict each other (Judd & Krosnick, 1982). Similarly, experts for whom relevant attitudes are likely to be important also show considerable consistency among their attitudes. People who know a lot about politics, report that they are politically interested, or follow political news are especially consistent (Judd & Krosnick, 1989). Important attitudes apparently are accessible (Bizer & Krosnick, 2001), persist over time, predict other choices, and connect to other attitudes (Judd & Krosnick, 1989).

Such attitudes show **centrality** (rich connection) to people's values. It would seem difficult, therefore, to change attitudes that people hold to be important. One intriguing strategy does seem to change attitudes about which people are highly certain (and therefore probably the attitudes are important ones). A communicator offers statements that are even more extreme than people's own attitudes and encourages people to endorse them. People who are certain about their attitudes recognize this apparent manipulation and resist the attempt to make them more extreme. In reaction, they change their attitude away from their own previous position. This paradoxical strategy (Swann, Pelham, & Chidester, 1988) works only with people who are certain of their attitudes. Attitudes about which one has **certainty** help to organize one's experience and matter to one's sense of self. Thus people attempt to self-verify (see Chapter 5) and reject the overly extreme positions by backing away from them.

Attitude Functions

Attitude functions can be divided in a few ways. Here we split them into knowledge, values, and sociality (Table 9.5). These newer approaches explicitly incorporate motivation, reexamining

Table 9.5   Functions of attitudes

---

1. *Object-appraisal* includes (a) cognitive knowledge function and often (b) utilitarian, instrumental, or goal function

(a) knowledge function is fundamentally cognitive and adaptive, making sense of the world
   - *understanding* motives make sense of the world
   - related: *internalization* of knowledge-based attitudes
(b) instrumental function is also adaptive, helping to avoid pain and receive rewards
   - *outcome-relevant involvement* is motivated by the ability to attain desirable outcomes
   - *response involvement* maximizes the rewards in a given situation
   - *task involvement* is concerned only with the consequences of a particular response
   - related: *compliance* as responding to rewards and punishments
2. *Value-expression* demonstrates and maintains long-term standards and orientations
   - *value-relevant involvement* is motivated by enduring values
   - *self-enhancement* motives protect and improve self-concept (here, as principled)
   - related: attitude *importance and conviction*
3. *Social-adjustment* functions for the self to signal interpersonal priorities, sensitivity to others, and getting along with people
   - *impression-relevant involvement* relates to need for affiliation, sensitivity to approval, awareness of self-presentation
   - *belonging* motives aim to fit into a group
   - related: attitude *identification* and conformity with a valued group
4. variously relevant:
   - *Ego involvement, issue involvement, personal involvement,* and *vested interest* all imply personal relevance or meaning, especially intrinsic importance for beliefs central to a person's identity.

---

traditional theories of attitudes' motivational functions (e.g., D. Katz, 1960; M. B. Smith, Bruner, & White, 1956), but with new cognitive twists.

Knowledge Functions

The most fundamental attitude function is an **object-appraisal function**, which prominently includes a cognitive *knowledge* function and often an *instrumental*, utilitarian, or goal function (Eagly & Chaiken, 1998; Greenwald, 1989; Pratkanis & Greenwald, 1989). The **knowledge function** of an attitude is fundamentally cognitive and adaptive. Attitudes help people to make sense of the world, to order and organize it. Moreover, attitudes can have **instrumental** and adaptive functions, helping people to avoid pain and receive rewards. The object-appraisal functions of attitudes may act as heuristics (Pratkanis, 1988), simple evaluative strategies for problem solving. For example, attitudes help define attitude-consistent information as true; liked people are assumed to have good qualities and disliked people to have bad ones. Attitudes affect a range of knowledge-related problem-solving activities: interpretation and explanation, reasoning, responses to persuasion, judgment, perceived consensus, identification of facts and errors, and prediction.

The knowledge function of attitudes may also serve schematic functions, shaping attitude-relevant memory. Attitudes can have a bipolar structure: Extreme material on either side is most easily judged and recalled (Judd & Kulik, 1980). Attitudes can also have a **unipolar** structure: Well-elaborated material supports one side, with little or nothing on the opposing side (Eagly & Chaiken, 1998; Pratkanis & Greenwald, 1989).

The motivational aspect of the knowledge function has been examined in an impressive series of studies designed to heighten people's need for cognitive clarity and structure (Jamieson & Zanna, 1989). Recall from Chapter 2 that the need for structure (Kruglanski, 1990; Kruglanski & Sheveland, 2012) induces people to cut short information seeking, which leads them to rely more heavily on their already-formed schemas and attitudes. People's need for structure can be enhanced by putting them under time pressure, stress, or increased arousal. Under these conditions, people form structurally simpler attitudes, and they rely more heavily on already-formed attitudes. Similar effects (simpler attitudes under pressure) can be observed in the real-world rhetoric of political leaders (Tetlock, 1985). The knowledge functions of attitudes relate to a variety of attitude operations.

Value Functions

The **value-expressive function** of attitudes describes the importance to people of demonstrating and maintaining their long-term standards and orientations. This is similar to B. T. Johnson and Eagly's (1989) **value-relevant involvement**, which inhibits persuasion based on mere argument strength. It also relates to attitude importance and conviction, just reviewed. People seem especially committed to attitudes that serve value-expressive functions, especially when they suffer or incur costs for holding those attitudes (Lydon & Zanna, 1990).

People differ in the value-expressive functions of their attitudes. For example, low **self-monitors** are people who do not regulate themselves with regard to the social situation but instead rely heavily on their inner thoughts and feelings to guide their behavior (M. Snyder, 1974; Chapter 15). Consequently, their own attitudes are more important to them than, say, the norms of the situation or the attitudes of their friends. Such people would be expected to have a stronger motivation for value expression than other people (M. Snyder & DeBono, 1985). Indeed, low self-monitors are especially likely to appeal selectively to their long-term values to justify their attitudes (Kristiansen & Zanna, 1988). Low self-monitors rely more heavily on appeals to important values (DeBono, 1987). Similarly, low self-monitors are particularly attentive to expert sources because they presumably provide reliable, value-relevant information (DeBono & Harnish, 1988).

People can have conflicting values about an attitude object, which potentially can cause problems when using an attitude to express their values. For example, White Americans often have ambivalent attitudes toward Black Americans, attitudes that elicit core values related to humanitarian and egalitarian values, on one hand, and to Protestant work ethic values, on the other hand (I. Katz & Hass, 1988). Depending on which is primed, White racial attitudes are correspondingly more positive or negative (see Dovidio & Gaertner, 1986, for related ideas).

Attitudes are likely to be more cognitively complex when they relate to core conflicting values (Tetlock, 1986). That is, assuming value expression is important, people work especially hard to reconcile important value conflicts, creating trade-offs that result in greater attitudinal and ideological complexity. An ideological position, such as liberalism, may entail (at least superficially) core conflicting values because of its emphasis on diversity; this attempt to reconcile conflicting values may result in more complex reasoning styles (Tetlock, 1984, 1986), which are not merely a function of rhetorical style (Tetlock, Hannum, & Micheletti, 1984; but see Sidanius, 1988). Upward shifts in complexity on both sides generally preceded major American–Soviet agreements, and downward shifts have preceded major military–political interventions (Tetlock, 1988). Value expression can have global effects.

Ideology expresses values through a set of related attitudes that define their preferred societal and political arrangements (Kay & Eibach, 2012). Ideology specifies both the fair distribution of resources (i.e., inequality, social safety nets) and moral authority (i.e., prescriptions and proscriptions). Ideology may be the ultimate in value-expressive function, which is why compromise seems unthinkable on both sides.

Social Functions

Attitudes also serve important **social-adjustive functions** for the self. Sometimes attitudes signal interpersonal priorities, sensitivity to others, and getting along with people in general. This function resembles B. T. Johnson and Eagly's (1989) **impression-relevant involvement**. This function tends to inhibit persuasion based on argument strength, which is presumably not the most important determinant of social-adjustive attitudes. Social-adjustive attitudes are most prominent for people with a high need for affiliation, sensitivity to approval, and well-developed awareness of their self-presentation to others (Herek, 1986). For example, prejudiced or egalitarian attitudes toward homosexuals can either promote acceptance by one's immediate peer group (social-adjustive functions) or demonstrate one's core moral stands (value-expressive functions). Again, self-monitoring differences show that high self-monitors, being more attuned to interpersonal settings, are more likely to have socially adjustive attitudes than are low self-monitors. High self-monitors more carefully process the message of an interpersonally attractive source (DeBono & Harnish, 1988), attend more to the images projected by consumer products (DeBono & Snyder, 1989; Snyder & DeBono, 1985), and rely more heavily on consensus information (DeBono, 1987; Snyder & DeBono, 1987).

The central empirical issue for functional theories has always been to identify a priori the functions served by particular attitudes for particular individuals. One approach, as we have seen, is to examine individual differences (i.e., self-monitoring) in the types of attitudes individuals are likely to hold. Another intriguing approach posits that certain attitude objects are intrinsically likely to elicit attitudes serving different functions (Shavitt, 1989). That is, the social-adjustive function of high-status clothing is more readily apparent than is the social-adjustive function of one's air conditioner. Moreover, people show some cross-domain consistency in the functions of their attitudes, values, and even possessions (Prentice, 1987). The bottom line is that certain individuals, in concert with certain attitudes and certain situations, hold attitudes for different functional reasons.

Summary

An attitude is a hypothetical mediating variable assumed to intervene between stimulus and response. Attitudes involve at least an evaluation of the attitude object, and many definitions also include cognitions and behavioral tendencies. Social cognition's contribution to the field began with a metatheoretical approach valuing a fine-grained analysis of the cognitive processes involved in attitude formation and change. Attitude research has also borrowed specific theories and methods from social cognition research.

Two traditional cognitive consistency theories have profited from newer social cognition insights. Dissonance theory's long-standing hypothesis of selective perception to support one's attitudes includes selective exposure (seeking attitude-consistent information), selective attention (heeding attitude-consistent information), and selective interpretation (perceiving ambiguous information to be attitude-consistent). Although evidence for selective exposure entails mostly *de facto* rather than deliberate exposure, evidence for selective attention and interpretation fully supports the premises of dissonance theory. In addition, dissonance theory has concerned selective learning and retention of attitude-relevant information. Incidental learning of attitude-consistent information demonstrates selectivity, but intentional learning and high degrees of motivation eliminate selectivity. People with high self-esteem, an internal locus of control, or a tendency to repress unpleasant experiences all show greater selectivity, which is consistent with dissonance theory.

Another consistency approach, balance theory, also posits that people selectively recall information, in this case information about the attitudes of self and others. People can most readily remember that friends agree (and perhaps that enemies disagree). A balanced triad of two friends who feel the same way about particular attitude objects creates a compact cognitive unit that is easier to imagine, comprehend, and remember. An unbalanced triad is more difficult and seems to be stored in separate pieces. Attitudes in general organize memory for relevant information to the extent that people may have difficulty remembering the evidence on which their attitudes were based.

Some social cognitive approaches emphasize people's everyday theories about persuasion. For example, attributional analyses of why the communicator is delivering a particular message influence persuasion. If a communicator delivers a particular message because of the audience or other situational factors, then it is suspect. Similarly, if a communicator is dispositionally biased in terms of knowledge or reporting motives, then the message is perceived as untrustworthy. Another lay theory approach examines attitude polarization in groups as a function of persuasive arguments raised by group members, social comparison information, or group identity.

Finally, people's implicit theories about stability and change encourage people to perceive or misperceive stability and change in their own attitudes and other dispositions. People do not typically expect their attitudes to change, so they misperceive stability, even when their attitudes have been altered by subtle means. Moreover, people misrecall their prior behavior to fit their current attitudes, again in line with the general belief that attitudes are stable and behavior accordingly follows. When people's theories suggest change, however, they also (mis)perceive change following a conversion, a self-help program, therapy, and the like.

People's attitudes vary along some dimensions important to social cognition. Conviction involves several components related to the importance of one's attitudes: emotional commitment, ego preoccupation, and cognitive elaboration. A related term for conviction is value-relevant involvement, and another related concept is strength. Whatever their name, such significant attitudes are few (for most people) and resist change. Such attitudes are stable, accessible, differentiate among attitude objects, and are consistent with other attitudes. They may be open to change only by paradoxical techniques.

People's attitudes serve several functions relevant to knowledge, values, and sociality. First, people's attitudes serve a knowledge function, providing heuristics for rapid responses and schemas for organizing knowledge. As people's need for structure increases, they are more likely to rely on their ready-made attitudes or on simple attitudes quickly constructed. Attitudes can also serve a self function of value expression, allowing people to demonstrate their prized standards and orientations. The attitudes of low self-monitors are especially likely to serve value-expressive functions. When people hold core conflicting values, their relevant attitudes become more complex with the necessity of integrating them. Finally, attitudes can also serve social-adjustive self functions. They help people to fit in with other people and to demonstrate interpersonal attunement. High self-monitors, who are oriented to the social environment, are more likely to hold social-adjustive attitudes. Apart from individual differences, some attitude objects may typically elicit attitudes with particular types of functions.

The various cognitive approaches to attitudes – those elaborating traditional theories and those positing altogether new processes, those emphasizing more thoughtful or more automatic processes, and those focusing almost entirely on cognition or more actively including motivation – have various implications for intergroup stereotyping and prejudice, for affect, and for the relationship between cognition and behavior, as the next chapters indicate.

FURTHER READING

Albarracín, D., & Vargas, P. (2010). Attitudes and persuasion: From biology to social responses to persuasive intent. In S. T. Fiske, D. T. Gilbert, & G. Lindzey (Eds.), *Handbook of social psychology* (5th edn, Vol. 1, pp. 394–427). Hoboken, NJ: Wiley.

Conrey, F. R., & Smith, E. R. (2007). Attitude representation: Attitudes as patterns in a distributed, connectionist representational system. *Social Cognition, 25(5),* 718–735.

Crano, W. D., & Prislin, R. (2006). Attitudes and persuasion. *Annual Review of Psychology, 57,* 345–374.

Eagly, A. H., & Chaiken, S. (2005). Attitude research in the 21st century: The current state of knowledge. In D. Albarracín, B. T. Johnson, & M. P. Zanna (Eds.), *The handbook of attitudes* (pp. 743–767). Mahwah, NJ: Erlbaum.

Ferguson, M. J., & Fukukura, J. (2012). Likes and dislikes: A social cognitive perspective on attitudes. In S. T. Fiske & C. N. Macrae (Eds.), *Sage handbook of social cognition* (pp. 165–190). Thousand Oaks, CA: Sage.

Kay, A. C., & Eibach, R. P. (2012). Ideological processes. In S. T. Fiske & C. N. Macrae (Eds.), *Sage handbook of social cognition* (pp. 495–516). Thousand Oaks, CA: Sage.

Kruglanski, A. W., & Sheveland, A. (2012). Thinkers' personalities: On individual differences in the processes of sense making. In S. T. Fiske & C. N. Macrae (Eds.), *Sage handbook of social cognition* (pp. 474–494). Thousand Oaks, CA: Sage.

Morling, B., & Masuda, T. (2012). Social cognition in real worlds: Cultural psychology and social cognition. In S. T. Fiske & C. N. Macrae (Eds.), *Sage handbook of social cognition* (pp. 429–450). Thousand Oaks, CA: Sage.

Cognitive Processing of Attitudes

10

- Heuristic versus Systematic Model
- Peripheral versus Central Routes to Persuasion: Elaboration Likelihood Model
- Motivation and Opportunity Determine Attitude Processes: The Mode Model
- Implicit Associations
- Embodied Attitudes
- Neural Correlates of Attitudes

In the previous chapter, we examined the explicitly cognitive aspects of several traditional attitude theories focused on attitude structure and function. One early attitude theory of process specially foreshadows modern cognitive approaches, proposing an expressly sequential information-processing model. Remember that Chapter 1 described early information-processing models as breaking mental operations into sequential stages. McGuire's (1969, 1976, 1985) **chain of cognitive responses** outlines the necessary conditions, many of them cognitive, for a persuasive communication to influence behavior; the steps include exposure, attention, comprehension, yielding, retention, retrieval, decision, and behavior (Table 10.1). Consider, as an example, political campaign literature. To be effective, not only must campaign managers expose voters to the literature, say, by distributing a leaflet under people's windshield wipers, but they also must ensure that the flyer grabs attention and conveys an understandable, convincing message. People have to retain their (presumably positive) new attitude, retrieve it, and decide to use it to determine the critical behavior: voting for Smedley rather than Smiley for dogcatcher. The entire sequence of carefully specified cognitive steps theoretically results in behavior. As such, the theory anticipates more recent cognitively oriented work in attitudes. Moreover, several of the stages specified by McGuire continue to be important (Eagly & Chaiken, 1984).

More broadly, several attitude theories of processing are themselves fundamentally cognitive in orientation. A review of the field of attitudes being prohibitive, in this chapter we examine cognitively oriented theories that explicitly build on social cognition ideas; each one specifies different

Table 10.1   Chain of cognitive responses: Necessary conditions for a persuasive communication to influence behavior

Stage	Political Campaign Example	Obstacles
Exposure	Encounter leaflet on windshields	Leaflet blows away
Attention	Captures more than a glance	Driver ignores; it's raining
Comprehension	Understand easily	Communication too difficult; font too small
Yielding	Convincing	Arguments are weak; failed to pretest
Retention	Memorable	Opinion fades
Retrieval	Recall favorable opinion	Too unimportant to remember dogcatcher
Decision	Choose to act on attitude	Unmotivated to act because uninvolved
Behavior	Able to act as intended	Cat's competing demands prevent action

Source: McGuire (1969, 1976, 1985)

modes of attitude processing based on cognitive principles. Foreshadowed in Chapter 2, the first three focus on dual modes of attitudinal processing and, in particular, on the degree to which people's attitudes form, change, and operate in relatively thoughtful or more automatic ways. After automatic responses, we briefly touch on implicit associations. The remaining two theories examine the interplay of attitudes and our physical beings: embodied attitudes and neural aspects of attitudes.

HEURISTIC VERSUS SYSTEMATIC MODEL

Many classic theories of attitudes posit that attitudes form and change based on thoughtful consideration of issue-relevant information. For example, McGuire's (1969) chain of persuasion assumed that people process and evaluate the arguments provided, accordingly agreeing or disagreeing with the persuasive communication. Similarly, the dominant framework for studying attitudes over a period of nearly two decades, the **Yale persuasive communications approach** (Hovland et al., 1953), emphasized learning message content and its conscious acceptance or rejection. Moreover, one of the most comprehensive theories of attitudes and behavior, the **theory of reasoned action** (Fishbein & Ajzen, 1974), later elaborated into the **theory of planned behavior** (Ajzen, 1987), stated that attitudes are importantly based on people's cognitive beliefs about the attitude object (Chapter 15). While not specifically a theory of cognitive processes, this theory does emphasize a deliberate, thoughtful process; namely, evaluating the strengths and weaknesses of one's particular beliefs, assessing their systematic implications for one's attitude, and ultimately, along with perceived norms and control, assessing their implications for one's behavior. These traditional theories essentially focus on a relatively controlled or systematic form of attitude formation and change.

The **heuristic-systematic model** (e.g., Chaiken, 1980; Chen & Chaiken 1999) proposes that people engage in such thoughtful processes only when they are sufficiently motivated and have the capacity to do so (Table 10.2). When people are relatively motivated, they indeed can engage in this thoughtful, effortful mode, termed **systematic processing**, which involves evaluating the pros and cons of a message's arguments. For example, systematic processing increases with various factors that increase motivation: receiving messages on topics of high personal relevance, making attitude judgments with important consequences, having sole responsibility for message evaluation, and discovering that one disagrees with the majority position (for a review, see Eagly & Chaiken, 1993). Systematic processing entails sensitivity to the valence and quality of a message, issue-relevant thoughts, enhanced recall for the arguments, and relatively lasting change (e.g., Axsom, Yates, & Chaiken, 1987; Mackie, 1987; McFarland, Ross, & Conway, 1984).

In contrast to this strategy that emphasizes relatively thoughtful processing of attitude-relevant information, people often engage in a more rapid, easy, **heuristic processing**. According to Chaiken's theory, people learn certain persuasion heuristics or rules (in arguments, long-is-strong; in communicators, believe-beauty and trust-an-expert); these shortcuts avoid effortful processing of the actual message contents. Learned from experience, the rules are often accurate enough. Equally important, heuristic processing makes relatively few capacity demands. People apparently use the heuristic strategy when they lack room for the more systematic type of processing. When cognitive capacity reduces, people are less likely to engage in systematic processing and more likely to engage in heuristic processing (e.g., Mackie & Worth, 1989; W. Wood, Kallgren, & Preisler, 1985).

One implication of the heuristic–systematic distinction in persuasion is that people may or may not carefully process message arguments, sometimes relying on shortcuts, sometimes engaging more comprehensive, analytic, systematic process. When they do each depends on various motives; for example, accuracy motives, defensive motives, and impression management motives all potentially influence the extent of heuristic or systematic processing (Chaiken, Liberman, & Eagly, 1989). These types of motives resemble those discussed in Chapter 2 as motives that encourage more automatic or controlled processes in general. For example, when motivated to be

Table 10.2 Heuristic-systematic model (Chaiken)

Mode	Processes	Moderators
Systematic processing	Consider message valence & quality Issue-relevant thoughts Recall arguments Lasting change	Personal interest Personal consequences Personal responsibility Lack of consensus
Heuristic processing	Use rapid, effortless informal rules Messages: long-is-strong Communicators: believe-beauty Communicators: trust-an-expert	Low cognitive capacity Low motivation

accepted by their partner, people use a go-along-to-get-along heuristic, expressing attitudes consistent with their partner's views (Chen, Shechter, & Chaiken, 1996).

PERIPHERAL VERSUS CENTRAL ROUTES TO PERSUASION: ELABORATION LIKELIHOOD MODEL

Another cognitively oriented model of persuasion also proposes two routes to attitude change (Petty & Cacioppo, 1981, 1986; Petty & Wegener, 1998). According to the **elaboration likelihood model**, the **central route** recruits active, careful thinking about (i.e., elaborating) the true merits of the message arguments and, in this sense, resembles the systematic route proposed by Chaiken's heuristic-systematic model. The **peripheral route** to persuasion includes any attitude change that occurs without much thought or elaboration. As such, this route includes Chaiken's heuristic mode as well as other types of superficial attitude change. For example, mere exposure effects on evaluations (Chapter 14) would be a peripheral (but not a heuristic) mode of persuasion.

One basic postulate of the elaboration likelihood model is that people are motivated to hold correct attitudes. With sufficient motivation and ability to process a message, people respond to argument quality. The balance of their favorable, unfavorable, and neutral thoughts then determines positive or negative attitude change by the central route, posited to be enduring. The amount and type of cognitive elaboration (issue-relevant thinking) depend on individual and situational factors. **Elaboration** includes making relevant associations, scrutinizing the arguments, inferring their value, and evaluating the overall message.

Methods

Elaboration is assessed in various ways (Petty & Cacioppo, 1986). One could ask people directly how much effort they invested in processing the message, but people cannot or will not always answer accurately. Two techniques have proved more successful in assessing degrees of cognitive elaboration. The first, **cognitive response analysis**, examines the recipient's cognitions (especially counterarguments) as the message is received (Brock, 1967); the favorability of the recipient's cognitive responses to persuasion directly relates to the degree of attitude change (Greenwald, 1968). The elaboration likelihood theory built on the earlier cognitive response technique by conceptualizing exactly how counterarguments and supporting arguments cause attitude change.

The cognitive response technique itself is a simple and elegant way to measure cognitive mediation. In general, cognitive **mediation** means that some stimulus causes a cognitive effect, which in turn causes an overt response (Chapter 3). In the case of persuasive communication, cognitive mediation entails a stimulus (low or high argument quality) causing a cognitive mediator (low or high counterarguing), which in turn causes a response (attitude change). In cognitive response research, participants not only give an opinion on the topic at hand but also list their thoughts during or just after receiving the communication. The cognitive responses are scored as reactions pro and con, and thus they presumably mediate attitude change. When researchers use the cognitive response method in concert with the elaboration likelihood model, they show that attitude change often is caused by one's personal responses to a message (Figure 10.1).

Cognitive response analysis is a method, but it is not a theory. As a technique, cognitive response analysis is compatible with various attitude theories (Petty, Ostrom, & Brock, 1981). Being a methodological technique, it does not guarantee theoretical advance by itself. The technique of cognitive response analysis has been applied to communicator, message, and audience variables.

Another method for assessing elaboration involves experimental manipulation rather than measurement of cognitive elaboration as the proposed mediator. By manipulating the quality of the message itself, one can see whether participants respond differently to the strong or weak arguments. If they are sensitive to argument quality, they are presumably thinking about what they received, so they are elaborating on it and, by definition, following the central route. If they are not sensitive to argument quality, then they are not elaborating much, and they are taking the more peripheral route. Much of the elaboration likelihood research program manipulates argument quality as well as some situational variable posited to affect elaboration, and then measures both cognitive responses and attitude change.

Armed with these methods, in particular cognitive response analysis and manipulations of argument strength, the elaboration likelihood model addresses many basic processes in persuasion (Petty & Cacioppo, 1981, 1986; Petty & Wegener, 1998). It emphasizes the *extent* and the *valence* (direction) of thinking to predict attitude change, and more recently, people's *confidence* in their thoughts has emerged as an important predictor (Petty, Briñol, & Tormala, 2002). The next few sections illustrate elaboration likelihood analyses of communicator, message, and audience. As we will see, many standard attitude change effects depend on the audience's (i.e., the participant's)

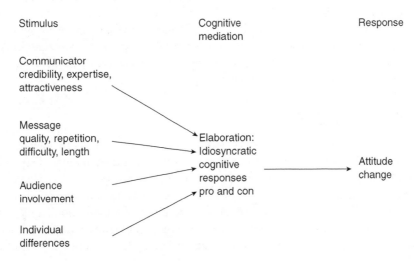

Figure 10.1   Cognitive response analysis

involvement with the persuasive message. In particular, outcome involvement, value involvement, and impression involvement all differ (B. T. Johnson & Eagly, 1989).

Communicator Effects

Who says it – the message source – heavily influences processes and outcomes of persuasion. The peripheral route often results from simple cues regarding the *expertise* and *attractiveness* of the communicator. For example, students were told that a mandatory comprehensive exam for all seniors was advocated by an expert source (Carnegie Commission on Higher Education) or by an inexpert source (a high-school class). When the issue was relevant to the students – because it would be instituted at their own school the next year – the students were more sensitive to the quality of the strong or weak arguments presented, as the elaboration likelihood model would predict. Moreover, when the issue was relevant, source expertise made little difference. However, when the issue was less relevant (the exam would be instituted elsewhere or much later) and students were, therefore, less outcome involved, source expertise essentially determined their attitudes, regardless of argument quality (Petty, Cacioppo, & Goldman, 1981). Under low **outcome involvement**, source expertise serves as a peripheral cue to persuasion, bypassing the need to process message arguments. Similar effects obtain for attractive or famous message sources (Chaiken, 1979; Pallak, 1983; Petty, Cacioppo, & Schumann, 1983). A caution: All persuasion variables can have multiple effects. Under the right conditions, source expertise could make one pay more attention and process the message more carefully (Petty & Wegener, 1998).

Overall, communicator credibility effects typically are strongest for recipients not involved in the outcomes at stake. Uninvolved recipients are most likely to respond to superficial indications of expertise. Of course, alleged expertise is not a totally reliable reason for agreeing with someone's arguments, but it is a convenient shortcut. Much research on communicator cues may represent only those recipients operating at fairly shallow levels. In support of this, highly outcome-involved subjects express more message-oriented thoughts (Chaiken, 1980). Cognitive response analysis distinguishes between people who are responding superficially and those who are thinking hard in response to a message, so it allows one to distinguish between outcome-involved and uninvolved participants' use of communicator cues.

Message Effects

What is said – the message – also influences persuasion, but not always in the obvious ways. The elaboration likelihood model applies to various features of the message: number of repetitions, difficulty, number of arguments, use of rhetorical questions, number of sources, and degree of distraction in context. In each of these areas, the model has emphasized the role of recipient thought.

The research on *message repetition* distinguishes two kinds of stimuli: nonlinguistic (e.g., the Coca-Cola logo) and linguistic (e.g., the persuasive message). Cognitive response analysis suggests that the differences are due to the amount and valence (direction pro or con) of thoughts generated in each case (A. Sawyer, 1981).

Researchers have long known that repeated exposures to nonlinguistic stimuli typically enhance liking in what is called the **mere exposure** effect (Stang, 1974; Zajonc, 1968a; for reviews, see Bornstein, 1989; Chapter 14). Two major qualifications on the mere exposure effect are that the stimulus is initially unfamiliar and that people's initial reaction to the stimulus is neutral or positive (Grush, 1976; Harrison, 1977). When the stimulus is initially negative, the exposure effect evaporates or reverses.

In line with the peripheral route of the elaboration likelihood model, the mere exposure effect on nonlinguistic stimuli operates most clearly when recipients are essentially unthinking; that is, they cannot be generating personal responses (pro or con) to the stimulus. Hence, the more you see the Coca-Cola logo, the more you like it, assuming you do not think about it much; the logo has become as familiar as the American flag. Even animals show the effect of exposure on preference. People show the effect of repetition quite plainly under circumstances of minimal cognitive processing, or as McGuire (1969) would say, when they are behaving as lazy organisms. Accordingly, the peripheral route to persuasion best describes message repetition effects with nonlinguistic stimuli.

Nonlinguistic stimuli make a strong case for nonconscious mere exposure effects on preference. Note its stark contrast to the central route of the elaboration likelihood model as a clearly peripheral route to persuasion. Chapter 14 reviews some mere exposure research supporting nonconscious mediation (also Zajonc's separate systems view of affect and cognition; Moreland & Zajonc, 1977; W. R. Wilson, 1979). Participants who do not even recognize stimuli as familiar still show exposure effects on liking (Zajonc, 1980b). Thus the simple mere exposure effect for nonlinguistic stimuli is unconsciously mediated. People show the effect without recognizing the stimulus, without awareness, and without thought. Because message repetition effects on nonlinguistic stimuli do not appear to be mediated by conscious cognitive responses, they exemplify the peripheral route.

The second kind of stimulus in research on message repetition is linguistic; that is, the persuasive message itself. This kind of material does elicit thought, and as the elaboration likelihood model would predict, amount of thought pro and con appears to determine whether or not the linguistic mere exposure effect occurs (Petty & Cacioppo, 1981). This point is illustrated by the difference between early work on message repetition and later work using cognitive response analysis. In a study predating cognitive response analysis, W. Wilson and Miller (1968) originally found repetition effects on persuasion with prose passages; in this case the prose concerned a lawsuit for damages. Students role-played being jury members receiving an attorney's arguments either one time or three times. More exposure led to more agreement. Repetition also markedly increased retention of the arguments after a week's delay. Because retention and attitude change were moderately correlated, Wilson and Miller concluded that at least some of the repetition effect was due to enhanced recall.

A decade after that effort, Cacioppo and Petty (1979) also tackled the question of what mediates message repetition effects. Armed with cognitive response analysis, they tapped participants' idiosyncratic responses to the communication immediately after hearing it. Participants retrospectively listed the thoughts they had had while listening to the communication and indicated whether each thought was pro (+), con (–), or neutral (0). In a separate measure, they were asked to recall the message's arguments. Agreement with the message was completely uncorrelated with recall, but highly correlated with both favorable thoughts (positively) and unfavorable thoughts (negatively). The number of irrelevant thoughts did not correlate with agreement. Thus cognitive responses pro and con – not recall – empirically mediated repetition effects on persuasion.

One important point is that the elaboration likelihood model supports a different sort of cognitive process model than does a model stressing recall as the mediating process. Cognitive response analysis looks at the individual's idiosyncratic reactions to the argument rather than at the person's ability simply to remember the argument as given. Cognitive response analysis successfully elucidates the processes intervening between exposure and agreement, consistent with the elaboration likelihood model's central route.

As elaboration likelihood model research on message repetition effects has continued, it specifies the exact nature of the mediating cognitive process. People's cognitive responses to repeated messages support a two-stage model in which uncertainty reduction and tedium counterbalance each other (Berlyne, 1970; Cacioppo & Petty, 1979). In other words, the first few times your friend explains his thesis to you, repetition aids understanding and convinces you the paper is right, assuming the arguments are cogent. But after that it is a bore, and you may begin to counterargue out of sheer perversity. In the Cacioppo and Petty study, for example, agreement first increased with exposure, as participants comprehended the message and thought about it. Then agreement decreased, presumably as tedium set in. Cognitive responses pro and con followed the same pattern as did agreement – positive at first and then negative – which supports the two-factor model. Of course, this model assumes that participants follow the central route (that is, they bother to think about the message), which presupposes at least some outcome involvement; uninvolved participants do not always initially agree, then disagree (A. Sawyer, 1981).

Conceptually, message repetition effects illustrate several crucial points about the elaboration likelihood model: the importance of whether the recipient is actively thinking, and if thinking, whether those thoughts are pro or con; the possibilities for nonconscious mediation in the various peripheral routes in contrast to the conscious cognitive mediation in the central route; and the role of the elaboration likelihood model as a well-specified theory that solves old puzzles in new ways (see Crano & Prislin, 2006; Petty & Wegener, 1998, for reviews). From an applied perspective, message repetition effects might inform advertisers who air the same television commercial several times during the late show; research suggests circumstances under which they are both right and wrong to do so.

Another type of message effect is its *difficulty*. As with repetition, the elaboration likelihood approach reveals that message difficulty effects are also influenced by outcome involvement. The number of supporting arguments and counterarguments people generate is a function of such involvement if the message is difficult. Consider trying to understand a difficult statistics lecture. A student who hates the course content, does not care much about the final grade, and has already given up working on the material will probably ignore the lecture and daydream. When acting as an uninvolved, lazy organism, one does not bother to absorb message content, regardless of its comprehensibility. At intermediate levels of outcome involvement, message difficulty should have maximum impact because a little added difficulty can make the critical difference between at least some processing and giving up. The majority of the statistics students presumably are at this intermediate level, and they would be sensitive to message difficulty. At high levels of outcome involvement, message difficulty again makes little difference to comprehension because people will be motivated to overcome message difficulty no matter what. (Ability helps, too, of course.) A new teaching assistant who has never heard the material before will make every effort to understand the lectures regardless of difficulty.

How, then, does message difficulty cause attitude change? An analysis that draws on cognitive response methods reveals the mediating factors to be the amount and valence of people's cognitive responses. Not surprisingly, comprehension encourages persuasion if the arguments are good (e.g., Eagly, 1974; see Eagly & Himmelfarb, 1978, for others). If you do not understand a message, you cannot easily repeat it to yourself, nor can you muster supporting arguments. People's own idiosyncratic supportive cognitive responses can strengthen the argued viewpoint, but only if people comprehend the message in the first place. The more comprehensible the message, the more the professor's audience can think positively about what he or she has said (assuming the arguments are good). Consequently, the more they comprehend the lecture's good arguments, the more they will agree with the professor (W. Wood & Eagly, 1981). In sum, message difficulty effects can be cognitively mediated (central route), as cognitive response evidence has indicated, but they need not always be (peripheral route).

Another important feature of messages is the sheer *number of arguments* that can act as a superficial cue for persuasion. Both the heuristic-systematic model (Chaiken, Liberman, & Eagly, 1989) and the elaboration likelihood model support this idea (Tormala, Petty, & Briñol, 2002). Under low personal relevance (i.e., low outcome involvement), number of arguments acts as a peripheral cue to persuasion, regardless of argument quality; under high relevance, argument quality and number of arguments together determine persuasion via the thoughtful central route (Petty & Cacioppo, 1984).

Cognitive responses explain many features of messages in addition to repetition, difficulty, and number of arguments (Petty & Cacioppo, 1981), for example: use of *rhetorical questions* (Petty, Rennier, & Cacioppo, 1987), *multiple sources* (Harkins & Petty, 1981), and *environmental distractions* (Petty, Wells, & Brock, 1976; for reviews, see Petty & Wegener, 1998; Petty, Wegener, & Fabrigar, 1997). In every case, the factor critical to persuasion is the amount of active cognitive elaboration, pro and con, done by the recipient. To generate favorable cognitive responses and to be maximally persuasive, a message should have good arguments, should be repeated a few times but not too many, should be comprehensible, and should be delivered in an atmosphere free of distraction. If the message has weak arguments (so could produce many counterarguments), distraction and a single exposure will inhibit those negative cognitive responses and accordingly enhance persuasion.

Overall, message effects depend on outcome involvement. Outcome involvement increases cognitive activity and subsequent attitude change for moderately repeated and comprehensible messages if the arguments are cogent. Related message effects occur for number of arguments, rhetorical questions, number of sources, and distractions.

Audience Involvement

In discussing the elaboration likelihood model, audience involvement combines with the effects of many other variables, in particular, communicator and message effects. Thus, at every step of the central persuasion process, the respondent's amount and valence of cognitive response determine the effect. Because cognitive responses demand an actively thinking recipient, audience involvement has influenced each effect so far.

However, different types of involvement have different effects. Early research operationalized involvement in various ways, without strong agreement. For example, students might be given a message advocating a change in dormitory visitation hours at their own school versus another school (Petty & Cacioppo, 1979). Or they might be told that a change in university policy will take place in one year versus in ten years (Petty, Ostrom, & Brock, 1981). The usual manipulations included some form of personal relevance and future consequence. A variant on involvement manipulated personal responsibility rather than relevance; participants were told they had sole responsibility for evaluating the message (Brickner, Harkins, & Ostrom, 1985; Petty, Harkins, & Williams, 1980).

Personal importance or relevance to one's self-concept seems to capture involvement's general conceptual meaning (Greenwald & Leavitt, 1984; B. T. Johnson & Eagly, 1989), but researchers have identified different types of involvement (Table 9.5). **Ego involvement** (M. Sherif & Hovland, 1961), **issue involvement** (C. A. Kiesler, Collins, & Miller, 1969), **personal involvement** (Apsler & Sears, 1968; C. W. Sherif, Kelly, Rodgers, Sarup, & Tittler, 1973), and **vested interest** (Sivacek & Crano, 1982) all imply that an issue has personal relevance or meaning, especially intrinsic importance for beliefs central to a person's identity. These terms contrast with **task involvement** (M. Sherif & Hovland, 1961), in which the individual is concerned only with the consequences of a particular response. If a person is interested in maximizing the rewards in a given situation, that is **response involvement** (Zimbardo, 1960). The different types of involvement illustrate the range of factors that might make a person respond more or less thoughtfully to a persuasion attempt that is personally important (see Chaiken & Stangor, 1987, for a discussion of involvement types).

A meta-analysis of this literature (B. T. Johnson & Eagly, 1989) concluded that the involvement effects on elaboration likelihood apply most to outcome involvement, which implicates people's ability to attain desired outcomes. High-involvement participants are more persuaded by strong arguments, consistent with the elaboration likelihood model, but not always less persuaded by weak arguments, despite elaboration likelihood predictions. Two other types of involvement do not obtain these effects: **Value involvement** (implicating one's enduring principles) generally inhibits persuasion, and the same is somewhat true of **impression involvement** (implicating one's concern for people's opinions of self). Proponents of the elaboration likelihood model prefer to include these latter two types, involvements based on outcomes and values, in one category (Petty & Cacioppo, 1990), invoking the elaboration likelihood model postulate that (value-)involved subjects process in a biased manner because of their prior knowledge, strong attitudes, or confidence (Petty & Cacioppo, 1986; for disagreement, see B. T. Johnson & Eagly, 1990). For present purposes, the distinction at least among outcome involvement, value involvement, and impression involvement is important.

Outcome involvement has an important impact on processing messages. Regardless of specific manipulations, outcome involvement stimulates thought, which increases or decreases persuasion, depending on the cognitive responses, which in turn depend on the strength of the arguments and on the recipient's preexisting attitudes. Levels of outcome involvement lead to different types of processing, which lead to greater or lesser reliance on superficial characteristics of the communication.

Overall, one way to think about the effects of outcome involvement on cognitive responses and on persuasion is that less involved people seem to operate "on automatic," with little conscious thought (Chaiken, 1980; Petty & Cacioppo, 1981; Chapter 2). Highly (outcome-) involved people operate in a relatively controlled mode, with more cognitive activity, and generate more cognitive responses that are sensitive to the message they encounter: The outcome-involved listener differentiates carefully between strong and weak arguments, and between pro- and counterattitudinal arguments (Petty & Cacioppo, 1979; Petty, Cacioppo, & Goldman, 1981). Given an airtight or pro-attitudinal message, the outcome-involved recipient will not bother to counterargue, but the outcome-involved person would tend to counterargue weak or counter-attitudinal communications. Someone less outcome-involved probably would generate few cognitions regardless of the message because the uninvolved person is attending only superficially. People who are outcome-involved use systematic, content-based processing strategies responsive to argument quality. Less-involved people rely on peripheral strategies, such as source likeability. Outcome involvement moderates communicator and message effects (as we have seen) as well as the persistence of attitude change (Cook & Flay, 1978; Hennigan, Cook, & Gruder, 1982).

However, note that outcome-involved people do not necessarily think more objectively or accurately; they just think more, sometimes in a more biased fashion (Howard-Pitney, Borgida, & Omoto, 1986). The motivation from their involvement causes them to think harder, but their motivation also biases their interpretation of what they process (Chen, Reardon, Rea, & Moore, 1992; Liberman & Chaiken, 1992).

Other types of involvement show other effects. According to a meta-analysis (B. T. Johnson & Eagly, 1989), involvement that implicates a person's centrally held values generally inhibits persuasion. Chapter 9's section on conviction and importance examined value involvement in more detail. Another type of involvement, impression relevance, which implicates people's self-presentational concerns, appears later.

Individual Differences in Cognitive Responses and Persuasion

So far we have examined situational factors that determine the amount of thought people give to persuasive communications. Most of these situational variables interact with a recipient variable, involvement, in determining the thoughtfulness of cognitive responding, as indicated. However, a more general dispositional factor also determines the amount of cognitive responses. Table 10.3 shows some of the items on the scale. **Need for cognition** (Cacioppo & Petty, 1982; Cacioppo, Petty, Feinstein, & Jarvis, 1996; Cacioppo, Petty, & Morris, 1983) refers to people's chronic level of thoughtfulness in response to external stimuli such as persuasive messages. People high on the need for cognition generate more cognitive responses, both pro and con, to persuasive communications and are consequently likely to be more or less persuaded depending on the message. People low in need for cognition are more likely to process communications heuristically (Chaiken, 1987). The need for cognition is an individual difference variable that specifically addresses the process (cognitive responses) presumed to mediate between external stimulus and attitude change.

Table 10.3 Subset of the need for cognition scale

---

1. I really enjoy a task that involves coming up with new solutions to problems.
2. I would prefer a task that is intellectual, difficult, and important to one that is somewhat important but does not require much thought.
3. Learning new ways to think doesn't excite me very much.*
4. The idea of relying on thought to make my way to the top does not appeal to me.*
5. I only think as hard as I have to.*
6. I like tasks that require little thought once I've learned them.*
7. I prefer to think about small, daily projects rather than long-term ones.*
8. I would rather do something that requires little thought than something that is sure to challenge my thinking abilities.*
9. I find little satisfaction in deliberating hard and for long hours.*
10. I don't like to have the responsibility of handling a situation that requires a lot of thinking.*

Notes: Entire scale has 34 items
*Reverse scoring was used on this item
Source: From Cacioppo & Petty (1982). Copyright 1982 by the American Psychological Association. Reprinted by permission

Another individual difference variable, **uncertainty orientation** (Sorrentino, Bobocel, Gitta, Olso, & Hewitt, 1988), also affects persuasion. Certainty-oriented people stay with the familiar and the predictable, avoiding threats to their current understanding of the world, whereas uncertainty-oriented people search for meaning, attempt to make sense of their environment, and seek novel situations. For example, East Asians fare best when personally matched to their culture's emphasis on certainty, whereas Westerners show the reverse (Sorrentino, Nezlek, Yasunaga, Kouhara, Otsubo, & Shuper, 2008). The standard elaboration likelihood effects – that personal relevance or outcome involvement leads to central processing – are predicted to hold only for uncertainty-oriented people. In contrast, certainty-oriented people apparently increase their use of heuristics under high relevance, contrary to the elaboration likelihood model. Uncertainty orientation differs from need for cognition in that need for cognition measures motivation to think, whereas uncertainty orientation measures when and what to think in the service of increasing certainty versus maintaining an open-minded uncertainty.

A third individual difference variable, the **need to evaluate** (Jarvis & Petty, 1996; Table 10.4), predicts holding more attitudes and having more pro and con thoughts in response to persuasive messages. It even predicts more pro–con thoughts in response just to considering a normal day. People high on this dimension spontaneously evaluate, forming attitudes quickly in the moment, compared to people who consult their memory for evidence (Tormala & Petty, 2001). Need to evaluate predicts consequential political effects: number of evaluative beliefs about candidates, intensity of emotional reactions toward candidates, using party identification and issues to determine candidate preferences, using the news media for gathering information, engaging in political activism, and voting or intending to vote (Bizer et al., 2004). Need to evaluate correlates moderately with the more general need for cognition, so they overlap somewhat.

Table 10.4   Need for evaluation

---

1. I form opinions about everything.
2. I often prefer to remain neutral about complex issues.*
3. I enjoy strongly liking and disliking new things.
4. There are many things for which I do not have a preference.*
5. It bothers me to remain neutral.
6. I like to have strong opinions even when I am not personally involved.
7. I have many more opinions than the average person.
8. I would rather have a strong opinion than no opinion at all.

Full test has 16 items.

Note: *Reverse scoring was used on this item

Source: From Jarvis & Petty (1996). Copyright 1996 by the American Psychological Association. Reprinted by permission

Conclusion about the ELM

Having spent considerable time on the elaboration likelihood model, we should note its limitations (Eagly & Chaiken, 1993; see the debate between Petty, Cacioppo, Kasmer, & Haugtvedt, 1987; Petty, Kasmer, Haugtvedt, & Cacioppo, 1987; and Stiff, 1986; Stiff & Boster, 1987). First, although it proposes that people's thoughts mediate attitude change, it does not explain why people support or counterargue what they encounter. In that sense, it leans on other theories of why people agree or disagree with communications to explain attitude change.

Second, it paints people as more oriented toward validating their attitudes than they may be. People are not only motivated to be accurate but also to feel secure, as the work on uncertainty orientation points out. Although Petty and Cacioppo noted that people are often only subjectively correct when they want to be rationally correct, even the attempt to be correct may not always be paramount. (One of us has a friend who defended his right to prefer a car that would make him feel foolish.) Just as elsewhere in social cognition, people are more and less motivated to be accurate, and future research will explain the when and how of accuracy motives in attitudes.

Similarly, when and how people actually are biased by prior attitudes, knowledge, value involvement, or impression-relevant involvement are still developing within this model's framework. Although the model does allow for biased information processing, its postulate that people are motivated to hold correct attitudes tended to limit its initial consideration of the conditions under which people are close-minded. One lead for studying both accuracy motivation and actual bias is people's naive theory of bias; people and situations vary in ability to identify and correct perceived biases. The flexible correction model (Wegener & Petty, 1995, 1997) assumes that overcoming bias requires more motivation and ability than failing to do so. Moreover, the direction of correction depends on one's naive theory specifying the direction of bias.

Third, persuasion variables all have multiple roles, so prediction is not simple. Some variables shift from encouraging central, "objective" processing to encouraging central but biased processing. Involvement's varying effects depend on its level (higher levels inducing more bias) or type (B. T. Johnson & Eagly, 1989). Similarly, some variables serve both as peripheral cues and as aids to central information processing (Petty & Wegener, 1998; Petty et al., 1997); number of arguments is one such variable (Petty & Cacioppo, 1986). Some of the moderating variables that determine specific effects of other variables have been identified, as this review indicates. Nevertheless, variables with multiple effects and multiple functions make it difficult to falsify the model, undermining its predictive power (Eagly & Chaiken, 1984). Future work will continue specifying the moderating variables that determine which of multiple possible effects a variable will demonstrate.

Fourth, some have questioned whether cognitive responses actually cause attitude change or merely correlate with it (Romer, 1979). That is, if attitudes change for other reasons such as reinforcement contingencies, people may justify the change with cognitive responses pro and con, but only after the fact. In this view, cognitive responses do not cause attitude change; they merely accompany it, justify it, or serve as an alternative measure of persuasion (Eagly & Chaiken, 1984). In a related vein, some have argued that the standard manipulations of argument quality (responsiveness to which reveals the central route) also manipulate argument valence (Areni & Lutz, 1988).

Finally, as its proponents admit, the elaboration likelihood model and cognitive response analysis are not well suited to the analysis of attitude change mediated by noncognitive or nonconscious processes. For example, cognitive response analysis does not account for persuasion based on mere exposure to nonlinguistic stimuli or based on negative affect spillover from a frustratingly difficult message. And the elaboration likelihood model does not, in general, detail peripheral processes of persuasion.

In summary, despite inevitable limitations, the elaboration likelihood model and cognitive response analysis are powerful theoretical and methodological tools. Methodologically, cognitive response analysis supplies the technique of having people list their thoughts pro and con during or just after a persuasive communication. Such cognitive responses presumably mediate the effects of traditional communicator, message, and audience variables on attitude change. Theoretically, the elaboration likelihood model builds on cognitive response analysis to propose that the amount and direction of people's idiosyncratic responses determine attitude change via the central or peripheral routes. The elaboration likelihood model summarizes effects of communicator, message, and audience on cognitive responses and on persuasion. In addition to these situational variables, individual differences in the need for cognition, uncertainty orientation, and need to evaluate each influence how much thought people devote to persuasive communications. Overall, cognitive response analysis and the elaboration likelihood model have had a major impact on the fine-grained understanding of long-standing issues in attitude research.

MOTIVATION AND OPPORTUNITY DETERMINE ATTITUDE PROCESSES: THE MODE MODEL

So far we have examined two attitude-processing models that focus on two different processes of persuasion: heuristic and systematic or peripheral and central, respectively. A third type of dual-process model examines the more automatic side in greater detail. This **MODE model** does not explain persuasion (i.e., how attitudes form or change); rather, it explains how attitudes, once formed, operate. It focuses on the automatic activation of attitudes.

This attitude accessibility model views an attitude as an association in memory between a given object and one's evaluation of it (Fazio, 1990; Fazio & Towles-Schwen, 1999). Associations between an attitude object and its evaluation vary in strength. The stronger the association, the more accessible one's attitude. The speed (latency) with which people can respond evaluatively to an attitude object is the most common way of measuring accessibility. For example, if people first see the priming word "cancer," they afterwards identify the stimulus word "crime" more quickly than "candy" because the first two concepts share a negative valence.

In one typical study (Fazio, Jackson, Dunton, & Williams, 1995), students saw color photographs of other students from various racial groups, which served as positive and negative primes, to the extent the student was prejudiced. After seeing each photograph, they saw a (race-irrelevant) positive or negative adjective and had to say "good" or "bad," according to its obvious valence. They responded more quickly when primed with a valence-matched photograph than with a mismatch. Their prejudice facilitated evaluatively matched responses immediately following the prime. This kind of research suggests that some attitudes activate upon mere observation of the attitude object.

Several factors contribute to the accessibility of an attitude, and they include, predictably, the same factors that contribute to the accessibility of any construct (Chapter 3). Recent and frequent expression of the attitude cause it to be activated more rapidly afterward (Fazio, Chen, McDonel, & Sherman, 1982; Houston & Fazio, 1989; Powell & Fazio, 1984). Reviewing one's prior attitude-congruent behavior and inferring the corresponding attitude, in a process consistent with self-perception theory (Chapter 5), also makes attitudes more accessible (Fazio, Herr, & Olney, 1984). Besides these situational factors that promote accessibility, individual differences also matter. Some people (namely, those low on **self-monitoring**, who are more attuned to their attitudes, Chapters 9, 15) may have chronically more accessible attitudes than others (Kardes, Sanbonmatsu, Voss, & Fazio, 1986).

Attitude accessibility has several practical implications. Accessible attitudes influence perceptions of the attitude object, facilitating attitude-consistent judgments about relevant information, such as the seemingly excellent debate performance of a favored candidate (Fazio & Williams, 1986) or the high quality of scientific evidence on one's own side of an issue (Houston & Fazio, 1989). Accessible attitudes resist contradiction (Houston & Fazio, 1989; cf. Wu & Shaffer, 1987), so they endure. In addition, accessible attitudes gloss over slight variations in the attitude object, making the attitude functionally robust for object appraisal (Fazio, Ledbetter, & Towles-Schwen, 2000). Finally, as we will see in Chapter 15, people more consistently act on their accessible attitudes.

The mere presentation of an object linked to an accessible attitude seems to trigger an automatic process whereby a strong evaluative association is activated (Fazio, 1990). For example, a classic set of studies primed people with a positive or negative attitude object immediately before presenting an evaluatively loaded adjective. The participants' task was to respond to the evaluative content of the adjectives (preselected to be unambiguous) by pressing a key marked "good" or "bad." Participants responded faster to the adjectives when the attitude prime and adjective stimulus were evaluatively congruent. This effect was biggest when their attitude was highly accessible (had previously elicited rapid responses) or had just been repeatedly expressed (Fazio, Sanbonmatsu, Powell, & Kardes, 1986).

Response facilitation observed in these studies may be relatively automatic. First, the sheer speed of people's responses to the adjective (less than a second) would seem to preclude controlled processing. That is, the facilitation provided by the evaluatively congruent, highly accessible attitude object in responding to the adjective was instantaneous. Second, the facilitation effect evaporates when the attitude prime and adjective stimulus are separated by a full second (rather than 300 msec, as in the successful priming condition). Thus the prime's evaluative congruence facilitates responses only if the stimulus appears within a fraction of a second of the prime's initial appearance. The short duration of its effectiveness suggests automatic processing. Third, participants are instructed to focus on identifying the positive or negative valence of the adjective rather than to focus on the attitude object, which they saw as irrelevant to their main goal. Hence, the facilitation apparently occurs without intent, another feature of relatively automatic processes.

The degree to which the facilitating effect of an attitude depends on sheer accessibility (measured as speed of response to the initial attitude object) has been contested (Bargh, Chaiken, Govender, & Pratto, 1992; Bargh, Chaiken, Raymond, & Hymes, 1996; see Fazio, 2001; Fazio & Olson, 2003 for reviews). Instead, the effect may generalize to a variety of attitudes under a variety of circumstances. Despite such complexities, at least some attitude objects – at a minimum those with a strong association between object and evaluation – apparently automatically elicit their corresponding evaluation (Ferguson & Zayas, 2009). This insight fits with some of the work on automatic category-based responses (Chapters 2 and 11), including schema-triggered affect (S. T. Fiske, 1982; Chapter 13; cf. Sanbonmatsu & Fazio, 1990). Although the precise boundaries of the effect are still being identified, the work identifies a relatively automatic form of attitude processing (see Table 10.5).

Table 10.5   MODE model

Determinant of accessibility	Mediator	Response
Recency of activation		Attitude-consistent interpretations
Frequency of activation	Automatic activation of attitude valence	Downplaying inconsistencies
Reviewing consistent behavior		Resistance to change
Low self-monitoring		Attitude-consistent behavior

IMPLICIT ASSOCIATIONS

Suppose you walk into a laboratory and the experimenter asks you to do a simple categorization task (Figure 10.2): Press the left key every time you see a word associated with older people *or* a word with unpleasant associations; press the right key every time you see a word associated with young people *or* a word with pleasant associations. You do dozens of these easy categorization pairs, and then the experimenter asks you to switch: Left key if older or pleasant; right key if younger or unpleasant. Suddenly it's harder. And suppose you learn that the order of these tasks would not have mattered (i.e., doing the second task first). (You can try this online if you search the term "implicit.") What does it mean about your attitudes toward older and younger people that the first, "congruent" task was easier?

People's simultaneous evaluative associations underlie another theory and measurement method, the **implicit association test** (IAT) (Greenwald et al., 2002; Greenwald, McGhee, & Schwartz, 1998). Consistent with ideas from balance theory, if people like themselves and link themselves with the ingroup, they will like their ingroup. The IAT posits this positive association to be strong on implicit measures that operate outside of normal explicit conscious responses. Most people show relatively automatic ingroup-favoring evaluations on the basis of common social categories such as gender, race, age, religion, nationality (Rudman, Greenwald, Mellott, & Schwartz, 1999), and merely minimal, arbitrary group memberships (Ashburn-Nardo, Voils, & Monteith, 2001). Even 4-year-olds can do it for objects commonly seen as good (flowers) or bad (insects) (Cvencek, Greenwald, & Meltzoff, 2011).

The IAT stimulated a staggering number of studies and also considerable controversy, both in short order. Although compatible techniques predated the IAT (e.g., the MODE model and others; see Fazio & Olson, 2003, for a review), IAT research provocatively argued that implicit associations – split-second speed of responding to evaluatively linked items – reveal unconscious prejudice. These **implicit attitudes**, measured by the IAT, have excellent predictive validity, correlating with reasonable criteria such as judgments, choices, behavior, and physiological responses (Greenwald, Poehlman, Uhlmann, & Banaji, 2009). What's more, the IAT works especially well in socially sensitive domains such as stereotyping and prejudice. Explicit self-reports do predict noncontroversial political and consumer choices, presumably topics where people have nothing to hide. And in cases where people are willing to report their (e.g., racial) prejudices explicitly, implicit measures correlate with those explicit admissions of prejudice (Wittenbrink, Judd, & Park, 1997). Implicit and explicit measures generally show small to medium correlations with each other, according to meta-analysis (Hofmann, Gawronski, Gschwendner, Le, & Schmitt, 2005). Correlations increase when explicit self-reports are more spontaneous and when the measures are conceptually most similar. Overall, the IAT may have particular utility for attitudes that people hesitate to report explicitly.

The IAT's prediction of overt behavior especially matters to convincing the critics, and the validity is comparable to explicit measures, but better on some issues, such as Black–White interracial responses (Greenwald, Poehlman, Uhlmann, & Banaji, 2009). Implicit measures best predict nonverbal behaviors, such as tone of voice (Dovidio, Kawakami, & Gaertner, 2002; Dovidio, Kawakami, Johnson, Johnson, & Howard, 1997; McConnell & Liebold, 2001), whereas explicit measures predict more overt behaviors, such as the content of speech. For example, European Americans' implicit associations predict early detection of threatening facial expressions in Black but not White faces (Hugenberg & Bodenhausen, 2003). The IAT also predicts financial discrimination (money allocation to ingroups and outgroups; Rudman & Ashmore, 2007). The IAT shows traditional consistency, stability, and convergent validity of measurement (Cunningham, Preacher, & Banaji, 2001).

(a) Read this list, tapping on your

LEFT if an OLD name   RIGHT if a YOUNG name

Rob
Mildred
Jennifer
Jessica
Edna
Brendan
Donald
Ruth

(b) Read this list, tapping on your

LEFT if **UNPLEASANT**   RIGHT if **PLEASANT**

truth
devil
assault
triumph
glory
brutal
talent
agony

(c) Now combine the two tasks, tapping on your

LEFT if **UNPLEASANT** or **OLD**   RIGHT if **PLEASANT** or **YOUNG**

Wendy
health
Derek
diamond
Stanley
devil
Alvin
triumph
Ethan
brutal

(d) Now switch sides for one list, tapping on your

LEFT if **UNPLEASANT** or **YOUNG**   RIGHT if **PLEASANT** or **OLD**

Harold
agony
Zach
family
Jessica
stink
Jeff
torture
Walter
peace

Figure 10.2   Sample IAT demonstration

Note: Task (d) (incongruent evaluative pairings) should be slower than Task (c) (congruent evaluative pairings). Sequence of (d) and (c) does not change the fundamental result. This demonstration is imperfect; go to the project implicit website for online demonstrations.

The core of the controversy revolves around whether to call the IAT a measure of attitudes. Arguably, if the IAT, clearly a measure of evaluative association, predicts related affect, cognition, and behavior, it is acting like an attitude. Indeed, it reliably does predict interpersonal affect, judgment, and behavior (Greenwald, Poehlman, Uhlmann, & Banaji, 2009). And the IAT gives people a palpable sense of the ease of certain (e.g., prejudiced) pairings over others (Ashburn-Nardo et al., 2001). At a minimum, it creates a teachable moment in seminars that sensitize people to the greater ease of prejudiced rather than unprejudiced associations.

In response, many have argued that the IAT merely assesses cultural beliefs (Arkes & Tetlock, 2004; Karpinski & Hilton, 2001; Kihlstrom, 2004; Olson & Fazio, 2004a; Uhlmann, Brescoll, & Paluck, 2006). However, people's attitudes do come partly from the larger culture, though they may also disagree with the culture, and the IAT should detect the difference in that case (Banaji, Nosek, & Greenwald, 2004; Lowery, Hardin, & Sinclair, 2001). This intrinsic mixing of cultural and personal associations sparked the idea of a personalized IAT, which correlates more strongly with explicit measures of attitudes and behavioral intentions (Olson & Fazio, 2004a). Instead of using generically pleasant and unpleasant words, this version uses the terms "I like" and "I don't like," paired with words associated with two contrasting societal groups, for example.

Another criticism of the IAT has been its malleability. That is, how implicit is it if people indeed can control their responses or if it changes with context? For example, race IAT results differ depending on whether people believe the IAT is assessing racism or is a nondiagnostic pilot test (Frantz, Cuddy, Burnett, Ray, & Hart, 2004). Moreover, people's IAT-assessed prejudice decreases after exposure to a variety of mitigating stimuli: positive minority and negative majority role models (Dasgupta & Greenwald, 2001), diversity training (Rudman, Ashmore, & Gary, 2001), counterstereotypic images (Blair, Ma, & Lenton, 2001; Wittenbrink, Judd, & Park, 2001b), social influence (Lowery, et al., 2001), and antiprejudice goals (Blair & Banaji, 1996). Nevertheless, faking is detectable (Cvencek, Greenwald, Brown, Snowden, & Gray, 2010).

How new is it? The IAT fits many standard social psychology findings but differs in several respects. One distinction between IAT pairings and MODE priming methods is that, for the IAT, people may be aware of the attitude involved, though not readily control the timing of their responses (Dasgupta, McGhee, Greenwald, & Banaji, 2000); with priming, people may not be aware of the prime, let alone its facilitating responses to a subsequent stimulus. Another distinction separates the IAT as a series of categorical judgments, whereas priming methods operate more readily on individual exemplars (Fazio & Olson, 2003). Implicit attitudes also generally may operate from a simple slow-learning (but durable and resistant) memory system, whereas explicit attitudes result more from a fast-learning (but flexible and context-sensitive) memory system (DeCoster, Banner, Smith, & Semin, 2006). Implicit attitudes are primarily associations, whereas explicit attitudes comprise propositions subjectively judged as true (Gawronski & Bodenhausen, 2006). And, more than many explicit attitudes, implicit attitudes may stem from early preverbal experiences, affective experiences, cultural associations, and cognitive consistency principles (Rudman, 2004; Sinclair, Dunn, & Lowery, 2005). Regardless of their special features, the impact of implicit evaluative associations is undeniable, both on individuals and on the field of attitudes.

EMBODIED ATTITUDES

The discovery of automatic or at least implicit attitudes supports other intriguing avenues for attitude research to avoid the problems of verbal self-reports, which are potentially plagued by people worrying about how they appear (**social desirability**). Embodied expressions of attitudes provide one route, as mentioned briefly earlier (Chapter 4): A few decades ago, experimental participants had to make arm movements to pull or push positive and negative stimuli (e.g., "smart," "stupid"; "tasty," "putrid"); they were faster to initiate compatible movements, such as pull toward positive and push away from negative (Solarz, 1960). Later results corroborated and expanded this result: Novel objects become progressively more positive or negative, respectively, with arm flexion versus extension (Cacioppo et al., 1993). This embodied valence affects novel more than familiar attitude objects (Priester, Cacioppo, & Petty, 1996). Embodied expression occurs even without a conscious goal to evaluate (Chen & Bargh, 1999), and simple exposure to novel (but valenced) stimuli speeds compatible movements (Duckworth, Bargh, Garcia, & Chaiken, 2002). Positive and negative stimuli, respectively, elicit approach (pull) and avoidance (push) responses (e.g., Neumann & Strack, 2000), and, conversely, the actions themselves facilitate compatible evaluations (Centerbar & Clore, 2006).

Other kinds of body movements may also reflect and reinforce valence. As noted (Chapter 4), people who nod their heads while listening to a strong persuasive communication will agree more than people who shake their heads (Briñol & Petty, 2003). But if the message is weak, the nodders react against it, disagreeing more. In this instance of embodied cognition, the movements increase people's confidence in their own thoughts (pro or con), self-validating their attitude. Going back to the arm flexion/extension work, the movement affects only attitudes (evaluations), not other types of judgments (Cacioppo et al., 1993), and it may partly do so by associations in memory (Förster & Strack, 1997, 1998).

People's facial expressions can also affect their evaluations (Laird, 1984). In one typical paradigm, participants are induced to adopt specific facial expressions (e.g., smile, frown) without labeling them as such. For example, one experiment instructed them to contract and hold the relevant muscles one-by-one, for supposed **electromyography** (EMG) recording, until they had inadvertently assumed an emotional expression (Laird, 1974; see also Strack, Martin, & Stepper, 1988; Chapter 4). Induced smiles facilitated positive reactions. Other researchers have obtained similar effects (e.g., Coan, Allen, & Harmon-Jones, 2001; Cupchik & Leventhal, 1974; Duncan & Laird, 1977; Lanzetta, Cartwright-Smith, & Kleck, 1976; Rhodewalt & Comer, 1979; Zuckerman, Klorman, Larrance, & Spiegel, 1981). Embodied attitudes are here to stay.

NEURAL CORRELATES OF ATTITUDES

If attitudes are embodied, then they should also have brain signatures (see Lieberman, 2007, for a review). We are not so far from being able to read people's evaluative reactions from their patterns of brain activation. When people explicitly express their attitudes, what they say does not always correspond to what their brains suggest. Neural patterns might reflect implicit responses rather than explicit expression of attitudes. For example, immediate attitude responses differ from deliberate ones in electrocortical responses (Crites, Cacioppo, Gardner, & Berntson, 1995). As another example, people do not report attending to negative more than positive information, although the attention literature indicates they do (Chapter 3). Similarly, the brain's evoked electrical activity (**event-related potential**; ERP) shows greater immediate impact of negative than comparably extreme positive stimuli (Ito et al., 1998). **Electroencephalography** (EEG) recordings sensitively measure neural time sequences. People respond incredibly rapidly to valenced inputs, as EEG data show (Chapter 3).

Brain imaging more sensitively indexes location than EEG does. Consider implicit responses: Frequently, implicit neural responses involve **amygdala** activation to negative attitude objects (W. A. Cunningham et al., 2003; Hart et al., 2000; Wheeler & Fiske, 2005). For example, Whites' amygdala activation to Black faces correlates with their prejudice scores as measured by the IAT (Phelps, Cannistraci, & Cunningham, 2003; Phelps et al., 2000). The race–amygdala effects are stronger when faces appear subliminally (Cunningham, Johnson, et al., 2004). However, implicit and explicit attitudes might seem to show contradictory neural responses. For example, African Americans show greater amygdala activity to Black faces, suggesting negativity, perhaps (Lieberman, Hariri, Jarcho, Eisenberger, & Bookheimer, 2005), but they also show more positive *explicit* attitudes toward Black faces (Nosek, Banaji, & Greenwald, 2002a).

Perhaps we need to broaden the idea of amygdala responses. The amygdala responds to emotionally significant cues that are extremely positive as well, such as photos of one's own versus someone else's child (Leibenluft, Gobbini, Harrison, & Haxby, 2004; see Zald, 2003, for a review). Hence, the amygdala responses seem not to indicate negative attitudes or emotions *per se* as much as general emotional significance, implicating vigilance. Vigilance, of course, is often needed in response to negative stimuli and sometimes in response to highly positive ones as well (such as one's own baby). Consistent with this interpretation, explicit ratings of emotional intensity correlate with amygdala response to socially relevant concepts, some negative, but also some positive, such as happiness (Cunningham, Raye, & Johnson, 2004).

A system of areas may provide a cleaner indicator of valence than mere evaluative/ emotional intensity (Figure 10.3). Part of this system may be the **insula**; in implicit attitudes, right insula correlates with negative valence ratings (Cunningham, Raye, & Johnson, 2004). Valence (e.g., reward and loss) relates to another likely area: the orbitofrontal cortex in this attitude study and in neuroeconomics research (O'Doherty, Kringelbach, Rolls, Hornack, & Andrews, 2001). A third part of this system follows from implicit activations of attitudes that implicate the ventral medial prefrontal cortex (Knutson et al., 2005; McClure et al., 2004; Milne & Grafman, 2001).

Explicit attitudes involve neural systems characteristic of more controlled processing, including the medial prefrontal cortex, lateral prefrontal cortex, and parietal cortex. People expressing attitudes toward topics that are not socially sensitive are more likely to express explicit attitudes that also fit their implicit attitudes, including those uncovered by neural activations. This pattern emerges toward, for example, socially relevant but not sensitive topics, such as welfare (Cunningham, Raye, & Johnson, 2004), politicians and cities (Zysset, Huber, Ferstl, & von Cramon, 2002), admired and detested famous names (Cunningham et al., 2003), novel abstract graphic patterns (Jacobsen, Schubotz, Hofel, & Cramon, 2006), and representational and abstract paintings (Vartanian & Goel, 2004).

a.

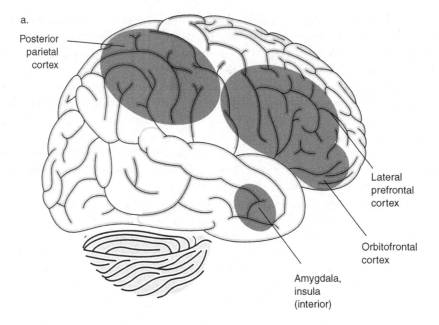

Posterior
parietal
cortex

Lateral
prefrontal
cortex

Orbitofrontal
cortex

Amygdala,
insula
(interior)

b.

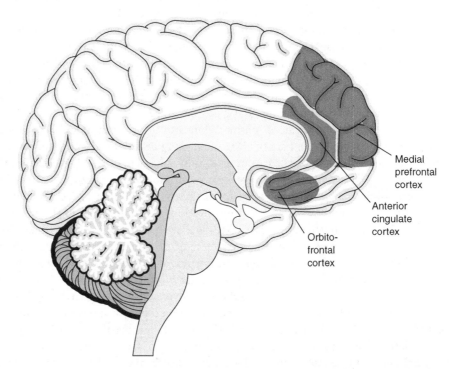

Medial
prefrontal
cortex

Anterior
cingulate
cortex

Orbito-
frontal
cortex

Figure 10.3   Brain areas implicated in implicit and explicit attitudes (see text)

An even more obviously controlled response, regulating a socially sensitive attitude (e.g., concerning race), first involves the dorsal anterior cingulate cortex (Amodio, Harmon-Jones, et al., 2004), which is often involved in discrepancy detection (Botvinick et al., 2004). Then, perhaps in sequence, the right lateral prefrontal cortex activates as people attempt to control the attitude expression (Cunningham, Johnson, et al., 2004; Cunningham, Raye, & Johnson, 2004; Richeson et al., 2003), consistent with the previous research. Activation in this right lateral PFC region apparently dampens amygdala responses (Cunningham, Johnson, et al., 2004).

Effortful control can dampen even seemingly automatic amygdala responses. Amygdala responses to emotionally negative stimuli are not inevitable, wired-in attitudes. For example, when people have to verbalize a person's racial category (Lieberman et al., 2005) or when they must infer the person's food preferences (Wheeler & Fiske, 2005), the race–amygdala effect evaporates. What's more, the amygdala effect inversely correlates with increased activity in the right ventrolateral prefrontal cortex, consistent with the idea of it being involved in controlling emotional responses.

Regardless of process – and across cultures – successful persuasion invokes a network of neural regions also broadly implicated in social cognition: dorsal medial prefrontal cortex, superior temporal sulcus, and temporal pole (Falk et al., 2010. This makes sense, because persuasion is a fundamentally social cognitive process, as these last two chapters have seen.

Summary

Perspectives on attitude processes – the heuristic-systematic model, the elaboration likelihood model, the MODE model, the IAT, embodied attitudes, and neural attitudes – integrate traditional attitude research and new insights from social cognition and social neuroscience. As such, they represent at least a "second generation" approach (S. J. Sherman, 1987). They insist that attitude formation, change, and operation are not entirely rational, in contrast to traditional approaches that presupposed recipients who necessarily learned and considered the message arguments, if persuasion was successful, and who necessarily consciously considered their attitudes when influenced by them. This older rational view failed in at least three ways. First, people do not have to learn and recall a message to be persuaded by it; they may instead react to it online, resulting in an attitude based on their own responses but not on the message arguments as given. Second, people can be persuaded by more cognitively economical methods, whether persuasion heuristics or other peripheral routes. Third, people access their attitudes in relatively automatic ways, indicated by cognitive (response latency), physical (movement), and neural (activation) data.

More recent attitude theories have drawn heavily on social cognition theories and methods. Some new theories examine different types of attitude processing; some relatively thoughtful and analytic, others relatively rapid and automatic. The heuristic-systematic model posits that attitudes are often changed by cognitive shortcuts or heuristics in the form of simple persuasion rules that avert the need to process message content. Attitudes can also change by more systematic processing of the message arguments. Considerable research supports these ideas.

The elaboration likelihood model also proposes that attitudes can change by two routes, but the more automatic peripheral route includes a variety of superficial strategies, all of which share the feature of being relatively inattentive to message quality. In contrast, the central route to persuasion, typical of more motivated recipients, involves thorough consideration of the merits of the arguments given. In response to message arguments, people engage in more or less cognitive elaboration; that is, idiosyncratic responses pro or con. These, as measured by cognitive response analysis, predict attitude change via the central route. Traditional variables, such as characteristics of the communicator (credibility, expertise, and attractiveness), the message (its quality, repetition, difficulty, and length), and the audience (its outcome involvement, need for cognition, uncertainty orientation, and need to evaluate), all contribute to the degree and direction of cognitive elaboration as well as the resulting attitude change. This approach has yielded quantities of data illuminating old problems with new sophistication.

The MODE approach concentrates on the automatic activation of attitudes, based on the mere encounter with the attitude object. Attitudes activate more easily when recently or frequently activated in the past or when one has just reviewed attitude-relevant behavior. Low self-monitors, who orient to their attitudes, also seem to have more accessible attitudes. Easily activated attitudes more dramatically influence judgments about attitude-relevant information, resist contradiction, endure longer, and affect behavior more directly. The process seems to be relatively automatic. Clearly, some attitudes can activate immediately upon perception of the pertinent attitude object.

Implicit associations share many features of attitudes, predicting behavior. Associations between categories of an attitude object and positive or negative words show reliability and validity. Implicit associations best predict attitudes in contested or sensitive domains, whereas more traditional self-reports may best predict attitudes in more ordinary domains.

Other novel approaches to relatively spontaneous or implicit attitudes include embodied attitudes, correlated with arm flexion or extension, head nodding or shaking, and facial muscle manipulation. And neural patterns of activation implicate the amygdala in attitude intensity and other areas in valence.

FURTHER READING

Albarracín, D., & Vargas, P. (2010). Attitudes and persuasion: From biology to social responses to persuasive intent. In S. T. Fiske, D. T. Gilbert, & G. Lindzey (Eds.), *Handbook of social psychology* (5th edn, Vol. 1, pp. 394–427). Hoboken, NJ: Wiley.

Crano, W. D., & Prislin, R. (2006). Attitudes and persuasion. *Annual Review of Psychology, 57,* 345–374.

Eagly, A. H., & Chaiken, S. (2005). Attitude research in the 21st century: The current state of knowledge. In D. Albarracín, B. T. Johnson, & M. P. Zanna (Eds.), *The handbook of attitudes* (pp. 743–767). Mahwah, NJ: Erlbaum.

Fazio, R. H., & Olson, M. A. (2003). Implicit measures in social cognition research: Their meaning and use. *Annual Review of Psychology, 54,* 297–327.

Ferguson, M. J., & Fukukura, J. (2012). Likes and dislikes: A social cognitive perspective on attitudes. In S. T. Fiske & C. N. Macrae (Eds.), *Sage handbook of social cognition* (pp. 165–190). Thousand Oaks, CA: Sage.

Kay, A. C., & Eibach, R. P. (2012). Ideological processes. In S. T. Fiske & C. N. Macrae (Eds.), *Sage handbook of social cognition* (pp. 495–515). Thousand Oaks, CA: Sage.

Nosek, B. A., Hawkins, C. B., & Frazier, R. S. (2012). Implicit social cognition. In S. T. Fiske & C. N. Macrae (Eds.), *Sage handbook of social cognition* (pp. 12–30). Thousand Oaks, CA: Sage.

Stereotyping
Cognition and Bias

11

- Blatant Stereotypes
- Subtle Stereotypes
- Effects of Bias

Casual forms of bias are everywhere, even in this new century, even in enlightened institutions of higher learning, as the following examples illustrate:

- A recent college graduate, who is a South Asian woman, was driving her modest new car to work when she was pulled over by a local police officer, who asked if the car was indeed hers. After he inspected her license and registration, she asked why she had been stopped. He admitted she had not been speeding, but said, ominously, "I'll be watching you." She drove on, deeply shaken.
- Another recent college graduate, who is a Black woman, was newly arrived at graduate school. As she was squeezing past some audience members to find a seat at a colloquium, one of them mumbled "affirmative action ..."
- A pregnant graduate student had just won a coveted fellowship. A male faculty member asked whether she could handle it.
- A White college freshman was moving into his first dorm room, which unexpectedly had no door knob. The White maintenance man, who arrived to remedy the situation, alluded to the just-finished summer program for students from underfunded public schools, saying "You just know it has to be *those people*."

These everyday incidents cumulatively cast a chill over people's experience, and in the long run, everyday bias taxes the physical and mental well-being of targets (Major & O'Brien, 2005; Schnittker & McLeod, 2005). Eventually, bias can, in fact, kill – just more slowly and indirectly than hate crimes do.

Social cognition has much to say about ordinary bias, exemplified by everyday intergroup hassles, and the extraordinary forms of bias, exemplified by hate crimes. This chapter and the next distinguish between, respectively, the cognitive side of intergroup bias (namely, **stereotypes**) and its affective side (namely, **prejudice**). Although they often correlate, distinct processes underlie each.

The most frequent intergroup distinctions in the United States at this time are gender, race, age, immigrant status, and sexual orientation. Most bias research in social psychology has focused on race and gender, assuming that the processes generalize across other social categories. This is both true and not true, as we shall see in these two chapters. Social cognition research has focused on stereotyping processes that often cut across social groups, although the contents of stereotypes and the specifics of emotional reactions do differ in accord with unique situations of biases directed toward each group.

Research on bias is abundant, even a dominant focus in the field, and we now known much (e.g., Bodenhausen, Kang, & Peery, 2012; R. J. Brown & Gaertner, 2001; Dovidio & Gaertner, 2010; S. T. Fiske, 1998, 2002; Quinn, Macrae, & Bodenhausen, 2003). In accord with the basic concepts of social cognition, intergroup bias takes both automatic and controlled forms. The most significant insight in the past few decades of bias research is that everyday bias is often subtle, automatic, and unintentional, contrary to people's commonsense intuitions about bias as overt bigotry. But today's subtle bias is not last century's blatant bias. This chapter first discusses cognitive aspects of **blatant bias**, which stem largely from perceived intergroup threats, both economic and value threats. Then we address **subtle bias**, which is automatic, ambiguous, and ambivalent; it stems from internal conflict. The chapter closes with the effects of bias, especially on targets.

As a preliminary note, the difference between blatant, intentional bias and subtle, perhaps unintentional bias matters quite a lot in practical terms as well as in theoretical ones. Ordinary perceivers and courts alike view intentional discrimination as far more serious and blameworthy than unintentional discrimination (S. T. Fiske, 1989; Swim, Scott, Sechrist, Campbell, & Stangor, 2003), even to the point of doubting whether people are legally responsible for unintentional discrimination and whether it can ever be avoided (Fiske & Borgida, 2008; Krieger & Fiske, 2006). We shall examine evidence relevant to these issues. But let's begin with the relatively rare case of extreme bigotry.

BLATANT STEREOTYPES

By some estimates, only 10% of the population in Western democracies hold extreme, blatant stereotypes. Nonetheless, they are a dangerous 10%, and they shape common knowledge about intergroup biases. Most people think that blatant bias results from realistic conflict over scarce resources, and it obviously can. Indeed, the intergroup conflict field began with this basic idea in a classic study randomly assigning summer campers to cabins and then pitting the cabins against each other for treats and privileges; conflict and bias quickly resulted (Sherif & Sherif, 1953). Other work linked economic downturns and lynching (Hovland & Sears, 1940). **Realistic group conflict** includes any kind of actual resource, such as prestige, money, or military power

(D. T. Campbell, 1965). Competition over actual resources does indeed matter both in the real world (Blake & Mouton, 1961; Bobo, 1983; Rabbie & Horowitz, 1969) and in the laboratory (Worchel, Axsom, Ferris, Samaha, & Schweitzer, 1978). Nonetheless, people have to perceive a conflict over resources, and the perceptions matter more than the reality as defined by some outside observer (Green, Glaser, & Rich, 1998; Green, Strolovitch, & Wong, 1998; Kinder & Sears, 1981; Sears & Kinder, 1985). Subjective perceptions clearly underlie conflict in the lab and in the field (R. J. Brown, Maras, Masser, Vivian, & Hewstone, 2001; Duckitt & Mphuthing, 1998; Hennessy & West, 1999; Huddy & Sears, 1995), and subjective perceptions are the stuff of social cognition.

Social Identity, Self-Categorization, and Other Identity Theories

To have intergroup conflict, people have to perceive themselves and other people as members of distinct groups. And they frequently do, although it's a subjective judgment that depends on circumstances. This section describes four group identity theories and their consequences for intergroup misunderstanding.

Theories

Groups compete more than individuals do (Schopler et al., 2001), and it takes only two to tango: A pair of individuals can compete as individuals or as members of opposing groups. The perception that two people may interact as individuals or as members of their respective groups is the essential insight of **social identity theory** (SIT), which argues that interactions – even between two people – range from interpersonal to intergroup (Tajfel, 1981; Tajfel & Turner, 1979). Social identity theory claims that people seek a positive social identity to maintain their self-esteem. Social identity turns on one's membership in a distinctive group that one views positively on subjectively important dimensions (called one's **ingroup**), *vis-à-vis* a comparison group (the **outgroup**). In this view, even members of societally devalued groups carve out a positive social identity by emphasizing certain dimensions of their identity as relative advantages.

Beyond the self-esteem assumption, SIT's most cognitive features specify that social identity is defined by the individual, society, and current context, so it rests on beliefs, which are cognitions. Moreover, categorization into ingroup and outgroups reduces perceived variability within the category while increasing perceived variability between categories. That is, any kind of categorization exaggerates both between-category differences (we're different from them) and within-category similarities (they're all alike, and in some important ways we are too).

This theory departs from the idea of group conflict and emphasizes the mere cognitive process of categorization into groups. The original goal was to find a **minimal group paradigm,** the base conditions for the experience of belonging in a group, and then to add progressively realistic conditions until biases emerged. To Tajfel's apparent surprise, even in experimentally created, explicitly arbitrary groups, people favored their ingroup over the outgroup when allocating limited resources (Table 11.1). Mere categorization created bias and, with it, the research enterprise

Table 11.1   Tajfel matrix: Ingroup/outgroup rewards

Ingroup	7	8	9	10	11	12	13	14	15	16	17	18	19
Outgroup	1	3	5	7	9	11	13	15	17	19	21	23	25

Participant has to choose one column's pair of numbers, determining rewards to ingroup and outgroup. Intergroup differentiation (e.g., 7 – 1 = 6 favoring ingroup) contrasts with fairness (13 each), maximizing joint outcomes (19 + 25 = 44 total, but relatively disadvantaging ingroup), and maximizing ingroup reward (19 is highest possible ingroup outcome, but then the outgroup is higher, 25). Each of several Tajfel matrices varies these trade-offs.

for an entire generation (for reviews, see Brewer & Brown, 1998; Hogg & Abrams, 2003; Yzerbyt & Demoulin, 2010).

As this research developed, the self-esteem hypothesis fell out of favor. The common lay assumption is that people discriminate in order to make themselves feel superior, but apparently it doesn't totally work. Discriminating does elevate **state self-esteem** – a temporary evaluative self-assessment – but it does not alter **trait self-esteem**, one's long-term view of oneself (Oakes & Turner, 1980; Rubin & Hewstone, 1998). What's more, low self-esteem does not directly motivate discrimination, despite common sense to the contrary (Aberson, Healy, & Romero, 2000; Hewstone, Rubin, & Willis, 2002). Temporary reductions in self-esteem among people highly identified with their group might well cause discrimination in the service of social change (Turner & Reynolds, 2001), but the global self-esteem hypothesis is not supported.

Self-categorization theory (SCT) extended social identity theory, without the self-esteem predictions (Turner, 1985). Aiming to predict actual behavior and not only perceived differences, SCT claims that people identified with a group will actually behave more like other ingroup members. From a cognitive perspective, self-categorization theory makes the point that the self is not fixed but depends on the salient intergroup context: One may think of oneself as a student (versus professors), a female (versus males), a White person (versus minorities), a psychology major (versus others), and so on. The operative group categorization depends on fit to the context. **Comparative fit** compares between-group differences to within-group differences in order to create a **meta-contrast ratio**. (In statistical terms, it is equivalent to an F or t-test, putting mean differences over within-group variance.) According to SCT, the best observed comparison determines the relevant categorization. For a demonstrator confronting the police, other category memberships matter less in that moment.

Self-categorization also depends on **normative fit**: socially shared meaning that defines the two categories. The consensus about characteristic group differences defines the relevant ingroup–outgroup categories. For example, students visiting a retirement home would likely self-categorize by age, whereas visiting a rival university would instead prompt self-categorization by school. Self-categorization emphasizes psychological group membership (Turner & Reynolds, 2001).

Entirely compatible, **optimal distinctiveness theory** (ODT) (Brewer, 1991) argues that people balance individual autonomy and distinctiveness against belonging to the right group in order to reach a self-affirming, satisfying identity. People value their group memberships, but they also value their individuality and need to strike a happy balance. This occurs across Western and non-Western cultures (Vignoles, Chryssochoou, & Breakwell, 2000) and for adolescents (Eckes, Trautner, & Behrendt, 2005) as well as undergraduates and adults (Hornsey & Jetten, 2004). People can achieve both individual differentiation and ingroup belonging by calibrating the distinctiveness of their ingroup identity.

Group distinctiveness also allays the tension of ambiguity. **Subjective uncertainty reduction theory** (Hogg, 2001) proposes that ingroup norms reduce anxiety, especially when people are unsure in self-relevant domains. Adopting the ingroup's values and norms creates certainty, as people assimilate to the group prototype, depersonalize themselves, and shed their uncertainty. As with SIT, SCT, and ODT, this theory has essential cognitive underpinnings in normal categorization processes, but with the crucial feature that the self occupies one of the two categories.

Ingroup Favoritism

People favor the ingroup when group membership is all the information they have, as SIT's minimal group paradigm demonstrates. People favor "us" more than they explicitly disfavor "them," except that, of course, then outgroup disadvantage occurs by exclusion (Brewer, 1999; Hewstone et al., 2002; Mullen, Brown, & Smith, 1992). Indeed, **ingroup favoritism** exploits the *relative* advantage of ingroup over outgroup, even to the detriment of self and own group's *absolute* outcomes. For example, participants prefer to give an ingroup member 7 points and the outgroup member 1 (maximizing difference), than giving both 13 (maximizing joint profit) or giving the ingroup 19 and the outgroup 25 (maximizing ingroup profit) (Tajfel, Billig, Bundy, & Flament, 1971). As another example, people value their ingroup even when they all are relatively deprived together and cannot reward each other personally (Rabbie & Horwitz, 1969). Ingroup favoritism over the outgroup (intergroup differentiation) occurs especially on dimensions favoring the ingroup and increases under conflict, social breakdown, and ingroup importance; all this points to ingroup favoritism as reducing subjective uncertainty when it matters most (Hogg, 1992).

People favor their ingroup because they are attracted to it, and attraction glues groups together (Hogg, 1992, 1993). Ingroup favoritism occurs automatically and increases with strong ingroup identification (Branscombe & Wann, 1994; Perreault & Bourhis, 1999), for those whose identity is under threat: embattled minorities (Mullen et al., 1992; Otten, Mummendey, & Blanz, 1996), distinctive groups (Jetten, Spears, & Manstead, 1998), and insecure high-status groups (Bettencourt, Charlton, Dorr, & Hume, 2001). The security of conforming to ingroup norms may contribute to the other cognitive feature of SIT, SCT, and related theories – namely, perceived group homogeneity.

Group Homogeneity

Categorization, as noted, reduces perceived variability within groups: "They" are all alike (Linville et al., 1989; Messick & Mackie, 1989; Mullen & Hu, 1989). **Group homogeneity** includes stereotyping but also perceived dispersion (spread of attributes) and similarity (Ostrom & Sedikides, 1992; Park & Judd, 1990). Outgroup homogeneity especially applies to groups that are real but unfamiliar and abstract, such as a national or ethnic group one has never encountered (Brewer & Brown, 1998; R. J. Brown, 2000; Devos, Comby, & Deschamps, 1996; Linville et al., 1989; Ostrom & Sedikides, 1992; Park, Ryan, & Judd, 1992). People think other people have more biases against outgroups than they themselves do (Judd, Park, Yzerbyt, Gordijn, & Muller, 2005). Thus people expect intergroup perceptions to be biased, with each side viewing the other side as homogeneous.

Sometimes, however, "we" are all alike too. Numerical minorities view themselves as relatively homogeneous, especially on identity-relevant dimensions (Kelly, 1989; Mullen & Hu, 1989; Simon, 1992). People who especially identify with their ingroup perceive greater ingroup homogeneity (Castano & Yzerbyt, 1998). A summary principle is that when intergroup distinctions are salient (because of threat or conflict), both ingroups and outgroups are seen as more homogeneous. And because people are especially likely to conform when ingroup identity matters most, perceived homogeneity may sometimes hold some truth.

Conclusion about Identity Theories

Identity approaches contribute essentially: Mere categorization is sufficient to produce overt bias. Ingroup favoritism may have automatic components, but it is largely conscious and overt, at least as measured in much of the research literature. Regardless, intergroup bias has cognitive underpinnings. Moreover, threat exaggerates category-based bias, and threat itself is determined by cognitions. The next theories describe two primary bases of threat, perceived economic threat and perceived value threat.

Intergroup Ideologies

Blatant bias can rest on motivated social cognition. Various political ideologies correlate with perceived threats to ingroup (Kay & Eibach, 2012). They all explain society's intergroup relations as inevitable, reasonable, and legitimate: social dominance theory, right-wing authoritarianism, terror management theory, system justification theory, and theories of essentialism (Table 11.2).

Social Dominance Theory

Groups compete for resources, and group hierarchies result. **Social dominance theory** (SDT) argues that group hierarchies are universal and even adaptive in societies beyond the hunter-gatherer stage. Some groups inevitably dominate others, and stable hierarchies regulate pointless conflict (however much the oppressed groups might wish it otherwise). Societies, groups, and individuals differ in their endorsement of social dominance (Sidanius & Pratto, 1999). With social dominance orientation come **legitimizing myths**, complex cognitions (beliefs and ideology) that support the status quo. Chief among those cognitions are stereotypes that keep groups in their respective places.

Individual differences in **social dominance orientation** (SDO) correlate with many blatant biases (e.g., Amiot & Bourhis, 2005; Pratto, Sidanius, Stallworth, & Malle, 1994; Sidanius, Pratto, & Bobo, 1996; for a list, see Sidanius & Pratto, 2003). Dominance interacts with intergroup contexts to reinforce the whole system in a variety of ways: High SDO predicts ingroup favoritism, not surprisingly among the powerful, but even among the powerless if they view the

Table 11.2 Ideologies as cognitive interpretations legitimating bias

Approach	Core beliefs	Threat to ingroup	Sample outgroup
Social dominance theory (SDT)	Inevitable group hierarchies	Zero-sum resources	Competitors
Right-wing authoritarianism	Dangerous world	Crumbling values	Deviants
Terror management theory	Own worldviews endure	Human mortality	Foreigners
System justification theory	Legitimate status quo	Unstable society	Resistors
Essentialism	Biology defines groups	Social construction	Race, gender

hierarchy as legitimate (Levin, Federico, Sidanius, & Rabinowitz, 2002). People individually high on SDO tend to choose careers that reinforce existing social dominance hierarchies (e.g., police, business, public prosecution), whereas people low on SDO tend to go into hierarchy-attenuating lines of work (social work, teaching, public defense). Once there, if the fit is good, they excel in their respective pursuits (Kemmelmeier, Danielson, & Basten, 2005; Pratto, Stallworth, Sidanius, & Siers, 1997; van Laar, Sidanius, Rabinowitz, & Sinclair, 1999).

Controversy over SDT centers on its claiming inevitability: For example, men's SDO scores always average higher than women's, hypothesized to account for the universality of men's greater political power in developed societies (Sidanius, Pratto, & Bobo, 1994). An SIT explanation argues that individual gender identification causes the SDO differences (Dambrun, Duarte, & Guimond, 2004; Wilson & Liu, 2003); maybe gender identification influences SDO, not the reverse. The more they identify with their gender group, the more they need to legitimate its fixed place in the hierarchy. Similarly, instead of SDO causing inequalities, SDO scores might reflect inequalities that are salient in a given context and even a temporarily privileged position (Schmitt, Branscombe, & Kappen, 2003). Overall, a group socialization model argues that dominant (privileged) positions motivate SDO attitudes, which in turn increase prejudice (Guimond, Dambrun, Michinov, & Duarte, 2003).

SDT agrees that chronic power differences – whether based on gender, class, or race – cause different intergroup orientations between socially constructed groups (e.g., Pratto, 1999; Sidanius & Pratto, 1999). Social dominance ideologies target the most salient groups that define the sharpest power hierarchies in given society. SDO legitimates and maintains existing intergroup relations.

From a cognitive perspective, SDO highlights the role of people's beliefs in a hierarchy that frequently advantages their own group's position. High SDO correlates with tough-minded views of the world as a dog-eat-dog competition (Duckitt, 2001). Its origins in unaffectionate parenting suggest a worldview in which people have to take care of themselves, and stronger groups inevitably must dominate weaker groups. Competitive threat motivates social dominance beliefs.

Right-Wing Authoritarianism

A different kind of perceived threat underlies a related dimension, namely, authoritarian beliefs. Specifically focused on perceived threat to cherished values is **right-wing authoritarianism** (RWA). The left wing does not test as authoritarian *per se*, although both left and right can be dogmatic (Rokeach, 1960). Individuals high on RWA conform to traditional values (conventions), obey powerful leaders (authoritarian submission), sanction nonconformists (authoritarian aggression), and derogate outgroups (prejudice) (Altemeyer, 1981, 1988; Duckitt, 1993; Meloen, Van der Linden, & De Witte, 1996).

Intense ingroup identification coupled with perceived value threat characterize RWA. If the ingroup is threatened by oppositional outsiders, then the ingroup must stick together, requiring cohesion and conformity to defend against the world's dangers. High RWA predicts bias against feminists and homosexuals, who are viewed as deviants (Haddock & Zanna, 1994; Haddock, Zanna, & Esses, 1993). High RWA correlates with various social attitudes that emphasize personal responsibility and punish deviance (relating to AIDS, abortion, child abuse, drugs, homelessness, trade deficits, and higher education; Peterson, Doty, & Winter, 1993). People high on RWA do not seek issue knowledge (Peterson, Duncan, & Pang, 2002) and deny the Holocaust (Yelland & Stone, 1996), perhaps because their values are unshakeable. Non-negotiable beliefs predict prejudice because tolerance requires a more relativist view of human group variety.

RWA correlates with punitive parenting, social conformity, and viewing the world as dangerous (Duckitt, 2001). The belief system represents a broad, cognitively coherent ideology. People who combine the highest levels of RWA and SDO are among the most prejudiced in society (Altemeyer, 2004) and are described as power-hungry, manipulative, amoral, dogmatic, ethnocentric, and anti-equality, positioning them as leaders of extremist fringe political groups, to society's peril.

Terror Management Theory

When people confront threats – intense uncertainty about an important negative possibility – they tend to take refuge in certainties, as RWA indicates. This cognitive-motivational mix also appears when people confront their own death, which itself is certain, though the timing is not. The uncertainty in mortality salience is key (van den Bos, Poortvliet, Maas, Miedema, & van den Ham, 2005). **Mortality salience** makes people cherish worldviews that will outlive them (a kind of vicarious immortality; Greenberg, Solomon, & Pyszczynski, 1997). People under threat of their own death validate the ideologies of their salient group identities (Halloran & Kashima, 2004). Conservatives want to conserve, and progressives want to progress, under threat (Greenberg, Simon, Pyszczynski, Solomon, & Chatel, 1992). People follow strong leaders, who reduce apparent uncertainty, under mortality salience (Landau et al., 2004).

Terror management theory (TMT) addresses how people cope with the dread of death when it comes to mind. Most relevant here, people seek to transcend death by identifying with their ingroups, which will outlive them (Castano & Dechesne, 2005). Under threat to self, people preserve the familiar, and this includes reacting against outgroups (Burris & Rempel, 2004). People respond harshly to deviant outgroups when mortality is salient (Castano, 2004; Greenberg et al., 1990; McGregor, Zanna, Holmes, & Spencer, 2001; Schimel et al., 1999), and this especially holds for people high in RWA. When the world is dangerous and threatening, conformity to bedrock values matters more. This orientation often punishes outgroups.

System Justification Theory

So far, several theories (SIT/SCT, SDT, RWA, and TMT) describe self-protective motivations influencing overt intergroup cognitions. Another theory similarly posits ideology as soothing negative reactions (anxiety, uncertainty, discomfort), but it flies in the face of the other theories' self-protection motives. **System justification theory** (SJT) posits that people seek to legitimate the status quo (e.g., Jost & Banaji, 1994; Jost & Hunyady, 2002). Unlike SDT, SJT not only argues that the advantaged do so, but provocatively argues that the disadvantaged do so as well. In this view, ego justification and even group justification give way to system justification because of its palliative effects. The idea that maintaining system stability outweighs individual and group interest receives varied support. Sometimes, at least, disadvantaged groups accept their status, feel less entitled, favor higher status groups, and support the system despite their own best interests (e.g., Jost, Pelham, Sheldon, & Sullivan, 2003; for reviews, see Jost, Banaji, & Nosek, 2004; Jost & Hunyady, 2002). Doubtless, under some circumstances, low-status groups do resist their status, however.

For high-status groups, justifying the status quo has obvious advantages. But for everyone the relationship between perceived status and perceived merit is surprisingly strong across cultures (Cuddy, Fiske, Kwan, et al., 2009; Fiske, 2011). Stereotyping generally supports the status quo. For example, people view even their *own* college group as more (or less) competent when they learn that it is high- (versus low-) achieving relative to a comparison college group (Haines & Jost, 2000; Jost & Burgess, 2000). People may be motivated to view high-power groups as deserving their status, to justify the system, but mainly when they personally feel they cannot change the situation (Dépret & Fiske, 1999; Pepitone, 1950; Stevens & Fiske, 2000). When one's group is devalued but boundaries are impermeable (one cannot leave), then one may under chronic or extreme circumstances internalize the inferiority (Ellemers, Spears, & Doosje, 2002).

Political conservatism, which by definition supports the status quo, fits a form of motivated social cognition – that is, a set of beliefs that correspond to various needs. (Liberalism does too, but it is to some extent the inverse of this analysis.) A meta-analysis of 88 studies (Jost, Glaser, Kruglanski, & Sulloway, 2003) found that conservative ideology correlated with death awareness (supporting terror management theory), concern with loss (supporting social dominance theory), perceived system instability (supporting system justification theory and right-wing authoritarianism), and intolerance of ambiguity (RWA) as well as aversion to novel experience, intolerance for uncertainty, and preference for order, structure, and closure. These last several motives support all of the theories, which jointly emphasize conservative cognitive structures that remove ambiguity in the face of threat and in the service of intergroup politics.

Entitativity and Its Heirs

The most reassuring group representation – most removing ambiguity, uncertainty, instability, and anxiety – makes the category seem objectively real. Social categories appear real, first, in being perceived as entities, that is, units in the Gestalt sense (Chapter 3). Once categorized, groups seem to possess **entitativity** (D. T. Campbell, 1958), the property of being a real thing. An entitative ingroup seems coherent, feels efficacious, meets one's needs, and motivates one's identity (Yzerbyt, Castano, Leyens, & Paladino, 2000). Entitativity tends to polarize intergroup relations (Castano, Sacchi, & Gries, 2003), strengthening belief systems: essentialism, multiculturalism, and infrahumanization/dehumanization.

Essentialism

Entitative groups are often endowed with an **essence** (Rothbart & Taylor, 1992; Yzerbyt, Corneille, & Estrada, 2001), which includes a foundational core often expressed as shared genes, blood, or nature. Perceived essence rests on interpretations of biology. People view biology as fixed (biologists, in contrast, understand its interactions with environment). People often view group categories as real biological phenomena instead of social constructions that change with history and culture.

Essentialism reinforces stereotypes. People who impute an essence to a social category also endorse stereotypes about it (Bastian & Haslam, 2006; Keller, 2005). Stereotypes help people to explain essentialized groups' characteristics as an enlightening Gestalt (Yzerbyt & Demoulin, 2010).

Group essentialism does vary by context. Both Western and East Asian cultures impute essence and entitativity to individual people more than to groups (Kashima et al., 2005), as basic person-perception principles would suggest. But when groups do seem especially essentialist (e.g., in East Asia), people impute more agency to these essentialist groups; that is, they view them as capable of taking action. One of us recalls overseas news reports that would impute agency to countries ("China intends …") in contrast to news reports that impute agency to individuals in the government ("The President announced that he intends….."); see Menon et al. (1999).

For majority members, minorities' group agency may threaten their own position. For minority members, their ingroup's perceived essence and agency may protect their own sense of integrity. And indeed, for Dutch majority adolescents, essentialist beliefs relate to resisting multiculturalism (Verkuyten & Brug, 2004). In contrast, for minority adolescents, a belief in group essence associates with endorsing multicultural beliefs, presumably because their own embattled group identity is a source of pride.

Multiculturalism

Multicultural beliefs endorse groups as essentially different and urge organizations to value those essential differences. **Multiculturalism**, in the extreme, implies biological essence, though moderate multiculturalism implies only chronic societal differences. A contrasting **colorblind** approach denies all differences and insists that everyone be treated identically, regardless of background. Multiculturalism fits social cognition's emphasis on intergroup categorization. Indeed, students primed with a multicultural (compared to colorblind) perspective do show stronger stereotypes and more category-based judgments of individuals (Wolsko, Park, Judd, & Wittenbrink, 2000), but they also are more accurate about statistical differences between the groups. Perceiving group differences may not necessarily lead to bias, instead recognizing multicultural differences (Park & Judd, 2005).

Infrahumanization and Dehumanization

The ultimate biological essence, of course, is being human. People ascribe human essence to their own group more than to other groups (Demoulin et al., 2004; Leyens et al., 2003). Human groups allegedly possess intelligence, language, and subtle emotions that differentiate us from animals.

Focusing on the emotions, people tend to ascribe raw **primary emotions** (anger, happiness) to their own groups and to others, just as they do to animals. But **secondary emotions** (sentiments such as regret, pride) are reserved for the ingroup. Subjective essentialism underlies this **infra-human** (less-than-human) perception of outgroup emotions, allowing people to sympathize less with infrahumanized groups. When a remote outgroup suffers a devastating hurricane or earth-quake, their grief for lost homes and family members seems less poignant than would be our own group's reaction to comparable losses, and people accordingly help them less (Cuddy, Rock, & Norton, 2007).

People regularly minimize the humanity of others in two major forms of **dehumanization** (Haslam, 2006; Table 11.3). First, people may treat others as animals, denying them the **uniquely human** culture, morality, logic, maturity, and refinement. Animalistic dehumanization most applies to outgroups based on ethnicity, immigration status, or disability. Or people may treat others as mechanistic objects, denying them **typical human nature**, such as warmth, emotional responsiveness, agency, curiosity, and depth. Mechanistic dehumanization most applies to some medical treatment of patients and to the objectification of women (Haslam, Bain, Douge, Lee, & Bastian, 2005). Referring to the two overall types as animals and androids, one study found art-ists to be viewed as curious, fun-loving, and emotional (more associated with animals), whereas businesspeople were viewed as organized, hard-hearted, and shallow (more associated with automata; Loughnan & Haslam, 2007).

Intergroup contexts are not the only setting for attributing humanity; people attribute more humanity to themselves than to other individuals (Haslam et al., 2005). But intergroup dehu-manization underlies some of humanity's worst mass crimes against humanity. Not only does dehumanization facilitate intergroup violence (it is easier to kill people you view as animals or machines), but ingroup violence against an outgroup also intensifies infrahumanization (Castano & Giner-Sorolla, 2006).

SUBTLE STEREOTYPES

Subtle stereotypes emerged in the later 20th century following dramatic changes in norms about acceptable beliefs. **Unobtrusive measures** show prejudice persisting even as overt attitudes

Table 11.3   Dehumanizing beliefs

Characteristics denied	Examples	Resulting stereotype	Sample outgroups
Uniquely human	Culture, morality, logic, maturity, refinement	Animalistic, primitive	Ethnicity, disability, immigration status, artists
Typically human nature	Warmth, emotion, agency, curiosity, depth	Mechanistic, robots	Medical patients, objectified women, business people

improved (Crosby, Bromley, & Saxe, 1980; Saucier, Miller, & Doucet, 2005). Just as people no longer blow secondhand smoke in other people's faces, so people no longer express insulting stereotypes in polite company. Using new, sophisticated measures, researchers now reveal these automatic, ambiguous, and ambivalent modern forms of stereotyping.

Automatic Stereotyping

Cognitive associations link to people's intergroup representations. The apparent organization of these stereotypic beliefs, as well as their valence, reveals automatic processes that make stereotypes readily accessible. Chapter 12 focuses on more explicitly emotional prejudices, but the more cognitive beliefs covered here also contain valence, so they relate to prejudice as well, although along more evaluative than explicitly emotional lines. Some relatively automatic cognitive processes here include category confusions, aversively racist associations, indirect racial priming, implicit associations, and cognitive load – but all subject to some motivated control.

Category Confusions

People rapidly identify each other's gender, race, and age, using these categories to sort people. As a result, people tend to confuse other people who fall into the same category, forgetting *which* woman, *which* Latino, or *which* elderly person contributed a suggestion. In the **who-said-what** experimental paradigm, people's spontaneous memory errors more often confuse people within category than between categories (Taylor, Fiske, Etcoff, & Ruderman, 1978). This confusion occurs within categories based on gender, race, age, sexual orientation, attitudes, attractiveness, skin tone, accent, and relationship type (e.g., Maddox & Chase, 2004; Maddox & Gray, 2002; Rakić, Steffens, & Mummendey, 2011; see S. T. Fiske, 1998, pp. 371–372). **Category confusions** happen even when controlling for related cognitive processes, such as guessing, especially when people respond rapidly (Klauer & Wegener, 1998), and concerning numerical minorities (Klauer, Wegener, & Ehrenberg, 2002). These memory errors occur without apparent intention, effort, or control, making them relatively automatic. And these confusions encourage stereotyping (Taylor et al., 1978).

Aversive Racism

Among the first to identify truly automatic bias, racial priming experiments (Chapter 10) revealed us–them categorization, as described by social identity theory, occurring instantly. Whites identify positive traits (e.g., smart) faster when primed with "Whites" than with "Blacks" (Dovidio, Evans, & Tyler, 1986; Gaertner & McLaughlin, 1983; Perdue et al., 1990). The same pattern occurs substituting "us" versus "them" for racial labels. People's automatically positive ingroup associations recur reliably over time (Kawakami & Dovidio, 2001) and predict nonverbal behavior in interracial interactions (Dovidio, Kawakami, & Gaertner, 2002). (Overt attitudes predict overt verbal behavior.) Ingroup positivity is clearer than outgroup negativity.

Ingroup positivity, of course, neglects the outgroup by exclusion. In zero-sum settings, such as hiring, even if overt biases improve, subtle biases persist, especially in ambiguous cases (Dovidio & Gaertner, 2000) and with only rare exceptions (Kawakami, Dovidio, & van Kamp, 2005). These instantaneous positive associations to the ingroup create a sense of comfort so that ingroup applicants just seem to fit in better.

According to meta-analysis, Whites help Blacks less when they can rationalize their decision as not pertaining to race: for example, when helping would be riskier, longer, harder, effortful, or distant (Saucier et al., 2005). **Aversive racism** describes most people as well intentioned and rejecting their own racist beliefs (Gaertner & Dovidio, 1986). They express their ingroup-favoring associations only when they have apparently nonracist reasons (excuses), as when information is ambiguous. Thus one way to override such associations is to remove ambiguity. Unfortunately, life is inherently ambiguous.

A more realistic option is to capitalize on the us–them effect, but to expand the "us" to include the previous "them." For example, after the terrorist attacks of September 11, 2001, many Americans noticed improved interracial relations as national identity trumped racial identity. Being reminded that the attacks targeted all Americans reduced Whites' prejudices against Blacks (Dovidio et al., 2004). This **common ingroup identity model** (Gaertner & Dovidio, 2005) works well, apparently by increased perspective-taking and awareness of injustice (Dovidio et al., 2004), plus shared interaction and common fate (Gaertner, Sedikides, & Graetz, 1999).

Indirect Racial Attitudes

Another early entrant in cognitive approaches to stereotyping is the **indirect priming** technique (Fazio et al., 1986, 1995). As with aversive racism measures, the technique assesses the speed-up in people's responses given a fit in the evaluation of a prime and a stimulus (Chapter 10).

The two tasks differ (Table 11.4), in the stimulus that follows the prime, and in the response required. In the aversive racism case, the ingroup or outgroup prime precedes a positive or negative race-relevant word or a meaningless string of letters. People make a **lexical decision** (i.e., is this a word or nonword?), which is speeded by a match between the racial prime and the valence of the stereotype-relevant word. In the indirect priming case, the initial racial prime (which could be a word or a photograph) precedes a positive or negative word *unrelated* to race, and the participant replies *good–bad* (instead of word–nonword). The aversive racism technique uses more conceptual processes because word meaning matters, whereas the indirect priming technique isolates the evaluative content because only valence matters. Conceptual versus evaluative priming does differ (Wittenbrink, Judd, & Park, 2001a). For example, conceptual processes link more to stereotyping, judgment, and impressions, whereas evaluative processes link more to affect, preferences, and social distance (Amodio & Devine, 2006). In both cases, however, the facilitation (speed-up) for some people's responses to negative or stereotypic terms following an outgroup prime provides an indirect index of racial attitudes. This cognitive facilitation places this measure alongside other measures of subtle bias.

Indirect priming measures do predict nonverbal behavior in interracial interactions, evaluations of an outgroup member's essay, emotional reactions to outgroup members, and other relevant attitudes (Fazio & Olson, 2003). Whether stereotypes and evaluations measured this way are the "real" attitude or not matters less than the observation that these upstream, relatively automatic indicators do correlate with downstream, more explicit attitudes and behaviors.

Consistent with this chapter's focus on stereotyping *per se*, automatically activated racial attitudes relate to Whites' trait inferences about Blacks (e.g., Graham & Lowery, 2004). But all is not lost. Even these relatively automatic reactions can diminish, depending on the individual's

Table 11.4　Comparison of three subtle bias measures

Approach	Timing	Prime	Stimulus	Task	Measure
Aversive racism	sequential	group name Black/White	stereotype-relevant word or nonword hostile/dsdjklfj	word? (yes/no)	speed

Prediction: "Black" speeds identifying "hostile" as a word; "White" speeds identifying "smart." Nonword (letter strings) show no speed-up.

Approach	Timing	Prime	Stimulus	Task	Measure
Indirect priming	sequential	group name Black/White	unrelated positive/ negative word garbage/ diamond	valence? (good/bad)	speed

Prediction: "Black" speeds judging "garbage" as bad; "White" speeds judging "diamond" as good.

Approach	Timing	Stimulus	Stimulus	Task	Measure
Implicit association	pairings	group name Black/White	unrelated positive/ negative word garbage/ diamond	match side (L/R)	speed

Prediction: People categorize "Black" and "garbage" faster on the same side, with "White" and "diamond" on the other side, compared to the reverse pairings.

Note: See text for task descriptions; for IAT, also see Figure 10.2, panels (c) and (d).

motivation to avoid prejudice (Dunton & Fazio, 1997; Olson & Fazio, 2002, 2004a; Towles-Schwen & Fazio, 2003).

Implicit Association Test

Chapter 10 introduced the **implicit association test** (IAT) (Nosek, Hawkins, & Frazier, 2012). Like the aversive racism and indirect priming measures just discussed, it has both an evaluative side and a more specific stereotype side. Here we focus on how it measures stereotypes *per se*, not the evaluative associations (attitudes) and not complex affective reactions (emotions). The basic IAT capitalizes on associations between ingroup (often, majority) and positive attitude objects, as well as between outgroup (often, minority) and negative attitude objects.

Separation of implicit stereotyping and implicit evaluation in race bias comes from possibly distinct underlying neural systems for semantic versus affective memory (Amodio & Devine, 2006). White participants evaluating an African American writer expressed less warmth and inclination to befriend as a function of their IAT evaluative bias. In contrast, their IAT stereotyping bias (on the hackneyed images of athletic, rhythmic, unintelligent) predicted their other stereotypic ratings (lazy, dishonest, untrustworthy). Whites' ratings of a prospective Black partner showed a similar correspondence. The evaluative IAT predicted how close they sat, reflecting the affective aspect, whereas the stereotype IAT predicted their expectancies for their partner's task performance, reflecting the more cognitive aspect (see also Neumann & Seibt, 2001).

Although mostly focused on evaluative attitudes, the implicit association test reveals stereotypes of gender-stereotyped appearance (e.g., petite), activities (e.g., football), objects (e.g., flowers), professions (e.g., mechanic), and roles (e.g., master; Blair & Banaji, 1996). Gender and strong gender identity combine with stereotyping math as male, to drive women away but men toward an implicit preference for math. As another example, women and men implicitly link their own gender to favorable trait stereotypes (Rudman, Greenwald, & McGhee, 2001).

Stereotyping and Cognitive Load

Category activation and **application** each depend on **cognitive load** (Chapter 4, memory representation; Gilbert & Hixon, 1991). After activation and application, later judgment also depends on cognitive load. Load plays different roles at each stage (Table 11.5).

Category activation (e.g., gender) emerges from faces faster than does individual identity (Cloutier, Mason, & Macrae, 2005; Macrae et al., 2005; Chapter 3). Although relatively automatic, category activation varies with load, task, and context. Merely encountering targets does not always prompt categorization (Macrae, Bodenhausen, Milne, Thorn, & Castelli, 1997). People apparently attend to cues relevant to multiple alternative categories (e.g., both gender and age), but activate only the currently most relevant category (Quinn & Macrae, 2005). Also, given multiple

Table 11.5 Cognitive load effects differ by stage

Stage	Favors	Effect of cognitive load
Activation	Relevant, accessible category over individual identity	Category may not activate
Interpretation	Stereotype-inconsistent cues, to explain or assimilate	Ignore stereotype-consistent cues' initial application
Recall	Stereotype-inconsistent cues, because attended to them	May not alter stereotypes
Later judgment	Stored stereotypes	Stereotype more

alternative categories, people activate the more accessible ones (Castelli, Macrae, Zogmaister, & Arcuri, 2004). Category activation also depends on context; for example, an African American at a family barbecue or a church cues different automatic responses than the same person on an urban street corner or with a gang (Wittenbrink, Judd, & Park, 2001b). Category activation is **conditionally automatic**, depending on goals and other contextual factors (Chapter 2).

Once the category is active, stereotype-consistent meanings absorb easily, requiring less cognitive capacity. Therefore, when cognitive resources are scarce, people selectively allocate attention to stereotype-inconsistent information. If prejudiced, they especially attend to stereotype-inconsistency, trying to explain it away (J. W. Sherman, Conrey, & Groom, 2004; J. W. Sherman, Lee, Bessenoff, & Frost, 1998; J. W. Sherman, Stroessner, Conrey, & Azam, 2005). At early stages of stereotype application, people prioritize coherent impressions, so they work on the inconsistencies; they then remember the inconsistent information that had required cognitive work to assimilate. However, having been explained or assimilated, inconsistency may well not undermine their stereotypes.

At later application, especially under load, people rely on stored stereotypes more when making judgments (e.g., Bodenhausen & Lichtenstein, 1987; Bodenhausen & Wyer, 1985; Macrae, Hewstone, & Griffiths, 1993; van Knippenberg, Dijksterhuis, & Vermeulen, 1999). Using stereotypes frees mental capacity (Macrae, Milne, & Bodenhausen, 1994). And people with a high need for cognitive economy are especially likely to engage intergroup categorization (Stangor & Thompson, 2002). Thus, although complex, the role of cognitive load in stereotype activation, application, and judgment generally favors stereotypes' efficient maintenance.

Stereotyping and Motivated Control

If stereotyping processes are so often automatic, how do people ever get past them? If stereotyping qualifies as conditionally automatic, then with sufficient motivation, capacity, and information, people can avert its impact. People more easily avoid relatively automatic stereotypic associations when they have enough motivation and time (Blair & Banaji, 1996; Macrae, Bodenhausen, Milne, & Ford, 1997). Practice helps diminish automatic stereotypic associations to a particular outgroup (Kawakami et al., 2000). So do perspective-taking (Galinsky & Moscowitz, 2000), guilt (Hing, Li, & Zanna, 2002), and self-focus (Dijksterhuis & van Knippenberg, 2000; Macrae, Bodenhausen, & Milne, 1998). The social influence of a minority experimenter makes a difference (Lowery et al., 2001), given affiliative motives (Sinclair, Lowery, Hardin, & Colangelo, 2005). People activate outgroup-relevant parts of self, as if preparing for harmonious interaction (Kawakami, Phills, Greenwald, Simard, Pontiero, Brnjas, Khan, Mills, & Dovidio, 2012). Altogether, goals and capacity allow individuating, beyond the most easily-used category (for review, see Fiske, Lin, & Neuberg, 1999).

The goal of merely suppressing stereotypes, without adding alternative information, can backfire, however. If people merely try to avoid stereotypes, when they relax their guard afterward, they may experience a **rebound**, with redoubled stereotypic associations later (Macrae, Bodenhausen, & Milne, 1998; Macrae, Bodenhausen, Milne, & Jetten, 1994; Wegner, 1994). Motivation and capacity influence rebound effects as well (Monteith, Sherman, & Devine, 1998; N. A. Wyer, Sherman, & Stroessner, 2000). Prejudice and goals combine to predict postsuppression rebound (Monteith, Spicer, & Tooman, 1998).

Controlling stereotypes uses up executive control, which may explain the rebound effect. In interracial interactions, when Whites are especially concerned about appearing prejudiced, they inhibit their behavior, with good effect for their Black partners. Unfortunately for Whites, they themselves do not enjoy the interaction as much (Shelton, 2003) and their executive control capacities are depleted afterward (Richeson et al., 2003; Richeson & Shelton, 2003). For Blacks trying to counteract the prejudices of a White partner, comparable damage occurs to their experience of themselves in the interaction and to their executive control afterward (Richeson, Trawalter, & Shelton, 2005; for a review, see Shelton & Richeson, 2006).

Ambiguous Stereotyping

The first prong of subtle stereotyping, its automaticity, rests on basic categorization and rapid association processes. Modern stereotyping is subtle not just in being fast but also slippery. Much depends on interpretation: People deal automatically with clearly stereotypic or counter-stereotypic information. But people also interpret ambiguous information to confirm their expectancies. In one classic, White people subliminally primed with Black stereotypic terms then interpreted ambiguous, race-unspecified behavior as more hostile (Devine, 1989). As described in Chapter 3 (Graham & Lowery, 2004), police and probation officers subliminally primed with Black-stereotypic words then read race-unspecified vignettes about shoplifting and assault. They subsequently rated the offenders' hostility and immaturity, culpability, expected recidivism, and deserved punishment more negatively. Stereotypic interpretations are not confined to race: People subliminally primed with rape-related terms read an ambiguous aggressive encounter between a man and a woman and then judged her more negatively afterward, especially if they endorsed beliefs in a just world, presumably because they were more likely to blame her for the ambiguous encounter (Murray, Spadafore, & McIntosh, 2005).

Nor are stereotypic interpretations of information only preconscious: People saw the same ambiguous angry-sad expression on a face that was made by hair and clothing to change gender; they then interpreted the facial expression as angry if male and sad if female, in line with gender stereotypes about emotion (Plant, Kling, & Smith, 2004). People interpret a construction worker hitting someone as punching, but a housewife as spanking (Kunda & Sherman-Williams, 1993). This occurs even when people are not asked for their interpretations but merely later misrecognize an inference as familiar (e.g., a nun's versus a rock star's reaction to the amount of liquor served at a party; Dunning & Sherman, 1997). These interpretations occur at encoding, so they become integral to people's impression of the other person.

People interpret not only the content of ambiguous information but its causal meaning. As Chapter 6 noted, the ingroup's positive action must reflect our inherent ability or goodness, but the outgroup's identical positive action must reflect chance or the situation. The reverse obtains for negative actions. Dubbed the **ultimate attribution error** (UAE) (Pettigrew, 1979), the effect appears in interethnic attributions (Hewstone, 1990) and in cross-gender attributions (Deaux & Emswiller, 1974; Swim & Sanna, 1996). Subtle and ambiguous, the UAE depends on interpreting the causes underlying group behavior. This has a practical impact: Jurors who believe African Americans are typically perpetrators readily interpret an interracial dispute as their fault, whereas viewing African Americans as victims leads to viewing Whites as guilty (Wittenbrink, Gist, & Hilton, 1997). Dispositional attributions stabilize negative outgroup stereotypes and positive ingroup ones, whereas situational attributions decrease the stability of their opposites (J. W. Sherman, Klein, Laskey, & Wyer, 1998). So-called **entity theorists** favor such fixed, entity attributions for negative stereotypes; **incremental theorists** take a more relative view (Levy, Plaks, Hong, Chiu, & Dweck, 2001).

Subjective judgments of ambiguous information do not always favor the dominant group. Because of **shifting standards**, for example, a woman may be viewed as performing well (for a woman) and praised. A man would have to perform well, for a man, to receive equal praise because the standards are higher. Praise is cheap, however. When allocating scarce resources, the two genders must compete, and then stereotypes create pro-male bias (Biernat & Vescio, 2002). One way to understand shifting standards is to contrast subjective judgments (rating people as "smart") versus apparently objective judgments (ranking the smartest people you know) (Table 11.6). These effects appear in contexts as varied as sports (Biernat & Vescio, 2002), military promotions (Biernat, Crandall, Young, Kobrynowicz, & Halpin, 1998), and hiring decisions (Biernat & Fuegen, 2001).

Stereotyping capitalizes on the ambiguity of the information given, so the influence of the stereotype itself is tacit and unexamined. People hide their stereotypic interpretations from themselves as well as from others. For example, in evaluating job applicants, people weight the credentials differently depending on how they want the decision to come out (Norton, Vandello, & Darley, 2004). What they value in one decision then carries over to subsequent decisions.

When the situation creates ambiguity – if prejudice is but one possible cause of a decision, but nonprejudiced reasons might excuse the action – the decision itself is ambiguous regarding prejudice. In aversive racism, Whites who score high on **modern racism** (see Table 11.7) hold various political opinions that all happen to disadvantage minorities. They also are less likely to help a Black person, but only when others are also present, diffusing responsibility for aid

Table 11.6 Shifting standards

Group	Expectation or standard	Actual performance	Subjective judgment	Objective judgment	Outcome
Subordinate (female, minority)	Low	Moderate	"Good, for a [subordinate]"	Moderate rank, relative to everyone not the fastest, compared with men	Praise only
Example:	Slow runner	Moderate	"Fast, for a woman"		
Dominant (male, majority)	High	Moderate	"Just OK, for a [dominant]"	Higher rank, relative to everyone, faster than the women	Reward only
Example:	Fast runner	Moderate	"Slow, for a guy"		

(Gaertner & Dovidio, 1986). Aggression, given nonracial excuses, works similarly; White participants aggressed against Black targets less than against White targets. But if they had the excuse of being insulted by the target, they aggressed more against Blacks than Whites (Rogers & Prentice-Dunn, 1981). Likewise, people who have proved their **moral credentials** as unprejudiced subsequently feel more free to express stereotypes and prejudices (Monin & Miller, 2001). What all these studies share is the ambiguity of expressing category-based cognitive biases.

Table 11.7 Modern racism scale, 2000

Denial of continuing racial discrimination

Generations of slavery and discrimination have created conditions that make it difficult for Blacks to work their way out of the lower class.*
Discrimination against Blacks is no longer a problem in the United States.

Blacks should work harder

It's really a matter of some people not trying hard enough; if Blacks would only try hard they could be just as well off as Whites.

Irish, Italian, Jewish, and many other minorities overcame prejudice and worked their way up. Blacks should do the same without any special favors.

Demands for special favors

Blacks are demanding too much from the rest of the society.

Blacks generally do not complain as much as they should about their situation in society.*

How much of the racial tension that exists in the United States today do you think Blacks are responsible for creating? All of it, most, or not much at all?

Undeserved outcomes

Over the past few years, Blacks have gotten more economically than they deserve.

Do Blacks get much more attention from the government than they deserve, more attention, about the right amount, less attention, or much less attention?

Note: * indicates reverse-scored items. Full scale has twice as many items.
Source: Sears & Henry (2003); reproduced by permission

Ambivalent Stereotyping

Besides being automatic and ambiguous, stereotyping can also be subtle in being ambivalent. Unlike automaticity, which became evident as more blatant, controlled biases receded, and unlike ambiguity, by which people excuse or disguise their aversive stereotyping, ambivalence is not new. As early as Americans' stereotypes were systematically measured, some groups elicited flat-out negative stereotypes (e.g., Turks were thought to be cruel and treacherous), and others all-out positive ones (e.g., the English were thought to be intelligent and good sports). But many others received mixed stereotypes: African Americans were allegedly lazy but musical, and Jews were allegedly industrious but mercenary (Katz & Braly, 1933). Stereotypes of Black people and Jewish people seemed inverse on competence and warmth, each high on one but low on the other (Allport, 1954). **Ambivalent stereotyping** turns out to be a general principle of their content over time (Bergsieker, Leslie, Constantine, & Fiske, 2012). Given improved anti-prejudice norms, people increasingly mention only the positive side and omit the negative side of ambivalent stereotypes, in effect, stereotyping by omission (in evaluating a job candidate: "Well, she's a really nice person..."). The innuendo is not lost on listeners, who infer the omitted negative dimension (Kervyn, Bergsieker, & Fiske, 2012), or on self-presenters, who present accordingly (Holoien & Fiske, 2012).

According to the **stereotype content model** (SCM), when people encounter an unfamiliar group, they must immediately answer two questions. First, as sentries demand, "friend or foe?" This describes the group's intention for good or ill (Are they competing and exploiting, or are they harmless, even cooperative?). Competitive intent predicts stereotypes of being unsociable, cold, and untrustworthy. Second, people want to know, "able or unable?" This answers whether the group can enact their intentions (Do they have the necessary resources?). High status predicts stereotypes of perceived competence and ability (see Fiske, Cuddy, & Glick, 2007, for a review).

This competence-by-warmth space describes two ambivalent combinations and two unambivalent combinations (Figure 11.1): In the United States, currently, people who are middle class, Christian, or heterosexual seem both warm and competent. Conversely, people who are homeless, drug-addicted, or poor (regardless of race) are stereotyped as neither warm nor competent. The ambivalent combinations reflect groups who are liked as warm but disrespected as incompetent (older people, disabled people) or groups who are disliked as not warm but respected as competent (Jews, Asians, rich people, professionals regardless of race or gender; Fiske, Xu, Cuddy, & Glick, 1999; Fiske, Cuddy, Glick, & Xu, 2002). These four combinations appear in representative US samples, in Europe, and in Asia (though the warm, competent reference groups appear more modest there; Cuddy, Fiske, & Glick, 2007; Cuddy, Fiske, Kwan, et al., 2009; Durante et al., 2012; Eckes, 2002).

The four clusters also describe various subtypes within larger categories: subgroups of men and women, subgroups of gay men, distinct mental illnesses, and categories of Black people within the Black community (respectively: Eckes, 2002; Clausell & Fiske, 2005; Fiske, 2012; Fiske, Bergsieker, Russell, & Williams, 2009). Because they seem to have intent and capability, even animals and corporate brands differentiate along warmth and competence dimensions (respectively: Sevillano, & Fiske, under review; Kervyn, Fiske, & Malone, 2012). Warmth-by-competence stereotypes predict specific emotional prejudices and discriminatory behaviors (Chapter 12; Cuddy, Fiske, & Glick, 2007; Fiske et al., 2002).

The SCM warmth-by-competence space operates in a wide range of social perception for both individual and group targets (see Fiske, Cuddy, & Glick, 2007, for a review). Related frameworks describe two similar stereotypic dimensions: competence or **agency**, as **self-profitable**, and morality/sociability or **communality**, as **other-profitable** (Abele & Wojciszke, 2007; Peeters, 1983).

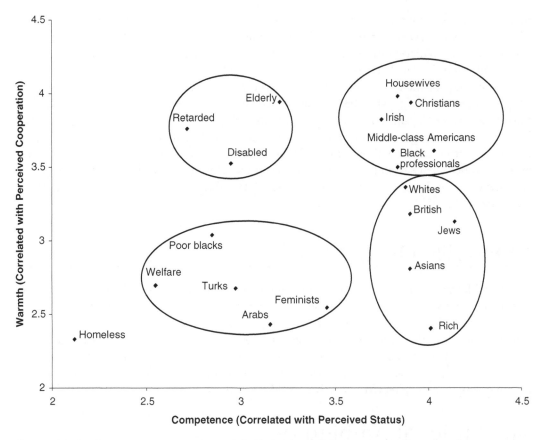

Figure 11.1   Stereotype content model: Data from US representative sample

Source: Cuddy, Fiske, & Glick (2007)

Being capable requires at least an initial focus on self, whereas being warm and trustworthy requires an orientation to others. In valuing the ingroup, with whom one interacts the most, people care most about morality (Leach, Ellemers, & Barreto, 2007). The overall self- and other-profitable framework applies to national groups (Phalet & Poppe, 1997) and values (Wojciszke, 1997). A third approach, **enemy images theory** (Alexander, Brewer, & Hermann, 1999), describes national stereotypes again in a framework that includes these competence and warmth dimensions plus power. The point here is that stereotypes have at least two dimensions, and groups can be viewed as positive on one and negative on the other, rendering the cognitions evaluatively ambivalent.

Stereotypes often evoke this tension between liking and respect. **Racial ambivalence** (Katz & Hass, 1988) reflects White liberals with mixed interracial reactions, pro and con, viewing Black people as disadvantaged alternatively because of external obstacles such as discrimination or because of internal obstacles such as values and motivation. **Ambivalent sexism** (Glick & Fiske, 1996, 2001) reflects two factors: First, **hostile sexism** resents women who pursue nontraditional roles, gaining respect but forfeiting affection; and second, subjectively **benevolent sexism** cherishes women who stay within prescribed gender roles, gaining protection but forgoing respect (Glick, Diebold, Bailey-Warner, & Zhu, 1997). This pattern, again, is not recent, holding up across cultures (Glick et al., 2000; see Glick & Fiske, 2001, for a review).

Another complementary ambivalent stereotype paints rich people as dishonest and poor people as honest (Kay & Jost, 2003). Exposing people to this stereotype increases their justification of the system. Praising winners on relevant dimensions (the rich as hard-working and intelligent) justifies the system, and praising losers on an irrelevant dimension (honest, happy) compensates the victims without undermining the system (Kay, Jost, & Young, 2005). In this view, everyone benefits from the system in at least some respects (Jost & Kay, 2005). Ambivalent stereotypes are especially useful in unequal societies, which have a lot of explaining to do (Durante et al., 2012).

EFFECTS OF BIAS

Whether blatant or subtle (automatic, ambiguous, ambivalent), stereotyping is best studied in interactions between people. Stereotyping research had emphasized Whites' perceptions of Blacks to the exclusion of Blacks' own racial attitudes and how they affect interracial encounters (Hebl & Dovidio, 2005; Shelton, 2000; Vorauer, 2006). The mutual interplay of expectancies is the stuff of social interaction. Much of the work on behavior appears in Chapter 15, but here we examine stereotypic expectancies and their effects on both sides. Targets of stereotypes have multiple options for coping (Miller & Kaiser, 2001), as do perpetrators.

Attributional Ambiguity

Precisely because so much stereotyping is subtle, targets often may be unsure whether negative reactions aim at them personally as unique individuals or collectively as interchangeable members of their group. This **attributional ambiguity** reflects the dilemma targets face (Crocker & Major, 1989). As with all negative events, experiences of bias typically provoke appraised threat and subsequent coping. When intergroup interactions go badly, targets may cope by blaming prejudice instead of their own behavior, thereby protecting their self-esteem (Major, Quinton, & McCoy, 2002).

Targets are, however, reluctant to attribute negative outcomes to prejudice because of the social as well as personal costs. Socially, people who make attributions to discrimination risk being labeled as complainers, troublemakers, or worse (Kaiser & Miller, 2001b, 2003; J. K. Swim & Hyers, 1999), especially by highly prejudiced people (Czopp & Monteith, 2003). An interaction is irrevocably altered when someone plays the prejudice card. People want to belong to their group (whether work or social), but alleged discrimination undermines belonging; hence, people high on a need to belong are less likely to make attributions to discrimination (Carvallo & Pelham, 2006).

Personally, also, attributions to discrimination undermine the target's sense of control. Although attributing negative outcomes to discrimination can buffer self-esteem, attributing positive outcomes to (bend-over-backwards positive) discrimination can undermine self-esteem as well, because one cannot take credit for the success (Crocker, Voelkl, Testa, & Major, 1991). Constant attribution to discrimination damages self-esteem (Major, Testa, & Blysma, 1991). And perceiving one's personal experience as an instance of pervasive discrimination is depressing (Schmitt, Branscombe, & Postmes, 2003).

Exaggerated **stigma consciousness** – heightened vigilance in interacting with outgroup members – can encompass a feedback loop of negativity: Expecting prejudice leads to acting negatively, which in turn elicits the expected negative experiences (Pinel, 1999, 2002). This paranoid perspective increases self-consciousness, sinister attributions, and negative perceptions of the other's attitudes (Santuzzi & Ruscher, 2002), none of them recipes for a successful interaction. Stigma consciousness, however, shows substantial individual differences.

Sometimes, expectations of discrimination reflect reality, and this is the target's predicament. People and situations vary in the extent to which they resolve attributional ambiguity by playing the discrimination card, and the pattern contradicts common sense. Low-status people (women, minorities) who endorse individual effort and the Protestant ethic are *less* likely to make attributions to discrimination (Major, Grazmow, McCoy, Levin, Schmader, & Sidanius, 2002). On the other hand, high-status people (men, Whites) who hold the same beliefs are *more* likely to attribute their own negative outcomes to discrimination against themselves. Women and minorities actually may be less likely than men and majorities to make attributions to discrimination, perhaps because their status is less legitimated, so frustration and disappointment are familiar. Again because of cultural ideologies about entitlement and blame, heavy-weight people are less likely to make attributions to discrimination, perhaps because of the cultural ethic that people can and should control their weight (Crocker, Cornwell, & Major, 1993). Attributions to discrimination interplay with expectations about who's to blame for negative outcomes and who's entitled to good ones.

Stereotype Threat

Expectations about groups' performance – success and failure – drive **stereotype threat**. Group stereotypes universally include a dimension of perceived competence or incompetence, as noted. Stereotypes target specific domains for specific groups: for example, women in math (Spencer, Steele, & Quinn, 1999), African Americans on standardized tests (Steele & Aronson, 1995), European Americans in sports (Stone, Lynch, Sjomeling, & Darley, 1999), men on emotional sensitivity (Koenig & Eagly, 2005; Leyens, Désert, Croizet, & Darcis, 2000), Whites on racism (Goff, Steele, & Davies, 2008), Latinos on math (Gónzales, Blanton, & Williams, 2002), older people on memory (Chasteen, Bhattacharyya, Horhota, Tam, & Hasher, 2005), previously mentally ill people on intellectual performance (Quinn, Kahng, & Crocker, 2004), and low-income people on ability testing (Croizet & Clare, 1998). In the relevant domain, if performance appears diagnostic of one's ability, then the stereotype poses a threat beyond the normal threat associated with high-pressure performance (e.g., Steele, 1997; for reviews, see Major & O'Brien, 2005; Steele, Spencer, & Aronson, 2002). If one fails, one suffers not only the personal humiliation of failure but also the shame of confirming stereotypes about the ingroup's intrinsic abilities.

Stereotype threat occurs only if one's relevant category is salient, the domain is relevant, the test is allegedly diagnostic, and one cares about it (Steele et al., 2002). (Table 11.8 summarizes.)

People cope with stereotype threat sometimes by disengaging from the domain. For example, many African Americans view intelligence testing as biased and unsuited to assessing important kinds of intelligence, so self-esteem is not contingent in the long or short term on that kind of performance (Major, Spencer, Schmader, Wolfe, & Crocker, 1998). Older adults (and others) may deny the relevance of a particular form of incompetence (von Hippel, von Hippel, Conway, Preacher, Schooler, & Radvansky, 2005). This **disidentification** with performance explains why some group members give up on domains in which others do not expect them to excel. It is not precisely a self-fulfilling prophecy because (a) they deny or avoid the domain altogether, so they do not actually underperform but instead refuse to perform, and (b) they do not actually have to meet a prejudiced person. Stereotype threat describes the impact of ambient stereotypes, that is, stereotypes "in the air," not necessarily stereotypes in a given encounter with a prejudiced person.

Table 11.8 Stereotype threat processes

Antecedents

- Relevant category is salient
- Self-relevant domain
- Allegedly diagnostic test
- Caring about it

Encounter

- Ambient stereotypes ("in the air")
- Performance demand

Respond cognitively and motivationally

- Vigilance and stress
- Arousal combined with attributions for that arousal
- Anxiety
- Negative thinking
- Impaired working memory
- Dejection

Result: Under-performance relative to ability

Solutions

- NOT: Trying to suppress stereotypes (which keeps them activated)
- Realizing intelligence is not fixed but is malleable (therefore context-dependent and improvable)
- Individuating oneself
- Affirming a distinct valued attribute
- Retraining
- Bifurcating one's identity
- Learning about stereotype threat and attributing one's anxiety to stereotypes

People suffer from stereotype threat when they are vulnerable to salient, important negative comparisons in a diagnostic domain. Everyone can fall prey to this, with even the same group underperforming in one comparison context and overperforming in another. Asian women do better on math in a comparative context when they identify as Asians and worse in a comparative context when they identify as women (Shih, Pittinsky, & Ambady, 1999). White men underperform in a comparative context with Asians but overperform in a comparative context with White women (Aronson, Lustina, Good, Keough, Steele, & Brown, 1999). Student-athletes perform differently depending on which identity is relevant (Yopyk & Prentice, 2005).

Stereotype threat emerges in specific contexts just noted (performance stereotypes, identity salience, test diagnosticity, domain importance); such contexts inadvertently heighten vigilance and stress (Steele et al., 2002). In these settings, cognition and motivation together undermine performance (Wheeler & Petty, 2001). For example, arousal combines with attributions for that arousal to sabotage performance (Ben-Zeev, Fein, & Inzlicht, 2005). Anxiety is subtle, measured either by physiological and nonverbal indicators or by self-reports (Bosson, Haymovitz, & Pinel, 2004; Croizet, Després, Gauzins, Huguet, Leyens, & Méot, 2004). Negative thinking and activated stereotypes may be one cognitive mechanism that interacts with motivation (Cadinu, Maass, Rosabianca, & Kiesner, 2005; Kray, Galinsky, & Thompson, 2002; Seibt & Förster, 2004; Stangor, Carr, & Kiang, 1998; Wheeler, Jarvis, & Petty, 2001). Trying to suppress the stereotypes does not work, precisely because suppression keeps the stereotype activated (Steele et al., 2002). On the cognitive side, working memory capacity suffers (Schmader & Johns, 2003), but on the motivation side, dejection also enters in (Keller & Dauenheimer, 2003). This mix of potential damage is daunting.

Fortunately, several antidotes work, such as individually realizing that intelligence is not fixed but is malleable and therefore context-dependent and improvable (Aronson, Fried, & Good, 2002). Other remedies include individuating oneself (Ambady, Paik, Steele, Owen-Smith, & Mitchell, 2004), affirming a distinct valued attribute (Martens, Johns, Greenberg, & Schimel, 2006), retraining (Forbes & Schmader, 2010), or bifurcating one's identity (Pronin, Steele, & Ross, 2004). Learning about stereotype threat and attributing one's anxiety to stereotypes also improve performance (Johns, Schmader, & Martens, 2005).

Structural remedies include not asking for demographic information before the test, presenting the test as fair or insensitive to group differences, emphasizing the organization's commitment to diversity, blurring group boundaries, and creating identity safety (Davies, Spencer, & Steele, 2005; O'Brien & Crandall, 2003; Rosenthal & Crisp, 2006; Steele et al., 2002). Between the personal and the structural remedies, stereotypes need not threaten people's performance, but only if people know about the phenomenon.

Minority Identity and Well-Being

Stereotype threat and attributional ambiguity help explain how stereotyped targets – despite the odds – avoid being crushed. People can reinterpret or ignore the relevance of public feedback. And indeed, public regard for one's group predicts nothing about self-esteem among African Americans (Rowley, Sellers, Chavous, & Smith, 1998), nor does public regard predict one's own private regard for one's group among African Americans, although it does for Asians

(Crocker, Luhtanen, Blaine, & Broadnax, 1994). Some aspects of **collective self-esteem** (Table 11.9) – namely, one's personal, private regard for one's group and one's own feelings of worth as a group member (living up to the group image) – do predict psychological well-being (e.g., life satisfaction, depression). Well-being is closely tied to private aspects of collective self-esteem (Crocker & Luhtanen, 1990).

Feeling contingent on others to validate the self generally is not healthy (Chapter 5; e.g., Crocker & Park, 2004). For example, an academic contingency for self-worth can make people depend on achievement for self-esteem, but this makes them especially vulnerable when they do fail, especially if they believe intelligence is fixed (not malleable; Niiya, Crocker, & Bartmess, 2004). All this can lead to further academic and even financial problems (Crocker & Luhtanen, 2003) as well as giving up on one's major (Crocker, Karpinski, Quinn, & Chase, 2003).

In a completely different domain – sexual satisfaction – basing one's self-esteem on others' approval of one's gender conformity also undermines relevant experiences (Sanchez, Crocker, & Boike, 2005). Investment of self in gender ideals is generally a bad idea for men and women alike (Sanchez & Crocker, 2005). Investment of self-esteem in others' approval of one's appearance is also bad for one's health, correlating with heavier alcohol use (Luhtanen & Crocker, 2005). For heavy-weight and poor people, perhaps because the culture blames them for their conditions, self-esteem suffers (Miller & Downey, 1999; Rudman, Feinberg, & Fairchild, 2002).

Table 11.9   Collective self-esteem sample items

Membership

I am a worthy member of the social groups I belong to.
I feel I don't have much to offer to the social groups I belong to.*

Private

I often regret that I belong to some of the social groups I do.*
In general, I'm glad to be a member of the social groups I belong to.

Public

Overall, my social groups are considered good by others.
Most people consider my social groups, on the average, to be more ineffective than other social groups.*

Identity

Overall, my group memberships have very little to do with how I feel about myself.*
The social groups I belong to are an important reflection of who I am.

Note: * indicates a reverse-coded item. Full scale has 16 items.
Source: Luhtanen & Crocker (1992); reproduced by permission

In various identity domains, **private regard** for one's identity seems more adaptive than relying on **public regard**. For example, among academically at-risk African American high-school students, private regard for Black people, coupled with a father's support, decreases alcohol use (Caldwell, Sellers, Bernat, & Zimmerman, 2004). Among African American college and high-school students generally, private regard for Blacks, combined with centrality of one's racial identity, preserves self-esteem (Rowley et al., 1998). Private regard correlates with maternal support; together they buffer against perceived stress, diminishing anxiety and depression (Caldwell, Zimmerman, Bernat, Sellers, & Notaro, 2002).

Identity also shapes perceived discrimination. Some minority individuals are more attuned to discrimination than others. For example, Blacks for whom race is central, whose ideology is Black nationalist, and who view public regard of the ingroup as generally negative are more likely to perceive discrimination but also to be buffered from its negative mental-health consequences (Sellers, Caldwell, Schmeelk-Cone, & Zimmerman, 2003; Sellers, Rowley, Chavous, Shelton, & Smith, 1997). Ethnic identity can sensitize people to discrimination (Operario & Fiske, 2001; Sellers & Shelton, 2003; Shelton & Sellers, 2000), but the types of identity, types of discrimination, and types of outcome matter.

On average, though, African Americans are more likely to detect subtle nonverbal indicators of prejudice than are European Americans, as indicated by accurately judging a White person's implicit and explicit prejudice (Richeson & Shelton, 2005). Monitoring an interaction for prejudice and managing it to produce positive outcomes can be depleting. The more they show ingroup favoritism (probably comparable to private regard of ingroup), the more African Americans experience loss of attentional resources *after* an interracial interaction (Richeson, Trawalter, & Shelton, 2005). African Americans who prioritize their ingroup may be particularly likely to monitor interracial interactions, which is depleting. Expecting another person to be prejudiced taints the interaction (Shelton, Richeson, & Salvatore, 2005). However, moderately prejudiced majority people who attempt to monitor their prejudice apparently can compensate: They are more engaged in the interaction. As a result, in this case a prejudiced interaction partner ironically may be preferable, at least in the short term (Shelton, Richeson, Salvatore, & Trawalter, 2005).

Perceiving discrimination is a multistep process, known as **ask-answer-announce** (Stangor, Swim, Secrist, DeCoster, Van Allen, & Ottenbreit, 2003). First, the idea that discrimination might be relevant has to occur to the target; one has to ask oneself the question. Contrary to dominant group intuitions, all stigmatized people do not think about discrimination at all times. Contexts and individual differences both can make the possibility of discrimination more or less accessible. Second, if the question is posed, one must answer: Judging a behavior as discrimination depends again on situational factors (e.g., amount and intent of harm), the role of affect, need for control, and protecting self-esteem (e.g., Sechrist, Swim, & Stangor, 2004; Swim et al., 2003). Third, even in concluding that discrimination occurred, one may or may not announce it. As noted earlier, the costs are high, and people often avoid drawing such conclusions publicly.

Lower-status (often minority) group members are most likely to have concerns related to evaluations of self when their outcomes depend on the high-status person (Vorauer, 2006). They may personalize negative behaviors and experience discomfort (Vorauer & Kumhyr, 2001). Lower-status group members can cope either by distancing themselves from the interaction, thereby damaging the impression they make (Kaiser & Miller, 2001a), or by overcompensating in the interaction, thereby improving the impression they make (Shelton, Richeson, & Salvatore, 2005).

Majority Concerns

Intergroup interactions have two sides, and higher-status groups (usually majorities) also worry about the impression they make (Shelton & Richeson, 2006; Vorauer, 2006). White students report wanting to have more interaction with Black peers but worry about being rejected, so they fail to initiate contact. They also attribute their Black peers' apparent lack of interest as rejection. Ironically, precisely the same process occurs for Black students regarding their White peers (Shelton & Richeson, 2005). Neither side understands the other, and this **pluralistic ignorance** prevents communication. When intergroup interactions do occur, low-prejudice majority people amplify their overtures to make their interest abundantly clear, whereas high-prejudice people (who are in fact less interested) tend to downplay the interest they convey (Vorauer, 2005). Dominant group members, when especially concerned about appearing prejudiced, may choke under pressure if they are low in prejudice. Conversely, if they are high in prejudice, their enhanced evaluative concerns allow them to shine – coming across as warm and friendly (Vorauer & Turpie, 2004). Ironically, minorities may prefer to interact with high-prejudice dominant group members, as noted, in the short term, at least when they are motivated.

Part of what may be annoying about well-intentioned but low-prejudice people is their self-absorption. Concerns with the other person's stereotypes of self (called **meta-stereotypes**) cause majority members to focus on themselves and how they are viewed (Vorauer, Hunter, Main, & Roy, 2000; Vorauer & Kumhyr, 2001). This public self-consciousness, as noted, depletes majority group members' executive function during and after the interaction (Richeson et al., 2003; Richeson & Shelton, 2003; Richeson & Trawalter, 2005), so interracial interactions between strangers can be exhausting for everyone.

Summary

Stereotyping is the cognitive aspect of bias – most frequently studied for gender, race, and age – and it comes in both blatant and subtle forms, a difference that matters in both practical and theoretical terms.

Blatant prejudice can begin with realistic intergroup conflict over tangible resources, but even under these circumstances, perceptions matter. People have to perceive conflict, and they have to perceive that they belong to separate groups in the first place. Social identity theory describes how people categorize self into an ingroup and others into outgroups, maximizing differences between them and minimizing difference within. Discriminating elevates short-term (state) self-esteem but not long-term (trait) self-esteem. Self-categorization theory jettisons the self-esteem hypothesis and focuses on comparative fit to describe behavior differences between groups and similarities within them. Normative fit incorporates groups' images. Optimal distinctiveness theory describes the balance between autonomy and belonging. Subjective uncertainty reduction theory describes the reassurance provided by group norms. The most cognitive features of these theories are ingroup favoritism (rewarding the ingroup relative to the outgroup) and perceived homogeneity (of outgroups most of the time and of ingroups under threat).

Threat enters into several theories of ideology, stereotyping, and bias. Social dominance theory describes endorsing group hierarchies under perceived economic threat to the ingroup. Right-wing authoritarianism describes endorsing status quo group boundaries under perceived threat to conventional values. Terror management theory describes adherence to cultural views that will outlast one's own lifetime, under mortality salience. System justification theory describes people's maintenance of hierarchies, even against their own self-interest, because stability may matter more. Essentialism imputes a biological basis to socially constructed groups, preserving the humanity of us and lessening the humanity of others. All these theories emphasize cognitions that resolve ambiguity, under threat, in the context of intergroup politics.

Subtle forms of stereotyping emerged as blatant forms of bias became taboo and as researchers developed more sophisticated measurement techniques based on cognitive psychology. Subtle stereotypes are automatic, ambiguous, and ambivalent. On the relatively automatic front, people unintentionally confuse other people within categories, and these confusions predict stereotyping. Aversive racism – bias abhorrent to the self – emerges in reaction time data showing instantly more favorable responses to ingroups and positive stereotypes, compared to outgroups. Aversive racism also emerges in discrimination when the prejudiced person can construct a nonracial excuse. Indirect priming also uses response times, but this technique focuses on valence matches between an outgroup and clearly positive or negative words. The implicit association test has an evaluative component (introduced in Chapter 10) and a conceptual (stereotype) component, the latter correlating with other stereotyping. All these reaction-time techniques correlate especially with nonverbal and other subtle, less-monitored behaviors.

Subtle forms of stereotyping also are ambiguous in that people interpret information to fit their expectations and hide these interpretations from themselves and others. Finally, subtle stereotyping is ambivalent: Many groups are liked but disrespected or respected but disliked. All these forms of subtle stereotyping result from internal conflicts between impulses to stereotype versus personal and social sanctions against it.

Bias affects dominant and minority group members alike. Attributional ambiguity describes the predicament of understanding when feedback reflects on oneself alone and when it reflects on biases regarding one's group membership. Stereotype threat describes the double risk of performance in a domain stereotypically poor for one's group; potential failure reflects not only on oneself but also on one's group. Hence, people may disidentify with the domain or may underperform when the task is diagnostic and important and one's relevant social category is salient. As a result of stereotypic biases, minority self-esteem is often disengaged from public regard for their ingroup, focusing instead on private regard, thereby buffering the ill effects of persistent bias. Although sensitive to bias, low-power groups rarely report bias because of the social and personal costs.

Dominant group members worry about how they are evaluated by minority groups, becoming self-conscious and self-absorbed in interactions. When both majority and minority group members make the effort to overcome prejudices, the effort can deplete executive control during and after the interaction. Nevertheless, interactions can often improve.

FURTHER READING

Bodenhausen, G. V., Kang, S. K., & Peery, D. (2012). Social categorization and the perception of social groups. In S. T. Fiske & C. N. Macrae (Eds.), *Sage handbook of social cognition* (pp. 311–329). Thousand Oaks, CA: Sage.

Dovidio, J. F., & Gaertner, S. L. (2010). Intergroup bias. In S. T. Fiske, D. T. Gilbert, & G. Lindzey (Eds.), *Handbook of social psychology* (5th edn, Vol. 2, pp. 1084–1121). Hoboken, NJ: Wiley.

Hewstone, M., Rubin, M., & Willis, H. (2002). Intergroup bias. *Annual Review of Psychology, 53*, 575–604.

Kay, A. C., & Eibach, R. P. (2012). Ideological processes. In S. T. Fiske & C. N. Macrae (Eds.), *Sage handbook of social cognition* (pp. 495–515). Thousand Oaks, CA: Sage.

Nosek, B. A., Hawkins, C. B., & Frazier, R. S. (2012). Implicit social cognition. In S. T. Fiske & C. N. Macrae (Eds.), *Sage handbook of social cognition* (pp. 31–53). Thousand Oaks, CA: Sage.

Yzerbyt, V., & Demoulin, S. (2010). Intergroup relations. In S. T. Fiske, D. T. Gilbert, & G. Lindzey (Eds.), *Handbook of social psychology* (5th edn, Vol. 2, pp. 1024–1083). Hoboken, NJ: Wiley.

Prejudice

Interplay of Cognitive and Affective Biases

12

- Intergroup Cognition and Emotion
- Racial Prejudice
- Gender Prejudice
- Age Prejudice
- Sexual Prejudice

Gut feelings drive behavior, but both interact with cognition. Affective parts of our brains evolved first and even today often respond first (Chapters 13–14). Intergroup relations especially illustrate the power of emotional prejudices; when people commit extreme discrimination – such as hate crimes, prisoner abuse, genocide, and terrorism – strong emotions underlie their behavior (Glaser, Dixit, & Green, 2002; Pettigrew & Meertens, 1995). Even in mundane cases, affective prejudices drive discrimination more than cognitive stereotyping does (Dovidio, Brigham, Johnson, & Gaertner, 1996; Talaska, Fiske, & Chaiken, 2008; Tropp & Pettigrew, 2005a). Stereotyping is not trivial; indeed, it occupies the majority of intergroup research. Stereotyping correlates with emotional prejudices and predicts intergroup behavior, but emotional prejudices are stronger predictors. Hence, this chapter covers the emotional prejudices that result from cognitive biases and interact with them.

Emotional prejudice goes beyond positive–negative evaluation (attitudes; see Chapters 9–10). It includes differentiated emotions such as fear, disgust, envy, pity, anxiety, and resentment, all qualitatively distinct. These specific emotions target specific groups and motivate specific behavior, so they matter in a practical way. But they also matter theoretically. Differentiated emotional prejudices not only describe the world but also predict and explain it (Giner-Sorolla, Mackie, & Smith, 2007). Note that intergroup emotion is not the traditional view of prejudice, which always focused more on attitudes. This chapter thus paves the way for the remaining chapters on the role of cognition in affect and behavior.

In social cognition, the angle on such affective biases is their interplay with cognition. The first section addresses several theories of intergroup cognition and emotion; in every case, a pattern of cognitions leads to a pattern of emotions and behaviors. The other parts of the chapter take seriously the idea that distinct emotional prejudices underpin reactions to different outgroups. Four sections focus in turn on categories that have received the most research attention from social psychologists: race and ethnicity, gender, age, and sexual orientation.

INTERGROUP COGNITION AND EMOTION

Why does the annoying driver blocking your way always come from some outgroup, not your own? Incidental affect irrelevant to the group (road rage) still perhaps affects the encounter. Although one might assume that people in bad moods stereotype more, which would be a straightforward valence assumption, instead different moods have distinct effects (Bodenhausen, Kramer, & Süsser, 1994; Bodenhausen, Sheppard, & Kramer, 1994). Angry moods do make people stereotype more, in accord with common sense. However, sad moods, although negative, actually make people stereotype less because they think harder. And people often stereotype more in happy moods than in neutral ones because they cannot be bothered to think hard. Chapter 14 returns to the more general influence of moods on cognition.

Groups do also elicit affect as an integral function of who they (apparently) are and the situations in which they appear. In contrast to incidental affect, different groups trigger different affective configurations as an integral feature of the encounter, according to several theories.

Stereotype Content Model

Two fundamental dimensions describe social perception – sociality and capability (Asch, 1946; Rosenberg & Sedlak, 1972; Wojciszke, 2005; see Fiske, Cuddy, & Glick, 2007, for a review). Intergroup perception is no exception (Chapter 11): Warmth and competence form the twin dimensions that differentiate social groups. According to the **stereotype content model** (SCM), stereotypes along these two dimensions result from structural relations between groups (Fiske, Cuddy, Glick, & Xu, 2002; see Table 12.1). Perceived *competition* for societal resources predicts *warmth* stereotypes; cooperative insiders and allies are warm and sincere, whereas allegedly exploitative outsiders are cold and untrustworthy. Perceived *status* predicts *competence* stereotypes; rich people are allegedly competent, whereas poor people are allegedly incompetent.

Stereotypes thus are circumstances of immigration, history, and geography, if social structural variables predict them. The group's position in society can vary over time and conditions, and the stereotypes will follow. For example (Cuddy, Fiske, Kwan, et al., 2009), many cultures identify a set of entrepreneurial outsiders, seen as capable but not especially warm (Jewish people and Chinese people, in their respective diasporas, have often been perceived this way). As another example, in a variety of cultures, older people are seen as incapable but warm. And in all cultures studied so far, poor people (homeless, welfare recipients, undocumented migrants, drug addicts) are seen as neither smart nor nice.

These SCM stereotypes matter because they correlate with intergroup emotions (Fiske et al., 2002) and with intergroup behavior (Cuddy, Fiske, & Glick, 2007). The **BIAS map** describes

Table 12.1 Stereotype content model: Examples

	STRUCTURAL VARIABLE: STATUS	
	↓ (+)	
	Stereotype: Competence	

STRUCTURAL VARIABLE: COMPETITION ↓ (−) Stereotype: Warmth		Low	High
High	Groups Prejudice Discrimination	Disabled, older people Pity Active help, passive harm	Middle-class, ingroup Pride Active help, passive support
Low	Groups Prejudice Discrimination	Poor, homeless Disgust Active harm, passive harm	Rich, Asians, Jews Envy Active harm, passive support

Source: After Cuddy, Fiske, & Glick (2007); Fiske, Cuddy, Glick, & Xu (2002)

stereotype-based clusters of emotions that directly predict intergroup behavior. Consider the outsider entrepreneurs (usually urban, and seen as rich, or at least mercenary). They elicit envy and jealousy, mixed emotions that say, "You have something we want and that we should have. We will take it if we can" (S. T. Fiske, 2011; Salovey, 1991; R. H. Smith, 2000). Envy breeds a volatile behavioral mix: (a) grudging association, going along to get along when the social order is stable, combined with (b) active attack when the chips are down. Genocides often take this form (Staub, 1999). Again, the cognitions about social structure (competitive, high-status) underlie the stereotypes (not warm but capable), which in turn elicit the emotions (envy, resentment) and the behaviors (passive accommodation but potential active harm).

Another unstable emotional combination targets older people and those with mental or physical handicaps, all seen as incapable but warm and trustworthy. They receive pity, a mixed emotion saying, "You are worse off than us, but as long as it's not your fault, we feel sorry." Pity motivates a confusing mix of helping and neglecting. Pity is demeaning because it involves unequal status and undermines the target's own control (R. H. Smith, 2000; Weiner, 2005). Many groups in this category are institutionalized. The typical behaviors directed toward these groups combine being helped but also abandoned, which again conveys an emotionally mixed message. As before, cognitions about social structure start this chain: Perceived noncompetition and low status convey incapacity and warmth, which elicit emotions (pity, sympathy) and corresponding behaviors (active helping but social neglect).

Finally, SCM's third outgroup cluster is the most extreme combination, less emotionally mixed but more straightforwardly awful. Poor people are stereotyped as having no redeeming features (neither warm nor competent), especially if they are homeless. The same is even more true of drug addicts. These groups receive contempt and even disgust, an emotion usually directed at things. Neuroimaging data support both the disgust reaction and the relative dehumanization of such extreme outgroups. When people look at photographs of homeless or addicted people, the normal social neural response (medial prefrontal cortex activation) simply falls below a significant baseline, and instead the insula (associated with disgust) activates (Harris & Fiske, 2006); these findings suggest that extreme outgroups seem somehow less human. Contempt and disgust both involve looking down, as does pity, but without any positive affect at all. Disgust evokes avoidance, expulsion, and fear of contamination (Rozin & Fallon, 1987), and contempt also is a distancing emotion. They result in both active attack and passive neglect.

In contrast to the outgroup emotions of envy, pity, and disgust are the ingroup/ally/reference-group emotions of pride and admiration. Pride assimilates the other to self, and admiration places the other above the self but still assimilates (rather than envy or contempt, which contrast self and other; R. H. Smith, 2000). Pride and admiration motivate both passive association (go along to get along) and active helping. Being an object of pride or admiration is all good, of course, and it stems from cognitions about social structure (high-status, noncompeting) and traits (competent, warm), resulting in both active and passive facilitation.

The SCM and its behavioral extension, the BIAS map, both turn crucially on distinct intergroup emotions. These emotional prejudices ultimately result from cognitions about structural features of society: who competes with whom, and who ranks above whom. Stereotypes link the perceived social structure to the expected emotions and behaviors. In emphasizing social structure, these models fit well with the next theory, focused on appraisals of "good for us" versus "bad for us."

Intergroup Emotions Theory

People's sense of self extends to their group membership (Chapters 5 and 11). **Intergroup emotions theory** (IET) goes one step further, to posit that people include the group in the self representation (E, R, Smith, 1993; E. R. Smith, Segar, & Mackie, 2007). The socially extended self-representation means that people respond more quickly and accurately to traits that match their self-concept *and* their ingroup concept, compared to mismatches; outgroup matches and mismatches do not show these effects (E. R. Smith, Coats, & Walling, 1999; E. R. Smith & Henry, 1996). To the extent that people treat the ingroup the way they treat the self, IET argues, their corresponding emotional reactions should also be similar.

For the self, **appraisal theories of emotions** describe people as evaluating stimuli initially as good-for-me versus bad-for-me, resulting in primitive positive–negative reactions. After this primary appraisal, more complex emotions result from analyzing the situation further for causes, certainty, and the like (Chapter 13). In the intergroup instance, the appraisals are stereotypes, and they entail perceived responsibility, fairness, and certainty. For example, people may stereotype government beneficiaries as demanding resources (tax money) from the ingroup. The intergroup appraisal would view the outgroup demands as inconsistent with ingroup motives: unfair, certain,

Table 12.2   Intergroup emotions theory: Example appraisal–emotion–action links

	Appraisals (all motive-inconsistent)	Emotion	Action tendency	Who
Certainty Cause Plus	Low Other or circumstance Perceiver weak	Fear	Avoid	Low status toward high status
Certainty Cause Plus	High Other or circumstance Norm violation	Disgust	Avoid	High status toward low status
Certainty Cause Plus	High Other's intent Perceiver weak Unfair	Contempt	Move against	Any
Certainty Cause Plus	High Other's intent Perceiver strong Unfair	Anger	Move against	High status toward demanding low status

Source: Adapted from E. R. Smith (1993)

intentional, but less powerful. The resulting emotional prejudice would be anger, and the associated action tendency (discrimination) would entail actively moving against the outgroup. As another example, suppose a similar appraisal (motive-inconsistent, unfair, certain, intentional) is made but the outgroup is more powerful as, for example, with some institution unfairly seizing your assets. Then one might feel intergroup fear. IET also generates predictions for intergroup disgust, contempt (dislike), and jealousy (see Table 12.2).

IET conceptualizes prejudice as a specific intergroup emotion that comes from a specific appraisal (stereotype) and creates specific emotional action tendencies (discrimination). IET focuses on intergroup particulars more than abstractions. That is, it analyzes specific intergroup experiences rather than general societal dimensions. As such, it fits an **exemplar**-based approach to intergroup representations (Mackie & Smith, 1998; E. R. Smith & DeCoster, 1998; Chapter 4). In this approach, people view each other as representing multiple group memberships, encountered in specific situations.

In one study, people categorized themselves as for or against gay marriage, then learned their attitudinal ingroup received either strong or weak support in several newspaper headlines. The study then measured anger and fear, as well as tendencies to attack or avoid the outgroup. Under these circumstances, ingroup weakness begets fear and avoidance, but ingroup strength begets anger and opposition (Mackie, Devos, & Smith, 2000). Intergroup emotions come from people's prior intergroup experiences and intergroup ideologies. Intergroup emotions then mediate between cognitive appraisals and evaluations (D. A. Miller, Smith, & Mackie, 2004).

Intergroup emotions also trigger defensive and offensive action tendencies in specific inter-group contexts (Devos, Silver, Mackie, & Smith, 2002). The intergroup emotions are functional in regulating behavior. When behavior is blocked, they intensify, but when behavior is implemented, they discharge (Maitner, Mackie, & Smith, 2006).

Image Theory

Enemy images theory identifies national images that result from perceived international context and perceived behavioral intentions (Alexander et al., 1999; Alexander, Brewer, & Livingston, 2005; Brewer & Alexander, 2002). The images result from, account for, and justify affective and behavioral orientations toward the other national group. The appraisal of the other nation as goal-compatible or goal-incompatible combines with its perceived status and perceived power. Out of many possible combinations, the five recurring images (Table 12.3) include two in which each side views the other symmetrically – *ally* (goal-compatible, equal), *enemy* (goal-incompatible, equal) – and three asymmetrical ones: *dependent* (perceiver goal-independent, lower status, and lower power), *imperialist* (other goal-independent, higher status, and higher power), and *barbarian* (goal-incompatible, lower status, but higher power).

Emotions enter this theory in two respects. First, high arousal readily cues arousal-related images (e.g., barbarian), given the right eliciting conditions (Alexander et al., 1999). Second, and consistent with IET and SCM, certain relationship patterns encourage particular intergroup emotions. Allies arouse admiration and trust, encouraging cooperation. Enemies arouse anger, facilitating containment or attack. Dependents arouse disgust and contempt, facilitating exploitation or paternalism. Imperialists arouse jealousy and resentment, facilitating resistance or rebellion. And barbarians arouse fear and intimidation, facilitating defensive protection (Alexander at al., 1999; Brewer & Alexander, 2002).

Table 12.3   Image theory: Examples

	OTHER'S STATUS		
Goals	Equal	Lower	Higher
Symmetrically compatible Symmetrically incompatible	Ally Enemy		
Other is dependent Perceiver is independent		Dependent (Low power)	
Other is independent Perceiver is dependent			Imperialist
Other is goal-incompatible		Barbarian (High power)	

Source: Adapted from Alexander et al. (1999)

In the closest test to date of the intergroup emotions prediction (Alexander et al., 2005), White urban high school students reported feeling more admiration (trust and respect) toward Whites and more fear and intimidation toward Blacks, consistent with their images of other Whites as allies and Blacks as enemies and barbarians. In turn, Black students reported feeling more admiration toward Black targets and more resentment (anger and disgust) toward White targets, consistent with their images of other Blacks as allies and Whites as enemies and imperialists. Overall, image theory complements the perspectives of SCM and IET, which together examine structural relations, stereotypes, emotions, and behavioral tendencies.

Biocultural Approach

A **biocultural approach**, like the previous theories, argues that discrete intergroup emotions result from discrete intergroup relations and predict discrete intergroup behaviors (Cottrell & Neuberg, 2005; Neuberg, Smith, & Asher, 2000). The starting point is neither social identity (as in the IET) nor social structural relations (as in the SCM and image theory), but intergroup threat viewed from a sociofunctional evolutionary perspective. The biocultural approach emphasizes human interdependence, effective group functioning, and individual adaptation to the benefits and threats of group life.

Threats to the group's integrity variously predict emotions and motivations. For example, obstacles (threats to ingroup property, freedom, coordination) produce anger and efforts at removal. Contamination (threats to health or values) produces disgust and prevention. Danger produces fear and protection, and so on. Consistent with these predictions, different outgroups evoke qualitatively distinct profiles of threat and emotion (Cottrell & Neuberg, 2005), so responses differentiate among ethnic groups (African Americans, Asian Americans, Native Americans) and social groups (gay men, activist feminists, fundamentalist Christians).

Other social-evolutionary approaches reinforce the underlying arguments. For example, they emphasize self-interest in social settings. Adaptive, self-promoting strategies include: dyadic cooperation, pursuing reliable partners for social exchange; coalitional exploitation, excluding others from the ingroup and exploiting the outgroup; and avoiding potential parasites, those who carry pathogens (Kurzban & Leary, 2001). The work on evolutionary origins of stigma all balances, on the one hand, adaptations for sociality, selecting appropriate partners, and on the other hand, limiting sociality to one's own advantage.

Anxiety: Integrated Threat Theory

Threats to the ingroup also shape **integrated threat theory** (ITT) (Stephan & Renfro, 2002). ITT incorporates many of the variables from the previous theories, but focuses on one major emotion, anxiety. ITT is a broad, generic, integrative model predicting attitudes (Table 12.4). Antecedents include intergroup relations (e.g., conflict, status inequality), individual differences (ingroup identity, contact experience), cultural dimensions (collectivism), and immediate situation (e.g., minority-majority in context).

Table 12.4   Integrated threat theory

Antecedents	Mediating threats	Consequences
Intergroup relations	Realistic threats	Psychological reactions (cognitive and affective)
Individual differences	Symbolic threats	Behavioral reactions
Cultural dimensions		
Immediate situation		

Source: Adapted from Stephan & Renfro (2002)

Threats mediate between these antecedents and attitudes. Threats primarily differ between the realistic and symbolic. Realistic threats are perceived tangible harms to ingroup resources, especially alleged economic threats (job competition, tax costs). Symbolic threats are abstract harms to ingroup ideals (values, religion, identity, language). In addition, anxiety and negative stereotypes relate to these threats differently in the early model and the later model (W. G. Stephan & Renfro, 2002; W. G. Stephan & Stephan, 2000). Essentially, the threats are a cognitive appraisal (as in IET), and the stereotypes a cognitive response (as in the SCM); anxiety is an emotional response common to all these theories.

The main claims of this theory are several. First, it focuses on anxiety, a negative emotion in response to uncertain threats. Anxiety facilitates usage of stereotypes (Wilder, 1993). By creating arousal and self-focus, anxiety diminishes the ability to distinguish among outgroup members. Distraction worsens the effects of anxiety, and anxious people especially assimilate differences within the outgroup, increasing its perceived homogeneity. ITT broadens this premise to include intergroup antecedents and consequences.

Second, ITT applies to a staggering array of intergroup settings, attitudes toward: immigrants (W. G. Stephan, Renfro, Esses, Stephan, & Martin, 2005; W. G. Stephan, Ybarra, & Bachman, 1999; Stephan, Ybarra, Martínez, Schwarzwald, & Tur-Kaspa, 1998), cancer and AIDS patients (Berrenberg, Finlay, Stephan, & Stephan, 2002), Blacks and Whites (W. G. Stephan et al., 2002), First Nations Canadians (Corenblum & Stephan, 2001), Mexicans and Americans (W. G. Stephan, Diaz-Loving, & Duran, 2000), and men as viewed by women (C. W. Stephan, Stephan, Demitrakis, Yamada, & Clason, 2000).

Third, ITT originally posed a simple causal chain: Antecedents → threats (symbolic, realistic, anxiety, stereotypes) → prejudiced attitudes. Various path analyses of survey data support threat as a mediator of antecedent effects on attitudes (Corenblum & Stephan, 2001; W. G. Stephan et al., 2002; W. G. Stephan, Diaz-Loving, & Duran, 2000), and experiments further support the causal importance of threats (W. G. Stephan et al., 2005).

Finally, ITT proposes a simple-sounding intervention to overcome anxiety and perceived intergroup threats – empathy. Of course, empathy with the outgroup is easier said than felt, but empathy has improved relationships between Blacks and Whites (Finlay & Stephan, 2000). Empathy can operate cognitively (perspective-taking) or emotionally (W. G. Stephan & Finlay, 1999) to reduce threat and anxiety.

Guilt: Various Theories

Guilt is a useful emotion because it tells you when you have done something you wish you hadn't done, encouraging you to change your future behavior and make amends, if possible. Guilt matters as a focal intergroup emotion, at least for powerful or majority groups viewed as oppressing less powerful or minority groups. Chapter 11 noted the difficulty of suppressing stereotypes, even with motivation and the capacity to do so (e.g., Monteith, Sherman, & Devine, 1998). So guilt does not easily improve intergroup responses.

Guilty feelings of compunction depend on the level of prejudice (Monteith, 1993, 1996). Low-prejudice respondents have high, internalized standards for their own interracial behavior, but when they do violate them, they feel conflicted and guilty. Discrepancies between what you should do and what you likely would do make low-prejudice people feel guilty (Voils, Ashbrun-Nardo, & Monteith, 2002). This guilt accordingly tempers their reactions to, for example, racist jokes (Monteith & Voils, 1998). For those who do experience prejudice-related conflict, guilt links to racial ambivalence (Chapter 11).

High-prejudice respondents have lower, more externalized standards, and when they violate them, they feel angry (Zuwerink, Devine, Monteith, & Cook, 1996). However, some high-prejudice people's standards do depend on a moral obligation to uphold equality of opportunity (Monteith & Walters, 1998). In either case, awareness of the discrepancy inhibits behavior, triggers guilt, and catalyzes retrospective reflection. Over time, the discrepancy-related stimuli and responses become associated with guilt, so they establish cues for control, such as behavioral inhibition and thinking ahead, which are potential control strategies (Monteith, Ashburn-Nardo, Voils, & Czopp, 2002). Guilt is indeed useful, even if not simple.

Not all standards are internal; activated social norms against prejudice can lower prejudiced responses by external incentives (Monteith, Deneen, & Tooman, 1996). Social norms and education change people by inducing guilt. For example, understanding White privilege and the prevalence of anti-Black discrimination leads to guilt, which in turn encourages favoring affirmative action as a remedy (Swim & Miller, 1999). Many Whites downplay White privilege because it undercuts their own feelings of personal merit (Lowery, Knowles, & Unzueta, 2007). Framing inequality in terms of dominant group advantage (instead of minority disadvantage) makes White people feel more guilty and more receptive to remedies such as affirmative action (Iyer, Leach, & Crosby, 2003). Conversely, people who oppose affirmative action often do so out of concern for protecting the ingroup rather than in showing direct hostility toward the outgroup (Lowery, Unzueta, Knowles, & Goff, 2006).

However, ingroup protection cannot be the whole story in attitudes toward affirmative action because it differs by target group. In these attitudes, racial threat to the White ingroup apparently outranks gender threat to the male ingroup. From the perspective of sheer numbers, the greater opposition to affirmative action benefiting a 13% racial minority (African Americans) makes less sense than opposition to its benefiting 50% of the population (women), if only ingroup protection were operating. So something more than ingroup protection is going on here. Perhaps people feel more guilty about female disadvantage because they feel more directly connected.

RACIAL PREJUDICE

American social psychologists have most often studied White racial prejudice against Blacks, probably because of Americans' particular history with regard to race. African Americans have uniquely survived the combination of two centuries' slavery, being counted as three-fifths a person; political turmoil around emancipation and reconstruction; a century's legalized segregation, known as Jim Crow; the last generation's civil rights movement; ongoing racial backlash; and continuing segregation and group disadvantage. (More detailed discussion lies beyond our scope here, but see, for example, Fredrickson, 2002; Jones, 1997; Sears, 1998.)[1]

Given the importance of racial prejudice, early social psychology studies immediately set to work measuring racial and ethnic attitudes (Bogardus, 1933; Katz & Braly, 1933; Thurstone, 1928; see Allport, 1935, for an early review). White–Black racial issues have persisted in the prejudice literature since that time, probably because racial prejudices are exceptional in several psychological respects: (a) This particular racial combination continues to carry strong emotions; (b) this type of prejudice is aversive to most of those who hold it; (c) it is not plausibly an evolved bias in itself, and ample evidence indicates social construction; and (d) racial groups remain hypersegregated, furthering the current divide in ordinary intergroup interactions. None of these features as pointedly characterizes other forms of prejudice, as we will see, but cognitive processes factor into each of them.

Racism is Emotionally Loaded

A previous section examined White guilt regarding racism. Let's here examine the strong emotional loading of racism and how it might relate to guilt. Guilt is an other-oriented moral emotion, showing concern that one's behavior harmed another person (Tangney, Stuewig, & Mashek, 2007). Regarding racism, White guilt reflects beliefs that one's group has harmed another group, about which Whites typically have no doubt, at least as regards the past. Racial guilt may be one reason that most White students do not identify strongly with their own race (although being the majority and therefore default group surely also matters to their lack of White racial identity).

Possibly, most Whites' emotionally loaded responses would better be described as shame rather than guilt. Shame is a self-directed moral emotion, being concerned with others' evaluations (Tangney et al., 2007). Many majority members are self-concerned in interracial interactions, which fits potential shame more than guilt. In contrast, many minorities are concerned for both self and other (Shelton & Richeson, 2006; Vorauer et al., 2000; Vorauer & Kumhyr, 2001). Many

---

[1] Arguably, African Americans are one of the most ill-treated ethnic groups in American history. This is not to diminish the importance of prejudice against Asians, Latinos, Jews, or Native Americans, which have variously resulted in internment, exclusionary immigration policies, employment discrimination, and genocide. Social psychologists in general and social cognition researchers in particular have studied these forms of ethnic prejudice less often (but for recent exceptions, see, e.g., Echebarria-Echabe & Fernández-Guede, 2006; Lin, Kwan, Cheung, & Fiske, 2005; van Laar, Levin, Sinclair, & Sidanius, 2005).

Whites are potentially worried by how they are evaluated because they think Blacks expect them to be racist. Avoiding shame is part of the emotional-cognitive matrix of contemporary race relations.

What's more, as we have seen, Whites are widely acquainted with negative cultural stereotypes about Blacks, and elements of these stereotypes are emotionally threatening. American cultural stereotypes of Blacks include elements of hostility and criminality (Devine, 1989; Devine & Elliot, 1995). These cultural stereotypes put Whites on their guard (Phelps et al., 2000), and this contributes to the emotionally loaded interaction.

But far worse, racial stereotypes and accompanying emotional prejudices create life-and-death consequences for Blacks. For example, race affects split-second shoot/don't-shoot decisions paralleling those made by police officers; racial bias lowers the threshold for shooting unarmed Black men (Correll, Park, Judd, & Wittenbrink, 2002; Correll, Park, Judd, Wittenbrink, Sadler, & Keesee, 2007; Figure 12.1). Cultural stereotypes and emotional prejudices affect neural responses as early as 200 msec, which in turn mediate the shooter bias (Correll, Urland, & Ito, 2006). More specifically, Black faces activate crime-related associations, including the early visual detection of weapons by both students and police officers. Conversely, stereotypic associations also facilitate detection of Black faces, especially faces that are prototypically Afrocentric (Eberhardt et al., 2004). The life-and-death consequences of the interplay between cultural stereotypes and visual processing extend beyond split-second decisions, all the way to death row. Higher likelihood of being sentenced to death for the murder of a White victim disproportionately punishes Black defendants who happen to have more stereotypically Black features (controlling for a variety of factors, including severity of crime; Eberhardt et al., 2006). Although race–crime associations are doubtless overridden by cues to social class, gender, and age, the connection remains. Most Black families have "the conversation" with their teenage sons about what to do (and not do) in an encounter with the police. Such issues heighten the emotional tensions even in crime-irrelevant interracial interactions, in part because the cultural associations are automatic.

Automatic interracial responses often reflect emotion-laden cultural associations, even if people do not personally endorse them. As Devine's (1989) **dissociation model** (Chapter 11) and the **implicit association test** (Chapters 10–11) show, people have automatic stereotypic thoughts, which are difficult to control. Whites' efforts to be egalitarian are widely shared, so most Whites try to avoid conveying their automatic associations. Of course, people differ on their **motivation to avoid prejudice**, a value that dates back to childhood experiences and parental values (Towles-Schwen & Fazio, 2001). Salient social norms also motivate Whites to inhibit prejudice, to acknowledge discrimination, and to resist hostile jokes (Crandall, Eshleman, & O'Brien, 2002). Indeed, under pressure of appearing racist, the best-intentioned people actually look even worse than the less well-intentioned people (Frantz et al., 2004; Vorauer & Turpie, 2004), and they feel worse about it (Fazio & Hilden, 2001). No wonder many Whites feel uncertain and anxious, especially in unstructured interracial interactions (Towles-Schwen & Fazio, 2003).

The speed of this emotional discomfort is breathtaking. As noted, people in general most rapidly evaluate each other's trustworthiness in less than 100 msec (Willis & Todorov, 2006), showing amygdala and right insula responses to people perceived as untrustworthy (Winston et al., 2002). As the attitudes research notes (Chapter 10), amygdala responses reflect emotionally significant and especially negative stimuli, whereas right insula responses reflect negative stimuli,

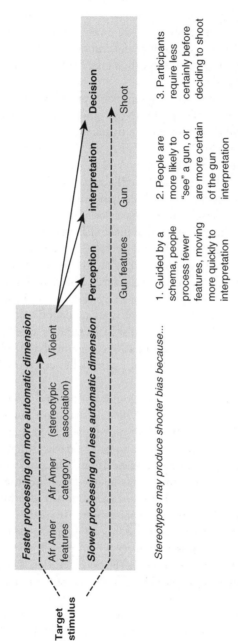

Figure 12.1 Shoot/don't-shoot decision processes: Faster more automatic processing on the irrelevant ethnic dimension may bias participants' (a) perception of targets, (b) interpretation of targets, or (c) the criterion of certainty required for the "shoot" response (Afr Amer = African American)

Source: Correll et al. (2002). Copyright American Psychological Association; reproduced by permission

often disgust. People rapidly register each other's race, also in less than 100 msec (Ito & Urland, 2003). Consistent with the speed of such responses, immediate neural responses fit affect-laden reactions on the basis of race (see Eberhardt, 2005, for a review).

In further support of the marked emotional loading of interracial interactions, some of the most provocative early work on the neuroscience of interracial reactions documented amygdala responses that correlate not only with negative implicit associations (IAT) but also with indicators of vigilance and arousal, especially in Whites responding to Blacks (Cunningham, Johnson, et al., 2004; Hart et al., 2000; Lieberman et al., 2005; Phelps et al., 2000; Wheeler & Fiske, 2005). Among Whites intrinsically concerned about prejudice (high in internal but low in external motivation to control their prejudice), immediate startle-eye-blink responses (indicators of arousal) to Black faces are low, indicating less arousal and vigilance; they also show lower delayed startle-eye-blink responses, indicating less negative affect (Amodio, Harmon-Jones, & Devine, 2003). People distinguish ingroup from outgroup and evaluate accordingly, all in half a second or less (Ito, Thompson, & Cacioppo, 2004).

Neural activity consistent with alerted control systems also occurs in Whites making unintentionally race-biased responses, especially those who can control such responses successfully (Amodio, Harmon-Jones, et al., 2004; Cunningham, Johnson, et al., 2004; Lieberman et al., 2005; Richeson et al., 2003). Thus Whites may respond immediately to Blacks as emotionally significant and perhaps negative, but they also invoke controlled processes fairly fast. In short, neural indicators endow racial cues with immediate emotional significance.

Other physiological evidence provides converging evidence of the immediate affective loading of interracial encounters, especially for Whites. Facial muscle activity (subtle expressive movements not yet visible but tracked electromyographically) indicates subtle racial bias (Vanman, Paul, Ito, & Miller, 1997). Whites interacting with Blacks show cardiovascular reactivity consistent with threat, especially if they have limited prior experience in cross-racial interactions (Blascovich, Mendes, Hunter, Lickel, & Kowai-Bell, 2001; Mendes, Blascovich, Lickel, & Hunter, 2002). Whites also perform poorly on subsequent cognitive tasks, consistent with other evidence that executive control over prejudiced responses has mental costs (Richeson & Shelton, 2003). The reverse is also true; Blacks who especially favor their ingroup incur cognitive costs after interracial interaction (Richeson, Trawalter, & Shelton, 2005).

Given all these emotional complexities, maybe it is not surprising that people avoid interracial interactions from the first moments of attention. People's face-sensitive fusiform gyrus activates less to cross-race than same-race faces and correlates with whether one remembers them (Golby, Gabrieli, Chiao, & Eberhardt, 2001). This is, in effect, a form of perceptual avoidance. And they avoid interactions deliberately as well, thinking that the other group will reject them (Shelton & Richeson, 2005). To summarize, the emotional loading of race relations has a heavy component of shame and anxiety for Whites, with life-or-death consequences for Blacks, based on automatic and more deliberate reactions, as shown by cognitive, social, and neural evidence.

Much Racism is Aversive

What is the role of deliberate control, and how is race exceptional in this regard? People are reminded of the need to watch their step when someone "plays the race card," an expression communicating that someone has upped the ante in an unpleasant way, bringing a fraught and taboo topic into an already contentious context. Whites watch themselves because being called a racist is such a potent interpersonal threat to most Whites. This is not an issue so much for the minority of blatant racists (Chapter 11), who experience simple but virulent disdain and dislike, potentially deadly but fortunately relatively rare in modern egalitarian democracies. Deliberate control over their racial attitudes is not their biggest issue.

Most racism instead concerns internal and external control, and even avoidance. **Aversive racism** reflects ambivalence that includes negative feelings and beliefs, coupled with paternalistic sympathy and denial of the negativity (Gaertner & Dovidio, 1986). Aversively racist Whites experience a variety of negative emotions toward Blacks – discomfort, uneasiness, and anxiety, predicting avoidance – but they experience more positive emotions toward the White ingroup, such as sympathy and admiration (Dovidio, Esses, Beach, & Gaertner, 2002). These subtle forms of discrimination also occur in Europe with regard to recent immigrants (Pettigrew & Meertens, 1995). Racism is aversive in two senses: (a) aversive racists reject its presence in themselves, and (b) it causes interracial interactions to be aversive, so they avoid them.

With regard to emotional prejudices, aversive racists theoretically show anxiety, discomfort, disgust, and fear. These emotions follow from a host of positive ingroup evaluations and negative outgroup ones (Chapters 10–11; Gaertner & Dovidio, 1986). Stephan's work on anxiety (just noted) corroborates this prediction, as do nonverbal indicators of discomfort (e.g., Dovidio et al., 1997; Word, Zanna, & Cooper, 1974).

The affective-evaluative, relatively automatic component of White racial attitudes predicts their behavior, particularly avoiding voluntary interracial contact (Dovidio, Kawakami, & Gaertner, 2002; Esses & Dovidio, 2002) and displaying uncomfortable nonverbal behavior (Chapters 10–11; Dovidio et al., 1997; Dovidio, Kawakami, & Gaertner, 2002; Figure 12.2). In contrast, the more cognitive component predicts verbal behavior and policy preferences. For example, conservative ideology predicts stereotypes about deservingness, which in turn predicts opposing affirmative action for Blacks but not for other groups such as women (Reyna, Henry, Korfmacher, & Tucker, 2006).

Turning to the targets of aversive racism, Blacks may approach interracial encounters with potential concern about being treated in a racist manner, although individuals differ and contexts differ in the extent to which this concern is uppermost (Hyers & Swim, 1998; Operario & Fiske, 2001; Sellers & Shelton, 2003; Shelton, 2000). Distrust stems from historic and current conditions, as well as Blacks' more common belief in the reality of discrimination compared to Whites (see Dovidio, Gaertner, Kawakami, & Hodson, 2002, for a review).

Explicit prejudice (usually cognitive channels) → verbal behavior → self-perception of interracial interaction

Implicit prejudice (usually affective/evaluative channels) → nonverbal behavior → partner & observer perceptions of behavior during interracial interaction

Figure 12.2   Dissociations between Whites' implicit and explicit prejudices in interracial interaction

Note: These independent pathways reflect both Devine's (1989) and Dovidio, Kawakami, & Gaertner's (2002) model and data.

Overall, besides its emotional loading, White aversive racism and Black distrust add to the exceptional features of race-based emotional prejudice, reflecting the cognitive-affective interplay. Next, we come to perceptions of biology and race.

Racial Prejudice is Not Plausibly Evolved

Perceived biological underpinnings are an issue in essentialist stereotypes (Chapter 11). Compared to many forms of prejudice, race prejudice claims an especially tenacious belief in biology. People greatly exaggerate the biology of racial differences. This essentialism persists despite (a) the dearth of biological evidence validating the genetics of racial groupings as currently, socially defined, and (b) the lack of evidence for an evolutionary predisposition to encode race automatically. Other social categories (gender, age) do have biological underpinnings and do fit an evolutionary explanation for rapid detection. So why are people so divided about the biology of race?

Because it seems so obvious to people, let's begin with the biological evidence for the genetics of race. The differences are surprisingly trivial. Genetic differences *within* races are about ten times greater than genetic differences *between* races (Lewontin, 1972; Nei & Roychoudhury, 1993). Moreover, even examining differences between races, no underlying genetic patterns reliably divide people into society's racial categories (Graves, 2001; Hirschfeld, 1996; Marks, 1995). Even skin color does not identify shared genetic heritage (Parra, Amado, Lambertucci, Rocha, Antunes, & Pena, 2003). In short, genetic markers for race do not support the commonsense view of race.

We divide people into races on the basis of a configuration of cues that are socially defined. The American definitions of race originated in and justified slavery. Think about why it was socially and economically convenient for slave-era Whites to define someone with one Black parent and one White parent as Black. Different American states even defined races differently, and a person's race was sometimes the tragic basis of otherwise absurd lawsuits: A great-grandparent's hair texture could determine if a later generation's marriage was interracial and therefore illegal (Banks & Eberhardt, 1998). From the law to everyday behavior, people resist believing that racial categories are not natural kinds (like species).

One might ask how the social construction of race and the exaggerated biology of race fit with race-related correlations to health. First, the majority of overall health disparities are due to wealth disparities (Wong, Shapiro, Boscardin, & Ettner, 2002). Race and income are correlated, of course, so effects due to the one can be mistakenly attributed to the other. Closer analysis indicates a greater influence of social class than racial classification. Independent of class, some race effects on health result from discrimination and its secondary effects on stress (Mays, Cochran, & Barnes, 2007). More specific, well-known examples of race–health correlations include sickle-cell anemia among Africans, cystic fibrosis among Europeans, and Tay-Sachs among Ashkenazi Jews. However, these diseases are extremely rare (most members of that population do not have the disease), and not everyone with the disease belongs to the population (Kittles & Weiss, 2003). Variations in disease rates correlate with biology, behavior, and environment, all of which are correlated with socially defined race. So even if socially defined race is not causal, it can be one cue to relative risks of specific diseases, along with other factors such as habits and environment. But people rely on race more readily than on other causes.

The second aspect of race and biology is evolutionary. That is, common wisdom often assumes that racial prejudice is a hard-wired adaptation to alien social groups. On closer inspection, however, the differentiation of other people as racial ingroup or outgroup does not fit a plausible evolutionary explanation (Cosmides, Tooby, & Kurzban, 2003). In ancestral times, people lived in racially homogeneous groups, within local walking distances, and even encounters with enemy groups would not have crossed racial boundaries. In contrast, sex and life stage would have been important (biological) categories to detect automatically.

If not part of an evolutionary module, race detection might be the by-product of another adaptation; for example, essentialist encoding of natural kinds. Essentialist encoding of plant or animal species makes evolutionary sense, and encoding systems could easily have adapted to detect natural kinds that differ both perceptually and in their underlying shared properties. This encoding system plausibly could be recruited to respond to human physical differences socially defined as racial differences as if they were natural kinds (Cosmides et al., 2003).

Race detection might also be the by-product of sensitivity to distinct social groups and their coalitions (Kurzban & Leary, 2001; Kurzban, Tooby, & Cosmides, 2001). Hunter-gatherers lived in small bands often in conflict with other bands, so mechanisms for tracking who belongs with whom would help. Ingroups coordinated action, so cues that predict an individual's membership in those groups would matter. Such cues might include otherwise arbitrary features such as clothing, decoration, or dialect. The mechanisms for imbuing these features with social meaning could transfer to other arbitrary features such as skin color or hair texture. The mechanism thus could be adaptive and automatic, but applied to features that have meaning in particular historical and social contexts. Cues to religion, for example, should have parallel properties to racial cues in places with long histories of denominational conflict. Race encoding is not mandatory, but socially constructed cues to coalitions (ingroups and outgroups) may be.

In contrast to the weakness of biological and evolutionary explanations for race as commonly understood, evidence for its social construction is strong. Much of it comes from facial recognition research showing that racial categorization is shaped by social context, not fixed features of faces. For example, European Americans recognize White faces more accurately than Black faces (Malpass & Kravitz, 1969), and the fusiform face area activates less to these cross-race faces (Golby et al., 2001), as noted. African Americans show this result to a lesser degree, presumably because as minorities they more often have to differentiate White faces. But contact alone does not drive this effect. Apparently, people process outgroup faces by racial category, noticing relevant cues, but do not code ingroup faces as having a race, instead noticing individuating cues (Levin, 2000). Whites' cross-race encoding deficit is not inevitable: For example, sports fans can prioritize team over race to individuate their team's members regardless of race (Cosmides et al., 2003). The importance of social context also emerges in findings that African Americans and African nationals differ in their encoding of Black and White faces.

Evidence for social construction also appears in the changing standards for judging race, and in biases that correlate with the typicality of racial features. Racial judgments operate by various routes, all socially constructed (Maddox, 2004). First, via a categorical route, a person's appearance (**phenotype**) determines racial category. This process can occur via a label: For example, racially ambiguous faces, morphed to be half and half, appear more "Black" or "White" depending on their label, and this especially occurs for entity theorists who believe in fixed traits

(Eberhardt, Dasgupta, & Banaszynski, 2003). Categorization can also operate mainly through a single feature, such as skin tone, combined with relevant cues such as a race-related discussion (Maddox & Chase, 2004; Maddox & Gray, 2002). Categorization can operate through a configuration of race-related features (Blair, Judd, Sadler, & Jenkins, 2002; Livingston & Brewer, 2002), not just a fixed set of defining features – hence, the lack of biological markers.

Racial categorization can also operate directly from individual race-related features associated with stereotypic traits (Blair et al., 2002) or evaluations (Livingston & Brewer, 2002). For example, heavy television news viewers report more emotional discomfort after a newscast featuring a darker-skinned Black perpetrator than a lighter-skinned one charged with the same crime (Dixon & Maddox, 2005). Given the importance of individual features, even a person typically viewed as White might have some Afrocentric facial features, which could carry stereotypic or affective associations independent of race (Blair et al., 2002). Consistent with the idea that specific features can have major consequences, Black defendants with more Afrocentric features are more likely to land on death row than those without such features (Eberhardt et al., 2006), as noted.

These routes to racial categorization interact with conceptual information, including semantic associations to light and dark, lay theories, cultural beliefs, and personal experiences, all of which help set the social context (Maddox, 2004). For example, racially prejudiced individuals care more about accurately categorizing racially ambiguous people (Blascovich, Wyer, Swart, & Kibler, 1997). How many times have ethnically ambiguous people heard, "What are you, anyway?" (We know someone who had it made into a T-shirt.)

Despite the lack of clear biological evidence for racial differences or evolutionary accounts of racial perception and the clear evidence for race as a social-cognitive construction, people cling to the notion of races as natural kinds. This may diminish, over time, as more people define themselves and others as multiracial (Bodenhausen & Peery, 2009). Meanwhile, conflicts over the races' perceived biological base versus evidence to the contrary feature prominently in racial prejudice. Biology implies determinism, in many people's minds, so this important issue contributes to the exceptional features of race as a categorization scheme.

Segregation

So far, we have seen that racial prejudice is psychologically exceptional because of its unique emotional load, its aversive quality, its (denied) social construction, and now, because of structural features of modern society that contribute to cognitive and affective biases. American society is more racially segregated than South Africa was under the legal system of apartheid (Massey & Denton, 1993; Massey, Rothwell, & Domina, 2009). This segregation occurs at all income levels, though not as much for middle-class Blacks, but their housing dollar goes less far as a result of segregation. Segregation is about race, not just social class. And it results from skin color, not just minority status. As an example of skin-color bias, Latinos who are Black are more segregated than Latinos who are White. Black Americans are more segregated and have remained segregated longer than any immigrant group, most of whom were somewhat segregated in the first generation but gradually less so over two generations. Why does segregation matter for the social cognition of race?

Segregation is not the reported preference of African Americans, who prefer a more racially balanced neighborhood than the average European American does. Neighborhood segregation operates through rental agents and real-estate agents, who steer and exclude people who do and do not fit the neighborhood. From segregation and the disproportionate poverty in the Black community comes concentrated poverty and all its ills (Massey & Denton, 1993). Schooling, employment prospects, health-care availability, exposure to social disorder, and constrained social networks all follow, with crucial population-level disadvantages.

The implications for social cognition and racial prejudice are many. At a social psychological level, one of the primary effects is limited interracial contact. The consequences of this differ for minorities and majorities. In general, equal-status **intergroup contact** reliably reduces prejudice across a variety of group divides: sexual orientation, physical disability, race and ethnicity, mental disability, and age (Pettigrew & Tropp, 2006; Table 12.5). The causality apparently goes from contact to prejudice reduction rather than just from low-prejudice people being more open to contact. The more the contact setting fits Allport's (1954) optimal conditions (equal status, common goals, intergroup cooperation, and authority sanction), the more effectively it reduces prejudice. Regarding the current context emphasizing affective prejudice, contact operates primarily by increasing outgroup friendships and intergroup closeness. These dynamics decrease affective prejudice more than cognitive biases such as stereotypes or beliefs (Tropp & Pettigrew, 2005a).

The effects of contact on prejudice especially operate for exposing White Americans to Black Americans, rather than vice versa, given their respective majority–minority status (Tropp & Pettigrew, 2005b). Minority members are well aware of the intergroup situation, the respective concerns of both sides, and the possibility of prejudice. Majority members are less likely to reflect on their own status, group identity, or problems of prejudice. Also, given relative numbers, minorities are more likely to have prior contact experience with majorities than vice versa. Hence, intergroup contact constitutes more of a novelty to majorities than minorities and perhaps is more of a shock to the emotional and cognitive systems, with more impact. Having experienced prejudice in the past, minorities are more likely to reserve judgment about whether contact conditions have truly been met (e.g., equal status). For example, minorities and majorities respond differently to explicit mention of group membership. Majorities feel discomfort, especially when an outgroup member brings it up, and they feel negative about the contact experience as a result (Tropp & Bianchi, 2006). For minorities, mentioning group membership does not break any taboos, but it can be interpreted positively or negatively depending on who does it and how it occurs. In particular, if it leads them to anticipate prejudice, it undermines trust and acceptance (Tropp, Stout, Boatswain, Wright, & Pettigrew, 2006). Each group's expectations about the other's prejudice depend on the salience of group membership and whether one will be viewed as typical (Tropp & Pettigrew, 2005b).

Exposure to prejudice understandably makes people feel anxious and hostile (Branscombe, Schmitt, & Harvey, 1999; Dion & Earn, 1975; Tropp, 2003). In any case, contact is a more dramatic issue in interracial prejudice than in sexism or ageism because people are more segregated by race than by gender or age. We turn to the distinctive features of these categories in the next sections.

Table 12.5   Effects of intergroup contact by target groups

Outgroup type	Correlation between contact and prejudice
Sexual orientation	−.27
Physical disability	−.24
Race, ethnicity	−.21
Mental disability	−.21
Mental illness	−.18
Elderly	−.18

Note: Higher numbers indicate greater reduction of prejudice; contact with homosexuals greatly reduces anti-gay prejudice, whereas contact with the elderly reduces prejudice to a lesser degree.

Source: Adapted from Pettigrew & Tropp (2006)

GENDER PREJUDICE

In contrast to racism, sexism has interested social psychologists only relatively recently (Deaux & LaFrance, 1998; Spence, Deaux, & Helmreich, 1985). These few decades of gender research reflect three particular aspects of American culture (and probably most developed cultures): gender polarization, categorical divides instead of overlapping continua; androcentrism, maleness as the neutral norm; and biological essentialism, focusing on genetic predispositions more than socialization (Bem, 1993). Although all these features also occur for race, they take a different form in gender prejudices. We shall see various notable features of gender prejudice and its interplay with cognition as this section moves from (a) men's and women's unique structural relationships of heterosexual interdependence and male power in society, to (b) the resulting mixed, prescriptive stereotypes and ambivalent prejudices, to (c) biological and social bases of gender prejudice.

Intimate Interdependence and Male Status

Compared to the intense segregation of interethnic contact, men and women certainly have plenty of contact, and of the most intimate kinds. As far as we know, no one proposes to overcome sexism by increased intergroup contact. Of course, only equal-status intergroup contact reduces prejudice, and the genders don't often have that. One exceptional feature of gender as an intergroup boundary is how much each ingroup needs the outgroup, more than any other societal groups. We could not very well measure this odd ingroup–outgroup relation by the classic Bogardus (1933) social distance scale, wherein allowing the group into one's country reflects superficial acceptance, and allowing members of the group into one's family by marriage reflects intimate acceptance. Certainly both men and women would endorse all levels of social interaction. Viewed this way, men and women accept each other completely. Male–female interdependence is a wonderful fact of life.

At the same time, every culture shows male status: In society at large, men dominate women, holding more positions of power in business and government and scoring higher on development indices such as education, health, and literacy (United Nations Entity, 2012). Even in the United States, women still earn far less than comparable men (82%) (United States Department of Labor, 2012), and in dual-career couples, women work a double shift – regular hours at work and longer hours at home than men do (Business and Professional Women's Foundation, 2005; Crosby, 1991; Deutsch, 1999). Female-headed households (even without children) are more likely to be in poverty than comparable male households. Women are injured and killed by men far more often than vice versa. Female fetuses are more often aborted, and female infants are more often killed at birth. For social cognition, what is remarkable is the combination of intimacy and status that creates the cognitive background for gender prejudice.

Expectations for male status but heterosexual intimacy particularly clash when the typical hierarchy reverses, as when women take leadership roles in traditionally male domains. Female leaders provide a case study of gender-role tension, expressed both cognitively and affectively. Perceived incongruity between the roles expected of leaders and women suggests that (a) it will be harder for women to become leaders because they will be viewed more negatively as potential leaders, and (b) when they are leaders, the same leaderlike behavior will be evaluated more negatively in a woman compared to a man (Eagly & Karau, 2002).

A remarkable series of meta-analyses supports this **role congruity theory**. Leadership is traditionally a male domain (Koenig, Eagly, Mitchell, & Ristikari, 2011; see Table 12.6), and gender roles are certainly expressed in behavior (Eagly & Carli, 2007). Regarding the emergence of leaders, men more often do lead initially leaderless groups in the laboratory and in the field (Eagly & Karau, 1991), especially in tasks that do not require complex social interaction. However, women more often emerge as social leaders, consistent with gender roles. When women do lead organizations, they do not differ from men on task versus interpersonal orientations, contrary to stereotypes. But they do lead in a more democratic and participatory, less autocratic or directive style than men (Eagly & Johnson, 1990). Moreover, they are equally as effective as men, though less so in masculine roles and in male-dominated settings (Eagly, Karau, & Makahijani, 1995). Consistent with the effectiveness data, women receive negative evaluations when they lead in a stereotypically masculine style (especially directive or autocratic) or in a male-dominated role, and particularly from male evaluators (Eagly, Makhijani, & Klonsky, 1992). Despite these barriers, women are nearly as motivated to manage as men are (Eagly, Karau, Miner, & Johnson, 1994). In one study, both implicit and explicit gender beliefs (associating men with high authority and women with low authority), respectively, correlated with implicit and explicit prejudice against female authority (Rudman & Kilianski, 2000). Thus people's expectations about gender reflect in part the statistical averages (more men in charge), but the expectations do not take account of variability around those means, nor do they acknowledge the nuances of leadership styles and the interplay of gender, behavior, and negative evaluations of role-incongruent behavior.

The incongruity between expectations about gender and job roles doubtless occurs beyond leadership. Women and men are differentially distributed into homemaker and employee roles, which guides gender stereotypes (Eagly & Steffen, 1984), maintaining both intimate interdependence and male status. Within employment, stereotypes of occupations fit two dimensions of

Table 12.6   Masculinity of leader stereotypes, from meta-analyses of three paradigms

Paradigm	Database	Result
Think manager–think male paradigm, compares gender & leader stereotypes (Schein, 1973)	40 studies, 51 effects	Leader-women similarity = .25 Leader-men similarity = .62
Agency–communion paradigm, compares stereotypes of leaders' agency & communion (Powell & Butterfield, 1979)	22 studies, 47 effects	Agency > communion
Masculinity–femininity paradigm, stereotypes of leader-related occupations (Shinar, 1975)	7 studies, 101 effects	Greater masculinity

Source: Koenig, Eagly, Mitchell, & Ristikari (2011)

gender and prestige (Glick, Wilk, & Perreault, 1995), and these images reflect the actual sex-segregation of employment (Cejka & Eagly, 1999). Women in nontraditional jobs probably face similar prejudice to that facing women leaders: difficulty entering the jobs and difficulty receiving fair evaluations. As a whole, this work engages cognitive factors, such as role expectations, stereotypes, and incongruity, with effects on attitudes (evaluations) but also on more complex affective responses.

Emotionally Mixed, Prescriptive Stereotypes and Ambivalent Prejudices

The backlash directed at men and women who do not conform to gender stereotypes suggests that people take their gender prejudices personally; these beliefs and emotions hit home. When women self-promote, for example, they may gain attributed competence, but they lose attributed social attractiveness (and hireability), an apparent backlash (Rudman, 1998). When either men or women succeed in gender-atypical ways, their competitors sabotage them as an excuse to repair their egos (Rudman & Fairchild, 2004). Such processes maintain cultural stereotypes as well as personal values.

Consequently, women must temper their "masculine" (**agentic**) side with "feminine" (**communal**) warmth (Rudman & Glick, 1999, 2001); Ann Hopkins learned this the hard way in a high-powered accounting firm, and social cognitive psychology explained why in her Supreme

Court case (Fiske, Bersoff, Borgida, Deaux, & Heilman, 1991). Women perhaps rightly believe that behaving in too masculine a manner would forfeit heterosexual romance (Rudman & Heppen, 2003). Prescriptions for female communality arguably reinforce the status quo (Jackman, 1994; Ridgeway, 2001). Emphasis on feminine warmth results from men depending on women for sexual relations and domestic duties, which require a loving and morally pure partner (Glick & Fiske, 2001). Stereotypes describe the typical woman as sentimental, superstitious, and emotional; the warmth aspect fits the **prescriptive** ideal whereas the sentimental aspect is merely a **descriptive stereotype** (Ruble & Ruble, 1982). Female stereotypic traits carry less economic value but form an important piece of the intimate interdependence. Female gender-deviants risk their heterosexual interdependence, according to these lines of research.

Conversely, stereotypically male traits carry more economic value (agency, competence) and reinforce male status because women traditionally depend on men for economic security and social prestige. Across cultures, the typical man is stereotyped as adventurous, independent, strong, and active; this descriptive stereotype also fits the prescriptive ideal (Ruble & Ruble, 1982). Prescriptive stereotypes reinforce heterosexual interdependence along with male societal dominance (Rudman & Glick, 2008).

Intimate interdependence and male status together create **ambivalent sexism** that incorporates hostility toward women who violate gender prescriptions and benevolence toward women who uphold them (Glick & Fiske, 2001; Chapter 11). One metaphor is the cultural carrot of benevolent sexism (BS) and the cultural stick of hostile sexism (HS). BS prescribes cherished but paternalistic stereotypes for women in traditional gender roles, liked but disrespected, whereas HS targets women who take nontraditional roles, respected but disliked. In line with these analyses of ambivalent sexism, more men than women on average do endorse hostile sexism in 19 countries (Glick et al., 2000). Men also on average endorse benevolent sexism more, although the gap is smaller, and in a few of the most sexist countries, women endorse it more. (In the worst settings, the benevolent sexism pedestal looks good, even if confining.)

All these patterns fit the idea that men have more to gain than women do from enforcing proscriptions against nontraditional roles for women (hostile sexism) because it helps to maintain their traditionally more powerful role. Conversely, women have less to lose from endorsing prescriptions for traditional roles (benevolent sexism) than they do from endorsing hostile sexism. BS has some advantages (e.g., chivalry), and women do not always view it as sexism (Barreto & Ellemers, 2005; Kilianski & Rudman, 1998), but it does undermine performance (Dardenne, Dumont, & Bollier, 2007; Dumont, Sarlet, & Dardenne, 2010). Hostile and benevolent sexism are correlated, but they have distinct meanings. BS predicts positive (likable, moral) stereotypes of traditional women, and HS predicts negative (cold, untrustworthy) stereotypes of nontraditional women, reflecting the fundamental ambivalence.

As a cognitive belief system, ambivalent sexism has consequences. Women as well as men endorse both forms of sexism to some extent, and national averages predict UN indices of gender inequality across nations. Prejudices about men also predict gender inequality across nations (Glick et al., 2004), probably because they stereotype men as less pleasant but more powerful than women; in effect, men are stereotypically designed for dominance. Regardless of the target, gender prejudice is not a simple form of antipathy but fundamentally an ambivalent, mixed set of emotions.

Gender prejudice has interpersonal consequences beyond its link to gender inequality on a national scale (wages, education, health, as noted). For example, gender prejudice creates everyday hassles. In a diary study, college women reported one or two weekly sexist incidents (defined as stereotyping, prejudice, degrading comments, sexual objectification), and these incidents undermined their psychological well-being (Swim, Hyers, Cohen, & Ferguson, 2001). Although women mostly do not respond directly, they stew about it in private (Swim & Hyers, 1999); this preoccupation could stress physical as well as mental health.

Biological and Social Bases of Gender Prejudice

Besides social structural perceptions of heterosexual interdependence and male status, with the resulting ambivalent prejudices, both biological-evolutionary and cultural explanations have been offered for the interplay of gender beliefs and feelings. In particular, sex differences in behavior and in mate preferences have attracted social-cognitive theories about why they occur and how they translate into stereotypes and prejudices. Here are some of the commonsense but provocative facts backed up by meta-analysis of sex differences: Girls show more effort at self-control (inhibition and perceptual sensitivity), whereas boys are more active and intense (Else-Quest, Hyde, Goldsmith, & Van Hulle, 2006). Men are more physically aggressive than women, who are more socially aggressive (Eagly & Steffen, 1986). Men are more heroically helpful than women, who are more helpful in long-term, caring ways (Eagly & Crowley, 1986). As noted earlier, men are more likely to emerge as leaders in task-oriented groups, whereas women are more likely to emerge as social leaders (Eagly & Karau, 1991). Women more often seek older mates with higher status and good earning capacity; men more often want younger mates who are physically attractive but also good housekeepers and cooks (Buss, 1989; Buss et al., 1990). Researchers, like other people, are fond of contrasting the sexes (for a sampling, see Eagly & Wood, 1991).

Some favor explaining such gender differences in evolutionary terms. In particular, derivations from the **parental investment models** argue that women have always had to invest more in reproduction because of pregnancy and nursing, whereas men's required biological investment is minimal (Trivers, 1985). From this, the argument runs, men are promiscuous, and women are choosy. Men seek fertile mates to maximize their reproductive capacity, and women seek mates with resources to ensure their reproductive success (Buss, 1989; Buss & Schmitt, 1993). Women do indeed weigh social class and ambition higher than men, who weigh attractiveness higher than women do (Feingold, 1992). The evolutionary explanations are appealing in their simplicity and apparent reliance on biology, though testing them is complicated (Buss & Kenrick, 1998). Also, unlike race, one can easily argue for the ancestral conditions that would have made automatically perceiving gender to be adaptive (Cosmides et al., 2003).

Other researchers favor explaining the same differences in sociocultural terms. **Social role theory** also addresses gender differences in social behavior. It starts with the division of labor between men and women, which guides both gender-role expectations and sex-typed skills and beliefs, which together guide sex differences in behavior (Eagly, 1987; Eagly & Wood, 1999). Cross-cultural variation in mate preferences, for example, correlates with cultural variations in social structure; namely, gender inequality. A **biosocial approach** acknowledges biological differences in average size and parental investment, as well as nearly universal but culturally moderated divisions of labor. The contrast with more evolutionary theories is that the biosocial approach argues for social forces as explaining most of the variance. This approach also highlights the enormous joint contributions that men and women make to child rearing and earning (Wood & Eagly, 2002).

The most comprehensive account of cognitions and prejudices about gender will require integrative approaches that combine biological and social realities. In the end, the gender similarities are greater than the differences, and most differences are small (Hyde, 2005). For example, regarding mate preference, across 37 cultures everyone first specifies kindness, intelligence, and social skills in a prospective mate (Buss, 1989). Both biological and cultural factors matter to gender differences in behavior, and both underlie gender stereotyping and prejudice.

AGE PREJUDICE

In this section we examine prejudice against older adults. (Age prejudice includes biases against children too, but scant research has addressed this topic.) Although a host of negative adjectives stereotype older adults (see Kite & Johnson, 1988, for a meta-analysis), age stigma is mixed (Richeson & Shelton, 2006), just as gender is. If women are weak but wonderful and men are bad but bold, older adults are doddering but dear according to prevailing stereotypes. The prejudices addressed to older adults, generically, are mainly pity and sympathy (Cuddy, Norton, & Fiske, 2005). This paternalism is reserved for groups with negative outcomes that are not their fault (Fiske et al., 2002). Generically, older people are viewed in a contradictory combination of condescension and compassion. Perhaps there are cultures where older people receive respect, but older people land in the pity area across several Western and Eastern cultures (Cuddy, Fiske, Kwan, et al., 2009).

Nevertheless, older people have images across the spectrum. One major difference divides the young-old (55–75 years) and the old-old (75 and up); prejudices spill over from the latter to the former (Neugarten, 1974; North & Fiske, 2013). Like both race and gender categories, meaningful subcategories represent relatively respected, disliked, and harmless elder subgroups (Brewer, Dull, & Lui, 1981; Hummert, Garstka, Shaner, & Strahm, 1994, 1995). Variations in valence, vitality, and maturity run through the different images (Hummert et al., 1994; Knox, Gekoski, & Kelly, 1995), which are cued by physiognomy (Hummert, 1994) and occur relatively automatically (Hummert, Garstka, O'Brien, Greenwald, & Mellott, 2002). Like gender and race, age is among the top three most rapidly perceived features of another person (Fiske, 1998).

Ageism is unique in several respects. Like gender, age divides people within families, but like race, different age groups live in segregated circumstances. Unlike either race or gender, ageism addresses a malleable intergroup boundary that most people hope to cross in their lifetime, but at the same time, people fear its implication of mortality. People, especially younger people, react to older people with some concern over resources – appropriate succession, shared consumption, and separate identities – and prescriptive stereotyping results (North & Fiske, 2012, under review).

Malleable Boundaries

Unlike gender and race, people resist their identity as older. The difference, of course, is that the gender and race are generally handed out at birth, whereas one acquires age gradually. As age creeps up on people, they do not necessarily internalize its negative stereotypes (for two contrasting views, see Levy & Langer, 1994; Zebrowitz, 2003). Older adults are viewed as incompetent socially, cognitively, and physically (e.g., Pasupathi, Carstensen, & Tsai, 1995; for reviews, see Nelson, 2002; North & Fiske, 2012 Richeson & Shelton, 2006), so people are in no hurry to believe themselves "old." Indeed, although people acknowledge their chronological age, they see "old age" as a moving target that recedes as they approach its boundary (Seccombe & Ishii-Kuntz, 1991). The malleable boundary perpetually resets as people resist membership in the old-person outgroup. Older adults associate themselves with young stereotypic terms faster than with old stereotypic terms (Hummert et al., 2002).

Older people are wise to reset and resist the malleable age boundary, for a youthful identity correlates with good mental and physical health, and even several years of longevity (Hummert et al., 2002; Levy, Slade, Kunkel, & Kasl, 2002; Tuckman & Lavell, 1957). The causality of the positivity–health correlation could go either way, but priming studies suggest that the stereotype itself can damage one's health and performance. For example, even subliminal exposure to age stereotypes increases older people's cardiovascular and skin conductance reactivity to the short-term stress of math and verbal challenges (Levy, Hausdorff, Hencke, & Wei, 2000). Negative self-stereotypes of aging impair older people's memory performance, self-efficacy, and even the will to live (Levy, Ashman, & Dror, 1999–2000); the ill effects are not just priming of elderly behavior *per se* because they do not affect younger adults, nor do positive stereotypes of aging impair older adults.

Acquired cultural beliefs shape the acquisition and damage due to age stereotypes. For example, older Chinese participants and older American deaf participants – presumably less exposed to negative age stereotypes – performed better than older, hearing Americans (Levy & Langer, 1994); comparable younger samples showed no culturally based performance differences. Within mainstream American culture, political correctness does not apply to ageism as it does to sexism and, especially, racism (Levy & Banaji, 2002), so people do not inhibit their age stereotypes as much as other kinds. Thus, when people finally enter the derogated category, they have fewer cognitive defenses to buffer the damage.

Mortality and Terror Management

Older people need buffers because aging stereotypes are uniquely related to death. Younger people may adopt negative stereotypes of older adults to distance and protect themselves (Snyder & Miene, 1994). **Terror management theory** (TMT) (Chapter 11) focuses on how people cope with the knowledge of their own ultimate death, so it applies well to age stereotypes and mortality salience (Greenberg, Schimel, & Mertens, 2002). Recall that TMT describes people's faith in their cultural worldviews as outlasting themselves, and thus soothing the threat posed by the certainty of their own death. One's ingroup values will endure, one hopes. Because outgroups hold different and hence challenging views, they undermine this buffer. Hence, according to TMT, people reminded of their own mortality derogate outgroups. One might expect older people to be the exception to this trend because, uniquely among outgroups, they represent precisely these comforting, familiar, traditional worldviews in most cultures. However, older people's traditional worldviews may pose a threat if those views seem outdated and obstructive. Regardless, the more fundamental threat posed by older people is their sheer existence – a reminder of one's own future decline.

TMT suggests various defenses against the mortality salience posed by older adults: Physical segregation, as in institutionalization, certainly characterizes the location of many old-old adults, and psychological segregation occurs through epithets and stereotypes. When these distancing attempts fail, exposure to older people may invoke the processes predicted by TMT: compensatory self-esteem-building efforts, endorsement of one's enduring worldview, derogation of outgroups, and favoring of ingroup. The mechanisms of TMT are essentially emotional prejudices, but this aspect remains to be more clearly demonstrated empirically with regard to ageism.

SEXUAL PREJUDICE

Prejudice against gay men and lesbians, which goes by the names heterosexism, homophobia, and sexual prejudice, differs from other prejudices in at least three primary respects. First, sexual orientation is not as visibly communicated as race, gender, and age, so its targets often control the extent to which they reveal their identity. Second, of the prejudices described so far, this one is among the most widespread. Third, whereas with race, gender, and age, the belief that "biology is destiny" tends to correlate with prejudice, in current American social construction, belief that homosexuality is biologically determined tends to correlate with tolerance (Hegarty, 2002). Finally, even more than sexism, heterosexism creates controversy. Not everyone agrees it is a problem. In part because of this, and because social psychological research on this topic is just beginning (Herek, 2000), our discussion of these issues will be relatively brief.

Some of the earliest studies of antigay prejudice drew on its quality of being a nonvisible, concealable identity. Early studies would tell one participant that another participant was gay and record self-report and nonverbal reactions (e.g., Farina, Allen & Saul, 1968). The reactions were uniformly negative. Consequently, much early work documented gay and lesbian people's strategies for managing their identity (Goffman, 1963). Both assumptions – that one can freely manipulate a person's apparent sexual identity and that homosexuality primarily concerns the target's stigma-management issues – raise ethical issues. (Is it really comparable to set up a straight person as gay? Is it OK to label a straight person gay or a gay person straight in a study? Is sexual prejudice really mainly about the target's stigma management or about the bias in the eye of the beholder?) More recent work avoids these ethical complexities by using surveys to document people's attitudes.

Antigay attitudes are among the most negative prejudices (Herek & McLemore, 2013; Yang, 1997), and most adult Americans report them (Herek & Capitanio, 1997). Women are less prejudiced than men, and lesbians are less targeted than gay men (Herek, 2002). Uniquely among the major prejudices, sexual prejudice most centrally entails disgust, an emotion directed toward human as well as nonhuman objects (Herek & Capitanio, 1999).

Hate crimes have targeted a fifth of lesbians and a quarter of gay men, resulting in depression, anger, anxiety, and stress, more than for comparable crime victims (Herek, Gillis, & Cogan, 1999). Sexual prejudice causes more unambiguous hate-crime violence toward gays and lesbians than the violence directed at heterosexual women and older adults. Those groups also face abuse and violence, but it is less obviously based on their social category *per se*. It is more likely to be intimate violence with complex causes. Like all common outgroups, gay men and lesbians also experience daily hassles with prejudice, which can undermine their mental and physical health (Swim, Pearson, & Johnston, 2006).

Summary

This chapter describes emotional prejudices and their interplay with cognitions on which they are based. Several recent theories describe specific emotions targeting particular outgroups, based on perceivers' beliefs about them. The stereotype content model predicts distinct emotional prejudices from stereotypes that themselves result from intergroup relations of status and competition. The intergroup emotions theory predicts distinct emotional prejudices from perceiver appraisals of the threat posed by each outgroup. Image theory examines structural relations between groups and posits types of outgroup images and associated emotions. The biocultural approach predicts different threats to group integrity and evolved emotional responses to preserve the group. All these theories posit intergroup behaviors stemming from outgroup emotional prejudices. Other theories focus on specific emotions of anxiety and guilt in intergroup encounters.

Taking seriously the idea that specific ingroup–outgroup prejudices reflect the unique circumstances of different groups, the chapter examines four specific kinds of prejudice. First, anti-Black racial prejudice is exceptional because it is more emotionally loaded in current society than is sexism or ageism. Racism is also more aversive to its agents than are other kinds of prejudice; people deny even to themselves that they hold these attitudes. Although people jump to biological explanations to explain racial issues, much evidence supports social cognitive construction as underlying this prejudice. Finally, Black Americans remain more segregated from the rest of society than any other outgroup, so contact is limited, and the prospects for going beyond racial prejudices are daunting.

Gender prejudice uniquely combines high status for one group with interdependence between the two groups. The result is ambivalent prescriptive stereotypes that mix positive and negative emotions, which together maintain the status quo. Both bio-evolutionary explanations and social role theory can explain prejudices that reinforce existing arrangements.

Ageism uniquely involves a moving target, in that people both hope and fear to join the outgroup category. As such, it raises issues of mortality and emotional distancing, as well as prescriptive stereotyping because of generational interdependence. Finally, sexual prejudice targets a concealable stigma, but it is widespread and simultaneously controversial, evoking strong reactions on all sides. We now turn to more general theories of the affect–cognition interplay.

FURTHER READING

Bodenhausen, G. V., & Peery, D. (2009). Social categorization and stereotyping *in vivo*: The VUCA challenge . *Social and Personality Psychology Compass, 3(2)*, 133–151.

Dovidio, J. F., & Gaertner, S. L. (2010). Intergroup bias. In S. T. Fiske, D. T. Gilbert, & G. Lindzey (Eds.), *Handbook of social psychology* (5th edn, Vol. 2, pp. 1084–1121). Hoboken, NJ: Wiley.

Eagly, A. H., & Carli, L. L. (2007). *Through the labyrinth: The truth about how women become leaders*. Boston, MA: Harvard Business School Press.

Fiske, S. T. (2011). *Envy up, scorn down: How status divides us*. New York: Russell Sage Foundation.

Herek, G. M., & McLemore, K. (2013). Sexual prejudice. *Annual Review of Psychology*.

North, M. S., & Fiske, S. T. (2012). An inconvenienced youth: Ageism and its potential intergenerational roots. *Psychological Bulletin*.

Ziv, T., & Banaji, M. R. (2012). Perceptions and preferences of social groups in the early years of life. In S. T. Fiske & C. N. Macrae (Eds.), *Sage handbook of social cognition* (pp. 372–389). Thousand Oaks, CA: Sage.

PART THREE

Beyond Social Cognition: Affect and Behavior

From Social Cognition to Affect 13

- Differentiating among Affects, Preferences, Evaluations, Moods, and Emotions
- Early Theories
- Physiological Theories of Emotion
- Social Cognitive Foundations of Affect

Emotion research has long struggled over the role of cognitive processes in affect (Cacioppo & Gardner, 1999; M. S. Clark & Fiske, 1982; V. Hamilton, Bower, & Frijda, 1988; Mesquita, Marinetti, & Delvaux, 2012; P. Shaver, 1984; Zajonc, 1998). The two questions that particularly concern us here – the influence of cognition on affect and the influence of affect on cognition – presuppose of course that the two can be usefully separated. However, the separation is not sustained, for example, by one's lived experience of affect and cognition as occurring in a simultaneous mix, not to mention the neuroscientific evidence. For analytic convenience, this chapter and the next divide affect and cognition, examining their reciprocal influences, but note that this separation is something of a fiction.

A final word of caution: The field of affect, and likewise affect-and-cognition, has spawned an encyclopedic array of theories, some tested by data and some remaining untested. This inevitably creates considerably uneven scientific status for the various theories, but it also presents opportunities for the enterprising researcher. Moreover, the sheer quantity of unrelated theories challenges the capacity of any neophyte (and even the seasoned affect expert). We organize and compare theories where possible, but let the reader beware that the review of theories inevitably resembles a laundry list to the extent that the literature has generated multiple unrelated and often untested explanations.

DIFFERENTIATING AMONG AFFECTS, PREFERENCES, EVALUATIONS, ATTITUDES, MOODS, AND EMOTIONS

Affect and Company

Defining terms forces one to think hard about what is meant by affect words used loosely in everyday language (cf. J. D. Mayer, 1986; H. A. Simon, 1982). **Affect** is a generic term for a whole range of preferences, evaluations, moods, and emotions. **Preferences** include relatively mild subjective reactions that are essentially either pleasant or unpleasant. The preferences most frequently studied by social psychologists are interpersonal evaluations; that is, simple positive and negative reactions to others, such as attraction, liking, prejudice, and so forth. Such positive and negative evaluations have obvious importance in social interaction, telling us whom to approach and whom to avoid. Such **evaluations** can also pertain to objects, and we already discussed them as attitudes.

Preferences and evaluations may be distinguished from affects that have a less specific target, that is, **moods**. One can have an evaluative reaction toward a person, but one does not typically have a mood directed toward someone. Moods affect a wide range of social cognitions and behaviors. Like preferences and evaluations, moods are primarily considered as simply positive or negative. Preferences, evaluations, and moods are not normally fleeting experiences but typically have some duration.

Simple positive and negative reactions do not capture all the intensity and complexity of affect. Think how limited our world would be if all we could say was, "I feel good (bad) right now" or "I feel positively (negatively) toward you." More sensitive terms differentiate between being elated and contented, between being sad and angry. For instance, one person we know insists on over a dozen distinct states of being emotionally drained: tired, fatigued, sleepy, exhausted, run down, wiped out, depleted, spent, weak, limp, blank, numb, spaced out, empty. Not all of us are so subtly attuned, but most of us need more than three or four terms to describe our affective reactions. **Emotion** refers to this complex assortment of affects, beyond merely good feelings and bad, to include delight, serenity, anger, sadness, fear, and more. Emotion also can imply intense feelings with physical manifestations, including physiological arousal. Emotions can be of short or long duration, but they do not usually last over periods as long as preferences and evaluations can last.

Differentiating Positive and Negative Responses

How to characterize the rich variety of affective responses is a long-standing problem in psychology (Barrett, 2009a, 2009b; Cacioppo & Gardner, 1999; Davitz, 1970; Ekman, 1984; Green,

Salovey, & Truax, 1999; Plutchik, 1980; Schlosberg, 1954; Wundt, 1897). Affects can be characterized in one of two ways that emerge consistently across analyses of the structure of emotion. The first structure emphasizes **bipolar** (positive–negative) evaluation, crossed with degree of arousal. This bipolar structure best fits behavioral responses of approach (e.g., to consume) or withdrawal (e.g., from a threat; Cacioppo & Gardner, 1999). Mostly, behavioral responses are physically constrained to be largely positive or negative.

The bipolar structure sometimes appears in verbal reports and classifications of emotions. As the solid lines in Figure 13.1 indicate, two common dimensions are pleasantness/unpleasantness and high/low arousal (engagement) (Barrett & Russell, 1999; Russell, 2003). When people describe how they feel right now, or when they sort emotion words according to their similarity, these two dimensions emerge reliably. Thus one might report feeling *content*, *happy*, and *pleased*,

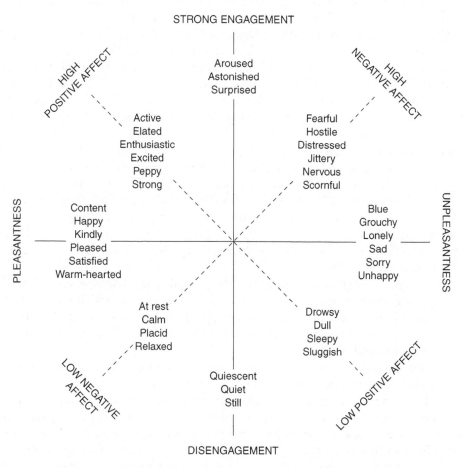

Figure 13.1 Two-factor solutions to the structure of affect

Source: After Watson & Tellegen, 1985

but at that same moment one is unlikely also to report feeling *blue*, *grouchy*, and *lonely* because those terms are at the opposite ends of the same dimension. Moreover, separately, one could also report feeling *aroused*, *astonished*, and *surprised*, but not simultaneously *quiescent*, *quiet*, and *still*. Apparently, people's commonsense theories of emotion are based on what one feels at any given point in time. In this short-run framework, the more one feels good, the less one feels bad, and this is especially true if emotions are intense (Diener & Iran-Nejad, 1986) or simple, but how aroused one feels is a separate matter. One can be happily or unhappily aroused, happily or unhappily quiescent. As noted, behavioral responses especially reflect this positive–negative bipolarity (Cacioppo & Gardner, 1999).

In contrast, suppose people are asked about their experience of emotion over time: for example, considering their life satisfaction in general, their feelings over the last year, how they feel in close relationships over time, and even their emotional reactions to presidential candidates over the course of the entire campaign (e.g., Abelson, Kinder, Peters, & Fiske, 1982; Bradburn & Caplovitz, 1965; Marcus & Mackuen, 1999; for reviews, see Barrett, Mesquita, Ochsner, & Gross, 2007; Cacioppo & Gardner, 1999; Diener, 1984; Izard, 2009; Keltner & Lerner, 2010; Mesquita, Marinetti, & Delvaux, 2012; Niedenthal & Brauer, 2012; Watson & Tellegen, 1985). In the case of a longer time frame, people's reports of positive and negative affect are curiously independent. That is, over time, whether one has felt distressed, fearful, or hostile is unrelated to whether one has also at other times felt elated, enthusiastic, and excited (Diener & Emmons, 1984). Over time, with less intense or more complex emotions, one can observe a structure of affect that is also apparent if you rotate Figure 13.1 by 45°, placing "high positive affect" at the top. In some cases, one can feel much or little "pure" positive affect, and that has little bearing on whether one also feels much or little "pure" negative affect. In short, one can feel both happy and sad, under some circumstances, especially looking back over a complex experience (Larsen, McGraw, & Cacioppo, 2001). This is termed a **bivalent** (two independent valences) structure.

What's more, the bivalent structure (separate, uncorrelated positive and negative dimensions, operating independently) goes beyond self-reported long-term experiences. The underlying psychophysiology reflects such independent positive and negative systems (Cacioppo & Berntson, 1999; see section on those theories).

People have many information sources for their emotion reports: experiential knowledge, episodic memory, situation-specific beliefs, and identity-related beliefs (Robinson & Clore, 2002a). People prioritize these information sources, preferring the most specific. People also use different processes to report current or recent emotions versus overall past patterns of emotion (Robinson & Clore, 2002b).

Time frame, intensity, and complexity jointly seem to determine which of two structures best captures people's emotional experiences. Intense, simple, short-term emotions show a negative correlation (i.e., inverse relation) between pleasant and unpleasant feelings, and thus a bipolar positive–negative structure. But longer-term summaries of complex and perhaps less intense emotional experience show no correlation between positive and negative emotions, and thus a bivalent or bivariate, independent variables structure. In both cases, however, a two-dimensional structure captures the most consensual understanding of the structure of emotion.

Positive and negative emotions differ in how they operate. Positive emotions are relatively limited but prevalent. Negative information especially captures attention, partly because it is so rare (Chapter 3). People mostly expect and experience slightly positive outcomes, so their baseline is slightly positive; the psychological neutral point is not zero but instead slightly right of zero. This represents a **positivity offset, Pollyanna effect**, or **positivity bias** (respectively: Cacioppo & Gardner, 1999; Matlin & Stang, 1978; Sears, 1983). Negative outcomes capture more attention and resources for coping with the threat. This represents a negativity bias as one mobilizes to the challenge, minimizes it, and then restores the moderately positive equilibrium (Cacioppo & Gardner, 1999; Fiske, 1980; Taylor, 1991).

Not only do they differ in their operating characteristics, but the two valences differ in complexity. Negative emotions, analyzed separately, seem to have a more complex dimensional structure than positive emotions analyzed separately (Averill, 1980; Ellsworth & Smith, 1988a, 1988b). Consider the differences among anger, sadness, fear, disgust, anxiety, shame, and hate. In contrast, love, serenity, pride, and joy seem more similar. Negative emotions vary in degree of human agency and situational control. For example, one feels more guilt when the human agent is self rather than another (the more responsible I feel, the more guilty), whereas the reverse is true for anger (the more responsible I feel, the less I am angry at other people; Ellsworth & Smith, 1988a). Negative emotions may also vary in degrees of certainty, attention, and anticipated effort more than positive emotions do. Positive emotions do have dimensional structure, but it tends to be simpler (Argyle & Crossland, 1987; Ellsworth & Smith, 1988b).

Basic Emotions?

The dimensional analyses of emotion are exceedingly useful, but how do we decide what is an emotion and what is not? Is pain an emotion? What about alienation, awe, challenge, or startle? No simple formula determines basic emotions, or even if basic emotions really exist (Barrett et al., 2007; Ortony & Turner, 1990; Russell, 2003). As a consequence, theorists have focused on an alternative way to characterize the concept of emotion. Deciding what is an emotion and what is not comes much more easily if one does not require emotion to be a classical concept with necessary and sufficient defining features. According to the **prototype** view of categories (Chapter 4), category membership is a matter of degree rather than being all or nothing. Some states are more obviously emotions (e.g., happiness, anger, sadness, love, fear, hate): They come to mind easily when people list emotions; they are likely to be labeled emotions; and they fit into the same contexts as other emotions ("He was overcome by ... [fill in the blank]"). Moreover, the better examples of emotion share many features with other prototypic category members (heart rate increase, perspiration, obsessive concern, tears; Fehr & Russell, 1984).

Prototypes also help define the meaning of particular emotions, which rigid definitions do not completely capture. What exactly is love, anger, or fear? In this view, people's categorization of particular emotional facial expressions, such as anger or fear, would reflect degree of fit, not an either-or decision (Russell & Bullock, 1985, 1986; Russell & Fehr, 1987; but see Ekman & O'Sullivan, 1988 versus Russell & Fehr, 1988). However, this prototype process may operate primarily to identify emotions, whereas lay theories about emotion concepts may help people reason about emotions (Clore & Ortony, 1991).

Taking some nominees for core emotions (love, joy, anger, sadness, and fear), people can specify prototypical emotion episodes characterized as **scripts** beginning with appraising events

Concept:

Appraising events → emotions → expressions, action tendencies,   subjective feelings, physiological states

Example:

Desired outcome, an achievement, or esteem, praise → prototypic joy → smile;	express enthusiasm; feel positive; seek others;	energetic, excited, bubbly

Figure 13.2   Emotion scripts

that elicit emotions, which then consist of expressions, action tendencies, subjective feelings, and physiological states (P. Shaver, Schwartz, Kirson, & O'Connor, 1987; Figure 13.2). The point here is that people conceive of a prototypic experience of joy such that a good example contains all these elements and less-good examples contain fewer of them but still might be classified as joy. In-depth analyses also have concentrated on prototypes for love and commitment (Fehr, 1988) and for loneliness (Horowitz, de Sales French, & Anderson, 1982; Cacioppo & Patrick, 2008).

More generally, people have **schemas** for the typical physiological changes that occur during particular emotions, and these schemas are similar across cultures (Rimé, Philippot, & Cisamolo, 1990). People also have rules for guessing other people's affective reactions (Karniol, 1986). In all this work, one cannot be certain whether common individual experiences cause shared prototypes or whether the culture defines certain experiences as certain emotions, which individuals then enact as emotions. That is, the direction of causality between individual emotional prototypes and cultural expectations is not clear.

Table 13.1   Social constructionist view of emotions

Emotions

(a) are constituted by social rules prescribed in cultural scripts,
(b) are importantly interpersonal phenomena that are interwoven with other actors as part of the larger "play,"
(c) are part of a cultural story or "plot" that gives them meaning,
(d) involve choice regarding one's participation as an actor,
(e) require training for skilled performance,
(f) require identification with the role to experience intensity, and
(g) entail interpretation of the role as it fits into the larger social context

---

Source: Averill (1990c)

One perspective embraces the cultural determination of emotion, holding that emotions are substantially defined by culture. This **social constructionist view** of emotions sees emotions as transitory social roles represented cognitively in members of a shared culture, as variations on a central (or prototypic) theme (e.g., Averill, 1983; 1990c; Table 13.1). As such, emotions entail a coherent, organized syndrome of responses (Averill, 1990b; cf. de Rivera, 1984; de Rivera & Grinkis, 1986), an entire set of characteristic responses that identify the emotion, within a certain fuzzy set of related reactions, just as prototypic features identify emotions in particular cases or emotions in general. At the psychological level, people construct their emotions from emotional meta-experience (Russell, 2003). That is, they combine features of their conscious experience of sensations, pleasantness, arousal, behavior, cognitions, and appraisal of the target of their emotions. The result is a labeled emotion, but it is fluid, and few pure instances of any given emotion (e.g., anger) occur. Some features are present; some are not, and people label emotions according to the features that accumulate and cohere.

A cautionary note in applying all these definitions to the remainder of the chapter: Many of these distinctions are not uniformly maintained by those working in the field. In fact, some of the best empirical work on affect ironically bears little relation to the best taxonomic work on affect.

EARLY THEORIES

The relationship between affect and cognition is a long-standing question. Over a century ago, William James (1890/1983) proposed that the feeling of **autonomic** feedback (heart rate, stomach tension) and muscular feedback (posture, facial expressions) itself constitutes emotion. Conrad Lange (1885/1922) invented a similar theory at the same time as James. In this **James–Lange view**, the physiological patterns unique to each emotion reveal to us what we are feeling. James stated that when we see a bear in the woods, we are afraid because we tremble and run away: The physical responses cause the emotion. The James–Lange theory of emotion downplayed the role of cognition or mental activity as a sole basis for emotion. In a similar manner, Charles Darwin (1872) had proposed that the relevant muscular activity can strengthen or inhibit emotion.

Decades later, the James–Lange theory was undermined by Walter Cannon's (1927) arguments that visceral sensations are too diffuse to account for all the different emotions and that the autonomic system responds too slowly to account for the speed of emotional response. Following this critique, many psychologists assumed that physiological contributions to emotion were limited to diffuse arousal and did not include specific patterns of bodily sensation. Assuming this undifferentiated view of arousal for the moment, a basic problem still remained: If arousal is diffuse, and simply ranges from high to low, how can one account for the rich texture of emotional experience? One set of answers is physiological, and the other is cognitive.

PHYSIOLOGICAL THEORIES OF EMOTION

Physiology might still provide the richness of emotional experience. Some noncognitive theories of emotion provide counterpoint to the cognitive theories.

Facial Feedback Theory

The original **facial feedback hypothesis** held that emotional events directly trigger certain innate configurations of muscles, and that we become aware of feelings only upon feedback from the face (Tomkins, 1962; cf. Gellhorn, 1964). Notice how compatible this view is with the James–Lange theory, yet without having to assume that arousal is fast and differentiated, only that facial responses are. According to facial feedback theory, development and upbringing constrain the range of expressions people adopt and so also the range of emotions they can feel (Izard, 1972, 1977). Over time people build up a repertoire of emotions on the basis of the facial muscles society allows them to use in expressing their emotions. Although variants exist, the core hypothesis is that feedback from facial expressions influences emotional experience and behavior (Buck, 1980; Winton, 1986).

Unfortunately, evidence for this intriguing idea is limited to pleasant versus unpleasant experiences and, perhaps, arousal. Facial expressions reflect both pleasantness and intensity, two basic dimensions of emotion (Schlosberg, 1954). Moreover, facial expressions are related to other physiological responses in emotion. The pleasantness of a person's facial expression (as rated by observers while the person is viewing evocative photographs) can directly relate to heart rate (extreme pleasantness with acceleration, extreme unpleasantness with deceleration; Winton, Putnam, & Krauss, 1984). And the rated intensity of expression can relate to **skin conductance** (i.e., minute differences in amount of perspiration). Visceral responses in facial expression, heart rate, and skin conductance correlate with basic dimensions of emotions (Winton et al., 1984) as part of an integrated configuration of physiological responses (cf. Ekman, Levenson, & Friesen, 1983; McCaul, Holmes, & Solomon, 1982; Zuckerman et al., 1981). Indeed, the face reliably reflects the pleasantness and intensity dimensions of emotion, even when overt expressions are not noticeable to observers. That is, electrodes attached to the face can detect tiny muscular (**electromyographic** or **EMG**) activity too subtle or fleeting to be seen, and this activity parallels the muscles used in overt facial expressions, reflecting two basic dimensions of emotion (Cacioppo, Petty, Losch, & Kim, 1986). For example, the lower cheek muscles that contract in a smile (**zygomaticus major**) and the muscles between the eyebrows that contract in a frown (**corrugator supercilii**) respectively index positive versus negative responses to affect-laden pictures, sounds, and words (Larsen, Norris, & Cacioppo, 2003).

Facial expressions do directly affect reported mood, emotion, and evaluations (Laird, 1984). In one typical paradigm, participants are induced to adopt positive or negative facial expressions (e.g., smile, frown) without labeling them as such. For example, one experiment instructed them to contract and hold the relevant muscles one by one for supposed EMG recording until they had inadvertently assumed an emotional expression (Laird, 1974). Supposedly to study the physical coping strategies of people with disabilities, another experiment asked participants to hold a pen in their teeth, without using their lips, thereby simulating a smile (Strack, Martin, & Stepper, 1988). As noted, participants then rated the funniness of cartoons, detecting more humor when they artificially maintained a smiling facial expression than when they inhibited a smile (see also Flack, 2006; Ito, Chiao, Devine, Lorig, & Cacioppo, 2006; Lanzetta et al., 1976; Rhodewalt & Corner, 1979; Zuckerman et al., 1981).

In pure form, the facial feedback hypothesis is controversial. The effect across studies appears small (Matsumoto, 1987). Moreover, some researchers do not replicate the finding that posed facial expressions change emotion (Buck, 1980; Ellsworth & Tourangeau, 1981; Tourangeau & Ellsworth, 1979; but see Hager & Ekman, 1981; Izard, 1981; Tomkins, 1981). Perhaps telling people simply to exaggerate their spontaneous facial expressions does change emotion, but rigidly posed expressions only sometimes produce changes in emotion, under conditions as yet unclear.

Another controversy revolves around whether or not facial feedback effects are cognitively mediated. Some maintain that facial feedback effects on emotion are cognitively mediated, as in self-attribution of attitudes (e.g., Laird, 1974); others argue that the effects are direct and cognitively unmediated (Gellhorn, 1964; Izard, 1972, 1977; Plutchik, 1962; Tomkins, 1962). Finally, throughout all the facial feedback research, even the most extreme precautions cannot completely silence critics who argue that subjects realize their expressions are being manipulated and so respond on the basis of experimental demand. Nevertheless, the facial feedback hypothesis – and related evidence regarding feedback from other nonverbal channels (Kellerman, Lewis, & Laird, 1989) – provides a physiological piece of the puzzle of complex differentiated emotions, probably most consistent with a constructionist account, whereby facial feedback provides mainly valence cues. Facial feedback also paves the way for embodied emotions (Niedenthal & Brauer, 2012).

Excitation Transfer

Affect could differentiate into discrete emotions without requiring that arousal be differentiated. That is, facial expressions could cue patterns of emotional experience, whereas arousal need only be a diffuse intensifier. If so, then how does arousal originate and influence emotion?

Arousal (that is, emotional excitation of the **sympathetic nervous system**) has both automatic and learned origins (Zillmann, 1988); for example, a startle response is unconditioned but fear of airplane travel is a conditioned response. The learned and unlearned features of arousal theoretically depend on three initially independent factors: dispositional, excitatory, and experiential (Table 13.2). The core of the theory, for our purposes, is that (a) arousal is nonspecific and slow to decay, (b) people are inept at partitioning the sources of their arousal, and (c) people cognitively interpret their arousal. Hence, arousal leftover from a previous setting can combine with arousal in a new situation and intensify one's emotional reaction. This idea is not without

Table 13.2   Excitation transfer

Immediate emotional arousal:

(a) *Dispositional* component: Learned and unlearned skeletal-motor reactions
    (e.g., startle responses, uncontrolled facial reactions, involuntary emotional gestures)
(b) *Excitatory* component: Learned and unlearned arousal reactions.
    (e.g., energizes the organism)

Subsequent reactions:

(c) *Experiential* aspect: Assessment of initial reactions and interpretation of the situation
    (can modify one's actions)

Source: Zillman (1988)

practical significance. Although plying one's date with alcohol is a traditional mode of seduction, in theory, plying the person with coffee or getting the person to yell at a basketball game could conceivably have better effects. Dancing, too, has its proponents.

Indeed, arousal from otherwise innocent sources can intensify affect toward seemingly irrelevant people, as in a classic study by Dutton and Aron (1974). They arranged for an attractive woman to interview men as they ventured across a scary suspension bridge or as they crossed a relatively sturdy wooden bridge nearby. Each man was asked to tell a story about an intentionally ambiguous picture of a young woman. As predicted, the men who crossed the scary bridge and who were presumably aroused had more sexual content in their stories than did the men who crossed the safe bridge. Moreover, they were more likely to telephone the attractive woman experimenter later than were the men from the safe bridge (for similar results, see Jacobs, Berscheid, & Walster, 1971; Stephan, Berscheid, & Walster, 1971). Thus arousal originally instigated by fear transferred to romantic or sexual attraction.

Fear and romantic attraction are not the only emotions that can function in this way. When one has been angered and then is exposed to erotic stories, nude pictures, or an attractive confederate, reports of heightened sexual arousal often occur (e.g., Barclay & Haber, 1965). Conversely, prior sexual arousal can increase the likelihood of aggression (e.g., Zillmann, 1971). For many men, a female companion's distress at a gory horror film intensifies their own enjoyment (Zillmann, Weaver, Mundorf, & Aust, 1986). Disgust can enhance humor (J. R. Cantor, Bryant, & Zillmann, 1974) or music (J. R. Cantor & Zillmann, 1973); the latter finding may explain the appeal of certain music videos. What is provocative about these findings is that the valence of the prior experience is irrelevant; only the arousal transfers (for dissenting views, see R. A. Baron, 1977; Branscombe, 1985).

By itself, simple physical arousal can intensify anger or sexual attraction. For example, people who have just exercised respond more aggressively or more angrily when provoked than do people not previously aroused (Zillmann, 1978; Zillmann & Bryant,1974; Zillmann, Katcher, & Milavsky, 1972). Arousal enhances romantic attraction (G. L. White, Fishbein, & Rutstein, 1981; G. L. White & Kight, 1984). Arousal even intensifies evaluations of one's alma mater (M. S. Clark, 1982), as well as one's egotistically satisfying attributions (Gollwitzer, Earle, & Stephan, 1982), and the likelihood of counterarguing a persuasive communication (Cacioppo, 1979). All these studies fit excitation transferring from one source to another, intensifying subsequent affect. Their implications are broadened by the finding that, even if unable to take immediate action under transferred excitation, people may commit themselves to future actions (e.g., revenge) while excited, so that the effects of excitation transfer can last long after the actual arousal dissipates (Bryant & Zillmann, 1979). Arousal, thus, polarizes both positive and negative reactions (Stangor, 1990).

A question of particular interest to social cognition research is whether the effects of arousal depend on being cognitively aware of it. People respond emotionally – and perhaps also can be aroused – by an affect-laden stimulus without even being fully aware of the stimulus (Corteen & Wood, 1972; Niedenthal & Cantor, 1986; Robles et al., 1987; Spielman, Pratto, & Bargh, 1988). Excitation transfer theory argues that arousal influences emotion even when people do not consciously feel aroused but physiological measures indicate that they are indeed aroused.

Note that this differs from Schachter and Singer's (1962) theory of emotion (Chapter 6), as well as its derivatives, which instead posit that emotion results when people label, interpret, and identify physiological arousal for which they have no immediate other explanation. The implication in Schachter's theory is that the arousal demands explanation because it has been consciously perceived. Evidence from people with spinal cord injuries indicates that the perception of arousal may not be necessary for emotional experience, as Schachter's theory assumes (Chwalisz, Diener, & Gallagher, 1988). Another important difference between the two theories is that Schachter's theory originally applied only when the initial source of arousal is ambiguous (Kenrick & Cialdini, 1977), which is not the case for the Zillmann theory. However, both theories describe roles for arousal when its current source is otherwise ambiguous.

Affective Neuroscience

The dimensions of emotion apparently include positivity and negativity and intensity/arousal. Neuroscience backs up these basic features and even hint at greater differentiation, though the evidence here is preliminary.

Some early affective neuroscience used **electroencephalography** (EEG) measures to identify the timing and approximate locations of positive and negative affect responses. Midfrontal activations on the left and right, respectively, generally correspond to positive and negative emotional reactions; mostly, these align with approach and avoidance behavioral tendencies (Coan & Allen, 2004; Davidson, 1993; Davidson & Irwin, 1999). Although first identified a couple of decades earlier than most current affective neuroscience, the simple idea of affective asymmetry is deceptive given the complexity of emotional processes. But still, the contrast between two broad motivational systems – positive (approach, reward, appetitive) and negative (avoidance, punishment, threat) – is convincing. The general neural patterns of course mask much complexity. For example, anger is a negative but approach-related emotion.

More recent neuroscience uses neuroimaging, which is worse at measuring time course but better at locating specific regions (Chapters 9–10; Figure 13.3); for example, the amygdala and possibly the insula participate in emotionally intense attitudes, especially negative ones. Emotions researchers also have emphasized the amygdala in emotionally intense experiences (beyond attitudes). The amygdala is implicated especially in recognizing fearful and other emotionally intense expressions as part of a larger system, including the orbitofrontal cortex (Adolphs, 2002). The amygdala is reliably implicated in fear conditioning and more broadly in intense emotional experiences (Phelps, 2006; for meta-analyses see Murphy, Nimmo-Smith, & Lawrence, 2003; Phan, Wager, Taylor, & Liberzon, 2002).

The insula is involved in disgust, at a minimum (Murphy et al., 2003; Phan et al., 2002). This certainly fits the idea that negative valence implicates the insula, as in attitudes. Beyond the amygdala and the insula, the two meta-analyses do not agree, although hints appear: Sadness

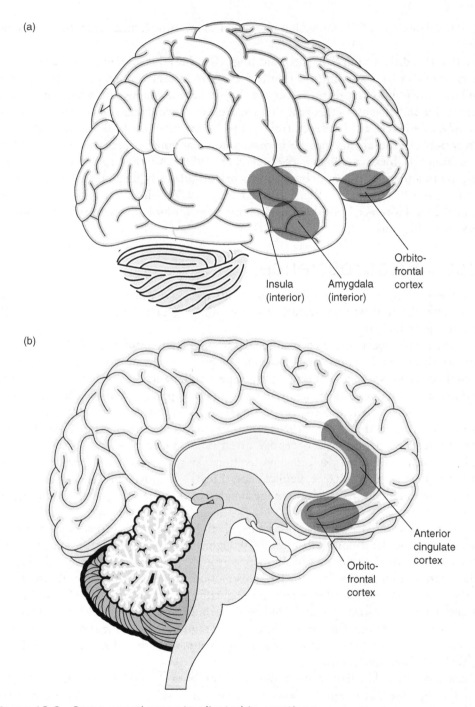

(a)

Insula
(interior)

Amygdala
(interior)

Orbito-
frontal
cortex

(b)

Anterior
cingulate
cortex

Orbito-
frontal
cortex

Figure 13.3   Some neural areas implicated in emotions

Table 13.3 Remedies for the seven sins of affective neuroscience

(1) Recognize the intermingling of affective and cognitive neural circuits;
(2) Acknowledge that affect involves the thinking cortex as well as the older brain's subcortical structures;
(3) Recognize that emotions correspond to measurable bodily responses, not just psychological constructions;
(4) Integrate knowledge of plausible neural circuits in the psychology of emotion;
(5) Realize that emotions differ with age;
(6) Avoid looking for emotions in discrete locations of the brain; and
(7) Include unconscious responses as part of emotion systems.

Source: Davidson (2003)

may implicate the anterior cingulate cortex, which also relates to attention and discrepancy-detection (Chapter 3).

Other basic kinds of emotions show less reliable results so far. This lack of consensus leads some to reject the relevance of neuroimaging data for detecting the essence of emotions (Barrett & Wager, 2006), but the disconnect may reflect research focused on self-reported emotional experience versus emotion-eliciting stimuli used in most affective neuroscience research.

Within social cognition and affect, the field is far from identifying differentiated "emotion areas," even if such a thing were possible. Indeed, one researcher identified this quest among the "seven sins" of affective neuroscience (Davidson, 2003; Table 13.3). The fast-moving work on affective neuroscience will continue to feed back to social cognition research as it develops (Cacioppo et al., 2007; Phelps, 2006).

All these theorists neglect cognition in emotional responses, compared to the theories covered next, but they increasingly recognize that emotions include components: conscious, unconscious, cognitive, affective, social, peripheral, subcortical, and cortical configurations. As noted, the brain is not divided up the way psychology departments are, with separate social, cognitive, affective areas. Instead, they all intertwine in form and function.

Before continuing, note that an apparently erroneous presumption motivated some of the theories just covered and some of those that follow. That is, some of the search for facial origins of emotion, some of the original excitation transfer ideas, and certainly the arousal-plus-cognition theories that follow all are based on Cannon's premise that arousal is too diffuse to account for emotional differentiation. Competing evidence indicates that this conclusion may have been premature; distinct patterns of arousal can indeed occur for different emotions (e.g., Ax, 1953; Derryberry & Rothbart, 1988; Lacey, 1959, 1967; Lacey & Lacey, 1958, 1970; G. E. Schwartz, Davidson, & Pugash, 1976; G. E. Schwartz, Weinberger, & Singer, 1981; Tourangeau & Ellsworth, 1979; Winton et al., 1984). Note, however, that Cannon (1927) and Schachter (1964) may well have been correct in describing these patterns as not easily distinguished on an experiential level; that question is still open. Nevertheless, ironically, solving a problem that ultimately may not require solving has been partly responsible for some of the most crucial contributions to emotion theory.

SOCIAL COGNITIVE FOUNDATIONS OF AFFECT

Return to an earlier question: How can emotions differentiate if physiological arousal does not? Clearly, a combination of physiological and neural response systems contribute to the variety of emotions. Nevertheless, physiology is by no means the whole story in emotion. In social psychology, the view of arousal as undifferentiated and inadequate to account for the variety of emotions led to a parallel effort to see how cognition could explain emotional complexity; these ideas worked essentially without reference to developing ideas about physiology.

In considering these ideas about how cognition leads to emotion, keep in mind that many social psychologists have assumed that cognition is a major basis for affective response: for example, in studying stereotyping as an origin of prejudice (Allport, 1954), in proposing cognitive inconsistency as causing arousal that instigates attitude change (Cooper, Zanna, & Taves, 1978), in examining self-concept discrepancies as creating affect (Higgins, 1987), and more. Because of this broad treatment of affect and cognition within the traditions of social psychology, what follows is necessarily selective. Table 13.4 helps organize four types of theory that follow.

Table 13.4 Theories relating cognitive structure to affect

Theories and theorists	Cognitive structure	Affective impact
Interruption		
Schachter	Unexplained arousal plus cognitive interpretation	Labeled emotion
Mandler	Interrupted application of schema (perceptual) or goal-directed action	Positive if fit, facilitate; negative if no fit, block
Berscheid	Interrupted interdependent goal sequence	Same
Matching		
Keltner	Expectations about power relations	Positive if high-power self; negative if low-power self
Fiske	Application of schema or category	Associated affect[1]
Linville	Complexity of representation	Moderation of affect[2]
Tesser	Elaboration of schema through thought	Extremity of affect[2]
Outcomes		
Weiner	Attribution for outcome (locus, stability)	Differentiated emotions

Theories and theorists	Cognitive structure	Affective impact
Kahneman & Miller	Comparing present outcome to norms	Amplify emotion if abnormal
Managing		
Simon	Change goal priority due to environment	Emotion as alert mechanism
Oatley & Johnson-Laird	Change goal priority due to probability of success	Same
Carver & Scheier	Discrepancy between current state and standard	Emotion cues effort or withdrawal

Notes:

[1] For attitudinal complements to schema-triggered affect, see Fazio's MODE model and Greenwald et al.'s IAT, covered in Chapter 10.

[2] To reconcile these apparently contradictory theories, see text.

Emotion as Cognition Plus Arousal: Interruption Theories

Most of us would like to think we are attracted to people because their unique personalities fit with our own unique personalities in significant, if not predestined, ways. We downplay seemingly incidental factors such as proximity (living in the same courtyard), timing (being divorced long enough to be ready for a new relationship), convenience (being on the same work schedule), or irrelevant sources of arousal (meeting after an intense workout). Yet all these factors can help establish a close relationship between two people. Moreover, as Schachter's theory of emotional lability proposed (Chapter 6), when people are aroused, they explain their arousal differently, depending on previous experience, socialization, and context (Schachter & Singer, 1962). Thus what one aroused person interprets as sexual attraction (Dutton & Aron, 1974), another may label love at first sight (Berscheid & Walster, 1978; Walster, 1971). Such misunderstandings have, no doubt, been the cause of much personal tragedy.

Schachter's two-component theory posits that diffuse physiological arousal catalyzes cognitive interpretation, so emotions are mediated by cognitive activity. Note how this differs from the previous views that focus more directly on unmediated physiological responses (e.g., some versions of facial feedback theory). Despite much controversy (Reisenzein, 1983), Schachter's theory had considerable impact on social psychological thinking about emotion (Chapter 6). Moreover, recent theories take the arousal-plus-cognition viewpoint several steps further.

Mind and Arousal in Emotion

Arousal-plus-mind theory (Mandler, 1975) resembles Schachter's in that physiological arousal combines with evaluative cognition to produce emotion. Visceral activation provides the intensity and particular emotional "feel" of the experience, while evaluative cognitions provide the quality of differentiated emotional experience.

This theory, unlike Schachter's, locates a mental origin for arousal; namely, in discrepancy and **interruption**. In this view, most arousal follows from perceptual or cognitive discrepancy or from interrupting or blocking ongoing action. Disruptions by definition violate expectations, preventing either the easy application of one's schemas or the smooth continuation of one's goal-directed activity. Perceptual-cognitive interruptions include musical or visual patterns that diverge from the expected, story lines with an unexpected twist, jokes, and the like. Similarly, disruptions of goal-directed activity can interfere with complex sequences of intended activity. (Recall the last time you were working to meet a deadline and you were asked to take out the garbage.) The complexity of the interrupted activity corresponds to the amount of arousal you feel: If you drop your keys while trying to get in the door, that interrupts a relatively simple goal, so it should cause only a small amount of arousal. If you drop your keys while trying to impress the date of your dreams, that interrupts a potentially more complex goal, so it should create more arousal. As in other theories, arousal intensifies emotion.

Arousal also sets off cognitive interpretation. The interruption may be interpreted positively or negatively, depending on the type of expectation disrupted and its interpretation. With complex action sequences, you may interpret the interruption as either hindering your goal or unexpectedly advancing it, with resulting respectively negative and positive emotions. That is, if your interpretation in the key-dropping episode is that you are a hopeless, clumsy oaf, you may feel ashamed and irritated. On the other hand, if your date communicates that your nervousness is endearing, you may interpret that as unexpectedly advancing you toward your goal and feel pleased. (Admittedly, the negative emotions resulting from interruption are more intuitively compelling than the positive emotions that could result.) Cognitive interpretation shapes not only the quality of one's immediate affect but also one's lasting mental representation of the event.

With perceptual-cognitive schemas, the effects of interruption are more subtle than for goal-directed action sequences. The degree of interruption (and therefore arousal) more directly determines the positivity of the response, with less need for complex interpretation (Gaver & Mandler, 1987). Disconfirmations of perceptual schemas (e.g., in music, visual arts, food) range from zero (total familiarity) to extreme (total chaos and discord). On the whole, (a) familiarity is pleasant but not intense; (b) a little novelty is good, for it requires slight assimilation and adds a bit of intensity to the pleasant recognition of the familiar; (c) more novelty is better if it can be reinterpreted in familiar terms, as the required adjustment adds more intensity; and (d) complete incongruity, unsuccessfully assimilated, leads to intense negative affect. One of us recently discovered how this operates, at a formal concert, as the string quartet combined the expected classical forms with jazz, causing a sizable portion of the audience to exit at intermission, presumably because the result simply did not fit their well-worn and comfortable perceptual-cognitive schemas. If asked, no doubt they would have simply reported disliking the music; interruptions and their resolutions need not be wholly conscious. In any case, a little novelty is a good thing (cf. Berlyne, 1970; D. W. Fiske & Maddi, 1961; Leventhal, 1984), but too much is hard to take.

Expectations, Goals, and Emotions in Close Relationships

Berscheid has presented a compelling case for the application of Mandler's theory to emotion in close relationships (Berscheid, 1982, 1983). The more intimate the relationship, the more two people's goals depend on each other (Kelley et al., 1983). The frequency, strength, diversity, and duration of dependencies on each other define the closeness of the relationship: The more intermeshed two people's daily and long-term goals, the more seriously each person can interrupt the other. Interruptions can include unexpected facilitation, causing relief, joy, and excitement, as well as unexpected hindrance, causing disappointment, frustration, and anger. Interdependent goals can range from simple behavior sequences, such as doing the laundry together, to complex behavior sequences, such as fully sharing child care or collaborating on work. The more complex the behavior sequence, the more intense the emotion when it is interrupted. The greater the interdependence, then, the greater the potential for intense negative emotion if one partner leaves, withdraws, or dies. Similarly, there is greater potential for positive emotions if one partner becomes suddenly more attuned, considerate, and helpful to the other and their shared goals. If the intermeshed sequence continues to function as usual, on the other hand, no interruptions and little emotion occur. As Berscheid notes, the paradox is that the most intimate, involved, and interdependent relationships may show as little emotion as distant, parallel, uninvolved relationships, simply because the intimate one is running smoothly. An intimate relationship is defined by the potential for – but not necessarily the experience of – emotional intensity, which results from interdependent goals.

The theory makes the interesting prediction that the sheer amount of emotion experienced in a relationship is negatively correlated with longevity; long-term relationships are least likely to show much emotion, either positive or negative. This prediction has been confirmed (Berscheid, Snyder, & Omoto, 1989). Consider the normal course of a long-term intimacy. At first emotions run high (both positive and negative) as two people learn all that they delightfully have in common – and all that tragically divides them. As they become better acquainted, surprises (disruptions) of both the pleasant and unpleasant sort are simply fewer. As the novelty wears off, emotions run less extreme, and either complacency or boredom may settle in. When the initial intensity fades, does that mean less potential for emotion? No. Quite the contrary. If the relationship broke up, emotional intensity would be extreme. Only when the long-term relationship functions smoothly do emotions seem flat and calm. The irony is that one can often only gauge the intensity of a long-term relationship when it is terminated or interrupted.

Cognitive Structures and Affect: Matching Theories

Interruptions of cognitive structures – schemas, goals, and relationship expectations – cue affect. Other theories emphasize matching world knowledge, examining cognitive structures such as social schemas, interpretations of obtained outcomes, and imagined outcomes. Emotions and goals have broad interplay, even without interruption. One note about the next theories: Here, the term **schema** refers to knowledge about concepts (Chapter 4), not people's schemas for the concept of emotion in general or for particular emotions. These more general schemas include other content that is then linked to affect by various processes (Table 13.4).

Expectations, Motives, and Emotions in Power Relations

One theory examines the interplay among emotions and cognitions in social relationships, specifically **power asymmetries** (Keltner, Gruenfeld, & Anderson, 2003). Powerful people experience a world in which they control resources (S. T. Fiske, 1993), so they expect both rewards and freedom to act. Low-power people experience a world in which others control resources, so they expect fewer positive outcomes and fear some negative ones.

These cognitions (experiences and expectancies) influence the people's emotions on each side of the power equation. High power is associated with approach emotions and behaviors, and thus with positive affect, as well as left frontal activity and the release of **dopamine**, a reward-related neurotransmitter. Specific high-power emotions include desire, enthusiasm, and pride. In the extreme case, the configuration would be mania. Attentional focus is flexible, and information processing is automatic. Behavior is relatively extraverted, less guarded, and more open to impulses (Keltner et al., 2003). Powerful people act on their goals (Guinote, 2007).

In contrast, low power is associated with avoidant, inhibited emotions and behaviors, and thus with negative affect, as well as right frontal activity and the release of **norepinephrine** and **cortisol**, stress-related responses in the neuroendocrine system. Specific low-power emotions include fear, shame, guilt, and embarrassment, as well as awe and gratitude. In the extreme case, the configuration would be anxiety and depression. Attentional focus is vigilant, and information-processing is narrowly focused. Behavior is relatively more inhibited and regulated. The contrasts between low-power and high-power cognitions, emotions, and behavior are, of course, theoretical extremes; actual responses are more nuanced and subtle.

The predicted associations among affect, cognition, and behavior emerge, for example, in correlational research: Dormitory peers nominated high-power men, who indeed reported higher baseline moods (Keltner et al., 2003). Similarly, self-reported social potency, dominance, assertiveness, and leadership correlate with positive mood (Watson & Clark, 1997). Experiments also show power having the predicted effects (Keltner et al., 2003). Moreover, this theory fits with other work showing effects of social expectations (cognitions) on emotions. For example, high-status people are expected to express more anger because of its relationship to control, whereas low-status people are expected to express more guilt and sadness (Tiedens, Ellsworth, & Mesquita, 2000).

Schema-Triggered Affect

Another matching approach stems from the observation that emotions can result from the successful application of affect-laden schemas. That is, some people (e.g., one's kindergarten teacher, a feared boss, judgmental clergy, intrusive outgroup members) and situations (giving a talk to a large audience, receiving a call from an old friend) inspire emotion without necessarily interrupting any goals. Originally called **schema-triggered affect** (S. T. Fiske, 1982), this idea was later incorporated into the broader distinction between **category-based responses** and **attribute-based responses** (e.g., S. T. Fiske & Neuberg, 1990; Chapter 2). The relevant point here is that schemas based on prior experiences can carry immediate affective tags. When a new instance fits the schema, not only does prior knowledge apply, but so also may prior affect. This matching effect has been demonstrated for a variety of person schemas: old flames, politicians, campus stereotypes (such as jock, nerd, artist, and gay), college majors (such as pre-med, engineering, theater), occupations (such as doctor, hotel maid, artist, loan shark), and the potentially stigmatized (schizophrenics, paraplegics) (S. T. Fiske, 1982; S. T. Fiske et al., 1987; S. T. Fiske & Pavelchak, 1986; Neuberg & Fiske, 1987; Pavelchak, 1989). More recently, the stereotype content model (Chapter 11) describes emotional prejudices triggered by particular outgroups (elderly cue pity, rich cue envy, poor cue contempt, ingroup cues pride).

The idea that old patterns match new people and situations, invoking feelings that are essentially holdovers from prior experience, also fits the literature on transference in psychotherapy (Singer, 1988; Westen, 1988). **Affective transference** occurs in close relationships when a new person resembles a previous significant other (Andersen & Chen, 2002; Andersen, Saribay & Przybylinski, 2012). People paired with a new person who matches their former liked partner express more positive affect than when paired with someone who matches a former disliked partner. Yoked controls do not show this difference when paired with someone else's former liked and disliked partners, so it is the unique match that matters (Berk & Andersen, 2000). Schema-triggered affect occurs in facial expressions as well (Andersen, Reznik, & Manzella, 1996). What's more, this transference occurs subliminally (Glassman & Andersen, 1999).

Schema-triggered affect describes people's affective reactions even to consumer products that fit familiar molds (Sujan, 1985) and to loaded political issues (Sears, Huddie, & Schaffer, 1986), so presumably, any affect-laden category. Indeed, prototypes associated with affect may be easier to learn than those that are not (J. D. Mayer & Bower, 1986).

Schema Complexity and Affective Extremity

Another set of approaches focuses on the features of the schema itself and their implications for affective responses. The **complexity-extremity hypothesis** (Linville, 1982a, 1982b; Linville, Fischer, & Salovey, 1989; Linville & Jones, 1980; Linville, Salovey, & Fischer, 1986; Chapters 4, 11) focuses on affective consequences of informational intricacy. People evaluate outgroup members (low complexity) more extremely than ingroup members (high complexity), all else being equal. More generally, the theory predicts that the greater the complexity of a schema, the more moderate the affect it typically elicits. For example, if you know a dozen dimensions that determine whether a given football team is good, your evaluation of any random team will include a lot of pluses and minuses. I can think of only two or three dimensions offhand, so any one bit of information about a team is more likely to sway my opinion to one extreme or the other. This analysis also applies to people with simple self-concepts (Chapter 5), who appear prone to mood swings, compared to those with more complex self-concepts (Linville, 1985). People differ considerably in their complexity about different domains of knowledge (de Vries & Walker, 1987) and in their complexity about people in general (Sommers, 1981), with similar results.

Another view of the link between knowledge structures and evaluation is that thought polarizes feelings by creating a tighter organization of the target's attributes in those people who possess a schema for thinking about it (Tesser, 1978; Chapter 3). A general preference for cognitive consistency predicts that the more you consider your team's chances for the league championship, the more likely you will fit all of your team's attributes into place as consistently pro or consistently con. Over time people can make an instance fit the schema, so evaluation becomes more extreme as the attributes become more organized. No amount of mere thought on my part about your team will polarize my evaluations of it, according to Tesser, because I have insufficient prior knowledge to rearrange and, according to Linville, because my opinion is already fairly extreme (being more easily swayed by random factors).

Linville's complexity-extremity hypothesis and Tesser's **thought-polarization hypothesis** may seem to make contradictory predictions, in that Linville claims that complexity moderates evaluations but Tesser claims that thought (which one might think makes schemas more complex) polarizes evaluations. However, several differences apply. First, Tesser's theory states that thought makes schemas more organized, internally consistent, and evaluatively uniform, so thought indeed makes the schema (evaluatively) simpler and, therefore, more polarized, which fits Linville's predictions. Second, the complexity-extremity hypothesis refers to initial evaluations at one point in time, whereas the thought-polarization hypothesis refers to changes over time (Linville, 1982b). Third, the thought-polarization effect occurs when people make an initial public commitment to their evaluations (perhaps because they are more motivated by pressures to be consistent), whereas the complexity-extremity effect obtains in the absence of such commitment (M. G. Millar & Tesser, 1986b). Finally, the thought-polarization effect occurs when the schema's dimensions are substantially correlated (i.e., ratings on one dimension predict ratings on other dimensions) because the schema's structure is more intrinsically coherent (M. G. Millar & Tesser, 1986b). The perceived correlation depends on one's familiarity with the group (Linville, Fischer, & Yoon, 1996). Hence, these thought-polarization and extremity effects are more likely for unfamiliar outgroups.

Obtained Outcomes and Affect

Just as schema theories emphasize matching prior expectations about events, so other theories focus on *post hoc* explanations for events (Table 13.4). Cognitions about one's outcomes underlie many common emotional experiences.

Attributions for Attained Outcomes

Weiner's attributional theory of achievement motivation (Weiner, 1985, 1986) describes basic dimensions that people use to understand their successes and failures: internal or external locus, stability over time, and controllability (Chapter 6). These dimensions, in turn, provoke basic emotions as well as expectations for future outcomes. Together the emotions and expectations guide behavior.

Specific emotions follow from specific causal attributions (Benesh & Weiner, 1982; Weiner, 1985; Table 13.5). The locus and controllability factors determine the quality of emotions, and the stability factor tends to exaggerate them. This framework has been applied, with considerable success, to cognitions and emotions in achievement settings (Weiner, 1985). The simple distinction between being responsible or not for one's bad outcome – that is, judged responsibility – determines anger or sympathy, which in turn determine aggression or helping (see meta-analysis by Rudolph, Roesch, Greitemeyer, & Weiner, 2004).

Table 13.5 Examples of Weiner's locus dimension with (controllable) positive and negative outcomes

	Own Negative Outcome	*Own Positive Outcome*
Attributed to self & controllable	Guilt	Pride
Attributed to another & controllable	Anger	Gratitude

Note: This example omits uncontrollable outcomes, as well as outcome stability, more generally, and other people's outcomes.

People implicitly understand these rules of attribution and emotion, so they use them to control the emotions of others. When providing excuses for interpersonal failures, people attribute their behavior to external, uncontrollable, and unintentional factors ("The dog ate my paper"; "My car broke down"). People do not provide the real reasons for being remiss when the real reasons are internal, controllable, and intentional ("I didn't feel like doing it") or unintentional ("I forgot"). People implicitly know which excuses provoke anger and which defuse it, and experimental manipulations of excuses' causal dimensions show that they are right (Folkes, 1982; Weiner, Amirkhan, Folkes, & Verette, 1987). People also try to control the emotions of others when hoping to elicit their help. If the cause of one's plight is controllable, one is likely to receive only anger, but if the cause is perceived as uncontrollable, then one is likely to receive both pity and help (Meyer & Mulherin, 1980; Reisenzein, 1986; G. Schmidt & Weiner, 1988; Weiner, 1980). General principles of the attribution-emotion-action relationships develop in the naive psychology of children as young as five years old (Graham & Weiner, 1986; Weiner & Handel, 1985).

This analysis extends to stigmatizing conditions, such as AIDS, mental illness, alcoholism, and physical disability. Physical stigmas are perceived to be stable and to have uncontrollable origins, so they elicit pity and helping, but mental and behavioral stigmas are perceived to be unstable (i.e., reversible) and to have controllable origins, so they elicit anger and neglect (Weiner, Perry, & Magnusson, 1988; cf. Brickman et al., 1982). Conflicts in people's implicit attributions about stigma doubtless cause much heartbreak; for example, depressed people sometimes view their condition as uncontrollable and expect pity while those around them often see it as controllable and feel anger (Weiner, 1987). A major issue in caring for persons who are HIV-positive or who have developed AIDS is the perception of others regarding the extent to which the person had control over contracting the disease; sufferers' perceived responsibility is one of the factors contributing to whether or not they receive help. Empirical tests of Weiner's attribution-emotion-behavior theory, as well as its clear applicability, support its usefulness as a cognitively based perspective on emotion resulting from cognitions (attributions) about already-obtained outcomes. Another theory (Ortony, Clore, & Collins, 1988) similarly emphasizes obtained outcomes, but addressing alternative possibilities (i.e., meeting personal goals or social standards).

Hypothetical Outcomes and Affect

Some psychologists studying emotion have focused on cognitions about outcomes that might have been or might yet be. This section considers two such theories, both of which concern the affective impact of people imagining alternatives to current reality.

One theory that is well developed conceptually and empirically relies on the **simulation** heuristic (Chapter 7), the ease of imagining alternative outcomes influences *post hoc* inferences of probability (Kahneman & Tversky, 1982). When one can easily imagine that things might have been otherwise, one's actual state of affairs seems like more of a fluke. In contrast, when it is more difficult to imagine how things could be other than what they are, the current situation seems inevitable. The emotional implications of these *post hoc* inferences are clear: Remember Chapter 7's example of whether it is more frustrating when one just barely misses the friend or the plane, or when one misses by a wide margin. Events that are retrospectively easier to undo mentally cause more intense emotion. When a person is killed by a freak accident, it somehow seems more tragic than when the person is killed in the normal course of a high-risk job or lifestyle.

Norm theory extends these and related ideas into a theory of how people decide what is normal and, by exclusion, what is surprising and therefore emotion producing (Chapter 7; Kahneman & Miller, 1986). An abnormal event has easily imagined alternative outcomes; these alternatives may be either constructed or remembered alternative scenarios. In either case, many possible alternatives make the actual events surprising. Consider the parallel between these ideas and ideas about expectancy effects. That is, an event inconsistent with one's implicit norms is perceived as unlikely in retrospect; an event inconsistent with one's expectations is perceived as unlikely in the future. Whereas schema and expectancy theories consider people's reasoning before the fact, which might be called anticipatory thinking, this theory concerns people's reasoning after the fact, which might be called backward thinking.

Norm theory's relevance for affect lies essentially in its emotional amplification hypothesis; namely, that events elicit stronger emotion when their causes are abnormal. This is especially evident for misfortunes, as in the just-missed planes and freak accidents, which are particularly upsetting. Similarly, a person who wins the lottery with a ticket bought minutes before the drawing – versus one bought weeks before – feels especially lucky and happy (D. T. Miller, Turnbull, & McFarland, 1990) and probably is especially envied as well. Abnormality influences emotional reactions to other people; one feels more sympathy for someone victimized by chance (D. T. Miller & McFarland, 1986). Again, the more easily imagined the counterfactual scenario, the more intense the emotion one experiences.

Emotions as Managers of Goals

Another set of approaches posits that emotions essentially manage people's priorities (Table 13.4). This perspective starts with the observation that many emotions occur when planned behavior is interrupted, as noted in Mandler's and Berscheid's theories, or could have been interrupted, as in Kahneman and Miller's theory. However, one can examine not only how interruptions cause emotion, as in those theories, but also the reverse: How emotions cause interruptions.

Emotions can control cognition, alerting people to important goals. In this view, emotions are alarm signals consisting of interruption and arousal, and they divert people from pursuing one goal and point them toward pursuing another goal that has meanwhile increased in importance (Simon, 1967, 1982). This view follows from the premise that people are capacity-limited information processors. That is, they can pursue basically only one goal at a time, whether listening to a lecture, thinking about a brilliant question to ask, planning what to have for dinner, playing an online game, or making eyes at the attractive person nearby. An information processor potentially could handle such multiple goals by ranking their relative importance and completing each in turn, at its leisure. Unfortunately, such an obsessive android might get run over by a truck if it were only attending to the goal of locomoting to work and not attending to the goal of staying intact. Survival depends on the organism being able to interrupt ongoing goals before completion if other environmental contingencies demand it. Emotions, such as fear of an onrushing moving van, can prompt attention to urgent goals. Examples of such high-priority items include environmental stimuli that warn of potential danger (e.g., producing fear), physiological stimuli that demand refueling (e.g., producing hunger or sleepiness), and internal cognitive stimuli that trigger unmet psychological needs (e.g., producing common negative emotions). In this view, the physiological arousal that accompanies emotion comes from the interruption itself. Note that the interrupting effect of emotion is to alter goals rather than to disorganize one's responses. Emotions merely indicate the changing importance of different goals (also see Oatley & Johnson-Laird, 1987; for commentary, see Frijda, 1987a).

Intense emotions do interrupt well-planned, ongoing cognitive activities. For example, emotionally salient material presented outside awareness quickly captures conscious attention (Nielsen & Sarason, 1981). Emotionally charged events are especially memorable (R. Brown & Kulik, 1977) and occupy much of people's daily thoughts (Klinger et al., 1980). Thus emotion may well interrupt both attention and memory.

Also related to emotion-as-interruption, the **cybernetic theory of self-attention** (Carver & Scheier, 1982; Chapter 5) describes self-focused people as noticing discrepancies between their current state and some goal or standard. When people notice the discrepancy, they attempt to adjust their behavior to reduce the discrepancy. The person may succeed and move on to another goal. If the person fails, the theory states that the person may try repeatedly and fail. Thus the theory must provide for the person to give up and change goals. Otherwise, it would portray the organism as marching into a corner, without knowing when it is beaten (Scheier & Carver, 1982; Scheier, Carver, & Gibbons, 1981). An affective feedback system could sense and regulate the organism's progress toward its goal (Carver & Scheier, 1990). Emotions interrupt ongoing behavior, causing a reassessment of one's probability of success, and one redoubles effort or withdraws accordingly. Thus emotions in general may lead to self-focused attention (Salovey & Rodin, 1985). However, feelings of pleasure indicate unexpected progress toward one's goals and that one may safely attend elsewhere (Carver, 2003).

Appraisal Theories

Other theories also link cognition and emotion, but focus less on information-processing details. Instead, they emphasize the interpretation of implications for oneself. When we walk into a gathering of people, most of us scan the room to see who is there (people we are glad to see, people we are not so glad to see, or people we do not know) and what has been arranged for us and the other participants (décor, food and drink, seating). In effect, we appraise the situation to see its possible significance for us. An older set of cognitively oriented emotion theories revolves around such a concept of environmental appraisal. The shared premise is that we evaluate our environment for its likely impact on us. The first to develop the term **appraisal** was Magda Arnold (e.g., 1945, 1970); her theory holds that we immediately and automatically appraise all that we encounter as a fundamental act of perception, producing tendencies to act. One basis for appraisal is memory of similar past experiences, along with associated affect, and an important element of our plans for action is expectation about the consequences of our actions. All of this appraisal process typically occurs quickly, intuitively, and innately. Although not developed with reference to recent ideas about cognition, Arnold's theory anticipates the more current approaches.

Personal Meaning

A subsequent proponent of the appraisal approach Lazarus (1966; Lazarus & Smith, 1988) viewed appraisal as evaluating any given stimulus according to its personal significance for one's own well-being. The assignment of personal meaning is viewed as a type of cognition, but not necessarily conscious, verbal, deliberate, or rational. Appraisal relates one's goals and beliefs to environmental realities.

The process begins with **primary appraisals**, in which people assess personal relevance (what is at stake for me). Primary appraisal determines both motivational relevance (regarding one's own goals and concerns) and motivational congruence (regarding whether the stimulus facilitates or thwarts one's goals). The emotional consequences of primary appraisal are relatively primitive, being simple avoidance or approach, respectively, to potential harm or benefit.

The consequences of **secondary appraisal** are more specific emotions whereby people consider how to cope (What can I do? What are my options?). Two primary kinds of secondary appraisal include **problem-focused coping**, which attempts to change the relationship between the person and the environment, or if that fails, **emotion-focused coping**, which attempts to adjust one's reactions through avoidant attentional strategies or changing the meaning of the threat. Examples of relevant secondary appraisal processes include attributions of past accountability (credit or blame) and expectancies about the future's perceived motivational congruence (maybe this cloud has a silver lining). The most effective secondary appraisal coping strategies depend on the degree of realistic control one has and on the stage of the threat involved (i.e., whether information gathering is still useful, whether one can realistically alter the situation, or whether it is too late to do anything). The core point is that appraisal leads to coping (through changes in attention, meaning, and actual circumstances), which changes person–environment relationships, which in turn lead to different emotions (Folkman & Lazarus, 1988a, 1988b). Lazarus's appraisal theory has primarily informed research on stress and coping (Lazarus, 2000), especially in health psychology, but also appears in Smith and Mackie's intergroup emotions theory (Chapter 12).

Cognitive Appraisals

Other appraisal theories focus more explicitly on people's knowledge of their circumstances and how these **cognitive appraisals** lead to emotion (Ellsworth & Smith, 1988a, 1988b; C. A. Smith &

Table 13.6 Locations of emotions along the appraisal components

Emotion	Pleasant[a]	Responsibility/ control[b]	Certain[c]	Attention[d]	Effort[e]	Situational- control[f]
Happiness	1.46		.46			
Sadness	−.87					1.15
Anger	−.85	−.94			.53	−.96
Boredom				−1.27	−1.19	
Challenge		.44		.52	1.19	
Hope	.50		−.46			
Fear	−.44		−.73		.63	.59
Interest	1.05			.70		.41
Contempt	−.89	−.50		.80		−.63
Disgust		−.50		−.96		
Frustration	−.88			.60	.48	
Surprise	1.35	−.94	−.73	.40	−.66	.15
Pride	1.25	.81				−.46
Shame	−.73	1.31				
Guilt	−.60	1.31				

Notes: Scores are standardized and scores below .40 are eliminated.
[a] Pleasantness: High scores indicate increased pleasantness.
[b] Responsibility/Control: High scores indicate increased self-responsibility/control.
[c] Certainty: High scores indicate increased certainty.
[d] Attentional activity: High scores indicate increased attentional activity.
[e] Effort: High scores indicate increased anticipated effort.
[f] Situational-control: High scores indicate increased situational control.
Source: C. A. Smith & Ellsworth (1985)

Ellsworth, 1985, 1987). Unlike the previous focus more specifically on personal motivational meaning (Lazarus & Smith, 1988), this approach is more explicitly cognitive. A core idea of the cognitive appraisal approach is that people appraise various dimensions of the situation, and these dimensions determine their specific emotional reaction. Once people appraise the pleasantness of the situation, more specific emotions result from evaluating, for example, agency (i.e., responsibility or control by self, other, or circumstances; how fair the situation is), uncertainty (how sure one is; how much understanding one has), and attention (heeding; thinking).

People do remember experiencing particular emotions and describe their corresponding appraisals, or vice versa, as well as reporting current emotions and their corresponding appraisals (Table 13.6). Among the negative emotions, for example, self-agency goes with shame and guilt; other-agency characterizes anger, contempt, and disgust; agency due to circumstances typifies sadness (cf. Weiner's theory, covered earlier). Thus one feels shame or guilt when responsible for an unpleasant situation, such as inadvertently ruining a dinner party by one's thoughtless behavior. However, one feels anger, contempt, and disgust when another is responsible in the same way.

Finally, one feels sadness when circumstances are responsible, as when the weather ruins an elaborate outdoor party. Other dimensions matter as well: For example, uncertainty characterizes fear, for one feels most intense fear in unpredictable and personally uncontrollable situations (a party at which several people become drunkenly violent). And the dimension of attention and thinking is important, for low levels of attention mark boredom and disgust; high levels of attention characterize frustration. (Consider the differences in one's attention to an interminable storyteller at a party; if the person is merely boring or disgusting, one ignores the conversational monopolist, but if the person is frustrating your attempt to tell your own story, you will attentively listen for any chance to break in.)

Among the positive emotions, people differentiate less clearly; a situation can be unpleasant in more ways than it can be pleasant, as noted earlier. Pleasant situations just make people generally happy. Nevertheless, one can distinguish some specific dimensions: Surprise is associated with uncertainty and external agency; interest fits with attention; hope correlates with perceived obstacles and anticipated effort; tranquility goes with certainty, an absence of obstacles, and a lack of effort; love is associated with importance, other-agency, and a lack of effort or obstacles. Moreover, particular appraisals influence physiological concomitants of emotion, specifically, that anticipated effort influences heart rate and that perceived obstacles influence eyebrow frown (C. A. Smith, 1989).

Various appraisal theories provide a daunting variety when considered in detail, but they do share some common themes (for integrations, see Frijda, 1988; Scherer, 1988). In particular, the theoretical taxonomies of appraisals for specific emotions overlap considerably in the dimensions viewed as important in distinguishing the emotions, namely, pleasantness, agency, certainty, and attention (see Fridja, 1987b; Roseman, 1984).

Another framework compares cross-cultural consensus in people's open-ended descriptions of specific emotional experiences, their antecedents, and bodily reactions (e.g., Scherer, 1984, 1988; Scherer, Wallbott, & Summerfield, 1986; Wallbott & Scherer, 1988). Dimensions of the **stimulus evaluation check** (similar to appraisal) aspect include novelty, intrinsic pleasantness, significance for goals and needs, and coping potential or degree of control; these dimensions serve both social and physiological functions.

Across all these cognitive appraisal theories, some central dimensions emerge: (a) pleasantness, motive consistency, and valence; (b) agency and responsibility; (c) certainty, probability, and control; and (d) attention, interest, and novelty. Accordingly, these compatible cognitive appraisal theories offer conceptual (and sometimes empirical) support for each other, suggesting that appraisal theorists home in on the crucial cognitive dimensions that result in distinct emotions.[1]

---

[1] Still other cognitively informed theories focus on more specific kinds of appraisal: For example, perceived self-efficacy as a cause of emotion (Bandura, 1982); illness cognitions and emotional coping (e.g., for empirical work, Ward, Leventhal, & Love, 1988; for the broader perceptual-motor theory of emotions, see Leventhal, 1982, 1984); or an accessible discrepancy between one's actual self and one's "ideal" or "ought" self (Higgins, 1987; Chapter 5). Relatedly, Epstein's (1984) cognitive-experiential self theory describes the preconscious construals of potential response options that give rise to specific emotions, with particular emphasis on fear, anger, sadness, joy, and affection in everyday life.

Affective Forecasting

A related theory suggests a final type of top-down determinant of affect. People have expectations about how they will feel (about a movie, for example), and if the actual experience fits their expectancy, their affective reactions are faster; if the experience is slightly discrepant, they may still assimilate it to the expectancy. When the experience is quite discrepant and they notice it, people have more trouble forming preferences (T. D. Wilson, Dunn, Kraft, & Lisle, 1989). This type of affective expectancy complements the previous work on affect-laden schemas and cognitive appraisals.

Taking affective expectancies further, a program of research indicates that people make wrong-headedly extreme **affective forecasts** of their own personal upcoming emotional weather (Wilson & Gilbert, 2005). People generally overestimate the impact of negative events, such as negative feedback, room assignments, romantic breakups, unfavorable election results, not getting hired, or not getting tenure (Dunn, Wilson, & Gilbert, 2003; Gilbert, Pinel, Wilson, Blumberg, & Wheatley, 1998; Wilson, Wheatly, Meyers, Gilbert, & Axsom, 2000). People especially fall prey when the anticipated events are emotionally intense (Gilbert, Lieberman, Morewedge, & Wilson, 2004).

Several cognitive mechanisms contribute. People fail to take account of their **psychological immune system** (i.e., self-protective mechanisms), which enables them to get past the blows that life deals. And their projections focus too much on the possible negative event, failing to account for other concurrent future events that will dilute its impact. People may be misled by their tendency to recall past events that were emotion-laden but atypical (Morewedge, Gilbert, & Wilson, 2005). People also overestimate the extent to which past events affected them (Wilson, Meyers, & Gilbert, 2003). Hence, people fall prey to **durability bias**, expecting negative events to affect them longer than they actually do.

People apparently learn little from experience (Wilson, Meyers, & Gilbert, 2001). What's more, when people do cope well, they do not credit their psychological immune systems but more typically tend to attribute their own coping to a powerful external agency such as a higher power (Gilbert, Brown, Pinel, & Wilson, 2000). Clearly, various types of cognition have a wide-ranging and discernable impact on affective responses, and moreover, no one explanation covers all types of affect.

Summary

The literature on affect and cognition is moving in numerous different directions simultaneously, some focusing on physiological responses and some on the ways that cognitive structures – either interrupted or successfully applied – influence affect. Some of these theoretical efforts are supported by considerably more empirical evidence than others. Nevertheless, some central themes emerge as directing research and theory.

Affect is a generic term encompassing all kinds of evaluations, moods, and emotion. Preferences include relatively mild subjective reactions that are essentially either pleasant or unpleasant. Moods typically do not have a specific target, are considered as simply positive or negative, and have some duration. Emotions are more complex and differentiated, often include physiological responses, and can be relatively brief. The two most common ways of distinguishing among emotions are along the two dimensions of pleasantness and arousal or along two independent dimensions of positive and negative emotions. Positive emotions, analyzed separately, have a simpler structure than negative emotions. Prototype and social-role approaches describe people's culturally shared categorization of specific emotions and the concept of emotion in general.

Early emotion theories asked whether physiological responses precede (James, Lange) or follow (Cannon) the experience of differentiated emotions. Subsequently, many physiological theories of emotion assumed that autonomic arousal was undifferentiated and that other mechanisms must account for the complexity of emotional experience. Facial feedback theory posits that the face's complex, subtle musculature provides the detailed patterns of feedback that underlie different emotions, particularly their valence and intensity.

Excitation transfer theory proposes that autonomic arousal from emotions or exercise decays slowly, and that people often cannot distinguish the source of their arousal. Consequently, prior excitation can spill over to intensify new affective responses, even those of a different valence. These physiological theories de-emphasize cognition's role in generating emotion.

In contrast, how might cognition contribute to affect? Some approaches examine the interplay between arousal and cognition, building on Schachter's two-component theory of emotion (Chapter 6; unexplained arousal leads people to search their environment for cognitive labels for their emotions). Mandler's theory of mind and emotion extends this analysis: Physiological arousal originates in the interruption of perceptual schemas or complex goal sequences. The degree of disconfirmation of a perceptual schema determines its experienced pleasantness. The interruption of a goal sequence also prompts cognitive interpretation that determines the nature of the experienced emotion. Berscheid's theory of emotion in close relationships extends this analysis to complex goal sequences in which people are interdependent: The more intimate the relationship, the more interdependence, and the more potential for interruption and, consequently, emotion.

Other social cognition theories focus on how cognitive structures impact affect. Keltner's theory posits that high power leads to positive affect. Fiske's theory of schema-triggered affect posits that affective values are stored at the top level of a schema, accessible immediately upon categorization of an instance as matching the schema. Linville analyzes how informational complexity influences affect; more complex knowledge structures often moderate affect, whereas simple ones allow more extreme affect. Over time, thought polarizes affect, in Tesser's analysis, if thought organizes the relevant schema, the schema contains correlated dimensions, and the person has publically committed to the initial affective response.

Other theories examine emotional reactions to own or others' obtained outcomes. Weiner's attributional dimensions theory proposes that different configurations – internal-external locus, stability over time, and controllability – result in specific emotional and behavioral responses.

Besides already-obtained outcomes, some theories emphasize alternative outcomes: What might have been or might yet be. Kahneman and Miller's norm theory describes an outcome's surprise-value compared to the ease of imagined alternatives, and then the intensity of emotional response. Thus, interruptions variously cause emotion.

Emotions also cause interruptions. Emotions may manage goal priorities, interrupting to cue changing priorities. In Simon's view and Oately and Johnson-Laird's related view, emotions serve as alarm signals, providing arousal and interruption that alert the organism to an unmet need that has shifted its urgency while the organism has been pursuing another goal. Carver and Scheier's cybernetic model posits an affective feedback system that regulates the rate at which the organism pursues the goal.

Finally, based on Arnold and Lazarus, cognition generates affect via appraisals: How people assess the environment to ascertain its significance for their concerns. The appraisal of personal meaning involves preconscious and conscious cognitive assessments of, first, personal relevance and, second, coping options. Cognitive appraisal assesses particular dimensions of the current situation, determining particular emotional responses. Other theories have identified similar dimensions of appraisal leading to emotion, in particular, pleasantness, agency, certainty, and attention. People's affective forecasts for the future tend to over-estimate the emotional impact of life events.

FURTHER READING

Andersen, S. M., Saribay, S. A., & Przybylinski, E. (2012). Social cognition in close relationships. In S. T. Fiske & C. N. Macrae (Eds.), *Sage handbook of social cognition* (pp. 350–371). Thousand Oaks, CA: Sage.

Barrett, L. F., Mesquita, B., Ochsner, K. N., & Gross, J. J. (2007). The experience of emotion. *Annual Review of Psychology, 58*, 373–403.

Hostetter, A. B., Alibali, M. W., & Niedenthal, P. M. (2012). Embodied social thought: Linking social concepts, emotion, and gesture. In S. T. Fiske & C. N. Macrae (Eds.), *Sage handbook of social cognition* (pp. 211–228). Thousand Oaks, CA: Sage.

Izard, C. E. (2009). Emotion theory and research: Highlights, unanswered questions, and emerging issues. *Annual Review of Psychology, 60*, 1–25.

Keltner, D., & Lerner, J. S. (2010). Emotion. In S. T. Fiske, D. T. Gilbert, & G. Lindzey (Eds.), *Handbook of social psychology* (5th edn, Vol. 1, pp. 317–352). Hoboken, NJ: Wiley.

Mesquita, B., Marinetti, C., & Delvaux, E. (2012). The social psychology of emotion. In S. T. Fiske & C. N. Macrae (Eds.), *Sage handbook of social cognition* (pp. 290–310). Thousand Oaks, CA: Sage.

Niedenthal, P. M., & Brauer, M. (2012). Social functionality of human emotion. *Annual Review of Psychology, 63*, 259–285.

From Affect to Social Cognition

14

- Affective Influences on Cognition
- Affect versus Cognition

Economists (at least the classic kind) like to believe that people make rational choices after weighing costs and benefits. Recent work on heuristics (Chapter 7; Kahneman, 2011) undermines the idea that these decisions are cognitively unbiased. Recent work on emotion undermines the idea that these decisions are mainly cognitive in the first place. In this chapter, we shall see that affect influences all manner of thoughts, memories, beliefs, and choices. But we will also see that people vary in their sensitivity to affective influences. Finally, as we will describe, some researchers argue that affect and cognition should be viewed as separate systems entirely. Certainly they have some distinct ways of operating.

AFFECTIVE INFLUENCES ON COGNITION

One woman, upon discovering she had lost weight, suddenly started being nicer to her dog. Another person, when tired, says "no" to virtually anything. Still another, just because the janitor unexpectedly washed out her coffee cup, felt her whole day was made. And we all have found, when we are feeling cheerful, that the ideas come thick and fast. These and related phenomena illustrate the many influences of affect on behavior, memory, judgment, decision making, and persuasion.

Before describing this research in detail, consider some bits of background. First, most studies have examined the effects of **mood** on cognition and social behavior; intense **emotions** have played a lesser role in this research. Second, and relatedly, experiments examining these effects typically utilize relatively minor mood manipulations, such as finding a quarter on the ground, not major life events, such as winning a million dollars in the lottery. It does not require a life-shaking affect-laden event for emotion to influence how we behave, think, decide, and create.

Third, people's perceptions and expectations have a positive bias, and people generally rate others' and their own lives as moderately positive (Chapters 2, 3, 13; Parducci, 1968; Sears, 1983); information processing is biased toward positive material, in the **Pollyanna effect** (Matlin & Stang, 1978). People remember and judge positive material more easily (e.g., Hampson & Dawson, 1985), and they make positively biased judgments. Thus, all else being equal, most people are moderately optimistic. This means that positive and negative moods are not simple opposites of each other, for positive moods fit what people feel more often and typically prefer. This asymmetry has important consequences.

The effects of positive moods are more clear-cut than are the effects of negative moods. Across research programs, the effects of positive moods are more predictable, consistent, and interpretable than are the effects of negative moods. Several reasons probably explain the uneven effects of negative moods. Positive affect is more common than negative, as just noted, so negative affect is a bigger change from the baseline, more interrupting and distracting. Moreover, negative moods can signal situations that threaten well-being (Chapter 13), so again, they are more disruptive. Negative emotions, in general, are more varied than positive ones, as demonstrated by the structure of negative and positive affect (Chapter 13). As a result, the effects of an angry mood and a sad mood may be less similar than the effects of a joyous mood and an excited one. In addition, negative moods are aversive, so people try to manage their negative feelings more than their positive feelings. All this results in negative moods having more variable effects than do positive moods.

Mood and Helping

Good moods lead people to help others (as shown by our friend who smothers the dog with affection just because she herself is feeling thin). An inspiring array of pleasant little experiences has been examined: success on a small task, finding a coin, receiving a free sample, being given a cookie or candy, viewing pleasant slides, listening to soothing music, being told one is helpful, experiencing good weather, and remembering positive events from the past (for review, see Forgas, 1995; Isen, 1987; J. D. Mayer & Salovey, 1988; Penner, Dovidio, Piliavin, & Schroeder, 2005). Even the fragrance of roasting coffee or baking cookies can make people more likely to change a dollar or retrieve a pen for a stranger in a shopping mall (R. A. Baron, 1997). These little rays of sunshine all have the salutary effect of making the world a better place: Recipients will mail a lost letter; help someone pick up dropped papers, packages, or books; donate to or solicit for charity; volunteer their time; agree to donate blood; give more positive advice; or make a phone call for a stranger. What's more, these effects generalize across age, social class, and ethnicity (Penner et al., 2005).

Several hypotheses have been proposed to account for these effects. In one analysis of the research, Carlson, Charlin, and Miller (1988) found strong evidence for four mechanisms, all of which bear on the principle that cheerful individuals are especially sensitive to concerns about positive reinforcement. People in a good mood will help if the situation makes salient their need for rewards and emphasizes the rewards of helping (Table 14.1).

Table 14.1 Mechanisms to explain how mood affects helping

Mechanism	Process	Distinguishes	Citation example
Attention	Focus on self or others	Good moods from own good fortune → help Good mood from other's good fortune → not	Rosenhan, Salovey, & Hargis, 1981
Separate process	Focus of request	Reward emphasis → help Guilt emphasis → not	M.R. Cunningham, Steinberg, & Grey, 1980; Gueguen & DeGail 2003; Perlow & Weeks, 2002
Social outlook	Focus of event	Human goodness, community benevolence → help Nonhuman causes → not	Holloway, Tucker, & Hornstein, 1977
Maintain mood	Focus on effects	Supports mood → help Ruin mood → not	Forest, Clark, Mills, & Isen, 1979; Isen & Simmonds, 1978

Mood can alter one's *focus of attention* such that one focuses on oneself or on other people. Good moods induced by focusing on one's own good fortune promote benevolence toward others, but focusing on someone else's good fortune does not increase helping and instead may provoke envy (e.g., Rosenhan, Salovey, & Hargis, 1981).

According to the *separate process view*, people in a positive mood will help mainly if the request emphasizes the rewards of helping rather than a guilt-inducing obligation to help (e.g., M. R. Cunningham, Steinberg, & Grey, 1980; Gueguen & DeGail 2003; Perlow & Weeks, 2002).

A third hypothesis holds that people can be placed in a good mood by having their *social outlook* improved (e.g., Holloway, Tucker, & Hornstein, 1977). When people are cheered by an interpersonal event, they are more likely to help because they focus on human goodness or community benevolence; an improved social outlook enhances prosocial values.

Finally, people are concerned with *mood maintenance,* so cheerful people are less likely to help if it would ruin their mood (e.g., Forest, Clark, Mills, & Isen, 1979; Isen & Simmonds, 1978). However, this does not mean that they help merely to boost or maintain their mood; people help for a variety of reasons, and cheerful people are simply sensitive to and avoidant of negative affect (Isen, 1987). Cheerful people help when they have salient concerns about rewards and when the rewards of helping are clear.[1]

In a related vein, cheerful people are more sociable: They initiate interactions, express liking, self-disclose more, give advice, aggress less, and cooperate more, and this does not seem to be due to their being generally more compliant when cheerful (e.g., M. R. Cunningham, 1988; for a review, see Isen, 1987). People even become more cooperative negotiators, using less contentious tactics and increasing joint benefits (Carnevale & Isen, 1986; Forgas, 1998). People are not only usually nicer to others, but they are also nicer to themselves when they are feeling good. They reward themselves and seek positive feedback, and this is not merely due to a loss of self-control (Isen, 1987). The beneficial effects of mood appear in a variety of good-citizen behaviors in the workplace (Brief & Weiss, 2002; Forgas & George, 2001). As the emotion-helping work progresses, it is likely to focus increasingly on specific positive emotions, such as gratitude (Bartlett & DeSteno, 2006).

What about people who are temporarily depressed? People in a bad mood are sometimes more helpful than people in a neutral mood, but only under particular conditions (for a review, see Carlson & Miller, 1987). In effect, the negative mood conditions that do encourage helping are those in which guilt rather than anger is operating. That is, according to the responsibility/**objective-self-awareness** view, unhappy people who perceive themselves to be the cause of a negative event (e.g., breaking an experimenter's equipment or being told they are responsible for their bad mood) are helpful, assuming prosocial norms are salient (e.g., M. Rogers, Miller, Mayer, & Dural, 1982).

---

[1] The concomitance hypothesis holds that happy people are helpful not in order to maintain their moods but rather as a side-effect of being happy; for instance, because of increased liking for others or increased optimism (Manucia, Baumann, & Cialdini, 1984). This hypothesis overlaps considerably with the social outlook hypothesis and others, so it is hard to evaluate it separately, particularly when mood maintenance concerns are also evident (Carlson, Charlin, & Miller, 1988).

In contrast, according to the focus-of-attention explanation, grumpy people who perceive a self-focused angle on a negative event (e.g., imagining their own personal reactions to a friend dying of cancer) are less helpful to others (e.g., W. Thompson, Cowan, & Rosenhan, 1980). The attentional explanation applies to helping that is instigated by both positive and negative moods; when helping focuses attention away from one's mood, the mood weakens, but when helping focuses attention on the conditions producing one's mood, the mood strengthens (M. G. Millar, Millar, & Tesser, 1988).

An additional explanation for the effects of bad moods on helping is more controversial. According to a **negative state-relief hypothesis**, unhappy people help when it could dispel their negative mood (e.g., Cialdini, Darby, & Vincent, 1973; Schaller & Cialdini, 1988). Even children are aware of the personally salutary effects of helping (Cialdini & Kenrick, 1976; Perry, Perry, & Weiss, 1986). Clearly, people attempt to regulate their moods (Baumgardner & Arkin, 1988; J. D. Mayer & Gaschke, 1988), so some version of this hypothesis is likely to hold. However, researchers disagree about the interpretation of such results (Carlson & Miller, 1987; cf. Schroeder, Davidio, Sibicky, Mathews, & Allen, 1988).

Mood and Memory

Have you ever received a piece of good news and found yourself mentally reviewing several other past experiences of being competent, good, and lovable? Present mood shapes memory for past experiences. Two essential phenomena have formed the core of research on mood and memory: mood-congruent memory and mood state-dependent memory.

Mood Congruence

Under many circumstances, people more easily remember material whose valence fits their current mood state (for reviews, see Blaney, 1986; Forgas, 1995; Isen, 1987; J. D. Mayer, 1986). Dozens of studies have induced moods experimentally by having participants undergo hypnosis, experience success and failure, read mood-relevant sentences (the **Velten procedure**), listen to mood-laden music, dwell on relevant past experiences, or assume positive and negative facial expressions (Blaney, 1986). In one study, moods were cued by odors picked to be pleasant (like almond essence) and unpleasant (like coal tar; Ehrlichman & Halpern, 1988). Across a variety of settings and procedures that demonstrate **mood-congruent memory**, people recall positive material in positive moods and sometimes recall negative material in negative moods (e.g., G. H. Bower, Gilligan, & Monteiro, 1981; Isen, Shalker, Clark, & Karp, 1978; Salovey & Singer, 1988; Teasdale & Russell, 1983).

Some argue that the effect is located primarily at retrieval (Blaney, 1986; Isen, 1987), but most argue that the evidence is stronger for effects at learning (G. H. Bower, 1987; J. D. Brown & Taylor, 1986; Fiedler, Nickel, Muehlfriedel, & Unkelbach, 2001; J. D. Mayer & Salovey, 1988; Nasby & Yando, 1982; J. A. Singer & Salovey, 1988). Consistent with this perspective, people more readily perceive emotion-congruent stimuli (Neidenthal & Setterlund, 1994). Most accounts assume that mood-congruence effects are fairly automatic, but some mood-congruence effects involve controlled, motivated processes (Blaney, 1986).

Table 14.2 Affect infusion model (AIM)

Processing mode	Affective influences	Precedents
Heuristic (automatic) perspective	Affect informs quick judgments ("if I am feeling good, I must like this")	Mood-as-information (e.g., Schwarz & Bless, 1991).
Substantive (controlled)	Affect primes judgments (selective attention, encoding, retrieval, association)	Traditional memory models (e.g., Bower, 1991)
Direct access to prior judgment	Little or no influence	Memory, judgment, behavior already channelled
Motivated processing	Little or no influence	Memory, judgment, behavior already channelled

Source: After Forgas (1995)

An integrative **affect infusion model** (AIM) proposes that, depending on the processing mode, affective influences may be relatively automatic, controlled, or absent altogether (Forgas, 1995; Table 14.2). That is, under *heuristic* processing, affect informs quick judgments (if I am feeling good, I must like this); this follows the **affect-as-information perspective** (e.g., Schwarz & Bless, 1991). Under more *substantive* (typically controlled) processing, affect primes judgments through selective attention, encoding, retrieval, and association; this follows more traditional memory models (e.g., Bower, 1991). However, affect may have little influence in two cases: either when people have *direct access* to a prior judgment or when they engage in *motivated* processing to further a preexisting goal. In these latter cases, memory, judgment, and behavior are already channeled, so they are less open to affective biases. In the context of memory, AIM describes how reactions to requests show a mood-congruent bias. In one study conducted at the library, students saw pictures or text eliciting positive moods (funny cartoons) or negative moods (car accidents); they then received polite or impolite requests for paper from another student. Negative moods made people more critical of requests and less likely to comply, but this was especially true for impolite requests, which were also more memorable, consistent with a substantive processing route (Forgas, 1998).

Most mood-congruence research finds uneven effects for negative moods, and motivated, controlled processes may account for these failures. That is, people try to repair negative moods, so the mood-inducing manipulations do not work as well (M. S. Clark & Isen, 1982; J. A. Singer & Salovey, 1988). Alternatively, the weakness of negative mood effects may result from the store of negative material in memory being less extensive and less integrated, so negative moods may not as effectively cue congruent material (Isen, 1987). Also, if negative material is less organized, it may be intrinsically harder to learn, so equating negative and positive stimuli is hard. Possibly, the weakness of negative mood effects is also due to the greater differentiation among negative moods (sadness, anger, fear) than among positive moods (happiness). If mood-congruence depends on matching more than just general valence but instead the specific emotion, then negative mood states would not match as easily. Also any one of them would tend to have fewer associations than would an overall happy glow (Laird et al., 1989).

Negative mood congruence does occur reliably in one important case: namely, for people who are depressed, for whom negative events are presumably mood-congruent and, therefore, memorable (Blaney, 1986; M. H. Johnson & Magaro, 1987). For example, when depressed and nondepressed people experience a series of experimenter-controlled successes and failures, depressed people underestimate successes relative to control participants (e.g., Craighead, Hickey, & DeMonbreun, 1979). The effect appears more likely to be a retrieval bias than an encoding deficit; that is, they notice the successes but just do not recall them easily. As another example, depressed people (compared to controls) underremember positive words and phrases or overrecall negative ones (e.g., Ingram, Smith, & Brehm, 1983). These negative mood-congruence effects may occur only when people focus on the applicability of the material to themselves (e.g., Bargh & Tota, 1988), but otherwise the conditions under which they have been obtained are numerous and varied. Depressed participants may deliberately focus on negative material to rebut it, to improve themselves, or to confirm their self-image, so the effects may or may not be automatic (i.e., unintentional, unconscious, and rapid; Chapter 2).

Besides individual differences in depression, people high on neuroticism also show exaggerated negative mood effects (Rusting, 1999). Extraverts show enhanced positive mood-memory effects. Either of two processes may explain personality's interplay with mood (Rusting, 1998). Mood can moderate (interact with) personality to affect cognition jointly. Or mood can mediate the personality-processing relationship such that certain personality traits predispose people to particular moods, which then affect cognition. A variety of studies support both these processes.

Altogether, considerable evidence supports the facilitating effects of congruence between mood and the material to be remembered. However, a few isolated examples of superior mood-incongruent memory complicate the usual mood-congruency effects (Fiedler, Pampe, & Scherf, 1986; Forgas, Burnham, & Trimboli, 1988; Mackie et al., 1989; Parrott & Sabini, 1990; Rusting & DeHart, 2000). As noted, people often regulate negative moods by reframing past negative events or by retrieving positive memories to counteract the bad mood, resulting in mood-incongruency effects for negative moods. Also, when people reflect on their moods, they are more likely to recall mood-incongruent events (McFarland & Buehler, 1998).

Mood-memory research is not without its problems: Within-participant designs may encourage participants to respond to **experimental demand** (i.e., telegraphing the hypothesis), and some research fails to include neutral-mood control groups (M. S. Clark & Williamson, 1989; J. A. Singer & Salovey, 1988). Nevertheless, some studies apparently circumvent demand by unobtrusively manipulating facial expressions rather than more overtly self-induced mood states, and these studies also show mood-congruent memory (Laird et al., 1989; Laird, Wagener, Halal, & Szegda, 1982). Embodied cognition research addresses similar issues in **offline cognition**, that is, recreating perception without the original targets being present (Chapter 4; Niedenthal, Barsalou, Winkielman, Krauth-Gruber, & Ric , 2005).

Moreover, the real-world effects are especially robust: Clinically depressed patients reliably show the mood-congruency effects, and real-life events show stronger mood-congruence effects than do experimenter-provided items (e.g., Mayer, McCormick, & Strong, 1995; see Ucros,

1989, for a meta-analysis). Overall, the findings of mood-congruence seem to outweigh the failures to find such effects.

Mood State-Dependent Memory

A separate mood-and-memory phenomenon concerns the congruence between the mood context in which material is learned and the mood context in which material is retrieved. That is, if one studies for an exam in a sad mood, one might best recall the material if taking the test also in a sad mood. **Mood state-dependent memory** would ignore the valence of the material itself, focusing only on the fit between the two contexts.

State-dependent memory apparently exists for drug-induced states (Eich, 1980); for example, something learned while intoxicated is easier to remember while intoxicated than while sober. (This should not be interpreted as a recommendation that people who cannot remember what they did while drunk should re-create the state merely in order to find out.) The reliability of drug-induced state-dependent memory led researchers to look for a similar phenomenon in mood states. Perhaps material learned while happy is best remembered while happy, regardless of the content of the particular material.

Although an effect that deserves to be true, evidence for it is weak (Blaney, 1986; G. H. Bower & Mayer, 1989; Isen, 1987). Studies that associate half the material with one mood (e.g., happy) and the other half with another mood (e.g., sad) have more frequently obtained effects. These within-participants designs rely on the interference between the different kind of items at the testing stage. However, systematic manipulations of interference do not reliably yield the effect (G. H. Bower & Mayer, 1989), and because all participants experience both moods, an obvious hypothesis and experimental demand then appear possible (Blaney, 1986; J. D. Mayer & Salovey, 1988; J. A. Singer & Salovey, 1988; Ucros, 1989). One might, therefore, think to examine naturally-occurring rather than experimenter-induced moods to minimize demand problems. However, mood dependence does not necessarily obtain for naturally occurring moods (Hasher, Rose, Zacks, Sanft, & Doren, 1985; J. D. Mayer & Bremer, 1985).

One remaining puzzle may be clarified. As noted at the outset, drugs reliably produce state-dependent effects, although mood does not. One possible explanation is that the state-dependency effects of drugs operate more like arousal-dependent memory, an effect that does appear to be reliable (M. S. Clark, Milberg, & Erber, 1988; M. S. Clark, Milberg, & Ross, 1983). That is, maybe not matching the valence (e.g., happy mood at learning and testing) but matching the arousal (e.g., excited at learning and testing) creates a specific form of mood congruence. Affective arousal improves memory by conveying events' importance (Storbeck & Clore, 2008).

Network Model of Mood and Memory

One theory originally proposed to account for the various effects of mood on memory was a network model (Chapter 4; J. A. Singer & Salovey, 1988, for a review). The theory posits that emotion is simply a retrieval cue like any other. This means that memories or events that come to mind at the same time as a given emotion are linked to that emotion, and hence (indirectly) to other emotion-congruent memories or events. Mood-congruent memory thus has an advantage because the emotion provides an additional route to the item in memory. In this view, mood-congruent memory would be based on the retrieval advantage of similar affect attached to

Table 14.3 Mood state-dependent memory moderators

Effects are stronger for	Possible reasons
Early studies	Less rigorous procedures and more enthusiastic experimenters
Longer studies	Stronger mood induction and re-creation, more time for forgetting
Older participants	More sophisticated? More forgetful?
Paid participants	More motivated
Smaller samples	More intense mood inductions

Source: Adapted from Ucros (1989)

the mood and the inherent valence of the item to be recalled. And mood state-dependent memory would rely on similar affect associated with the item at learning and at retrieval.

However, subsequent research was disappointing in its attempts to support the facilitating effects of mood on perception of similarly toned material (G. H. Bower, 1987) and on mood state-dependent retrieval, as just noted. Moreover, the combined effect of conceptual and emotional relatedness in memory networks is not well supported (E. J. Johnson & Tversky, 1983). Overall, the network model of mood and memory "has not fared well: . . . a few successes and several glaring failures" (G. H. Bower, 1987, p. 454), suggesting that new frameworks are needed.

In general, mood state-dependent memory effects have been stronger given more possibility of experimental demand – more likelihood of the experimental participants accurately perceiving and responding to the investigators' hypotheses. Effects have been larger for (a) the earlier studies that perhaps involved less rigorous procedures and more enthusiastic experimenters, (b) studies involving longer experimental sessions, (c) studies with older and perhaps more sophisticated participants, (d) participants recruited for money rather than for course credit or on a voluntary basis, and (e) studies involving fewer participants and more intense mood inductions (Ucros, 1989; Table 14.3). One interpretation of the overall pattern of mood and memory results is that the studies work better when the induced moods are intense (J. D. Mayer & Salovey, 1988; Ucros, 1989); results are also stronger when participants are selected according to their responsiveness to the mood induction or when both naturally occurring moods and real-life events are used.

Conclusions about Mood and Memory

As we have seen, the evidence for mood-congruent memory is strong, while the evidence for mood state-dependent memory is weak. Despite the distinctions conventionally drawn (as here) between mood congruence and mood dependence, the distinction is not always clear in real life (Blaney, 1986; Ucros, 1989). Positive material often is acquired when one is in a positive mood or takes its positive interpretation from a positive context, thereby confounding the mood at learning with the valence of the material to be learned. Nevertheless, the two are at least conceptually distinct, and mood-congruence effects are far more reliable than mood-dependence effects.

Mood and Judgment

Politicians who smile can put their viewers in a good mood, and this translates to positive feelings about the officeholder or seeker; those who cry, scream, or frown risk negative mood-congruent responses (for a review, see Glaser & Salovey, 1998). Legal decision making is affected by emotion as well (for examples, see Bornstein & Wiener, 2006). One of the clearest effects in the mood literature is that cheerful people like just about everything better: themselves, their health, their cars, other people, the future, and even politics and criminal defendants (for reviews, see Bodenhausen, Kramer, & Süsser, 1994; Bodenhausen, Sheppard, & Kramer, 1994; Clore, Schwarz, & Conway, 1994; Crano & Prislin, 2006; Forgas, 1995; Petty, Wegener, & Fabrigar, 1997; Schwarz & Clore, 1996; Zajonc, 1998). Consider an interpersonal example: People viewing their behavior in replayed social interactions rate themselves more positively when happy (Forgas, Bower, & Krantz, 1984). This effect provides new perspective on those imaginary replays of one's behavior after a party, the interpretation of which apparently depends on the hour and condition in which one engages in such self-assessment.

The variety of cheery mood-based benevolence effects have led to the suggestion that one has multiple personalities, depending on one's current mood (G. H. Bower, 1990; cf. Epstein, 1990b). However, this phenomenon has some limits; for example, cheerful people do not overvalue the criminal and the unattractive (Forgas & Moylan, 1987; G. L. White, Fishbein, & Rutstein, 1981), and high levels of personal involvement may moderate mood-congruence effects (Branscombe & Cohen, 1990).

Is the converse true? Do unhappy people dislike everything? Sometimes, but the evidence is more mixed for many of the same reasons it is mixed for studies of negative mood and memory (M. S. Clark & Williamson, 1989; J. D. Mayer & Salovey, 1988). Accordingly, studies that include neutral control groups are more informative than studies that merely contrast positive and negative moods. That is, if one compares only positive and negative moods and obtains a difference, one does not know which mood had an effect relative to baseline. Frequently, negative mood effects do not differ from neutral mood effects, and sometimes they are even equivalent to positive mood effects, as people attempt to repair their negative moods. Hence, to detect negative mood effects, having a neutral control group is essential. Some effects have emerged from negative mood studies: For example, negative moods increase the perceived likelihood of future negative events (E. J. Johnson & Tversky, 1983). People judge other people according to negative applicable traits more when temporarily depressed than when in a neutral mood (Erber, 1991). Similarly, both temporary depression and a chronic negative outlook lead people to perceive themselves as having less social support (L. H. Cohen, Towbes, & Flocco, 1988; Vinokur, Schul, & Caplan, 1987). Other examples throughout this literature show negative mood-congruent judgments.

Some other intriguing puzzles remain in this line of work. For example, not only do positive (and sometimes negative) moods show congruence in judgments, but aroused moods show judgmental congruence effects as well (M. S. Clark, Milberg, & Erber, 1984; Stangor, 1990). That is, when people are physiologically aroused (e.g., by exercise), they make arousal-congruent judgments, viewing another's ambiguously positive facial expression as more joyous than serene and interpreting an ambiguous statement ("Just look at that sunset") as an exclamation rather than a sign of contentment.

Mood researchers are moving beyond valence and arousal to complex emotions. For example, two negative and potentially aroused emotions – anger and fear – have distinct effects on judgment (Lerner & Gonzalez, 2005; Lerner & Keltner, 2001). Fear increases the perceived risk of terrorist attacks, whereas anger decreases the perceived possibility (Fischhoff, Gonzalez, Lerner, & Small, 2005). When it comes to their own choices, fearful people are pessimistic and see increased risks; fear instills a prevention or avoidance orientation. In contrast, fitting its approach orientation, anger makes people optimistic and risk-seeking. Anger produces relatively pleasant judgments only when people appraise the future, not the past (Lerner & Tiedens, 2006).

When it comes to other people, angry people can be a menace, and sad people can be more careful and thoughtful. Anger facilitates automatic prejudices, whereas sadness neutralizes intergroup bias (DeSteno, Dasgupta, Bartlett, & Cajdric, 2004; cf. Bodenhausen, Sheppard, & Kramer, 1994). Anger fits intergroup competition, so it encourages prejudice. Similarly, angry and sad communications, respectively, persuade angry and sad recipients (DeSteno, Petty, Rucker, Wegener, & Braverman, 2004). Sadness and anger differentially bias the perceived likelihood of saddening and angering events (DeSteno, Petty, Wegener, & Rucker, 2000). In general, if the moods match the message, events, or recipient, then the affect-cognition effects appear strong.

Specific emotions matter in specific types of judgment. For example, many moral judgments respond to disgust. One study induced disgust by seating some participants on an old chair with a dirty, torn cushion, at a stained, sticky desk, with a chewed pen and a dried-up leftover smoothie, next to a trash can overflowing with a greasy pizza box and used tissues. Other participants landed in newer, cleaner surroundings. All then made moral judgments, reported various emotions, and completed a scale of **private body consciousness** (PBC) (e.g., responsive to own physical sensations of hunger, illness, mood; Table 14.4; L. C. Miller, Murphy, & Buss, 1981). For people high on PBC, disgust led to more severe moral judgments (Schnall, Haidt, Clore, & Jordan, 2008). Inducing disgust by hypnosis has the same effect (Wheatley & Haidt, 2005). People differ in their sensitivity to disgust across domains, including food, vermin, bodily products, and death (Haidt, McCauley, & Rozin, 1994). And cultures differ on the role of disgust in moral judgments. For example, cleaning a toilet with the country's flag might be seen by elite American college students as a matter of arbitrary convention, but by some other Americans and by Brazilian adults as intrinsically disgusting and immoral (Haidt, Koller, & Dias, 1993). Political conservatives have a multifaceted moral agenda predicted by disgust (e.g., viewing homosexuality as immoral). Liberals have a narrower moral agenda, emphasizing perceived threats to autonomy (e.g., degree of harm to others) versus, for example, threats to community or divinity (Haidt & Hersh, 2001). All these moral judgments rely on **intuition**, which includes sudden, conscious, emotional reactions, without awareness of having gone through prior calculations (Haidt, 2001).

Emotions in general influence a wide range of judgments, more than traditional decision-making research had acknowledged. In the words of one moral judgment theorist: "Moral emotions and intuitions drive moral reasoning, just as surely as a dog wags its tail" (Haidt, 2001, p. 830).

Open questions remain. Children, curiously, do not always show the same effects of positive and negative moods that adults do (Forgas, Burnham, & Trimboli, 1988; Masters & Furman,

Table 14.4   Body consciousness, private and public, sample items

Private body consciousness

I know immediately when my mouth or throat gets dry.
I can often feel my heart beating.

Public body consciousness

It's important for me that my skin looks nice
I like to make sure that my hair looks right.

Source: L. C. Miller, Murphy, & Buss (1981)

1976; cf. Barden, Garber, Leiman, Ford, & Masters, 1985). Why this is the case is not yet clear. Is it because the arousal component of their mood overwhelms its valence? Is it because they have less developed networks of associations? Is it because they are less well socialized into the culturally shared effects of moods? It remains to be seen.

Another challenge for research on mood and judgment is specifying the effects of mood-incongruent stimuli. For example, mood-incongruent stimuli may interfere with information processing, causing people to evaluate others via shortcuts such as **illusory correlation** (Mackie et al., 1989). Similarly, mood itself may distract people from elaborative processing (Asuncion & Lam, 1995). Certainly, some theories of emotion as an interruption (Chapter 13) would suggest that affect, regardless of congruence, can be disruptive. The role of moods – congruent or incongruent – as interfering with judgments is not well understood. Moreover, it would be reasonable to expect some incidence of mood-incongruent judgment effects, with the mood creating a contrast to the judged objects, although we have not seen clear demonstrations of this.

Another avenue for future research is specifying the neuroscience of emotion in decision making (Figure 14.1). In one model (Naqvi, Shiv, & Bechara, 2006), the amygdala is recruited in the sensory experience of rewards and punishments, consistent with its role in vigilance for emotionally significant events. Internal representations of the behavioral choices that brought about positive and negative experiences implicate the ventromedial prefrontal cortex (vmPFC). During subsequent decision making, the vmPFC and dorsolateral PFC re-create these representations. The mapping of these emotional-bodily states during decision making activates the insular cortex. For example, this area activates when participants evaluate the fairness of offers by another participant (Sanfey et al., 2003; Chapter 8). This type of insula activation may underlie visceral reactions or "gut feelings" about choices. Mesolimbic areas are implicated in the unconscious emotional biasing of choices in decision making. Moral decisions may be especially prone to emotional influences, as suggested by neuroimaging data (Greene, Somerville, Nystrom, Darley, & Cohen, 2001; Valdesolo & DeSteno, 2006).

Also, some people are more emotionally reactive than others. For example, an early family environment characterized by stress (e.g., harsh parenting) can carry over to dampen the typical amygdala response to fearful and angry faces (Taylor, Eisenberger, Saxbe, Lehman, & Lieberman, 2006). What's more, typically the amygdala is regulated through activation in the rvlPFC when people label their emotions, but this regulation does not occur for adults from risky families.

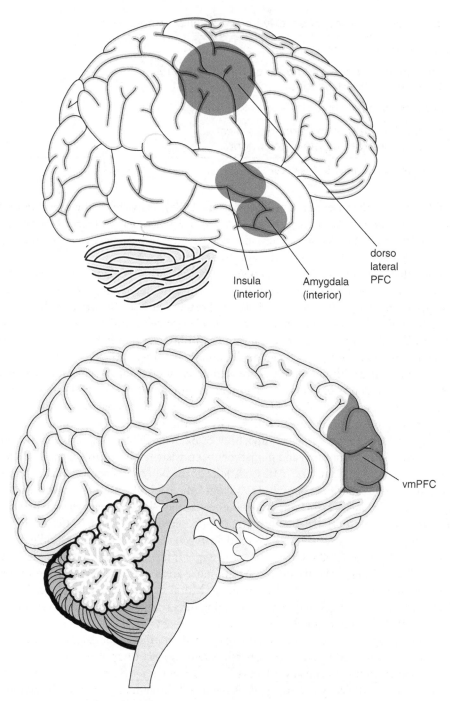

Figure 14.1   Brain areas implicated in choices

Thus, early experiences shape neural responses to emotional stimuli, and cognitive processes (labeling) can regulate (or fail to regulate) these reactions. These hypothesized mechanisms remain to be developed, and they are eliciting active research attention that will clarify the emotion–decision interaction.

Mood and Decision-Making Style

Mood not only influences what we remember and how positively we evaluate our world, but it also influences the manner in which we make judgments (for reviews, see Fiedler, 1988; Forgas, 1995; Isen, 1987). As early work indicated, elated people are expansive, inclusive, and somewhat impulsive; they make decisions quickly (Isen & Means, 1983), they work quickly at simple tasks (J. D. Mayer & Bremer, 1985), they group more varied things into the same category (Isen & Daubman, 1984), they see more unusual connections among things (Isen, Johnson, Mertz, & Robinson, 1985), they have looser and less-organized associations (Fiedler, 1988), they have more associations to positive words (J. D. Mayer, Mamberg, & Volanth, 1988), they are willing to take more risks if the possible losses are small (Isen & Geva, 1987), but losses loom larger to them (Isen, Nygren, & Ashby, 1988). Altogether, positive moods apparently are associated with factors conducive to creativity, and people will even claim a bad mood as an excuse for failure (Baumgardner, Lake, & Arkin, 1985).

As this work has continued, happy people emerge as especially flexible decision makers. Probably, happy people are not so much unmotivated or unable to process carefully as they are likely to interpret their mood as information indicating that all is well (Isbell, 2004), which is consistent with the **affect-as-information** approach (Schwarz, Bless, & Bohner, 1991). Admittedly, they often are satisfied with a quick, heuristic judgment (including stereotypes), but when motivated, they are perfectly capable of more detailed, controlled processing. Still, their tendency toward quick decisions may lead them astray, more readily relying on misinformation (Forgas, Laham & Vargas, 2005), more easily falling prey to the **fundamental attribution error** (Forgas, 1998), and being vulnerable to recognition errors from guessing (Bless et al., 1996). When personally uninvolved, happy people are more likely to discriminate impulsively, but when involved, they can be thoughtful (Forgas & Fiedler, 1996).

Sad people, on the other hand, are more likely to be careful and to mull over their decisions. For example, sad people feel alerted that something is amiss, so they correct their stereotypes (Lambert, Khan, Lickel, & Fricke, 1997). Guilt also makes people reconsider their stereotypic judgments (Chapter 11). But sad people in particular focus on details, neglecting the big picture (Gasper & Clore, 2002). Sad people attend to details such as being polite (Forgas, 1998), but they can also discriminate because their thoughtful processing leaves them open to the negative mood-congruent processing of detailed information (Forgas & Fiedler, 1996).

Mood and Persuasion

Along with being expansive and inclusive and generally pleasant to others, cheerful people are more compliant with persuasive communications, whereas angry or uncomfortable people are generally less compliant (see McGuire, 1985; Petty, Cacioppo, & Kasmer, 1988, for reviews). The positive mood results may explain the effectiveness of free samples, soothing music, and friendly banter in marketing, all of which increase positive moods and therefore, perhaps, persuasion. (But the effects of anger on noncompliance oddly do not seem to discourage the relentless programs of telephone charity appeals.)

Much of the mood and persuasion research was originally conducted under a **classical conditioning** paradigm, but subsequent studies have suggested some roles for cognitive processes. For example, not all persuasion is automatically enhanced by positive mood; perhaps positive mood enhances persuasion only under conditions of low involvement and low cognitive activity (Petty, Cacioppo, & Kasmer, 1988; Petty, Cacioppo, Sedikides, & Strathman, 1988; Petty, Gleicher, & Baker, 1991). Positive moods themselves can be distracting and reduce cognitive capacity, leading participants to superficial but still cognitively mediated processing of messages (Mackie & Worth, 1989; Worth & Mackie, 1987). Under conditions of moderate involvement, however, affect may enhance thought because of affect's arousing and attention-getting impact. Under conditions of high involvement, mood may serve an informative function relevant to one's possible reactions, or it may bias retrieval of relevant supporting information (Petty et al., 1988). Affect as information about the state of oneself and one's environment depends on ability and motivation to process a communication (Albarracín, 2002; Albarracín & Kumkale, 2003; Albarracín & Wyer, 2001). The effect may be curvilinear, with low levels of processing making affect unnoticed and high levels making it recognizably irrelevant. Moderate levels of affect would be noticed but not recognized as irrelevant (Figure 14.2).

As this work develops, more of it will likely focus on discrete emotions, not just general moods. Specific emotional states cue expectations for events that match that emotion. Hence, emotion-matching persuasion should be most effective (DeSteno et al., 2004). So far, though, most of the work focuses on positive or negative moods.

Mood affects attitudes through multiple processes (Petty, Wegener, & Fabrigar, 1997). Mood can act as an incidental, peripheral cue, but mood can also bias detailed processing of

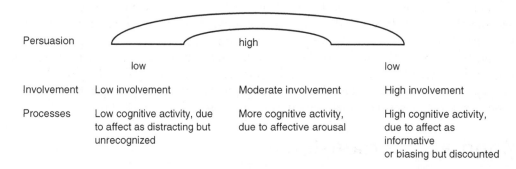

Figure 14.2　Hypothetical curvilinear effects of positive affect on persuasion

an argument, or even the sheer amount of processing that occurs. Multiple roles for mood thus aptly summarize a variety of mood effects on memory, judgment, decision-making style, and persuasion.

Mood and Well-Being

Cheerful people have a variety of advantages, as we have seen. These culminate in a wide array of general life outcomes: Being happy improves health, friendships, marriage, income, and performance (Lyubomirsky, King, & Diener, 2005). The evidence includes cross-sectional designs in which happiness–success correlations leave open the alternative possibility that success causes happiness. But the data also include numerous studies that are longitudinal (happiness precedes success) and experimental (manipulated happiness causes success). Frequent positive affect results from genetic set points in temperament, life circumstances, and specific activities (Lyubomirsky, Sheldon, & Schkade, 2005). Presumably, one has the most control over one's activities, habits, and practices, so these offer the best avenues for intervention. Positive affect specifically motivates effort on one's positive and active behavioral goals (Custers & Aarts, 2005), so this cognitive-affective mechanism might well account for the salutary effects of happiness.

AFFECT VERSUS COGNITION

We have examined research investigating some cognitive bases of emotional responses (last chapter) and some affective (mood) influences on cognition (this chapter). In the final section of this chapter, we examine the relationship between affect and cognition more explicitly, starting with the possibility that they are largely independent.

The Separate-Systems View

Despite the scientific and commonsense idea that we think about things in order to know how we feel, there is a case for affect preceding cognition rather than vice versa (Zajonc, 1980b). Indeed, some of us are constantly amazed at our own ability to make major life decisions on the basis of emotional preferences guided by no apparently relevant cognitive data. (Consider how you fell into your first serious romantic involvement or your earliest image of your career; some of us can find not one iota of rational cognitive analysis in those choices.) Affective processes may operate independently of cognitive processes in this view. Note that this is a controversial perspective, and it depends at a minimum on how one defines the terms *affect* and *cognition*. Before detailing the objections, it is useful to present the Zajonc argument and its evidence.

The **separate-systems view** suggests that affective and cognitive processes proceed in parallel paths without influencing each other much, under at least some circumstances. Affective processes are argued to occur at a more basic level than cognitive processes in several respects (Zajonc, 1980b):

- Affective reactions are primary. Evaluations are made and then justified; decisions are based on preference rather than computation. (Romantic involvements are a prime example of not choosing based on a cognitive list of pros and cons.)
- Affect is basic. Evaluation is a major and universal component of virtually all perception and meaning. It is difficult to understand something without evaluating it. (Consider a lonely person scouting for a mate, unable to meet anyone in any context without evaluating the person's potential availability.)
- Affective reactions are inescapable. They are demandingly present in a way that simple knowledge is not. (Attraction is harder to ignore than the other person's career plans.)
- Affective reactions tend to be irrevocable, in contrast to cognitive judgments. One's feelings cannot be wrong, but one's beliefs can be; hence, affect is less vulnerable to persuasion than cognition. (As parents of adolescents constantly discover, other people's feelings of love and anger do not respond well to counterargument.)
- Affect implicates the self. While cognitive judgments rest on features inherent in the object, affective judgments describe one's own reactions to the object. (One's affective response to another has everything to do with one's relationship to the other, but one's knowledge of the person does not necessarily.)
- Affective judgments are difficult to verbalize. Much emotional response is communicated nonverbally; words for affective reactions always seem to fall short of the experience. (Describing the superficial features of the loved one is easy, but communicating one's actual feeling of love challenges even the poets.)
- Affective reactions may not depend on cognition. The features that people use to discriminate a stimulus may not be the same features that they use to decide whether or not they like it. (Totaling up the lover's pros and cons does not necessarily predict one's feelings.)
- Affective reactions may be separated from content knowledge. One sometimes remembers how one feels about a person but cannot remember the details of where or how the person was previously encountered. (One may feel strongly about someone without remembering all the reasons why.)

Overall, this stimulating line of argument has proved controversial, so we will examine some of the relevant evidence and then some of the objections.

Evidence from Mere Exposure Research

The last pair of arguments – that affect may not depend on cognition and may be separated from knowledge of content – underlie a research program demonstrating that people can know how they feel about an object before they can recognize it. The opening bars of a classic old song on the radio may be enough to let us know whether or not this is a golden oldie we like, but many of us cannot identify it right away or even be completely certain we have heard it before. Many studies document this phenomenon of feeling a warm familiar glow that is accompanied by a total lack of recognition. More generally, people grow to like an initially unobjectionable stimulus the more frequently it is encountered; this is called the **mere exposure** effect (Zajonc, 1968a; Chapter 10).

In mere exposure studies, recall that people typically see a series of nonsense words, Chinese characters, or yearbook photographs, either many times or few times. The more often people are exposed to the stimulus, the more they favor it, and this effect replicates consistently (Kunst-Wilson & Zajonc, 1980; for a review, see Bornstein, 1989). People prefer the frequent stimuli to the less frequent stimuli, even when they can only recognize them both at levels approximating chance guessing. One study found that mere exposure to Japanese ideographs influenced affect, independent of recognition for them (Moreland & Zajonc, 1977; for debate, see Birnbaum & Mellers, 1979a, 1979b; Moreland & Zajonc, 1979). Liking for frequently heard tone sequences was found consistently, even though the tones were recognized as familiar only at approximately chance levels (W. R. Wilson, 1979). Further evidence came from a study using a **dichotic listening task** in which the experimenter presented the tones in one ear but focused participants' attention on a literary passage presented to the other ear. Using this task, one can virtually eliminate recognition for the tone sequences, leaving affective reactions intact (Figure 14.3). Similar results have been obtained with more engaging stimuli, such as the photographs and interests of fellow students (Moreland & Zajonc, 1982). The effects are generally strongest for meaningful words (including names), polygons, and photographs, and they do not occur reliably for paintings, drawings, and matrices (Bornstein, 1989). Moreover, the effects are stronger for **subliminal** than for supraliminal presentation (Bornstein & D'Agostino, 1992; Janiszewski, 1993; cf. Murphy et al., 1995).

Apparently, affective processes more than cognitive ones underlie the mere exposure effect. A dissenting view has suggested, however, that brief repeated exposure activates a simple schema, which affects judgments of familiarity and liking, but also brightness, darkness, or any other stimulus-relevant judgment (G. Mandler, Nakamura, & Van Zandt, 1987); this view rejects the idea that mere exposure effects are noncognitive.

Related to this idea is perceptual **fluency**. That is, a stimulus is more easily processed after an initial exposure, and people sometimes correctly attribute that ease of processing to indeed having seen it before (see Koriat, Goldsmith, & Pansky, 2000, for a review). But sometimes people just have a feeling of familiarity from fluency, not being explicitly aware of having seen it before. The fluency mechanism in this case would not be strictly cognition or affect, just the ease of encoding, which presumably increases with mere exposure. In support of this mechanism, perceptual fluency is experienced as affectively positive (Winkielman & Cacioppo, 2001) and is attributed to positive features (Reber, Schwarz, & Winkielman, 2004; Reber, Winkielman, & Schwarz, 1998), increasing liking. Indeed, perceptual fluency increases mere exposure effects, but only if the person does not attribute the ease of processing to prior exposure (Bornstein & D'Agostino, 1994). Clearly, mere exposure effects on liking (and perhaps on other judgments) do not depend on conscious recognition of the stimuli, itself an impressive effect.

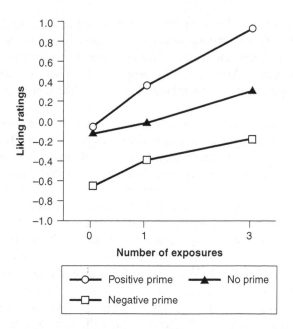

Figure 14.3   Liking as a function of suboptimal affective primes and number of exposures

Source: From S. T. Murphy et al. (1995). Copyright 1995 by the American Psychological Association. Reprinted by permission

Evidence from Person Perception, Attribution, and Attitude Research

A wide range of affective variables are independent of seemingly relevant cognitive variables. For example, evaluative impressions (one kind of affect) can be independent of memory for the details on which they were based (one kind of relevant cognition). This occurs when impressions are formed online, at the time of the initial encounter (N. H. Anderson & Hubert, 1963; Bargh & Thein, 1985; Dreben, Fiske, & Hastie, 1979; Riskey, 1979; for a review, see Hastie & Park, 1986). Thus, as you are forming an impression of someone at a party, your affective response is likely to occur independently of your later ability to remember details about the person. The exception to this apparent independence of affective responses and memory for the data on which they were based occurs when people are overloaded at the time of the encounter and do not have the motivation or the individual capacity to form an evaluative impression; in this case, their impression is memory based (Bargh & Thein, 1985). More generally, though, other social judgments and recall are often uncorrelated (Chapter 4; S. T. Fiske, Kenny, & Taylor, 1982; S. T. Fiske, Taylor, Etcoff, & Laufer, 1979).

Affective judgments are not necessarily based on recallable cognitions; instead they often are based on evaluations formed online. This implies that some affective reactions are better characterized as immediate responses. One must then entertain the related possibility that affective responses are also relatively direct and noncognitive. The concept of separate stores for evaluative and cognitive content (N. H. Anderson & Hubert, 1963) is one description of this process. The notion of affective reactions as a direct result of initial categorization (S. T. Fiske, 1982; S. T. Fiske & Neuberg, 1990) is another. The idea that attitude objects can directly cue the relevant attitude is also pertinent (Fazio, Powell, & Herr, 1983). Affect may have primacy in evaluative judgments (Cervellon & Dubé, 2002; Huskinson & Haddock, 2004), although this may be most true for extreme attitudes (Giner-Sorolla, 1999, 2001). Much other relevant work demonstrates the importance of online processes in affective responses (Chapters 2–3), and at least some emotional responses (startle and pupil dilation) are not preceded by identifying and judging stimuli (Schmidt-Atzert, 1988).

Objections

Quite a few theorists have responded to Zajonc's (1980b) view of emotion as a system separate from cognition. The objections have centered around the existence of nonconscious cognitive processes, the possibility of subsuming affect under other forms of cognition, the definitions of both cognition and affect, and the problems in empirically comparing the two.

Among the first to respond to Zajonc was Lazarus (1982, 1984), whose emotion theory depends on the appraisal of personal meaning (Chapter 13). Lazarus argued that cognition, defined as appraisal, is necessary for emotion; appraisal interprets meaningful stimuli in terms of their significance for personal well-being. In this view, appraisal is not regarded as deliberate, rational, and conscious because it occurs from the very beginning of perceiving environmental inputs, not at the end of a long chain of serial, complete, thorough information processing. Similarly, Epstein (1983, 1984) argued that preconscious cognitions usually precede emotions, and that the Zajonc approach implicitly defines cognition as conscious, when it need not be. Thus, some form of intuitive, preconscious, unintentional cognitive appraisal is seen as an integral part of all emotion. Zajonc (1984) argued that this definition of cognitive appraisal blurs the distinction between perception and cognition and that the Lazarus concept of emotion arbitrarily requires cognitive appraisal by definition. Clearly, the two viewpoints differ as to the defining features of emotion and of cognition and therefore differ as to the separation between the two.

Two other critiques of the Zajonc definitions of cognition and affect begin with the observation that cognitions can be rapid, unconscious, and automatic, just as affect is presumed to be; further, like affect, cognition can be irrational and can be tied to motor involvement (Holyoak & Gordon, 1984). In this view, the distinctions are less important than the possibility of subsuming both cognition and affect within one mental system.

A related proposal specifically relies on the procedural view of memory (Chapter 4); this view of memory depends on highly practiced mental activities that become more rapid as they are repeated. In this view, emotion can result from unconscious pattern-matching to emotional procedures, as well as from consciously accessible nonprocedural knowledge (Branscombe, 1988). Both of these efforts subsume affect under traditionally cognitive frameworks. Others have similarly argued that affect should be treated just like all other kinds of information (N. H. Anderson, 1981).

Another possible resolution comes from recognizing two meanings of cognition (Averill, 1990a). The first, **cognition₁**, is intellective knowledge acquisition, which is the everyday (dictionary) meaning of cognition. The contrast to intellective cognition is value-laden, intuitive, or irrational thinking. The other meaning, **cognition₂**, subsumes all mental activity, as compared to behavior. This second meaning of cognition – that is, any nonbehavioral mental activity – is closer to the meaning of cognition as discussed, for example, by Lazarus in defining appraisal as a form of cognitive activity. Emotions are noncognitive in the first sense only, being nonintellective cognition – that is, being more value-laden, intuitive, and irrational. Emotions are, however, cognitive₂ in the sense of being generic mental processes.

The most useful point is that emotions as mental processes tend to be distinguished from intellective cognition, in typical ways:

- Emotion concerns the person's own experience as subject or origin rather than focusing on the object itself out there.
- Emotion tends to influence perceived "reality," whereas thinking to a greater extent accommodates to reality.
- Emotion views the target as important for its relationship to the person, but intellective cognition emphasizes an object's relationship to other external objects.
- Emotion involves physiological experiences, not just environmental inputs.
- Emotion regulates the intensity and style of behavior rather than the goal-directed efficiency of behavior.
- Emotion is experienced passively or as a reaction to the stimulus, but people experience themselves as the source of intellective cognition.
- Emotion commits one to action more than does the cost–benefit calculation of intellective cognition.
- Emotion norms are moral and aesthetic, whereas intellective norms are rational.
- Emotion helps define the self, rather than the world.

This is not to say that intellective cognition is necessarily rational, merely that it displays all these features less often than does emotion (cf. Epstein, 1990a).

So far, we have focused on definitional issues regarding cognition and emotion or cognition *per se*. Of course, the resolution to this debate also depends on how one defines **emotion**. For example, the original Zajonc article focused on **preferences** (**evaluations**, affective judgments, liking) rather than on **moods** or on full-blown emotional episodes (J. A. Russell & Woudzia, 1986). Moods and emotions, many would argue, do intrinsically depend on cognitively driven appraisal processes (e.g., see theories of Lazarus, and Ellsworth & Smith, in Chapter 13). Preferences are relatively simple affective responses, distinguished mainly by valence, so some of the Zajonc results may pertain primarily to simple preferences and not so much to full-blown complex emotions.

Others suggest that the entire distinction is largely definitional and therefore not constructively pursued (Leventhal, 1984; Leventhal & Scherer, 1987). Instead, they suggest viewing emotion as developing from sensory–motor processes to complex cognitive–emotional patterns. Each level along this continuum entails distinct levels of memory and information processing. Each level also involves continuous appraisals (checks on the organism–environment relationship).

To all this, we would add only that comparing cognition and affect has inherent problems. Implicit in our discussion so far has been the idea that affect and cognition are somehow comparable. Judgments representing affect have included evaluation, preference, and differentiated emotions, while reactions representing cognition have included attention, inference, and memory. How does one decide what are the relevant cognitions and what are the comparable affective responses?

One study illustrates the complexity of this problem. In a mere exposure experiment, participants rated their recognition and liking for random polygons that had been presented at varying frequencies. Although recognition accuracy was only at chance levels, participants liked the familiar polygons better than the unfamiliar ones, confirming the standard mere exposure effect and that liking need not depend on accurate memory (Kunst-Wilson & Zajonc, 1980). But in what sense is recognition accuracy comparable to liking? The study assessed two other variables that help answer this question. Affective judgments were made more confidently and somewhat faster than recognition judgments.

Nevertheless, speed and confidence may not be the appropriate dimensions for comparing affect and cognition. The appropriate empirical tests depend on the conceptual definitions of affect and cognition, matters of some controversy, as noted. For example, affect and cognition have been distinguished, respectively, as sensory versus inferential, physiological versus mental, motor versus perceptual, innate versus learned, preference versus knowledge, and liking versus discrimination. How one defines and compares affect and cognition will depend on which of these dimensions one emphasizes.

One can also question whether these are fair tests because people can be wrong about a recognition judgment but not about an affective judgment. One can also argue that recognition judgments are more complex. But the two types of judgment intrinsically differ in these ways, and one cannot make them more similar without destroying them as realistic judgments of their type. Affective judgments are by their nature subjective, simple, and direct. Trying to specify a cognitive response that is truly equivalent to a given affective response may be a losing proposition.

Trying to establish the independence of affect and cognition is also, essentially, trying to establish the **null hypothesis**. To the extent one argues that they are independent, one is trying to establish the absence of a relationship. This is a thankless task, as any statistics professor will insist if someone tries to prove the null hypothesis of no relationship. The more sensible task is to show on what each is based, if not entirely on each other (Zajonc, Pietromonaco, & Bargh, 1982). And because the separation is not complete, another task is to show the ways in which they do relate. The work reviewed in this and the previous chapter does just that.

Summary

In addition to considering the various influences of cognition on affect (Chapter 13), a considerable body of research has considered the influences of affect on cognition, and in particular, the influences of mood. This research finds clear effects even of small mood manipulations on a variety of cognitive processes. The effects for positive mood are more clear-cut than the effects of negative mood in general. Positive moods lead to more prosocial behavior. These robust effects may be explained by the cheerful person's sensitivity to positive reinforcement; helping in a good mood is enhanced by focus of attention on oneself, requests emphasizing the rewards of helping, an emphasis on a positive social outlook, and the opportunity to maintain one's positive mood. People in a negative mood may or may not be helpful, depending on the circumstances.

Mood reliably increases people's memory for mood-congruent material due to both automatic and controlled processes. Effects for positive moods are stronger than those for negative moods, with the exception of people who are chronically depressed, who also show strong mood-congruent memory. Another mood-memory phenomenon, mood state-dependent memory, posited that people would best recall material that was learned and retrieved in the same mood state; this hypothesis has little support.

Mood generally influences judgment in a mood-congruent direction as well. Arousal similarly creates arousal-congruent judgments. Again, the effects of positive mood are more reliable than the effects of negative moods. Moreover, the effects on adults are more reliable than the effects on children. Various explanations for the effects have been proposed but, for the most part, remain to be tested. Mood also affects people's style of decision making, with positive moods making people more expansive, inclusive, impulsive, and perhaps creative. Positive moods also make people more compliant toward attempts at persuasion, at least under low involvement.

The contrast between affect and cognition has been hotly debated, leading to a proposal that they are separate systems with affect being primary. Evidence from mere exposure and person perception research is cited in support of this perspective; people report liking frequently encountered stimuli they cannot discriminate as familiar, and people's evaluative judgments are often made online, without recall for the data on which they were based. Objections to this perspective have focused on the possibility of nonconscious cognitive processes, the role of affect within broader (cognitive) representational systems, the problems of defining both affect and cognition, and empirical tests of the differences. The most constructive course seems to be to examine the bases of each and to investigate the multiple ways in which they do relate, as reviewed here.

FURTHER READING

Hostetter, A. B., Alibali, M. W., & Niedenthal, P. M. (2012). Embodied social thought: Linking social concepts, emotion, and gesture. In S. T. Fiske & C. N. Macrae (Eds.), *Sage handbook of social cognition* (pp. 211–228). Thousand Oaks, CA: Sage.

Keltner, D., & Lerner, J. S. (2010). Emotion. In S. T. Fiske, D. T. Gilbert, & G. Lindzey (Eds.), *Handbook of social psychology* (5th edn, Vol. 1, pp. 317–352). Hoboken, NJ: Wiley.

Mesquita, B., Marinetti, C., & Delvaux, E. (2012). The social psychology of emotion. In S. T. Fiske & C. N. Macrae (Eds.), *Sage handbook of social cognition* (pp. 290–310). Thousand Oaks, CA: Sage.

Niedenthal, P. M., Barsalou, L. W., Winkielman, P., Krauth-Gruber, S., & Ric, F. (2005). Embodiment in attitudes, social perception, and emotion. *Personality and Social Psychology Review, 9*, 184–211.

Zajonc, R. B. (1980b). Feeling and thinking: Preferences need no inferences. *American Psychologist, 35*, 151–175.

Behavior and Cognition   15

- Goal-Directed Behavior
- When are Cognitions and Behavior Related?
- Using Behavior for Impression Management
- Using Behavior to Test Hypotheses about Others

Most social cognition research assumes that cognitions develop partly so that people will know how to behave: Thinking is for doing (Fiske, 1992). For example, if a supervisor is rude to a coworker, one tries to infer whether the supervisor is a disagreeable person, it has been a bad day, or the coworker has done something to deserve the treatment. Through this kind of analysis, one infers whether or not to stay out of the way of the supervisor. In this sense, cognitions give rise to behavior. Daily interactions with others also provide a constant source of information, some redundant and much new, that must be incorporated into cognitive representations. Hence, behavior also gives rise to cognitions. This chapter explores relationships between cognitions and behavior.

GOAL-DIRECTED BEHAVIOR

Chapter 5 introduced **self-regulation**, how people control and direct their behavior. **Goals** are clearly central to this process. How individuals behave depends on how they define their situation with respect to personal interests and goals. For example, two people can attend an office party with different goals in mind: One person may have the goal of impressing the boss; another may regard the same occasion as an opportunity to grab a couple of quick drinks with friends before going home. The different behaviors of these two people depend on the goals they have constructed and the strategies and plans devised for meeting those goals.

Despite the close relationship between personal goals and behavior in a given social setting, people show remarkable flexibility in adjusting as situations change. They can take active control of their thoughts and their plans; they can review several alternatives for interpreting the same event; and they change their knowledge through feedback from new experiences, reworking existing beliefs, values, and goals (Showers & Cantor, 1985). For example, the woman intent on impressing her boss may shift her goal to impressing her coworkers if she learns that her boss has been called away from the office party. Similarly, the man planning to have a couple of drinks with friends may leave the party early if none of his friends attend. This behavioral flexibility provides an antidote to some research on cognitive representations, which implicitly suggests that behavior is always automatically enacted in response to preexisting conceptions.

Affective states and emotional responses to situations also influence behavior (Chapters 13–14). People in a good mood behave to further that mood, whereas those in a bad mood often try to improve their mood. More generally, people in a positive mood appear to have more flexibility and awareness of multiple ways of dealing with situations, whereas poor mood is tied to more rigid strategies of social interaction. In these ways, then, cognitions and affect can have powerful joint regulatory effects on behavior (Ickes, Robertson, Tooke, & Teng, 1986; Showers & Cantor, 1985). Cognitive and affective influences on behavior are often functionally inseparable and difficult to distinguish, reciprocally influencing each other and changing in response to behavioral feedback (Aarts, 2012).

Planning and Behavior

In social situations people implicitly ask questions such as: What is going on here? Who are these people? What are they doing, and what do they want of me? What are my own goals? Do my goals conflict with theirs, and if so, how do I choose? How can I achieve the goals that I select, and how do I pick among the available strategies? What are the consequences for being wrong, and how can I recover from my mistakes? What consequences will my choices have for others, and what can I do about their reactions? The wealth of knowledge, plans, and strategies that people bring to answering these questions in social interactions is **social intelligence**. It consists of concept knowledge, such as facts about situations and people, and rule knowledge, including how we categorize, judge and infer, solve problems, and perform actions (Cantor & Kihlstrom, 1985; cf. S. J. Read & Miller, 1989).[1] The specific cognitions people use to self-regulate their behavior are idiosyncratic, given individual differences in memories, concepts, and rules for self, social situations, and people, based on past personal experience.

So far, we have implied that people manage their behavior by defining their situations and by developing appropriate plans for realizing whatever goals might be achieved. But remember that people actively choose and construct situations as well. Thus, for example, an employee who wishes to impress his boss need not wait for an office party. He may arrange a dinner party for boss, ask the boss out for lunch, hang around the men's room waiting for him to show up, or

---

[1] Note that Cantor and Kihlstrom's use of the term **social intelligence** includes the various knowledge, talents, plans, and strategies, as well as interpersonal skills, that people bring to social situations. Others (e.g., Allport, 1935; S. J. Read & Miller, 1989) reserve the same term only for social, expressive, and communicative skills, a more restricted use of the term.

otherwise actively create situations in service of his goals (Showers & Cantor, 1985; M. Snyder, 1982). As these examples suggest, personal goals often entail conscious planning (Aarts, 2012).

To understand how people construct situations that meet personal goals, divide the process into stages, motivational and volitional (Gollwitzer, 1990; Heckhausen & Gollwitzer, 1987; Table 15.1). The initial motivation phase involves a **deliberative mindset** focused on incentives and expectations, choosing among alternative goals and their implied courses of action. An employee at an office party may, for example, regard the party as an opportunity to impress her boss, to make an advance on a coworker, or to coordinate problem-solving with her office team. Each goal would provide different incentives and different behavior during the party.

The motivational, deliberative mindset ends with a decision, a more or less conscious choice that then leads to a volitional, **implementational mindset**. Volition involves the consideration of when and how to act so as to implement the intended course of action. Selection among alternative paths depends on volitional strength, including how feasible, desirable, and urgent a particular goal is, and on how much the situation favors realizing a goal. Recognizing that the boss is already launched in conversation and that the attractive coworker keeps looking at his watch as if ready to leave, the employee may decide to use the party as an opportunity to brainstorm with the fellow team member. After this decision, she may be oblivious to any further actions of her boss or the attractive coworker, instead deploying her efforts to the goal she has chosen to pursue. As these observations imply, selecting a focal goal leads to **goal-shielding**, whereby the activated focal goal inhibits alternative goals' accessibility. When focal-goal commitment is high, so is goal-related tenacity and goal pursuit. Thus, goal-shielding has beneficial consequences for goal attainment (Shah, Friedman, & Kruglanski, 2002). However, if alternative goals (e.g., impressing a coworker) become subgoals of a larger goal (e.g., increasing one's visibility at work), people do not goal-shield but simultaneously pursue the secondary, complementary goal (Fishbach, Dhar, & Zhang, 2006).

Deliberative (motivational) and implementational (volitional) mindsets prompt different cognitions. In a deliberative mindset, for example, people weigh alternatives in a relatively even-handed manner, considering factors that both favor and oppose an action (Taylor & Gollwitzer, 1995). Open-minded, they attend to both incidental and diagnostic information (Fujita, Gollwitzer, & Oettingen, 2007). Once having selected a course of action, however, the

Table 15.1 Mindsets for planning behavior

Stage:	Deliberative	Implementational
Mindset:	Motivation	Volition
Focus:	Incentives	Feasibility
	Expectancies	Desirability
		Urgency
Process:	Choose among alternatives	Pursue chosen goal
Approach:	Even-handed balance	Goal-shielding

Note: For details, see e.g. Gollwitzer & Sheeran (2006).

implementation mindset assesses situational contingencies that favor the selected action. For example, in one study, participants were induced either to deliberate the merits of participating in a scavenger hunt or to imagine implementing a plan to complete the task (Armor & Taylor, 2003). Participants then participated in the scavenger hunt. Those in a deliberative mindset initially formed more pessimistic expectations about how many objects they might find and subsequently found fewer objects, relative to implementational-mindset participants, who formed overly optimistic expectations about their likely performance but actually performed well.

What accounts for persistence toward activated goals? Is it the goal itself? During implementation, the affect associated with anticipated goal attainment may transfer to the means for achieving those goals. Thus, if invested in a particular goal, and seeing particular means as essential to achieving the goal, the affect associated with the goal will likely transfer to the means, and this will further efforts to pursue goal-related activities (e.g., Fishbach, Shah, & Kruglanski, 2004).

Sometimes goal intentions are not enough. Even though we hold goals for ourselves, our behavior fails to correspond with those goals. A number of factors may bring behavior in line with personal goals. One of these is the explicit formation of **implementation intentions**; that is, people not only formulate their goals but make explicit if–then plans that specify how to realize a goal. When a person makes an explicit implementation intention, this enhances the likelihood of making progress toward that goal. For example, consider a graduate student who wants to write a research paper, but thus far has been only somewhat successful in doing so. One possibility for making progress is to create implementation intentions that produce automatic action control. If you make writing the first task you undertake each morning and pursue it for two hours before undertaking other tasks (such as teaching, meeting with undergraduates, and going to classes), then you no longer have to rely on conscious planning to write. Writing each morning becomes automatically under the control of situational cues. Implementation intentions may further goals (Sheeran, Webb, & Gollwitzer, 2005). More than 94 studies indicate that forming implementation intentions fosters goal attainment (Gollwitzer & Sheeran, 2006).

Planning for achieving goals is not without pitfalls. Typically people are overly optimistic about how quickly they will accomplish their goals. Many of us make a daily to-do list, created in a fit of unrealistic optimism at the beginning of the day, only to discover that most tasks remain undone at the end of the day. For example, we may habitually take home a load of work to do over the weekend and bring most of it back again on Monday. Demonstrating this **planning fallacy** in one study (Buehler, Griffin, and Ross (1994), students completing senior theses estimated when the thesis would be completed and when it would be completed if the worst possible problems intervened. Only one third of the students finished their projects by their predicted completion times, and many remaining students went well beyond the worst possible completion date. Nonetheless, everyone completed the project, and perhaps could not have done so without the initially overly optimistic expectations. Although making expectations more realistic might seem useful, overly optimistic expectations ensure that people accomplish more in a given time than they would otherwise (Armor & Taylor, 1998).

Following goal pursuit, a person may evaluate goal success and whether outcomes match their expected value. Such post-action evaluations contribute to future goal setting. Thus, goals relate to behavior across time, with different cognitive activities directing action at different points in the motivation–action–evaluation sequence.

Automatic Goal Pursuit

Although goal-related self-regulation sometimes involves conscious choices, much self-regulatory activity proceeds mindlessly without awareness (Bargh, 1997; Bargh, Gollwitzer, Lee-Chai, Barndollar, & Trötschel, 2001; Dijksterhuis & Bargh, 2001; Macrae & Miles, 2012). Some goals that influence behavior are chronic concerns, such as the desire to be liked, which may automatically elicit smiling and deferential behavior (Levesque & Pelletier, 2003). Indeed, a habit may be partly an association between a goal and an action, so that if the goal is primed, the action will occur automatically. You may have had the experience of thinking about something you needed to do at school and discovered that you are now driving in that direction even though you were headed somewhere else. Or perhaps you made late dinner plans with friends and found yourself accidentally cooking at your usual time. Many habits do indeed seem to be a result of goal-dependent automatic behavior (Aarts, 2012; Aarts & Dijksterhuis, 2000; Wood, Quinn, & Kashy, 2002), including those related to seemingly complex social interactions with others (Bargh & Williams, 2006). The fact that our behavior often occurs as automatic responses to cues that are rapidly, effortlessly, and unconsciously processed helps explain how people go about the tasks of daily living with so little apparent thought, so often creatures of our own habits.

Essentially, years of practice responding to cues in the environment automate our emotional, cognitive, and behavioral responses to many situations (Aarts & Dijksterhuis, 2003). We respond to evaluative cues in the environment without needing to attend to them or think about them (Roser & Gazzaniga, 2004; Chapters 9–10, 13–14). For example, we have had so many experiences with social occasions that we can regulate our behavior with respect to our goals quite unconsciously, and it may take a flaw in the plan to make salient and conscious both our personal goals for a situation and the strategies designed to achieve them. Familiar situations tend to inspire mindless behavior, whereas unfamiliar situations are more likely to evoke conscious, self-regulatory efforts (Cantor & Kihlstrom, 1985). For example, the process of meeting new acquaintances in Japan may prompt an American to become intensely aware of the dynamics of social situations, inasmuch as most Westerners do not have well-developed knowledge of the norms and appropriate behaviors for many Japanese social settings.

Expertise also determines how self-consciously and how successfully people self-regulate. People who feel uncertain are more likely to try to identify the prototypic actions that are successful in social situations, compared with people who are more aware of the competencies required in any given setting (Cantor, Mackie, & Lord, 1983–1984; Showers & Cantor, 1985; Wicklund & Braun, 1987). Uncertain, confused people are also more likely to characterize others through the ascription of dispositional attributions, typing them as particular sorts of people. This rigidity in perceptions may give their own behavior a certain flat, unresponsive quality, compared to those able to maintain a more flexible fit between their cognitive-behavioral repertoire and the environment (Wicklund, 1986).

Nonverbal behavior can also reflect social goals automatically. People often nonconsciously mimic the postures, mannerisms, and facial expressions of the people with whom they are interacting. This is easy to demonstrate on your own. Smile at a person with whom you are speaking and see if your smile isn't reciprocated. Then cross your arms and see if your partner doesn't mirror that behavior. Nonconscious mimicry shows how we use environmental cues as bases for our own behavior without awareness or intention (Chartrand & Bargh, 1999).

These examples illustrate that links between perception and action are automatic bases not only of social understanding but also of social interaction (Knoblich & Sebanz, 2006). Mirror neurons (e.g., Rizzolatti, Fogassi, & Gallese, 2001; Figure 15.1), located in the premotor cortex, activate both when a person watches someone else act and when performing the action. For example, people show mirror neuron activation (as well as muscle twitches) reflecting the action sequences they observe another person doing, and the activation is stronger the more expert they are in the activity (e.g., Calvo-Merino, Glaser, Grezes, Passingham, & Haggard, 2005); this activation is strongest when one observes one's own past performance. Mirror neurons appear to link situational cues to the automatic performance of behavior in socially interactive settings.

Automatic evaluation occurs rapidly, within milliseconds (Chapter 10). For example, in one study participants were presented with word-pair sequences and asked to judge whether target adjectives were negative or positive (Fazio, Sanbonmatsu, Powell, & Kardes, 1986). The first, a prime, appeared for 200 msec, and the second, the target word, appeared 100 msec after the

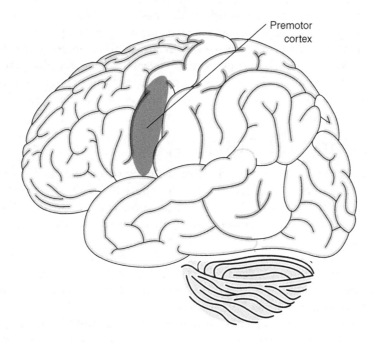

Figure 15.1 Mirror neurons

prime had disappeared. Despite the speed at which this task had to be accomplished, participants' ratings of the target word as positive or negative were much faster when the prime and the target had the same evaluative content (i.e., both words were negative or both were positive) than when they were incongruent.

Automatic evaluation can affect seemingly complex behavioral sequences as well. In one study, participants were given word puzzles to solve that contained words suggesting either rudeness or politeness (Bargh, Chen, & Burrows, 1996). Following the puzzle task, participants were sent down the hall to a room to get credit for the experiment. However, the person who was to give the credit was involved in a lengthy personal phone conversation with a friend and did not respond to the participant. Priming affected how long it took the participant to interrupt the ongoing conversation. Whereas 63% of the group primed with "rude" words interrupted, only 17% of the "polite" group did.

Not only can cues in the environment automatically prime behavior, but also evaluative cues may be among the most potent influences on subsequent information and behavior. When people have clear goals, goal-relevant cues become positive, suggesting that automatic evaluation can help to maintain goal pursuit (Custers & Aarts, 2005; Ferguson & Bargh, 2004b). Evaluatively toned latent stimuli are quickly noticed and prompt behavioral tendencies toward approach or avoidance (Chen & Bargh, 1999; Wentura, Rothermund, & Bak, 2000). Recall that participants responded faster to positive attitude statements by moving a lever toward them or and faster to negative ones by pushing it away (Chen & Bargh, 1999; Neumann & Strack, 2000; Chapter 4). Relatedly, when people face temptations they want to avoid, they are quick to push away temptation-related stimuli and faster to pull toward their approach goals (Fishbach & Shah, 2006).

In similar ways, unobtrusively primed stereotypes can influence subsequent behaviors (Mussweiler, 2006). In one study, participants were unobtrusively induced to move in the ungainly manner that is stereotypic of overweight people. Subsequently, when presented with an ambiguous target to evaluate, they attributed more overweight-stereotypic characteristics to the target than did participants in the control condition. Thus, not only do unobtrusive primes affect behavior, the feedback from one's own behavior may inadvertently influence subsequent cognitions.

Assimilation and Contrast

Many automatic behaviors do show **assimilation** to environmental cues. When an elderly stereotype is primed, we walk more slowly, or when induced to walk as an overweight person, we ascribe overweight stereotypic attributes to an ambiguous target. Sometimes, however, seeing one thing leads to doing another: **contrast** effects in automatic behavior (Dijksterhuis et al., 1998). For example, participants who had positive attitudes toward the elderly walked more slowly after being primed with the elderly stereotype, but participants who had negative attitudes toward the elderly actually walked faster (e.g., Cesario, Plaks, & Higgins, 2006). Hence, contrast effects may also occur in automatic behavior, and these contrast effects may be due to the cognitive processes of preparing for joint action.

Whereas traits and stereotypes tend to elicit assimilation, **exemplars** (that is, typical or good examples) appear to elicit judgmental contrast by evoking social comparison. In one study, participants were primed either with stereotypes of professors or supermodels or they were primed with exemplars of those categories (Albert Einstein and Claudia Schiffer, respectively). Being primed by the stereotypes led to behavioral assimilation: Participants got more answers right on a subsequent knowledge test if they had been primed with the "professor" stereotype and fewer items correct if they had been primed with the "model" stereotype. However, participants primed with the exemplars demonstrated contrast effects; that is, those primed with Albert Einstein did more poorly, and those primed with Claudia Schiffer did better. When presented with the specific exemplars, participants apparently engaged in social comparison, concluding "I could never do as well as Albert Einstein" or "I can certainly do better than Claudia Schiffer." When only the stereotype was primed, no social comparison was evoked, and assimilation of performance to the stereotype occurred (Dijksterhuis & van Knippenberg, 1998).

Individual Differences and Goals

Different people relate a situational cue to their own circumstances in different ways, and thus the same prime can have quite different effects. In a sequential priming paradigm (Mussweiler & Förster, 2000), men first primed with aggression-related words (e.g., violence) and then primed with sex-related words responded more aggressively (throwing darts at faces), but only if the target face was female; however, parallel effects did not occur for women.

Whether one adopts a **promotion** or **prevention focus** influences behavior toward a goal (Chapter 5). Promotion focus involves aspiration, and goal-attainment brings a sense of accomplishment (e.g., getting a high grade in a course). By contrast, other goals have a prevention focus (e.g., not failing a course), which involves a sense of responsibility, and goal-attainment brings a sense of security. Commitment to promotion-goal accomplishment encourages performance to reach the goal, whereas prevention-goal commitment to security goals is characterized by doing what is necessary (Shah, Higgins, & Friedman, 1998). Whether one adopts a promotion or a prevention focus also influences emotional responses to goals. Under promotion focus, goal attainment yields greater cheerfulness and less dejection, whereas under prevention focus, goal attainment yields greater calm and less agitation (Higgins, Shah, & Friedman, 1997).

Goals can be idiosyncratically primed by activating representations of a significant other. Which regulatory goals are activated will be influenced by the expectations those others are perceived to have with respect to one's own personal goals. For example, suppose your father believes that achieving as much as you can in your chosen field is important, but your mother believes that what matters is not making others look bad. Priming representations of your mother or father could affect your achievement-related behavior. If you are in a debate with a colleague and your father is salient, you might go all out to win, whereas if your mother is sitting in the front row, you might moderate your behavior so that your opponent does not look bad (Shah, 2003a, 2003b). Priming significant others can influence goal appraisal, the appraisal of the difficulty of the task, and reactions to one's own performance (Shah, 2003b). It can influence the perceived value of goal attainment, persistence toward the goal, and actual performance. For example, if a significant other, such as a romantic partner, has high expectations for your performance, you would be likely to believe that you can attain the goal, you will persist at the goal, and you will perform better (Shah, 2003b). Another person's behavior directed toward attractive goals especially cues pursuing the same goal (Aarts, Gollwitzer, & Hassin, 2004; Shah, 2003a).

Neural Underpinnings of Goal-Directed Behavior

How exactly do goals influence behavior? The cognitive control of behavior stems from the active maintenance of patterns of activity in the prefrontal cortex that represent goals and the means to achieve them (E. K. Miller & Cohen, 2001). These representations are updated regularly by experience through feedback from brain stem neuromodulatory systems. The activity in the PFC brain regions signals other brain structures that guide the flow of activity along neural pathways and establish mappings between inputs of internal states and outputs needed to perform a particular task (E. K. Miller & Cohen, 2001).

Although the prefrontal cortex is not implicated for simple automatic behavior, such as reacting to a sudden sound or movement, it *is* implicated when behavior must be guided by intentions, goals, or other internal states. Thus a primary task of the prefrontal cortex appears to be representing goals and the means to achieve them for top-down regulation of activity. Increasing the personal relevance of stimuli and the intensity of approach motivation, especially, increases left frontal activation, consistently tied to positive and approach motivational affect, whereas right frontal activation associates with negative or withdrawal motivational affect (Harmon-Jones et al., 2006).

So far, goals seem to imply consistency between cognitions and behavior. Yet a striking aspect of behavior is that under some circumstances, it does not correspond to what one would expect on the basis of apparently predominant cognitions. For example, most people are horrified by the prospect of a nuclear war, mass starvation, or global warming, and yet very few people take any action to attempt to reduce their likelihood. We next address cognition-behavior (in)consistency.

WHEN ARE COGNITIONS AND BEHAVIOR RELATED?

The question is not easy to answer, at least not simply. First, scant social cognition research includes behavioral dependent measures, limiting opportunities to examine the relationship, and when they do, results are mixed. To address the cognition–behavior relationship, one may turn to related literatures addressing similar problems. For example, those aware of social psychological history should find the cognition–behavior problem all too familiar. Attitude change research of the 1950s and 1960s produced a similar situation: Researchers initially failed to examine the attitude–behavior relationship, and when it was examined, the evidence was inconsistent. Some reported relatively weak relationships between cognitions and behavior (Nisbett & Wilson, 1977b; Wicker, 1969), whereas others maintained that the consistency is strong when moderating factors are taken into account (Quattrone, 1985; Schuman & Johnson, 1976). The literature on the correspondence between personality traits and behavior, although not cognitive in its origins, is also a useful source of hypotheses: The relationship between personality traits (which have important cognitive components) and behaviors that would theoretically be expected to follow from them sometimes proves to be weak and unreliable (Mischel, 1968). Drawing on these literatures, the attempt to clarify when cognitions and behavior go together can take several routes, as in the next sections.

Which Behaviors are Related to Cognition?

Perhaps we expect too many and too varied behaviors to relate to any given cognition. Consider the self-perception of friendliness as an example. Some people think of themselves as friendly; others do not. Considering only the people who consider themselves friendly, should we expect them to be friendly in all situations? Certainly we would expect them to be more friendly than people who consider themselves unfriendly, but they will not be friendly every minute of the day. To consider oneself a friendly person, perhaps one need only show a high degree of consistency in **prototypic** behaviors (Chapter 4) and not on behaviors less centrally related to friendliness.

In fact, research supports this contention (Mischel, 1984; Mischel & Peake, 1982): Undergraduates who considered themselves conscientious (or not) were studied in a wide variety of relevant situations. An independent group of raters judged each situation for how prototypic it was for conscientiousness. The investigators then calculated cross-situational consistency. Individuals who rated themselves high and low in conscientiousness did not behave differently in situations that were low in prototypicality for conscientiousness. However, in prototypic conscientiousness situations, the highly conscientious individuals showed significantly greater consistency in their behavior as compared with the individuals low in conscientiousness (Mischel & Peake, 1982; Schutte, Kenrick, & Sadalla, 1985).

A similar argument appears in the context of attitudes. Attitudes often represent general beliefs about categories of people, things, or events. Whether an attitude predicts behavior toward any particular category member is influenced by the match of that instance to the category prototype. When people hold stereotypes about particular groups (Lord, Lepper, & Mackie, 1984), they manifest that attitude in interactions with a particular group member primarily if that person matches their prototype of the group.

What are the implications for the cognition–behavior relationship generally? They suggest that consistency will be highest when one examines behaviors prototypically related to particular cognitions.

Measuring Cognitions and Behaviors

Another problem with assessing the cognition–behavior relationship concerns whether cognitions and behavior are measured at the same level of specificity. If asked whether you feel needy people should be helped through charity, you may well answer yes. If you are then accosted by a persistent panhandler begging for spare change, you may well decline. Although your attitudes and behavior would appear inconsistent, have you violated your attitudes? Not necessarily. You may, for example, feel that charity should be managed by institutions, not individuals, or that begging should be discouraged. The apparent inconsistency of your attitude and behavior is caused by the fact that your attitude was assessed generally, but your behavior was measured in a specific situation. When attitudes and behaviors are assessed at different levels of specificity, they may show low corre-spondence. How, then, can attitude and behavior assessment be more comparable?

One solution is to measure behavior through general behavioral tendencies, employing a **multiple-act criterion** (e.g., Epstein, 1979; Fishbein & Ajzen, 1974). That is, instead of examin-ing the relationship between a general attitude (i.e., toward charity in the abstract) and a single act (i.e., giving money to a specific beggar), one would measure a number of specific acts to get a general behavioral measure. For example, one might measure money given to various causes, time volunteered to help the needy, and so on. Although your general belief about charity may not predict your specific response to a particular panhandler, it should predict your charitable behavior more generally if we examine how much money, time, or effort you volunteer to each of several relevant causes.

The multiple-act criterion may succeed in demonstrating attitude–behavior consistency because (a) multiple actions better estimate the individual's typical behavior, (b) employing mul-tiple actions includes at least one situation predicted by attitudes (cf. Monson, Hesley, & Chernick, 1982), or (c) multiple actions include at least two situations the individual sees as similar to each other and relevant to the attitude, thus warranting similar behavior (cf. Lord, 1982). For which-ever reason, correspondence is higher when multiple-act measures of behavior relate to global attitudes (for a similar view in personality psychology, see Buss & Craik, 1980, 1981).

A second solution to assessing cognition–behavior correspondence is to measure cognitions more specifically. For example, if you had been asked about how you feel about giving money to beggars instead of how you feel about charity generally, correspondence between your attitude and behavior might well have been high. Many efforts to examine the attitude–behavior relationship have adopted this approach by assessing attitudes as intentions to behave in specific ways (Ajzen & Fishbein, 1977; Fishbein & Ajzen, 1974, 1975). The **theory of reasoned action** (Chapters 2, 10) predicts people's behavior directly from their intentions, which are, in turn, a function of atti-tudes toward the behavior, subjective norms about what others think one should do, and the relative importance of the attitudinal and normative considerations. The theory of reasoned action predicts a broad array of behaviors, especially in health (S. E. Taylor, 2006a). When intentions are stable, they predict behaviors, but when they are unstable, past behavior better predicts current behavior (Conner & Abraham, 2001; Sheeran, Orbell, & Trafimow, 1999).

In addition to knowing people's attitudes, subjective norms, and behavioral intentions with respect to a given behavior, one needs to know their perceived behavioral control over that action (Ajzen, 2001; Chapters 2, 10). A test of this revised model found that participants not only need to hold a behavioral intention toward a particular attitude object but also needed to feel that they were capable of performing the action contemplated. Thus feelings of perceived control or self-efficacy appear to be important in demonstrating attitude–behavior consistency, even with a clear behavioral intention to act upon an attitude.

Which Cognitions Predict Behavior?

One of the most frustrating aspects of the attitude–behavior relationship is that one can change cognitions that would seem to be highly related to behavior without necessarily changing those corresponding behaviors. For example, beliefs about women in the workplace show, increasingly, both men and women are more egalitarian. However, most indicators of discrimination and harassment suggest that women still experience far more of these adverse effects than men (Barreto & Ellemers, 2005). Behavior might not match attitudes for many reasons. In this example (Kahn & Crosby, 1987), attitudes may reflect ideal or socially desirable ways of responding, but behavior may be influenced by other factors, such as other attitudes (i.e., seniority should determine pay), situational factors (i.e., the characteristics of a particular woman under consideration for a particular position), individual differences in the propensity to use attitudes as guides for behavior, and the possibility of getting away with harassment and discrimination (cf. Crosby, Bromley, & Saxe, 1980). This section considers further the various factors that determine which cognitions are most likely to predict behavior.

One condition for a strong relation between cognition and behavior is that the cognition be held strongly and clearly. This is most evident in attitude research, where **strength** of attitudes predicts their stability: They have personal implications, and they concern personally important issues about which a person feels extremely certain. When attitudes and behaviors are inconsistent, the attitudes often are weak or ambivalent (Armitage & Conner, 2000). Strongly-held attitudes are more likely to be accessible and, thus, influence behavior (Bizer & Krosnick, 2001; Posavac, Sanbonmatsu, & Fazio, 1997).

Attitudes generally influence behavior if **accessible** (e.g., Aldrich, Sullivan, & Borgida, 1989; Fazio & Williams, 1986; Kallgren & Wood, 1986; Kiesler, Nisbett, & Zanna, 1969). Accessible attitudes seem important (Roese & Olson, 1994). Sometimes we hold attitudes as general values but are not able to access them readily to influence our behavior. For example (Kallgren & Wood, 1986), participants reported attitudes toward the preservation of the environment and also displayed accessibility of those attitudes by how many facts they could remember relevant to the attitude and how many past behaviors they could remember consistent with the attitude. Two weeks later, the participants were asked to sign and circulate a petition and to participate in a recycling project. Only those able to access their prior attitudes showed substantial congruence between their attitudes and behavior.

Related to accessibility, cognitions are more likely to influence behavior when they have been rehearsed and practiced. When people hold attitudes that are highly embedded – that is, tied to other beliefs that they hold – those **embedded attitudes** are more strongly related to behavior than less embedded attitudes (Prislin & Oullette, 1996).

Cognitions are more likely to influence behavior if they concern a domain of people's relative expertise and considerable knowledge. For example, being asked to sign a petition to protect the environment would be more likely to occur among people who not only hold pro-environmental attitudes but who are knowledgeable about preserving the environment (Armitage & Conner, 2000; Kallgren & Wood, 1986). In longitudinal data (A. R. Davison, Yantis, Norwood, & Montano, 1985), more information about an attitude object produced greater attitude–behavior congruence, even after controlling for prior experience with the attitude and for attitude certainty.

Another factor that determines whether attitudes will predict behavior is how they developed. Attitudes formed from **direct experience** predict behavior better than do attitudes based on indirect experience (Fazio & Zanna, 1981). In one study, college students reported their attitudes regarding their university's housing shortage. Only those participants whose attitudes had been formed through relevant experience (i.e., sleeping on cots in dorm lounges for several weeks because there were no rooms) showed strong attitude–behavior relationships. Relevant personal experience encourages people to think and talk about the issue, so the attitude is more likely to influence behavior than if we just hear or read about the issue. In addition, when people have the time and motivation to deliberate on their attitudes, they are more likely to consider the relevance of those attitudes to their behavior before deciding to act on them (Fabrigar, Petty, Smith, & Crites, 2006). Overall, attitudes that are formed through relevant experience are more accessible (ready to guide behavior), more specific (behavior-relevant), more confidently held (less hesitant), more stable (more consistent) and robust (resist counterargument), more than attitudes not based on relevant experience (Borgida & Campbell, 1982 Fazio & Zanna, 1978, 1981; Table 15.2). Consequently, they predict behavior.

Another factor that influences attitude–behavior consistency is **vested interest**. To the extent that a person's attitude involves self-interest, the person is more likely to act on it. For example, 18-year-olds are more likely to canvass against a referendum that would raise the drinking age to 21 than are 22-year-olds also against it (Sivacek & Crano, 1982). Vested interest is more likely to predict behavior for attitudes that are personally important to an individual than for attitudes that are low in personal importance (Young, Borgida, Sullivan, & Aldrich, 1987). When values relevant to the desired behavior change are salient, behavior change occurs as well (Homer & Kahle, 1988; Schwartz & Inbar-Saban, 1988).

Stable cognitions that are easily remembered are more likely to predict behavior than those that are less stable (Kraus, 1995). When attitudes are unstable, salient environmental cues or competing casually held beliefs may predict behavior instead. A primary factor that determines whether a cognition is stable and accessible is frequency of expression. For example, if a group of friends debate foreign policy on a regular basis, those attitudes are more likely to influence behavior. Moreover, attitudes often become more extreme when they are expressed more frequently (Downing, Judd, & Brauer, 1992). Thus, if you have multiple opportunities to express your attitudes about a war, you may come to feel strongly about it in the process.

The preceding factors suggest that importance determines whether an attitude will influence behavior. **Important attitudes** reflect fundamental values, self-interest, or identification with individuals or groups that one values (Boninger, Krosnick, & Berent, 1995). Such attitudes both resist persuasion and predict behavior. **Self-schemas** also determine the attitude–behavior relationship. Those whose attitudes represent strongly held beliefs about their personal qualities are more likely to behave consistently with those attitudes than are people who hold attitudes that are not central to self-schemas (Milburn, 1987).

Overall, attitudes that matter to a person, being accessible, stable, and important, show a stronger relationship to behavior than those that matter little. The implication for the cognition–behavior relationship more generally is that cognitions emerging from personal experience and mattering for one's life predict behavior better than do cognitions developed from mild curiosity, passing interest, or secondhand sources. Table 15.2 summarizes factors that affect the attitude–behavior relation and cognition–behavior relations more generally.

Table 15.2   Attitudes that contribute to high attitude–behavior consistency

Characteristic	Sample mechanisms and overlap
Attitude is strong	Accessible, stable, important
Attitude is accessible	Ready to use, important
Attitude is embedded	Rehearsed, practiced
Attitude draws on expertise	Information about attitude object
Attitude is based on direct personal experience with attitude object	Accessible, specific, confident, stable, robust
Attitude is stable over time	Frequent expression
Attitude reflects vested interests	Consistent with values & goals
Attitude is important	Relevant to goals and values, identity, self-schema
Attitude has consistent affective and cognitive components	Unconflicted implications

Thinking about Reasons Underlying Attitudes

Is deliberation always good for attitude–behavior consistency? When do people spontaneously come up with reasons for their attitudes? When people encounter unexpected reactions from others or have unexpected feelings about their attitude objects, they are motivated to engage in a reasons analysis (T. D. Wilson, Dunn, Kraft, & Lisle, 1989). Being induced to think about the reasons underlying one's attitudes actually reduces attitude–behavior consistency (T. D. Wilson, Dunn, et al., 1989; T. D. Wilson & Hodges, 1992). Essentially, **analyzing reasons** that underlie one's attitudes changes those attitudes temporarily (T. D. Wilson, Hodges, & LaFleur, 1995; T. D. Wilson & LaFleur, 1995), especially if the attitudes have little cognitive support (Maio & Olson, 1998) from other beliefs that buttress the attitude. People do not normally think a lot about their attitudes, and when induced, they often focus on particular aspects of the attitudes that then become more salient. In doing so, they fail to discriminate important from unimportant information or properly perceive the relevance of particular information (Tordesillas & Chaiken, 1999). When trying to come up with reasons for their attitudes, people often bring to mind thoughts that are available in memory but that may not represent their attitude. The reasons they come up with may come from salient situational factors or from recent experiences that imply a new attitude, leading at least temporarily to attitude change.

   What is the impact of assessing the reasons for one's attitudes on behavior? If behavior is measured shortly after people have expressed new attitudes, then the behavior is consistent with those new attitudes. If behavior is measured some time after attitudes have been analyzed for reasons, the behavior seems to "snap back" to the original attitude and thus is inconsistent with the attitude reported after the reasons analysis (T. D. Wilson, Kraft, & Dunn, 1989). Also, behavior may be more under the control of affective aspects of an attitude than cognitive aspects. Because self-reports of attitudes are cognitively driven and behavior may be more affectively driven, under conditions when one has focused on the reasons underlying one's attitudes, self-reports of attitudes and behaviors may be discrepant.

As the previous analysis implies, some attitudes are more vulnerable than others to the disruption produced by focusing on reasons. Attitudes that are difficult to access, weakly held, based on scant knowledge, or affectively based are more vulnerable to reasons analysis disruption than are attitudes that are easily accessed, strongly held, based on lots of knowledge, and cognitively based (T. D. Wilson, Dunn, et al., 1989; T. D. Wilson, Kraft, & Dunn, 1989).

Affective versus Cognitive Impacts of Attitudes

The type of behavior influences how exactly an affective or cognitive focus influences the cognition–behavior relationship (M. G. Millar & Tesser, 1986a). In its simplest form: Behavior engaged in for its own sake (**consummatory behavior**) seems driven by affect, but behavior in service of goals (**instrumental behavior**) seems driven by cognition. Thus if one focuses on the cognitive component of an attitude, attitude–behavior congruence should increase if the behavior is instrumental. On the other hand, focusing on the emotional component of an attitude would increase the attitude–behavior relationship if the behavior is engaged in for its own sake (consummatory).

To test this hypothesis (Millar & Tesser, 1986b), participants solved difficult puzzles while focused either on the cognitive component of the attitude (why the participant felt that way about the puzzles) or the affective aspect of the attitude (how the participant felt about the puzzles). In addition, participants learned that they would later either take a test of analytic ability (making their puzzle-solving activity instrumental) or take a test of social sensitivity (making puzzle solving an activity undertaken in its own right, a consummatory behavior). As predicted, participants who engaged in the puzzle instrumentally showed consistency between evaluations and time spent only in the cognitive-focus condition; those playing with the puzzles for their own sake showed high attitude–behavior congruence only in the affective focus condition. These results emerge only if the affective and cognitive components disagree (M. G. Millar & Tesser, 1989).

Action Identification

How people label their actions changes their subsequent behavior. Specifically, people may identify their actions at low levels of behavior (making idle conversation) or at high levels in the service of some goal (trying to create a positive impression); this phenomenon is **action identification** (Vallacher & Wegner, 1987). The theory assumes that act identities – different levels of thinking about a particular action – systematically relate to each other hierarchically. Low levels identify the specifics of the action, whereas higher levels indicate a more abstract understanding of the action, indicating why and for what purposes. Putting one's feet successively in front of each other represents a low-level action identity; going for a walk represents a middle-level action identity;

walking through a neighborhood to judge its suitability would be a high-level action identity; and planning one's future would be an even higher-level action identity.

People use action identification to organize implementing that action, monitoring its occurrence, and reflecting on its maintenance. Higher level identities tend to dominate enacting and evaluating the action. When people have only low-level understandings of what they are doing, they are predisposed to accept any higher-level identity suggested by the context (Wegner, Vallacher, Kiersted, & Dizadji, 1986; Wegner, Vallacher, Macomber, Wood, & Arps, 1984). In one study, participants were induced to drink coffee from a strangely shaped cup, thereby focusing their attention on low-level aspects of the action (actually getting the coffee to their mouths); other participants drank from normal cups. Those drinking from the unusual cups were more receptive to a suggestion that they were seeking (or avoiding) self-stimulation, a higher-level action identification than simply "drinking coffee." Moreover, they generalized the self-stimulation action identification, turning up (or down) the volume of music in the room (Wegner et al., 1984).

When an action cannot maintain a higher level, it drops to a lower one. For example, those skilled in the use of chopsticks can consider consuming a Chinese meal as a delightful experience, whereas those inexperienced in the use of chopsticks may regard it primarily as a task of getting food from plate to mouth. When the higher-level identities of an action cannot be automatically enacted, action identifications move to lower levels. More generally, actions that are successful tend to be identified and maintained at relatively high levels, whereas unsuccessful actions tend to be identified at lower levels (Vallacher, Wegner, & Frederick, 1987).

Action identification depends on several factors, including the context, the action's difficulty, and the person's prior experience (Table 15.3). With respect to context, situational cues often guide identifying an action at high or low levels. For example, the presence of one's boss at a social gathering may define one's comments about the future directions of the company as an

Table 15.3 The effects of action identification

	Low level of identification	High level of identification
Example	Bike riding	Getting exercise
Flexibility	Low (There is only one way to ride a bike)	High (There are many ways to get exercise)
Stability	Low (Action identification subject to context effects)	High
Impact of context	Context may move identification to higher level (e.g., bike riding becomes labeled as getting exercise)	Little impact of context on level of identification
Difficulty of behavior (maintenance indicators)	Disruption less likely to occur; when it does, action identification may move to lower level	Disruption shifts action identification to lower level
Likelihood of emergent action	High, because low-level behavior is responsive to context effects	Low

Source: After Vallacher & Wegner (1987)

opportunity to impress one's boss, whereas if the boss were not present, one's observations about the company's future might simply remain gratuitous observations.

With respect to action difficulty, five factors, termed **maintenance indicators**, determine the potential disruption of an action identity: They are the action's difficulty, familiarity, complexity, time to enact, and time to learn to do it well. Waiting for a bus, for example, is not difficult to enact; it is familiar to most people, it is simple, it may take a short time, and it is not hard to learn. Consequently, the likelihood that waiting for a bus would drop to an even lower level of action identification is small. However, flagging down a taxi may be somewhat more difficult to enact, being less familiar, more complex, under some circumstances taking longer, and in particular cities requiring an inordinate amount of learning time. The novice cab-flagger in New York City, for example, may shift the identification of the task from flagging a cab down to getting into the street with one's hand up to attract attention before other people do. Actions seen as easy, familiar, short, and requiring little learning time tend to be maintained at their initial level.

As individuals develop experience with a particular action sequence, they will come to identify it at a higher level than if they have little experience with the action sequence. Well-practiced actions chunked at higher levels can often be enacted automatically. To the extent that this is true, they tend to be maintained at higher rather than lower levels (Vallacher, Wegner, & Frederick, 1987).

Whether an action is identified at a high or low level has a number of implications. As noted, behaviors enacted at a higher level of action identification tend to be more stable than those enacted at low levels of action identification. Action identification also influences the flexibility of that action. Actions identified at a higher level, such as getting exercise, may be enacted in any of several ways, such as jogging, riding a bike, or swimming, whereas actions identified at a lower level, such as riding a bike, will show less flexibility. Actions performed at the wrong level are subject to performance impairments. Specifically, difficult tasks are performed best when identified in low-level terms, whereas easy tasks are performed best when they are identified in high-level terms. An action typically performed at a high level may be disrupted if one moves it to a lower level. We know a broad jumper who claims that, by asking one of her opponents why she places her right foot in a particular way, she can knock two feet off the opponent's jump. Conversely, when a behavior can be enacted automatically at a relatively low level of action identification (e.g., shaking hands), contextual effects that suggest a higher level of action identification (making a good impression) can disrupt the performance of the behavioral sequence because the higher level of identification forces attention to the components (right amount of pressure? sweaty hands? eye contact?).

Under some circumstances, action identities produce **emergent action**. Emergent action is behavior that people find themselves doing that they did not intend to do. Given that low-level action identities respond to contexts suggesting higher-level action identities, emergent action occurs for low-level action identification. In one study, participants thought about participating in an experiment in its details or more generally (Wegner et al., 1986). Those who concentrated on the details were more susceptible to suggestions from others that they were either helping the experimenter by behaving altruistically or being selfish by seeking extra course credit. These participants who initially thought of their participation at relatively low levels came to accept these action identifications, and moreover, continued the emergent action by choosing to participate in subsequent activities that were consistent with the emergent action identity.

Action identification theory relates to other social cognition topics. Action identification may influence the attributions made for performance. For example, when people enact behaviors at relatively low levels, they attend to situational contexts that may change the behavior's meaning. Consequently, they more often make situational attributions for behavior. In contrast, when people identify action at a high level, they may perceive it as dispositionally based because of seeing it as initiated and maintained by higher-level personal goals rather than situational constraints (Vallacher & Wegner, 1987). Relatedly, when we identify another person's actions at high-level action identities, the attribution of intentionality is especially strong (Kozak, Marsh, & Wegner, 2006).

The theory also predicts that cross-situational inconsistency in behavior need not always lead to situational attributions. If individuals identify an action at a high level, they can view that behavior dispositionally, despite cross-situational flexibility in enacting the goal. The theory also explains the apparent consistency versus malleability of the self-concept (Chapter 5), specifically how people maintain stable self-concept stability despite behavioral variability. Action identification theory suggests that only behaviors enacted at high levels seem related to self-conceptions, so much behavior apparently inconsistent with the self-concept will not be perceived as such when enacted at low levels and thereby judged to have few implications for the self-concept. In one study (Wegner et al., 1986), participants generated five one-sentence descriptions of their behavior in either relatively low-level or high-level terms. They then received false feedback indicating that they were either cooperative or competitive. Participants led to think about their behavior at lower levels agreed with the bogus feedback.

Finally, action identification theory also illuminates measurement of traits, specifically, the relatively modest success that personality researchers have had in predicting behavior from traits. Action identification theory argues that people may perform an action for any of many reasons. Some will be high level, which may correspond to particular traits or other dispositional qualities, but others of them will be low level, not necessarily related to traits (Vallacher & Wegner, 1987).

Situational Factors Mediate Cognition–Behavior Consistency

Situational factors influence the cognition–behavior relationship by making salient particular cognitions as guides for behavior. Suppose a friend approaches you to help collect signatures on a petition that allows first-year students to have cars on campus. What do you do? If the friend tells you he is desperate because he promised to have 100 signatures by noon and has only 60 at 10 in the morning, you might help out of friendship because the friend is salient. If a classmate then walks by muttering about insufficient parking for the cars already on campus, you might reconsider, so as not to alienate peers. Similarly, if parking is billed as an individual right, you might help, but if you have just read an editorial decrying local air pollution, you might not. This example illustrates that, in trying to examine the consistency question, one must ask, "Consistent with what? Social norms? Attitudes? Which attitudes?" Behavior is influenced by situational factors highlighting one set of cognitions over others, and one must know which concerns are salient before inferring consistency.

Attitude–behavior consistency thus will be affected by which meaning of a particular attitude or behavior is made salient by situational cues. One study (Prislin, 1987) measured participants' attitudes toward capital punishment and then asked them to make a decision in a fictitious jury case. Participants were reminded to act either in line with their attitudes (high attitude relevance) or in line with the facts (low attitude relevance). They were also told that their decision could or could not influence the decision of a real jury (high versus low behavior relevance). When external factors made neither the implications of the attitude nor the behavior especially relevant, attitude–behavior relationships were strong. However, when external factors made attitude or behavior relevant, the correlation decreased. Context effects on behavior can be subtle, induced even by prior subliminal priming (Herr, 1986; Neuberg, 1989).

Social norms can situationally determine behavior, overwhelming relevant attitudes (e.g., Bentler & Speckart, 1981; Fishbein & Ajzen, 1975; LaPiere, 1934; Pagel & Davidson, 1984; S. H. Schwartz & Tessler, 1972). For example, asked if you would allow Sleazy Sam into your home, you may respond with some indignation that you would not, but if he shows up at your party as a guest's date, you will probably not turn him away. Your behavior will be consistent with the norms surrounding the host role, although inconsistent with your attitudes about Sam. Norms are especially salient before an audience and when one's attention is directed outward toward the situation (rather than self); self-presentational concerns affect behavior (Cialdini, Levy, Herman, & Evenbeck, 1973).

Other situational factors favor prior attitudes as a basis for behavior. If situational factors focus attention inward, people base their behavior on enduring attitudes (Wicklund, 1975): Attention to the self minimizes external influences and makes prior attitudes more salient (see S. E. Taylor & Fiske, 1978). When past behaviors suggesting a particular attitude are salient, subsequent attitude–behavior consistency is high.

Priming particular constructs also affects behavior. Making extraversion salient, for example, increases expressions of extraversion among most people. However, people also differ in the extent to which a primed construct may fit their own self-concept. For example, an introverted person may behave in a more extraverted way if the primed norm for a situation calls for extraverted behavior, but as the salience of the norm of extraversion declines, the person may revert more to more chronically accessible self-perception of introversion. A person who considers the self neither extraverted nor introverted might, instead, remain sensitive to the behavior normative for the situation, even when the salience of that norm declines (see Bargh, Lombardi, & Higgins, 1988).

Overall, attention to often random situational cues can reduce attitude–behavior consistency. Consistent with this viewpoint are the effects of neural laterality on attitude–behavior consistency. Specifically, when the brain's left hemisphere is activated in right-handed participants, attitude–behavior consistency is low, whereas with right-induced hemispheric activation, the attitude–behavior relation increases (Drake & Sobrero, 1987). This may occur because attention to the self increases with relative left hemisphere activation, whereas attention to external stimuli is enhanced during right hemisphere activation (Drake, 1986).

Why should seemingly trivial aspects of a situation influence people's behavior? Situationally induced salience foregrounds relevant attitudes or norms, making them more accessible guides to action (Borgida & Campbell, 1982; C. A. Kiesler, Collins, & Miller, 1969; M. Snyder, 1977). Salience defines the situation for the individual, reducing ambiguity (R. Norman, 1975); it tells you what should be relevant to your behavior if you are uncertain. Finally, when global attitudes or values are salient, responsibility for behaving consistently looms large (C. A. Kiesler, 1971; S. H. Schwartz, 1978). If cognition–behavior linkages are salient, cognitions and behaviors typically cohere, but when situational cues are salient, behavior may be consistent with those cues.

Individual Differences Mediate Consistency

The question, "Consistent with what?" becomes even more important when examining individual differences in cognition–behavior consistency. Some people behave consistently with social norms, whereas others behave consistently with their attitudes. Some people have an overriding social goal manifested chronically in their behavior, whereas others show more behavioral flexibility. We now turn to these individual difference factors.

A basic question in trait–behavior and attitude–behavior relations concerns how much people actually think about themselves in trait terms and see behavior as stable across situations. Both children and adults tend to view predispositions as condition–behavior contingencies rather than as invariants that apply across a broad array of situations (J. C. Wright & Mischel, 1988). For example, adults make dispositional attributions about others' behaviors but also modify them with conditional statements ("George is outgoing except with people he doesn't know."). Hence, people may see no need to behave according to their personal dispositions, if they perceive those dispositions as only conditionally relevant to particular situations. Thus one may believe that one is a friendly person but believe that returning the greeting of a roadside vagrant is not required by the disposition "friendly."

People who are inexperienced, incompetent, or unsure of their abilities within a given performance context are more concerned with the appropriate traits and characteristics for that performance than are experienced, capable performers (Cantor, Mackie, & Lord, 1983–1984). This focus on competencies required in a given performance context encourages attempts to match situational demands, though not necessarily successful performance, which also depends on competence (Mischel, 1984; Wicklund, 1986; Wicklund & Braun, 1987).

Self-Monitoring

We all know people who blend into social situations easily. They seem to know exactly what to do or say with each person. We also know people who are emphatically themselves, regardless of situation, rarely bending to the norms of the social setting. Such different patterns are respectively termed high and low **self-monitoring** (M. Snyder, 1979). Those who act as the situation demands monitor themselves with respect to the situation. Those who act on their own internal demands are not monitoring themselves with respect to the situation; they are low self-monitors

(M. Snyder, 1974; M. Snyder & Campbell, 1982; M. Snyder & Monson, 1975; M. Snyder & Tanke, 1976).

Self-monitoring describes how individuals plan, act out, and regulate social behavior (M. Snyder & Cantor, 1980). Behavioral choices utilize various information, including knowledge of particular social settings and knowledge of one's own abilities, resources, and stable qualities. High self-monitors are particularly sensitive to social norms, situations, and interpersonal cues regarding appropriate behavior (M. Snyder, 1974). Low self-monitors, in contrast, respond less to these environmental cues and instead draw on information from their internal selves to decide how to behave. In essence, when faced with a new situation, high self-monitors ask, "What is the ideal person for this situation and how can I be it?" whereas low self-monitors ask, "How can I best be me in this situation?" (M. Snyder, 1974, 1979; Table 15.4).

High self-monitors are indeed more socially skilled than low self-monitors (Ickes & Barnes, 1977): communicating a wider range of emotions, learning more quickly how to behave in new situations, initiating more conversations, and having good self-control (see M. Snyder, 1979). When asked to adopt the behavior of another type of person – for example, a reserved, withdrawn, introverted type – high self-monitors are better at it than low self-monitors (Lippa, 1976), and they also appear to be better at discerning the meaning of nonverbal behavior (M. Snyder, 1979). When their social outcomes depend on another person, such as a potential date, high self-monitors remember more about the other person and make more confident, extreme inferences about the other (Berscheid et al., 1976). To the observer, the high self-monitor appears more friendly and less anxious than the low self-monitor (Lippa, 1976).

High self-monitors are interested in social information, apparently because it is useful to them. They remember information about another person with whom they will interact better than do low self-monitors (M. Snyder, 1974). High self-monitors are particularly able to construct images of prototypic individuals in particular domains (e.g., the classic extravert or the

Table 15.4 Sample items measuring self-monitoring

Answer the following items true or false.		
1. I find it hard to imitate the behavior of other people.	T	F
2. I would probably make a good actor.	T	F
3. In a group of people, I am rarely the center of attention.	T	F
4. I may deceive people by being friendly when I really dislike them.	T	F
5. I can only argue for ideas which I already believe.	T	F
6. I can make impromptu speeches even on topics about which I have almost no information.	T	F

First, answer the items in the table. If you answered "false" to items 1, 3, and 5, and "true" to items 2, 4, and 6, you would tend toward the high self-monitoring side. On the other hand, if the reverse pattern characterizes your answers, you tend to be a low self-monitor.

Source: After M. Snyder (1974). Copyright 1974 by the American Psychological Association. Adapted by permission

perfect princess) than are low self-monitors and are more likely to enter a social situation when norms are clear; low self-monitors, on the other hand, are more skilled at constructing images of themselves in particular situations (e.g., how they would behave in situations calling for extravertedness), and they are more likely to enter a social situation if it fits their self-conception (M. Snyder & Cantor, 1980).

Given differences in the styles and informational preferences of high and low self-monitors, their behavior is under the control of different forces. High self-monitors describe themselves as flexible, adaptive, shrewd individuals; when asked to explain the cause of their own behavior, they are likely to point to situational factors.[2] Low self-monitors, in contrast, see themselves as more consistent and principled, and they offer dispositional explanations for their behavior (M. Snyder, 1976). Low self-monitors show more effects of temporary mood states or fatigue on their behavior than do high self-monitors, who are better able to mask these sources of internal interference (e.g., Ajzen, Timko, & White, 1982). High self-monitors also respond more to manipulations of public self-awareness (Chapter 5), whereas low self-monitors are more sensitive to manipulations of private self-awareness (Webb, Marsh, Schneiderman, & Davis, 1989).

These differences in self-perception also appear behaviorally, so self-monitoring helps unravel the cognition–behavior relationship. Because they behave consistently with social norms that vary from situation to situation, high self-monitors show little consistency across situations. After being induced to perform a counterattitudinal behavior, high self-monitors are less likely to infer new attitudes from the counterattitudinal behavior than are low self-monitors. Low self-monitors, on the other hand, show less situational variability in their behavior, and their future behavior can be better predicted from knowledge of their relevant cognitions (M. Snyder & Swann, 1976). Their attitudes appear more accessible than those of high self-monitors in that their response latencies to attitudinal inquiries are faster, suggesting that low self-monitors have stronger object-evaluation associations (Kardes et al., 1986). However, high self-monitors sometimes do show attitude–behavior consistency. When the relevance of personal attitudes to behavior is salient, they are consistent presumably because it is socially desirable to act on one's attitudes (M. Snyder & Kendzierski, 1982; cf. M. Snyder, 1982).

High and low self-monitors differ in what they value in personal relationships. High self-monitoring individuals are more influenced by physical attractiveness of the potential partners, romantic and nonromantic, whereas low self-monitors are influenced more by the personality characteristics of potential partners. High self-monitoring individuals report more romantic partners than low self-monitoring individuals, and low self-monitoring individuals reported having dated their current partner for longer. Similarly, high self-monitoring individuals are more willing to terminate current relationships in favor of alternative partners. Finally, low self-monitors' relationships appear to be more intimate, suggesting more commitment to their relationships (M. Snyder & Simpson, 1984).

---

[2] Described this way, high self-monitoring individuals appear to be quite Machiavellian. However, Ickes, Reidhead, and Patterson (1986) have suggested that people high in Machiavellianism are self-oriented in their impression management efforts, whereas self-monitoring reflects an other-oriented accommodation to situations.

USING BEHAVIOR FOR IMPRESSION MANAGEMENT

People use their behavior to create certain impressions in others' minds (Nezlek & Leary, 2002). Sometimes people know the image they wish to present and conscientiously go about creating it (Kowalski & Leary, 1990). Often people desire to convey to others that they are successful, attractive, and likeable. There are many reasons for wanting to create a good impression, such as increasing one's personal power, obtaining desired results, gaining approval, and experiencing the intrinsic satisfaction of a positive image (Table 15.5).

Making a Positive Impression

How are positive impressions created? One strategy is **behavioral matching**. If another person behaves modestly, usually the impression manager will do so as well, but if the other is self-promoting, so will the impression manager (Newtson & Czerlinsky, 1974). Behavioral matching is often automatic and beyond personal control, as when people automatically mimic the non-verbal behaviors of others (Chartrand & Bargh, 1999), and this kind of behavioral matching contributes to a positive impression.

Conforming to situational norms also helps to create an appropriate impression. A wedding reception, for example, permits a ribald toast, but a funeral typically does not, unless it's an Irish one.

Table 15.5   Strategies of self-presentation

Type of impression effort	Possible motives	Representative strategies
Creating a positive impression	Increase one's power, obtain resources; obtain approval; validate a positive self-image; be liked	Match target's behavior; convey most positive image possible; conform to norms; appreciate or flatter target; appear to be consistent
Creating an ambiguous impression	Avoid stereotyping by others; maintain behavioral freedom; maintain self-esteem; save face	Engage in inconsistent behavior; provide multiple reasons for behavior; proclaim that everyone does it (i.e., muster consensus); leave the field; avoid evaluations
Controlling a negative impression	Control one's own and others' attributions for failure; avoid low-ability attributions; avoid own or others' disappointment over future anticipated failure	Exaggerate impediments to success; exert little effort; self-handicap (i.e., engage in self-destructive behavior, such as using drugs or drinking); proclaim one's failure to be due to external and/or unstable factors; make one's attributes ambiguous

Ingratiation, or flattery, refers to saying positive things about the target other (Jones & Pittman, 1982). On the whole, this is a successful strategy for making a positive impression, although not when one's ingratiating motive is transparently clear or when the ingratiation is excessive or prolonged. Flattery is most successful if it is centered on attributes that the target person values but on which the target questions his or her standing. For example, telling a prize-winning scientist that she is smart will likely have little effect because she already knows it, but telling her that she is charming may well have an intended effect if she values but doubts her social skills.

Self-presentation is not always effective. **Self-promotion** – conveying positive information about one's ability to others – can be a positive impression strategy, although it can sometimes backfire (Chapter 5); people may see one as arrogant or conceited instead.

Sometimes the impression manager does the wrong thing. You may call a current romantic partner by the name of your previous partner, or spill your soup in your lap while having lunch with a boss. One way to handle a less than stellar behavioral performance is to give excuses (Kernis & Grannemann, 1990; C. R. Snyder & Higgins, 1988). Attributing one's failure to external, uncontrollable causes (such as blaming a late arrival on a flat tire) is typically a better strategy for managing an ineffective self-presentation than causes that are internal and under your control (such as not setting the alarm clock).

Self-Handicapping

A more desperate strategy for managing failure is **self-handicapping** (Baumeister & Scher, 1988; Berglas & Jones, 1978). People sometimes engage in actions that provide obstacles to success so that failure can later be attributed to those obstacles. The student who stays up all night before an exam can attribute a low grade to fatigue, not to lack of ability (McCrea & Hirt, 2001).

Self-handicapping strategy has two versions. One is behavioral self-handicapping–creating genuine handicaps such as fatigue, alcohol abuse, tardiness, and inattention to excuse failures. The other strategy is self-reported handicaps–claiming to be ill, anxious, shy, or a victim of a traumatic incident in the hopes that such states might excuse poor performance.

Other people are not easily persuaded by self-handicapping strategies (Rhodewalt, Sanbonmatsu, Tschanz, Feick, & Waller, 1995). Self-handicapping makes a poor impression. Although one may avoid a low-ability attribution, the price can be high: One may instead look lazy, anxious, drunk, or stoned. Moreover, a further risk of poor self-presentation is that often impression management efforts are internalized: People come to believe that they are the way they act.

Other Strategies of Impression Management

Social anxiety, depression, shyness, and low self-esteem also influence self-presentational styles by evoking a self-protective style (Arkin, 1987; Baumeister, Tice, & Hutton, 1989; Schlenker, 1987). This style is characterized by withdrawing in social interaction, specifically: initiating fewer conversations, talking less frequently, avoiding topics that might reveal ignorance, minimizing self-disclosure, and providing modest self-descriptions. This interaction style centers on pleasant behaviors such as agreeing with others or smiling and avoids disagreeing.

Sometimes people choose to obscure others' impressions of them. Being typed as a particular sort of person can reduce a sense of personal control over one's outcomes because it implies that one is no longer free to do the opposite. Under certain circumstances, people will muddy the waters by making their attributes ambiguous. A person might engage in an inconsistent behavior or provide reasons for a behavior so that others will discount the importance of stable personality factors. For example, if you organize a successful party for your dorm, you might want to indicate that luck was on your side and you happened to have some free time, to avoid being handed the same responsibility a few months later.

USING BEHAVIOR TO TEST HYPOTHESES ABOUT OTHERS

We learn about other people in many ways: from other people, their situations, or assembling evidence. Regardless, we quickly develop hypotheses concerning the person. How will the hypotheses influence our interaction? People often act to corroborate their hypotheses, eliciting confirmatory information.

For example, suppose you learn that Ed has just returned from Tahiti, and you quickly view him as a carefree adventurer who seeks exotic places. Upon inquiring, you learn that he once sailed the Virgin Islands and had a job feeding sharks at Sea World, all fairly exotic. But note that you solicited the information that confirmed this image. All of us have at least a few little things about us that make us quasi-exotic, and when those bits are elicited from us in their entirety, we look much more exciting than we really are. After dating Exotic Ed for several weeks, it may emerge that his company flew him to Tahiti for the conference; his uncle, manager of Sea World, got him the summer job; and he sailed the Virgin Islands with his grandparents. Because people have a repertoire, when sampled preferentially, they may fit whatever hypothesis that selective questioning supports.

In one study (M. Snyder & Swann, 1978a), students interviewed another student; half were told to find out if the other was an extravert (e.g., outgoing, sociable), and half were told to find out if the other was an introvert (e.g., shy, retiring). Given various questions measuring introversion and extraversion, the students picked questions to ask. If told to assess extraversion, they disproportionately selected extraversion questions ("What would you do if you wanted to liven things up at a party?"); told to assess introversion, they disproportionately chose introversion questions ("What factors make it really hard for you to open up to people?"). These questions, in turn, made the target appear particularly extraverted or introverted, respectively, providing only the sample of behavior relevant to the questions. **Confirmatory hypothesis testing** (Slowiaczek, Klayman, Sherman, & Skov, 1992; Snyder, Campbell, & Preston, 1982) occurs whether the hypothesis concerns an individual's personality traits or stereotypic characteristics based on race, gender, or sexual orientation. It occurs regardless of how the hypothesis originated, how likely it is to be true, and whether incentives for accuracy are offered to the hypothesis tester (Klayman & Ha, 1987; Skov & Sherman, 1986).

Confirmatory hypothesis testing goes beyond casual social settings. In courtrooms, leading questions (Swann, Giuliano, & Wegner, 1982) – such as "Tell the jury about the last time you got into a fight" – assume a history of aggressive behavior, whether true or not. Conjectures within such leading questions can themselves be interpreted as evidence for the behavior in question. Having to answer such a leading question forces you to provide information that further confirms the behavior. Assuming you were in at least one fight in your life, you must now tell the jury about its details. Hence, leading questions are doubly biasing: The question itself implies the behavior (Wegner, Wenzlaff, Kerker, & Beattie, 1981), and the answer provides evidence.

Although confirmatory hypothesis testing emerges across circumstances, certain methods contribute to demonstrating it. First, the to-be-tested hypothesis often entails detailed description, for example, a portrait of extraversion (Trope & Bassok, 1982). Thus people may select questions that tend to confirm preexisting hypotheses primarily because that hypothesis is especially salient. Second, the questions provided may presuppose the to-be-tested hypothesis (e.g., extraversion). Instead of neutral questions ("Do you like parties?", a question extraverts might answer yes and introverts no), the list includes biased questions ("What would you do to liven up a party?", a question that virtually forces both introverts and extraverts to provide answers supporting extraversion). When participants create their own questions, they rarely choose such biased ones. Thus, moderating factors include task framing, the questions available, hypothesis certainty, and availability of alternatives (Kruglanski & Mayseless, 1988; Skov & Sherman, 1986; Swann & Giuliano, 1987; Trope & Mackie, 1987). Nevertheless, hypothesis confirmation bias exemplifies the more general tendency to test cases expected to have a property of interest rather than cases that will not (Klayman & Ha, 1987; Chapter 7).

Self-Fulfilling Prophecies: When Behavior Creates Reality

Confirmatory hypothesis testing misrepresents others in the social perceiver's mind by selectively favoring particular attributes. When this hypothesis testing also alters the target's behavior to support the hypothesis, a **self-fulfilling prophecy** occurs. An initially false definition, then, evokes behaviors that subsequently make it true (Merton, 1957), also known as **behaviorial confirmation** – the tendency of the target to adopt behaviors related to the expectations held by the perceiver.

A classic classroom demonstration (Rosenthal & Jacobson, 1968) told teachers at the term's start that certain students were potential late bloomers who, with proper nurturing and guidance, would excel. In fact, nothing distinguished these students: They were randomly selected. However, months later, the so-called late bloomers' schoolwork improved, and even their IQs increased. This **Pygmalion effect** is robust (Rosenthal, 1974) across positive and negative expectations, varied targets and situations. Table 15.6 describes factors that abet the Pygmalion effect.

Perceivers convey expectations to targets through nonverbal behaviors such as eye contact, posture, smiling, nodding, and body angle. In a classic study (Word, Zanna, & Cooper, 1974), negative

Table 15.6   Some classroom factors leading to the Pygmalion effect

Positive expectancies for a specific student create

Warmer socioemotional climate
More feedback, both positive and negative
Input: More and more difficult material taught
Output: Greater opportunity for responding

Note: An expectation is also more likely to lead to a self-fulfilling prophecy if held by a high-status person (e.g., an authority figure or older, male individual) (Darley & Fazio, 1980).

expectations communicated nonverbally by an interviewer actually caused interviewees to perform more poorly (see also M. Snyder, Tanke, & Berscheid, 1977). Such effects are common (Darley & Fazio, 1980) but require several critical steps (Figure 15.2): perceiver expectation and consistent behavior, target interpretation and response, perceiver interpretation as consistent (Darley & Fazio, 1980). As this sequence implies, either perceivers or targets can undermine self-fulfilling prophecies.

Perceivers moderate their self-fulfilling behavior especially given negative expectations, sometimes compensating for, rather than reciprocating, expected negative behavior. For example,

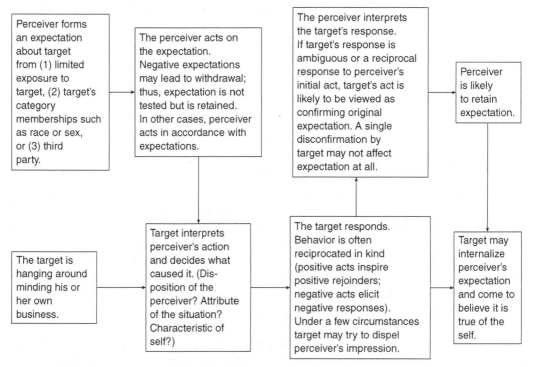

Figure 15.2 Development of a self-fulfilling prophecy

Source: After Darley & Fazio (1980)

if you expect hostility, rather than being hostile yourself (reciprocating), you may decide to be extra nice (compensating), hoping that you may thereby minimize the other's unpleasant behavior (M. H. Bond, 1972; Ickes, Patterson, Rajecki, & Tanford, 1982; Major, Cozzarelli, Testa, & McFarlin, 1988; Shelton & Richeson, 2005; Swann & Snyder, 1980). A perceiver's accuracy goal also undoes some behaviors associated with expectancy-based interactions (Neuberg, 1989).

Perceivers moderate their expectations depending on their own and targets' respective certainty. Behavior confirmation occurs only when perceivers are certain of their expectancies but targets are uncertain of their self-conception. In contrast, target **self-verification** (Chapter 5) occurred when targets are certain of their self-conceptions, and it tends to occur when both perceivers and targets are uncertain of their beliefs (Swann & Ely, 1984). Thus, target individuals themselves can also prevent the enactment of a self-fulfilling prophecy by refusing to be miscast into some role they feel does not fit. Each of us has no doubt had the experience.

Targets especially try to dispel perceivers' false impressions when they are aware of them (Hilton & Darley, 1985), when targets think their own behavior might have contributed to the misperception (Darley & Fazio, 1980), when the false impressions especially contradict targets' own self-views (Baumeister & Jones, 1978), and when they matter a lot to the target. However, under some circumstances, the target may find the perceiver's false impression to be so desirable that the target will attempt to fit it and come to see the self as the perceiver does. This extreme case of the self-fulfilling prophecy shows not only the target's behavior but own self-concept coming to fit the perceiver's initially false impression (Fazio, Effrein, & Falender, 1981; M. Snyder & Swann, 1978b).

Summary

Behavior depends on how people define a situation and adopt relevant personal goals, showing considerable flexibility. Sometimes self-regulation proceeds consciously by making explicit goals and plans, evenhandedly deliberating alternatives, but then implementing too optimistically. Nonetheless, cognitions serve goal pursuit, affecting persistence and ultimate achievement. Other goal-related self-regulation occurs automatically. However, people change from conscious deliberation to automatic behavior in part by forming explicit if–then implementation intentions that use situational cues to shift action control into automaticity.

Automatic evaluation of situational cues (including significant others) can occur rapidly and evoke complex action sequences. Sometimes we assimilate our behavior to situational cues, for example, becoming more achievement oriented when others do. But contrast effects also occur when people do the opposite of situational cues.

The cognition–behavior relationship has been especially explored by research on attitude–behavior consistency. Attitudes fit behaviors that are prototypic and measured at a comparable level of specificity. Attitudes formed from direct experience, accessible, and reflecting self-interest or values predict behavior. Focusing on the reasons underlying one's attitudes can reduce attitude–behavior consistency.

How behavior is labeled influences attitude–behavior consistency. Actions may be identified at relatively low levels or higher levels. High-level behaviors tend to seem dispositionally based, but also behaviorally flexible. Low-level actions, in contrast, show stability across situations but may not seem to reflect underlying dispositions. Situational factors moderate cognition–behavior consistency by making such factors as social norms or prior attitudes salient. Finally, individual differences in how people approach social situations (e.g., self-monitoring and self-consciousness) influence attitude salience and link to behavior.

People manage others' impressions of them. Typically, people strive to convey positive impressions through matching others' behaviors, flattering them, self-promoting, or conforming to situational norms. When a poor impression seems likely, people make excuses or self-handicap, engaging in or claiming liabilities to account for their failure.

Behavior can test hypotheses about both self and others, but people are often biased, seeking confirmatory information; even tentative hypotheses may look more true than they really are. Testing a hypothesis can lead even targets to confirm the hypothesis in self-fulfilling prophecies. Potential self-fulfilling prophecies can be undermined if perceivers compensate or targets resist.

FURTHER READING

Aarts, H. (2012). Goals, motivated social cognition and behavior. In S. T. Fiske & C. N. Macrae (Eds.), *Sage handbook of social cognition* (pp. 75–95). Thousand Oaks, CA: Sage.

Chartrand, T. L., & Bargh, J. A. (1999). The chameleon effect: The perception–behavior link and social interaction. *Journal of Personality and Social Psychology, 76*, 893–910.

Gollwitzer, P. M., & Sheeran, P. (2006). Implementation intentions and goal achievement: A meta-analysis of effects and processes. In M. P. Zanna (Ed.), *Advances in Experimental Psychology* (Vol. 38, pp. 69–119). San Diego, CA: Academic Press.

Macrae, C. N., & Miles, L. K. (2012). Revisiting the sovereignty of social cognition: Finally some action. In S. T. Fiske & C. N. Macrae (Eds.), *Sage handbook of social cognition* (pp. 1–11). Thousand Oaks, CA: Sage.

Word, C. O., Zanna, M. P., & Cooper, J. (1974). The nonverbal mediation of self-fulfilling prophecies in interracial interaction. *Journal of Experimental Social Psychology, 10*, 109–120.

Glossary

Abnormal conditions   are circumstances of apparent failure, especially unexpected ones.

Accessibility   describes how attention is primed for categories and concepts that fit what people have thought about recently or frequently.

Accountability   is the need to justify one's judgments to others.

Action identification   labels a specific action at levels ranging from low level (concrete) to higher level (abstract).

Actions   are voluntary behaviors that are always internally caused, consisting of two subtypes: endogenous acts (ends) and exogenous acts (means).

Activated actor   approaches, prominent in the 2000s, view social environments as rapidly cuing perceivers' social concepts, without awareness, and almost inevitably triggering associated cognitions, evaluations, affect, motivation, and behavior.

Actor–observer effect   maintains that people explain other people's behavior as due to dispositional factors but their own behavior as due to situational factors.

Affect   is a generic term for a whole range of preferences, evaluations, moods, and emotions.

Affect as information   proposes that affective valence tells the self how it should evaluate a stimulus, even when the affect has an irrelevant source.

Affect infusion model (AIM)   proposes that, depending on the processing mode, affective influences may be relatively automatic, controlled, or absent altogether.

Affective forecasting   describes people's attempt to anticipate how events will make them feel.

Affective transference   describes emotional responses to a person who resembles a significant other.

Affordances   describe perceived action possibilities for a specific perceiver in a specific setting.

Agency   describes personal authorship of an outcome, the ability to intend and take autonomous action (generally human, but often associated with male stereotypes).

Agent-based modeling,   usually in a computer simulation, represents the distributions of individual units with particular characteristics (various attitudes, knowledge, goals, physical positions) all interacting with each other as autonomous actors to produce emergent outcome patterns.

Algebraic model,   described but not endorsed by Asch, evaluates each individual trait, in isolation, and combines the evaluations into a summary evaluation (see **elemental approach**).

Amae   is the Japanese experience of being lovingly cared for and dependent on another's indulgence.

Ambivalent sexism theory   posits that anti-female prejudices include not only **hostile sexism** but also subjectively **benevolent sexism**.

Ambivalent stereotyping   describes a group as high on one dimension (e.g., competence) but low on another (e.g., warmth).

Amygdala   is one of a pair of small brain regions (often described as almond-shaped and sized), implicated in emotions and motivational relevance, but most clearly in fear.

Analyzing reasons   refers to the phenomenon of considering (and constructing) rationale underlying one's attitudes, often with little bearing on their actual origins.

Anchor   describes, when judging under uncertainty, people reducing ambiguity by using an initial reference point, and adjusting it to reach a final conclusion.

Anchoring and adjustment   describes basing a judgment on an arbitrary starting point and failing to move far enough away from it.

ANOVA model   is Kelley's normative model of causal inference, drawing on distinctiveness, consensus, and consistency (also called the **covariation model**).

Anterior   describes relatively forward areas of the brain (relative to **posterior** ones).

Anterior cingulate cortex (ACC),   the forward part of the brain's cingulate cortex, which itself wraps around the corpus callosum connecting the two hemispheres. The ACC is implicated in social-cognition-relevant tasks such as discrepancy detection and shifting from automatic to controlled processes in regulating behavior, shown in both social and physical pain.

Appraisal theories of emotions   describe people as evaluating stimuli initially as good-for-me versus bad-for-me, resulting in primitive positive–negative reactions.

Arousal (that is, emotional excitation of the **sympathetic nervous system**) controls bodily functions such as heart-rate and breathing.

Arousal-plus-mind theory (our term for Mandler's emotion theory) combines physiological arousal with evaluative cognition to produce emotion.

Ask–answer–announce is a sequence of steps in considering, judging, and confronting prejudice.

Assimilation describes fitting a specific occasion, instance, or behavior to a more general prior concept.

Associated systems theory (AST) is a person memory model positing that representations of other people develop through the use of four primary mental systems: (a) the visual system, (b) the verbal/semantic system, (c) the affective system, and (d) the action system.

Associative meaning perceives two items as belonging together because they fit prior expectations (e.g., bacon–eggs).

Associative models of memory most refer to connections between nodes linked to other nodes.

Associative-propositional evaluation model of attitudes combines implicit associative and deliberative propositional representations of attitudes.

Attention focuses on the contents of consciousness, including encoding external material and retrieving material from memory, characterized by both direction (selectivity) and intensity (effort).

Attitude is an evaluation, though definitions vary. Attitudes broadly dispose people to respond positively or negatively, as inferred from their specific cognitive, affective, and behavioral responses.

Attribute-based responses, in contrast to **category-based** ones, describe piecemeal impression formation that incorporates the details of the individual.

Attribution attempts to identify what factors give rise to what outcomes, describing how people infer other people's dispositions and mental states from behavior and its causes.

Attribution theories describe people's causal analyses of (attributions about) the social world, mostly as due to the target's dispositions or situations.

Attributional ambiguity describes the dilemma of understanding whether a negative interpersonal outcome is a reaction to one's personal attributes or bias against one's social category.

Attributional theory of motivated behavior, largely in the domains of achievement behavior and helping, articulates dimensions (locus, stability, and controllability) for understanding causal inference's effects on expectations, emotions, and behavior.

Attributions of responsibility concern who or what is accountable for an event, especially if negatively valenced.

Attunement describes perceiver sensitivity to particular stimulus properties that afford action.

Augmenting principle maintains that people increase the value of a cause given no alternative causes.

Automaticity, in pure form, is unintentional, uncontrollable, efficient, autonomous, and outside awareness (see **preconscious automaticity**).

Auto-motives describe situations automatically cuing certain motives.

Autonomic describes the part of the nervous system that controls the visceral or involuntary bodily functions (heart rate, breathing), including the parasympathetic and **sympathetic nervous systems**.

Availability denotes either (a) whether information has been stored at all or (b) (for heuristic inferences) ease of bringing information to mind.

Availability heuristic evaluates the likelihood of an event based on how quickly instances or associations come to mind.

Aversive racism describes most people's good intentions regarding race and their rejection of their own potentially racist beliefs. It results from negative reactions, simultaneously coupled with denial of the negativity, causing interracial interactions to be aversive.

Balance theory describes structures in the perceiver's mind representing the perceiver (P), another person (0), and the mutual attitude object (X).

Basal ganglia are located at the base of the forebrain and implicated in motor control; relevant to social cognition, this area includes the **striatum**, itself implicated in automatic monitoring of reward.

Base rates are population characteristics (averages, prior probabilities, or proportions), or other broad-based general prior data, normatively but not descriptively used to estimate particular instances.

Bayes' theorem   draws on the prior overall odds (**base rates**) and a focal event's likelihood to estimate probabilities of the event, given the prior odds.

Behavioral activation system (BAS)   is an appetitive system, promoting approach-oriented rewarding goals.

Behavioral confirmation   describes a target acting as a perceiver expects just because of that expectation (see **Pygmalion effect**).

Behavioral inhibition system (BIS)   is an aversive system, preventing negative outcomes by avoiding action.

Behavioral matching   imitates another person, in order to smooth the interaction.

Behaviorist   approaches, especially to learning, examine stimulus–response relationships without positing intervening cognitions; only overt, measurable acts are sufficiently valid objects for empirical scrutiny.

Belonging   is a motive to have relationships and be accepted by other people, especially one's group.

Benevolent sexism   describes a subjectively positive but controlling and paternalistic attitude toward women, cherishing them only if they stay in traditional roles, subordinate to men.

BIAS (Behaviors from Intergroup Affect and Stereotypes) map   extends the **stereotype content model** into discriminatory actions.

Biocultural approach   views intergroup threat from a sociofunctional evolutionary perspective, emphasizing human interdependence, effective group functioning, and individual adaptation to the benefits and threats of group life.

Biosocial approach   takes into account both genetic, physical differences among people and societal norms shaping their behavior, most applied to explaining gender roles, stereotypes, and prejudices.

Bipolar   means having two poles (opposite ends), and in affect and attitude scales, most often meaning positive and negative endpoints, although bipolar scales could involve agree–disagree (see **unipolar**).

Bivalent   implies two independent valences, often separate, uncorrelated positive and negative dimensions, operating independently.

Blatant bias is overtly expressed ingroup favoritism or outgroup derogation, largely from perceived intergroup threats, both economic and value-oriented.

Bottom-up processes include sensory motor perceptions or any relatively concrete starting point, stimulus-driven, or data-driven.

C system (reflective) involves the lateral prefrontal cortex, **medial prefrontal cortex**, rostral **anterior cingulate,** posterior parietal cortex, and the medial temporal lobe regions, all implicated in controlled processing.

Cardiovascular activity (CV) indexes cardiac output, ventricle activity, total peripheral resistance.

Categories describe expectations about clusters of people, entities, or social groups.

Categorization stage, as an initial relatively automatic part of the attribution process, perceives the stimulus configuration as characteristic of certain types of behavior.

Category gathers subjectively similar members into a conceptually related group.

Category activation reflects, in response to an individual, the initial, relatively automatic access to group-level expectations.

Category application reflects, in response to an individual, the use of group expectations to form an impression.

Category-based responses include cognition, affect, and behavior that react to an individual on the basis of perceived social group membership.

Category confusions describe perceivers mixing up individuals who belong to the same social group (e.g., remembering only that the person was a woman but misremembering which one).

Central route describes the **elaboration likelihood model'**s deliberate thoughtful mode of persuasion, evaluating the merits of arguments pro and con.

Certainty of an attitude reflects its properties of mattering to one's sense of self and organizing one's experience.

Chain of cognitive responses outlines the necessary conditions for a persuasive communication to influence behavior.

Characterization stage, as an initial relatively automatic part of the attribution process, attributes dispositional qualities to an action.

Chronically accessible concepts   reflect individual differences in how people habitually code other people, especially particular trait dimensions that tend to capture attention and repeatedly surface in impressions.

Chronicity   reflects dimensions that are frequently accessed or permanently primed, which may become central aspects of one's personality.

Circumscribed accuracy   provides valid predictions of another person's behavior in specific situations, often ones where perceiver and target overlap.

Classical conditioning   associates stimuli and responses through repeated pairings; stimuli and responses commonly include valence.

Cognition$_1$ is intellective knowledge acquisition, the everyday (dictionary) meaning of cognition, in contrast to value-laden, intuitive, or irrational thinking.

Cognition$_2$ subsumes all mental activity, as compared to behavior.

Cognitive busyness   model splits a first automatic stage into *categorization* of behavior and its *characterization* in dispositional terms, followed by a controlled *correction* for situational factors only if the perceiver is not cognitively busy.

Cognitive consistency theories   posit that inconsistencies – among cognitions, among affects, or between cognitions and affects – cause attitude change; cognitions may be general beliefs or beliefs about behavior.

Cognitive load (or **busyness**),   which may involve the simultaneous performance of other tasks or attentional diversion to other stimuli, operates on the assumption that perceivers have limited on-line capacity.

Cognitive miser   model, prominent in the 1980s, holds that people are limited in their capacity to process information, so they take shortcuts, which lead to often good-enough but sometimes deeply flawed results.

Cognitive process   concerns how mental elements form, operate, and change over time.

Cognitive response analysis   is a method that examines the recipient's reported cognitions (especially counterarguments) as the message is received.

Collective self-esteem   is one's belief about one's own private and others' public regard for one's group and one's worth as a group member.

Colorblind   approaches deny group differences and insists that everyone be treated identically, regardless of background.

Common ingroup identity model   describes going beyond group boundaries by including an (e.g., ethnic) outgroup, alongside the ingroup, in an overarching ingroup (e.g., citizens).

Commonsense psychology   (see also **naive psychology**) is ordinary people's everyday theories about each other.

Communality   describes an orientation to the welfare of specific and generalized others.

Comparative fit   compares between-group differences to within-group differences in **self-categorization theory**.

Competition   among cognitive links favors the successful (frequent) links strengthened at the expense of the less successful (less frequent) ones.

Complexity-extremity hypothesis   posits that representations with more dimensions will usually have more moderate evaluations that those with fewer dimensions.

Compliance   operates to gain rewards and avoid punishments.

Conception   entails knowing without consciously retrieving visual (or other sensory motor) details.

Conditional automaticity   is automatic responding that depends on context, including but not limited to goals.

Configural model,   developed by Asch, hypothesizes that people form a unified overall impression of other people; the Gestalt unifying forces shape individual elements to fit together (see **Holistic approach**).

Confirmatory hypothesis testing   is selective information-seeking biased to support one's expectations.

Conjunction fallacy   overestimates the likelihood that any two or more events will co-occur, compared to their isolated likelihood; because their joint probability is the product of their probabilities of occurring alone, their joint probability cannot exceed the probability of the least probable event.

Connection strengths   represent the type and magnitude of association among features.

Connectionist models   use parallel distributed processing ideas to focus on simultaneous activation of knowledge systems that depend on dynamic links more than rigid nodes. Only the strengths of connections are stored, so that the pattern can be re-created by activating parts of it and waiting for the connections to reverberate throughout the system until the entire pattern is activated.

Connectionist model of impression formation is a parallel distributed model of both social perception and social learning.

Conscious will is experienced when a thought precedes, fits, and explains a subsequent action.

Consciousness is variously defined as: stream of thought; attention; being aware of a cognition; being aware that it reflects one's behavior even though one might not be able to report on it; an epiphenomenon irrelevant to ongoing mental processes; an executive that directs mental structures; a necessary condition for human understanding and intent; a constructed device; allowing the formation of new associations; the internal stimulus field composed of thoughts, emotional experiences, and body sensations; being awake and mindful; having a subjective experienced available for report and intentional use.

Consensus described whether other actors besides the particular actor behave similarly toward this entity.

Consistency described whether a person's behavior toward an entity occurs reliably across time and modality.

Consistency seeker view, a 1950s–60s perspective on social thinkers, in this case primarily motivated by perceived discrepancies among their cognitions, as in dissonance theory.

Consolidation in a connectionist model describes adjusting long-term linkages in memory,

Constraints determine what units activate depending on the entire pattern of links.

Consummatory behavior is enacted for its own sake, perhaps driven by affect.

Contingencies of self-worth describe people being selective about the domains on which they base their self-esteem.

Continuum model of impression formation compares immediate relatively automatic categorization based on sex, race, age, etc., with intermediate processing by subtypes, going toward full individuation by attributes.

Contrast describes a specific reaction opposite to a more general prior concept.

Controllability as a dimension of causality relates to whether a person can influence the outcome at will.

Controlled processes entail the perceiver's conscious intent substantially determining their operation.

Controlling   motives strive to influence one's own outcomes that depend on other people.

Conviction   about an attitude includes emotional commitment, preoccupation, and cognitive elaboration.

Correction phase,   as a late relatively controlled part of the attribution process, uses situational and other information to discount or augment the initial dispositional attribution.

Correspondence bias (see also **fundamental attribution error**),   over-attributes another person's behavior to dispositional causes, rather than taking account of situational factors.

Correspondent inference   is Jones and Davis's theory of how people infer other people's intents and dispositions.

Corrugator supercilii   are the muscles between the eyebrows that contract in a frown.

Cortisol   is a hormone that is produced in response to stress, increasing protein and carbohydrate metabolism to increase blood sugar, while suppressing immune system and bone formation processes.

Counterfactual reasoning   is the mental simulation of how events might otherwise have occurred.

Covariation   judgments estimate how strongly two events are related.

Covariation model of attribution (also called the **ANOVA model**)   is a normative model of causal inference, drawing on distinctiveness, consensus, and consistency information.

Cybernetic theory of self-regulation   describes the feedback process by which people try to conform to a salient standard, evaluate own behavior against it, decide that the behavior either matches the standard or does not, and continue adjusting and comparing until meeting the standard or giving up.

De facto selective exposure   describes an environment biased toward attitude-consistent information.

Declarative memory   assumes an associative long-term store of network concepts, the "what" of memory; it includes both **semantic memory** and **episodic memory**.

Defensive attribution   refers to the idea that people attribute more human responsibility for actions that produce severe rather than mild consequences.

Dehumanization   treats another individual or group as not fully human, closer to an object.

Deliberative mindset is the (motivational) focus on incentives and expectations, choosing among alternative goals and their implied courses of action.

Depth of processing accounts maintain that self-relevant information (or any more involving process) leaves a richer, more interconnected, and more enduring memory trace than a simpler more superficial form of processing.

Descriptive stereotypes specify what a group allegedly is.

Dichotic listening task involves piping two separate series of inputs to each ear, with instructions to attend only to one, and measures of reactions to the unattended ear.

Dilution effect is the finding that extreme predictions can be attenuated by the presence of irrelevant information; when diagnostic information is weakened by nondiagnostic information, inferences are less extreme.

Direct experience describes an occasion of attitude formation based on personal events rather than second-hand information.

Direct perception, unmediated by cognitive processing, is local, feature-oriented, piecemeal.

Discount rate describes the diminishing utility of an outcome when extended over time.

Discounted utility theory (DU) adds to the **expected utility theory** (EU) that the utility of any given choice diminishes as consequences are spread over time, called the **discount rate**.

Discounting principle maintains that people reduce the importance of any one cause, given another sufficient cause.

Disidentification describes removing a domain from relevance to one's personal or social identity.

Dispositions are people's enduring personality or intentions, invariances across behaviors.

Dissociation model of prejudice first contrasted automatic and controlled attitudes toward outgroups.

Dissonance theory focuses on how inconsistency among cognitions causes a motivational state (dissonance) directed toward resolving that inconsistency.

Distinctiveness describes whether a person's behavior occurs only in the presence of a particular target (entity) or is directed toward many such entities.

Dopamine is a neurotransmitter implicated in rewards and reward learning.

Dorsal describes the brain's upper surface and areas located upward relative to another area (e.g., **ventral**).

Downward social comparisons judge self against less-fortunate others, either enhancing the self as superior or threatening the self with a fall.

Dual attitudes comprise an older, automatic attitude and the newer, explicitly accessible attitude.

Dual-process model of impression formation contrasts choice points that result in relatively automatic processes such as initial identification or categorization using images versus more deliberate personalized concepts or individuated subtypes and exemplars.

Dual-process model of overconfident attributions contrasts relatively automatic identification of behavior with more controlled explanations.

Dual-process models generally compare more automatic and more controlled modes.

Durability bias is people's tendency to overestimate how long an adverse event will affect them.

Dynamical perspective describes social cognition in a **connectionist model** following **Gestalt** principles where for example concepts or people are adjacent nodes linked by mutual influence.

Ecological perception (Gibsonian) approach emphasizes adapted, accurate perceivers interacting with their environments and embedded in their own characteristic niche; "perceiving is for doing," in this view.

Ecological perspective examines how people make specific inferences from physical features of the stimulus configuration, unmediated by cognition.

Ego involvement is exemplified by one's attitude toward a controversial social issue. (Roughly equivalent to **issue involvement, personal involvement, vested interest.**)

Elaboration includes making relevant associations, for example, scrutinizing arguments, inferring their value, and evaluating the overall message.

Elaboration likelihood model (ELM), a dual-process model of attitude change, describes two routes to persuasion: the central route, via thoughtful evaluation of message arguments, and the peripheral route, via relatively automatic use of superficial cues.

Electrodermal responses (EDR) measures electro-conductance to assess skin moisture (also galvanic skin response (GSR), **skin conductance**).

Electroencephalography (EEG) records neural **event-related potentials,** that is voltage fluctuation on the scalp, detecting neural activity.

Electromyography (EMG) in social cognition, mostly facial) records voltage changes on skin over muscles, so their activity.

Elemental approaches break scientific problems down into pieces and analyze the pieces in separate detail before combining them.

Embedded attitudes link to other beliefs.

Embodied representation includes both external stimuli and bodily responses, preparing the perceiver for appropriate action.

Emergent action is defined as behavior that people find themselves doing that they did not set out to do.

Emotion refers to a complex assortment of affects, beyond merely good and bad feelings, and can imply intense feelings with physical manifestations, including physiological arousal.

Emotional lability theory models how people self-attribute emotion from labeling arousal according to environmental circumstances.

Emotional prejudices, beyond positive–negative evaluation (attitudes), include distinct emotions such as fear, disgust, envy, pity, anxiety, and resentment.

Emotion-focused coping attempts to deal with the affective impact of a threat or adverse event.

Empathy gap describes people in a cool mindset inaccurately imagining people, including themselves, acting in a hot mindset.

Encoding transforms a perceived external stimulus into an internal representation.

Endogenous acts are voluntary actions committed as ends in themselves.

Enemy images theory posits that national and ethnic stereotypes fit dimensions of relative status, relative power, and goal compatibility.

Entitativity is the property of being a real thing.

Entity theorists have lay beliefs that personal attributes (e.g., intelligence) are relatively fixed, in contrast to **incremental theorists**.

Epinephrine   (alternately, adrenaline) acts as both a hormone and a neurotransmitter affecting the **sympathetic nervous system**, increasing heart rate, constricting blood vessels, dilating air passages, as well as more generally stress and the fight-or-flight response.

Episodic memory   represents specific events as part of declarative long-term memory.

Epistemic   relates to acquiring knowledge or understanding.

Essence   endorses categories as having a foundational core often expressed as shared genes, blood, or nature.

Evaluations   are simple positive and negative reactions telling us whom (and what) to approach and avoid.

Event-related potential (ERP)   describes the brain's localized evoked electrical activity, measured by **electroencephalography** (EEG).

Executive   processes control other processes, especially prioritizing them.

Exemplar   approaches suggest remembering separate instances or exemplars actually encountered rather than prototypes abstracted from experience.

Exogenous acts   are voluntary actions committed in service of other goals.

Expected utility (EU) **theory**   maintains that inferential behavior can be conceptualized as choices among alternatives, each with a probability of occurrence and a designated value. According to the model, people assess available alternatives for their likelihood and the worth of the outcomes that they promise (i.e., probability and value), calculate the utility of each outcome (the product of the probability of each outcome and its value), and choose the option that maximizes utility.

Experience-sampling   methods query respondents for self-reports at random moments during daily life.

Experimental demand   describes a variety of ways that a method, setting, or personnel may inadvertently communicate the hypothesis or otherwise channel participant responses to confirm the hypothesis. Features of the situation, experimenter–participant interaction, or measures can inadvertently constrain expected behavior.

Expertise   as a cognitive concept encompasses considerable experience, coded as organized prior knowledge, both declarative and procedural, enabling efficiency.

Extrinsic motivation   results from rewards external to the task, as in payment for performance.

Facial feedback hypothesis holds that emotional events directly trigger certain configurations of muscles, and that we become aware of feelings only upon feedback from the face.

False alarms mistakenly identify distracter items on the test as being part of the original set.

False consensus effect describes people's tendency to assume that under the same circumstances other people would react in the same way.

Family resemblance describes any given pair of category members sharing some features with each other and other features with other category members.

Fantasy envisions the future as filled with bountiful (unrealistic) possibilities (wishful thinking).

Feared selves are selves we are afraid of becoming.

Feature-oriented processing of a face entails separate focus on each aspect (e.g., eyes, mouth).

Fluency describes the ease of perceiving or processing information.

Frame, within the **perceptual symbol systems** (PSS) **simulator,** integrates across experiences within a category, to create the **simulations** of the experience of a particular example on a particular occasion.

Frame of reference, or frame in judgment and decision making, is the way the problem is described (see **reference point**).

Framing is how a decision's background context of the choice is described, and in **prospect theory,** often contrasting gain versus loss.

Frontal lobe encompasses the anterior (forward) regions of the brain.

Functional magnetic resonance imaging (fMRI) records re-oxygenizing blood flow to just-activated brain areas.

Fundamental attribution error (see also **correspondence bias**) over-attributes another person's behavior to dispositional causes, rather than taking account of situational factors.

Fusiform face area (FFA), part of the brain's temporal lobe, is known in social cognition for its sensitivity to human faces.

Fuzzy sets reflect the idea that natural categories do not have necessary and sufficient attributes.

Genetic analyses, combined with environment, detect their interactive links to social cognition.

Gestalt representation   emphasizes perception of configurations in context.

Global   processing is configural and holistic, perceptually integrating across the whole (e.g., face).

Goal-dependent automaticity   is initially intentional and often conscious, but also partially automatic, according to some criteria: lack of awareness of the process itself, not needing to monitor the process to completion, and lack of intending all the specific outcomes.

Goal-inconsistent automaticity   occurs when a person's own unwanted responses are governed by cognitive factors outside control and awareness (see **thought suppression**).

Goals   are mental representations of desired outcomes; they include intended behavior sequences with preferred outcomes.

Goal-shielding   describes how activating the focal goal inhibits alternative goals' accessibility.

Group homogeneity   is the perception, often applied to outgroups, that they do not vary much; this includes stereotyping but also dispersion (perceived spread of attributes) and similarity.

Group polarization (one direction being a **risky shift**)   describes a group decision more extreme than the average of the individual decisions, as a result of discussion.

Group-serving bias (see **ultimate attribution error**)   refers to the tendency of group members to attribute positive actions committed by their own group to positive ingroup qualities, and negative actions committed by the ingroup to external causes, and vice versa for the outgroup.

Guided induction   involves a learning-through-examples approach.

Habits   are behavior repeated frequently, without much thought.

Hard interface   is an early term anticipating embodied representations.

Hebbian learning   describes associative learning by changing the strength of links between nerve cells; simultaneous activation strengthens the links, but does not provide for inhibition of unactivated links.

Hedonic emotions   explicitly reflect on short-term concerns of the self, as in shame.

Hedonic relevance   is whether another person's action bears on (obstructs or promotes) the perceiver's own self-interest and goals.

Heuristic processing   describes the **heuristic-systematic model**'s rapid, easy shortcuts to attitude change.

Heuristics are one kind of shortcut people use for judgments under uncertainty, generally used for strategies identified by Kahneman and Tversky, mostly relying on ease of bringing instances to mind, to reduce complex problem solving to simpler judgmental operations and meet the pressing demands of the environment.

Heuristic-systematic model (HSM), a dual-process theory of attitude change, contrasts relatively automatic processes of persuasion driven by shortcuts versus relatively controlled systematic processes. It proposes thoughtful processes, only given sufficient motivation and capacity; otherwise, people use faster, easier cognitive shortcuts.

Hindsight bias (see **twenty-twenty hindsight**) indicates the difficulty of ignoring knowledge of an actual outcome to generate unbiased inferences about what could or should have happened.

Holistic approaches analyze the pieces in the context of other pieces and focus on the entire configuration of relationships among them.

Hormone levels (e.g., **cortisol, testosterone, oxytocin**) variously link to sociality.

Hostile sexism resents nontraditional women, who are seen as unfairly competing with men, trying to control men sexually, and resisting conventional roles.

Hypothetical mediating variables are constructs theorized as a mechanism to explain the link between a cause and an outcome, for example, an attitude intervening between an observable stimulus (S) and an observable response (R), providing the necessary connection.

Ideal self is who one wants to be (goals, hopes, and dreams).

Identification operates toward attitudes that enhance belonging with valued groups.

Identification stage in attribution processes describes initial labeling of a behavior.

Illusory correlation expects a relationship between two variables when none actually exists; people often overestimate their correlation or impose a relationship because of **associative meaning** or **paired distinctiveness**.

Imagery representations are conscious and specific about the sensory motor features.

Immune functioning assays track-specific immune cells and system operation.

Implementation intentions are explicit if–then plans that specify how to realize a goal in a specific situation.

Implementational mindset   is the (volitional) focus on when and how to enact the intended course of action.

Implicit association test (IAT)   is a method contrasting evaluative associations between categories.

Implicit attitudes   are typically assessed by the **implicit association test** (IAT), at least partially automatic and uncontrolled.

Implicit memory   describes the influence of past judgmental processes on current judgments and reactions.

Implicit self-esteem   is measured by indirect indicators of self-value.

Implicit theories   of personal histories are people's construction of their own stability and change over time.

Importance   of an attitude indicates a person's interest or concern.

Important attitudes   reflect fundamental values, self-interest, or identification with valued individuals or groups.

Impression-relevant involvement   reflects people's need for attitudes that promote a positive public image, affiliation, and social approval (see also **social-adjustive functions**).

Inconsistency advantage   describes superior memory for expectancy-incongruent information because of extra attention, its being surprising; this produces extra associative linkages for those items, increasing their alternative retrieval paths and probability of recall.

Incremental theorists   have lay beliefs that personal attributes (e.g., intelligence) are malleable, in contrast to **entity theorists**.

Independence   models view people as autonomous actors without much social connection.

Independent self   sees the self as a unique, autonomous, agentic (originator of action), bounded, coherent whole, contrasting with other individuals and with the context; this view occurs most clearly in Western settings.

Indirect primimg   assesses indirect attitudes by response-time facilitation from a valenced prime to an attitude object.

Inference   most means judgment and decision making on the basis of uncertain, incomplete, or ambiguous evidence. Processes are often **controlled** but may include **heuristics** or other **shortcuts**.

Information processing breaks down mental operations into sequential cognitive stages.

Informational influence describes attitude (or behavior) change that relies on a cognitive interpretation of the group's beliefs.

Infrahuman perception views another group or individual as essentially less-than-human.

Ingratiation is a self-presentational strategy designed to make one seem likeable.

Ingroup is one's own group, often viewed as distinctive and positive on subjectively important dimensions.

Ingroup favoritism exploits the relative advantage of ingroup over outgroup, even to the detriment of self and own group's absolute outcomes.

Instrumental behavior is enacted in service of goals, perhaps driven by cognition.

Instrumental functions of an attitude are adaptive, helping people to avoid pain and gain rewards.

Insula are "islands" deep within each hemisphere of the brain, between the **frontal lobe** and **temporal lobe**; they are reliably implicated in disgust but also other automatic, intense negative responses, for example, attitudes.

Integrated threat theory (ITT) incorporates many intergroup variables but focuses on one major emotion, anxiety, to predict attitudes.

Intentional thought is characterized by having options, most obviously by making the hard choice, and enacted by paying attention to implementing the intent.

Interdependence models recognize people's connection to each other as needing each other for important outcomes (see **outcome dependency**).

Interdependent self sees oneself as part of encompassing social relationships and adjusts one's behavior to what one perceives to be the thoughts, feelings, and actions of others in the relationship; this occurs most clearly in Asian, Southern European, and Latin American cultures.

Intergroup contact describes encountering an outgroup – under certain conditions, reducing prejudice.

Intergroup emotions theory (IET) describes emotional assessments on behalf of one's ingroup, as an extension of **appraisal theories** of emotion.

Intermediate memory in some models falls temporally between short-term and long-term memory.

Internalization operates to store attitude-relevant knowledge.

Interpreter is a hypothetical neural module that integrates diverse self-relevant processing in different parts of the brain to create that sense of self that most of us experience subjectively; it appears to emerge from the functions of the left hemisphere.

Interruption describes the disruption of an expected perceptual pattern or a goal-directed behavior sequence.

Intrinsic motivation results from the rewards inherent to the task, such as enjoyment.

Introspection is a method that relies on people's own reports of their internal cognitive processes (the how, not the what or contents, for which see **think-aloud protocols**).

Introspective access describes people's ability to report accurately on the processes (not simply contents) of their minds.

Intuition, variously defined, includes sudden, conscious, emotional reactions, without awareness of having gone through prior calculations.

Invariances are factors such as dispositional properties that reliably account especially for stable patterns of behavior.

Issue involvement reflects personal motivation tied to an attitude. (Roughly equivalent to **ego involvement, personal involvement, vested interest**.)

James-Lange view of emotions holds that behavioral reactions and physiological patterns reveal to us what emotion we are feeling.

Knowledge function of an attitude is fundamentally cognitive and adaptive, related to object appraisal.

Lateral describes the sides of the brain (relative to **medial** areas).

Law of large numbers is the statistical principle that small samples produce poor estimates of a population's characteristics, whereas larger samples are more reliable.

Legitimizing myths are complex cognitions (beliefs and ideology) that support the status quo.

Lexical decision task is a common cognitive method asking participants to judge a sequence of letter strings as words or nonwords, often to assess response time after relevant primes.

Linear model   describes a combinatorial rule using a weighted average or sum of components, for example, when the total impression is an additive combination of the available information.

Locus   as a dimension of causality concerns whether an individual attributes an outcome to internal or external factors; it links to changes in self-esteem-related emotions such as pride and shame in self-attributions and to admiration or pity in other-attributions.

Long-term memory   comprises the vast store of information potentially brought to mind.

Loss aversion   describes the subjective value (**preference**) curve as steeper for losses than for gains: the same objective (e.g., monetary) difference looms larger as a loss than as a gain.

Maintenance indicators   include an action's difficulty, familiarity, complexity, time to enact, and time to learn to do it well.

Medial   describes the interior midline of the neocortex (relative to **lateral** areas).

Medial prefrontal cortex   is an **anterior** neocortical brain region along the vertical midline, implicated in many, if not most, social cognition processes, as well as other tasks, and perhaps the resting state, in which participant thoughts are unmanipulated and unknown.

Mediation   connects between stimulus inputs or other antecedents and response outputs or other consequences.

Memory-based impression   constructs a coherent representation of another person, based on retrieval of previously received information.

Mental addition   describes simulations that increase the perceived likelihood of a potential outcome, easier than mental subtraction.

Mental subtraction   describes simulations that reduce the perceived likelihood of a potential consequence.

Mentalism   is the belief in the importance of cognitive representations.

Mere exposure   describes repeated encounters (especially with nonlinguistic stimuli), which typically enhance liking.

Meta-cognition   is a second-order form of consciousness, people's beliefs about their own thinking processes.

Meta-contrast ratio,   in statistical terms, is equivalent to an F or t-test, putting mean differences between groups over within-group variance in **self-categorization theory**.

Meta-stereotypes   are people's beliefs about what outgroups think of the ingroup.

Metatheoretical   stands are major, overarching conceptual frameworks common to several theories of a certain type.

Mind perception   encompasses everyday mindreading: inferences about another's mental states, including beliefs, but also intentions, desires, and feelings.

Mindlessness   describes a cognitively dis-engaged, generally clueless, uncritical, essentially automatic responding.

Mind-wandering   is stimulus-independent thought.

Minimal group paradigm   creates the least necessary conditions for the experience of belonging in a group.

Misattribution effect   shows that arousal or emotional reactions induced by one source can potentially be reattributed to another source; arousal due to threat, for example, can be reattributed to a neutral source, thereby reducing anxiety.

MODE model   (motivation and opportunity as determinants) is an attitude accessibility model focusing on an attitude as an association in memory between a given object and one's evaluation of it. It describes how motivation and opportunity to process attitude-relevant information together determine behavior.

Modern racism   describes a form of subtle bias that focuses on attitudes, ideology, and symbols that all advantage the dominant majority over minorities.

Mood state-dependent memory   occurs when a matching mood at learning and retrieval facilitates memory.

Mood-congruent memory   describes a retrieval advantage for material with the same affective loading as one's current mood.

Moods   are positive and negative affect without a specific target, but typically with some duration.

Moral credentials   establish evidence for a person's apparent lack of prejudice, freeing the person subsequently to act in prejudiced ways.

Mortality salience   occurs when people confront their own death.

Motivated tactician   refers to people's tendency to rely on relatively automatic processes or alternatively on more effortful ones, depending on the situational and motivational demands.

The motivated tactician models view people as fully engaged thinkers with multiple cognitive strategies available, who (consciously or unconsciously) choose among them based on goals, motives, and needs.

Motivation to avoid prejudice   is a value-based compunction not to expresses intergroup biases.

mPFC (see **medial prefrontal cortex**).

Multiculturalism   endorses the idea that groups differ in essential ways and that organizations should value those essential differences.

Multiple necessary causal schemas   are characterized by the need for the presence of several contributing causes to produce an effect.

Multiple sufficient causal schemas   are characterized by conditions in which a behavior may be due to any of several present causes.

Multiple-act criterion   refers to measuring behavior's consistency with an attitude, trait, or cognition by using several instances of the relevant action.

Naive epistemology   describes the ways people think about and infer meaning from what occurs around them.

Naive psychology   (see also **commonsense psychology**) is ordinary people's everyday theories about each other.

Naive realism   describes people's idea that other people in general, especially those who disagree with them, are more susceptible to bias than they are themselves.

Naive scientist   describes the normative (idealized) assumption that people are essentially rational problem solvers with a few acknowledged biases. This view of social thinker, prominent in the 1970s, constructed optimal models of people as logical information-seekers, to assess whether and when they approximate the ideal.

Naturalistic social cognition   studies ask participants to view tapes of their own spontaneous interaction and report what they were thinking and feeling at specific moments.

Need for cognition   refers to people's chronic level of thoughtfulness in response to external stimuli.

Need to evaluate   is an individual difference that predicts spontaneous pro and con thoughts in response to stimuli, including persuasive messages.

Negative state-relief hypothesis   posits that people help other people in order to mitigate the personally aversive experience of seeing them suffer.

Neuroeconomics   brings together insights from the three disciplines of economics, neuroscience, and psychology to understand decision making.

Neuropsychology   considers personal and social lives of patients with brain impairments.

Noncommon effects   are the unique or at least distinctive outcomes of a particular choice or behavior.

Norepinephrine   (alternately, noradrenaline) acts as both a neurotransmitter and a hormone affecting the **sympathetic nervous system,** including heart rate, and the **amygdala**, as well as more generally stress and fight-or-flight responses.

Norm theory   focuses on *post hoc* interpretation based on an encounter with a particular stimulus in a particular context, with the aim of judging whether the stimulus was normal or surprising; **category** and **schema** theories describe reasoning forward, norm theory describes reasoning backward.

Normative fit   describes socially shared meaning that differentiates groups in **self-categorization**.

Normative influences   describe attitude (or behavior) change due to perceived norms and values.

Normative model   of inference is a formal, idealized set of rules for validating attributions.

Norm   has two distinct meaning in psychology: (a) informal rules for conduct (normative influences) in a given group; and (b) ideal (normative-model) responses to a decision problem, using all relevant information in unbiased fashion. Respectively, one is a social ideal; the other is an **epistemic** ideal.

Null hypothesis   is a statistical term for the prediction of no difference.

Object-appraisal function   of an attitude governs approach-avoidance decisions and includes a cognitive knowledge function and often a utilitarian, instrumental, or goal function.

Objective self-awareness   describes the experience of self as the target of other's perception, often experiencing self as failing to live up to ideal standards.

Occurrences   are behaviors that are involuntary or not completely voluntary, potentially caused by either internal/personal or external/situational factors.

Offline cognition is a term related to embodied cognition, when recreating perception without the original targets being present; it operates in the absence of the considered social object, in contrast to **online cognition** during interaction. Person memory research refers to this as a **memory-based impression,** but the hypothesized mechanism differ.

Online cognition occurs in the presence of the stimulus, rather than being **memory-based impression** (also in contrast to **offline cognition**).

Online impression formation develops a coherent representation of another person, while a perceiver receives information.

Operant thought is instrumental and problem-solving, goal-directed, volitional, progress-monitoring, protected against external and internal distractions, contrasted with respondent thought.

Optimal distinctiveness theory (ODT) argues that people balance individual autonomy and distinctiveness against belonging to the right group in order to reach a self-affirming and satisfying identity.

Optimizers make the choice that maximizes expected utility (see **expected utility** (EU) **model**), reaching the best possible inferences and decisions.

Orbitofrontal cortex is the prefrontal cortex area just behind the eyes, implicated in reward processing.

Other-profitable describes a person's attributes (e.g., friendliness, morality, communality) that further others' interests.

Ought self is who one thinks one should be (obligations and duties).

Outcome dependency describes the **interdependence** structure of relying on another person for valued outcomes, sometimes referred to as being low **power**.

Outcome involvement describes concern with what a persuasive communication implies for one's own future experiences and interests.

Outgroup is any group to which one does not belong.

Oxytocin is a hormone associated with social attachment.

Paired distinctiveness perceives two things as belonging together because they share some unusual feature.

Parallel constraint satisfaction theory is a single-mode alternative to dual-mode models, in which perceivers interpret and integrate a variety of incoming information simultaneously with accessing the relevant knowledge base, balancing mutual and immediate influence of both concrete and abstract inputs.

Parallel distributed processing (PDP) models the structure of cognition wherein each basic unit participates in representing many different concepts, which are retrieved when the appropriate pattern of activation occurs across the basic units; developed as an alternative to serial models of mental structure.

Parallel processes proceed simultaneously, for example, activating many related pathways at once.

Parallel processes model of impressions posits that all kinds of information, whether categorical or individuated, are integrated simultaneously, without a priori privileging some.

Parental investment model posits that women commit more resources to parenthood because of pregnancy, lactation, and the opportunity costs they entail for reproduction.

Parietal lobe is a major region of neocortex, located behind the **frontal lobe,** and above the **temporal lobe** and **occipital lobe.**

Perceptual symbol systems (PSS) encode both external and internal experience in a memory representation that incorporates both bottom-up perceptual processes and top-down sensory motor representations that include **conception** and imagery.

Peripheral route describes the **elaboration likelihood model**'s rapid, effortless route to persuasion, occurring without much thought or elaboration.

Permanence motivates lasting decisions.

Person memory model is an associative network model of social memory.

Personal control or a sense of general mastery enables people to plan, cope with setbacks, and pursue self-regulatory activities.

Personal involvement reflects general relevance of an attitude to self. (Roughly equivalent to **ego involvement, issue involvement, vested interest**.)

Personalism is the perceiver's perception that the actor has intentionally targeted behavior to benefit or harm the perceiver.

Person-situation interaction describes the combination of individual and contextual contributions, including different impressions of someone in particular contexts.

Persuasive arguments theory proposes that attitudes in groups polarize toward relatively extreme (cautious or risky) alternatives when people are exposed to new information.

Phenomenology describes systematically how ordinary people say they experience their world.

Phenotype (appearance) often determines racial categorization.

Planning fallacy describes people's optimistic tendency to overestimate how much they can accomplish in a given timeframe, underestimating the obstacles and the required effort.

Pluralistic ignorance describes individuals believing their opinions to be unique, when in fact they are shared.

PM-1 (Person Memory One) is an associative network model of social memory.

Pollyanna effect refers to people's tendency to interpret, rate, and remember entities more positively than not (see **positivity offset, positivity bias**).

Positive illusions are self-perceptions that are falsely positive and somewhat exaggerated with respect to one's actual abilities, talents, and social skills; overestimating control; and unrealistically optimistic about the future.

Positivity bias describes people's tendency to emphasize the good over the bad (see **positivity offset, Pollyanna effect**).

Positivity offset refers to the displacement of neutral judgments in a slightly positive direction (see **Pollyanna effect, positivity bias**).

Possible selves represent whom we could become, especially whom we would like to be.

Postconscious automaticity entails conscious perception of the prime but no awareness of its effects on subsequent reactions.

Posterior describes relatively far back areas of the brain (relative to **anterior** ones).

Power is most often defined as asymmetrical control over valued resources.

Power asymmetry theory holds that the affective experiences of powerful people tend to be more positive than those of less powerful people.

Preconscious automaticity requires that people are not aware of the priming cue, or of its effects on their reaction to a relevant stimulus.

Preferences   include relatively mild subjective reactions that are essentially either pleasant or unpleasant.

Prejudice   is the affective side of intergroup bias, evaluations of, and feelings about groups.

Prescriptive stereotypes   describe what a group should be.

Prevention focus   avoids negative outcomes and inhibits behavior.

Primacy effect   describes early information most influencing an evaluation or being most memorable.

Primary appraisal   is the initial automatic assessment of the object as good-bad for self.

Primary emotions   are the primitive, simple emotions felt by either animals or humans.

Priming   describes the effects of prior context on the interpretation of new information, that is, the impact of a recently or frequently activated category on the processing of category-relevant information, typically interpreted in terms of category accessibility, within declarative (associative network) memory.

Private body consciousness   describes sensitivity to one's internal physical reactions.

Private regard   describes one's personal beliefs about the worth of one's social category.

Probes   are experimenter-determined signals to respond according to previous instructions, such as reporting what one is currently thinking, feeling, or doing.

Problem-focused coping   attempts to deal directly with mitigating a threat or adverse event.

Procedural knowledge   represents condition–action pairs, if–then statements, called productions.

Procedural memory,   sometimes contrasted with **declarative memory**, is one form of automaticity, the "how" stored in memory.

Procedural priming   makes some relevant processes more accessible than others.

Proceduralization   is the practice process that develops automaticity; it generalizes processes from specific repeated experiences, sometimes viewed as the second step of a two-step process of compilation.

Productions   are procedural knowledge represented as condition–action pairs, or if–then statements.

Promotion focus   follows goals and involves behavioral activation.

Propositions   in memory consist of nodes (an idea: noun, verb, adjective) and link of relations between ideas.

Proprioception   is the sense of one's own bodily position from internal feedback.

Prospect theory   describes the decision processes involved when people compare options, focusing on frame of reference and subjective value function.

Prototype   is the central tendency or average (mean or mode) of category members.

Psychological field   is a configuration of subjectively driving and restraining motivational forces.

Psychological immune system   comprises people's coping processes that mitigate the effects of adversity.

Public regard   describes one's beliefs about how society values one's social category.

Pygmalion effect   describes a target acting as a perceiver expects just because of that expectation (see **behavioral confirmation**).

Racial ambivalence   describes Whites as simultaneously believing the Blacks are collectively disadvantaged due to circumstances and due to personal attributes and choices.

Realistic group conflict   includes any competition over actual resources, such as prestige, money, or military power.

Rebound   describes increased accessibility of a concept after attempted **thought suppression**.

Recency   effect describes later information most influencing an evaluation or being most memorable.

Reference point (also termed **frame of reference**)   is the internal standard with which people compare the objective value of an option so as to classify the option as positive (i.e., better than the reference point) or as negative (i.e., worse than the reference point); objectively identical options can be framed positively or negatively, such that an option perceived as a gain in one frame can be perceived as a loss in another frame.

Regression to the mean   refers to the statistical fact that extreme events will, on average, be less extreme when reassessed later.

Regulatory fit   describes a match between the goals pursued (activation/inhibition) and regulatory orientation (promotion/prevention).

Relational self   links the self-concept to mental representations of significant others.

Representativeness heuristic   makes inferences about probability by matching information about a specific instance against a general category to determine the likelihood by the goodness of fit.

Respondent thought   is neither volitional nor effortful but receptive; it constitutes all the ordinary distractions of unbidden images, contrasted with operant thought.

Response involvement   reflects a person interested in maximizing the rewards in a given situation.

Retrieval routes   proceed along node–link pathways; more links to a given node create more alternative paths.

Right-wing authoritarianism (RWA)   is an individual–difference ideology that endorses conventional values, obedience to leaders, aggression toward nonconformists, and derogating outgroups.

Risk-aversion   strategies avoid uncertainty when dealing with possible gains (e.g., money added or lives saved).

Risk-seeking   strategies approach uncertainty when dealing with possible losses (e.g., money subtracted or lives lost).

Risky shift (one direction of **group polarization**)   describes a group decision riskier than the average of the individual decisions, as a result of discussion.

Role congruity theory   describes how observing the correlation between gender and roles leads to prejudices against women (and men) in nontraditional roles.

Role-play participation   asks participants to imagine themselves in a partial or overheard interaction and report reactions to it.

Rumination   is repetitive, counterproductive thinking.

Salience   describes how much particular stimuli stand out relative to others in their environment.

Satisficers   make good-enough, adequate inferences and decisions.

Schema   describes an abstract representation, including the concept's attributes and the relations among them.

Schema-triggered affect   posits that some categories automatically link to affect.

Scripts are prototypic or schematic sequences of familiar events.

Secondary appraisal occurs, after primary appraisal, as a subsequent assessment based on analyzing the object and its relevance to self.

Secondary emotions are the complex, subtle sentiments felt by humans but not animals.

Selective accessibility model of assimilation and contrast, addressing conscious comparisons, assumes accessibility is flexible (controllable) and specific to the current judgment (rather than general semantic priming).

Selective attention heeds attitude-consistent information already present.

Selective exposure seeks attitude-consistent information not already present.

Selective interpretation translates ambiguous information to be consistent with attitudes.

Selective perception posits that attitudes shape encoding; it divides into **selective exposure**, **selective attention**, and **selective interpretation**.

Self-affirmation maintains that people cope with threats to their self-worth by endorsing other, unrelated aspects of themselves, thereby addressing self-enhancement needs.

Self-awareness describes the state of being focused on self, thereby evaluating behavior against a standard and subsequently adjusting to meet the standard.

Self-categorization theory (SCT) builds on **social identity theory** (without the self-esteem predictions); proposing that people categorize themselves and others into distinct social groups, ingroup and outgroup members. SCT posits that social identities determine intergroup behavior because people act as group members, categorized by **normative fit**, and **comparative fit** in the **meta-contrast ratio**.

Self-centered attribution bias consists of taking more than one's share of credit or responsibility for a jointly produced outcome.

Self-concept is the collection of beliefs we hold about ourselves.

Self-conscious emotions reflect on the long-term concerns of the self (as in guilt).

Self-discrepancy theory focuses on the gap between pairs of self-guides, that is, what people perceive to be their actual self and their ideal self (whom they want to be) or their ought self (whom they should be).

Self-efficacy beliefs refer to specific expectations about one's own abilities to accomplish specific tasks.

Self-enhancement is the tendency to seek and maintain a favorable or at least improvable **self-concept**.

Self-enhancing motivates viewing the self positively or at least sympathetically as improvable.

Self-esteem is the evaluation we make of ourselves; see **state self-esteem** and **trait self-esteem**.

Self-evaluation maintenance suggests that people facilitate and maintain their positive self-regard when they deal with the performance of people around them with whom they might compare themselves.

Self-fulfilling prophecy describes the process by which one person's expectations become reality in a social interaction.

Self-guides influence gaps that result from a shortfall between one's current self and one's ideal self, or one's ought self.

Self-handicapping employs actual or constructed liabilities to explain under-performance.

Self-monitoring describes individual differences in the extent to which people use the social situation (as opposite to their inner predispositions) to guide their behavior. High self-monitoring people regulate themselves with regard to others, instead of relying more heavily on their inner thoughts and feelings.

Self-perception theory is a model of how people infer their own attitudes from their behavior and situational forces.

Self-profitable describes a person's attributes (e.g., competence, agency) that further own interests.

Self-promotion is a self-presentational strategy designed to make one seem competent.

Self-regulation refers to the ways people control and direct their own actions, emotions, and thoughts, especially how people formulate and pursue goals; it includes higher-order executive control of lower-order processes responsible for the planning and execution of behavior.

Self-schemas are cognitive-affective structures that represent the self's qualities in a given domain with clarity and certainty.

Self-serving attributional bias is the tendency to take credit for success and deny responsibility for failure.

Self-verification describes people seeking other people, situations, and interpretations that confirm their preexisting self-conceptions.

Semantic memory represents facts, word meaning, and encyclopedic knowledge as part of **declarative** long-term memory.

Separate-systems view of affect and cognition posits that they operate as parallel independent processes.

Serial processes proceed sequentially, for example, in the overall processes of encoding, memory retrieval, and response generally viewed as ordered steps.

Set-size effect reflects the sheer result of acquiring more confirming information over less of it.

Shifting standards contrast evaluating an individual relative to the social category versus everyone else.

Shortcuts are a general term for any social perceiver strategy that substitutes simpler processes for more complex, effortful ones.

Short-term memory (also called **working memory**) comprises information being considered at any given moment, contents of attention; in many memory models, the activated portion of long-term memory represents short-term memory or consciousness. The contents of short-term memory can be consolidated for storage in long-term memory.

Simulation, in **perceptual symbol systems** (PSS), recreates a particular experience of a particular category member. More generally, in social cogntion it means imagining experiences or events.

Simulation heuristic makes inferences by constructing hypothetical scenarios to estimate outcomes, running events through in the mind chronologically to assess likely consequences.

Simulation theory describes people inferring the mental states of others by imagining their own thoughts, emotions, or behaviors in a similar setting.

Simulator, in **perceptual symbol systems** (PSS), first registers and later re-creates a perceptual experience, the pattern of brain activation created by selective attention at the perceptual stage. The simulator contains two kinds of structures: the underlying **frame** that integrates across categories of experience, and the **simulation** that creates the experience of a particular example on a particular occasion.

Situated action depends entirely on the ecological context.

Situational constraint   describes whether contextual forces determine the behavior of the actor (versus the actor's choice).

Skin conductance   measures minute amounts of perspiration (see also **electrodermal response** (EDR), galvanic skin response (GSR)).

Social cognition   comprises all the processes that people use to make sense of each other, in order to coordinate in their social world.

Social comparison   produces feedback from comparing self with others.

Social comparison theory   posits that people evaluate their position relative to similar others doing better or worse.

Social constructivist view   of emotions interprets emotions as culturally shared, temporary roles.

Social desirability   describes people's concern about how they appear to others, so it reflects the response valued by society.

Social dominance orientation   (SDO) is an individual difference perspective on group hierarchy that correlates with a wide range of blatant biases.

Social dominance theory   (SDT) argues that group hierarchies are universal and even evolutionarily adaptive in societies beyond the hunter-gatherer stage; some groups inevitably dominate others, and stable hierarchies regulate pointless conflict.

Social identity theory   (SIT) proposes that people interact along a continuum from interpersonal to intergroup identities.

Social intelligence   is variously defined as the array of knowledge, plans, and strategies that people use in social interactions, but sometimes just as specific social, expressive, and communicative skills.

Social projection   refers to people estimating their own preferences, traits, problems, activities, and attitudes to be characteristic of others, or at least more characteristic of others than the evidence warrants.

Social role   is the set of behavior expected of someone in a particular position.

Social role theory   describes how observing the correlation between gender and roles leads to gender stereotypes.

Social validation   describes being accepted for who we are.

Social-adjustive functions   of attitudes signal interpersonal priorities, sensitivity to others, and getting along with people in general (see also **impression-relevant involvement**).

Sociometer   describes self-esteem as a general indicator of how one is doing in the eyes of others.

Spontaneous trait inferences,   describe accessible trait attributions coming to mind when interpreting behavior; they bind the trait implications of a behavior to the person committing the behavior.

Spreading the alternatives,   a dissonance-reduction process, describes how people justify their choices by reinterpreting their chosen alternative as clearly superior, emphasizing its virtues and downplaying its flaws while doing the reverse for nonchosen alternatives.

Stability   as a dimension of causality indicates whether the cause will change and is strongly associated with subsequent expectations of success or failure.

State self-esteem   is a temporary affective self-assessment, but it does not alter **trait self-esteem**, one's long-term view of oneself

Stereotype content model   posits two fundamental dimensions of social cognition, warmth (friendly, trustworthy) and competence (capability), with groups arrayed across the two-dimensional space.

Stereotype threat   describes people's reaction to performance demands in domains that stereotype their social category as inferior.

Stereotypes   are the cognitive side of intergroup bias, beliefs about groups.

Striatum,   part of the brain's **basal ganglia**, has in its **ventral** (lower) aspect been implicated in automatic reward processing.

Stigma consciousness   describes individual differences in stereotyped group members' heightened vigilance in interacting with outgroup members.

Stimulus evaluation check   is a process similar to **primary appraisal**, immediately assessing a target's implications for self.

Stimulus-dependent thoughts   relate to the current environment.

Stimulus-independent thought (or **mind-wandering**)   does not relate to the current environment.

Strength   of a link between nodes, is a function of prior joint activations (e.g., frequent rehearsal).

Strength   of an attitude includes various interrelated components, for example, **importance** and **certainty**.

Subjective uncertainty reduction theory   proposes that ingroup norms reduce anxiety, especially when people are unsure in self-relevant domains.

Subjective value function   plots perceived value against objective outcomes; the curve is S-shaped – concave for gains (reflecting **risk aversion**) and convex for losses (reflecting **risk seeking**), as well as steeper for losses than for gains (reflecting **loss aversion**).

Subliminal priming   occurs when a concept is activated by the environment, but at exposure times below consciousness; it registers on the senses but not on awareness.

Subtle bias   is automatic, ambiguous, and ambivalent, typically, from internal conflict between anti-prejudice norms and cultural stereotypes.

Subtractive rule   holds that inhibiting situational inducements augment and facilitating situational inducements attenuate the diagnostic value of the identified behavior regarding the corresponding disposition.

Superior temporal sulcus   (STS) is the indentation in the temporal lobe that separates its upper (superior) and middle areas; STS is implicated in perceptions of biological motion, trajectory, and intent,

Sympathetic nervous system   controls bodily functions such as heart-rate and breathing.

System 1 versus System 2,   developed by Kahneman, contrast intuition versus reason in decision-making.

System justification theory   posits that people seek to preserve and legitimate the status quo.

Systematic processing   describes the **heuristic-systematic model**'s thoughtful, effortful mode, which involves evaluating the pros and cons of a message's arguments.

Task involvement   reflects an individual concerned only with the consequences of a particular response.

Temporal construal theory   describes how the greater the temporal, physical, or mental distance to an event, the more abstractly one considers that event, focusing in high-level features that convey the event's essence.

Temporal lobe, one of the major lobes of the neocortex; the temporal lobe is located approximately at the level of the ears.

Temporal parietal junction (TPJ) is the intersection between the **temporal lobe** and **parietal lobe**, implicated in theory of mind related to self-other differences in beliefs.

Temporal self-appraisal theory holds that people distance themselves from their negative past selves and reduce the distance to their positive past selves.

Tensor-product model is a connectionist group memory approach using Hebbian learning.

Terror management theory (TMT) addresses how people cope with the dread of death when it comes to mind. TMT holds that people are biologically driven for self-preservation, and the threat of death is managed at both the cultural level, by developing worldviews that provide meaning and purpose, and at the individual level, through self-esteem.

Testosterone, a hormone linked to masculine characteristics, also relates to risk-taking and physical aggression.

Theory of mind describes people's (especially children's) everyday understanding of the contents of another's mind, especially beliefs and knowledge. It focuses on ordinary people's perception that other people have beliefs, intentions, and personalities distinct from their own minds.

Theory of planned behavior predicts attitude-relevant behavior from intent, itself predicted by beliefs, subjective social norms, and perceived behavioral control. Developed by Ajzen, it builds on Fishbein & Ajzen's **theory of reasoned action**, adding perceived behavioral control as a predictor variable.

Theory of reasoned action proposes that beliefs (subjective values and their likelihood) and norms (perceived norms and their probability) together determine behavioral intentions, which predict behavior (see **theory of planned behavior** for a later version.)

Thin slices of behavior describe people seeing brief (typically under a minute) samples of a person's actions and drawing remarkably accurate inferences about enduring characteristics.

Think-aloud protocols ask participants to voice their thoughts as they perform a laboratory task.

Thought suppression involves the failure to prevent unwanted cognition, through the ironic process of monitoring their occurrence.

Thought-polarization hypothesis   posits that thinking about an attitude object will often polarize evaluations of it.

Top-down   processes include conception and imagery or any other relatively abstract, generalized starting point, conceptually-driven or theory-driven processes, heavily influenced by organized prior knowledge.

Trait self-esteem   is a long-term, chronic predisposition to evaluate self positively or negatively.

Transcranial magnetic stimulation   (TMS) uses electromagnetic induction that stimulates or inhibits brain regions, allowing causal inferences from the experimental manipulation.

Transference   occurs when activation of the mental representations of a significant other evokes the relational self with that significant other, including expectations that a person resembling the significant other will be similar and evoke similar emotions and behavior.

Trusting   motivates viewing people, at least in one's own group, positively until proven otherwise.

Twenty-twenty hindsight   indicates the difficulty of ignoring knowledge of an actual outcome to generate unbiased inferences about what could or should have happened (see **hindsight bias**).

Twofold retrieval by associative pathways (TRAP) model   is a person memory model positing separate heuristic and exhaustive retrieval strategies, consistent with other dual-process models.

Typical human nature   includes warmth, emotional responsiveness, agency, curiosity, and depth.

Ultimate attribution error (see **group-serving bias**)   refers to the tendency of group members to attribute positive actions committed by their own group to positive ingroup qualities, and negative actions committed by the ingroup to external causes, and vice versa for the outgroup.

Uncertainty orientation   is an individual difference ranging from certainty-oriented preference for the familiar and predictable, to uncertainty-oriented preference for meaning search, sense-making, and novelty.

Understanding   motives aim for socially shared cognition, the belief that one's views correspond to those of one's group.

Unimode model   builds on lay **epistemic** theory of ordinary knowledge to propose that people's subjective understanding essentially tests their everyday hypotheses using available evidence, not needing to differentiate more automatic and more controlled modes.

Unipolar   means having only one end, as in ranging from zero to much, or *not-at-all* to *extremely* in an attitude scale.

Uniquely human   attributes include culture, morality, logic, maturity, and refinement.

Unobtrusive measures   assess psychological variables without interfering with participants' ordinary activities, often without their awareness.

Upward social comparisons   judge self against more fortunate others, at best inspiring and at worst, demoralizing.

Urgency   motivates quick decisions.

Valence   is the positive or negative evaluation attached to an entity.

Value-expressive function   of attitudes describes the importance to people of demonstrating and maintaining their long-term standards and orientations (see also **value-relevant involvement**).

Value-relevant involvement   in an attitude indicates its importance to a person's social or moral standards.

Velten procedure   manipulates mood by having participants read mood-relevant statements.

Ventral   describes the brain's lower surface and areas located downward relative to another area (e.g., **dorsal**).

Verbal overshadowing   invokes a local, feature-by-feature process in describing a face, which ironically interferes with recognizing it later.

Vested interest   implies that an issue has personal relevance or meaning, especially intrinsic importance for beliefs central to a person's identity. (Roughly equivalent to **ego involvement, issue involvement, personal involvement**.)

Vividness   constitutes the inherent attention-getting features of a stimulus regardless of environment, predicted to be emotionally interesting, imagery-provoking, and proximate.

WEIRD,   acronym critiquing psychology's predominant research samples as Western, Educated, Industrialized, Rich, Democratic, and therefore culturally unrepresentative of most of the human population.

Who-said-what   experimental paradigm assesses how people's memories confuse other people more *within* social category (e.g., two women) than *between* social categories (e.g., a man and a woman) (see **category confusions**).

Working memory   (see **short-term memory**).

Working self-concept   is the currently active aspect of the self-concept that influences ongoing thought and behavior depending on which aspect of the self is accessible.

X system (reflexive)   involves the **amygdala**, dorsal **anterior cingulate**, basal ganglia, ventro **medial prefrontal cortex**, and lateral temporal cortex, all regions implicated in automatic processing.

Yale persuasive communications approach   emphasizes learning message content and its conscious acceptance or rejection.

Zygomaticus major   is the cheek's smile muscle on either side of the lower nose.

References

Aarts, H. (2012). Goals, motivated social cognition and behavior. In S. T. Fiske & C. N. Macrae (eds.), *Sage handbook of social cognition* (pp. 75–95). Thousand Oaks, CA: Sage.

Aarts, H., Custers, R., & Wegner, D. M. (2005). On the inference of personal authorship: Enhancing experienced agency by priming effect information. *Consciousness and Cognition: An International Journal, 14,* 439–458.

Aarts, H., & Dijksterhuis, A. (2000). Habits as knowledge structures: Automaticity in goal-directed behavior. *Journal of Personality and Social Psychology, 78,* 53–63.

Aarts, H., & Dijksterhuis, A. (2003). The silence of the library: Environment, situational norm, and social behavior. *Journal of Personality and Social Psychology, 84,* 18–28.

Aarts, H., Gollwitzer, P. M., & Hassin, R. R. (2004). Goal contagion: Perceiving is for pursuing. *Journal of Personality and Social Psychology, 87,* 23–37.

Abele, A. E., & Wojciszke, B. (2007). Agency and communion from the perspective of self versus others. *Journal of Personality and Social Psychology, 93(5),* 751–763.

Abelson, R. P. (1981). The psychological status of the script concept. *American Psychologist, 36,* 715–729.

Abelson, R. P. (1988). Conviction. *American Psychologist, 43,* 267–275.

Abelson, R. P., Aronson E., McGuire, W. J., Newcomb, T. M., Rosenberg, M. J., & Tannebaum, P. H. (Eds.). (1968). *Theories of cognitive consistency: A sourcebook.* Chicago: Rand McNally.

Abelson, R. P., & Gross, P. H. (1987). The strength of conjunctive explanations. *Personality and Social Psychology Bulletin, 13,* 141–155.

Abelson, R. P., Kinder, D. R., Peters, M. D., & Fiske, S. T. (1982). Affective and semantic components in political person perception. *Journal of Personality and Social Psychology, 42,* 619–630.

Abelson, R. P., & Levi, A. (1985). Decision making. In G. Lindzey & E. Aronson (Eds.), *Handbook of social psychology* (pp. 231–309). New York: Random House.

Aberson, C. L., Healy, M., & Romero, V. (2000). Ingroup bias and self-esteem: A meta-analysis. *Personality and Social Psychology Review, 4,* 157–173.

Ackerman, J. M., Huang, J. Y., & Bargh, J. A. (2012). Evolutionary perspectives on social cognition. In S. T. Fiske & C. N. Macrae (Eds.), *Sage handbook of social cognition* (pp. 451–474). Thousand Oaks, CA: Sage.

Ackerman, J. M., Shapiro, J. R., Neuberg, S. L., Kenrick, D. T., Becker, D. V., Griskevicius, V., Maner, J. K., & Schaller, M. (2006). They all look the same to me (unless they're angry): From out-group homogeneity to out-group heterogeneity. *Psychological Science, 17,* 836–840.

Adolphs, R. (2002). Recognizing emotion from facial expressions: Psychological and neurological mechanisms. *Behavioral and Cognitive Neuroscience Reviews, 1,* 21–62.

Adorno, T. W., Frenkel-Brunswik, E., Levinson, D. J., & Sanford, R. N. (1950). *The authoritarian personality.* New York: Harper.

Agostinelli, G., Sherman, S. J., Presson, C. C., & Chassin, L. (1992). Self-perception and self-enhancement biases in estimates of population prevalence. *Personality and Social Psychology Bulletin, 18,* 631–642.

Ajzen, I. (1977). Intuitive theories of events and the effects of baserate information on prediction. *Journal of Personality and Social Psychology, 35,* 303–314.

Ajzen, I. (1987). Attitudes, traits, and actions: Dispositional prediction of behavior in personality and social psychology. In L. Berkowitz (Ed.), *Advances in experimental social psychology* (Vol. 20, pp. 1–64). San Diego, CA: Academic Press.

Ajzen, I. (2001). Nature and operation of attitudes. *Annual Review of Psychology, 52,* 27–58.

Ajzen, I., & Fishbein, M. (1977). Attitude-behavior relations: A theoretical analysis and review of empirical research. *Psychological Bulletin, 84,* 888–918.

Ajzen, I., & Sexton, J. (1999). Depth of processing, belief congruence, and attitude-behavior correspondence. In S. Chaiken & Y. Trope (Eds.), *Dual-process theories in social psychology* (pp. 117–138). New York: Guilford Press.

Ajzen, I., Timko, C., & White, J. B. (1982). Self-monitoring and the attitude-behavior relation. *Journal of Personality and Social Psychology, 42,* 426–435.

Albarracín, D. (2002). Cognition in persuasion: An analysis of information processing in response to persuasive communications. In M. P. Zanna (Ed.), *Advances in experimental social psychology* (Vol. 34, pp. 61–130). San Francisco, CA: Academic Press.

Albarracín, D., Johnson, B. T., & Zanna, M. P. (Eds). (2005). *The handbook of attitudes.* Hillsdale, NJ: Erlbaum.

Albarracín, D., & Kumkale, G. T. (2003). Affect as information in persuasion: A model of affect identification and discounting. *Journal of Personality and Social Psychology, 84,* 453–469.

Albarracín, D., & Vargas, P. (2010). Attitudes and persuasion: From biology to social responses to persuasive intent. In S. T. Fiske, D. T. Gilbert, & G. Lindzey (Eds.), *Handbook of social psychology* (5th edn, Vol. 1, pp. 394–427). Hoboken, NJ: Wiley.

Albarracín, D., & Wyer, R. S., Jr. (2001). Elaborative and nonelaborative processing of a behavior-related communication. *Personality and Social Psychology Bulletin, 27,* 691–705.

Aldrich, J. H., Sullivan, J. L., & Borgida, E. (1989). Foreign affairs and issue voting: Do presidential candidates "waltz before a blind audience"? *American Political Science Review, 83,* 123–141.

Alexander, M. G., Brewer, M. B., & Hermann, R. K. (1999). Images and affect: A functional analysis of out-group stereotypes. *Journal of Personality and Social Psychology, 77,* 78–93.

Alexander, M. G., Brewer, M. B., & Livingston, R. W. (2005). Putting stereotype content in context: Image theory and interethnic stereotypes. *Personality and Social Psychology Bulletin, 31,* 781–794.

Alicke, M. D. (1985). Global self-evaluations as determined by the desirability and controllability of trait adjectives. *Journal of Personality and Social Psychology, 49,* 1621–1630.

Alicke, M. D., & Largo, E. (1995). The role of self in the false consensus effect. *Journal of Experimental Social Psychology, 31,* 28–47.

Allison, S. T., & Messick, D. M. (1988). The feature-positive effect, attitude strength, and degree of perceived consensus. *Personality and Social Psychology Bulletin, 14,* 231–241.

Alloy, L. B., & Tabachnik, N. (1984). Assessment of covariation by humans and animals: The joint influence of prior expectations and current situational information. *Psychological Review, 91,* 112–149.

Allport, G. W. (1935). Attitudes. In C. Murchison (Ed.), *Handbook of social psychology* (pp. 798–844). Worcester, MA: Clark University Press.

Allport, G. W. (1954). *The nature of prejudice.* Reading, MA: Addison-Wesley.

Altemeyer, B. (1981). *Right-wing authoritarianism.* Winnipeg, Canada: University of Manitoba Press.

Altemeyer, B. (1988). *Enemies of freedom: Understanding right-wing authoritarianism.* San Francisco, CA: Jossey-Bass.

Altemeyer, B. (2004). Highly dominating, highly authoritarian personalities. *Journal of Social Psychology, 144,* 421–447.

Ambady, N., Paik, S. K., Steele, J., Owen-Smith, A., & Mitchell, J. P. (2004). Deflecting negative self-relevant stereotype activation: The effects of individuation. *Journal of Experimental Social Psychology, 40,* 401–408.

Ambady, N., & Rosenthal, R. (1993). Half a minute: Predicting teacher evaluations from thin slices of nonverbal behavior and physical attractiveness. *Journal of Personality and Social Psychology, 64,* 431–441.

Ames, D. R. (2004a). Inside the mind reader's tool kit: Projection and stereotyping in mental state inference. *Journal of Personality and Social Psychology, 87,* 340–353.

Ames, D. R. (2004b). Strategies for social inference: A similarity contingency model of projection and stereotyping in attribute prevalence estimates. *Journal of Personality and Social Psychology, 87,* 573–585.

Ames, D. R., & Mason, M. F. (2012). Mind perception. In S. T. Fiske & C. N. Macrae (Eds.), *Sage handbook of social cognition* (pp. 115–137). Thousand Oaks, CA: Sage.

Amiot, C. E., & Bourhis, R. Y. (2005). Ideological beliefs as determinants of discrimination in positive and negative outcome distributions. *European Journal of Social Psychology, 35,* 581–598.

Amodio, D. M., & Devine, P. G. (2006). Implicit stereotyping vs. evaluative race bias. *Journal of Personality and Social Psychology, 91,* 652–661.

Amodio, D. M., & Frith, C. D. (2006). Meeting of minds: The medial frontal cortex and social cognition. *Nature Reviews Neuroscience, 7,* 268–277.

Amodio, D. M., Harmon-Jones, E., & Devine, P. G. (2003). Individual differences in the activation and control of affective race bias as assessed by startle eyeblink response and self-report. *Journal of Personality and Social Psychology, 84,* 738–753.

Amodio, D. M., Harmon-Jones, E., Devine, P. G., Curtin, J. J., Hartley, S. L., & Covert, A. E. (2004). Neural signals for the detection of unintentional race bias. *Psychological Science, 15,* 88–93.

Amodio, D. M., Shah, J. Y., Sigelman, J., Brazy, P. C., & Harmon-Jones, E. (2004). Implicit regulatory focus associated with asymmetrical frontal cortical activity. *Journal of Experimental Social Psychology, 40,* 225–232.

Andersen, S. M., & Chen, S. (2002). The relational self: An interpersonal social-cognitive theory. *Psychological Review, 109,* 619–645.

Andersen, S. M., & Klatzky, R. L. (1987). Traits and social stereotypes: Levels of categorization in person perception. *Journal of Personality and Social Psychology, 53,* 235–246.

Andersen, S. M., Reznik, I., & Manzella, L. M. (1996). Eliciting facial affect, motivation, and expectancies in transference: Significant–other representations in social relations. *Journal of Personality and Social Psychology, 71,* 1108–1129.

Andersen, S. M., Saribay, S. A., & Przybylinski, E. (2012). Social cognition in close relationships. In S. T. Fiske & C. N. Macrae (Eds.), *Sage handbook of social cognition* (pp. 350–371). Thousand Oaks, CA: Sage.

Anderson, A. K., & Phelps, E. A. (2001). Lesions of the human amygdala impair enhanced perception of emotionally salient events. *Nature, 411,* 305–309.

Anderson, C. A. (1983). Abstract and concrete data in the perseverance of social theories: When weak data lead to unshakeable beliefs. *Journal of Experimental Social Psychology, 19,* 93–108.

Anderson, C. A., & Godfrey, S. S. (1987). Thoughts about actions: The effects of specificity and availability of imagined behavioral scripts on expectations about oneself and others. *Social Cognition, 5,* 238–258.

Anderson, C. A., Lepper, M. R., & Ross, L. D. (1980). Perseverance of social theories: The role of explanation in the persistence of discredited information. *Journal of Personality and Social Psychology, 39,* 1037–1049.

Anderson, J. R. (1976). *Language, memory, and thought.* Hillsdale, NJ: Erlbaum.

Anderson, J. R., Bothell, D., Byrne, M. D., Douglass, S., Lebiere, C., & Qin, Y. (2004). An integrated theory of the mind. *Psychological Review, 111,* 1036–1060.

Anderson, N. H. (1981). *Foundations of information integration theory.* New York: Academic Press.

Anderson, N. H., & Hubert, S. (1963). Effects of concomitant verbal recall on order effects in personality impression formation. *Journal of Verbal Learning and Verbal Behavior, 2,* 379–391.

Anik, L., Aknin, L. B., Norton, M. I., & Dunn, E. W. (2011). Feeling good about giving: The benefits (and costs) of self-interested charitable behavior. In D. M. Oppenheimer & C. Y. Olivola (Eds.), *The science of giving: Experimental approaches to the study of charity* (pp. 3–13). Society for judgment and decision making series. New York: Psychology Press.

Antrobus, J. S., Singer, J. L., Goldstein, S., & Fortgang, M. (1970). Mindwandering and cognitive structure. *Transactions of the New York Academy of Sciences, 32,* 242–252.

Apsler, R. & Sears, D. O. (1968). Warning, personal involvement, and attitude change. *Journal of Personality and Social Psychology, 9,* 162–166.

Areni, C. S., & Lutz, R. J. (1988). The role of argument quality in the elaboration likelihood model. *Advances in Consumer Research, 15,* 197–203.

Argyle, M., & Crossland, J. (1987). The dimensions of positive emotions. *British Journal of Social Psychology, 26,* 127–137.

Aristotle. (1931). On memory and recollection. In W. D. Ross (Ed.), J. I. Beare (trans.), *The works of Aristotle.* Oxford: Clarendon Press.

Arkes, H. R., & Harkness, A. R. (1980). Effect of making a diagnosis on subsequent recognition of symptoms. *Journal of Experimental Social Psychology: Human Learning and Memory, 6,* 568–575.

Arkes, H. R., & Tetlock, P. E. (2004). Attributions of implicit prejudice, or "Would Jesse Jackson 'Fail' the Implicit Association Test?" *Psychological Inquiry, 15,* 257–278.

Arkin, R. M. (1987). Shyness and self-presentation. In K. Yardley & T. Honess (Eds.), *Self and identity: Psychosocial perspectives* (pp. 187–195). London: Wiley.

Arkin, R. M., Cooper, H. M., & Kolditz, T. A. (1980). A statistical review of the literature concerning the self-serving attribution bias in interpersonal influence situations. *Journal of Personality, 48,* 435–448.

Armitage, C. J., & Conner, M. (2000). Attitudinal ambivalence: A test of three key hypotheses. *Personality and Social Psychology Bulletin, 26,* 1421–1432.

Armor, D. A., & Sackett, A. M. (2006). Accuracy, error, and bias in predictions for real versus hypothetical events. *Journal of Personality and Social Psychology, 91,* 583–600.

Armor, D. A., & Taylor, S. E. (1998). Situated optimism: Specific outcome expectancies and self-regulation. In M. P. Zanna (Ed.), *Advances in experimental social psychology* (Vol. 30, pp. 309–379). New York: Academic Press.

Armor, D. A., & Taylor, S. E. (2003). The effects of mindset on behavior: Self-regulation in deliberative and implemental frames of mind. *Personality and Social Psychology Bulletin, 29,* 86–95.

Arndt, J., Schimel, J., Greenberg, J., & Pyszczynski, T. (2002). The intrinsic self and defensiveness: Evidence that activating the intrinsic self reduces self-handicapping and conformity. *Personality and Social Psychology Bulletin, 28,* 671–683.

Arnold, M. B. (1945). Physiological differentiation of emotional states. *Psychological Review, 52,* 35–48.

Arnold, M. B. (1970). Perennial problems in the field of emotion. In M. B. Arnold (Ed.), *Feelings and emotions: The Loyola Symposium.* New York: Academic Press.

Aronson, J., Blanton, H., & Cooper, J. (1995). From dissonance to disidentification: Selectivity in the self-affirmation process. *Journal of Personality and Social Psychology, 68,* 986–996.

Aronson, J., Fried, C. B., & Good, C. (2002). Reducing the effects of stereotype threat on African American college students by shaping theories of intelligence. *Journal of Experimental Social Psychology, 38,* 113–125.

Aronson, J., Lustina, M. J., Good, C., Keough, K., Steele, C. M., & Brown, J. (1999). When White men can't do math: Necessary and sufficient factors in stereotype threat. *Journal of Experimental Social Psychology, 35,* 29–46.

Asch, S. E. (1946). Forming impressions of personality. *Journal of Abnormal and Social Psychology, 41,* 1230–1240.

Ashburn-Nardo, L., Voils, C. I., & Monteith, M. J. (2001). Implicit associations as the seeds of intergroup bias: How easily do they take root? *Journal of Personality and Social Psychology, 81,* 789–799.

Ashby, F. G., & Maddox, W. T. (2005). Human category learning. *Annual Review of Psychology, 56,* 149–178.

Aspinwall, L. G., & Brunhart, S. M. (1996). Distinguishing optimism from denial: Optimistic beliefs predict attention to health threats. *Personality and Social Psychology Bulletin, 22,* 993–1003.

Asuncion, A. G., & Lam, W. F. (1995). Affect and impression formation: Influence of mood on person memory. *Journal of Experimental Social Psychology, 31,* 437–464.

Augoustinos, M., & Walker, I. (1995). *Social cognition: An integrated introduction.* Thousand Oaks, CA: Sage.

Averill, J. R. (1980). On the paucity of positive emotions. In K. Blankstein, P. Pliner, & J. Polivy (Eds.), *Advances in the study of communication and affect, Vol. 6. Assessment and modification of emotional behavior* (pp. 7–45). New York: Plenum Press.

Averill, J. R. (1983). Studies on anger and aggression: Implications for theories of emotion. *American Psychologist, 38,* 1145–1160.

Averill, J. R. (1990a). Emotions as episodic dispositions, cognitive schemas, and transitory social roles: Steps toward an integrated theory of emotion. In D. J. Ozer, J. M. Healy Jr., & A. J. Stewart (Eds.), *Perspectives in personality, Vol. 3a: Self and emotion.* Greenwich, CT: JAI Press.

Averill, J. R. (1990b). Emotions in relation to systems of behavior. In N. L. Stein, B. Leventhal, & T. Trabasso (Eds.), *Psychological and biological approaches to emotion.* Hillsdale, NJ: Erlbaum.

Averill, J. R. (1990c). Inner feelings, works of the flesh, the beast within, diseases of the mind, driving force, and putting on a show: Six metaphors of emotion and their theoretical extensions. In D. Leary (Ed.), *Metaphors in the history of psychology.* Cambridge, MA: Harvard University Press.

Ax, A. F. (1953). Physiological differentiation of emotional states. *Psychosomatic Medicine, 15,* 433–442.

Axsom, D., Yates, S., & Chaiken, S. (1987). Audience response as a heuristic cue in persuasion. *Journal of Personality and Social Psychology, 53,* 30–40.

Babey, S. H., Queller, S., & Klein, S. B. (1998). The role of expectancy violating behaviors in the representation of trait knowledge: A summary-plus-exception model of social memory. *Social Cognition, 16,* 287–339.

Baddeley, A. (2012) Working memory: Theories, models, and controversies. *Annual Review of Psychology, 63,* 1–30.

Bahrick, H. P., Bahrick, P. O., & Wittlinger, R. P. (1975). Fifty years of memory for names and faces: A cross-sectional approach. *Journal of Experimental Psychology: General, 104(1),* 54–75.

Baldwin, D. A., & Baird, J. A. (2001). Discerning intentions in dynamic human action. *Trends in Cognitive Sciences, 5(4),* 171–178.

Banaji, M. R., Nosek, B. A., & Greenwald, A. G. (2004). No place for nostalgia in science: A response to Arkes and Tetlock. *Psychological Inquiry, 15,* 279–310.

Bandura, A. (1982). Self-efficacy mechanism in human agency. *American Psychologist, 37,* 122–147.

Bandura, A. (2006). Toward a psychology of human agency. *Perspectives on Psychological Science, 1,* 164–180.

Banfield, J. F., Wyland, C. L., Macrae, C. N., Münte, T. F., & Heatherton, T. F. (2004). The cognitive neuroscience of self-regulation. In R. F. Baumeister & K. D. Vohs (Eds.), *Handbook of self-regulation: Research, theory, and applications* (pp. 62–83). New York: Guilford Press.

Banks, R. R., & Eberhardt, J. L. (1998). Social psychological processes and the legal bases of racial categorization. In J. L. Eberhardt & S. T. Fiske (Eds.), *Confronting racism: The problem and the response* (pp. 54–75). Thousand Oaks, CA: Sage.

Bar, M., Neta, M., & Linz, H. (2006). Very first impressions. *Emotion, 6,* 269–278.

Barclay, A. M., & Haber, R. N. (1965). The relation of aggressive to sexual motivation. *Journal of Personality, 33,* 462–475.

Barden, R. C., Garber, J., Leiman, B., Ford, M. E., & Masters, J. C. (1985). Factors governing the effective remediation of negative affect and its cognitive and behavioral consequences. *Journal of Personality and Social Psychology, 49,* 1040–1053.

Bargh, J. A. (1984). Automatic and conscious processing of social information. In R. S. Wyer Jr. & T. K. Srull (Eds.), *Handbook of social cognition* (Vol. 3, pp. 1–44). Hillsdale, NJ: Erlbaum.

Bargh, J. A. (1997). The automaticity of everyday life. In R. S. Wyer Jr. (Ed.), *The automaticity of everyday life* (pp. 1–62). Mahwah, NJ: Erlbaum.

Bargh, J. A. (1999). The cognitive monster: The case against the controllability of automatic stereotype effects. In S. Chaiken & Y. Trope (Eds.), *Dual-process theories in social psychology* (pp. 361–382). New York: Guilford Press.

Bargh, J. A., Bond, R. N., Lombardi, W. J., & Tota, M. E. (1986). The additive nature of chronic and temporary sources of construct accessibility. *Journal of Personality and Social Psychology, 50,* 869–879.

Bargh, J. A., Chaiken, S., Govender, R., & Pratto, F. (1992). The generality of the automatic attitude activation effect. *Journal of Personality and Social Psychology, 62,* 893–912.

Bargh, J. A., Chaiken, S., Raymond, P., & Hymes, C. (1996). The automatic evaluation effect: Unconditional automatic attitude activation with a pronunciation task. *Journal of Experimental Social Psychology, 32,* 104–128.

Bargh, J. A., Chen, M., & Burrows, L. (1996). Automaticity of social behavior: Direct effects of trait construct and stereotype activation on action. *Journal of Personality and Social Psychology, 71*, 230–244.

Bargh, J. A., Gollwitzer, P. M., Lee-Chai, A., Barndollar, K., & Trötschel, R. (2001). The automated will: Nonconscious activation and pursuit of behavioral goals. *Journal of Personality and Social Psychology, 81*, 1014–1027.

Bargh, J. A., Lombardi, W. J., & Higgins, E. T. (1988). Automaticity of chronically accessible constructs in person X situation effects on person perception: It's just a matter of time. *Journal of Personality and Social Psychology, 55*, 599–605.

Bargh, J. A., & Pietromonaco, P. (1982). Automatic information processing and social perception: The influence of trait information presented outside of conscious awareness on impression formation. *Journal of Personality and Social Psychology, 43*, 437–449.

Bargh, J. A., & Pratto, F. (1986). Individual construct accessibility and perceptual selection. *Journal of Experimental Social Psychology, 22*, 293–311.

Bargh, J. A., & Thein, R. D. (1985). Individual construct accessibility, person memory, and the recall–judgment link: The case of information overload. *Journal of Personality and Social Psychology, 49*, 1129–1146.

Bargh, J. A., & Tota, M. E. (1988). Context-dependent automatic processing in depression: Accessibility of negative constructs with regard to self but not others. *Journal of Personality and Social Psychology, 54*, 925–939.

Bargh, J. A., & Williams, E. L. (2006). The automaticity of social life. *Current Directions in Psychological Science, 15*, 1–4.

Bar-Hillel, M. (1980). The base-rate fallacy in probability judgments. *Acta Psychologica, 44*, 211–233.

Bar-Hillel, M., & Fischhoff, B. (1981). When do base rates affect predictions? *Journal of Personality and Social Psychology, 41*, 671–680.

Baron, R. A. (1977). *Human aggression.* New York: Plenum Press.

Baron, R. A. (1997). The sweet smell of . . . helping: Effects of pleasant ambient fragrance on prosocial behavior in shopping malls. *Personality and Social Psychology Bulletin, 23*, 498–503.

Baron, R. M. (1980). Contrasting approaches to social knowing: An ecological perspective. *Personality and Social Psychology Bulletin, 6*, 590–600.

Barreto, M., & Ellemers, N. (2005). The burden of benevolent sexism: How it contributes to the maintenance of gender inequalities. *European Journal of Social Psychology, 35(5)*, 633–642.

Barrett, L. F. (2006). Solving the emotion paradox: Categorization and the experience of emotion. *Personality and Social Psychology Review, 10*, 20–46.

Barrett, L. F. (2009a). Variety is the spice of life: A psychological construction approach to understanding variability in emotion. *Cognition and Emotion, 23(7)*, 1284–1306.

Barrett, L. F. (2009b). The future of psychology: Connecting mind to brain. *Perspectives on Psychological Science, 4(4)*, 326–339.

Barrett, L. F., Mesquita, B., Ochsner, K. N., & Gross, J. J. (2007). The experience of emotion. *Annual Review of Psychology, 58*, 373–403.

Barrett, L. F., & Russell, J. A. (1999). The structure of current affect: Controversies and emerging consensus. *Current Directions in Psychological Science, 8*, 10–14.

Barrett, L. F., Tugade, M. M., & Engle, R. W. (2004). Individual differences in working memory capacity and dual-process theories of the mind. *Psychological Bulletin, 130*, 553–573.

Barrett, L. F., & Wager, T. D. (2006). The structure of emotion: Evidence from neuroimaging studies. *Current Directions in Psychological Science, 15*, 79–83.

Barsalou, L. W. (1985). Ideals, central tendency, and frequency of instantiation as determinants of graded structure in categories. *Journal of Experimental Psychology: Learning, Memory, and Cognition, 11*, 629–654.

Barsalou, L. W. (1999). Perceptual symbol systems. *Behavioral and Brain Sciences, 22*, 577–660.

Bartlett, M. Y., & DeSteno, D. (2006). Gratitude and prosocial behavior: Helping when it costs you. *Psychological Science, 17*, 319–325.

Bassili, J. N., & Krosnick, J. A. (2000). Do strength-related attitude properties determine susceptibility to response effects? New evidence from response latency, attitude extremity, and aggregate indices. *Political Psychology, 21,* 107–132.

Bastian, B., & Haslam, N. (2006). Psychological essentialism and stereotype endorsement. *Journal of Experimental Social Psychology, 42,* 228–235.

Baumeister, R. F., Campbell, J. D., Krueger, J. I., & Vohs, K. D. (2003). Does high self-esteem cause better performance, interpersonal success, happiness, or healthier lifestyles? *Psychological Science in the Public Interest, 4,* 1–44.

Baumeister, R. F., DeWall, C. N., Ciarocco, N. J., & Twenge, J. M. (2005). Social exclusion impairs self-regulation. *Journal of Personality and Social Psychology, 88,* 589–604.

Baumeister, R. F., & Jones, E. E. (1978). When self-presentation is constrained by the target's knowledge. *Journal of Personality and Social Psychology, 36,* 608–618.

Baumeister, R. F., & Leary, M. R. (1995). The need to belong: Desire for interpersonal attachments as a fundamental human motivation. *Psychological Bulletin, 117,* 497–529.

Baumeister, R. F., & Scher, S. J. (1988). Self-defeating behavior patterns among normal individuals: Review and analysis of common self-destructive tendencies. *Psychological Bulletin, 104,* 3–22.

Baumeister, R. F., Smart, L., & Boden, J. M. (1996). Relation of threatened egotism to violence and aggression: The dark side of high self-esteem. *Psychological Review, 103,* 5–33.

Baumeister, R. F., Tice, D. M., & Hutton, D. G. (1989). Self-presentational motivations and personality differences in self-esteem. *Journal of Personality, 57,* 547–579.

Baumeister, R. F., & Vohs, K. D. (Eds.). (2004). *Handbook of self-regulation: Research, theory, and applications* New York: Guilford Press.

Baumgardner, A. H., & Arkin, R. M. (1988). Affective state mediates causal attributions for success and failure. *Motivation and Emotion, 12,* 99–111.

Baumgardner, A. H., Lake, E. A., & Arkin, R. M. (1985). Claiming mood as a self-handicap: The influence of spoiled and unspoiled public identities. *Personality and Social Psychology Bulletin, 11,* 349–357.

Beauregard, K. S., & Dunning, D. (1998). Turning up the contrast: Self-enhancement motives prompt egocentric contrast effects in social judgments. *Journal of Personality and Social Psychology, 74,* 606–621.

Bechara, A., Damasio, A. R., Damasio, H., & Anderson, S. W. (1994). Insensitivity to future consequences following damage to human prefrontal cortex. *Cognition, 50,* 7–15.

Beer, J. S. (2012). Self-evaluation and self-knowledge. In S. T. Fiske & C. N. Macrae (Eds.), *Sage handbook of social cognition* (pp. 330–349). Thousand Oaks, CA: Sage.

Beer, J. S., Heerey, E. A., Keltner, D., Scabini, D., & Knight, R. T. (2003). The regulatory function of self-conscious emotion: Insights from patients with orbitofrontal damage. *Journal of Personality and Social Psychology, 85,* 594–604.

Bem, D. J. (1967). Self-perception: An alternative interpretation of cognitive dissonance phenomena. *Psychological Review, 74,* 183–200.

Bem, D. J. (1972). Self-perception theory. In L. Berkowitz (Ed.), *Advances in experimental social psychology* (Vol. 6, pp. 1–62). New York: Academic Press.

Bem, D. J., & McConnell, H. K. (1970). Testing the self-perception explanation of dissonance phenomena: On the salience of premanipulation attitudes. *Journal of Personality and Social Psychology, 14,* 23–31.

Bem, S. L. (1993). *The lenses of gender: Transforming the debate on sexual inequality.* New Haven, CT: Yale University Press.

Benesh, M., & Weiner, B. (1982). On emotion and motivation: From the notebooks of Fritz Heider. *American Psychologist, 37,* 887–895.

Bentler, P. M., & Speckart, G. (1981). Attitudes cause behaviors: A structural equation analysis. *Journal of Personality and Social Psychology, 40,* 226–238.

Ben-Zeev, T., Fein, S., & Inzlicht, M. (2005). Arousal and stereotype threat. *Journal of Experimental Social Psychology, 41,* 174–181.

Berger, S. M., & Lambert, W. W. (1968). Stimulus–response theory in contemporary social psychology. In G. Lindzey & E. Aronson (Eds.), *The handbook of social psychology* (2nd edn, Vol. 1). Reading, MA: Addison-Wesley.

Berglas, S., & Jones, E. E. (1978). Drug choice as a self-handicapping strategy in response to noncontingent success. *Journal of Personality and Social Psychology, 36,* 405–417.

Bergsieker, H. B., Leslie, L. M., Constantine, V. S., & Fiske, S. T. (2012). Stereotyping by omission: Eliminate the negative, accentuate the positive. *Journal of Personality and Social Psychology.*

Berk, M. S., & Andersen, S. M. (2000). The impact of past relationships on interpersonal behavior: Behavioral confirmation in the social-cognitive process of transference. *Journal of Personality and Social Psychology, 79,* 546–562.

Berkowitz, L. (1974). Some determinants of impulsive aggression: Role of mediated associations with reinforcements for aggression. *Psychological Review, 81,* 165–176.

Berlyne, D. E. (1970). Novelty, complexity, and hedonic value. *Perception and Psychophysics, 8,* 279–286.

Bernstein, D. M., Erdfelder, E., Meltzoff, A. N., Peria, W., & Loftus, G. R. (2011). Hindsight bias from 3 to 95 years of age. *Journal of Experimental Psychology: Learning, Memory, and Cognition, 37(2),* 378–391.

Berrenberg, J. L., Finlay, K. A., Stephan, W. G., & Stephan C. (2002). Prejudice toward people with cancer or AIDS: Applying the integrated threat model. *Journal of Applied Biobehavioral Research, 7,* 75–86.

Berry, D. S., & McArthur, L. Z. (1986). Perceiving character in faces: The impact of age-related craniofacial changes on social perception. *Psychological Bulletin, 100,* 3–18.

Berry, D. S., & Zebrowitz-McArthur, L. (1988). What's in a face? Facial maturity and the attribution of legal responsibility. *Personality and Social Psychology Bulletin, 14,* 23–33.

Berscheid, E. (1982). Attraction and emotion in interpersonal relationships. In M. S. Clark & S. T. Fiske (Eds.), *Affect and cognition: The 17th Annual Carnegie Symposium on Cognition* (pp. 37–54). Hillsdale, NJ: Erlbaum.

Berscheid, E. (1983). Emotion. In H. H. Kelley, E. Berscheid, A. Christensen, J. Harvey, T. Huston, G. Levinger, E. McClintock, A. Peplau, & D. Peterson (Eds.), *Close relationships* (pp. 110–168). San Francisco: Freeman.

Berscheid, E., Graziano, W. G., Monson, T. C., & Dermer, M. (1976). Outcome dependency: Attention, attribution, and attraction. *Journal of Personality and Social Psychology, 34,* 978–989.

Berscheid, E., Snyder, M., & Omoto, A. M. (1989). Issues in studying close relationships: Conceptualizing and measuring closeness. In C. Hendrick (Ed.), *Close relationships.* Newbury Park, CA: Sage.

Berscheid, E., & Walster, E. H. (1978). *Interpersonal attraction.* Reading, MA: Addison-Wesley.

Bettencourt, B. A., Charlton, K., Dorr, N., & Hume, D. L. (2001). Status differences and in-group bias: A meta-analytic examination of the effects of status stability, status legitimacy, and group permeability. *Psychological Bulletin, 127,* 520–542.

Biernat, M., Crandall, C. S., Young, L. V., Kobrynowicz, D., & Halpin, S. M. (1998). All that you can be: Stereotyping of self and others in a military context. *Journal of Personality and Social Psychology, 75,* 301–317.

Biernat, M., & Fuegen, K. (2001). Shifting standards and the evaluation of competence: Complexity in gender-based judgment and decision making. *Journal of Social Issues, 57,* 707–724.

Biernat, M., & Vescio, T. K. (2002). She swings, she hits, she's great, she's benched: Implications of gender-based shifting standards for judgment and behavior. *Personality and Social Psychology Bulletin, 28,* 66–77.

Birnbaum, M. H., & Mellers, B. A. (1979a). One-mediator model of exposure effects is still viable. *Journal of Personality and Social Psychology, 37,* 1090–1096.

Birnbaum, M. H., & Mellers, B. A. (1979b). Stimulus recognition may mediate exposure effects. *Journal of Personality and Social Psychology, 37,* 391–394.

Bizer, G. Y., & Krosnick, J. A. (2001). Exploring the structure of strength-related attitude features: The relation between attitude importance and attitude accessibility. *Journal of Personality and Social Psychology, 81,* 566–586.

Bizer, G. Y., Krosnick, J. A., Holbrook, A. L., Wheeler, S. C., Rucker, D. D., & Petty, R. E. (2004). The impact of personality on cognitive, behavioral, and affective political processes: The effects of need to evaluate. *Journal of Personality, 72,* 995–1027.

Blackwood, N. J., Bentall, R. P., ffytche, D. H., Simmons, A., Murray, R. M., & Howard, R. J. (2003). Self-responsibility and the self-serving bias: An fMRI investigation of causal attributions. *NeuroImage, 20,* 1076–1085.

Blair, I. V., & Banaji, M. R. (1996). Automatic and controlled processes in stereotype priming. *Journal of Personality and Social Psychology, 70,* 1142–1163.

Blair, I. V., Judd, C. M., & Chapleau, K. M. (2004). The influence of Afrocentric facial features in criminal sentencing. *Psychological Science, 15,* 674–679.

Blair, I. V., Judd, C. M., Sadler, M. S., & Jenkins, C. (2002). The role of Afrocentric features in person perception: Judging by features and categories. *Journal of Personality and Social Psychology, 83,* 5–25.

Blair, I. V., Ma, J. E., & Lenton, A. P. (2001). Imagining stereotypes away: The moderation of implicit stereotypes through mental imagery. *Journal of Personality and Social Psychology, 81,* 828–841.

Blake, R. R., & Mouton, J. S. (1961). Reactions to intergroup competition under win–lose conditions. *Management Science, 7,* 420–435.

Blaney, P. H. (1986). Affect and memory: A review. *Psychological Bulletin, 99,* 229–246.

Blanton, H., Cooper, J., Skurnik, I., & Aronson, J. (1997). When bad things happen to good feedback: Exacerbating the need for self-justification with self-affirmations. *Personality and Social Psychology Bulletin, 23,* 684–692.

Blascovich, J., & Mendes, W. B. (2010). Social psychophysiology and embodiment. In S. T. Fiske, D. T. Gilbert, & G. Lindzey (Eds.), *Handbook of social psychology* (5th edn, pp. 194–227). Hoboken, NJ: Wiley.

Blascovich, J., Mendes, W. B., Hunter, S. B., Lickel, B. A., & Kowai-Bell, N. (2001). Perceiver threat in social interactions with stigmatized others. *Journal of Personality and Social Psychology, 80,* 253–267.

Blascovich, J., Wyer, N. A., Swart, L. A., & Kibler, J. L. (1997). Racism and racial categorization. *Journal of Personality and Social Psychology, 72,* 1364–1372.

Bless, H., Clore, G. L., Schwarz, N., Golisano, V., et al. (1996). Mood and the use of scripts: Does a happy mood really lead to mindlessness? *Journal of Personality and Social Psychology, 71,* 655–679.

Bless, H., Fiedler, K., & Strack, F. (2004). *Social cognition: How individuals construct social reality.* New York: Psychology Press.

Bobo, L. D. (1983). Whites' opposition to busing: Symbolic racism or realistic group conflict? *Journal of Personality and Social Psychology, 45,* 1196–1210.

Bobrow, D. G., & Norman, D. A. (1975). Some principles of memory schemata. In D. G. Bobrow & A. G. Collins (Eds.), *Representation and understanding: Studies in cognitive science* (pp. 131–150). New York: Academic Press.

Bochner, S. (1994). Cross-cultural differences in the self concept: A test of Hofstede's individualism/collectivisn distinction. *Journal of Cross-Cultural Psychology, 25,* 273–283.

Bodenhausen, G. V., Kang, S. K., & Peery, D. (2012). Social categorization and the perception of social groups. In S. T. Fiske & C. N. Macrae (Eds.), *Sage handbook of social cognition* (pp. 311–329). Thousand Oaks, CA: Sage.

Bodenhausen, G. V., Kramer, G. P., & Süsser, K. (1994). Happiness and stereotypic thinking in social judgment. *Journal of Personality and Social Psychology, 66,* 621–632.

Bodenhausen, G. V., & Lichtenstein, M. (1987). Social stereotypes and information processing strategies: The impact of task complexity. *Journal of Personality and Social Psychology, 52,* 871–880.

Bodenhausen, G. V., & Macrae, C. N. (1998). In R. S. Wyer Jr. (Ed.), *Advances in social cognition, Vol. 11: Stereotype activation and inhibition.* Mahwah, NJ: Erlbaum.

Bodenhausen, G. V., Macrae, C. N., & Sherman, J. S. (1999). On the dialectics of discrimination: Dual processes in social stereotyping. In S. Chaiken & Y. Trope (Eds.), *Dual-process theories in social psychology* (pp. 271–290). New York: Guilford Press.

Bodenhausen, G. V., & Peery, D. (2009). Social categorization and stereotyping in vivo: The VUCA challenge. *Social and Personality Psychology Compass, 3(2),* 133–151.

Bodenhausen, G. V., Sheppard, L. A., & Kramer, G. P. (1994). Negative affect and social judgment: The differential impact of anger and sadness. *European Journal of Social Psychology, 24(1),* 45–62.

Bodenhausen, G. V., & Wyer, R. S., Jr. (1985). Effects of stereotypes on decision making and information-processing strategies. *Journal of Personality and Social Psychology, 48,* 267–282.

Bogardus, E. S. (1933). A social distance scale. *Sociology and Social Research, 17,* 265–271.

Bonano, G. A., Field, N. P., Kovacevic, A., & Kaltman, S. (2002). Self-enhancement as a buffer against extreme adversity: Civil war in Bosnia and traumatic loss in the United States. *Personality and Social Psychology Bulletin, 28,* 184–196.

Bond, M. H. (1972). Effect of an impression set on subsequent behavior. *Journal of Personality and Social Psychology, 24,* 301–305.

Boney-McCoy, S., Gibbons, F. X., & Gerrard, M. (1999). Self-esteem, compensatory self-enhancement, and the consideration of health risk. *Personality and Social Psychology Bulletin, 25,* 954–965.

Boninger, D. S., Krosnick, J. A., & Berent, M. K. (1995). Origins of attitude importance: Self-interest, social identification, and value relevance. *Journal of Personality and Social Psychology, 68,* 61–80.

Borgida, E., & Campbell, B. (1982). Attitude–behavior consistency: The moderating role of personal experience. *Journal of Personality and Social Psychology, 42,* 239–247.

Borgida, E., & Howard-Pitney, B. (1983). Personal involvement and the robustness of perceptual salience effects. *Journal of Personality and Social Psychology, 45,* 560–570.

Boring, E. G. (1950). *A history of experimental psychology* (2nd edn). Englewood Cliffs, NJ: Prentice-Hall.

Bornstein, R. F. (1989). Exposure and affect: Overview and meta-analysis of research, 1968–1987. *Psychological Bulletin, 106,* 265–289.

Bornstein, R. F., & D'Agostino, P. R. (1992). Stimulus recognition and the mere exposure effect. *Journal of Personality and Social Psychology, 63,* 545–552.

Bornstein, R. F., & D'Agostino, P. R. (1994). The attribution and discounting of perceptual fluency: Preliminary tests of a perceptual fluency/attributional model of the mere exposure effect. *Social Cognition, 12,* 103–128.

Bornstein, B. H., & Wiener, R. L. (2006). Introduction to the special issue on emotion in legal judgment and decision making. *Law and Human Behavior, 30,* 115–118.

Bosson, J. K., Haymovitz, E. L., & Pinel, E. C. (2004). When saying and doing diverge: The effects of stereotype threat on self-reported versus non-verbal anxiety. *Journal of Experimental and Social Psychology, 40,* 247–255.

Botvinick, M. M., Cohen, J. D., & Carter, C. S. (2004). Conflict monitoring and anterior cingulate cortex: An update. *Trends in Cognitive Sciences, 8,* 539–546.

Bower, G. H. (1987). Commentary on mood and memory. *Behavior Research Therapy, 25,* 443–455.

Bower, G. H. (1990). Awareness, the unconscious, and repression: An experimental psychologist's perspective. In. J. A. Singer (Ed.), *Repression: Defense mechanism and personality style* (pp. 209–231). Chicago, IL: University of Chicago Press.

Bower, G. H. (1991). *The psychology of learning and motivation: Advances in research and theory* (Vol. 27). San Diego, CA: Academic Press.

Bower, G. H., Gilligan, S. G., & Monteiro, K. P. (1981). Selectivity of learning caused by affective states. *Journal of Experimental Psychology: General, 110,* 451–473.

Bower, G. H., & Mayer, J. D. (1989). In search of mood-dependent retrieval. *Journal of Social Behavior and Personality, 4,* 121–156.

Bradburn, N. M., & Caplovitz, D. (1965). *Reports on happiness.* Chicago: Aldine.

Bramel, D. (1963). Selection of a target for defensive projection. *Journal of Abnormal and Social Psychology, 66,* 318–324.

Brandstätter, V., & Frank, E. (2002). Effects of deliberative and implemental mindsets on persistence in goal-directed behavior. *Personality and Social Psychology Bulletin, 28,* 365–375.

Branscombe, N. R. (1985). Effects of hedonic valence and physiological arousal on emotion: A comparison of two theoretical perspectives. *Motivation and Emotion, 9,* 153–169.

Branscombe, N. R. (1988). Conscious and unconscious processing of affective and cognitive information. In K. Fiedler & J. Forgas (Eds.), *Affect, cognition, and social behavior: New evidence and integrative attempts* (pp. 3–24). Toronto, Canada: Hogrefe.

Branscombe, N. R., & Cohen, B. M. (1990). Motivation and complexity levels as determinants of heuristic use in social judgment. In J. Forgas (Ed.), *Emotion and social judgment.* Oxford: Pergamon Press.

Branscombe, N. R., Schmitt, M. T., & Harvey, R. D. (1999). Perceiving pervasive discrimination among African Americans: Implications for group identification and well-being. *Journal of Personality and Social Psychology, 77,* 135–149.

Branscombe, N. R., & Wann, D. L. (1994). Collective self-esteem consequences of outgroup derogation when a valued social identity is on trial. *European Journal of Social Psychology, 24,* 641–657.

Braverman, J. (2005). The effect of mood on detection of covariation. *Personality and Social Psychology Bulletin, 31,* 1487–1497.

Brehm, J. W. (1956). Postdecision changes in the desirability of alternatives. *Journal of Abnormal and Social Psychology, 52,* 384–389.

Brehm, J. W., & Cohen, A. R. (1962). *Explorations in cognitive dissonance.* New York: Wiley.

Brewer, M. B. (1988). A dual process model of impression formation. In T. K. Srull & R. S. Wyer Jr. (Eds.), *Advances in social cognition* (Vol. 1, pp. 1–36). Hillsdale, NJ: Erlbaum.

Brewer, M. B. (1991). The social self: On being the same and different at the same time. *Personality and Social Psychology Bulletin, 17,* 475–482.

Brewer, M. B. (1999). The psychology of prejudice: Ingroup love or outgroup hate? *Journal of Social Issues, 55,* 429–444.

Brewer, M. B., & Alexander, M. G. (2002). Intergroup emotions and images. In D. M. Mackie & E. R. Smith (Eds.), *From prejudice to intergroup emotions* (pp. 209–225). New York: Psychology Press.

Brewer, M. B., & Brown, R. J. (1998). Intergroup relations. In D. T. Gilbert, S. T. Fiske, & G. Lindzey (Eds.), *Handbook of social psychology* (4th edn, Vol. 2, pp. 554–594). New York: McGraw-Hill.

Brewer, M. B., Dull, V., & Lui, L. (1981). Perceptions of the elderly: Stereotypes as prototypes. *Journal of Personality and Social Psychology, 41,* 656–670.

Brewer, M. M., & Harasty Feinstein, A. S. (1999). Dual processes in the cognitive representation of persons and social categories. In S. Chaiken & Y. Trope (Eds.), *Dual-process theories in social psychology* (pp. 255–270). New York: Guilford Press.

Brickman, P., Rabinowitz, V. C., Karuza, J. Jr., Coates, D., Cohn, E., & Kidder, L. (1982). Models of helping and coping. *American Psychologist, 37,* 368–384.

Brickner, M. A., Harkins, S. G., & Ostrom, T. M. (1985). The effects of personal involvement: Thought provoking implications of social loafing. *Journal of Personality and Social Psychology, 51,* 763–770.

Brief, A. P., & Weiss, H. M. (2002). Organizational behavior: Affect in the workplace. *Annual Review of Psychology, 53,* 279–307.

Briñol, P., & Petty, R. E. (2003). Overt head movements and persuasion: A self-validation analysis. *Journal of Personality and Social Psychology, 84,* 1123–1139.

Briñol, P., Petty, R. E., & Wheeler, S. C. (2006). Discrepancies between explicit and implicit self-concepts: Consequences for information processing. *Journal of Personality and Social Psychology, 91,* 154–170.

Broadbent, D. (1958). *Perception and communication.* London: Pergamon Press.

Brock, T. C. (1967). Communication discrepancy and intent to persuade as determinants of counterargument production. *Journal of Experimental Social Psychology, 3,* 269–309.

Brock, T. C., Albert, S. M., & Becker, L. A. (1970). Familiarity, utility, and supportiveness as determinants of information receptivity. *Journal of Personality and Social Psychology, 14,* 292–301.

Brock, T. C., & Balloun, J. L. (1967). Behavioral receptivity to dissonant information. *Journal of Personality and Social Psychology, 6,* 413–428.

Brockner, J., Wiesenfeld, B. M., & Martin, C. L. (1995). Decision frame, procedural justice, and survivors' reactions to job layoffs. *Organizational Behavior and Human Decision Processes, 63,* 59–68.

Bronfenbrenner, U. (1977). Lewinian space and ecological substance. *Journal of Social Issues, 33,* 199–212.

Brown, J. D. (1990). Evaluating one's abilities: Shortcuts and stumbling blocks on the road to self-knowledge. *Journal of Experimental Social Psychology, 26,* 149–167.

Brown, J. D., & Dutton, K. A. (1995). Truth and consequences: The costs and benefits of accurate self-knowledge. *Personality and Social Psychology Bulletin, 21,* 1288–1296.

Brown, J. D., & Marshall, M. A. (2001). Self-esteem and emotion: Some thoughts about feelings. *Personality and Social Psychology Bulletin, 27,* 575–584.

Brown, J. D., & Taylor, S. E. (1986). Affect and the processing of personal information: Evidence for mood-activated self-schemata. *Journal of Experimental Social Psychology, 22,* 436–452.

Brown, R. (1986). *Social psychology* (2nd edn). New York: Free Press.

Brown, R., & Kulik, J. A. (1977). Flashbulb memories. *Cognition, 5,* 73–99.

Brown, R. J. (2000). Social identity theory: Past achievements, current problems, and future challenges. *European Journal of Social Psychology, 30,* 745–778.

Brown, R. J., & Gaertner, S. L. (2001). *Blackwell handbook of social psychology: Intergroup processes.* London: Blackwell.

Brown, R. J., Maras, P., Masser, B., Vivian, J., & Hewstone, M. (2001). Life on the ocean wave: Testing some intergroup hypotheses in a naturalistic setting. *Group Processes and Intergroup Relations, 4,* 81–97.

Bruce, V., & Young, A. (1986). Understanding face recognition. *British Journal of Psychology, 77,* 305–327.

Bruner, J. S. (1957). On perceptual readiness. *Psychological Review, 64,* 123–152.

Bruner, J. S. (1958). Social psychology and perception. In E. E. Maccoby, T. M. Newcomb, & E. L. Hartley (Eds.), *Readings in social psychology* (3rd edn). New York: Holt, Rinehart, & Winston.

Brunswik, E. (1956). *Perception and the representative design of psychological experiments* (2nd edn). Berkeley and Los Angeles: University of California Press.

Bryant, J., & Zillmann, D. (1979). Effect of intensification of annoyance through unrelated residual excitation on substantially delayed hostile behavior. *Journal of Experimental Social Psychology, 15,* 470–480.

Buck, R. (1980). Nonverbal behavior and the theory of emotion: The facial feedback hypothesis. *Journal of Personality and Social Psychology, 38,* 811–824.

Buckner, R. L., Kelley, W. M., & Petersen, S. E. (1999). Frontal cortex contributes to human memory formation. *Nature Neuroscience, 2,* 311–314.

Buehler, R., Griffin, D., & Ross, M. (1994). Exploring the "planning fallacy": Why people underestimate their task completion times. *Journal of Personality and Social Psychology, 67,* 366–381.

Burger, J. M. (1981). Motivational biases in the attribution of responsibility for an accident: A meta-analysis of the defensive-attribution hypothesis. *Psychological Bulletin, 90,* 496–512.

Burgess, E. W. (1941). An experiment in the standardization of the case study method. *Sociometry, 4,* 329–348.

Burnstein, E., & Vinokur, A. (1973). Testing two classes of theories about group-induced shifts in individual choice. *Journal of Experimental Social Psychology, 9,* 123–137.

Burnstein, E., & Vinokur, A. (1975). What a person thinks upon learning he has chosen differently from others: Nice evidence for the persuasive-arguments explanation of choice shifts. *Journal of Experimental Social Psychology, 11,* 412–426.

Burris, C. T., & Rempel, J. K. (2004). "It's the end of the world as we know it:" Threat and the spatial-symbolic self. *Journal of Personality and Social Psychology, 86,* 19–42.

Bush, G., Luu, P., & Posner, M. (2000). Cognitive and emotional influences in anterior cingulate cortex. *Trends in Cognitive Science, 4,* 215–222.

Business and Professional Women's Foundation. (2005, July). 101 facts on the status of working women. Retrieved July 31, 2006, from www.bpwusa.org.

Buss, D. M. (1989). Sex differences in human mate preferences: Evolutionary hypothesis tested in 37 cultures. *Behavioral and Brain Sciences, 12,* 1–49.

Buss, D. M., Abbott, M., Angleitner, A., Asherian, A., et al. (1990). International preferences in selecting mates: A study of 37 cultures. *Journal of Cross-Cultural Psychology, 21,* 5–47.

Buss, D. M., & Craik, K. H. (1980). The frequency concept of disposition: Dominance and prototypically dominant acts. *Journal of Personality, 43,* 379–392.

Buss, D. M., & Craik, K. H. (1981). The act frequency analysis of interpersonal dispositions: Aloofness, gregariousness, dominance, and submissiveness. *Journal of Personality, 49,* 175–192.

Buss, D. M., & Kenrick, D. T. (1998). Evolutionary social psychology. In D. T. Gilbert, S. T. Fiske, & G. Lindzey (Eds.), *Handbook of social psychology* (4th edn, Vol. 2, pp. 982–1026). New York: McGraw-Hill.

Buss, D. M., & Schmitt, D. P. (1993). Sexual strategies theory: An evolutionary perspective on human mating. *Psychological Review, 100,* 204–232.

Cacioppo, J. T. (1979). Effects of exogenous changes in heart rate on facilitation of thought and resistance to persuasion. *Journal of Personality and Social Psychology, 37,* 489–498.

Cacioppo, J. T., Amaral, D., Blanchard, J. J., Cameron, J. L., Carter, C. S., Crews, D. P., et al. (2007). Social neuroscience: Progress and implications for mental health. *Perspectives on Psychological Science, 2,* 99–123.

Cacioppo, J. T., & Berntson, G. G. (1992). Social psychological contributions to the decade of the brain: Doctrine of multilevel analysis. *American Psychologist, 47,* 1019–1028.

Cacioppo, J. T., & Berntson, G. G. (1999). The affect system: Architecture and operating characteristics. *Current Directions in Psychological Science, 8,* 133–137.

Cacioppo, J. T., & Gardner, W. L. (1999). Emotions. *Annual Review of Psychology, 50,* 191–214.

Cacioppo, J. T., & Patrick, W. (2008). *Loneliness: Human nature and the need for social connection.* New York: Norton.

Cacioppo, J. T., & Petty, R. E. (1979). Effects of message repetition and position on cognitive response, recall, and persuasion. *Journal of Personality and Social Psychology, 37,* 97–109.

Cacioppo, J. T., & Petty, R. E. (1982). The need for cognition. *Journal of Personality and Social Psychology, 42,* 116–131.

Cacioppo, J. T., Petty, R. E., Feinstein, J. A., & Jarvis, W. B. G. (1996). Dispositional differences in cognitive motivation: The life and times of individuals varying in need for cognition. *Psychological Bulletin, 119(2),* 197–253.

Cacioppo, J. T., Petty, R. E., Losch, M. E., & Kim, H. S. (1986). Electromyographic activity over facial muscle regions can differentiate the valence and intensity of affective reactions. *Journal of Personality and Social Psychology, 50,* 260–268.

Cacioppo, J. T., Petty, R. E., & Morris, K. J. (1983). Effects of need for cognition on message evaluation, recall, and persuasion. *Journal of Personality and Social Psychology, 45,* 805–818.

Cacioppo, J. T., Priester, J. R., & Berntson, G. G. (1993). Rudimentary determinants of attitudes: II. Arm flexion and extension have differential effects on attitudes. *Journal of Personality and Social Psychology, 65,* 5–17.

Cadinu, M., Maass, A., Rosabianca, A., & Kiesner, J. (2005). Why do women underperform under stereotype threat? Evidence for the role of negative thinking. *Psychological Science, 16,* 572–578.

Caldwell, C. H., Sellers, R. M., Bernat, D. H., & Zimmerman, M. A. (2004). Racial identity, parental support, and alcohol use in a sample of academically at-risk African American high school students. *American Journal of Community Psychology, 34,* 71–82.

Caldwell, C. H., Zimmerman, M. A., Bernat, D. H., Sellers, R. M., & Notaro, P. C. (2002). Racial identity, maternal support and psychological distress among African American adolescents. *Child Development, 73,* 1322–1336.

Calvo-Merino, B., Glaser, D. E., Grezes, J., Passingham, R. E., & Haggard, P. (2005). Action observation and acquired motor skills. *Cerebral Cortex, 15,* 1243–1249.

Camerer, C. (2003). Strategizing in the brain. *Science, 300,* 1673–1675.

Campbell, D. T. (1958). Common fate, similarity, and other indices of the status of aggregates of persons as social entities. *Behavioral Science, 3,* 14–25.

Campbell, D. T. (1965). Ethnocentric and other altruistic motives. In D. Levine (Ed.), *Nebraska Symposium on Motivation* (pp. 283–311). Lincoln, NB: University of Nebraska Press.

Campbell, J. D. (1986). Similarity and uniqueness: The effects of attribute type, relevance, and individual differences in self-esteem and depression. *Journal of Personality and Social Psychology, 50,* 281–294.

Cannon, W. B. (1927). The James-Lange theory of emotions: A critical examination and an alternative theory. *American Journal of Psychology, 39,* 106–124.

Cantor, J. R., Bryant, J., & Zillmann, D. (1974). Enhancement of humor appreciation by transferred excitation. *Journal of Personality and Social Psychology, 30,* 812–821.

Cantor, J. R., & Zillmann, D. (1973). The effect of affective state and emotional arousal on music appreciation. *Journal of General Psychology, 89,* 97–108.

Cantor, N., & Kihlstrom, J. F. (1985) Social intelligence: The cognitive basis of personality. In P. Shaver (Ed.), *Review of personality and social psychology* (Vol. 6, pp. 15–34). Beverly Hills, CA: Sage.

Cantor, N., & Kihlstrom, J. F. (1987). *Personality and social intelligence.* Englewood Cliffs, NJ: Prentice-Hall.

Cantor, N., Mackie, D. M., & Lord, C. G. (1983–1984). Choosing partners and activities: The social perceiver decides to mix it up. *Social Cognition, 2,* 256–272.

Cantor, N., & Mischel, W. (1979). Prototypes in person perception. In L. Berkowitz (Ed.), *Advances in experimental social psychology* (Vol. 12, pp. 3–52). New York: Academic Press.

Carlson, M., Charlin, V., & Miller, N. (1988). Positive mood and helping behavior: A test of six hypotheses. *Journal of Personality and Social Psychology, 55,* 211–229.

Carlson, M., & Miller, N. (1987). Explanation of the relation between negative mood and helping. *Psychological Bulletin, 102,* 91–108.

Carlston, D. E. (1994). Associated systems theory: A systematic approach to the cognitive representation of persons and events. In R. S. Wyer (Ed.), *Advances in social cognition: Associated systems theory* (Vol. 7, pp. 1–78). Hillsdale, NJ: Erlbaum.

Carlston, D. E., & Skowronski, J. J. (1994). Savings in the relearning of trait information as evidence for spontaneous inference generation. *Journal of Personality and Social Psychology, 66,* 840–856.

Carlston, D. E., Skowronski, J. J., & Sparks, C. (1995). Savings in relearning II: On the formation of behavior-based trait associations and inferences. *Journal of Personality and Social Psychology, 69,* 420–436.

Carnevale, P. J. D., & Isen, A. M. (1986). The influence of positive affect and visual access on the discovery of integrative solutions in bilateral negotiation. *Organizational Behavior and Human Decision Processes, 37,* 1–13.

Carney, D. R., Cuddy, A. J. C., & Yap, A. J. (2010). Power posing: Brief nonverbal displays affect neuroendocrine levels and risk tolerance. *Psychological Science, 21*(10), 1363–1368.

Carroll, J. S. (1978). The effect of imagining an event on expectations for the event: An interpretation in terms of the availability heuristic. *Journal of Experimental Social Psychology, 14,* 88–96.

Carvallo, M., & Pelham, B. W. (2006). When fiends become friends: The need to belong and perceptions of personal and group discrimination. *Journal of Personality and Social Psychology, 90,* 94–108.

Carver, C. S. (1979). A cybernetic model of self-attention processes. *Journal of Personality and Social Psychology, 37,* 1251–1281.

Carver, C. S. (2003). Pleasure as a sign you can attend to something else: Placing positive feelings within a general model of affect. *Cognition and Emotion, 17,* 241–261.

Carver, C. S., la Voie, L., Kuhl, J., & Ganellen, R. J. (1988). Cognitive concomitants of depression: A further examination of the roles of generalization, high standards, and self-criticism. *Journal of Social and Clinical Psychology, 7,* 350–365.

Carver, C. S., & Scheier, M. F. (1982). Outcome expectancy, locus of attribution for expectancy, and self-directed attention as determinants of evaluations and performance. *Journal of Experimental Social Psychology, 18,* 184–200.

Carver, C. S., & Scheier, M. F. (1990). Origins and functions of positive and negative affect: A control-process view. *Psychological Review, 97,* 19–35.

Carver, C. S., & Scheier, M. F. (1998). *On the self-regulation of behavior.* New York: Cambridge University Press.

Carver, C. S., Sutton, S. K., & Scheier, M. F. (2000). Action, emotion, and personality: Emerging conceptual integration. *Personality and Social Psychology Bulletin, 26,* 741–751.

Carver, C. S., & White, T. L. (1994). Behavioral inhibition, behavioral activation, and affective responses to impending reward and punishment: The BIS/BAS scales. *Journal of Personality and Social Psychology, 67,* 319–333.

Castano, E. (2004). In case of death, cling to the ingroup. *European Journal of Social Psychology, 34,* 375–384.

Castano, E., & Dechesne, M. (2005). On defeating death: Group reification and social identification as immortality strategies. In W. Strobe & M. Hewstone (Eds.), *European Review of Social Psychology* (Vol. 16, pp. 221–256). New York: Psychology Press.

Castano, E., & Giner-Sorolla, R. (2006). Not quite human: Infra-humanization in response to collective responsibility for intergroup killing. *Journal of Personality and Social Psychology, 90,* 804–818.

Castano, E., Sacchi, S., & Gries, P. H. (2003). The perception of the other in international relations: Evidence for the polarizing effect of entitativity. *Political Psychology, 24,* 449–468.

Castano, E., & Yzerbyt, V. Y. (1998). The highs and lows of group homogeneity. *Behavioural Processes, 42,* 219–238.

Castelli, F., Happé, F., Frith, U., & Frith, C. (2000). Movement and mind: A functional imaging study of perception and interpretation of complex intentional movement patterns. *NeuroImage, 12,* 314–325.

Castelli, L., Macrae, C. N., Zogmaister, C., & Arcuri, L. (2004). A tale of two primes: Contextual limits on stereotype activation. *Social Cognition, 22,* 233–247.

Cejka, M. A., & Eagly, A. H. (1999). Gender-stereotypic images of occupations correspond to the sex segregation of employment. *Personality and Social Psychology Bulletin, 25,* 413–423. [Erratum: *25,* 1059.]

Centerbar, D. B., & Clore, G. L. (2006). Do approach-avoidance actions create attitudes? *Psychological Science, 17,* 22–29.

Cervellon, M. C., & Dubé, L. (2002). Assessing the cross-cultural applicability of affective and cognitive components of attitude. *Journal of Cross Cultural Psychology, 33,* 346–357.

Cesario, J., Grant, H., & Higgins, E. T. (2004). Regulatory fit and persuasion: Transfer from "feeling right." *Journal of Personality and Social Psychology, 86,* 388–404.

Cesario, J., Plaks, J. E., & Higgins, E. T. (2006). Automatic social behavior as motivated preparation to interact. *Journal of Personality and Social Psychology, 90,* 893–910.

Chaiken, S. (1979). Communicator physical attractiveness and persuasion. *Journal of Personality and Social Psychology, 37,* 1387–1397.

Chaiken, S. (1980). Heuristic versus systematic information processing and the use of source versus message cues in persuasion. *Journal of Personality and Social Psychology, 39,* 752–766.

Chaiken, S. (1987). The heuristic model of persuasion. In M. P. Zanna, J. M. Olson, & C. P. Herman (Eds.), *Social influence: The Ontario Symposium* (Vol. 5, pp. 3–40). Hillsdale, NJ: Erlbaum.

Chaiken, S., & Eagly, A. H. (1976). Communication modality as a determinant of message persuasiveness and message comprehensibility. *Journal of Personality and Social Psychology, 34,* 605–614.

Chaiken, S., & Eagly, A. H. (1983). Communication modality as a determinant of persuasion: The role of communicator salience. *Journal of Personality and Social Psychology, 45,* 41–56.

Chaiken, S., Liberman, A., & Eagly, A. H. (1989). Heuristic and systematic information processing within and beyond the persuasion context. In J. S. Uleman & J. A. Bargh (Eds.), *Unintended thought* (pp. 212–252). New York: Guilford Press.

Chaiken, S., & Stangor, C. (1987). Attitudes and attitude change. *Annual Review of Psychology, 38,* 575–630.

Chaiken, S., & Trope, Y. (Eds.). (1999). *Dual-process theories in social psychology.* New York: Guilford Press.

Chaiken, S., & Yates, S. (1985). Affective-cognitive consistency and thought-induced attitude polarization. *Journal of Personality and Social Psychology, 49,* 1470–1481.

Chajut, E., & Algom, D. (2003). Selective attention improves under stress: Implications for theories of social cognition. *Journal of Personality and Social Psychology, 86,* 231–248.

Chang, C., & Hitchon, J. C. B. (2004). When does gender count? Further insights into gender schematic processing of female candidates' political advertisements. *Sex Roles, 51,* 197–208.

Chaplin, W. F., John, O. P., & Goldberg, L. R. (1988). Conceptions of states and traits: Dimensional attributes with ideals as prototypes. *Journal of Personality and Social Psychology, 54,* 541–557.

Chapman, L. J. (1967). Illusory correlation in observational report. *Journal of Verbal Learning and Verbal Behavior, 6,* 151–155.

Chartrand, T. L., & Bargh, J. A. (1999). The chameleon effect: The perception–behavior link and social interaction. *Journal of Personality and Social Psychology, 76,* 893–910.

Chasteen, A. L., Bhattacharyya, S., Horhota, M., Tam, R., & Hasher, L. (2005). How feelings of stereotype threat influence older adults' memory performance. *Experimental Aging Research, 31,* 235–260.

Chen, H. C., Reardon, R., Rea, C., & Moore, D. J. (1992). Forewarning of content and involvement: Consequences for persuasion and resistance to persuasion. *Journal of Experimental and Social Psychology, 28,* 523–541.

Chen, M., & Bargh, J. A. (1999). Consequences of automatic evaluation: Immediate behavioral predispositions to approach or avoid the stimulus. *Personality and Social Psychology Bulletin, 25,* 215–224.

Chen, S., & Chaiken, S. (1999). The heuristic-systematic model in its broader context. In S. Chaiken & Y. Trope (Eds.), *Dual-process theories in social psychology* (pp. 73–96). New York: Guilford Press.

Chen, S., Schechter, D., & Chaiken, S. (1996). Getting at the truth or getting along: Accuracy-versus impression-motivated heuristic and systematic processing. *Journal of Personality and Social Psychology, 71,* 262–275.

Cheng, P. W., Holyoak, K. J., Nisbett, R. E., & Oliver, L. M. (1986). Pragmatic versus syntactic approaches to training deductive reasoning. *Cognitive Psychology, 18,* 293–328.

Chiao, J. Y., Cheon, B. K., Bebko, G. M., Livingston, R. L., & Hong, Y.-y. (2012). Gene x environment interaction in social cognition. In S. T. Fiske & C. N. Macrae (Eds.), *Sage handbook of social cognition* (pp. 516–534). Thousand Oaks, CA: Sage.

Choi, I., & Choi, Y. (2002). Culture and self-concept flexibility. *Personality and Social Psychology Bulletin, 28,* 1508–1517.

Choi, I., Dalal, R., Kim-Prieto, C., & Park, H. (2003). Culture and judgment of causal relevance. *Journal of Personality and Social Psychology, 84,* 46–59.

Chomsky, N. (1959). Verbal behavior. [Review of Skinner's book.] *Language, 35,* 26–58.

Christensen, T. C., Wood, J. V., & Barrett, L. F. (2003). Remembering everyday experience through the prism of self-esteem. *Personality and Social Psychology Bulletin, 29,* 51–62.

Christensen-Szalanski, J. J., & Willham, C. F. (1991). The hindsight bias: A meta-analysis. *Organizational Behavior and Human Decision Processes, 48,* 147–168.

Chun, M. M., Golomb, J. D., & Turk-Browne, N. B. (2011). A taxonomy of external and internal attention. *Annual Review of Psychology, 62,* 73–101.

Chun, W. Y., & Kruglanski, A. W. (2006). The role of task demands and processing resources in the use of base-rate and individuating information. *Journal of Personality and Social Psychology, 91,* 205–217.

Chun, W. Y., Spiegel, S., & Kruglanski, A. W. (2002). Assimilative behavior identification can also be resource dependent: The unimodel perspective on personal-attribution phases. *Journal of Personality and Social Psychology, 83,* 542–555.

Chwalisz, K., Diener, E., & Gallagher, D. (1988). Autonomic arousal feedback and emotional experience: Evidence from the spinal cord injured. *Journal of Personality and Social Psychology, 54,* 820–828.

Cialdini, R. B., Darby, B. L., & Vincent, J. E. (1973). Transgression and altruism: A case for hedonism. *Journal of Experimental Social Psychology, 9,* 502–516.

Cialdini, R. B., & Kenrick, D. T. (1976). Altruism as hedonism: A social development perspective on the relationship of negative mood state and helping. *Journal of Personality and Social Psychology, 34,* 907–914.

Cialdini, R. B., Levy, A., Herman, C. P., & Evenbeck, S. (1973). Attitudinal politics: The strategy of moderation. *Journal of Personality and Social Psychology, 25,* 100–108.

Cikara, M., Botvinick, M. M., & Fiske, S. T. (2011). Us versus them: Social identity shapes neural responses to intergroup competition and harm. *Psychological Science, 22,* 306–313.

Clark, M. S. (1982). A role for arousal in the link between feeling states, judgments, and behavior. In M. S. Clark & S. T. Fiske (Eds.), *Affect and cognition: The 17th Annual Carnegie Symposium on Cognition* (pp. 263–290). Hillsdale, NJ: Erlbaum.

Clark, M. S., & Fiske, S. T. (Eds.). (1982). *Affect and cognition: The 17th Annual Carnegie Symposium on Cognition.* Hillsdale, NJ: Erlbaum.

Clark, M. S., & Isen, A. M. (1982). Toward understanding the relationship between feeling states and social behavior. In A. Hastorf & A. Isen (Eds.), *Cognitive social psychology* (pp. 73–108). New York: Elsevier North-Holland.

Clark, M. S., Milberg, S., & Erber, R. (1984). Effects of arousal on judgments of others' emotions. *Journal of Personality and Social Psychology, 46,* 551–560.

Clark, M. S., Milberg, S., & Erber, R. (1988). Arousal-state-dependent memory: Evidence and implications for understanding social judgments and social behaviors. In K. Fiedler & J. Forgas (Eds.), *Affect, cognition, and social behavior: New evidence and integrative attempts.* Toronto, Canada: Hogrefe.

Clark, M. S., Milberg, S., & Ross, J. (1983). Arousal cues material stored in memory with a similar level of arousal: Implications for understanding the effects of mood on memory. *Journal of Verbal Learning and Verbal Behavior, 22,* 633–649.

Clark, M. S., & Williamson, G. M. (1989). Moods and social judgments. In H. L. Wagner & A. S. R. Manstead (Eds.), *Handbook of psychophysiology: Emotion and social behavior.* Chichester, England: Wiley.

Clark, N. K., & Rutter, D. R. (1985). Social categorization, visual cues, and social judgements. *European Journal of Social Psychology, 15,* 105–119.

Clausell, E., & Fiske, S. T. (2005). When do subgroup parts add up to the stereotypic whole? Mixed stereotype content for gay male subgroups explains overall ratings. *Social Cognition, 23,* 161–181.

Clore, G. L., & Ortony, A. (1991). What more is there to emotion concepts than prototypes? *Journal of Personality and Social Psychology, 60,* 48–50.

Clore, G. L., Schwarz, N., & Conway, M. (1994). Affective causes and consequences of social information processing. In R. S. Wyer Jr. & T. K. Srull (Eds.), *Handbook of social cognition, Vol. 1: Basic processes.* (2nd edn, pp. 323–417). Hillsdale, NJ: Erlbaum.

Cloutier, J., Mason, M. F., & Macrae, C. N. (2005). The perceptual determinants of person construal: Reopening the social-cognition toolbox. *Journal of Personality and Social Psychology, 88,* 885–894.

Coan, J. A., & Allen, J. J. B. (2004). Frontal EEG asymmetry as a moderator and mediator of emotion. *Biological Psychology, 67,* 7–49.

Coan, J. A., Allen, J. J. B., & Harmon-Jones, E. (2001). Voluntary facial expression and hemispheric asymmetry over the frontal cortex. *Psychophysiology, 38,* 912–925.

Cohen, A. R., Brehm, J. W., & Latané, B. (1959). Choice of strategy and voluntary exposure to information under public and private conditions. *Journal of Personality, 27,* 63–73.

Cohen, C. E., & Ebbesen, E. B. (1979). Observational goals and schema activation: A theoretical framework for behavior perception. *Journal of Experimental Social Psychology, 15,* 305–329.

Cohen, J. B., & Basu, K. (1987). Alternative models of categorization: Toward a contingent processing framework. *Journal of Consumer Research, 13,* 455–472.

Cohen, L. H., Towbes, L. C., & Flocco, R. (1988). Effects of induced mood on self-reported life events and perceived and received social support. *Journal of Personality and Social Psychology, 55,* 669–674.

Collins, A. M., & Loftus, E. F. (1975). A spreading-activation theory of semantic processing. *Psychological Review, 82,* 407–428.

Collins, R. L., Taylor, S. E., Wood, J. V., & Thompson, S. C. (1988). The vividness effect: Elusive or illusory? *Journal of Experimental Social Psychology, 24,* 1–18.

Coman, A., & Hirst, W. (2012). Cognition through a social network: The propagation of induced forgetting and practice effects. *Journal of Experimental Psychology: General, 141*(2), 321–336.

Coman, A., Maner, D., & Hirst, W. (2009). Forgetting the unforgettable through conversation: Socially shared retrieval-induced forgetting of September 11 memories. *Psychological Science, 20(5),* 627–633.

Conner, M., & Abraham, C. (2001). Conscientiousness and the theory of planned behavior: Toward a more complete model of the antecedents of intentions and behavior. *Personality and Social Psychology Bulletin, 27,* 1547–1561.

Conrey, F. R., & Smith, E. R. (2007). Attitude representation: Attitudes as patterns in a distributed, connectionist representational system. *Social Cognition, 25(5),* 718–735.

Conway, M., & Ross, M. (1984). Getting what you want by revising what you had. *Journal of Personality and Social Psychology, 47,* 738–748.

Cook, T. D., & Flay, B. R. (1978). The persistence of experimentally induced attitude change. In L. Berkowitz (Ed.), *Advances in experimental social psychology* (Vol. 11, pp. 1–57). New York: Academic Press.

Cooley, C. H. (1902). *Human nature and the social order.* New York: Scribners.

Cooper, J., & Cooper, G. (2002). Subliminal motivation: A story revisited. *Journal of Applied Social Psychology, 32,* 2213–2227.

Cooper, J., & Fazio, R. H. (1984). A new look at dissonance theory. In L. Berkowitz (Ed.), *Advances in experimental social psychology* (Vol. 17, pp. 229–266). New York: Academic Press.

Cooper, J., Zanna, M. P., & Taves, P. A. (1978). Arousal as a necessary condition for attitude change following induced compliance. *Journal of Personality and Social Psychology, 36,* 1101–1106.

Corenblum, B., & Stephan, W. G. (2001). White fears and native apprehensions: An integrated threat theory approach to intergroup attitudes. *Canadian Journal of Behavioral Science, 33,* 251–268.

Correll, J., Park, B., Judd, C. M., & Wittenbrink, B. (2002). The police officer's dilemma: Using ethnicity to disambiguate potentially threatening individuals. *Journal of Personality and Social Psychology, 83,* 1314–1329.

Correll, J., Park, B., Judd, C. M., Wittenbrink, B., Sadler, M. S., & Keesee, T. (2007). Across the thin blue line: Police officers and racial bias in the decision to shoot. *Journal of Personality and Social Psychology, 92(6),* 1006–1023.

Correll, J., Urland, G. R., & Ito, T. A. (2006). Event-related potentials and the decision to shoot: The role of threat perception and cognitive control. *Journal of Experimental Social Psychology, 42,* 120–128.

Corteen, R. S., & Wood, B. (1972). Automatic responses to shock-associated words in an unattended channel. *Journal of Experimental Psychology, 94,* 308–313.

Cosmides, L., Tooby, J., & Kurzban, R. (2003). Perception of race. *Trends in Cognitive Sciences, 7,* 173–179.

Cottrell, C. A., & Neuberg, S. L. (2005). Different emotional reactions to different groups: A sociofunctional threat-based approach to "prejudice." *Journal of Personality and Social Psychology, 88,* 770–789.

Cottrell, N. B., Ingraham, L. A., & Monfort, F. W. (1971). The retention of balanced and unbalanced cognitive structures. *Journal of Personality, 39,* 112–131.

Cousins, S. D. (1989). Culture and self-perception in Japan and the United States. *Journal of Personality and Social Psychology, 56,* 124–131.

Couzin, I. D., Krause, J., Franks, N. R., & Levin, S. A. (2005). Effective leadership and decision making in animal groups on the move. *Nature, 433,* 513–516.

Craighead, W. E., Hickey, K. S., & DeMonbreun, B. G. (1979). Distortion of perception and recall of neutral feedback in depression. *Cognitive Therapy and Research, 3,* 291–298.

Crandall, C. S., Eshleman, A., & O'Brien, L. T. (2002). Social norms and the expression and suppression of prejudice: The struggle for internalization. *Journal of Personality and Social Psychology, 82,* 359–378.

Crandall, C. S., & Greenfield, B. S. (1986). Understanding the conjunction fallacy: A conjunction of effects? *Social Cognition, 4,* 408–419.

Crano, W. D., & Prislin, R. (2006). Attitudes and persuasion. *Annual Review of Psychology, 57,* 345–374.

Crary, W. G. (1966). Reactions to incongruent self-experiences. *Journal of Consulting Psychology, 30,* 246–252.

Creswell, J. D., Welch, W. T., Taylor, S. E., Sherman, D. K., Gruenewald, T. L., & Mann, T. (2005). Affirmation of personal values buffers neuroendocrine and psychological stress responses. *Psychological Science, 16,* 846–851.

Crisp, R. J., & Husnu, S. (2011). Attributional processes underlying imagined conflict effects. *Group Processes and Intergroup Relations, 14(2),* 275–287.

Crites, S. L., Cacioppo, J. T., Gardner, W. L., & Berntson, G. G. (1995). Bioelectrical echoes from evaluative categorization: II. A late positive brain potential that varies as a function of attitude registration rather than attitude report. *Journal of Personality and Social Psychology, 68,* 997–1013.

Crocker, J. (1981). Judgment of covariation by social perceivers. *Psychological Bulletin, 90,* 272–292.

Crocker, J., Cornwell, B., & Major, B. (1993). The stigma of overweight: Affective consequences of attributional ambiguity. *Journal of Personality and Social Psychology, 64,* 60–70.

Crocker, J., Karpinski, A., Quinn, D. M., & Chase, S. K. (2003). When grades determine self-worth: Consequences of contingent self-worth for male and female engineering and psychology majors. *Journal of Personality and Social Psychology, 85,* 507–516.

Crocker, J., & Knight, K. M. (2005). Contingencies of self-worth. *Current Directions in Psychological Science, 14,* 200–203.

Crocker, J., & Luhtanen, R. K. (1990). Collective self-esteem and ingroup bias. *Journal of Personality and Social Psychology, 58,* 60–67.

Crocker, J., & Luhtanen, R. K. (2003). Level of self-esteem and contingencies of self-worth: Unique effects on academic, social and financial problems in college students. *Personality and Social Psychology Bulletin, 29,* 701–712.

Crocker, J., Luhtanen, R. K., Blaine, B., & Broadmax, S. (1994). Collective self-esteem and psychological well-being among White, Black, and Asian college students. *Personality and Social Psychology Bulletin, 20,* 503–513.

Crocker, J., & Major, B. (1989). Social stigma and self-esteem: The self-protective properties of stigma. *Psychological Review, 96,* 608–630.

Crocker, J., & McGraw, K. M. (1984). What's good for the goose is not good for the gander: Solo status as an obstacle to occupational achievement for males and females. *American Behavioral Scientist, 27,* 357–369.

Crocker, J., & Park, L. E. (2004). The costly pursuit of self-esteem. *Psychological Bulletin, 130,* 392–414.

Crocker, J., Voelkl, K., Testa, M., & Major, B. (1991). Social stigma: The affective consequences of attributional ambiguity. *Journal of Personality and Social Psychology, 60,* 218–228.

Croizet, J. C., & Claire, T. (1998). Extending the concept of stereotype threat to social class: The intellectual underperformance of students from low socioeconomic backgrounds. *Personality and Social Psychology Bulletin, 24,* 588–594.

Croizet, J. C., Després, G., Gauzins, M. E., Huguet, P., Leyens, J.-Ph., & Méot, A. (2004). Stereotype threat undermines intellectual performance by triggering a disruptive mental load. *Personality and Social Psychology Bulletin, 30,* 721–731.

Crosby, F. J. (1991). *Juggling: The unexpected advantages of balancing career and home for women and their families.* New York: Free Press.

Crosby, F. J., Bromley, S., & Saxe, L. (1980). Recent unobtrusive studies of Black and White discrimination and prejudice: A literature review. *Psychological Bulletin, 87,* 546–563.

Cross, S. E., Bacon, P. L., & Morris, M. L. (2000). The relational-interdependent self-construal and relationships. *Journal of Personality and Social Psychology, 78,* 791–808.

Cross, S. E., & Vick, N. V. (2001). The interdependent self-construal and social support: The case of persistence in engineering. *Personality and Social Psychology Bulletin, 27,* 820–832.

Csikszentmihalyi, M. (1978). Attention and the holistic approach to behavior. In K. S. Pope & J. L. Singer (Eds.), *The stream of consciousness* (pp. 335–358). New York: Plenum Press.

Csikszentmihalyi, M., & Larson, R. (1984). *Being adolescent: Conflict and growth in the teenage years.* New York: Basic Books.

Cuddy, A. J. C., Fiske, S. T., & Glick, P. (2007). The BIAS map: Behaviors from intergroup affect and stereotypes. *Journal of Personality and Social Psychology, 92,* 631–648.

Cuddy, A. J. C., Fiske, S. T., Kwan, V. S. Y., Glick, P., Demoulin, S., Leyens, J.-Ph., et al. (2009). Is the stereotype content model culture-bound? A cross-cultural comparison reveals systematic similarities and differences. *British Journal of Social Psychology, 48,* 1–33.

Cuddy, A. J. C., Norton, M. I., & Fiske, S. T. (2005) This old stereotype: The pervasiveness and persistence of the elderly stereotype. *Journal of Social Issues, 61,* 265–283.

Cuddy, A. J. C., Rock, M. S., & Norton, M. I. (2007). Aid in the aftermath of Hurricane Katrina: Inferences of secondary emotions and intergroup helping. *Group Processes and Intergroup Relations, 10,* 107–118.

Cunningham, M. R. (1988). Does happiness mean friendliness? Induced mood and heterosexual self-disclosure. *Personality and Social Psychology Bulletin, 14*, 283–297.

Cunningham, M. R., Steinberg, J., & Grey, R. (1980). Wanting to and having to help: Separate motivations for positive mood and guilt-induced helping. *Journal of Personality and Social Psychology, 38*, 181–192.

Cunningham, W. A., Johnson, M. K., Gatenby, J. C., Gore, J. C., & Banaji, M. R. (2003). Neural components of social evaluation. *Journal of Personality and Social Psychology, 85*, 639–649.

Cunningham, W. A., Johnson, M. K., Raye, C. L., Gatenby, J. C., Gore, J. C., & Banaji, M. R. (2004). Separable neural components in the processing of Black and White faces. *Psychological Science, 15*, 806–813.

Cunningham, W. A., Preacher, K. J., & Banaji, M. R. (2001). Implicit attitude measures: Consistency, stability, and convergent validity. *Psychological Science, 12*, 163–170.

Cunningham, W. A., Raye, C. L., & Johnson, M. K. (2004). Implicit and explicit evaluation: fMRI correlates of valence, emotional intensity, and control in the processing of attitudes. *Journal of Cognitive Neuroscience, 16*, 1717–1729.

Cupchik, G. C., & Leventhal, H. (1974). Consistency between expressive behavior and the evaluation of humorous stimuli: The role of sex and self-observation. *Journal of Personality and Social Psychology, 30*, 429–442.

Custers, R., & Aarts, H. (2005). Positive affect as implicit motivator: On the nonconscious operation of behavioral goals. *Journal of Personality and Social Psychology, 89*, 129–142.

Cvencek, D., Greenwald, A. G., Brown, A., Snowden, R., & Gray, N. (2010). Faking of the Implicit Association Test is statistically detectable and partly correctable. *Basic and Applied Social Psychology, 32*, 302–314.

Cvencek, D., Greenwald, A. G., & Meltzoff, A, N. (2011). Measuring implicit attitudes of 4-year-old children: The Preschool Implicit Association Test. *Journal of Experimental Child Psychology, 109*, 187–200.

Czopp, A. M., & Monteith, M. J. (2003). Confronting prejudice (literally): Reactions to confrontations of racial and gender bias. *Personality and Social Psychology Bulletin, 29*, 532–544.

Dambrun, M., Duarte, S., & Guimond, S. (2004). Why are men more likely to support group-based dominance than women? The mediating role of gender identification. *British Journal of Social Psychology, 43*, 287–297.

Dardenne, B., Dumont, M., & Bollier, T. (2007). Insidious dangers of benevolent sexism: Consequences for women's performance. *Journal of Personality and Social Psychology, 93(5)*, 764–779.

Darley, J. M., & Fazio, R. H. (1980). Expectancy confirmation processes arising in the social interaction sequence. *American Psychologist, 35*, 867–881.

Darwin, C. R. (1872). *The expression of emotions in man and animals.* London: John Murray.

Dasgupta, N., & Greenwald, A. G. (2001). On the malleability of automatic attitudes: Combating automatic prejudice with images of admired and disliked individuals. *Journal of Personality and Social Psychology, 81*, 800–814.

Dasgupta, N., McGhee, D. E., Greenwald, A. G., & Banaji, M. R. (2000). Automatic preference for White Americans: Eliminating the familiarity explanation. *Journal of Experimental Social Psychology, 36*, 316–328.

Davidson, R. J. (1993). Parsing affective space: Perspectives from neuropsychology and psychophysiology. *Neuropsychology, 7*, 464–475.

Davidson, R. J. (2003). Seven sins in the study of emotion: Correctives from affective neuroscience. *Brain and Cognition, 52*, 129–132.

Davidson, R. J., & Irwin, W. (1999). The functional neuroanatomy of emotion and affective style. *Trends in Cognitive Neuroscience, 3*, 11–21.

Davies, P. G., Spencer, S. J., & Steele, C. M. (2005). Clearing the air: Identity safety moderates the effects of stereotype threat on women's leadership aspirations. *Journal of Personality and Social Psychology, 88*, 276–287.

Davis, J. L., & Rusbult, C. E. (2001). Attitude alignment in close relationships. *Journal of Personality and Social Psychology, 81*, 65–84.

Davison, A. R., Yantis, S., Norwood, M., & Montano, D. E. (1985). Amount of information about the attitude object and attitude-behavior consistency. *Journal of Personality and Social Psychology, 49*, 1184–1198.

Davison, G. C., Robins, C., & Johnson, M. K. (1983). Articulated thoughts during simulated situations: A paradigm for studying cognition in emotion and behavior. *Cognitive Therapy and Research, 7*, 17–40.

Davison, G. C., & Zighelboim, V. (1987). Irrational beliefs in the articulated thoughts of college students with social anxiety. *Journal of Rational-Emotive Therapy, 5*, 238–254.

Davitz, J. R. (1970). A dictionary and grammar of emotion. In M. B. Arnold (Ed.), *Feelings and emotion: The Loyola Symposium.* New York: Academic Press.

Dawes, R. M. (1980). You can't systematize human judgment: Dyslexia. In R. A. Shweder (Ed.), *New directions for methodology of social and behavioral science* (Vol. 4, pp. 67–78). San Francisco: Jossey-Bass.

Dawes, R. M, Faust, D., & Meehl, P. E. (1989). Clinical versus actuarial judgment. *Science, 243*, 1668–1674.

Deaux, K., & Emswiller, T. (1974). Explanations of successful performance on sex-linked tasks: What is skill for the male is luck for the female. *Journal of Personality and Social Psychology, 29*, 80–85.

Deaux, K., & LaFrance, M. (1998). Gender. In D. T. Gilbert, S. T. Fiske, & G. Lindzey (Eds.), *The handbook of social psychology* (4th edn, Vol. 1, pp. 788–827). New York: McGraw-Hill.

Deaux, K., & Major, B. (1977). Sex-related patterns in the unit of perception. *Personality and Social Psychology Bulletin, 3*, 297–300.

Deaux, K., Winton, W. M., Crowley, M., & Lewis, L. L. (1985). Level of categorization and content of gender stereotypes. *Social Cognition, 3*, 145–167.

DeBono, K. G. (1987). Investigating the social-adjustive and value-expressive functions of attitudes: Implications for persuasion processes. *Journal of Personality and Social Psychology, 52*, 279–287.

DeBono, K. G., & Harnish, R. J. (1988). Source expertise, source attractiveness, and the processing of persuasive information: A functional approach. *Journal of Personality and Social Psychology, 55*, 541–546.

DeBono, K. G., & Snyder, M. (1989). Understanding consumer decision-making processes: The role of form and function in product evaluation. *Journal of Applied Social Psychology, 19*, 416–424.

Decéty, J., & Chaminade, T. (2003). Neural correlates of feeling sympathy. *Neuropsychologia. Special Issue on Social Cognition, 41*, 127–138.

DeCoster, J., Banner, M. J., Smith, E. R., & Semin, G. R. (2006). On the inexplicity of the implicit: Differences in the information provided by implicit and explicit tests. *Social Cognition, 24*, 5–21.

Delle Fave, A., & Massimini, F. (2004). Parenthood and the quality of experience in daily life: A longitudinal study. *Social Indicators Research, 67*, 75–106.

Demoulin, S., Torres, R. R., Perez, A. R., Vaes, J., Paladino, M. P., Gaunt, R., Pozo, B. C., & Leyens, J.-Ph. (2004). Emotional prejudice can lead to infra-humanisation. In W. Stroebe & M. Hewstone (Eds.), *European review of social psychology* (Vol. 15, pp. 259–296). Hove, UK: Psychology Press/Taylor & Francis.

Dépret, E. F., & Fiske, S. T. (1999). Perceiving the powerful: Intriguing individuals versus threatening groups. *Journal of Experimental Social Psychology, 35*, 461–480.

de Rivera, J. (1984). The structure of emotional relationships. In P. Shaver (Ed.), *Review of personality and social psychology* (Vol. 5, pp. 116–145). Beverly Hills, CA: Sage.

de Rivera, J., & Grinkis, C. (1986). Emotions as social relationships. *Motivation and Emotion, 10*, 351–369.

Derryberry, D., & Rothbart, M. K. (1988). Arousal, affect, and attention as components of temperament. *Journal of Personality and Social Psychology, 55*, 958–966.

Desimone, R., & Duncan, J. (1995). Neural mechanisms of selective visual attention. *Annual Review of Neuroscience, 18*, 193–222.

DeSteno, D., Dasgupta, N., Bartlett, M. Y., & Cajdric, A. (2004). Prejudice from thin air: The effect of emotion on automatic intergroup attitudes. *Psychological Science, 15*, 319–324.

DeSteno, D., Petty, R. E., Rucker, D. D., Wegener, D. T., & Braverman, J. (2004). Discrete emotions and persuasion: The role of emotion-induced expectancies. *Journal of Personality and Social Psychology, 86*, 43–56.

DeSteno, D., Petty, R. E., Wegener, D. T., & Rucker, D. D. (2000). Beyond valence in the perception of likelihood: The role of emotion specificity. *Journal of Personality and Social Psychology, 78*, 397–416.

Deutsch, F. M. (1999). *Halving it all: How equally shared parenting works.* Cambridge, MA: Harvard University Press.

Deutsch, M. A. (1968). Field theory in social psychology. In G. Lindzey & E. Aronson (Eds.), *The handbook of social psychology* (2nd edn, Vol. 1). Reading, MA: Addison-Wesley.

Devine, P. G. (1989). Stereotypes and prejudice: Their automatic and controlled components. *Journal of Personality and Social Psychology, 56*, 5–18.

Devine, P. G., & Elliot, A. J. (1995). Are racial stereotypes really fading? The Princeton trilogy revisited. *Personality and Social Psychology Bulletin, 21*, 1139–1150.

Devine, P. G., & Monteith, M. J. (1999). Automaticity and control in stereotyping. In S. Chaiken & Y. Trope (Eds.), *Dual-process theories in social psychology* (pp. 339–360). New York: Guilford Press.

Devos, T., Comby, L., & Deschamps, J. C. (1996). Asymmetries in judgments of ingroup and outgroup variability. In W. Stroebe & M. Hewstone (Eds.), *European review of social psychology* (Vol. 7, pp. 95–104). Chichester, UK: Wiley.

Devos, T., Silver, L. A., Mackie, D. M., & Smith, E. R. (2002). Experiencing intergroup emotions. In D. M. Mackie & E. R. Smith (Eds.), *From prejudice to intergroup emotions* (pp. 111–134). New York: Psychology Press.

de Vries, B., & Walker, L. J. (1987). Conceptual/integrative complexity and attitudes toward capital punishment. *Personality and Social Psychology Bulletin, 13*, 448–457.

Dickerson, S. S., & Kemeny, M. E. (2004). Acute stressors and cortisol responses: A theoretical integration and synthesis of laboratory research. *Psychological Bulletin, 130*, 355–391.

Dickerson, S. S., Kemeny, M. E., Aziz, N., Kim, K. H., & Fahey, J. L. (2004). Immunological effects of induced shame and guilt. *Psychosomatic Medicine, 66*, 124–131.

Diener, E. (1984). Subjective well-being. *Psychological Bulletin, 95*, 542–575.

Diener, E., & Diener, M. (1995). Cross-cultural correlates of life satisfaction and self-esteem. *Journal of Personality and Social Psychology, 68*, 653–663.

Diener, E., & Emmons, R. A. (1984). The independence of positive and negative affect. *Journal of Personality and Social Psychology, 47*, 1105–1117.

Diener, E., & Iran-Nejad, A. (1986). The relationship in experience between various types of affect. *Journal of Personality and Social Psychology, 50*, 1031–1038.

Dietrich, E., & Markman, A. B. (2003). Discrete thoughts: Why cognition must use discrete representations. *Mind & Language, 18(1)*, 95–119.

Dijksterhuis, A. (2004). Think different: The merits of unconscious thought in preference development and decision making. *Journal of Personality and Social Psychology, 87*, 586–598.

Dijksterhuis, A., & Bargh, J. A. (2001). The perception-behavior expressway: Automatic effects of social perception on social behavior. In M. P. Zanna (Ed.), *Advances in experimental and social psychology* (Vol. 33, pp. 1–40). San Diego, CA: Academic Press.

Dijksterhuis, A., Bos, M. W., Nordgren, L. F., & van Baaren, R. B. (2006). On making the right choice: The deliberation-without-attention effect. *Science, 311*, 1005–1007.

Dijksterhuis, A., Spears, R., Postmes, T., Stapel, D. A., Koomen, W., van Knippenberg, A., et al. (1998). Seeing one thing and doing another: Contrast effects in automatic behavior. *Journal of Personality and Social Psychology, 75*, 862–871.

Dijksterhuis, A., & van Knippenberg, A. (1998). The relation between perception and behavior, or how to win a game of Trivial Pursuit. *Journal of Personality and Social Psychology, 74*, 865–877.

Dijksterhuis, A., & van Knippenberg, A. (2000). Behavioral indecision: Effects of self-focus on automatic behavior. *Social Cognition, 81*, 55–74.

Dimitrov, M., Grafman, J., Soares, A. H., & Clark, K. (1999). Concept formation and concept shifting in frontal lesion and Parkinson's disease patients assessed with the California Card Sorting Test. *Neuropsychology, 13*, 135–143.

Dion, K. L., & Earn, B. M. (1975). The phenomenology of being a target of prejudice. *Journal of Personality and Social Psychology, 32*, 944–950.

Di Paula, A., & Campbell, J. D. (2002). Self-esteem and persistence in the face of failure. *Journal of Personality and Social Psychology, 83*, 711–724.

Dixon, T. L., & Maddox, K. B. (2005). Skin tone, crime news, and social reality judgments: Priming the stereotype of the dark and dangerous Black criminal. *Journal of Applied Social Psychology, 35*, 1555–1570.

Dolan, R. J. (1999). On the neurology of morals. *Nature Neuroscience, 2*, 927–929.

Dovidio, J. F., Brigham, J. C., Johnson, B. T., & Gaertner, S. L. (1996). Stereotyping, prejudice, and discrimination: Another look. In C. N. Macrae, C. Stangor, & M. Hewstone (Eds.), *Stereotypes and stereotyping*. New York: Academic Press.

Dovidio, J. F., Esses, V. M., Beach, K. R., & Gaertner, S. L. (2002). The role of affect in determining intergroup behavior: The case of willingness to engage in intergroup contact. In D. M. Mackie & E. R. Smith (Eds.), *From prejudice to intergroup emotions* (pp. 153–172). New York: Psychology Press.

Dovidio, J. F., Evans, N., & Tyler, R. B. (1986). Racial stereotypes: The contents of their cognitive representations. *Journal of Experimental Social Psychology, 22*, 22–37.

Dovidio, J. F., & Gaertner, S. L. (Eds.). (1986). *Prejudice, discrimination, and racism.* Orlando, FL: Academic Press.

Dovidio, J. F., & Gaertner, S. L. (2000). Aversive racism and selection decisions: 1989 and 1999. *Psychological Science, 11*, 315–319.

Dovidio, J. F., & Gaertner, S. L. (2010). Intergroup bias. In S. T. Fiske, D. T. Gilbert, & G. Lindzey (Eds.), *Handbook of social psychology* (5th edn, Vol. 2, pp. 1084–1121). Hoboken, NJ: Wiley.

Dovidio, J. F., Gaertner, S. E., Kawakami, K., & Hodson, G. (2002). Why can't we just get along? Interpersonal biases and interracial distrust. *Cultural Diversity and Ethnic Minority Psychology, 8*, 88–102.

Dovidio, J. F., Kawakami, K., & Gaertner, S. L. (2002). Implicit and explicit prejudice and interracial interaction. *Journal of Personality and Social Psychology, 82*, 62–68.

Dovidio, J. F., Kawakami, K., Johnson, C., Johnson, B., & Howard, A. (1997). On the nature of prejudice: Automatic and controlled processes. *Journal of Experimental Social Psychology, 33*, 510–540.

Dovidio, J. F., ten Vergert, M., Stewart, T. L., Gaertner, S. L., Johnson, J. D., Esses, V. M., et al. (2004). Perspective and prejudice: Antecedent and mediating mechanisms. *Personality and Social Psychology Bulletin, 30*, 1537–1549.

Downing, J. W., Judd, C. M., & Brauer, M. (1992). Effects of repeated expressions on attitude extremity. *Journal of Personality and Social Psychology, 63*, 17–29.

Drake, R. A. (1986). Lateral asymmetry of impression formation. *International Journal of Neuroscience, 30*, 121–126.

Drake, R. A., & Sobrero, A. P. (1987). Lateral orientation effects upon trait-behavior and attitude-behavior consistency. *Journal of Social Psychology, 127*, 639–651.

Dreben, E. K., Fiske, S. T., & Hastie, R. (1979). The independence of evaluative and item information: Impression and recall order effects in behavior-based impression formation. *Journal of Personality and Social Psychology, 37*, 1758–1768.

Duckitt, J. (1993). Right-wing authoritarianism among white South American students: Its measurement and correlates. *Journal of Social Psychology, 133*, 553–563.

Duckitt, J. (2001). A dual-process cognitive-motivational theory of ideology and prejudice. In M. P. Zanna (Ed.), *Advances in experimental social psychology* (Vol. 33, pp. 41–113). New York: Academic Press.

Duckitt, J., & Mphuthing, T. (1998). Group identification and intergroup attitudes: A longitudinal analysis in South Africa. *Journal of Personality and Social Psychology, 74*, 80–85.

Duckworth, K. L., Bargh, J. A., Garcia, M., & Chaiken, S. (2002). The automatic evaluation of novel stimuli. *Psychological Science, 13*, 513–519.

Duclos, S. E., Laird, J. D., Schneider, E., Sexter, M., Stern, L., & Van Lighten, O. (1989). Emotion-specific effects of facial expressions and postures on emotional experience. *Journal of Personality and Social Psychology, 57*, 100–108.

Duguid, M. (2011). Female tokens in high-prestige work groups: Catalysts or inhibitors of group diversification? *Organizational Behavior and Human Decision Processes, 116(1)*, 104–115.

Dumont, M., Sarlet, M., & Dardenne, B. (2010). Be too kind to a woman, she'll feel incompetent: Benevolent sexism shifts self-construal and autobiographical memories toward incompetence. *Sex Roles, 62(7–8)*, 545–553.

Dunbar, R. I. M. (2003). The social brain: Mind, language, and society in evolutionary perspective. *Annual Review of Anthropology, 32*, 163–181. doi: 10.1146/annurev.anthro.32.061002.093158.

Dunbar, R. I. M. (2012). The social brain meets neuroimaging. *Trends in Cognitive Sciences, 16(2)*, 101–102.

Duncan, J. W., & Laird, J. D. (1977). Cross-modality consistencies in individual differences in self-attribution. *Journal of Personality, 45*, 191–196.

Dunn, E. W., Wilson, T. D., & Gilbert, D. T. (2003). Location, location, location: The misprediction of satisfaction in housing lotteries. *Personality and Social Psychology Bulletin, 29*, 1421–1432.

Dunn, J. R., & Schweitzer, M. R. (2005). Feeling and believing: The influence of emotion on trust. *Journal of Personality and Social Psychology, 88*, 736–748.

Dunning, D. (1999). A newer look: Motivated social cognition and the schematic representation of social concepts. *Psychological Inquiry, 10*, 1–11.

Dunning, D. (2003). The zealous self-affirmer: How and why the self lurks so pervasively behind social judgment. In S. J. Spencer & S. Fein (Eds.), *Motivated social perception: The Ontario Symposium* (Vol. 9, pp. 45–72). Mahwah, NJ: Erlbaum.

Dunning, D. (2012). Judgment and decision-making. In S. T. Fiske & C. N. Macrae (Eds.). *Sage handbook of social cognition* (pp. 251–272). Thousand Oaks, CA: Sage.

Dunning, D., & Hayes, A. F. (1996). Evidence for egocentric comparison in social judgment. *Journal of Personality and Social Psychology, 71*, 213–229.

Dunning, D., Meyerowitz, J. A., & Holzberg, A. D. (1989). Ambiguity and self-evaluation: The role of idiosyncratic trait definitions in self-serving assessments of ability. *Journal of Personality and Social Psychology, 57*, 1082–1090.

Dunning, D., & Parpal, M. (1989). Mental addition versus subtraction in counterfactual reasoning: On assessing the impact of personal actions and life events. *Journal of Personality and Social Psychology, 57*, 5–15.

Dunning, D., Perie, M., & Story, A. L. (1991). Self-serving prototypes of social categories. *Journal of Personality and Social Psychology, 30*, 349–359.

Dunning, D., & Sherman, D. A. (1997). Stereotypes and tacit inference. *Journal of Personality and Social Psychology, 73*, 459–471.

Dunton, B. C., & Fazio, R. H. (1997). An individual difference measure of motivation to control prejudiced reactions. *Personality and Social Psychology Bulletin, 23*, 316–326.

Durante, F., Fiske, S. T., Cuddy, A. J. C., Kervyn, N., et al. (in press). Nations' income inequality predicts ambivalence in stereotype content: How societies mind the gap. *British Journal of Social Psychology*.

Dutton, D. G., & Aron, A. P. (1974). Some evidence for heightened sexual attraction under conditions of high anxiety. *Journal of Personality and Social Psychology, 30*, 510–517.

Duval, S., & Wicklund, R. A. (1972). *A theory of objective self-awareness*. New York: Academic Press.

Eagly, A. H. (1974). Comprehensibility of persuasive arguments as a determinant of opinion change. *Journal of Personality and Social Psychology, 29*, 758–773.

Eagly, A. H. (1987). *Sex differences in social behavior: A social-role interpretation*. Mahwah, NJ: Erlbaum.

Eagly, A. H., & Carli, L. L. (2007). *Through the labyrinth: The truth about how women become leaders*. Boston, MA: Harvard Business School Press.

Eagly, A. H., & Chaiken, S. (1975). An attribution analysis of the effect of communication characteristics on opinion change: The case of communicator attractiveness. *Journal of Personality and Social Psychology, 32*, 136–144.

Eagly, A. H., & Chaiken, S. (1984). Cognitive theories of persuasion. In L. Berkowitz (Ed.), *Advances in experimental social psychology* (Vol. 17, pp. 267–359). New York: Academic Press.

Eagly, A. H., & Chaiken, S. (1993). *The psychology of attitudes*. Orlando, FL: Harcourt Brace Jovanovich.

Eagly, A. H., & Chaiken, S. (1998). Attitude structure and function. In D. T. Gilbert, S. T. Fiske, & G. Lindzey (Eds.), *Handbook of social psychology* (4th edn, Vol. l, pp. 269–322). New York: McGraw-Hill.

Eagly, A. H., & Chaiken, S. (2005). Attitude research in the 21st century: The current state of knowledge. In D. Albarracín, B. T. Johnson, & M. P. Zanna (Eds.), *The handbook of attitudes* (pp. 743–767). Mahwah, NJ: Erlbaum.

Eagly, A. H., & Chaiken, S. (2007). The advantages of an inclusive definition of attitude. *Social Cognition, 25(5),* 582–602.

Eagly, A. H., Chaiken, S., & Wood, W. (1981). An attribution analysis of persuasion. In J. H. Harvey, W. J. Ickes, & R. F. Kidd (Eds.), *New directions in attribution research* (Vol. 3, pp. 37–62). Hillsdale, NJ: Erlbaum.

Eagly, A. H., Chen, S., Chaiken, S., & Shaw-Barnes, K. (1999). The impact of attitudes on memory: An affair to remember. *Psychological Bulletin, 125,* 64–89.

Eagly, A. H., & Crowley, M. (1986). Gender and helping behavior: A meta-analytic review of the social psychological literature. *Psychological Bulletin, 100,* 283–308.

Eagly, A. H., & Himmelfarb, S. (1978). Attitudes and opinions. *Annual Review of Psychology, 29,* 517–554.

Eagly, A. H., & Johnson, B. T. (1990). Gender and leadership style: A meta-analysis. *Psychological Bulletin, 108,* 233–256.

Eagly, A. H., & Karau, S. J. (1991). Gender and the emergence of leaders: A meta-analysis. *Journal of Personality and Social Psychology, 60,* 685–710.

Eagly, A. H., & Karau, S. J. (2002). Role congruity theory of prejudice toward female leaders. *Psychological Review, 109,* 573–598.

Eagly, A. H., Karau, S. J., & Makhijani, M. G. (1995). Gender and the effectiveness of leaders: A meta-analysis. *Psychological Bulletin, 117,* 125–145.

Eagly, A. H., Karau, S. J., Miner, J. B., & Johnson, B. T. (1994). Gender and motivation to manage in hierarchic organizations: A meta-analysis. *Leadership Quarterly, 5,* 135–159.

Eagly, A. H., Kulesa, P., Brannon, L. A., Shaw-Barnes, K., & Hutson-Comeaux, S. (2000). Why counterattitudinal messages are as memorable as proattitudinal messages: The importance of active defense against attack. *Personality and Social Psychology Bulletin, 26,* 1392–1408.

Eagly, A. H., Kulesa, P., Chen, S., & Chaiken, S. (2001). Do attitudes affect memory? Tests of the congeniality hypothesis. *Current Directions in Psychological Science, 10,* 5–9.

Eagly, A. H., Makhijani, M. G., & Klonsky, B. G. (1992). Gender and the evaluation of leaders: A meta-analysis. *Psychological Bulletin, 111,* 3–22.

Eagly, A. H., & Steffen, V. J. (1984). Gender stereotypes stem from the distribution of women and men into social roles. *Journal of Personality and Social Psychology, 46,* 735–754.

Eagly, A. H., & Steffen, V. J. (1986). Gender and aggressive behavior: A meta-analytic review of the social psychological literature. *Psychological Bulletin, 100,* 309–330.

Eagly, A. H., & Wood, W. (1991). Explaining sex differences in social behavior: A meta-analytic perspective. *Personality and Social Psychology Bulletin, 17,* 306–315.

Eagly, A. H., & Wood, W. (1999). The origins of sex differences in human behavior: Evolved dispositions versus social roles. *American Psychologist, 54,* 408–423.

Eagly, A. H., Wood, W., & Chaiken, S. (1978). Causal inferences about communicators and their effect on opinion change. *Journal of Personality and Social Psychology, 36,* 424–435.

Ebbesen, E. B. (1980). Cognitive processes in understanding ongoing behavior. In R. Hastie, T. M. Ostrom, E. B. Ebbesen, R. S. Wyer, D. L. Hamilton, & D. E. Carlston (Eds.), *Person memory: The cognitive basis of social perception* (pp. 179–226). Hillsdale, NJ: Erlbaum.

Ebbinghaus, H. (1964). *Memory: A contribution to experimental psychology.* H. A. Ruger & C. E. Bussenius (trans.). New York: Dover. (Originally published 1885.)

Eberhardt, J. L. (2005). Imaging race. *American Psychologist, 60,* 181–190.

Eberhardt, J. L., Dasgupta, N., & Banaszynski, T. L. (2003). Believing is seeing: The effects of racial labels and implicit beliefs on face perception. *Personality and Social Psychology Bulletin, 29,* 360–370.

Eberhardt, J. L., Davies, P. G., Purdie-Vaughns, V. J., & Johnson, S. L. (2006). Looking deathworthy: Perceived stereotypically of Black defendants predicts capital sentencing outcomes. *Psychological Science, 17,* 383–386.

Eberhardt, J. L., Goff, P. A., Purdie, V. J., & Davies, P. G. (2004). Seeing Black: Race, crime, and visual processing. *Journal of Personality and Social Psychology, 87,* 876–893.

Echebarria-Echabe, A., & Fernández-Guede, E. (2006). Effects of terrorism on attitudes and ideological orientation. *European Journal of Social Psychology, 36,* 259–265.

Eckes, T. (2002). Paternalistic and envious gender stereotypes: Testing predictions from the stereotype content model. *Sex Roles, 47,* 99–114.

Eckes, T., Trautner, H. M., & Behrendt, R. (2005). Gender subgroups and intergroup perception: Adolescents' views of own-gender and other-gender groups. *Journal of Social Psychology, 145,* 85–111.

Ehrlichman, H., & Halpern, J. N. (1988). Affect and memory: Effects of pleasant and unpleasant odors on retrieval of happy and unhappy memories. *Journal of Personality and Social Psychology, 55,* 769–779.

Ehrlinger, J., & Dunning, D. (2003). How chronic self-views influence (and potentially mislead) estimates of performance. *Journal of Personality and Social Psychology, 84,* 5–17.

Ehrlinger, J., Gilovich, T., & Ross, L. D. (2005). Peering into the bias blind spot: People's assessments of bias in themselves and others. *Personality and Social Psychology Bulletin, 31,* 680–692.

Eich, J. E. (1980). The cue-dependent nature of state-dependent retrieval. *Memory & Cognition, 8(2),* 157–173.

Einhorn, H. J., & Hogarth, R. M. (1981). Behavioral decision theory: Processes of judgment and choice. *Annual Review of Psychology, 32,* 53–88.

Einhorn, H. J., & Hogarth, R. M. (1986). Judging probable cause. *Psychological Bulletin, 99,* 3–19.

Eisen, S. V., & McArthur, L. Z. (1979). Evaluating and sentencing a defendant as a function of his salience and the observer's set. *Personality and Social Psychology Bulletin, 5,* 48–52.

Eisenberger, N. I., Jarcho, J. M., Lieberman, M. D., & Naliboff, B. D. (2006). An experimental study of shared sensitivity to physical pain and social rejection. *Pain, 126,* 132–138.

Eisenberger, N. I., Lieberman, M. D., & Williams, K. D. (2003). Does rejection hurt? An fMRI study of social exclusion. *Science, 302,* 290–292.

Eiser, J., Fazio, R. H., Stafford, T., & Prescott, T. J. (2003). Connectionist simulation of attitude learning: Asymmetries in the acquisition of positive and negative evaluations. *Personality and Social Psychology Bulletin, 29,* 1221–1235.

Ekman, P. (1984). Expression and the nature of emotion. In K. Scherer & P. Ekman (Eds.), *Approaches to emotion* (pp. 319–343). Hillsdale, NJ: Erlbaum.

Ekman, P., Levenson, R. W., & Friesen, W. V. (1983). Autonomic nervous system activity distinguishes among emotions. *Science, 221,* 1208–1210.

Ekman, P., & O'Sullivan, M. (1988). Comment on Russell and Fehr. *Journal of Experimental Psychology: General, 117,* 86–88.

Elio, R., & Anderson, J. R. (1981). The effects of category generalizations and instance similarity on schema abstraction. *Journal of Experimental Psychology: Human Learning and Memory, 7,* 397–417.

Ellemers, N., Spears, R., & Doosje, B. (2002). Self and social identity, *Annual Review of Psychology, 53,* 161–186.

Elliot, A. J., & Devine, P. G. (1994). On the motivational nature of cognitive dissonance: Dissonance as psychological discomfort. *Journal of Personality and Social Psychology, 67,* 382–394.

Ellsworth, P. C., & Smith, C. A. (1988a). From appraisal to emotion: Differences among unpleasant feelings. *Motivation and Emotion, 12,* 271–302.

Ellsworth, P. C., & Smith, C. A. (1988b). Shades of joy: Patterns of appraisal differentiating pleasant emotions. *Emotion and Cognition, 2,* 302–331.

Ellsworth, P. C., & Tourangeau, R. (1981). On our failure to disconfirm what nobody ever said. *Journal of Personality and Social Psychology, 40,* 363–369.

Else-Quest, N. M., Hyde, J. S., Goldsmith, H. H., & Van-Hulle, C. A. (2006). Gender differences in temperament: A meta-analysis. *Psychological Bulletin, 132,* 33–72.

Enquist, C., Newtson, D., & LaCross, K. (1979). Prior expectations and the perceptual segmentation of ongoing behavior. Unpublished manuscript, University of Virginia.

Epley, N., & Dunning, D. (2000). Feeling "holier than thou": Are self-serving assessments produced by errors in self- or social prediction? *Journal of Personality and Social Psychology, 79,* 861–875.

Epley, N., & Gilovich, T. (2001). Putting adjustment back in the anchoring and adjustment heuristic: Differential processing of self-generated and experimenter-provided anchors. *Psychological Science, 12,* 391–396.

Epley, N., Keysar, B., Van Boven, L., & Gilovich, T. (2004). Perspective taking as egocentric anchoring and adjustment. *Journal of Personality and Social Psychology, 87,* 327–339.

Epley, N., Morewedge, C., & Keysar, B. (2004). Perspective taking in children and adults: Equivalent egocentrism but differential correction. *Journal of Experimental Social psychology, 40,* 760–768.

Epley, N., & Waytz, A. (2010). Mind perception. In S. T. Fiske, D. T. Gilbert, & G. Lindzey (Eds.), *Handbook of social psychology* (5th edn, Vol. 1, pp. 498–541). Hoboken, NJ: Wiley.

Epley, N., Waytz, A., & Cacioppo, J. T. (2007). On seeing human: A three-factor theory of anthropomorphism. *Psychological Review, 114,* 864–886.

Epstein, S. (1979). The stability of behavior: I. On predicting most of the people much of the time. *Journal of Personality and Social Psychology, 37,* 1097–1126.

Epstein, S. (1983). The unconscious, the preconscious, and the self-concept. In J. Suls & A. Greenwald (Eds.), *Psychological perspectives on the self* (Vol. 2, pp. 220–247). Hillsdale, NJ: Erlbaum.

Epstein, S. (1984). Controversial issues in emotion theory. In P. Shaver (Ed.), *Review of personality and social psychology* (Vol. 5, pp. 64–88). Beverly Hills, CA: Sage.

Epstein, S. (1990a). Cognitive experiential self-theory. In L. Pervin (Ed.), *Handbook of personality theory and research* (pp. 165–192). New York: Guilford Press.

Epstein, S. (1990b). The self-concept, the traumatic neurosis, and the structure of personality. In D. Ozer, J. M. Healy Jr., & A. J. Stewart (Eds.), *Perspectives on personality* (Vol. 3). Greenwich, CT: JAI Press.

Erber, R. (1991). Affective and semantic priming: Effects of mood on category accessibility and inference. *Journal of Experimental Social Psychology, 27,* 480–498.

Erber, R., & Fiske, S. T. (1984). Outcome dependency and attention to inconsistent information. *Journal of Personality and Social Psychology, 47,* 709–726.

Erdley, C. A., & D'Agostino, P. R. (1988). Cognitive and affective components of automatic priming effects. *Journal of Personality and Social Psychology, 54,* 741–747.

Ericsson, K. A., & Kintsch, W. (1995). Long-term working memory. *Psychological Review, 102,* 211–245.

Ericsson, K. A., & Simon, H. A. (1980). Verbal reports as data. *Psychological Review, 87,* 215–251.

Esses, V. M., & Dovidio, J. F. (2002). The role of emotions in determining willingness to engage in intergroup contact. *Personality and Social Psychology Bulletin, 28,* 1202–1214.

Evans, L. M., & Petty, R. E. (2003). Self-guide framing and persuasion: Responsibly increasing message processing to ideal levels. *Personality and Social Psychology Bulletin, 29,* 313–324.

Eyal, T., Liberman, N., Trope, Y., & Walther, E. (2004). The pros and cons of temporally near and distant action. *Journal of Personality and Social Psychology, 86,* 781–795.

Fabrigar, L. R., Petty, R. E., Smith, S. M., & Crites, S. L., Jr. (2006). Understanding knowledge effects on attitude-behavior consistency: The role of relevance, complexity, and amount of knowledge. *Journal of Personality and Social Psychology, 90,* 556–577.

Falk, E. B., Rameson, L., Berkman, E. T., Liao, B., Kang, Y., Inagaki, T. K., & Lieberman, M. D. (2010). The neural correlates of persuasion: A common network across cultures and media. *Journal of Cognitive Neuroscience, 22(11),* 2447–2459.

Farah, M. J. (1994). Neuropsychological inferences with an interactive brain: A critique of the "locality" assumption. *Behavioral and Brain Sciences, 22,* 287–288.

Farina, A., Allen, J. G., & Saul, B. B. (1968). The role of the stigmatized person in affecting social relationships. *Journal of Personality, 36,* 169–182.

Fazio, R. H. (1990). Multiple processes by which attitudes guide behavior: The MODE model as an integrative framework. In M. P. Zanna (Ed.), *Advances in experimental social psychology* (Vol. 23, pp. 75–110). New York: Academic Press.

Fazio, R. H. (2001). On the automatic activation of associated evaluations: An overview. *Cognition and Emotion, 15,* 115–141.

Fazio, R. H., Chen, J., McDonel, E. C., & Sherman, S. J. (1982). Attitude accessibility, attitude-behavior consistency, and the strength of the object-evaluation association. *Journal of Experimental Social Psychology, 18,* 339–357.

Fazio, R. H., & Cooper, J. (1983). Arousal in the dissonance process. In J. T. Cacioppo & R. E. Petty (Eds.), *Social psychophysiology* (pp. 122–152). New York: Guilford Press.

Fazio, R. H., Effrein, E. A., & Falender, V. J. (1981). Self-perceptions following social interaction. *Journal of Personality and Social Psychology, 41,* 232–242.

Fazio, R. H., Herr, P. M., & Olney, T. J. (1984). Attitude accessibility following a self-perception process. *Journal of Personality and Social Psychology, 47,* 277–286.

Fazio, R. H., & Hilden, L. E. (2001). Emotional reactions to a seemingly prejudiced response: The role of automatically activated racial attitudes and motivation to control prejudiced reactions. *Personality and Social Psychology Bulletin, 27,* 538–549.

Fazio, R. H., Jackson, J. R., Dunton, B. C., & Williams, C. J. (1995). Variability in automatic activation as an unobtrusive measure of racial attitudes: A bona fide pipeline? *Journal of Personality and Social Psychology, 69,* 1013–1027.

Fazio, R. H., Ledbetter, J. E., & Towles-Schwen, T. (2000). On the costs of accessible attitudes: Detecting that the attitude object has changed. *Journal of Personality and Social Psychology, 78,* 197–210.

Fazio, R. H., & Olson, M. A. (2003). Implicit measures in social cognition research: Their meaning and use. *Annual Review of Psychology, 54,* 297–327.

Fazio, R. H., Powell, M. C., & Herr, P. M. (1983). Toward a process model of attitude-behavior relation: Accessing one's attitude upon mere observation of the attitude object. *Journal of Personality and Social Psychology, 44,* 723–735.

Fazio, R. H., Sanbonmatsu, D. M., Powell, M. C., & Kardes, F. R. (1986). On the automatic activation of attitudes. *Journal of Personality and Social Psychology, 50,* 229–238.

Fazio, R. H., & Towles-Schwen, T. (1999). The MODE model of attitude-behavior process. In S. Chaiken & Y. Trope (Eds.), *Dual-process theories in social psychology* (pp. 97–116). New York: Guilford Press.

Fazio, R. H., & Williams, C. J. (1986). Attitude accessibility as a moderator of the attitude-perception and attitude-behavior relations: An investigation of the 1984 presidential election. *Journal of Personality and Social Psychology, 51,* 505–514.

Fazio, R. H., & Zanna, M. P. (1978). Attitudinal qualities relating to the strength of the attitude-behavior relationship. *Journal of Experimental Social Psychology, 14,* 398–408.

Fazio, R. H., & Zanna, M. P. (1981). Direct experience and attitude-behavior consistency. In L. Berkowitz (Ed.), *Advances in experimental social psychology* (Vol. 14, pp. 162–203). New York: Academic Press.

Fazio, R. H., Zanna, M. P., & Cooper, J. (1977). Dissonance and self-perception: An integrative view of each theory's proper domain of application. *Journal of Experimental Social Psychology, 13,* 464–479.

Feather, N. T. (1969). Attitude and selective recall. *Journal of Personality and Social Psychology, 12,* 310–319.

Feeney, B. C., & Cassidy, J. (2003). Reconstructive memory related to adolescent–parent conflict interactions: The influence of attachment-related representations on immediate perceptions and changes in perceptions over time. *Journal of Personality and Social Psychology, 85,* 945–955.

Fehr, B. (1988). Prototype analysis of the concepts of love and commitment. *Journal of Personality and Social Psychology, 55,* 557–579.

Fehr, B., & Russell, J. A. (1984). Concept of emotion viewed from a prototype perspective. *Journal of Experimental Psychology: General, 113,* 464–486.

Fein, S., Hilton, J. L., & Miller, D. T. (1990). Suspicion of ulterior motivation and the correspondence bias. *Journal of Personality and Social Psychology, 58,* 753–764.

Fein, S., & Spencer, S. J. (1997). Prejudice as self-image maintenance: Affirming the self through derogating others. *Journal of Personality and Social Psychology, 73,* 31–44.

Feingold, A. (1992). Gender differences in mate selection preferences: A test of the parental investment model. *Psychological Bulletin, 112,* 125–139.

Ferguson, M. J., & Bargh, J. A. (2004a). How social perception can automatically influence behavior. *Trends in Cognitive Science, 8,* 33–39.

Ferguson, M. J., & Bargh, J. A. (2004b). Liking is for doing: The effects of goal pursuit on automatic evaluation. *Journal of Personality and Social Psychology, 87,* 557–572.

Ferguson, M. J., & Fukukura, J. (2012). Likes and dislikes: A social cognitive perspective on attitudes. In S. T. Fiske & C. N. Macrae (Eds.), *Sage handbook of social cognition* (pp. 165–190). Thousand Oaks, CA: Sage.

Ferguson, M. J., & Zayas, V. (2009). Automatic evaluation. *Current Directions in Psychological Science, 18(6),* 362–366.

Festinger, L. (1954). A theory of social comparison processes. *Human Relations, 7,* 117–140.

Festinger, L. (1957). *A theory of cognitive dissonance.* Stanford, CA: Stanford University Press.

Fiedler, K. (1988). Emotional mood, cognitive style, and behavior regulation. In K. Fiedler & J. P. Forgas (Eds.), *Affect, cognition, and social behavior* (pp. 100–119). Toronto, Canada: Hogrefe.

Fiedler, K., & Freytag, P. (2004). Pseudocontingencies. *Journal of Personality and Social Psychology, 87,* 453–467.

Fiedler, K., Nickel, S., Muehlfriedel, T., & Unkelbach, C. (2001). Is mood congruency an effect of genuine memory or response bias? *Journal of Experimental Social Psychology, 37,* 201–214.

Fiedler, K., Pampe, H., & Scherf, U. (1986). Mood and memory for tightly organized social information. *European Journal of Social Psychology, 16,* 149–164.

Fiedler, K., Walther, E., & Nickel, S. (1999). Explaining asymmetric intergroup judgment through differential aggregation: Computer simulations and some new evidence. *European Review of Social Psychology, 10,* 1–40.

Finlay, K. A., & Stephan, W. G. (2000). Improving intergroup relations: The effects of empathy on racial attitudes. *Journal of Applied Social Psychology, 30,* 1720–1737.

Fischer, P., Jonas, E., Frey, D., & Schulz-Hardt, S. (2005). Selective exposure to information: The impact of information limits. *European Journal of Social Psychology, 35,* 469–492.

Fischhoff, B. (1980). For those condemned to study the past: Reflections on historical judgment. In R. A. Shweder (Ed.), *New directions for methodology of social and behavioral science* (Vol. 4, pp. 79–93). San Francisco: Jossey-Bass.

Fischhoff, B. (1982). Debiasing. In D. Kahneman, P. Slovic, & A. Tversky (Eds.), *Judgment under uncertainty: Heuristics and biases* (pp. 422–444). New York: Cambridge University Press.

Fischhoff, B., & Beyth, R. (1975). "I knew it would happen" – Remembered probabilities of once-future things. *Organizational Behavior and Human Performance, 13,* 1–16.

Fischhoff, B., Gonzalez, R. M., Lerner, J. S., & Small, D. A. (2005). Evolving judgments of terror risks: Foresight, hindsight, and emotion. *Journal of Experimental Psychology: Applied, 11,* 124–139.

Fischhoff, B., Slovic, P., & Lichtenstein, S. (1977). Knowing with certainty: The appropriateness of extreme confidence. *Journal of Experimental Psychology: Human Perception and Performance, 3,* 552–564.

Fishbach, A., Dhar, R., & Zhang, Y. (2006). Subgoals as substitutes or complements: The role of goal accessibility. *Journal of Personality and Social Psychology, 91,* 232–242.

Fishbach, A., & Shah, J. Y. (2006). Self-control in action: Implicit dispositions toward goals and away from temptations. *Journal of Personality and Social Psychology, 90,* 820–832.

Fishbach, A., Shah, J. Y., & Kruglanski, A. W. (2004). Emotional transfer in goal systems. *Journal of Experimental Social Psychology, 40,* 723–738.

Fishbein, M. (1963). An investigation of the relationship between beliefs about an object and the attitude toward that object. *Human Relations, 16,* 233–240.

Fishbein, M., & Ajzen, I. (1974). Attitudes toward objects as predictors of single and multiple behavioral criteria. *Psychological Review, 81,* 59–74.

Fishbein, M., & Ajzen, I. (1975). *Belief, attitude, intention, and behavior: An introduction to theory and research.* Reading, MA: Addison-Wesley.

Fiske, A. P., Haslam, N., & Fiske, S. T. (1991). Confusing one person with another: What errors reveal about the elementary forms of social relations. *Journal of Personality and Social Psychology, 60,* 656–674.

Fiske, A. P., Kitayama, S., Markus, H. R., & Nisbett, R. E. (1998). The cultural matrix of social psychology. In D. T. Gilbert, S. T. Fiske, & G. Lindzey (Eds.), *The handbook of social psychology* (4th edn, pp. 915–981). New York: McGraw-Hill.

Fiske, D. W., & Maddi, S. R. (1961). *Functions of varied experience.* Oxford, England: Dorsey.

Fiske, S. T. (1980). Attention and weight in person perception: The impact of negative and extreme behavior. *Journal of Personality and Social Psychology, 38,* 889–906.

Fiske, S. T. (1982). Schema-triggered affect: Applications to social perception. In M. S. Clark & S. T. Fiske (Eds.), *Affect and cognition: The 17th Annual Carnegie Symposium on Cognition* (pp. 55–78). Hillsdale, NJ: Erlbaum.

Fiske, S. T. (1988). Compare and contrast: Brewer's dual-process model and Fiske et al.'s continuum model. In T. K. Srull & R. S. Wyer (Eds.), *Advances in social cognition: A dual model of impression formation* (Vol. 1, pp. 65–76). Hillsdale, NJ: Erlbaum.

Fiske, S. T. (1989). Examining the role of intent: Toward understanding its role in stereotyping and prejudice. In J. S. Uleman & J. A. Bargh (Eds.), *Unintended thought* (pp. 253–283). New York: Guilford Press.

Fiske, S. T. (1992). Thinking is for doing: Portraits of social cognition from daguerreotype to laserphoto. *Journal of Personality and Social Psychology, 63,* 877–889.

Fiske, S. T. (1993). Social cognition and social perception. In M. R. Rosenzweig & L. W. Porter (Eds.), *Annual review of psychology* (Vol. 44, pp. 155–194). Palo Alto, CA: Annual Reviews.

Fiske, S. T. (1998). Stereotyping, prejudice, and discrimination. In D. T. Gilbert, S. T. Fiske, & G. Lindzey (Eds.), *Handbook of social psychology* (4th edn, Vol. 2, pp. 357–411). New York: McGraw-Hill.

Fiske, S. T. (2002). Five core social motives, plus or minus five. In S. J. Spencer, S. Fein, M. P. Zanna, & J. Olson (Eds.), *Motivated social perception: The Ontario Symposium* (Vol. 9, pp. 233–246). Mahwah, NJ: Erlbaum.

Fiske, S. T. (2008). Core social motivations, a historical perspective: Views from the couch, consciousness, classroom, computers, and collectives. In J. Y. Shah & W. L. Gardner (Eds.), *Handbook of motivation science* (pp. 3–22). New York: Guilford.

Fiske, S. T. (2010). *Social beings: Core motives in social psychology* (2nd edn). New York: Wiley.

Fiske, S. T. (2011). *Envy up, scorn down: How status divides us.* New York: Russell Sage Foundation.

Fiske, S. T. (2012). Warmth and competence: Stereotype content issues for clinicians and researchers. *Canadian Psychologist/ Psychologie canadienne, 53(1),* 14–20.

Fiske, S. T., Bergsieker, H., Russell, A. M., & Williams, L. (2009). Images of Black Americans: Then, "them" and now, "Obama!" *DuBois Review: Social Science Research on Race, 6,* 83–101.

Fiske, S. T., Bersoff, D. N., Borgida, E., Deaux, K., & Heilman, M. E. (1991). Social science research on trial: The use of sex stereotyping research in *Price Waterhouse v. Hopkins. American Psychologist, 46,* 1049–1060.

Fiske, S. T., & Borgida, E. (2008). Providing expert knowledge in an adversarial context: Social cognitive science in employment discrimination cases. *Annual Review of Law and Social Science, 4,* 123–148.

Fiske, S. T., Cuddy, A. J. C., & Glick, P. (2007). Universal dimensions of social perception: Warmth and competence. *Trends in Cognitive Science, 11,* 77–83.

Fiske, S. T., Cuddy, A. J. C., Glick, P., & Xu, J. (2002). A model of (often mixed) stereotype content: Competence and warmth respectively follow from perceived status and competition. *Journal of Personality and Social Psychology, 82,* 878–902.

Fiske, S. T., Kenny, D. A., & Taylor, S. E. (1982). Structural models for the mediation of salience effects on attribution. *Journal of Experimental Social Psychology, 18,* 105–127.

Fiske, S. T., Lin, M. H., & Neuberg, S. L. (1999). The continuum model: Ten years later. In S. Chaiken & Y. Trope (Eds.), *Dual-process theories in social psychology* (pp. 231–254). New York: Guilford Press.

Fiske, S. T., & Linville, P. W. (1980). What does the schema concept buy us? Symposium on social knowing. *Personality and Social Psychology Bulletin, 6,* 543–557.

Fiske, S. T., & Neuberg, S. L. (1990). A continuum of impression formation, from category-based to individuating processes: Influences of information and motivation on attention and interpretation. In M. P. Zanna (Ed.), *Advances in experimental social psychology* (Vol. 23, pp. 1–74). New York: Academic Press.

Fiske, S. T., Neuberg, S. L., Beattie, A. E., & Milberg, S. J. (1987). Category-based and attribute-based reactions to others: Some informational conditions of stereotyping and individuating processes. *Journal of Experimental Social Psychology, 23,* 399–427.

Fiske, S. T., & Pavelchak, M. A. (1986). Category-based versus piecemeal-based affective responses: Developments in schema-triggered affect. In R. M. Sorrentino & E. T. Higgins (Eds.), *Handbook of motivation and cognition: Foundations of social behavior* (pp. 167–203). New York: Guilford Press.

Fiske, S. T., & Ruscher, J. B. (1989). On-line processes in category-based and individuating impressions: Some basic principles and methodological reflections. In J. N. Bassili (Ed.), *On-line cognition in person perception* (pp. 141–174). Hillsdale, NJ: Erlbaum.

Fiske, S. T., Taylor, S. E., Etcoff, N. L., & Laufer, J. K. (1979). Imaging, empathy, and causal attribution. *Journal of Experimental Social Psychology, 15,* 356–377.

Fiske, S. T., Xu, J., Cuddy, A. C., & Glick, P. (1999). (Dis)respecting versus (dis)liking: Status and interdependence predict ambivalent stereotypes of competence and warmth. *Journal of Social Issues, 55,* 473–491.

Flack, W. F., Jr. (2006). Peripheral feedback effects of facial expressions, bodily postures, and vocal expressions on emotional feelings. *Cognition and Emotion, 20,* 177–195.

Flory, J. D., Räikkönen, K., Matthews, K. A., & Owens, J. F. (2000). Self-focused attention and mood during everyday social interactions. *Personality and Social Psychology Bulletin, 26,* 875–883.

Folkes, V. S. (1982). Communicating the causes of social rejection. *Journal of Experimental Social Psychology, 18,* 235–252.

Folkman, S., & Lazarus, R. S. (1988a). Coping as a mediator of emotion. *Journal of Personality and Social Psychology, 54,* 466–475.

Folkman, S., & Lazarus, R. S. (1988b). The relationship between coping and emotion: Implications for theory and research. *Social Science Medicine, 26,* 309–317.

Fong, G. T., Krantz, D. H., & Nisbett, R. E. (1986). The effects of statistical training on thinking about everyday problems. *Cognitive Psychology, 18,* 253–292.

Fong, G. T., & Markus, H. R. (1982). Self-schemas and judgments about others. *Social Cognition, 1,* 191–205.

Forbes, C. E., & Schmader, T. (2010). Retraining attitudes and stereotypes to affect motivation and cognitive capacity under stereotype threat. *Journal of Personality and Social Psychology, 99(5),* 740–754.

Forest, D., Clark, M. S., Mills, J., & Isen, A. M. (1979). Helping as a function of feeling state and nature of the helping behavior. *Motivation and Emotion, 3,* 161–169.

Forgas, J. P. (1995). Mood and judgment: The affect infusion model (AIM). *Psychological Bulletin, 117,* 39–66.

Forgas, J. P. (1998). On being happy and mistaken: Mood effects on the fundamental attribution error. *Journal of Personality and Social Psychology, 75,* 318–331.

Forgas, J. P., Bower, G. H., & Krantz, S. E. (1984). The influence of mood on perceptions of social interactions. *Journal of Experimental Social Psychology, 20,* 497–513.

Forgas, J. P., Burnham, D. K., & Trimboli, C. (1988). Mood, memory, and social judgments in children. *Journal of Personality and Social Psychology, 54,* 697–703.

Forgas, J. P., & Fiedler, K. (1996). Us and them: Mood effects on intergroup discrimination. *Journal of Personality and Social Psychology, 70,* 28–40.

Forgas, J. P., & George, J. M. (2001). Affective influences on judgments and behavior in organizations: An information processing perspective. *Organizational Behavior and Human Decision Processes, 86,* 3–34.

Forgas, J. P., Laham, S., & Vargas, P. (2005). Mood effects on eyewitness memory: Affective influences on susceptibility to misinformation. *Journal of Experimental Social Psychology, 41,* 574–588.

Forgas, J. P., & Moylan, S. (1987). After the movies: Transient mood and social judgments. *Personality and Social Psychology Bulletin, 13,* 467–477.

Förster, J., Friedman, R. S., & Liberman, N. (2004). Temporal construal effects on abstract and concrete thinking: Consequences for insight and creative cognition. *Journal of Personality and Social Psychology, 87,* 177–189.

Förster, J., Higgins, T. E., & Idson, L. C. (1998). Approach and avoidance strength during goal attainment: Regulatory focus and the "goal looms larger" effect. *Journal of Personality and Social Psychology, 75,* 1115–1131.

Förster, J., & Liberman, N. (2007). Knowledge activation. In A. W. Kruglanski & E. T. Higgins (Eds.), *Social psychology: Handbook of basic principles* (2nd edn, pp. 201–231). New York: Guilford Press.

Förster, J., & Strack, F. (1997). Motor actions in retrieval of valenced information: A motor congruence effect. *Perceptual and Motor Skills, 85,* 1419–1427.

Förster, J., & Strack, F. (1998). Motor actions in retrieval of valenced information: II. Boundary conditions for motor congruence effects. *Perceptual and Motor Skills, 86,* 1423–1426.

Fragale, A. R., & Heath, C. (2004). Evolving informational credentials: The (mis)attribution of believable facts to credible sources. *Personality and Social Psychology Bulletin, 30,* 225–236.

Frantz, C. M., Cuddy, A. J. C., Burnett, M., Ray, H., & Hart, A. J. (2004). A threat in the computer: The race implicit association test as a stereotype threat experience. *Personality and Social Psychology Bulletin, 30,* 1611–1624.

Frederick, S., Loewenstein, G., & O'Donoghue, T. (2002). Time discounting and time preference: A critical review. *Journal of Economic Literature, 40,* 351–401.

Fredrickson, G. M. (2002). *Racism: A short history.* Princeton, NJ: Princeton University Press.

Freedman, J. L., & Sears, D. O. (1965). Selective exposure. In L. Berkowitz (Ed.), *Advances in experimental social psychology* (Vol. 2, pp. 57–97). San Diego, CA: Academic Press.

Freitas, A. L., Liberman, N., Salovey, P., & Higgins, E. T. (2002). When to begin? Regulatory focus and initiating goal pursuit. *Personality and Social Psychology Bulletin, 28,* 121–130.

Frey, D. (1986). Recent research on selective exposure to information. In L. Berkowitz (Ed.), *Advances in experimental social psychology* (Vol. 19, pp. 41–80). New York: Academic Press.

Frijda, N. H. (1987a). Comment on Oatley and Johnson-Laird's "Towards a cognitive theory of emotions." *Cognition and Emotion, 1,* 51–58.

Frijda, N. H. (1987b). Emotion, cognitive structure, and action tendency. *Cognition and Emotion, 1,* 115–143.

Frijda, N. H. (1988). The laws of emotion. *American Psychologist, 43,* 349–358.

Frith, U., & Frith, C. (2001). The biological basis of social interaction. *Current Directions in Psychological Science, 10,* 151–155.

Fu, P. O., Kennedy, J., Tata, J., Yukl, G., Bond, M. H., et al. (2004). The impact of societal cultural values and individual social beliefs on the perceived effectiveness of managerial influence strategies: A meso approach. *Journal of International Business Studies, 35,* 284–305.

Fujita, K., Eyal, T., Chaiken, S., Trope, Y., & Liberman, N. (2008). Influencing attitudes toward near and distant objects. *Journal of Experimental Social Psychology, 44(3),* 562–572.

Fujita, K., Gollwitzer, P. M., & Oettingen, G. (2007). Mindsets and pre-conscious open-mindedness to incidental information. *Journal of Experimental Social Psychology, 43,* 48–61.

Fujita, K., Henderson, M. D., Eng, J., Trope, Y., & Liberman, N. (2006). Spatial distance and mental construal of social events. *Psychological Science, 17,* 278–282.

Funder, D. C. (1987). Errors and mistakes: Evaluating the accuracy of social judgment. *Psychological Bulletin, 101,* 75–90.

Funder, D. C. (1995). On the accuracy of personality judgment: A realistic approach. *Psychological Review, 102,* 652–670.

Gable, S. L., Reis, H. T., & Elliot, A. J. (2000). Behavioral activation and inhibition in everyday life. *Journal of Personality and Social Psychology, 78,* 1135–1149.

Gabrielcik, A., & Fazio, R. H. (1984). Priming and frequency estimation: A strict test of the availability heuristic. *Personality and Social Psychology Bulletin, 10,* 85–89.

Gaertner, S. L., & Dovidio, J. F. (1986). The aversive form of racism. In J. F. Dovidio & S. L. Gaertner (Eds.), *Prejudice, discrimination, and racism* (pp. 61–90). Orlando, FL: Academic Press.

Gaertner, S. L., & Dovidio, J. F. (2005). Understanding and addressing contemporary racism: From aversive racism to the common ingroup identity model. *Journal of Social Issues, 61,* 615–639.

Gaertner, S. L., & McLaughlin, J. P. (1983). Racial stereotypes: Associations and ascriptions of positive and negative characteristics. *Social Psychology Quarterly, 46,* 23–40.

Gaertner, S. L., Sedikides, C., & Graetz, K. (1999). In search of self-definition: Motivational primacy of the individual self, motivational primacy of the collective self, or contextual primacy? *Journal of Personality and Social Psychology, 76,* 5–18.

Gailliot, M. T., Schmeichel, B. J., & Baumeister, R. F. (2006). Self-regulatory processes defend against the threat of death: Effects of self-control depletion and trait self-control on thoughts and fears of dying. *Journal of Personality and Social Psychology, 91,* 49–62.

Galanis, C. M. B., & Jones, E. E. (1986). When stigma confronts stigma: Some conditions enhancing a victim's tolerance of other victims. *Personality and Social Psychology Bulletin, 12,* 169–177.

Galinsky, A. D., Ku, G., & Mussweiler, T. (2009). To start low or to start high? The case of auctions versus negotiations. *Current Directions in Psychological Science, 18(6),* 357–361.

Galinsky, A. D., & Moskowitz, G. B. (2000). Perspective-taking: Decreasing stereotype expression, stereotype accessibility, and in-group favoritism. *Journal of Personality and Social Psychology, 78,* 708–724.

Gallagher, H. L., & Frith, C. D. (2003). Functional imaging of "theory of mind." *Trends in Cognitive Sciences, 7,* 77–83.

Gallagher, H. L., Jack, A., Roepstorff, A., & Frith, C. D. (2002). Imaging the intentional stance in a competitive game. *NeuroImage, 16,* 814–821.

Garcia-Marques, L., & Hamilton, L. (1996). Resolving the apparent discrepancy between the incongruency effect and the expectancy-based illusory correlation effect: The TRAP model. *Journal of Personality and Social Psychology, 71,* 845–860.

Garcia-Marques, L., Hamilton, L., & Maddox, K. B. (2002). Exhaustive and heuristic retrieval processes in person cognition: Further tests of the TRAP model. *Journal of Personality and Social Psychology, 82,* 193–207.

Gardner, W. L., Gabriel, S., & Hochschild, L. (2002). When you and I are "we," you are not threatening: The role of self-expansion in social comparison. *Journal of Personality and Social Psychology, 82(2),* 239–251.

Gasper, K., & Clore, G. L. (2002). Attending to the big picture: Mood and global versus local processing of visual information. *Psychological Science, 13,* 34–40.

Gauthier, I., Skudlarski, P., Gore, J. C., & Anderson, A. W. (2000). Expertise for cars and birds recruits brain areas involved in face recognition. *Nature Neuroscience, 3,* 191–197.

Gaver, W. W., & Mandler, G. (1987). Play it again, Sam: On liking music. *Cognition and Emotion, 1,* 259–282.

Gawronski, B., & Bodenhausen, G. V. (2006). Associative and propositional processes in evaluation: An integrative review of implicit and explicit attitude change. *Psychological Bulletin, 132,* 692–731.

Gawronski, B., & Bodenhausen, G. V. (2007). Unraveling the processes underlying evaluation: Attitudes from the perspective of the APE model. *Social Cognition, 25(5),* 687–717.

Gazzaniga, M. S. (2000). Cerebral specialization and interhemispheric communication: Does the corpus callosum enable the human condition? *Brain, 123,* 1293–1326.

Geertz, C. (1975). On the nature of anthropological understanding. *American Scientist, 63,* 47–53.

Gellhorn, E. (1964). Motion and emotion: The role of proprioception in the physiology and pathology of emotions. *Psychological Review, 71,* 457–472.

Genero, N., & Cantor, N. (1987). Exemplar prototypes and clinical diagnosis: Toward a cognitive economy. *Journal of Social and Clinical Psychology, 5,* 59–78.

Gernsbacher, M. A., & Kaschak, M. P. (2003). Neuroimaging studies of language production and comprehension. *Annual Review of Psychology, 54,* 91–114.

Gibson, J. J. (1966). *The senses considered as perceptual systems.* Boston, MA: Houghton Mifflin.

Gibson, J. J. (1979). *The ecological approach to visual perception.* Boston, MA: Houghton Mifflin.

Gilbert, D. T. (1991). How mental systems believe. *American Psychologist, 46,* 107–119.

Gilbert, D. T. (1998). Ordinary personology. In D. T. Gilbert, S. T. Fiske, & G. Lindzey (Eds.), *The handbook of social psychology* (4th edn, Vol. 2, pp. 89–150). New York: McGraw-Hill.

Gilbert, D. T. (1999). What the mind's not. In S. Chaiken & Y. Trope (Eds.), *Dual-process theories in social psychology* (pp. 3–11. New York: Guilford Press.

Gilbert, D. T., Brown, R. P., Pinel, E. C., & Wilson, T. D. (2000). The illusion of external agency. *Journal of Personality and Social Psychology, 79,* 690–700.

Gilbert, D. T., & Hixon, J. G. (1991). The trouble of thinking: Activation and application of stereotypic beliefs. *Journal of Personality and Social Psychology, 60,* 509–517.

Gilbert, D. T., Krull, D. S., & Pelham, B. W. (1988). Of thoughts unspoken: Social inference and the self-regulation of behavior. *Journal of Personality and Social Psychology, 55,* 685–694.

Gilbert, D. T., Lieberman, M. D., Morewedge, C. K., & Wilson, T. D. (2004). The peculiar longevity of things not so bad. *Psychological Science, 15,* 14–19.

Gilbert, D. T., & Malone, P. S. (1995). The correspondence bias. *Psychological Bulletin, 117,* 21–38.

Gilbert, D. T., Pelham, B. W., & Krull, D. S. (1988). On cognitive busyness: When person perceivers meet persons perceived. *Journal of Personality and Social Psychology, 54,* 733–739.

Gilbert, D. T., Pinel, E. C., Wilson, D., Blumberg, S. J., & Wheatley, T. P. (1998). Immune neglect: A source of durability bias in affective forecasting. *Journal of Personality and Social Psychology, 75,* 617–638.

Gilovich, T. (1981). Seeing the past in the present: The effect of associations to familiar events on judgments and decisions. *Journal of Personality and Social Psychology, 40,* 797–808.

Giner-Sorolla, R. (1999). Affect in attitude: Immediate and deliberative perspectives. In S. Chaiken & Y. Trope (Eds.), *Dual-process theories in social psychology* (pp. 441–461). New York: Guilford Press.

Giner-Sorolla, R. (2001). Affective attitudes are not always faster: The moderating role of extremity. *Personality and Social Psychology Bulletin, 27,* 666–677.

Giner-Sorolla, R., Mackie, D. M., & Smith, E. R. (Eds.). (2007). Special issue: Intergroup emotions. *Group Processes and Intergroup Relations, 10,* 5–136.

Ginossar, Z., & Trope, Y. (1980). The effects of base rates and individuating information on judgments about another person. *Journal of Experimental Social Psychology, 16,* 228–242.

Ginossar, Z., & Trope, Y. (1987). Problem solving in judgment under uncertainty. *Journal of Personality and Social Psychology, 52,* 464–474.

Gladwell, M. (2005). *Blink: The power of thinking without thinking.* New York: Little, Brown.

Glaser, J., Dixit, J., & Green, D. P. (2002). Studying hate crime with the internet: What makes racists advocate racial violence? *Journal of Social Issues, 58,* 177–193.

Glaser, J., & Salovey, P. (1998). Affect in electoral politics. *Personality and Social Psychology Review, 2,* 156–172.

Glass, A. L., & Holyoak, K. J. (1986). *Cognition* (2nd edn). New York: Random House.

Glassman, N. S., & Andersen, S. M. (1999). Activating transference without consciousness: Using significant-other representations to go beyond what is subliminally given. *Journal of Personality and Social Psychology, 77,* 1146–1162.

Gleicher, F. H., Kost, K. A., Baker, S. M., Strathman, A. J., Richman, S. A., & Sherman, S. J. (1990). The role of counterfactual thinking in judgments of affect. *Personality and Social Psychology Bulletin, 16,* 284–295.

Glick, P., Diebold, J., Bailey-Werner, B., & Zhu, L. (1997). The two faces of Adam: Ambivalent sexism and polarized attitudes toward women. *Personality and Social Psychology Bulletin, 23,* 1323–1334.

Glick, P., & Fiske, S. T. (1996). The Ambivalent Sexism Inventory: Differentiating hostile and benevolent sexism. *Journal of Personality and Social Psychology, 70,* 491–512.

Glick, P., & Fiske, S. T. (2001). Ambivalent sexism. In M. P. Zanna (Ed.), *Advances in experimental social psychology* (Vol. 33, pp. 115–188). San Diego, CA: Academic Press.

Glick, P., Fiske, S. T., Mladinic, A., Saiz, J. L., Abrams, D., Masser, B., et al. (2000). Beyond prejudice as simple antipathy: Hostile and benevolent sexism across cultures. *Journal of Personality and Social Psychology, 79,* 763–775.

Glick, P., Lameriras, M., Fiske, S. T., Eckes, T., Masser, B., Volpato, C., et al. (2004). Bad but bold: Ambivalent attitudes toward men predict gender inequality in 16 nations. *Journal of Personality and Social Psychology, 86,* 713–728.

Glick, P., Wilk, K., & Perrault, M. (1995). Images of occupations: Components of gender and status in occupational stereotypes. *Sex Roles, 32,* 9–10.

Glimcher, P. D. (2003). *Decisions, uncertainty, and the brain: The science of neuroeconomics.* Cambridge, MA: MIT Press.

Glimcher, P. W., & Rustichini, A. (2004). Neuroeconomics: The consilience of brain and decision. *Science, 306,* 447–452.

Goethals, G. R. (1976). An attributional analysis of some social influence phenomena. In J. H. Harvey, W. J. Ickes, & R. F. Kidd (Eds.), *New directions in attribution research* (Vol. 1, pp. 291–310). Hillsdale, NJ: Erlbaum.

Goethals, G. R., & Reckman, R. F. (1973). The perception of consistency in attitudes. *Journal of Experimental Social Psychology, 9,* 491–501.

Goethals, G. R., & Zanna, M. P. (1979). The role of social comparison in choice shifts. *Journal of Personality and Social Psychology, 37,* 1469–1476.

Goff, P. A., Steele, C. M., & Davies, P. G. (2008). The space between us: Stereotype threat and distance in interracial contexts. *Journal of Personality and Social Psychology, 94(1),* 91–107.

Goffman, E. (1963). *Stigma: Notes on the management of spoiled identity.* New York: Prentice-Hall.

Golby, A. J., Gabrieli, J. D. E., Chiao, J. Y., & Eberhardt, J. L. (2001). Differential responses in the fusiform region to same-race and other-race faces. *Nature Neuroscience, 4,* 845–850.

Goldberg, E. (2001). *The executive brain: Frontal lobes and the civilized mind.* New York: Oxford University Press.

Goldberg, L. R. (1968). Simple models or simple processes? Some research on clinical judgments. *American Psychologist, 23,* 483–496.

Goldberg, L. R. (1970). Man versus model of man: A rationale, plus some evidence, for a method of improving on clinical inferences. *Psychological Bulletin, 73,* 422–432.

Goldberg, L. R. (1986). The validity of rating procedures to index the hierarchical level of categories. *Journal of Memory and Language, 25,* 323–347.

Gollwitzer, P. M. (1990). *Action phases and mindsets.* New York: Guilford Press.

Gollwitzer, P. M., Earle, W. B., & Stephan, W. G. (1982). Affect as a determinant of egotism: Residual excitation and performance attributions. *Journal of Personality and Social Psychology, 43,* 702–709.

Gollwitzer, P. M., & Sheeran, P. (2006). Implementation intentions and goal achievement: A meta-analysis of effects and processes. In M. P. Zanna (Ed.), *Advances in experimental psychology* (Vol. 38, pp. 69–119). San Diego, CA: Academic Press.

Gónzales, P. M., Blanton, H., & Williams, K. J. (2002). The effects of stereotype threat and double-minority status on the test performance of Latino women. *Personality and Social Psychology Bulletin, 28,* 659–670.

Gosling, S. D., Ko, S. J., Mannarelli, T., & Morris, M. E. (2002). A room with a cue: Judgments of personality based on offices and bedrooms. *Journal of Personality and Social Psychology, 82,* 379–398.

Graham, S., & Lowery, B. S. (2004) Priming unconscious racial stereotypes about adolescent offenders. *Law and Human Behavior, 28,* 483–504.

Graham, S., & Weiner, B. (1986). From an attributional theory of emotion to developmental psychology: A round-trip ticket? *Social Cognition, 4,* 152–179.

Granberg, D., & Brent, E. (1980). Perceptions of issue positions of presidential candidates. *American Scientist, 68,* 617–625.

Graves, J. (2001). *The emperor's new clothes: Biological theories of race at the millennium.* New Brunswick, NJ: Rutgers University Press.

Gray, J. A. (1990). Brain systems that mediate both emotion and cognition. *Cognition and Emotion, 4,* 269–288.

Graziano, W. G., Moore, J. S., & Collins, J. E., II. (1988). Social cognition as segmentation of the stream of behavior. *Developmental Psychology, 24,* 568–573.

Greaves, G. (1972). Conceptual system functioning and selective recall of information. *Journal of Personality and Social Psychology, 21,* 327–332.

Green, D. P., Glaser, J., & Rich, A. (1998). From lynching to gay bashing: The elusive connection between economic conditions and hate crime. *Journal of Personality and Social Psychology, 75,* 82–92.

Green, D. P., Salovey, P., & Truax, K. M. (1999). Static, dynamic, and causative bipolarity of affect. *Journal of Personality and Social Psychology, 76,* 856–867.

Green, D. P., Strolovitch, D. Z., & Wong, J. S. (1998). Defended neighborhoods, integration, and racially motivated crime. *American Journal of Sociology, 104,* 372–403.

Greenberg, J., Arndt, J., Schimel, J., Pyszczynski, T., & Solomon, S. (2001). Clarifying the function of mortality salience-induced worldview defense: Renewed suppression or reduced accessibility of death-related thoughts? *Journal of Experimental Social Psychology, 37,* 70–76.

Greenberg, J., Porteus, J., Simon, L., Pyszczynski, T., & Solomon, S. (1995). Evidence of a terror management function of cultural icons: The effects of mortality salience on the inappropriate use of cherished cultural symbols. *Personality and Social Psychology Bulletin, 21,* 1221–1228.

Greenberg, J., & Pyszczynski, T. (1985). The effects of an overheard ethnic slur on evaluations of the target: How to spread a social disease. *Journal of Experimental Social Psychology, 21,* 61–72.

Greenberg, J., Pyszczynski, T., & Solomon, S. (1986). The causes and consequences of a need for self-esteem: A terror management theory. In R. F. Baumeister (Ed.), *Public self and private self* (pp. 189–212). New York: Springer-Verlag.

Greenberg, J., Pyszczynski, T., Solomon, S., Rosenblatt, A., Veeder, M., Kirkland, S., & Lyon, D. (1990). Evidence for terror management theory II: The effects of mortality salience on reactions to those who threaten or bolster the cultural worldview. *Journal of Personality and Social Psychology, 58,* 308–318.

Greenberg, J., Schimel, J., & Meertens, A. (2002). Ageism: Denying the face of the future. In T. D. Nelson (Ed.), *Ageism: Stereotyping and prejudice against older persons* (pp. 27–48). Cambridge, MA: MIT Press.

Greenberg, J., Simon, L., Pyszczynski, T., Solomon, S., & Chatel, D. (1992). Terror management and tolerance: Does mortality salience always intensify negative reactions to others who threaten one's worldview? *Journal of Personality and Social Psychology, 63,* 212–220.

Greenberg, J., Solomon, S., & Pyszczynski, T. (1997). Terror management theory of self-esteem and cultural worldviews: Empirical assessments and conceptual refinements. In M. P. Zanna (Ed.), *Advances in experimental social psychology* (Vol. 29, pp. 61–139). San Diego, CA: Academic Press.

Greenberg, J., Williams, K. D., & O'Brien, M. K. (1986). Considering the harshest verdict first: Biasing effects on mock juror verdicts. *Personality and Social Psychology Bulletin, 12,* 41–50.

Greene, J. D., Somerville, R. B., Nystrom, L. E., Darley, J. M., & Cohen, J. D. (2001). An fMRI investigation of emotional engagement in moral judgment. *Science, 293,* 2105–2108.

Greenwald, A. G. (1968). Cognitive learning, cognitive response to persuasion and attitude change. In A. G. Greenwald, T. C. Brock, & T. M. Ostrom (Eds.), *Psychological foundations of attitudes* (pp. 147–170). New York: Academic Press.

Greenwald, A. G. (1975). Consequences of prejudice against the null hypothesis. *Psychological Bulletin, 82,* 1–20.

Greenwald, A. G. (1989). Why attitudes are important: Defining attitude and attitude theory 20 years later. In A. R. Pratkanis, S. J. Breckler, & A. G. Greenwald (Eds.), *Attitudes structure and function* (pp. 429–440). Hillsdale, NJ: Erlbaum.

Greenwald, A. G., Banaji, M. R., Rudman, L. A., Farnham, S. D., Nosek, B. A., & Mellott, D. S. (2002). A unified theory of implicit attitudes, stereotypes, self-esteem, and self-concept. *Psychological Review, 109,* 3–25.

Greenwald, A. G., Klinger, M. R., & Liu, T. J. (1989). Unconscious processing of dichotically masked words. *Memory and Cognition, 17,* 35–47.

Greenwald, A. G., & Leavitt, C. (1984). Audience involvement in advertising: Four levels. *Journal of Consumer Research, 11,* 581–592.

Greenwald, A. G., McGhee, D. E., & Schwartz, J. L. K. (1998). Measuring individual differences in implicit cognition: The implicit association test. *Journal of Personality and Social Psychology Bulletin, 74,* 1464–1480.

Greenwald, A. G., Poehlman, T. A., Uhlmann, E., & Banaji, M. R. (2009). Understanding and using the Implicit Association Test: III. Meta-analysis of predictive validity. *Journal of Personality and Social Psychology, 97*, 17–41.

Grice, H. P. (1975). Logic and conversation. In P. Cole & J. L. Morgan (Eds.), *Syntax and semantics 3: Speech acts* (pp. 95–113). New York: Academic Press.

Griffiths, T. L., & Tenenbaum, J. B. (2006). Optimal predictions in everyday cognition. *Psychological Science, 17*, 767–773.

Grill-Spector, K., & Kanwisher, N. (2005). Visual recognition: As soon as you know it is there, you know what it is. *Psychological Science, 16*, 152–160.

Groom, C. J., Sherman, J. W., Lu, L., Conrey, F. R., & Keijzer, S. C. (2005). Judging compound social categories: Compound familiarity and compatibility as determinants of processing mode. *Social Cognition, 23*, 291–323.

Grush, J. E. (1976). Attitude formation and mere exposure phenomena: A nonartificial explanation of empirical findings. *Journal of Personality and Social Psychology, 33*, 281–290.

Guadagno, R. E., Rhoads, K. v. L., & Sagarin, B. J. (2011). Figural vividness and persuasion: Capturing the "elusive" vividness effect. *Personality and Social Psychology Bulletin, 37(5)*, 626–638.

Gueguen, N., & DeGail, M. (2003). The effect of smiling on helping behavior: Smiling and good Samaritan behavior. *Communication Report, 16*, 133–140.

Guimond, S., Chatard, A., Martinot, D., Crisp, R. J., & Redersdorff, S. (2006). Social comparison, self-stereotyping, and gender differences in self-construals. *Journal of Personality and Social Psychology, 90*, 221–242.

Guimond, S., Dambrun, M., Michinov, N., & Duarte, S. (2003). Does social dominance generate prejudice? Integrating individual and contextual determinants of intergroup cognitions. *Journal of Personality and Social Psychology, 84*, 697–721.

Guinote, A. (2001). The perception of group variability in a non-minority and a minority context: When adaptation leads to out-group differentiation. *British Journal of Social Psychology, 40*, 117–132.

Guinote, A. (2007). Power and goal pursuit. *Personality and Social Psychology Bulletin, 33(8)*, 1076–1087.

Haddock, G., & Zanna, M. P. (1994). Preferring "housewives" to "feminists": Categorization and the favorability of attitudes toward women. *Psychology of Women Quarterly, 18*, 25–52.

Haddock, G., Zanna, M. P., & Esses, V. M. (1993). Assessing the structure of prejudicial attitudes: The case of attitudes toward homosexuals. *Journal of Personality and Social Psychology, 65*, 1105–1118.

Hager, J. C., & Ekman, P. (1981). Methodological problems in Tourangeau and Ellsworth's study of facial expression and experience of emotion. *Journal of Personality and Social Psychology, 40*, 358–362.

Haidt, J. (2001). The emotional dog and its rational tail: A social intuitionist approach to moral judgment. *Psychological Review, 108*, 814–834.

Haidt, J., & Hersh, M. A. (2001). Sexual morality: The cultures and emotions of conservatives and liberals. *Journal of Applied Social Psychology, 31*, 191–221.

Haidt, J., Koller, S. H., & Dias, M. G. (1993). Affect, culture, and morality, or is it wrong to eat your dog? *Journal of Personality and Social Psychology, 65*, 613–628.

Haidt, J., McCauley, C. & Rozin, P. (1994). Individual differences in sensitivity to disgust: A scale sampling seven domains of disgust elicitors. *Personality and Individual Differences, 16*, 701–713.

Haines, E. L., & Jost, J. T. (2000). Placating the powerless: Effects of legitimate and illegitimate explanation on affect, memory, and stereotyping. *Social Justice Research, 13*, 219–236.

Halloran, M. J., & Kashima, E. S. (2004). Social identity and worldview validation: The effects of ingroup identity primes and mortality salience on value endorsement. *Personality and Social Psychology Bulletin, 30*, 915–925.

Hamill, R., Wilson, T. D., & Nisbett, R. E. (1980). Insensitivity to sample bias: Generalizing from atypical cases. *Journal of Personality and Social Psychology, 39*, 578–589.

Hamilton, D. L. (1979). A cognitive-attributional analysis of stereotyping. In L. Berkowitz (Ed.), *Advances in experimental social psychology* (Vol. 12, pp. 53–84). New York: Academic Press.

Hamilton, D. L., Driscoll, D. M., & Worth, L. T. (1989). Cognitive organization of impressions: Effects of incongruency in complex representations. *Journal of Personality and Social Psychology, 57*, 925–939.

Hamilton, D. L., Dugan, P. M., & Trolier, T. K. (1985). The formation of stereotypic beliefs: Further evidence for distinctiveness-based illusory correlations. *Journal of Personality and Social Psychology, 48,* 5–17.

Hamilton, D. L., & Gifford, R. K. (1976). Illusory correlation in interpersonal perception: A cognitive basis of stereotypic judgments. *Journal of Experimental Social Psychology, 12,* 392–407.

Hamilton, D. L., & Rose, T. L. (1980). Illusory correlation and the maintenance of stereotypic beliefs. *Journal of Personality and Social Psychology, 39,* 832–845.

Hamilton, V., Bower, G. H., & Frijda, N. H. (Eds.). (1988). *Cognitive perspectives on emotion and motivation.* Norwood, MA: Kluwer Academic.

Hampson, S. E., & Dawson, W. J. M. (1985). Whatever happened to Pollyanna? The effects of evaluative congruence on speed of trait inference. *Personality and Social Psychology Bulletin, 11,* 106–117.

Hampson, S. E., Goldberg, L. R., & John, O. P. (1987). Category-breadth and social-desirability values for 573 personality terms. *European Journal of Personality, 1,* 241–258.

Hampson, S. E., John, O. P., & Goldberg, L. R. (1986). Category breadth and hierarchical structure in personality: Studies of asymmetries in judgments of trait implications. *Journal of Personality and Social Psychology, 51,* 37–54.

Hansen, C. H., & Hansen, R. D. (1988a). Finding the face in the crowd: An anger superiority effect. *Journal of Personality and Social Psychology, 54,* 917–924.

Hansen, C. H., & Hansen, R. D. (1988b). How rock music videos can change what is seen when boy meets girl: Priming stereotypic appraisal of social interactions. *Sex Roles, 19,* 287–316.

Hansen, J., & Wänke, M. (2010). Truth from language and truth from fit: The impact of linguistic concreteness and level of construal on subjective truth. *Personality and Social Psychology Bulletin, 36(11),* 1576–1588.

Harkins, S. G., & Petty, R. E. (1981). Effects of source magnification of cognitive effort on attitudes: An information-processing view. *Journal of Personality and Social Psychology, 40,* 401–413.

Harkness, A. R., DeBono, K. G., & Borgida, E. (1985). Personal involvement and strategies for making contingency judgments: A stake in the dating game makes a difference. *Journal of Personality and Social Psychology, 49,* 22–32.

Harmon-Jones, E., Lueck, L., Fearn, M., & Harmon-Jones, C. (2006). The effect of personal relevance and approach-related action expectation on relative left frontal cortical activity. *Psychological Science, 17,* 434–440.

Harris, L. T., & Fiske, S. T. (2006). Dehumanizing the lowest of the low: Neuro-imaging responses to extreme outgroups. *Psychological Science, 17,* 847–853.

Harris, L. T., McClure, S. M., van den Bos, W., Cohen, J. D., & Fiske, S. T. (2007). Regions of MPFC differentially tuned to social and non-social affective evaluation. *Cognitive and Behavioral Neuroscience, 7,* 309–316.

Harris, L. T., Todorov, A., & Fiske, S. T. (2005). Attributions on the brain: Neuro-imaging dispositional inferences, beyond theory of mind. *NeuroImage, 28,* 763–769.

Harris, R. J., Teske, R. R., & Ginns, M. J. (1975). Memory for pragmatic implications from courtroom testimony. *Bulletin of the Psychonomic Society, 6,* 494–496.

Harrison, A. A. (1977). Mere exposure. In L. Berkowitz (Ed.), *Advances in experimental social psychology* (Vol. 10, pp. 39–83). New York: Academic Press.

Hart, A. J., Whalen, P. J., Shin, L. M., McInerney, S. C., Fischer, H., & Rauch, S. L. (2000). Differential response in the human amygdala to racial outgroup vs. ingroup face stimuli. *Neuroreport: For Rapid Communication of Neuroscience Research, 11,* 2351–2355.

Hartley, D. (1966). *Observations on man, his frame, his duty, and his expectations.* Delmar, NY: Scholastic Facsimiles. (Originally published 1749.)

Harvey, J. H., Yarkin, K. L., Lightner, J. M., & Town, J. P. (1980). Unsolicited interpretation and recall of interpersonal events. *Journal of Personality and Social Psychology, 38,* 551–568.

Hasher, L., Rose, K. C., Zacks, R. T., Sanft, H., & Doren, B. (1985). Mood, recall, and selectivity effects in normal college students. *Journal of Experimental Psychology: General, 114,* 104–118.

Haslam, N. (2006). Dehumanization: An integrative review. *Personality and Social Psychology Review, 10,* 252–264.

Haslam, N., Bain, P., Douge, L., Lee, M., & Bastian, B. (2005). More human than you: Attributing humanness to self and others. *Journal of Personality and Social Psychology, 89,* 937–950.

Hastie, R. (1988a). Causes and effects of causal attribution. *Journal of Personality and Social Psychology, 46,* 44–56.

Hastie, R. (1988b). A computer simulation model of person memory. *Journal of Experimental Social Psychology, 24,* 423–447.

Hastie, R., & Dawes, R. M. (2001). *Rational choice in an uncertain world: The psychology of judgment and decision making.* Thousand Oaks, CA: Sage.

Hastie, R., & Park, B. (1986). The relationship between memory and judgment depends on whether the judgment task is memory-based or on-line. *Psychological Review, 93,* 258–268.

Hastorf, A. H., & Cantril, H. (1954). They saw a game: A case study. *Journal of Abnormal and Social Psychology, 49,* 129–134.

Hawkley, L. C., Burleson, M. H., Berntson, G. G., & Cacioppo, J. T. (2003). Loneliness in everyday life: Cardiovascular activity, psychosocial context, and health behaviors. *Journal of Personality and Social Psychology, 85,* 105–120.

Haxby, J. V., Gobbini, M. I., & Montgomery, K. J. (2004). Spatial and temporal distribution of face and object representations in the human brain. In M. S. Gazzaniga (Ed.), *The cognitive neurosciences* (3rd edn, pp. 889–904). Cambridge, MA: MIT Press.

Haxby, J. V., Hoffman, E. A., & Gobbini, M. I. (2000). The distributed human neural system for face perception. *Trends in Cognitive Science, 4,* 223–233.

Hayes-Roth, B., & Hayes-Roth, F. (1977). Concept learning and the recognition and classification of exemplars. *Journal of Verbal Learning and Verbal Behavior, 16,* 321–338.

Heatherton, T. F., Macrae, C. N., & Kelley, W. M. (2004). What the social brain sciences can tell us about the self. *Current Directions in Psychological Science, 13,* 190–193.

Heatherton, T. F., & Vohs, K. D. (2000). Interpersonal evaluations following threats to self: Role of self-esteem. *Journal of Personality and Social Psychology, 78,* 726–736.

Heatherton, T. F., Wyland, C. L., Macrae, C. N., Demos, K. E., Denny, B. T., & Kelley, W. M. (2006). Medial prefrontal activity differentiates self from close others. *Social Cognitive and Affective Neuroscience, 1,* 18–25.

Hebl, M. R., & Dovidio, J. F. (2005). Promoting the "social" in the examination of social stigmas. *Personality and Social Psychology Review, 9,* 156–182.

Heckhausen, H., & Gollwitzer, P. M. (1987). Thought contents and cognitive functioning in motivational versus volitional states of mind. *Motivation and Emotion, 11,* 101–120.

Hegarty, P. (2002). "It's not a choice, it's the way we're built": Symbolic beliefs about sexual orientation in the US and Britain. *Journal of Community and Applied Social Psychology, 12(3),* 153–166.

Heider, F. (1958). *The psychology of interpersonal relations.* New York: Wiley.

Heilman, M. E. (1980). The impact of situational factors on personnel decisions concerning women: Varying the sex composition of the applicant pool. *Organizational Behavior and Human Performance, 26,* 386–395.

Heine, S. J., Kitayama, S., Lehman, D. R., Takata, T., Ide, E., Leung, C., et al. (2001). Divergent consequences of success and failure in Japan and North America: An investigation of self-improving motivations and malleable selves. *Journal of Personality and Social Psychology, 81,* 599–615.

Heine, S. J., & Lehman, D. R. (1997). Culture, dissonance, and self-affirmation. *Personality and Social Psychology Bulletin, 23,* 389–400.

Heine, S. J., & Renshaw, K. (2002). Interjudge agreement, self-enhancement, and liking: Cross-cultural divergences. *Personality and Social Psychology Bulletin, 28,* 578–587.

Heine, S. J., Takata, T., & Lehman, D. R. (2000). Beyond self-presentation: Evidence for self-criticism among Japanese. *Personality and Social Psychology Bulletin, 26,* 71–78.

Henderson, M. D., Fujita, K., Trope, Y., & Liberman, N. (2006). Transcending the "here": The effect of spatial distance on social judgment. *Journal of Personality and Social Psychology, 91,* 845–856.

Henderson, M. D., & Wakslak, C. J. (2010). Over the hills and far away: The link between physical distance and abstraction. *Current Directions in Psychological Science, 19(6),* 390–394.

Hennessey, J., & West, M. A. (1999). Intergroup behavior in organizations: A field test of social identity theory. *Small Group Research, 30,* 361–382.

Hennigan, K. M., Cook, T. D., & Gruder, C. L. (1982). Cognitive tuning set, source credibility, and the temporal persistence of attitude change. *Journal of Personality and Social Psychology, 42,* 412–425.

Henrich, J., Heine, S. J., & Norenzayan, A. (2010). The weirdest people in the world? *Behavioral and Brain Sciences, 33(2–3),* 61–83.

Herek, G. M. (1986). The instrumentality of ideologies: Toward a neofunctional theory of attitudes. *Journal of Social Issues, 42,* 99–114.

Herek, G. M. (2000). The psychology of sexual prejudice. *Current Directions in Psychological Science, 9,* 19–22.

Herek, G. M. (2002). Gender gaps in public opinion about lesbians and gay men. *Public Opinion Quarterly, 66,* 40–66.

Herek, G. M., & Capitanio, J. P. (1997). AIDS stigma and contact with persons with AIDS: Effects of direct and vicarious contact. *Journal of Applied Social Psychology, 27,* 1–36.

Herek, G. M., & Capitanio, J. P. (1999). Sex differences in how heterosexuals think about lesbians and gay men: Evidence from survey context effects. *Journal of Sex Research, 36,* 348–360.

Herek, G. M., Gillis, J. R., & Cogan, J. C. (1999). Psychological sequelae of hate-crime victimization among lesbian, gay, and bisexual adults. *Journal of Consulting and Clinical Psychology, 67,* 945–951.

Herek, G. M., & McLemore, K. (2013). Sexual prejudice. *Annual Review of Psychology.*

Herr, P. M. (1986). Consequences of priming: Judgment and behavior. *Journal of Personality and Social Psychology, 51,* 1106–1115.

Herr, P. M., Sherman, S. J., & Fazio, R. H. (1983). On the consequences of priming: Assimilation and contrast effects. *Journal of Experimental Social Psychology, 19,* 323–340.

Hewstone, M. (1990). The "ultimate attribution error"? A review of the literature on intergroup causal attribution. *European Journal of Social Psychology, 20,* 311–335.

Hewstone, M., Benn, W., & Wilson, A. (1988). Bias in the use of base rates: Racial prejudice in decision-making. *European Journal of Social Psychology, 18,* 161–176.

Hewstone, M., & Jaspers, J. (1987). Covariation and causal attribution: A logical model of the intuitive analysis of variance. *Journal of Personality and Social Psychology, 53,* 663–672.

Hewstone, M., Rubin, M., & Willis, H. (2002). Intergroup bias. *Annual Review of Psychology, 53,* 575–604.

Higgins, E. T. (1987). Self-discrepancy: A theory relating self and affect. *Psychological Review, 94,* 319–340.

Higgins, E. T. (1989). Self-discrepancy theory: What patterns of self-beliefs cause people to suffer? In L. Berkowitz (Ed.), *Advances in experimental social psychology* (pp. 93–136). San Diego: Academic Press.

Higgins, E. T. (1996). Knowledge activation: Accessibility, applicability, and salience. In E. T. Higgins & A. W. Kruglanski (Eds.), *Social psychology: Handbook of basic principles* (pp. 133–168). New York: Guilford Press.

Higgins, E. T. (2005). Value from regulatory fit. *Current Directions in Psychological Science, 14,* 209–213.

Higgins, E. T., & Bargh, J. A. (1987). Social cognition and social perception. *Annual Review of Psychology, 38,* 369–425.

Higgins, E. T., Bargh, J. A., & Lombardi, W. J. (1985). The nature of priming effects on categorization. *Journal of Experimental Psychology: Learning, Memory, and Cognition, 11,* 59–69.

Higgins, E. T., Bond, R. N., Klein, R., & Strauman, T. J. (1986). Self-discrepancies and emotional vulnerability: How magnitude, accessibility, and type of discrepancy influence affect. *Journal of Personality and Social Psychology, 51,* 5–15.

Higgins, E. T., & Chaires, W. M. (1980). Accessibility of interrelational constructs: Implications for stimulus encoding and creativity. *Journal of Experimental Social Psychology, 16,* 348–361.

Higgins, E. T., Idson, L. C., Freitas, A. L., Spiegel, C., & Molden, D. C. (2003). Transfer of value from fit. *Journal of Personality and Social Psychology, 84,* 1140–1153.

Higgins, E. T., & King, G. A. (1981). Accessibility of social constructs: Information-processing consequences of individual and contextual variability. In N. Cantor & J. F. Kihlstrom (Eds.), *Personality, cognition, and social interaction* (pp. 69–122). Hillsdale, NJ: Erlbaum.

Higgins, E. T., King, G. A., & Mavin, G. H. (1982). Individual construct accessibility and subjective impressions and recall. *Journal of Personality and Social Psychology, 43,* 35–47.

Higgins, E. T., Klein, R., & Strauman, T. J. (1985). Self-concept discrepancy theory: A psychological model for distinguishing among different aspects of depression and anxiety. *Social Cognition, 3,* 51–76.

Higgins, E. T., Kuiper, N. A., & Olson, J. M. (1981). Social cognition: A need to get personal. In E. T. Higgins, C. P. Herman, & M. P. Zanna (Eds.), *Social cognition: The Ontario Symposium* (Vol. 1, pp. 395–420). Hillsdale, NJ: Erlbaum.

Higgins, E. T., Rholes, W. S., & Jones, C. R. (1977). Category accessibility and impression formation. *Journal of Experimental Social Psychology, 13,* 141–154.

Higgins, E. T., Shah, J. Y., & Friedman, R. S. (1997). Emotional responses to goal attainment: Strength of regulatory focus as moderator. *Journal of Personality and Social Psychology, 72,* 515–525.

Highhouse, S., & Paese, P. W. (1996). Problem domain and prospect frame: Choice under opportunity versus threat. *Personality and Social Psychology Bulletin, 22,* 124–132.

Hilton, D. J., & Slugoski, B. R. (1986). Knowledge-based causal attribution: The abnormal conditions focus model. *Psychological Review, 93,* 75–88.

Hilton, J. L., & Darley, J. M. (1985). Constructing other persons: A limit on the effect. *Journal of Experimental Social Psychology, 21,* 1–18.

Hing, L. S., Li, W., & Zanna, M. P. (2002). Inducing hypocrisy to reduce prejudicial responses among aversive racists. *Journal of Experimental Social Psychology, 38,* 71–78.

Hinsz, V. B., & Davis, J. H. (1984). Persuasive arguments theory, group polarization, and choice shifts. *Personality and Social Psychology Bulletin, 10,* 260–268.

Hirschberger, G. (2006). Terror management and attributions of blame to innocent victims: Reconciling compassionate and defensive responses. *Journal of Personality and Social Psychology, 91,* 832–844.

Hirschfeld, L. (1996). *Race in the making.* Cambridge, MA: MIT Press.

Hirst, W., & Echterhoff, G. (2012). Remembering in conversations: The social sharing and reshaping of memories. *Annual Review of Psychology, 63,* 55–79.

Hoffman, E. A., & Haxby, J. V. (2000). Distinct representations of eye gaze and identity in the distributed human neural system for face perception. *Nature Neuroscience, 3,* 80–84.

Hofmann, W., Gawronski, B., Gschwendner, T., Le, H., & Schmitt, M. (2005). A meta-analysis on the correlation between the implicit association test and explicit self-report measures. *Personality and Social Psychology Bulletin, 31,* 1369–1385.

Hogg, M. A. (1992). *The social psychology of group cohesiveness: From attraction to social identity.* London: Harvester Wheatsheaf.

Hogg, M. A. (1993). Group cohesiveness: A critical review and some new directions. *European Review of Social Psychology, 4,* 85–111.

Hogg, M. A. (2001). A social identity theory of leadership. *Personality and Social Psychology Review, 5*(3), 184-200.

Hogg, M. A., & Abrams, D. (2003). Intergroup behavior and social identity. In M. A. Hogg & J. Cooper (Eds.), *The Sage handbook of social psychology* (pp. 407–431). Thousand Oaks, CA: Sage.

Hogg, M. A., Turner, J. C., & Davidson, B. (1990). Polarized norms and social frames of reference: A test of the self-categorization theory of group polarization. *Basic and Applied Social Psychology, 11,* 77–100.

Holbrook, A. L., Berent, M. K., Krosnick, J. A., Visser, P. S., & Boninger, D. S. (2005). Attitude importance and the accumulation of attitude-relevant knowledge in memory. *Journal of Personality and Social Psychology, 88,* 749–769.

Holloway, S., Tucker, L., & Hornstein, H. A. (1977). The effects of social and nonsocial information on interpersonal behavior of males: The news makes news. *Journal of Personality and Social Psychology, 35,* 514–522.

Holmes, D. S. (1978). Projection as a defense mechanism. *Psychological Bulletin, 69,* 248–268.

Holyoak, K. J., & Gordon, P. C. (1984). Information processing and social cognition. In R. S. Wyer Jr. & T. K. Srull (Eds.), *Handbook of social cognition* (Vol. 1, pp. 39–70). Hillsdale, NJ: Erlbaum.

Holmes, D. S. (1978). Projection as a defense mechanism. *Psychological Bulletin, 69,* 248–268.

Homer, P. M., & Kahle, L. R. (1988). A structural equation test of the value–attitude–behavior hierarchy. *Journal of Personality and Social Psychology, 54,* 638–646.

Hood, B. M., Macrae, C. N., Cole-Davies, V., & Dias, M. (2003). Eye remember you: The effects of gaze direction on face recognition in children and adults. *Developmental Science, 6,* 67–71.

Hornsey, M. J., & Jetten, J. (2004). The individual within the group: Balancing the need to belong with the need to be different. *Personality and Social Psychology Review, 8,* 248–264.

Horowitz, L. M., de Sales French, R., & Anderson, C. A. (1982). The prototype of a lonely person. In L. A. Peplau & D. Perlman (Eds.), *Loneliness: A sourcebook of current theory, research and therapy* (pp. 183–205). New York: Wiley.

Hoshino-Browne, E., Zanna, A. S., Spencer, S. J., Zanna, M. P., Kitayama, S., & Lackenbauer, S. (2005). On the cultural guises of cognitive dissonance: The case of the Easterners and Westerners. *Journal of Personality and Social Psychology, 89,* 294–310.

Hostetter, A. B., Alibali, M. W., & Niedenthal, P. M. (2012). Embodied social thought: Linking social concepts, emotion, and gesture. In S. T. Fiske & C. N. Macrae (Eds.), *Sage handbook of social cognition* (pp. 211–228). Thousand Oaks, CA: Sage.

House, J. S., Landis, K. R., & Umberson, D. (1988). Social relationships and health. *Science, 241,* 540–545.

Houston, D. A., & Fazio, R. H. (1989). Biased processing as a function of attitude accessibility: Making objective judgments subjectively. *Social Cognition, 7,* 51–66.

Hovland, C. I., Janis, I. L., & Kelley, H. H. (1953). *Communication and persuasion.* New Haven, CT: Yale University Press.

Hovland, C. I., Lumsdaine, A. A., & Sheffield, F. D. (1949). *Experiments in mass communication.* Princeton, NJ: Princeton University Press.

Hovland, C. I., & Sears, R. R. (1940). Minor studies of aggression: VI. Correlation of lynchings with economic indices. *Journal of Psychology, 9,* 301–310.

Howard-Pitney, B., Borgida, E., & Omoto, A. M. (1986). Personal involvement: An examination of processing differences. *Social Cognition, 4,* 39–57.

Hsu, M., Bhatt, M., Adolphs, R., Tranel, D., & Camerer, C. F. (2005). Neural systems responding to degrees of uncertainty in human decision-making. *Science, 310,* 1680–1683.

Hübner, R., Steinhauser, M., & Lehle, C. (2010). A dual-stage two-phase model of selective attention. *Psychological Review, 117(3),* 759–784.

Huddy, L., & Sears, D. O. (1995). Opposition to bilingual education: Prejudice or the defense of realistic interests? *Social Psychology Quarterly, 58,* 133–145.

Hugenberg, K., & Bodenhausen, G. V. (2003). Facing prejudice: Implicit prejudice and the perception of facial threat. *Psychological Science, 14,* 640–643.

Hume, D. (1978). *A treatise on human nature being an attempt to introduce the experimental method of reasoning into moral subjects.* Fair Lawn, NJ, and Oxford: Oxford University Press. (Originally published 1739.)

Hummert, M. L. (1994). Physiognomic cues to age and the activation of stereotypes of the elderly in interaction. *International Journal of Aging and Human Development, 39,* 5–19.

Hummert, M. L., Garstka, T. A., O'Brien, L. T., Greenwald, A. G., & Mellott, D. S. (2002). Using the implicit association test to measure age differences in implicit social cognitions. *Psychology and Aging, 17,* 482–495.

Hummert, M. L., Garstka, T. A., Shaner, J. L., & Strahm, S. (1994). Stereotypes of the elderly held by young, middle-aged, and elderly adults. *Journals of Gerontology, 49,* 240–249.

Hummert, M. L., Garstka, T. A., Shaner, J. L., & Strahm, S. (1995). Judgments about stereotypes of the elderly: Attitudes, age associations, and typicality ratings of young, middle-aged, and elderly adults. *Research on Aging, 17,* 168–189.

Huskinson, T. L. H., & Haddock, G. (2004). Individual differences in attitude structure: Variance in the chronic reliance on affective and cognitive information. *Journal of Experimental and Social Psychology, 40,* 82–90.

Hyde, J. S. (2005). The gender similarities hypothesis. *American Psychologist, 60,* 581–592.

Hyers, L. L., & Swim, J. K. (1998). A comparison of the experiences of dominant and minority group members during an intergroup encounter. *Group Processes and Intergroup Relations, 1,* 143–163.

Hymes, R. W. (1986). Political attitudes as social categories: A new look at selective memory. *Journal of Personality and Social Psychology, 51,* 233–241.

Iacoboni, M., Lieberman, M. D., Knowlton, B. J., Molnar-Szakacs, I., Moritz, M., Throop, C. J., & Fiske, A. P. (2004). Watching social interactions produces dorsomedial prefrontal and medial parietal BOLD fMRI signal increases compared to a resting baseline. *NeuroImage, 21,* 1167–1173.

Ickes, W. J. (1984). Compositions in Black and White: Determinants of interaction in interracial dyads. *Journal of Personality and Social Psychology, 47,* 230–241.

Ickes, W. J., & Barnes, R. D. (1977). The role of sex and self-monitoring in unstructured dyadic interactions. *Journal of Personality and Social Psychology, 35,* 315–330.

Ickes, W. J., Patterson, M. L., Rajecki, D. W., & Tanford, S. (1982). Behavioral and cognitive consequences of reciprocal versus compensatory responses to preinteraction expectancies. *Social Cognition, 1,* 160–190.

Ickes, W. J., Reidhead, S., & Patterson, M. (1986). Machiavellianism and self-monitoring: As different as "me" and "you." *Social Cognition, 4,* 58–74.

Ickes, W. J., Robertson, E., Tooke, W., & Teng, G. (1986). Naturalistic social cognition: Methodology, assessment, and validation. *Journal of Personality and Social Psychology, 51,* 66–82.

Ickes, W. J., Tooke, W., Stinson, L., Baker, V. L., & Bissonnette, V. (1988). Naturalistic social cognition: Intersubjectivity in same-sex dyads. *Journal of Nonverbal Behavior, 12,* 58–84.

Idson, L. C., & Mischel, W. (2001). The personality of familiar and significant people: The lay perceiver as a social-cognitive theorist. *Journal of Personality and Social Psychology, 80,* 585–596.

IJzerman, H., & Semin, G. R. (2010). Temperature perceptions as a ground for social proximity. *Journal of Experimental Social Psychology, 46(6),* 867–873.

Ingram, R. E., Smith, T. W., & Brehm, S. S. (1983). Depression and information processing: Self-schemata and the encoding of self-referent information. *Journal of Personality and Social Psychology, 45,* 412–420.

Insko, C. A., & Cialdini, R. B. (1969). A test of three interpretations of attitudinal verbal reinforcement. *Journal of Personality and Social Psychology, 12,* 333–341.

Isaacowitz, D. M. (2005). The gaze of the optimist. *Personality and Social Psychology Bulletin, 31,* 407–415.

Isbell, L. M. (2004). Not all happy people are lazy or stupid: Evidence of systematic processing in happy moods. *Journal of Experimental Social Psychology, 40,* 341–349.

Isen, A. M. (1987). Positive affect, cognitive processes, and social behavior. In L. Berkowitz (Ed.), *Advances in experimental social psychology* (Vol. 20, pp. 203–253). New York: Academic Press.

Isen, A. M., & Daubman, K. A. (1984). The influence of affect on categorization. *Journal of Personality and Social Psychology, 47,* 1206–1217.

Isen, A. M., & Geva, N. (1987). The influence of positive affect on acceptable level of risk: The person with a large canoe has a large worry. *Organizational Behavior and Human Decision Processes, 39,* 145–154.

Isen, A. M., Johnson, M. M. S., Mertz, E., & Robinson, G. F. (1985). The influence of positive affect on the unusualness of word associations. *Journal of Personality and Social Psychology, 48,* 1413–1426.

Isen, A. M., & Means, B. (1983). The influence of positive affect on decision-making strategy. *Social Cognition, 2,* 18–31.

Isen, A. M., & Noonberg, A. (1979). The effects of photographs of the handicapped on donation to charity: When a thousand words may be too much. *Journal of Applied Social Psychology, 9,* 426–431.

Isen, A. M., Nygren, T. E., & Ashby, F. G. (1988). Influence of positive affect on the subjective utility of gains and losses: It is just not worth the risk. *Journal of Personality and Social Psychology, 55,* 710–717.

Isen, A. M., Shalker, T. E., Clark, M. S., & Karp, L. (1978). Affect, accessibility of material in memory and behavior: A cognitive loop? *Journal of Personality and Social Psychology, 36,* 1–12.

Isen, A. M., & Simmonds, S. F. (1978). The effect of feeling good on a helping task that is incompatible with good mood. *Social Psychology, 41,* 346–349.

Isenberg, D. J. (1986). Group polarization: A critical review and meta-analysis. *Journal of Personality and Social Psychology, 50,* 1141–1151.

Ishii, K., Reyes, J. A., & Kitayama, S. (2003). Spontaneous attention to word content versus emotional tone: Differences among three cultures. *Psychological Science, 14,* 39–46.

Ito, T. A., Chiao, K. W., Devine, P. G., Lorig, T. S., & Cacioppo, T. (2006). The influence of facial feedback on race bias. *Psychological Science, 17,* 256–261.

Ito, T. A., Larsen, J. T., Smith, N. K., & Cacioppo, J. T. (1998). Negative information weighs more heavily on the brain: The negativity bias in evaluative categorizations. *Journal of Personality and Social Psychology, 75,* 887–900.

Ito, T. A., Thompson, E., & Cacioppo, J. T. (2004). Tracing the timecourse of social perception: The effects of racial cues on event-related brain potentials. *Personality and Social Psychology Bulletin, 30,* 1–14.

Ito, T. A., & Urland, G. R. (2003). Race and gender on the brain: Electrocortical measures of attention to the race and gender of multiple categorizable individuals. *Journal of Personality and Social Psychology, 85,* 616–626.

Ito, T. A., & Urland, G. R. (2005). The influence of processing objectives on the perception of faces: An ERP study of race and gender perception. *Cognitive Affective and Behavioral Neuroscience, 5(1),* 21–36.

Iyengar, S., & Kinder, D. R. (1987). *News that matters: Television and American opinion.* Chicago: University of Chicago Press.

Iyengar, S. S., & Lepper, M. R. (1999). Rethinking the value of choice: A cultural perspective on intrinsic motivation. *Journal of Personality and Social Psychology, 76,* 349–366.

Iyer, A., Leach, C. W., & Crosby, F. J. (2003). White guilt and racial compensation: The benefits and limits of self-focus. *Personality and Social Psychology Bulletin, 29,* 117–129.

Izard, C. E. (1972). *The face of emotion.* New York: Appleton-Century-Crofts.

Izard, C. E. (1977). *Human emotions.* New York: Plenum Press.

Izard, C. E. (1981). Differential emotions theory and the facial feedback hypothesis of emotion activation: Comments on Tourangeau and Ellsworth's "The role of facial response in the experience of emotion." *Journal of Personality and Social Psychology, 40,* 350–354.

Izard, C. E. (2009). Emotion theory and research: Highlights, unanswered questions, and emerging issues. *Annual Review of Psychology, 60,* 1–25.

Jackman, M. R. (1994). *The velvet glove: Paternalism and conflict in gender, class, and race relations.* Berkeley, CA: University of California Press.

Jacobs, L., Berscheid, E., & Walster, E. (1971). Self-esteem and attraction. *Journal of Personality and Social Psychology, 17,* 84–91.

Jacobsen, T., Schubotz, R. I., Hofel, L., & Cramon, D. Y. (2006). Brain correlates of aesthetic judgment of beauty. *NeuroImage, 29,* 276–285. [Erratum: *32,* 486–487.]

Jacoby, L. L., & Kelley, C. M. (1987). Unconscious influences of memory for a prior event. *Personality and Social Psychology Bulletin, 13,* 314–336.

James, K. (1986). Priming and social categorizational factors: Impact on awareness of emergency situations. *Personality and Social Psychology Bulletin, 12,* 462–467.

James, W. (1907). *Pragmatism.* New York: Longmans-Green.

James, W. (1983). *The principles of psychology.* Cambridge, MA: Harvard University Press. (Originally published 1890.)

Jamieson, D. W., & Zanna, M. P. (1989). Need for structure in attitude formation and expression. In A. R. Pratkanis, S. J. Breckler, & A. G. Greenwald (Eds.), *Attitude structure and function* (pp. 383–406). Hillsdale, NJ: Erlbaum.

Janis, I. L. (1972). *Victims of groupthink.* Boston, MA: Houghton Mifflin.

Janis, I. L. (1989). *Crucial decisions: Leadership in policymaking and crisis management.* New York: Free Press.

Janiszewski, C. (1993). Preattentive mere exposure effects. *Journal of Consumer Research, 20,* 376–392.

Janoff-Bulman, R., Timko, C., & Carli, L. L. (1985). Cognitive biases in blaming the victim. *Journal of Experimental Social Psychology, 21,* 161–177.

Jarvis, W. G. G., & Petty, R. E. (1996). The need to evaluate. *Journal of Personality and Social Psychology, 70,* 172–194.

Jaspers, J. M. F., Hewstone, M., & Fincham, F. D. (1983). Attribution theory and research: The state of the art. In J. Jaspars, D. Fincham, & M. Hewstone (Eds.), *Attribution theory and research: Conceptual, developmental, and social dimensions* (pp. 3–36). London: Academic Press.

Jecker, J. D. (1964). The cognitive effects of conflict and dissonance. In L. Festinger (Ed.), *Conflict, decision, and dissonance.* Stanford, CA: Stanford University Press.

Jennings, D., Amabile, T. M., & Ross, L. D. (1982). Informal covariation assessment: Data-based vs. theory-based judgments. In A. Tversky, D. Kahneman, & P. Slovic (Eds.), *Judgment under uncertainty: Heuristics and biases* (pp. 211–230). New York: Cambridge University Press.

Jervis, R. (1976). *Perception and misperception in international politics.* Princeton, NJ: Princeton University Press.

Jetten, J., Spears, R., & Manstead, A. S. R. (1998). Defining dimensions of distinctiveness: Group variability makes a difference to differentiation. *Journal of Personality and Social Psychology, 74,* 1481–1492.

Johns, M., Schmader, T., & Martens, A. (2005). Knowing is half the battle: Teaching stereotype threat as a means of improving women's math performance. *Psychological Science, 16,* 175–179.

Johnson, B. T., & Eagly, A. H. (1989). The effects of involvement on persuasion: A meta-analysis. *Psychological Bulletin, 106,* 290–314.

Johnson, B. T., & Eagly, A. H. (1990). Involvement and persuasion: Types, traditions, and the evidence. *Psychological Bulletin, 107,* 375–384.

Johnson, E. J., & Tversky, A. (1983). Affect generalization and the perception of risk. *Journal of Personality and Social Psychology, 45,* 20–31.

Johnson, M. H., & Magaro, P. A. (1987). Effects of mood and severity on memory processes in depression and mania. *Psychological Bulletin, 101,* 28–40.

Johnson, M. K., Raye, C. L., Mitchell, K. J., Touryan, S. R., Greene, E. J., & Nolen-Hoeksema, S. (2006). Dissociating medial frontal and posterior cingulate activity during self-reflection. *Social Cognitive and Affective Neuroscience, 1,* 56–64.

Jolly, E. J., & Reardon, R. (1985). Cognitive differentiation, automaticity, and interruptions of automatized behaviors. *Personality and Social Psychology Bulletin, 11,* 301–314.

Jonas, E., Greenberg, J., & Frey, D. (2003). Connecting terror management and dissonance theory: Evidence that mortality salience increases the preference for supporting information after decisions. *Personality and Social Psychology Bulletin, 29,* 1181–1189.

Jonas, E., Schulz-Hardt, S., Frey, D., & Thelen, N. (2001). Confirmation bias in sequential information search after preliminary decisions: An expansion of dissonance theoretical research on selective exposure to information. *Journal of Personality and Social Psychology, 80,* 557–571.

Jones, E. E. (1990). *Interpersonal perception.* New York: Freeman.

Jones, E. E., & Davis, K. E. (1965). From acts to dispositions: The attribution process in person perception. In L. Berkowitz (Ed.), *Advances in experimental social psychology* (Vol. 2, pp. 220–266). New York: Academic Press.

Jones, E. E., & Goethals, G. R. (1972). Order effects in impression formation: Attribution context and the nature of the entity. In E. E. Jones, D. E. Kanouse, H. H. Kelley, R. E. Nisbett, S. Valins, & B. Weiner (Eds.), *Attribution: Perceiving the causes of behavior* (pp. 27–46). Morristown, NJ: General Learning Press.

Jones E. E., & Harris, V. A. (1967). The attribution of attitudes. *Journal of Experimental Social Psychology, 3,* 1–24.

Jones E. E., & McGillis, D. (1976). Correspondent inferences and the attribution cube: A comparative reappraisal. In J. H. Harvey, W. J. Ickes, & R. F. Kidd (Eds.), *New directions in attribution research* (Vol. 1, pp. 389–420). Hillsdale, NJ: Erlbaum.

Jones, E. E., & Nisbett, R. E. (1972). The actor and the observer: Divergent perceptions of the causes of behavior. In E. E. Jones, D. E. Kanouse, H. H. Kelley, R. E. Nisbett, S. Valins, & B. Weiner (Eds.), *Attribution: Perceiving the causes of behavior* (pp. 79–94). Morristown, NJ: General Learning Press.

Jones, E. E., & Pittman, T. S. (1982). Toward a general theory of strategic self-presentation. In J. Suls (Ed.), *Psychological perspectives on the self* (pp. 231–262). Hillsdale, NJ: Erlbaum.

Jones, J. M. (1997). *Prejudice and racism* (2nd edn). New York: McGraw-Hill.

Jones, J. T., Pelham, B. W., Mirenberg, M. C., & Hetts, J. J. (2002). Name letter preferences are not merely mere exposure: Implicit egotism as self-regulation. *Journal of Experimental Social Psychology, 38,* 170–177.

Jordan, C. H., Spencer, S. J., & Zanna, M. P. (2003). "I love me . . . I love me not": Implicit self-esteem, explicit self-esteem, and defensiveness. In S. J. Spencer, S. Fein, M. P. Zanna, & J. M. Olson (Eds.), *Motivated social perception: The Ontario Symposium* (Vol. 9, pp. 117–145). Mahwah, NJ: Erlbaum.

Jordan, C. H., Spencer, S. J., & Zanna, M. P. (2005). Types of high self-esteem and prejudice: How implicit self-esteem relates to ethnic discrimination among high explicit self-esteem individuals. *Personality and Social Psychology Bulletin, 31,* 693–702.

Josephs, R. A., Bosson, J. K., & Jacobs, C. G. (2003). Self-esteem maintenance processes: Why low self-esteem may be resistant to change. *Personality and Social Psychology Bulletin, 29,* 920–933.

Jost, J. T., & Banaji, M. R. (1994). The role of stereotyping in system-justification and the production of false consciousness. *British Journal of Social Psychology, 33,* 1–27.

Jost, J. T., Banaji, M. R., & Nosek, B. A. (2004). A decade of system justification theory: Accumulated evidence of conscious and unconscious bolstering of the status quo. *Political Psychology, 25,* 881–920.

Jost, J. T., & Burgess, D. (2000). Attitudinal ambivalence and the conflict between group and system justification motives in low status groups. *Personality and Social Psychology Bulletin, 26,* 293–305.

Jost, J. T., Glaser, J., Kruglanski, A. W., & Sulloway, F. J. (2003). Political conservatism as motivated social cognition. *Psychological Bulletin, 129,* 339–375.

Jost, J. T., & Hunyady, O. (2002). The psychology of system justification and the palliative function of ideology. In W. Stroebe & M. Hewstone (Eds.), *European review of social psychology* (Vol. 13, pp. 111–153). Hove, England: Psychology Press/Taylor & Francis.

Jost, J. T., & Kay, A. C. (2005). Exposure to benevolent sexism and complementary gender stereotypes: Consequences for specific and diffuse forms of system justification. *Journal of Personality and Social Psychology, 88,* 498–509.

Jost, J. T., Pelham, B. W., Sheldon, O., & Sullivan, B. N. (2003). Social inequality and the reduction of ideological dissonance on behalf of the system: Evidence of enhanced system justification among the disadvantaged. *European Journal of Social Psychology, 33,* 13–36.

Judd, C. M., & Krosnick, J. A. (1982). Attitude centrality, organization, and measurement. *Journal of Personality and Social Psychology, 42,* 436–447.

Judd, C. M., & Krosnick, J. A. (1989). The structural bases of consistency among political attitudes: Effects of political expertise and attitude importance. In A. R. Pratkanis, S. J. Breckler, & A. G. Greenwald (Eds.), *Attitude structure and function* (pp. 99–128). Hillsdale, NJ: Erlbaum.

Judd, C. M., & Kulik, J. A. (1980). Schematic effects of social attitudes on information processing and recall. *Journal of Personality and Social Psychology, 38,* 569–578.

Judd, C. M., & Park, B. (1988). Out-group homogeneity: Judgments of variability at the individual and group levels. *Journal of Personality and Social Psychology, 54,* 778–788.

Judd, C. M., Park, B., Yzerbyt, V. Y., Gordijn, E. H., & Muller, D. (2005). Attributions of intergroup bias and outgroup homogeneity to ingroup and outgroup others. *European Journal of Social Psychology, 35,* 677–704.

Kahn, W. A., & Crosby, F. J. (1987) Discriminating between attitudes and discriminatory behaviors. In L. Larwood, B. A. Gutek, & A. H. Stromberg (Eds.), *Women and work: An annual review* (Vol. 1, pp. 215–328). Beverly Hills, CA: Sage.

Kahneman, D. (2003). A perspective on judgment and choice. *American Psychologist, 58,* 697–720.

Kahneman, D. (2011). *Thinking, fast and slow.* New York: Farrar, Straus & Giroux.

Kahneman, D., & Frederick, S. (2002). Representativeness revisited: Attribute substitution in intuitive judgment. In T. Gilovich, D. Griffin, & D. Kahneman (Eds.), *Heuristics and biases: The psychology of intuitive judgment* (pp. 49–81). New York: Cambridge University Press.

Kahneman, D., & Miller, D. T. (1986). Norm theory: Comparing reality to its alternatives. *Psychological Review, 93,* 136–153.

Kahneman, D., & Tversky, A. (1972). Subjective probability: A judgment of representativeness. *Cognitive Psychology, 3,* 430–454.

Kahneman, D., & Tversky, A. (1973). On the psychology of prediction. *Psychological Review, 80,* 237–251.

Kahneman, D., & Tversky, A. (1979). Prospect theory: An analysis of decision under risk. *Econometrica, 47,* 263–292.

Kahneman, D., & Tversky, A. (1982). The simulation heuristic. In D. Kahneman, P. Slovic, & A. Tversky (Eds.), *Judgment under uncertainty: Heuristics and biases* (pp. 201–208). New York: Cambridge University Press.

Kahneman, D., & Tversky, A. (1984). Choices, values, and frames. *American Psychologist, 39,* 341–350.

Kaiser, C. R., & Miller, C. T. (2001a). Reacting to impending discrimination: Compensation for prejudice and attributions to discrimination. *Personality and Social Psychology Bulletin, 27,* 1357–1367.

Kaiser, C. R., & Miller, C. T. (2001b). Stop complaining! The social costs of making attributions to discrimination. *Personality and Social Psychology Bulletin, 27,* 254–263.

Kaiser, C. R., & Miller, C. T. (2003). Derogating the victim: The interpersonal consequences of blaming events on discrimination. *Group Processes and Intergroup Relations, 6,* 227–237.

Kallgren, C. A., & Wood, W. (1986). Access to attitude-relevant information in memory as a determinant of attitude-behavior consistency. *Journal of Experimental Social Psychology, 22,* 328–338.

Kammrath, L. K., Mendoza-Denton, R., & Mischel, W. (2005). Incorporating if . . . then . . . personality signatures in person perception: Beyond the person–situation dichotomy. *Journal of Personality and Social Psychology, 88,* 605–618.

Kanagawa, C., Cross, S. E., & Markus, H. R. (2001). "Who am I?" The cultural psychology of the conceptual self. *Personality and Social Psychology Bulletin, 27,* 90–103.

Kanazawa, S. (1992). Outcome or expectancy? Antecedent of spontaneous causal attribution. *Personality and Social Psychology Bulletin, 18,* 659–668.

Kant, I. (1969). *Critique of pure reason.* New York: St. Martin's Press. (Originally published 1781.)

Kanter, R. (1977). *Men and women of the corporation.* New York: Basic Books.

Kanwisher, N., & Wojciulik, E. (2000). Visual attention: Insights from brain imaging. *Nature Reviews, 1,* 91–100.

Kardes, F. R., Sanbonmatsu, D. M., Voss, R. T., & Fazio, R. H. (1986). Self-monitoring and attitude accessibility. *Personality and Social Psychology Bulletin, 12,* 468–474.

Karniol, R. (1986). What will they think of next? Transformation rules used to predict other people's thoughts and feelings. *Journal of Personality and Social Psychology, 51,* 932–944.

Karpinski, A., & Hilton, J. L. (2001). Attitudes and the implicit associations test. *Journal of Personality and Social Psychology, 81,* 774–788.

Kashima, K., & Davison, G. C. (1989). Functional consistency in the face of topographical change in articulated thoughts. *Journal of Rational-Emotive and Cognitive-Behavior Therapy, 7,* 131–139.

Kashima, Y., Kashima, E., Chiu, C.-y., Farsides, T., Gelfand, M., Hong, Y.-y., Kim, U., Strack, F., Werth, L., Yuki, M., & Yzerbyt, V. Y. (2005). Culture, essentialism, and agency: Are individuals universally believed to be more real entities than groups? *European Journal of Social Psychology, 35,* 147–169.

Kashima, Y., Woolcock, J., & Kashima, E. S. (2000). Group impressions as dynamic configurations: The tensor product model of group impression formation and change. *Psychological Review, 107,* 914–942.

Kasser, T., & Ryan, R. M. (1996). Further examining the American dream: Differential correlates of intrinsic and extrinsic goals. *Personality and Social Psychology Bulletin, 22,* 280–287.

Kassin, S. M., & Baron, R. M. (1986). On the basicity of social perception cues: Developmental evidence for adult processes? *Social Cognition, 4,* 180–200.

Katz, D. (1960). The functional approach to the study of attitudes. *Public Opinion Quarterly, 24,* 163–204.

Katz, D., & Braly, K. (1933). Racial stereotypes of one hundred college students. *Journal of Abnormal and Social Psychology, 28,* 280–290.

Katz, E. (1968). On reopening the question of selectivity in exposure to mass media. In R. P. Abelson et al. (Eds.), *Theories of cognitive consistency: A sourcebook.* Chicago: Rand-McNally.

Katz, I., & Hass, R. G. (1988). Racial ambivalence and American value conflict: Correlational and priming studies of dual cognitive structures. *Journal of Personality and Social Psychology, 55,* 893–905.

Kawakami, K., & Dovidio, J. F. (2001). The reliability of implicit stereotyping. *Personality and Social Psychology Bulletin, 27,* 212–225.

Kawakami, K., Dovidio, J. F., & Dijksterhuis, A. (2003). Effect of social category priming on personal attitudes. *Psychological Science, 14,* 315–319.

Kawakami, K., Dovidio, J. F., Moll, J., Hermsen, S., & Russin, A. (2000). Just say no (to stereotyping): Effects of training in the negation of stereotypic associations on stereotype activation. *Journal of Personality and Social Psychology, 78,* 871–888.

Kawakami, K., Dovidio, J. F., & van Kamp, S. (2005). Kicking the habit: Effects of nonstereotypic association training and correction processes on hiring decisions. *Journal of Experimental Social Psychology, 41,* 68–75.

Kawakami, K., Phills, C. E., Greenwald, A. G., Simard, D., Pontiero, J., Brnjas, A., Khan, B., Mills, J., & Dovidio, J. F. (2012). In perfect harmony: Synchronizing the self to activated social categories. *Journal of Personality and Social Psychology, 102,* 562–575.

Kay, A. C., & Eibach, R. P. (2012). Ideological processes. In S. T. Fiske & C. N. Macrae (Eds.), *Sage handbook of social cognition* (pp. 495–515). Thousand Oaks, CA: Sage.

Kay, A. C., & Jost, J. T. (2003). Complementary justice: Effects of "poor but happy" and "poor but honest" stereotype exemplars on system justification and implicit activation of the justice motive. *Journal of Personality and Social Psychology, 85,* 823–837.

Kay, A. C., Jost, J. T., & Young, S. (2005). Victim derogation and victim enhancement as alternate routes to system justification. *Psychological Science, 16,* 240–246.

Keller, J. (2005). In genes we trust: The biological component of psychological essentialism and its relationship to mechanisms of motivated social cognition. *Journal of Personality and Social Psychology, 88,* 686–702.

Keller, J., & Dauenheimer, D. (2003). Stereotype threat in the classroom: Dejection mediates the disrupting threat effect on women's math performance. *Personality and Social Psychology Bulletin, 29,* 371–381.

Kellerman, J., Lewis, J., & Laird, J. D. (1989). Looking and loving: The effects of mutual gaze on feelings of romantic love. *Journal of Research in Personality, 23,* 145–161.

Kelley, H. H. (1967). Attribution theory in social psychology. In D. Levine (Ed.), *Nebraska Symposium on Motivation* (Vol. 15, pp. 192–240). Lincoln, NB: University of Nebraska Press.

Kelley, H. H. (1972a). Attribution in social interaction. In E. E. Jones, D. E. Kanouse, H. H. Kelley, R. E. Nisbett, S. Valins, & B. Weiner (Eds.), *Attribution: Perceiving the causes of behavior* (pp. 1–26). Morristown, NJ: General Learning Press.

Kelley, H. H. (1972b). Causal schemata and the attribution process. In E. E. Jones, D. E. Kanouse, H. H. Kelley, R. E. Nisbett, S. Valins, & B. Weiner (Eds.), *Attribution: Perceiving the causes of behavior* (pp. 151–174). Morristown, NJ: General Learning Press.

Kelley, H. H., Berscheid, E., Christensen, A., Harvey, J. H., Huston, T. L., Levinger, G., et al. (1983). Analyzing close relationships. In H. H. Kelley, E. Berscheid, A. Christensen, J. H. Harvey, T. L. Huston, G. Levinger, E. McClintock, L. A. Peplau, & D. R. Peterson (Eds.), *Close relationships* (pp. 20–67). New York: Freeman.

Kelley, H. H., & Michela, J. L. (1980). Attribution theory and research. *Annual Review of Psychology, 31,* 457–501.

Kelley, W. M., Macrae, C. N., Wyland, C. L., Caglar, S., Inati, S., & Heatherton, T. F. (2002). Finding the self? An event-related fMRI study. *Journal of Cognitive Neuroscience, 14,* 785–794.

Kelly, C. (1989). Political identity and perceived intra-group homogeneity. *British Journal of Social Psychology, 28,* 239–250.

Kelman, H. C. (1958). Compliance, identification, and internalization: Three processes of attitude change. *Journal of Conflict Resolution, 2,* 51–60.

Keltner, D., Gruenfeld, D. H., & Anderson, C. (2003). Power, approach, and inhibition. *Psychological Review, 110,* 265–284.

Keltner, D., & Lerner, J. S. (2010). Emotion. In S. T. Fiske, D. T. Gilbert, & G. Lindzey (Eds.), *Handbook of social psychology* (5th edn, Vol. 1, pp. 317–352). Hoboken, NJ: Wiley.

Kemler-Nelson, D. G. (1984). The effect of intention on what concepts are acquired. *Journal of Verbal Learning and Verbal Behavior, 23,* 734–759.

Kemmelmeier, M., Danielson, C., & Basten, J. (2005). What's in a grade? Academic success and political orientation. *Personality and Social Psychology Bulletin, 31,* 1386–1399.

Kenny, D. A., & Acitelli, L. K. (2001). Accuracy and bias in the perception of the partner in a close relationship. *Journal of Personality and Social Psychology, 80,* 439–448.

Kenrick, D. T., & Cialdini, R. B. (1977). Romantic attraction: Misattribution versus reinforcement explanations. *Journal of Personality and Social Psychology, 35,* 381–391.

Kernis, M. H. (2003). Toward a conceptualization of optimal self-esteem. *Psychological Inquiry, 4,* 1–26.

Kernis, M. H., & Grannemann, B. D. (1990). Excuses in the making: A test and extension of Darley and Goethals' attributional model. *Journal of Experimental Social Psychology, 26,* 337–349.

Kernis, M. H., Paradise, A. W., Whitaker, D. J., Wheatman, S. R., & Goldman, B. N. (2000). Master of one's psychological domain? Not likely if one's self-esteem is unstable. *Personality and Social Psychology Bulletin, 26,* 1297–1305.

Kervyn, N., Bergsieker, H. B., & Fiske, S. T. (2012). The innuendo effect: Hearing the positive but inferring the negative. *Journal of Experimental Social Psychology, 48(1),* 77–85.

Kervyn, N., Fiske, S. T., & Malone, C. (2012). Brands as intentional agents framework: Warmth and competence map brand perception. *Journal of Consumer Psychology.*

Kiesler, C. A. (1971). *The psychology of commitment: Experiments linking behavior to belief.* New York: Academic Press.

Kiesler, C. A., Collins, B. E., & Miller, N. (1969). *Attitude change: A critical analysis of theoretical approaches.* New York: Wiley.

Kiesler, C. A., Nisbett, R. E., & Zanna, M. P. (1969). On inferring one's beliefs from one's behavior. *Journal of Personality and Social Psychology, 11,* 321–327.

Kihlstrom, J. F. (2004). Implicit methods in social psychology. In C. Sansone, C. C. Morf, & A. T. Panter (Eds.), *The Sage handbook of methods in social psychology* (pp. 195–212). Thousand Oaks, CA: Sage.

Kilianski, S. E., & Rudman, L. A. (1998). Wanting it both ways: Do women approve of benevolent sexism? *Sex Roles, 39,* 333–352.

Killeen, P. R. (2009). An additive-utility model of delay discounting. *Psychological Review, 116(3),* 602–619.

Kim, H.-S., & Baron, R. S. (1988). Exercise and the illusory correlation: Does arousal heighten stereotypic processing? *Journal of Experimental Social Psychology, 24,* 366–380.

Kinder, D. R., & Sears, D. O. (1981). Prejudice and politics: Symbolic racism versus racial threats to the good life. *Journal of Personality and Social Psychology, 40,* 414–431.

Kircher, T. T. J., Brammer, M., Bullmore, E., Simmons, A., Bartels, M., & David, A. S. (2002). The neural correlates of intentional and incidental self processing. *Neuropsychologia, 40,* 683–692.

Kitayama, S., Duffy, S., Kawamura, T., & Larsen, J. T. (2003). Perceiving an object and its context in different cultures: A cultural look at New Look. *Psychological Science, 14,* 201–206.

Kitayama, S., & Karasawa, M. (1997). Implicit self-esteem in Japan: Name letters and birthday numbers. *Personality and Social Psychology Bulletin, 23,* 736–742.

Kitayama, S., Markus, H. R., Matsumoto, H., & Norasakkunkit, V. (1997). Individual and collective processes in the construction of the self: Self-enhancement in the United States and self-criticism in Japan. *Journal of Personality and Social Psychology, 72,* 1245–1267.

Kitayama, S., Snibbe, A. C., Markus, H. R., & Suzuki, T. (2004). Is there any "free choice"? Self and dissonance in two cultures. *Psychological Science, 15,* 527–533.

Kite, M. E., & Johnson, B. T. (1988). Attitudes toward older and younger adults: A meta-analysis. *Psychology and Aging, 3,* 233–244.

Kittles, R. A., & Weiss, K. M. (2003). Race, ancestry, and genes: Implications for defining disease risk. *Annual Review of Geonomics and Human Genetics, 4,* 33–67.

Klar, Y., & Giladi, E. E. (1999). Are most people happier than their peers, or are they just happy? *Personality and Social Psychology Bulletin, 25,* 585–594.

Klauer, K. C., & Meiser, T. (2000). A source-monitoring analysis of illusory correlations. *Personality and Social Psychology Bulletin, 26,* 1074–1093.

Klauer, K. C., & Wegener, I. (1998). Unraveling social categorization in the "Who said what?" paradigm. *Journal of Personality and Social Psychology, 75,* 1155–1178.

Klauer, K. C., Wegener, I., & Ehrenberg, K. (2002). Perceiving minority members as individuals: The effects of relative group size in social categorization. *European Journal of Social Psychology, 32,* 223–245.

Klayman, J., & Ha, Y.-W. (1987). Confirmation, disconfirmation, and information in hypothesis testing. *Psychological Review, 94,* 211–228.

Klein, S. B., Cosmides, L., Tooby, J., & Chance, S. (2001). Priming exceptions: A test of the scope hypothesis in naturalistic trait judgments. *Social Cognition, 19,* 443–468.

Klein, S. B., & Kihlstrom, J. F. (1998). On bridging the gap between social-personality psychology and neuropsychology. *Personality and Social Psychology Review, 2(4),* 228–242.

Kleinhesselink, R. R., & Edwards, R. E. (1975). Seeking and avoiding belief-discrepant information as a function of its perceived refutability. *Journal of Personality and Social Psychology, 31,* 787–790.

Klinger, E. (1977). *Meaning and void: Inner experience and the incentives in people's lives.* Minneapolis, MN: University of Minnesota Press.

Klinger, E. (1978). Modes of normal conscious flow. In K. S. Pope & J. L. Singer (Eds.), *The stream of consciousness: Scientific investigations into the flow of human experience.* New York: Plenum Press.

Klinger, E., Barta, S. G., & Maxeiner, M. E. (1980). Motivational correlates of thought content frequency and commitment. *Journal of Personality and Social Psychology, 39,* 1222–1237.

Knäuper, B., Kornik, R., Atkinson, K., Guberman, C., & Aydin, C. (2005). Motivation influences the underestimation of cumulative risk. *Personality and Social Psychology Bulletin, 31,* 1511–1523.

Knoblich, G., & Sebanz, N. (2006). The social nature of perception and action. *Current Directions in Psychological Science, 15,* 99–104.

Knowles, E. D., Morris, M. W., Chiu, C.-y., & Hong, Y.-y. (2001). Culture and the process of person perception: Evidence for automaticity among East Asians in correcting for situational influences on behavior. *Personality and Social Psychology Bulletin, 27,* 1344–1356.

Knox, V. J., Gekoski, W. L., & Kelly, L. E. (1995). The age group evaluation and description (AGED) Inventory: A new instrument for assessing stereotypes of and attitudes toward age groups. *International Journal of Aging and Human Development, 40,* 31–55.

Knudsen, E. I. (2007). Fundamental components of attention. *Annual Review of Neuroscience, 30,* 57–78.

Knutson, B., Taylor, J., Kaufman, M., Peterson, R., & Glover, G. (2005). Distributed neural representation of expected value. *Journal of Neuroscience, 25,* 4806–4812.

Koenig, A. M., & Eagly, A. H. (2005). Stereotype threat in men on a test of social sensitivity. *Sex Roles, 52,* 489–496.

Koenig, A. M., Eagly, A. H., Mitchell, A. A., & Ristikari, T. (2011). Are leader stereotypes masculine? A meta-analysis of three research paradigms. *Psychological Bulletin, 137(4),* 616–642.

Koffka, K. (1935). *Principles of Gestalt psychology.* New York: Harcourt, Brace, & World.

Kohler, W. (1976). *The place of value in a world of facts.* New York: Liveright. (Originally published 1938.)

Koole, S. L., Dijksterhuis, A., & van Knippenberg, A. (2001). What's in a name: Implicit self-esteem and the automatic self. *Journal of Personality and Social Psychology, 80,* 669–685.

Koole, S. L., Smeets, K., van Knippenberg, A., & Dijksterhuis, A. (1999). The cessation of rumination through self-affirmation. *Journal of Personality and Social Psychology, 77,* 111–125.

Koriat, A., Goldsmith, M., & Pansky, A. (2000). Toward a psychology of memory accuracy. *Annual Review of Psychology, 51,* 481–537.

Kossan, N. E. (1981). Developmental differences in concept acquisition strategies. *Child Development, 52,* 290–298.

Kowalski, R. M., & Leary, M. R. (1990). Strategic self-presentation and the avoidance of aversive events: Antecedents and consequences of self-enhancement and self-depreciation. *Journal of Experimental Social Psychology, 26,* 322–336.

Kozak, M. N., Marsh, A. A., & Wegner, D. M. (2006). What do I think you're doing? Action identification and mind attribution. *Journal of Personality and Social Psychology, 90,* 543–555.

Kraus, S. J. (1995). Attitudes and the prediction of behavior: A meta-analysis of the empirical literature. *Personality and Social Psychology Bulletin, 21,* 58–75.

Kray, L. J., Galinsky, A. D., & Thompson, L. (2002). Reversing the gender gap in negotiations: An exploration of stereotype regeneration. *Organizational Behavior and Human Decision Processes, 87,* 386–409.

Kray, L. J., George, L. G., Liljenquist, K. A., Galinsky, A. D., Tetlock, P. E., & Roese, N. J. (2010). From what might have been to what must have been: Counterfactual thinking creates meaning. *Journal of Personality and Social Psychology, 98(1),* 106–118.

Krieger, L. H., & Fiske, S. T. (2006). Behavioral realism in employment discrimination law: Implicit bias and disparate treatment. *California Law Review, 94,* 997–1062.

Kristiansen, C. M., & Zanna, M. P. (1988). Justifying attitudes by appealing to values: A functional perspective. *British Journal of Social Psychology, 27,* 247–256.

Krosnick, J. A. (1988a). Attitude importance and attitude change. *Journal of Experimental Social Psychology, 24,* 240–255.

Krosnick, J. A. (1988b). The role of attitude importance in social evaluation: A study of policy preferences, presidential candidate evaluations, and voting behavior. *Journal of Personality and Social Psychology, 55,* 196–210.

Krosnick, J. A. (1989). Attitude importance and attitude accessibility. *Personality and Social Psychology Bulletin, 15,* 297–308.

Krueger, J. I. (1998). Enhancement bias in descriptions of self and others. *Personality and Social Psychology Bulletin, 24,* 505–516.

Krueger, J. I., & Clement, R. W. (1994). The truly false consensus effect: An ineradicable and egocentric bias in social perception. *Journal of Personality and Social Psychology, 67,* 596–610.

Krueger, J. I., & Stanke, D. (2001). The role of self-referent and other referent knowledge in perceptions of group characteristics. *Personality and Social Psychology Bulletin, 27,* 878–888.

Krueger, J. I., Wirtz, D., & Miller, D. T. (2005). Counterfactual thinking and the first instinct fallacy. *Journal of Personality and Social Psychology, 88,* 725–735.

Kruglanski, A. W. (1975). The endogenous–exogenous partition in attribution theory. *Psychological Review, 82,* 387–406.

Kruglanski, A. W. (1980). Lay epistemo-logic-process and contents: Another look at attribution theory. *Psychological Review, 87,* 70–87.

Kruglanski, A. W. (1989). The psychology of being "right": On the problem of accuracy in social perception and cognition. *Psychological Bulletin, 106,* 395–409.

Kruglanski, A. W. (1990). Motivations for judging and knowing: Implications for causal attribution. In E. T. Higgins & R. M. Sorrentino (Eds.), *Handbook of motivation and cognition: Foundations of social behavior* (Vol. 2, pp. 333–368). New York: Guilford Press.

Kruglanski, A. W., & Mayseless, O. (1988). Contextual effects in hypothesis testing: The role of competing alternatives and epistemic motivations. *Social Cognition, 6,* 1–20.

Kruglanski, A. W., & Sheveland, A. (2012). Thinkers' personalities: On individual differences in the processes of sense making. In S. T. Fiske & C. N. Macrae (Eds.), *Sage handbook of social cognition* (pp. 474–494). Thousand Oaks, CA: Sage.

Kruglanski, A. W., Thompson, E. P., & Spiegel, S. (1999). Separate or equal? Bimodal notions of persuasion and a single-process "unimodel." In S. Chaiken & Y. Trope (Eds.), *Dual-process theories in social psychology* (pp. 293–313). New York: Guilford Press.

Kruglanski, A. W., & Webster, D. M. (1996). Motivated closing of the mind: "Seizing" and "freezing." *Psychological Review, 103,* 263–283.

Kühnen, U., Hannover, B., & Schubert, B. (2001). The semantic–procedural interface model of the self: The role of self-knowledge for context-dependent versus context-independent modes of thinking. *Journal of Personality and Social Psychology, 80,* 397–409.

Kunda, Z. (1987). Motivated inference: Self-serving generation and evaluation of causal theories. *Journal of Personality and Social Psychology, 53,* 636–647.

Kunda, Z. (1990). The case for motivated reasoning. *Psychological Bulletin, 108,* 480–498.

Kunda, Z. (1999). *Social cognition: Making sense of people.* Cambridge, MA: MIT Press.

Kunda, Z., & Nisbett, R. E. (1986). Prediction and the partial understanding of the law of large numbers. *Journal of Experimental Social Psychology, 22,* 339–354.

Kunda, Z., & Nisbett, R. E. (1988). Predicting individual evaluations from group evaluations and vice versa: Different patterns for self and other? *Personality and Social Psychology Bulletin, 14,* 326–334.

Kunda, Z., & Sherman-Williams, B. (1993). Stereotypes and the construal of individuating information. *Personality and Social Psychology Review, 9,* 2–16.

Kunda, Z., & Thagard, P. (1996). Forming impressions from stereotypes, traits, and behaviors: A parallel-constraint-satisfaction theory. *Psychological Review, 103,* 284–308.

Kunst-Wilson, W. R., & Zajonc, R. B. (1980). Affective discrimination of stimuli that cannot be recognized. *Science, 207,* 557–558.

Kurman, J. (2001). Self-enhancement: Is it restricted to individualistic cultures? *Personality and Social Psychology Bulletin, 27,* 1705–1716.

Kurzban, R., & Leary, M. R. (2001). Evolutionary origins of stigmatization: The functions of social exclusion. *Psychological Bulletin, 127,* 187–208.

Kurzban, R., Tooby, J., & Cosmides, L. (2001). Can race be erased? Coalitional computation and social categorization. *Proceedings of the National Academy of Sciences of the United States of America, 98,* 15387–15392.

Kwan, V. S. Y., John, O. P., Kenny, D. A., Bond, M. H., & Robins, R. W. (2004). Reconceptualizing individual differences in self-enhancement bias: An interpersonal approach. *Psychological Review, 111,* 94–110.

Lacey, J. I. (1959). Psychophysiological approaches to the evaluation of psychotherapeutic process and outcome. In E. A. Rubinstein & M. B. Parloff (Eds.), *Research in psychotherapy.* Washington, DC: American Psychological Association.

Lacey, J. I. (1967). Somatic response patterning and stress: Some revisions of activation theory. In M. H. Appley & R. Trumbull (Eds.), *Psychological stress: Issues in research.* New York: Appleton-Century-Crofts.

Lacey, J. I., & Lacey, B. C. (1958). The relationship of resting autonomic activity to motor impulsivity. In H. C. Solomon, S. Cobb, & W. Pennfield (Eds.), *The brain and human behavior* (Vol. 36). Baltimore, MD: Williams & Wilkins.

Lacey, J. I., & Lacey, B. C. (1970). Some autonomic-central nervous system interrelationships. In P. Black (Ed.), *Physiological correlates of emotion.* New York: Academic Press.

Laird, J. D. (1974). Self-attribution of emotion: The effects of expressive behavior on the quality of emotional experience. *Journal of Personality and Social Psychology, 29,* 475–486.

Laird, J. D. (1984). The real role of facial response in the experience of emotion: A reply to Tourangeau and Ellsworth, and others. *Journal of Personality and Social Psychology, 47,* 909–917.

Laird, J. D., Cuniff, M., Sheehan, K., & Shulman, D., et al. (1989). Emotion specific effects of facial expressions on memory for life events. *Journal of Social Behavior and Personality, 4,* 87–98.

Laird, J. D., Wagener, J., Halal, M., & Szegda, M. (1982). Remembering what you feel: Effects of emotion on memory. *Journal of Personality and Social Psychology, 42,* 646–657.

Lambert, A. J., Khan, S. R., Lickel, B. A., & Fricke, K. (1997). Mood and the correction of positive versus negative stereotypes. *Journal of Personality and Social Psychology, 72,* 1002–1016.

Lambird, K. H., & Mann, T. (2006). When do ego threats lead to self-regulation failure? Negative consequences of defensive high self-esteem. *Personality and Social Psychology Bulletin, 32,* 1177–1187.

Landau, M. J., Solomon, S., Greenberg, J., Cohen, F., Pyszczynski, T., Arndt, J., Miller, C. H., Ogilvie, D. M., & Cook, A. (2004). Deliver us from evil: The effects of mortality salience and reminders of 9/11 on support for President George W. Bush. *Personality and Social Psychology Bulletin, 30,* 1136–1150.

Landman, J. (1988). Regret and elation following action and inaction: Affective responses to positive versus negative outcomes. *Personality and Social Psychology Bulletin, 13,* 524–536.

Lange, C. G. (1922). *The emotions.* Baltimore, MD: Williams & Wilkins. (Originally published 1885.)

Langer, E. J., Blank, A., & Chanowitz, B. (1978). The mindlessness of ostensibly thoughtful action: The role of "placebic" information in interpersonal interaction. *Journal of Personality and Social Psychology, 36,* 635–642.

Langer, E. J., Taylor, S. E., Fiske, S. T., & Chanowitz, B. (1976). Stigma, staring, and discomfort: A novel stimulus hypothesis. *Journal of Experimental Social Psychology, 12,* 451–463.

Lanzetta, J. T., Cartwright-Smith, J., & Kleck, R. E. (1976). Effects of nonverbal dissimilation on emotional experience and autonomic arousal. *Journal of Personality and Social Psychology, 33,* 354–370.

LaPiere, R. T. (1934). Attitudes versus actions. *Social Forces, 13,* 230–237.

Larsen, J. T., McGraw A. P., & Cacioppo, J. T. (2001). Can people feel happy and sad at the same time? *Journal of Personality and Social Psychology, 81,* 684–696.

Larsen, J. T., Norris, C., & Cacioppo, J. T. (2003). Effects of positive and negative affect on electromyographic activity over zygomaticus major and corrugator supercilli. *Psychophysiology, 40,* 776–785.

Lassiter, G. D. (1988). Behavior perception, affect, and memory. *Social Cognition, 6,* 150–176.

Lassiter, G. D. (2002). Illusory causation in the courtroom. *Current Directions in Psychological Science, 11,* 204–208.

Lassiter, G. D., Munhall, P. J., Berger, I. P., Weiland, P. E., Handley, I. M., & Geers, A. L. (2005). Attributional complexity and the camera perspective bias in videotaped confessions. *Basic and Applied Social Psychology, 27(1),* 27–35.

Lassiter, G. D., & Stone, J. I. (1984). Affective consequences of variation in behavior perception: When liking is in the level of analysis. *Personality and Social Psychology Bulletin, 10,* 253–259.

Lassiter, G. D., Stone, J. I., & Rogers, S. L. (1988). Memorial consequences of variation in behavior perception. *Journal of Experimental Social Psychology, 24,* 222–239.

Lasswell, H. D. (1948). The structure and function of communication in society. In L. Byron (Ed.), *Communication of ideas.* New York: Harper.

Latané, B., & Bourgeois, M. J. (2001). Dynamic social impact and the consolidation, clustering, correlation, and continuing diversity of culture. In M. A. Hogg & R. S. Tindale (Eds.), *Blackwell handbook of social psychology: Group processes* (pp. 235–258). Malden, MA: Blackwell.

Lazarus, R. S. (1966). *Psychological stress and the coping process.* New York: McGraw-Hill.

Lazarus, R. S. (1982). Thoughts on the relations between emotion and cognition. *American Psychologist, 37,* 1019–1024.

Lazarus, R. S. (1984). On the primacy of cognition. *American Psychologist, 39,* 124–129.

Lazarus, R. S. (2000). Toward better research on stress and coping. *American Psychologist, 55,* 665–673.

Lazarus, R. S., & Smith, C. A. (1988). Knowledge and appraisal in the cognition–emotion relationship. *Cognition and Emotion, 2,* 281–300.

Leach, C. W., Ellemers, N., & Barreto, M. (2007). Group virtue: The importance of morality (vs. competence and sociability) in the positive evaluation of in-groups. *Journal of Personality and Social Psychology, 93(2),* 234–249.

Leary, M. R. (1990). Responses to social exclusion: Social anxiety, jealousy, loneliness, depression, and low self-esteem. *Journal of Social and Clinical Psychology, 9,* 221–229.

Leary, M. R., & Baumeister, R. F. (2000). The nature and function of self-esteem: Sociometer theory. In M. P. Zanna (Ed.), *Advances in experimental social psychology* (Vol. 32, pp. 1–62). San Diego, CA: Academic Press.

Leary, M. R., Tambor, E. S., Terdal, S. K., & Downs, D. L. (1995). Self-esteem as an interpersonal monitor: The sociometer hypothesis. *Journal of Personality and Social Psychology, 68,* 518–530.

Leddo, J., Abelson, R. P., & Gross, P. H. (1984). Conjunctive explanations: When two reasons are better than one. *Journal of Personality and Social Psychology, 47,* 933–943.

Ledgerwood, A., Trope, Y., & Chaiken, S. (2010). Flexibility now, consistency later: Psychological distance and construal shape evaluative responding. *Journal of Personality and Social Psychology, 99(1),* 32-51.

Lee, A. Y., & Aaker, J. L. (2004). Bringing the frame into focus: The influence of regulatory fit on processing fluency and persuasion. *Journal of Personality and Social Psychology, 86,* 205–218.

Lee, A. Y., Aaker, J. L., & Gardner, W. L. (2000). The pleasures and pain of distinct self-construals: The role of interdependence in regulatory focus. *Journal of Personality and Social Psychology, 78,* 1122–1134.

Lehman, D. R., Lempert, R. O., & Nisbett, R. E. (1988). The effects of graduate training on reasoning: Formal discipline and thinking about everyday-life events. *American Psychologist, 43,* 431–442.

Leibenluft, E., Gobbini, M. I., Harrison, T., & Haxby, J. V. (2004). Mothers' neural activation in response to pictures of their children and other children. *Biological Psychiatry, 56,* 225–232.

Leonardelli, G. J., Lakin, J. L., & Arkin, R. M. (2007). A regulatory focus model of self-evaluation. *Journal of Experimental Social Psychology, 43(6),* 1002–1009.

Lepper, M. R., Greene, D., & Nisbett, R. E. (1973). Undermining children's intrinsic interest with extrinsic rewards: A test of the "overjustification" hypothesis. *Journal of Personality and Social Psychology, 28,* 129–137.

Lerner, J. S., & Gonzalez, R. M. (2005). Forecasting one's future based on fleeting subjective experiences. *Personality and Social Psychology Bulletin, 31,* 454–466.

Lerner, J. S., & Keltner, D. (2001). Fear, anger, and risk. *Journal of Personality and Social Psychology, 81,* 146–159.

Lerner, J. S., & Tiedens, L. Z. (2006). Portrait of the angry decision maker: How appraisal tendencies shape anger's influence on cognition. *Journal of Behavioral Decision Making, 19,* 115–137.

Leslie, A. M. (1994). Pretending and believing: Issues in the theory of mind. *Cognition, 50,* 211–238.

Leung, K., & Bond, M. H. (2004). Social axioms: A model for social beliefs in multicultural perspective. In M. P. Zanna (Ed.), *Advances in experimental social psychology* (Vol. 35, pp. 119–197). San Diego, CA: Academic Press.

Leventhal, H. (1982). The integration of emotion and cognition: A view from the perceptual-motor theory of emotion. In M. S. Clark & S. T. Fiske (Eds.), *Affect and cognition: The 17th Annual Carnegie Symposium on Cognition* (pp. 121–156). Hillsdale, NJ: Erlbaum.

Leventhal, H. (1984). A perceptual-motor theory of emotion. In L. Berkowitz (Ed.), *Advances in experimental social psychology* (Vol. 17, pp. 118–182). Orlando, FL: Academic Press.

Leventhal, H., & Scherer, K. (1987). The relationship of emotion to cognition: A functional approach to a semantic controversy. *Cognition and Emotion, 1,* 3–28.

Levesque, C., & Pelletier, L. G. (2003). On the investigation of primed and chronic autonomous and heteronomous motivational orientations. *Personality and Social Psychology Bulletin, 29,* 1570–1584.

Levin, D. (2000). Race as a visual feature: Using visual search and perceptual discrimination tasks to understand face categories and the cross-race recognition deficit. *Journal of Experimental Psychology: General, 129,* 559–574.

Levin, I. P., & Gaeth, G. J. (1988). How consumers are affected by the framing of attribute information before and after consuming the product. *Journal of Consumer Research, 15,* 374–378.

Levin, I. P., Schneider, S. L., & Gaeth, G. J. (1998). All frames are not created equal: A typology and critical analysis of framing effects. *Organizational Behavior and Human Decision Processes, 76,* 149–188.

Levin, I. P., Schnittjer, S. K., & Thee, S. L. (1988). Information framing effects in social and personal decisions. *Journal of Experimental Social Psychology, 24,* 520–529.

Levin, S., Federico, C. M., Sidanius, J., & Rabinowitz, J. L. (2002). Social dominance orientation and inter-group bias: The legitimation of favoritism for high-status groups. *Personality and Social Psychology Bulletin, 28,* 144–157.

Levine, J. M., & Murphy, G. (1943). The learning and forgetting of controversial material. *Journal of Abnormal and Social Psychology, 38,* 507–517.

Levinger, G., & Breedlove, J. (1966). Interpersonal attraction and agreement. *Journal of Personality and Social Psychology, 3,* 367–372.

Levy, B., Ashman, O., & Dror, I. (1999–2000). To be or not to be: The effects of aging stereotypes on the will to live. *Omega: Journal of Death and Dying, 40,* 409–420.

Levy, B. R., & Banaji, M. R. (2002). Implicit ageism. In T. D. Nelson (Ed.), *Ageism: Stereotyping and prejudice against older persons* (pp. 49–75). Cambridge, MA: MIT Press.

Levy, B. R., Hausdorf, J. M., Hencke, R., & Wei, J. Y. (2000). Reducing cardiovascular stress with positive self-stereotypes of aging. *Journals of Gerontology: Series B: Psychological Sciences and Social Issues, 55B,* 205–213.

Levy, B. R., & Langer, E. J. (1994). Aging free from negative stereotypes: Successful memory in China and among the American deaf. *Journal of Personality and Social Psychology, 66,* 989–997.

Levy, B. R., Slade, M. D., Kunkel, S. R., & Kasl, S. V. (2002). Longevity increased by positive self-perceptions of aging. *Journal of Personality and Social Psychology, 83,* 261–270.

Levy, S. R., Plaks, J. E., Hong, Y.-y., Chiu, C.-y., & Dweck, C. S. (2001). Static versus dynamic theories and the perception of groups: Different routes to different destinations. *Personality and Social Psychology Review, 5,* 156–168.

Lewicki, P. (1985). Nonconscious biasing effects of single instances on subsequent judgments. *Journal of Personality and Social Psychology, 48,* 563–574.

Lewicki, P., Czyzewska, M., & Hoffman, H. (1987). Unconscious acquisition of complex procedural knowledge. *Journal of Experimental Psychology: Learning, Memory, and Cognition, 13,* 523–530.

Lewin, K. (1951). *Field theory in social psychology.* New York: Harper.

Lewontin, R. (1972). The apportionment of human diversity. *Evolutionary Biology, 6,* 381–398.

Leyens, J.-Ph., Cortes, B., Demoulin, S., Dovidio, J. F., Fiske, S. T., Gaunt, R., et al. (2003). Emotional prejudice, essentialism, and nationalism: The 2002 Tajfel Lecture. *European Journal of Social Psychology, 33,* 703–717.

Leyens, J.-Ph., Désert, M., Croizet, J. C., & Darcis, C. (2000). Stereotype threat: Are lower status and history of stigmatization preconditions of stereotype threat? *Personality and Social Psychology Bulletin, 26,* 1189–1199.

Libby, L. K., Eibach, R. P., & Gilovich, T. (2005). Here's looking at me: The effect of memory perspective on assessments of personal change. *Journal of Personality and Social Psychology, 88,* 50–62.

Liberman, A., & Chaiken, S. (1992). Defensive processing of personally relevant health messages. *Personality and Social Psychology Bulletin, 18,* 669–679.

Lieberman, M. D. (2007). Social cognitive neuroscience: A review of core processes. *Annual Review of Psychology, 58,* 259–289.

Lieberman, M. D. (2010). Social cognitive neuroscience. In S. T. Fiske, D. T. Gilbert, & G. Lindzey (Eds.), *Handbook of social psychology* (5th edn, Vol. 1, pp. 143–193). Hoboken, NJ: Wiley.

Lieberman, M. D., Gaunt, R., Gilbert, D. T., & Trope, Y. (2002). Reflexion and reflection: A social cognitive neuroscience approach to attributional inference. In M. P. Zanna (Ed.), *Advances in experimental social psychology* (Vol. 34, pp. 199–249). San Diego, CA: Academic Press.

Lieberman, M. D., Hariri, A., Jarcho, J. M., Eisenberger, N. I., & Bookheimer, S. Y. (2005). An fMRI investi-gation of race-related amygdala activity in African-American and Caucasian-American individuals. *Nature Neuroscience, 8,* 720–722.

Lieberman, M. D., Jarcho, J. M., & Satpute, A. B. (2004). Evidence-based and intuition-based self-knowledge: An fMRI study. *Journal of Personality and Social Psychology, 87,* 421–435.

Lieberman, M. D., Ochsner, K. N., Gilbert, D. T., & Schacter, D. L. (2001). Do amnesiacs exhibit cognitive disso-nance reduction? The role of explicit memory and attention in attitude change. *Psychological Science, 12,* 135–140.

Lin, M. H., Kwan, V. S. Y., Cheung, A., & Fiske, S. T. (2005). Stereotype content model explains prejudice for an envied outgroup: Scale of anti-Asian American stereotypes. *Personality and Social Psychology Bulletin, 31,* 34–47.

Lingle, J. H., Altom, M. W., & Medin, D. L. (1984). Of cabbages and kings: Assessing the extendibility of natural object concept models to social things. In R. S. Wyer Jr. & T. K. Srull (Eds.), *Handbook of social cognition* (Vol. 1, pp. 71–117). Hillsdale, NJ: Erlbaum.

Lingle, J. H., Geva, N., Ostrom, T. M., Leippe, M. R., & Baumgardner, M. H. (1979). Thematic effects of person judgments on impression organization. *Journal of Personality and Social Psychology, 37,* 674–687.

Lingle, J. H., & Ostrom, T. M. (1979). Retrieval selectivity in memory-based impression judgments. *Journal of Personality and Social Psychology, 37,* 180–194.

Linville, P. W. (1982a). Affective consequences of complexity regarding the self and others. In M. S. Clark & S. T. Fiske (Eds.), *Affect and cognition: The 17th Annual Carnegie Symposium on Cognition* (pp. 79–109). Hillsdale, NJ: Erlbaum.

Linville, P. W. (1982b). The complexity-extremity effect and age-based stereotyping. *Journal of Personality and Social Psychology, 42,* 193–211.

Linville, P. W. (1985). Self-complexity and affective extremity: Don't put all your eggs in one cognitive basket. *Social Cognition, 3,* 94–120.

Linville, P. W., Fischer, G. W., & Fischhoff, B. (1993). AIDS risk perceptions and decision biases. In J. B. Pryor & G. D. Reeder (Eds.), *The social psychology of HIV infection* (pp. 5–38). Hillsdale, NJ: Erlbaum.

Linville, P. W., Fischer, G. W., & Salovey, P. (1989). Perceived distributions of the characteristics of ingroup and outgroup members: Empirical evidence and a computer simulation. *Journal of Personality and Social Psychology, 57,* 165–188.

Linville, P. W., Fischer, G. W., & Yoon, C. (1996). Perceived covariation among the features of ingroup and outgroup members: The outgroup covariation effect. *Journal of Personality and Social Psychology, 70,* 421–436.

Linville, P. W., & Jones, E. E. (1980). Polarized appraisals of outgroup members. *Journal of Personality and Social Psychology, 38,* 689–703.

Linville, P. W., Salovey, P., & Fischer, G. W. (1986). Stereotyping and perceived distributions of social characteristics: An application to ingroup-outgroup perception. In J. F. Dovidio & S. L. Gaertner (Eds.), *Prejudice, discrimination, and racism* (pp. 165–208). Orlando, FL: Academic Press.

Lippa, R. (1976). Expressive control and the leakage of dispositional introversion-extraversion during role-playing teaching. *Journal of Personality, 44,* 541–559.

Liu, J., Harris, A., & Kanwisher, N. (2002). Stages of processing in face perception: An MEG study. *Nature Neuroscience, 5,* 910–916.

Livingston, R. W., & Brewer, M. B. (2002). What are we really priming? Cue-based versus category-based processing of facial stimuli. *Journal of Personality and Social Psychology, 82,* 5–18.

Locher, P., Unger, R., Sociedade, P., & Wahl, J. (1993). At first glance: Accessibility of the physical attractiveness stereotype. *Sex Roles, 28,* 729–743.

Locke, J. (1979). *Essay concerning human understanding.* New York: Oxford University Press. (Originally published 1690.)

Loewenstein, G. (1996). Out of control: Visceral influences on behavior. *Organizational Behavior and Human Decision Processes, 65,* 272–292.

Loftus, E. F. (2004). Memories of things unseen. *Current Directions in Psychological Science, 13,* 145–147.

Loftus, E. F., & Davis, D. (2006). Recovered memories. *Annual Review of Clinical Psychology, 2,* 469–498.

Loken, B. (1984). Attitude processing strategies. *Journal of Experimental Social Psychology, 20,* 272–296.

Lombardi, W. J., Higgins, E. T., & Bargh, J. A. (1987). The role of consciousness in priming effects on categorization: Assimilation versus contrast as a function of awareness of the priming task. *Personality and Social Psychology Bulletin, 13,* 411–429.

Lopes, L. L. (1982). *Towards a procedural theory of judgment.* (Tech. Rep. No. 17, pp. 1–49). Madison, WI: Information Processing Program, University of Wisconsin.

Lord, C. G. (1982). Predicting behavioral consistency from an individual's perception of situational similarities. *Journal of Personality and Social Psychology, 42,* 1076–1088.

Lord, C. G., Lepper, M. R., & Mackie, D. M. (1984). Attitude prototypes as determinants of attitude-behavior consistency. *Journal of Personality and Social Psychology, 46,* 1254–1266.

Lord, C. G., & Saenz, D. S. (1985). Memory deficits and memory surfeits: Differential cognitive consequences of tokenism for tokens and observers. *Journal of Personality and Social Psychology, 49,* 918–926.

Lord, C. G., Saenz, D. S., & Godfrey, D. K. (1987). Effects of perceived scrutiny on participant memory for social interactions. *Journal of Experimental Social Psychology, 23,* 498–517.

Losch, M. E., & Cacioppo, J. T. (1990). Cognitive dissonance may enhance sympathetic tonus, but attitudes are changed to reduce negative affect rather than arousal. *Journal of Experimental Social Psychology, 26,* 289–304.

Loughnan, S., & Haslam, N. (2007). Animals and androids: Implicit associations between social categories and nonhumans. *Psychological Science, 18,* 116–121.

Lowe, C. A., & Kassin, S. M. (1980). A perceptual view of attribution: Theoretical and methodological implications. *Personality and Social Psychology, 6,* 532–542.

Lowery, B. S., Hardin, C. D., & Sinclair, S. (2001). Social influence effects on automatic racial prejudice. *Journal of Personality and Social Psychology, 81,* 842–855.

Lowery, B. S., Knowles, E. D., & Unzueta, M. M. (2007). Framing inequity safely: The motivated denial of White privilege. *Personality and Social Psychology Bulletin, 33*(9) 1237–1250.

Lowery, B. S., Unzueta, M. M., Knowles, E. D., & Goff, P. A. (2006). Concern for the ingroup and opposition to affirmative action. *Journal of Personality and Social Psychology, 90,* 961–974.

Luhtanen, R., & Crocker, J. (1992). A collective self-esteem scale: Self-evaluation of one's social identity. *Personality and Social Psychology Bulletin, 18(3),* 302–318.

Luhtanen, R. K., & Crocker, J. (2005). Alcohol use in college students: Effects of level of self-esteem, narcissism, and contingencies of self-worth. *Psychology of Addictive Behaviors, 1,* 99–103.

Lun, J., Sinclair, S., Whitchurch, E. R., & Glenn, C. (2007). (Why) do I think what you think? Epistemic social tuning and implicit prejudice. *Journal of Personality and Social Psychology, 93(6),* 957–972.

Lydon, J. E., & Zanna, M. P. (1990). Commitment in the face of adversity: A value-affirmation approach. *Journal of Personality and Social Psychology, 58,* 1040–1047.

Lydon, J., Zanna, M. P., & Ross, M. (1988). Bolstering attitudes by autobiographical recall: Attitude persistence and selective memory. *Personality and Social Psychology Bulletin, 14,* 78–86.

Lynn, M., Shavitt, S., & Ostrom, T. M. (1985). Effects of pictures on the organization and recall of social information. *Journal of Personality and Social Psychology, 49,* 1160–1168.

Lyubomirsky, S., King, L., & Diener, E. (2005). The benefits of frequent positive affect: Does happiness lead to success? *Psychological Bulletin, 131,* 803–855.

Lyubomirsky, S., Sheldon, K. M., & Schkade, D. (2005). Pursuing happiness: The architecture of sustainable change. *Review of General Psychology, 9,* 111–131.

Mackie, D. M. (1986). Social identification effects in group polarization. *Journal of Personality and Social Psychology, 50,* 720–728.

Mackie, D. M. (1987). Systematic and nonsystematic processing of majority and minority persuasive communications. *Journal of Personality and Social Psychology, 53,* 41–52.

Mackie, D. M., & Cooper, J. (1984). Attitude polarization: Effects of group membership. *Journal of Personality and Social Psychology, 46,* 575–585.

Mackie, D. M., Devos, T., & Smith, E. R. (2000). Intergroup emotions: Explaining offensive action tendencies in an intergroup context. *Journal of Personality and Social Psychology, 79,* 602–616.

Mackie, D. M., & Gastardo-Conaco, M. C. (1988). The impact of importance accorded an issue on attitude inferences. *Journal of Experimental Social Psychology, 24,* 543–570.

Mackie, D. M., Hamilton, D. L., Schroth, H. A., Carlisle, C. J., Gersho, B. F., Meneses, L. M., Nedler, B. F., & Reichel, L. D. (1989). The effects of induced mood on illusory correlations. *Journal of Experimental Social Psychology, 25,* 524–544.

Mackie, D. M., & Smith, E. R. (1998). Intergroup relations: Insights from a theoretically integrative approach. *Psychological Review, 105,* 499–529.

Mackie, D. M., & Worth, L. T. (1989). Cognitive deficits and the mediation of positive affect in persuasion. *Journal of Personality and Social Psychology, 57,* 27–40.

MacLeod, C., & Campbell, L. (1992). Memory accessibility and probability judgment: An experimental evaluation of the availability heuristic. *Journal of Personality and Social Psychology, 63,* 890–902.

MacLeod, M. D., & Macrae, C. N. (2001). Gone but not forgotten: The transient nature of retrieval-induced forgetting. *Psychological Science, 12,* 148–152.

Macrae, C. N., & Bodenhausen, G. V. (2000). Social cognition: Thinking categorically about others. *Annual Review of Psychology, 51,* 93–120.

Macrae, C. N., & Bodenhausen, G. V. (2001). Social cognition: Categorical person perception. *British Journal of Psychology, 92,* 239–255.

Macrae, C. N., Bodenhausen, G. V., & Milne, A. B. (1998). Saying no to unwanted thoughts: Self-focus and the regulation of mental life. *Journal of Personality and Social Psychology, 74,* 578–589.

Macrae, C. N., Bodenhausen, G. V., Milne, A. B., & Ford, R. L. (1997). On the regulation of recollection: The intentional forgetting of stereotypical memories. *Journal of Personality and Social Psychology, 72,* 709–719.

Macrae, C. N., Bodenhausen, G. V., Milne, A. B., & Jetten, J. (1994). Out of mind but back in sight: Stereotypes on the rebound. *Journal of Personality and Social Psychology, 67,* 808–817.

Macrae, C. N., Bodenhausen, G. V., Milne, A. B., Thorn, T. M. J., & Castelli, L. (1997). On the activation of social stereotypes: The moderating role of processing objectives. *Journal of Experimental Social Psychology, 33,* 471–489.

Macrae, C. N., Bodenhausen, G. V., Schloerscheidt, A. M., & Milne, A. B. (1999). Tales of the unexpected: Executive function and person perception. *Journal of Personality and Social Psychology, 76,* 200–213.

Macrae, C. N., Hewstone, M., & Griffiths, R. J. (1993). Processing load and memory for stereotype-based information. *European Journal of Social Psychology, 23,* 77–87.

Macrae, C. N., Hood, B. M., Milne, A. B., Rowe, A. C., & Mason, M. F. (2002). Are you looking at me? Eye gaze and person perception. *Psychological Science, 13,* 460–464.

Macrae, C. N., & Lewis, H. L. (2002). Do I know you? Processing orientation and face recognition. *Psychological Science, 13,* 194–196.

Macrae, C. N., & Miles, L. K. (2012). Revisiting the sovereignty of social cognition: Finally some action. In S. T. Fiske & C. N. Macrae (Eds.), *Sage handbook of social cognition* (pp. 1–11). Thousand Oaks, CA: Sage.

Macrae, C. N., Milne, A. B., & Bodenhausen, G. V. (1994). Stereotypes as energy-saving devices: A peek inside the cognitive toolbox. *Journal of Personality and Social Psychology, 66,* 37–47.

Macrae, C. N., Moran, J. M., Heatherton, T. F., Banfield, J. F., & Kelley, W. M. (2004). Medial prefrontal activity predicts memory for self. *Cerebral Cortex, 14,* 647–654.

Macrae, C. N., Quinn, K. A., Mason, M. F., & Quadflieg, S. (2005). Understanding others: The face and person construal. *Journal of Personality and Social Psychology, 89,* 686–695.

Macrae, C. N., Schloerscheidt, A. M., Bodenhausen, G. V., & Milne, A. B. (2002). Creating memory illusions: Expectancy-based processing and the generation of false memories. *Memory, 10,* 63–80.

Maddox, K. B. (2004). Perspectives on racial phenotypicality bias. *Personality and Social Psychology Review, 8,* 383–401.

Maddox, K. B., & Chase, S. G. (2004). Manipulating subcategory salience: Exploring the link between skin tone and social perception of Blacks. *European Journal of Social Psychology, 34,* 533–546.

Maddox, K. B., & Gray, S. A. (2002). Cognitive representations of Black Americans: Re-exploring the role of skin tone. *Personality and Social Psychology Bulletin, 28,* 250–259.

Madon, S., Smith, A., Jussim, L., Russel, D. W., Eccles, J., Palumbo, P., et al. (2001). Am I as you see me or do you see me as I am? Self-fulfilling prophecies and self-verification. *Personality and Social Psychology Bulletin, 27,* 1214–1224.

Maguire, E. A., Gadian, D. G., Johnsrude, I. S., Good, C. D., Ashburner, J., Frackowiak, R. S. J., & Frith, C. D. (2000). Navigation-related structural change in the hippocampi of taxi drivers. *Proceedings of the National Academy of Sciences, 97,* 4398–4403.

Maio, G. R., & Olson, J. M. (1998). Values as truisms: Evidence and implications. *Journal of Personality and Social Psychology, 74,* 294–311.

Maitner, A. T., Mackie, D. M., & Smith, E. R. (2006). Evidence for the regulatory function of intergroup emotion: Emotional consequences of implemented or impeded intergroup action tendencies. *Journal of Experimental Social Psychology, 42,* 720–728.

Major, B., Cozzarelli, C., Testa, M., & McFarlin, D. B. (1988). Self-verification versus expectancy confirmation in social interaction: The impact of self-focus. *Personality and Social Psychology Bulletin, 14,* 346–359.

Major, B., Gramzow, R. H., McCoy, S. K., Levin, S., Schmader, T., & Sidanius, J. (2002). Perceiving personal discrimination: The role of group status and legitimizing ideology. *Journal of Personality and Social Psychology, 82,* 269–282.

Major, B., & O'Brien, L. T. (2005). The social psychology of stigma. *Annual Review of Psychology, 56,* 393–421.

Major, B., Quinton, W. J., & McCoy, S. K. (2002). Antecedents and consequences of attributions to discrimination: Theoretical and empirical advances. In M. P. Zanna (Ed.), *Advances in experimental social psychology* (Vol. 34, pp. 251–330). New York: Academic Press.

Major, B., Spencer, S., Schmader, T., Wolfe, C. T., & Crocker, J. (1998). Coping with negative stereotypes about intellectual performance: The role of psychological disengagement. *Personality and Social Psychology Bulletin, 24,* 34–50.

Major, B., Testa, M., & Blysma, W. H. (1991). Responses to upward and downward social comparisons: The impact of esteem-relevance and perceived control. In J. Suls & T. A. Wills (Eds.), *Social comparison: Contemporary theory and research* (pp. 237–260). Hillsdale, NJ: Erlbaum.

Malle, B. F. (2006). The actor–observer asymmetry in attribution: A (surprising) meta-analysis. *Psychological Bulletin, 132,* 895–919.

Malle, B. F., & Knobe, J. (1997). Which behaviors do people explain? A basic actor–observer asymmetry. *Journal of Personality and Social Psychology, 72,* 288–304.

Malle, B. F., Knobe, J., O'Laughlin, M. J., Pearce, G. E., & Nelson, S. E. (2000). Conceptual structure and social functions of behavior explanations: Beyond person–situation attributions. *Journal of Personality and Social Psychology, 79,* 309–326.

Mallon, E. B., Pratt, S. C., & Franks, N. R. (2001). Individual and collective decision-making during nest site selection by an ant, *Leptothorax albipennis. Behavioral Ecology and Sociobiology, 50,* 352–359.

Malpass, R. S. (1969). Effects of attitude on learning and memory: The influence of instruction-induced sets. *Journal of Experimental Social Psychology, 5,* 441–453.

Malpass, R. S., & Kravitz, J. (1969). Recognition for faces of own and other race. *Journal of Personality and Social Psychology, 13,* 330–334.

Mandler, G. (1975). *Mind and emotion.* New York: Wiley.

Mandler, G., & Nakamura, Y. (1987). Aspects of consciousness. *Personality and Social Psychology Bulletin, 13,* 299–313.

Mandler, G., Nakamura, Y., & Van Zandt, B. J. S. (1987). Nonspecific effects of exposure on stimuli that cannot be recognized. *Journal of Experimental Psychology: Learning, Memory, and Cognition, 13,* 646–648.

Manis, M. (1977). Cognitive social psychology. *Personality and Social Psychology Bulletin, 3,* 550–566.

Manis, M., Dovalina, I., Avis, N. E., & Cardoze, S. (1980). Base rates can affect individual predictions. *Journal of Personality and Social Psychology, 38,* 231–248.

Manis, M., Shedler, J., Jonides, J., & Nelson, T. E. (1993). Availability heuristic in judgments of set size and frequency of occurrence. *Journal of Personality and Social Psychology, 65,* 448–457.

Manucia, G. K., Baumann, D. J., & Cialdini, R. B. (1984). Mood influences on helping: Direct effects or side effects? *Journal of Personality and Social Psychology, 46,* 357–364.

Marcel, A. J. (1983a). Conscious and unconscious perception: An approach to the relations between phenomenal experience and perceptual processes. *Cognitive Psychology, 15,* 238–300.

Marcel, A. J. (1983b). Conscious and unconscious perception: Experiments on visual masking and word recognition. *Cognitive Psychology, 15,* 197–237.

March, J. G., & Simon, G. A. (1958). *Organizations.* New York: Wiley.

Marchand, M. A. G., & Vonk, R. (2005). The process of becoming suspicious of ulterior motives. *Social Cognition, 23,* 242–256.

Marcus, G. E., & Mackuen, M. B. (1999). Anxiety, enthusiasm, and the vote: The emotional underpinnings of learning and involvement during presidential campaigns. *American Political Science Review, 87,* 672–685.

Marks, J. (1995). *Human biodiversity: Genes, races, and history.* New York: Aldine de Gruyter.

Marks, G., & Miller, N. (1982). Target attractiveness as a mediator of assumed attitude similarity. *Personality and Social Psychology Bulletin, 8,* 728–735.

Markus, H. R. (1977). Self-schemata and processing information about the self. *Journal of Personality and Social Psychology, 35,* 63–78.

Markus, H. R., & Kitayama, S. (1991). Culture and the self: Implications for cognition, emotion, and motivation. *Psychological Review, 98,* 224–253.

Markus, H. R., & Kunda, Z. (1986). Stability and malleability of the self concept. *Journal of Personality and Social Psychology, 51,* 858–866.

Markus, H. R., & Nurius, P. (1986). Possible selves. *American Psychologist, 41,* 954–969.

Markus, H. R., & Wurf, E. (1987). The dynamic self-concept: A social psychological perspective. *Annual Review of Psychology, 38,* 299–337.

Marshall, G. D., & Zimbardo, P. G. (1979). Affective consequences of inadequately explained physiological arousal. *Journal of Personality and Social Psychology, 37,* 970–988.

Martens, A., Johns, M., Greenberg, J., & Schimel, J. (2006). Combating stereotype threat: The effect of self-affirmation on women's intellectual performance. *Journal of Experimental Social Psychology, 42,* 236–243.

Martin, D., & Macrae, C. N. (2007). A boy primed Sue: Feature-based processing and person construal. *European Journal of Social Psychology, 37,* 793–805.

Martin, L. L. (1986). Set/reset: Use and disuse of concepts in impression formation. *Journal of Personality and Social Psychology, 51,* 493–504.

Martin, L. L., & Tesser, A. (1989). Toward a motivational and structural theory of ruminative thought. In J. S. Uleman & J. A. Bargh (Eds.), *Unintended thought* (pp. 306–326). New York: Guilford Press.

Maslach, C. (1979). Negative emotional biasing of unexplained arousal. *Journal of Personality and Social Psychology, 37,* 953–969.

Mason, M. F., Hood, B. M., & Macrae, C. N. (2004). Look into my eyes: Gaze direction and person memory. *Memory, 12,* 637–643.

Mason, M. F., & Macrae, C. N. (2004). Categorizing and individuating others: The neural substrates of person perception. *Journal of Cognitive Neuroscience, 16,* 1785–1795.

Mason, M. F., Norton, M. I., Van, J. D., Wegner, D. M., Grafton, S. T., & Macrae, C. N. (2007). Wandering minds: The default network and stimulus independent thought. *Science, 315,* 393–395.

Mason, M. F., Tatkow, E. P., & Macrae, C. N. (2005). The look of love: Gaze shifts and person perception. *Psychological Science, 16,* 236–239.

Mason, W. A., Conrey, F. R., & Smith, E. R. (2007). Situating social influence processes: Dynamic, multi-directional flows of influence within social networks. *Personality and Social Psychology Review, 11(3),* 279–300.

Massad, C. M., Hubbard, M., & Newtson, D. (1979). Selective perception of events. *Journal of Experimental Social Psychology, 15,* 513–532.

Massey, D. S., & Denton, N. A. (1993). *American apartheid: Segregation and the making of the underclass.* Cambridge, MA: Harvard University Press.

Massey, D. S., Rothwell, J., & Domina, T. (2009). The changing bases of segregation in the United State. *The ANNALS of the American Academy of Political and Social Science, 626,* 74–90.

Masters, J. C., & Furman, W. (1976). Effects of affective states on noncontingent outcome expectancies and beliefs in internal or external control. *Developmental Psychology, 12,* 481–482.

Masuda, T., & Nisbett, R. E. (2001). Attending holistically vs. analytically: Comparing the context sensitivity of Japanese and Americans. *Journal of Personality and Social Psychology, 81,* 922–934.

Matlin, M., & Stang, D. J. (1978). *The Pollyanna principle.* Cambridge, MA: Schenkman.

Matsumoto, D. (1987). The role of facial response in the experience of emotion: More methodological problems and a meta-analysis. *Journal of Personality and Social Psychology, 52,* 769–774.

Mayer, J. D. (1986). How mood influences cognition. In N. E. Sharkey (Ed.), *Advances in cognitive science* (pp. 290–314). Chichester: Ellis Horwood.

Mayer, J. D., & Bower, G. H. (1986). Learning and memory for personality prototypes. *Journal of Personality and Social Psychology, 51,* 473–492.

Mayer, J. D., & Bremer, D. (1985). Assessing mood with affect-sensitive tasks. *Journal of Personality Assessment, 49,* 95–99.

Mayer, J. D., & Gaschke, Y. N. (1988). The experience and meta-experience of mood. *Journal of Personality and Social Psychology, 55,* 102–111.

Mayer, J. D., Mamberg, M. H., & Volanth, A. J. (1988). Cognitive domains of the mood system. *Journal of Personality, 56,* 453–486.

Mayer, J. D., McCormick, L. J., & Strong, S. E. (1995). Mood-congruent memory and natural mood: New evidence. *Personality and Social Psychology Bulletin, 21,* 736–746.

Mayer, J. D., & Salovey, P. (1988). Personality moderates the interaction of mood and cognition. In K. Fiedler & J. Forgas (Eds.), *Affect, cognition, and social behavior* (pp. 87–99). Toronto, Canada: Hogrefe.

Mays, V. M., Cochran, S. D., & Barnes, N. W. (2007). Race, race-based discrimination, and health outcomes among African Americans. *Annual Review of Psychology, 58,* 201–225.

McArthur, L. Z. (1972). The how and what of why: Some determinants and consequences of causal attribution. *Journal of Personality and Social Psychology, 22,* 171–193.

McArthur, L. Z. (1981). What grabs you? The role of attention in impression formation and causal attribution. In E. T. Higgins, C. P. Herman, & M. P. Zanna (Eds.), *Social cognition: The Ontario Symposium* (Vol. 1, pp. 201–246). Hillsdale, NJ: Erlbaum.

McArthur, L. Z., & Baron, R. M. (1983). Toward an ecological theory of social perception. *Psychological Review, 90,* 215–238.

McArthur, L. Z., & Berry, D. S. (1987). Cross-cultural agreement in perceptions of babyfaced adults. *Journal of Cross-Cultural Psychology, 18,* 165–192.

McArthur, L. Z., & Ginsberg, E. (1981). Causal attribution to salient stimuli: An investigation of visual fixation mediators. *Personality and Social Psychology Bulletin, 7,* 547–553.

McArthur, L. Z., & Post, D. L. (1977). Figural emphasis and person perception. *Journal of Experimental Social Psychology, 13,* 520–535.

McArthur, L. Z., & Solomon, L. K. (1978). Perceptions of an aggressive encounter as a function of the victim's salience and the perceiver's arousal. *Journal of Personality and Social Psychology, 36,* 1278–1290.

McCabe, K., Houser, D., Ryan, L., Smith, V., & Trouard, T. (2001). A functional imaging study of cooperation in two-person reciprocal exchange. *Proceedings of the National Academy of Sciences, 98,* 11832–11835.

McCaul, K. D., Holmes, D. S., & Solomon, S. (1982). Voluntary expressive changes and emotion. *Journal of Personality and Social Psychology, 42,* 145–152.

McCauley, C., Stitt, C. L., Woods, K., & Lipton, D. (1973). Group shift to caution at the race track. *Journal of Experimental Social Psychology, 9,* 80–86.

McClelland, J. L., McNaughton, B. L., & O'Reilly, R. C. (1995). Why there are complementary learning systems in the hippocampus and neocortex: Insights from the successes and failures of connectionist models of learning and memory. *Psychological Review, 102,* 419–457.

McClelland, J. L., Rumelhart, D. E., & Hinton, G. E. (1986). The appeal of parallel distributed processing. In D. E. Rumelhart, J. L. McClelland, & the PDP Research Group, *Parallel distributed processing: Explorations in the microstructure of cognition* (Vol. 1, pp. 3–44). Cambridge, MA: MIT Press.

McClosky, M. E., & Glucksberg, S. (1978). Natural categories: Well-defined or fuzzy sets. *Memory and Cognition, 6,* 462–472.

McClure, S. M., Daw, N. D., & Montague, P. R. (2003). A computational substrate for incentive salience. *Trends in Neuroscience, 26,* 423–428.

McClure, S. M., Li, J., Tomlin, D., Cypert, K. S., Montague, L. M., & Montague, P. R. (2004). Neural correlates of behavioral preference for culturally familiar drinks. *Neuron, 44,* 379–387.

McConnell, A. R., & Leibold, J. M. (2001). Relations among the implicit association test, discriminatory behavior, and explicit measures of racial attitudes. *Journal of Experimental Social Psychology, 37,* 435–442.

McCrea, S. M., & Hirt, E. R. (2001). The role of ability judgments in self-handicapping. *Personality and Social Psychology Bulletin, 27,* 1378–1389.

McFarland, C., & Buehler, R. (1998). The impact of negative affect on autobiographical memory: The role of self-focused attention to moods. *Journal of Personality and Social Psychology, 75,* 1424–1440.

McFarland, C., & Ross, M. (1987). The relation between current impressions and memories of self and dating partners. *Personality and Social Psychology Bulletin, 13,* 228–238.

McFarland, C., Ross, M., & Conway, M. (1984). Self-persuasion and self-presentation as mediators of anticipatory attitude change. *Journal of Personality and Social Psychology, 46,* 529–540.

McGarty, C., Turner, J. C., Hogg, M. A., Davidson, B., & Wetherell, M. S. (1992). Group polarization as conformity to the prototypical group member. *British Journal of Social Psychology, 31,* 11–19.

McGregor, H., Lieberman, J. D., Solomon, S., Greenberg, T., Arndt, J., Simon, L., et al. (1998). Terror management and aggression: Evidence that mortality salience motivates aggression against worldview threatening others. *Journal of Personality and Social Psychology, 74,* 590–605.

McGregor, I., Zanna, M. P., Holmes, J. G., & Spencer, S. J. (2001). Compensatory conviction in the face of personal uncertainty: Going to extremes and being oneself. *Journal of Personality and Social Psychology, 80,* 472–488.

McGuire, W. J. (1969). Nature of attitudes and attitude change. In G. Lindzey & E. Aronson (Eds.), *The handbook of social psychology* (2nd edn, Vol. 3, pp. 136–314). Reading, MA: Addison-Wesley.

McGuire, W. J. (1976). Some internal psychological factors influencing consumer choice. *Journal of Consumer Research, 2,* 302–309.

McGuire, W. J. (1985). Attitudes and attitude change. In G. Lindzey & E. Aronson (Eds.), *The handbook of social psychology* (3rd edn, Vol. 2, pp. 233–346). New York: Random House.

McKenzie-Mohr, D., & Zanna, M. P. (1990). Treating women as sexual objects: Look to the (gender schematic) male who has viewed pornography. *Personality and Social Psychology Bulletin, 16,* 296–308.

McKone, E., Kanwisher, N., & Duchaine, B. C. (2007). Can generic expertise explain special processing for faces? *Trends in Cognitive Sciences, 11,* 8–15.

McLachlan, A. (1986). Polarization and discussion context. *British Journal of Social Psychology, 25,* 345–347.

McMullen, M. N., & Markman, K. D. (2000). Downward counterfactuals and motivation: The "wake-up call" and the "Pangloss" effect. *Personality and Social Psychology Bulletin, 26,* 575–584.

Mead, G. H. (1934). *Mind, self, and society.* Chicago: University of Chicago Press.

Medin, D. L., Altom, M. W., & Murphy, T. D. (1984). Given versus induced category representations: Use of prototype and exemplar information in classification. *Journal of Experimental Psychology: Learning, Memory, and Cognition, 10,* 333–352.

Medin, D. L., & Atran, S. (2004). The native mind: Biological categorization and reasoning in development and across cultures. *Psychological Review, 111(4),* 960–983.

Medin, D. L., Waxman, S., Woodring, J., & Washinawatok, K. (2010). Human-centeredness is not a universal feature of young children's reasoning: Culture and experience matter when reasoning about biological entities. *Cognitive Development, 25(3),* 197–207.

Meehl, P. E. (1954). *Clinical versus statistical prediction: A theoretical analysis and review of the literature.* Minneapolis, MN: University of Minnesota Press.

Meloen, J. D., Van der Linden, G., & De Witte, H. (1996). A test of the approaches of Adorno et al., Lederer, and Altemeyer of authoritarianism in Belgian Flanders: A research note. *Political Psychology, 17,* 643–656.

Mendes, W. B., Blascovich, J., Lickel, B. A., & Hunter, S. (2002). Challenge and threat during social interaction with White and Black men. *Personality and Social Psychology Bulletin, 28,* 939–952.

Mendoza-Denton, R., Ayduk, O., Mischel, W., Shoda, Y., & Testa, A. (2001). Person X situation interactionism in self-encoding (I am . . . when . . .): Implications for affect regulation and social information. *Journal of Personality and Social Psychology, 80,* 533–544.

Menon, T., Morris, M. W., Chiu, C.-y., & Hong, Y.-y. (1999). Culture and the construal of agency: Attribution to individual versus group dispositions. *Journal of Personality and Social Psychology, 76,* 701–717.

Merton, R. K. (1957). *Social theory and social structure.* New York: Free Press.

Mervis, C. B., & Rosch, E. H. (1981). Categorization of natural objects. *Annual Review of Psychology, 32,* 89–115.

Mesquita, B. (2001). Emotions in collectivist and individualist contexts. *Journal of Personality and Social Psychology, 80,* 68–74.

Mesquita, B., Marinetti, C., & Delvaux, E. (2012). The social psychology of emotion. In S. T. Fiske & C. N. Macrae (Eds.), *Sage handbook of social cognition* (pp. 290–310). Thousand Oaks, CA: Sage.

Messick, D. M., & Mackie, D. M. (1989). Intergroup relations. *Annual Review of Psychology, 40,* 45–81.

Meyer, J. P., & Mulherin, A. (1980). From attribution to helping: An analysis of the mediating effects of affect and expectancy. *Journal of Personality and Social Psychology, 39,* 201–210.

Milburn, M. A. (1987). Ideological self-schemata and schematically induced attitude consistency. *Journal of Experimental Social Psychology, 23,* 383–398.

Mill, J. S. (1869). *The analysis of the phenomena of the human mind.* New York: Kelley.

Mill, J. S. (1974). *System of logic, ratiocinative and inductive.* Toronto, Canada: University of Toronto Press. (Originally published 1843.)

Millar, M. G., Millar, K. U., & Tesser, A. (1988). The effects of helping and focus of attention on mood states. *Personality and Social Psychology Bulletin, 14,* 536–543.

Millar, M. G., & Tesser, A. (1986a). Effects of attitude and cognitive focus on the attitude-behavior relation. *Journal of Personality and Social Psychology, 51,* 270–276.

Millar, M. G., & Tesser, A. (1986b). Thought-induced attitude change: The effects of schema structure and commitment. *Journal of Personality and Social Psychology, 51,* 259–269.

Millar, M. G., & Tesser, A. (1989). The effects of affective-cognitive consistency and thought on the attitude-behavior relationship. *Journal of Experimental Social Psychology, 25,* 189–202.

Millar, M. G., Tesser, A., & Millar, K. U. (1988). The effects of a threatening life event on behavior sequences and intrusive thought: A self-disruption explanation. *Cognitive Therapy and Research, 12,* 441–457.

Miller, C. T., & Downey, K. T. (1999). A meta-analysis of heavyweight and self-esteem. *Personality and Social Psychology Review, 3,* 68–84.

Miller, C. T., & Kaiser, C. R. (2001). A theoretical perspective on coping with stigma. *Journal of Social Issues, 57,* 73–92.

Miller, D. A., Smith, E. R., & Mackie, D. M. (2004). Effects of intergroup contact and political dispositions on prejudice: Role of intergroup emotions. *Group Processes and Intergroup Relations, 7,* 221–237.

Miller, D. T., & McFarland, C. (1986). Counterfactual thinking and victim compensation: A test of norm theory. *Personality and Social Psychology Bulletin, 12,* 513–519.

Miller, D. T., & Prentice, D. A. (1999). Some consequences of a belief in group essence: The category divide hypothesis. In D. A. Prentice & D. T. Miller (Eds.), *Cultural divides: Understanding and overcoming group conflict* (pp. 213–238). New York: Russell Sage Foundation.

Miller, D. T., & Ross, M. (1975). Self-serving biases in the attribution of causality: Fact or fiction? *Psychological Bulletin, 82,* 213–225.

Miller, D. T., Turnbull, W., & McFarland, C. (1990). Counterfactual thinking and social perception: Thinking about what might have been. In M. P. Zanna (Ed.), *Advances in experimental social psychology* (Vol. 23, pp. 305–331). New York: Academic Press.

Miller, D. T., Visser, P. S., & Staub, B. D. (2005). How surveillance begets perceptions of dishonesty: The case of the counterfactual sinner. *Journal of Personality and Social Psychology, 89,* 117–128.

Miller, E. K., & Cohen, J. D. (2001). An integrative theory of prefrontal cortex function. *Annual Review of Neuroscience, 24,* 167–202.

Miller, G. A. (1956). The magical number seven, plus or minus two: Some limits on our capacity for processing information. *Psychological Review, 63,* 81–97.

Miller, L. C., Murphy, R., & Buss, A. H. (1981). Consciousness of body: Private and public. *Journal of Personality and Social Psychology, 41(2),* 397–406.

Mills, J. (1968). Interest in supporting and discrepant information. In R. P. Abelson, E. Aronson, W. J. McGuire, T. M. Newcomb, M. J. Rosenberg, & P. H. Tannenbaum (Eds.), *Theories of cognitive consistency: A sourcebook.* Chicago: Rand-McNally.

Milne, E., & Grafman, J. (2001). Ventromedial prefrontal cortex lesions in humans eliminate implicit gender stereotyping. *Journal of Neuroscience, 21,* 1–6.

Mischel, W. (1968). *Personality and assessment.* New York: Wiley.

Mischel, W. (1984). Convergences and challenges in the search for consistency. *American Psychologist, 39,* 351–364.

Mischel, W. (1997). Was the cognitive revolution just a detour on the road to behaviorism? On the need to reconcile situational control and personal control. In R. S. Wyer Jr. (Ed.), *The automaticity of everyday life* (pp. 181–186). Mahwah, NJ: Erlbaum.

Mischel, W., & Peake, P. K. (1982). Beyond déjà vu in the search for cross-situational consistency. *Psychological Review, 89,* 730–755.

Mitchell, J. P., Banaji, M. R., & Macrae, C. N. (2005a). General and specific contributions of the medial prefrontal cortex to knowledge about mental states. *NeuroImage, 28,* 757–762.

Mitchell, J. P., Banaji, M. R., & Macrae, C. N. (2005b). The link between social cognition and self-referential thought in the medial prefrontal cortex. *Journal of Cognitive Neuroscience, 17*(8), 1306–1315.

Mitchell, J. P., Heatherton, T. F., & Macrae, C. N. (2002). Distinct neural systems subserve person and object knowledge. *Proceedings of the National Academy of Sciences, 99,* 15238–15243.

Mitchell, J. P., Macrae, C. N., & Banaji, M. R. (2005). Forming impressions of people versus inanimate objects: Social-cognitive processing in the medial prefrontal cortex. *NeuroImage, 26,* 251–257.

Miyamoto, Y., & Kitayama, S. (2002). Cultural variation in correspondence bias: The critical role of attitude diagnosticity of socially constrained behavior. *Journal of Personality and Social Psychology, 83,* 1239–1248.

Monin, B. (2003). The warm glow heuristic: When liking leads to familiarity. *Journal of Personality and Social Psychology, 85,* 1035–1048.

Monin, B., & Miller, D. T. (2001). Moral credentials and the expression of prejudice. *Journal of Personality and Social Psychology, 81,* 33–43.

Monson, T. C., Hesley, J. W., & Chernick, L. (1982). Specifying when personality traits can and cannot predict behavior: An alternative to abandoning the attempt to predict single-act criteria. *Journal of Personality and Social Psychology, 43,* 385–399.

Monteith, M. J. (1993). Self-regulation of prejudiced responses: Implications for progress in prejudice-reduction efforts. *Journal of Personality and Social Psychology, 65,* 469–485.

Monteith, M. J. (1996). Contemporary forms of prejudice-related conflict: In search of a nutshell. *Personality and Social Psychology Bulletin, 22,* 461–473.

Monteith, M. J., Ashburn-Nardo, L., Voils, C. I., & Czopp, A. M. (2002). Putting the brakes on prejudice: On the development and operation of cues for control. *Journal of Personality and Social Psychology, 83,* 1029–1050.

Monteith, M. J., Deneen, N. E., & Tooman, G. D. (1996). The effect of social norm activation on the expression of opinions concerning gay men and Blacks. *Basic and Applied Social Psychology, 18,* 267–288.

Monteith, M. J., Sherman, J. W., & Devine, P. G. (1998). Suppression as a stereotype control strategy. *Personality and Social Psychology, 36,* 125–154.

Monteith, M. J., Spicer, C. V., & Tooman, G. D. (1998). Consequences of stereotype suppression: Stereotypes on and not on the rebound. *Journal of Experimental Social Psychology, 34,* 355–377.

Monteith, M. J., & Voils, C. I. (1998). Proneness to prejudiced responses: Toward understanding the authenticity of self-reported discrepancies. *Journal of Personality and Social Psychology, 75,* 901–916.

Monteith, M. J., & Walters, G. L. (1998). Egalitarianism, moral obligation, and prejudice-related personal standards. *Personality and Social Psychology Bulletin, 24,* 186–199. [Erratum: *24,* 442.]

Montepare, J. M., & Zebrowitz-McArthur, L. (1986). The influence of facial characteristics on children's age perceptions. *Journal of Experimental Child Psychology, 42,* 303–314.

Montepare, J. M., & Zebrowitz-McArthur, L. (1987). Perceptions of adults with childlike voices in two cultures. *Journal of Experimental Social Psychology, 23,* 331–349.

Mor, N., & Winquist, J. (2002). Self-focused attention and negative affect: A meta-analysis. *Psychological Bulletin, 128,* 638–662.

Moreland, R. L., & Zajonc, R. B. (1977). Is stimulus recognition a necessary condition for the occurrence of exposure effects? *Journal of Personality and Social Psychology, 35,* 191–199.

Moreland, R. L., & Zajonc, R. B. (1979). Exposure effects may not depend on stimulus recognition. *Journal of Personality and Social Psychology, 37,* 1085–1089.

Moreland, R. L., & Zajonc, R. B. (1982). Exposure effects in person perception: Familiarity, similarity, and attraction. *Journal of Experimental Social Psychology, 18,* 395–415.

Moretti, M., & Higgins, E. T. (1990). Relating self-discrepancy beyond actual self-ratings. *Journal of Experimental Social Psychology, 26,* 108–123.

Morewedge, C. K., Gilbert, D. T., & Wilson, T. D. (2005). The least likely of times: How remembering the past biases forecasts of the future. *Psychological Science, 16,* 626–630.

Morier, D. M., & Borgida, E. (1984). The conjunction fallacy: A task specific phenomenon? *Personality and Social Psychology Bulletin, 10,* 243–252.

Morling, B., & Masuda, T. (2012). Social cognition in real worlds: Cultural psychology and social cognition. In S. T. Fiske & C. N. Macrae (Eds.), *Sage handbook of social cognition* (pp. 429–450). Thousand Oaks, CA: Sage.

Morris, J. S., Ohman, A., & Dolan, R. J. (1998). Conscious and unconscious emotional learning in the human amygdala. *Nature, 393,* 467–470.

Morris, M. W., & Peng, K. (1994). Culture and cause: American and Chinese attributions for social and physical events. *Journal of Personality and Social Psychology, 67,* 949–971.

Moskalenko, S., & Heine, S. J. (2003). Watching your troubles away: Television viewing as a stimulus for subjective self-awareness. *Personality and Social Psychology Bulletin, 29,* 76–85.

Moskowitz, G. B. (2005). *Social cognition: Understanding self and others.* New York: Guilford Press.

Mullen, B., Brown, R. J., & Smith, C. (1992). Ingroup bias as a function of salience, relevance, and status: An integration. *European Journal of Social Psychology, 22,* 103–122.

Mullen, B., & Goethals, G. R. (1990). Social projection, actual consensus, and valence. *British Journal of Social Psychology, 29,* 279–282.

Mullen, B., & Hu, L. (1989). Perceptions of ingroup and outgroup variability: A meta-analytic integration. *Basic and Applied Social Psychology, 10,* 233–252.

Mullen, B., & Johnson, C. (1990). Distinctiveness-based illusory correlations and stereotyping: A meta-analytic integration. *British Journal of Social Psychology, 29,* 11–27.

Mullen, B., & Riordan, C. A. (1988). Self-serving attributions for performance in naturalistic settings: A meta-analytic review. *Journal of Applied Social Psychology, 18,* 3–22.

Murphy, F. C., Nimmo-Smith, I., & Lawrence, A. D. (2003). Functional neuroanatomy of emotions: A meta-analysis. *Cognitive Affective and Behavioral Neuroscience, 3,* 207–233.

Murphy, G. L., & Medin, D. L. (1985). The role of theories in conceptual coherence. *Psychological Review, 92,* 289–316.

Murphy, N. A. (2012). Nonverbal perception. In S. T. Fiske & C. N. Macrae (Eds.), *Sage handbook of social cognition* (pp. 191–210). Thousand Oaks, CA: Sage.

Murphy, S. T., Monahan, J. L., & Zajonc, R. B. (1995). Additivity of nonconscious affect: Combined effects of priming and exposure. *Journal of Personality and Social Psychology, 69,* 589–602.

Murray, J. D., Spadafore, J. A., & McIntosh, W. D. (2005). Belief in a just world and social perception: Evidence for automatic activation. *Journal of Social Psychology, 145,* 35–47.

Musen, G., & Squire, L. R. (1993). Implicit learning of color-word associations using a Stroop paradigm. *Journal of Experimental Psychology: Learning, Memory, and Cognition, 19,* 789–798.

Mussweiler, T. (2003). Comparison processes in social judgment: Mechanisms and consequences. *Psychological Review, 110,* 472–489.

Mussweiler, T. (2006). Doing is for thinking! *Psychological Science, 17,* 17–21.

Mussweiler, T., & Bodenhausen, G. (2002). I know you are but what am I? Self-evaluative consequences of judging in-group and out-group members. *Journal of Personality and Social Psychology, 82,* 19–32.

Mussweiler, T., & Förster, J. (2000). The sex → aggression link: A perception–behavior dissociation. *Journal of Personality and Social Psychology, 79,* 507–520.

Mussweiler, T., & Strack, F. (1999). Hypothesis-consistent testing and semantic priming in the anchoring paradigm: A selective accessibility model. *Journal of Experimental Social Psychology, 35,* 136–164.

Mussweiler, T., & Strack, F. (2000). Numeric judgments under uncertainty: The role of knowledge in anchoring. *Journal of Experimental Social Psychology, 36,* 495–518.

Mussweiler, T., Strack, F., & Pfeiffer, T. (2000). Overcoming the inevitable anchoring effect: Considering the opposite compensates for selective accessibility. *Personality and Social Psychology Bulletin, 26,* 1142–1150.

Naqvi, N., Shiv, B., & Bechara, A. (2006). The role of emotion in decision making: A cognitive neuroscience perspective. *Current Directions in Psychological Science, 15,* 260–264.

Nasby, W., & Yando, R. (1982). Selective encoding and retrieval of affectively-valent information: Two cognitive consequences of mood. *Journal of Personality and Social Psychology, 43,* 1244–1253.

Nei, M., & Roychoudhury, A. (1993). Evolutionary relationships of human populations on a global scale. *Molecular Biology Evolution, 10,* 927–943.

Neisser, U. (1980). On "social knowing." *Personality and Social Psychology Bulletin, 6,* 601–605.

Nelson, T. D. (Ed.). (2002). *Ageism: Stereotyping and prejudice against older persons.* Cambridge, MA: MIT Press.

Nesdale, A. R., Dharmalingam, S., & Kerr, G. K. (1987). Effect of subgroup ratio on stereotyping. *European Journal of Social Psychology, 17,* 353–356.

Neuberg, S. L. (1988). Behavioral implications of information presented outside of conscious awareness: The effect of subliminal presentation of trait information on behavior in the prisoner's dilemma game. *Social Cognition, 6,* 207–230.

Neuberg, S. L. (1989). The goal of forming accurate impressions during social interactions: Attenuating the impact of negative expectancies. *Journal of Personality and Social Psychology, 56,* 374–386.

Neuberg, S. L., & Fiske, S. T. (1987). Motivational influences on impression formation: Outcome dependency, accuracy-driven attention, and individuating processes. *Journal of Personality and Social Psychology, 53,* 431–444.

Neuberg, S. L., & Newsom, J. T. (1993). Personal need for structure: Individual differences in the desire for simpler structure. *Journal of Personality and Social Psychology, 65,* 113–131.

Neuberg, S. L., Smith, D. M., & Asher, T. (2000). Why people stigmatize: Toward a biocultural framework. In T. F. Heatherton, R. E. Kleck, & M. R. Hebl (Eds.), *The social psychology of stigma* (pp. 31–61). New York: Guilford Press.

Neugarten, B. (1974). Age groups in American society and the rise of the young-old. *Annals of the American Academy of Political and Social Science,* September, 187–198.

Neumann, R., & Seibt, B. (2001). The structure of prejudice: Associative strength as a determinant of stereotype endorsement. *European Journal of Social Psychology, 31,* 609–620.

Neumann, R., & Strack, F. (2000). Approach and avoidance: The influence of proprioceptive and exteroceptive cues on encoding of affective information. *Journal of Personality and Social Psychology, 79,* 39–48.

Newell, A., & Simon, H. A. (1972). *Human problem solving.* Englewood Cliffs, NJ: Prentice-Hall.

Newman, L. S., & Uleman, J. S. (1990). Assimilation and contrast effects in spontaneous trait inference. *Personality and Social Psychology Bulletin, 16,* 224–240.

Newtson, D. (1973). Attribution and the unit of perception of ongoing behavior. *Journal of Personality and Social Psychology, 28,* 28–38.

Newtson, D. (1980). An interactionist perspective on social knowing. *Personality and Social Psychology Bulletin, 6,* 520–531.

Newtson, D., & Czerlinsky, T. (1974). Adjustment of attitude communications for contrasts by extreme audiences. *Journal of Personality and Social Psychology, 30,* 829–837.

Newtson, D., & Enquist, G. (1976). The perceptual organization of ongoing behavior. *Journal of Experimental Social Psychology, 12,* 436–450.

Newtson, D., Enquist, G., & Bois, J. (1977). The objective basis of behavior units. *Journal of Personality and Social Psychology, 35,* 847–862.

Newtson, D., Hairfield, J., Bloomingdale, J., & Cutino, S. (1987). The structure of action and interaction. *Social Cognition, 5,* 191–237.

Nezlek, J. B., & Leary, M. R. (2002). Individual differences in self-presentational motives in daily social interaction. *Personality and Social Psychology Bulletin, 28,* 211–223.

Niedenthal, P. M., Barsalou, L. W., Winkielman, P., Krauth-Gruber, S., & Ric, F. (2005). Embodiment in attitudes, social perception, and emotion. *Personality and Social Psychology Review, 9,* 184–211.

Niedenthal, P. M., & Brauer, M. (2012). Social functionality of human emotion. *Annual Review of Psychology, 63,* 259–285.

Niedenthal, P. M., & Cantor, N. (1986). Affective responses as guides to category-based inferences. *Motivation and Emotion, 10,* 217–232.

Niedenthal, P. M., & Setterlund, M. B. (1994). Emotion congruence in perception. *Personality and Social Psychology Bulletin, 20,* 401–411.

Nielson, S. L., & Sarason, S. G. (1981). Emotion, personality, and selective attention. *Journal of Personality and Social Psychology, 41,* 945–960.

Niiya, Y., Crocker, J., & Bartmess, E. N. (2004). From vulnerability to resilience: Learning orientations buffer contingent self-esteem from failure. *Psychological Science, 15,* 801–805.

Nilsson, I., & Ekehammar, B. (1987). Person-positivity bias in political perception? *European Journal of Social Psychology, 17,* 247–252.

Nisbett, R. E., Krantz, D. H., Jepson, C., & Fong, G. T. (1982). Improving inductive inference. In D. Kahneman, P. Slovic, & A. Tversky (Eds.), *Judgment under uncertainty: Heuristics and biases* (pp. 445–462). New York: Cambridge University Press.

Nisbett, R. E., Peng, K., Choi, I., & Norenzayan, A. (2001). Culture and systems of thought: Holistic versus analytic cognition. *Psychological Review, 108,* 291–310.

Nisbett, R. E., & Ross, L. D. (1980). *Human inference: Strategies and shortcomings of social judgment.* Englewood Cliffs, NJ: Prentice-Hall.

Nisbett, R. E., & Valins, S. (1972). Perceiving the causes of one's own behavior. In E. E. Jones, E. E. Kanouse, H. H. Kelley, R. E. Nisbett, S. Valins, & B. Weiner (Eds.), *Attribution: Perceiving the causes of behavior* (pp. 63–78). Morristown, NJ: General Learning Press.

Nisbett, R. E., & Wilson, T. D. (1977a). The halo effect: Evidence for unconscious alteration of judgments. *Journal of Personality and Social Psychology, 35,* 250–256.

Nisbett, R. E., & Wilson, T. D. (1977b). Telling more than we can know: Verbal reports on mental processes. *Psychological Review, 84,* 231–259.

Nisbett, R. E., Zukier, H., & Lemley, R. E. (1981). The dilution effect: Non-diagnostic information weakens the implications of diagnostic information. *Cognitive Psychology, 13,* 248–277.

Nordgren, L. F., McDonnell, M.-H. M., & Loewenstein, G. (2011). What constitutes torture?: Psychological impediments to an objective evaluation of enhanced interrogation tactics. *Psychological Science, 22(5),* 689–694.

Nordgren, L. F., van der Pligt, J., & van Harreveld, F. (2006). Visceral drives in retrospect: Explanations about the inaccessible past. *Psychological Science, 17(7)*, 635–640.

Norenzayan, A., Choi, I., & Nisbett, R. E. (2002). Cultural similarities and differences in social inference: Evidence from behavioral predictions and lay theories of behavior. *Personality and Social Psychology Bulletin, 28*, 109–120.

Norman, D. A., & Shallice, T. (1986). Attention to action: Willed and automatic control of behavior. In R. J. Davidson, G. E. Schwartz, & D. Shapiro (Eds.), *Consciousness and self regulation: Advances in research and theory* (Vol. 4, pp. 1–18). New York: Plenum Press.

Norman, K. A., & O'Reilly, R. C. (2003). Modeling hippocampal and neocortical contributions to recognition memory: A complementary-learning systems approach. *Psychological Review, 110*, 611–646.

Norman, R. (1975). Affective-cognitive consistency, attitudes, conformity, and behavior. *Journal of Personality and Social Psychology, 32*, 83–91.

North, M. S., & Fiske, S. T. (2012). Social cognition. In A. W. Kruglanski & W. Stroebe (Eds.), *Handbook of the history of social psychology* (pp. 81–100). New York: Psychology Press.

North, M. S., & Fiske, S. T. (2012). An inconvenienced youth: Ageism and its potential intergenerational roots. *Psychological Bulletin*.

North, M. S., & Fiske, S. T. (2013). Subtyping ageism: Policy issues in succession and consumption. *Social Issues and Policy Review*.

North, M. S., & Fiske, S. T. (under review). The young and the ageist: Intergenerational tensions over succession, identity, and consumption.

Norton, M. I., Vandello, J. A., & Darley, J. M. (2004). Casuistry and social category bias. *Journal of Personality and Social Psychology, 87*, 817–831.

Nosek, B. A., Banaji, M., & Greenwald, A. G. (2002a). Harvesting implicit group attitudes and beliefs from a demonstration web site. *Group Dynamics: Theory, Research, and Practice, 6*, 101–115.

Nosek, B. A., Banaji, M. R., & Greenwald, A. G. (2002b). Math = male, me = female, therefore math = me. *Journal of Personality and Social Psychology, 83*, 44–59.

Nosek, B. A., Hawkins, C. B., & Frazier, R. S. (2012). Implicit social cognition. In S. T. Fiske & C. N. Macrae (Eds.), *Sage handbook of social cognition* (pp. 31–53). Thousand Oaks, CA: Sage.

Nowak, A., Vallacher, R. R., Tesser, A., & Borkowski, W. (2000). Society of self: The emergence of collective properties in self-structure. *Psychological Review, 107*, 39–61.

Nussbaum, S., Trope, Y., & Liberman, N. (2003). Creeping dispositionism: The temporal dynamics of behavior prediction. *Journal of Personality and Social Psychology, 84*, 485–497.

Oakes, P. J., & Turner, J. C. (1980). Social categorization and intergroup behaviour: Does minimal intergroup discrimination make social identity more positive? *European Journal of Social Psychology, 10*, 295–301.

Oakes, P., & Turner, J. C. (1986). Distinctiveness and the salience of social category memberships: Is there an automatic perceptual bias towards novelty? *European Journal of Social Psychology, 16*(4), 325-344.

Oatley, K., & Johnson-Laird, P. N. (1987). Towards a cognitive theory of emotions. *Cognition and Emotion, 1*, 29–50.

O'Brien, L. T., & Crandall, C. S. (2003). Stereotype threat and arousal: Effects on women's math performance. *Personality and Social Psychology Bulletin, 29*, 782–789.

Ochsner, K. N., Beer, J. S., Robertson, E. R., Cooper, J. C., Gabrieli, J. D. E., Kihlstrom, J. F., et al. (2005). The neural correlates of direct and reflected self-knowledge. *NeuroImage, 28*, 797–814.

Ochsner, K. N., & Lieberman, M. D. (2001). The emergence of social cognitive neuroscience. *American Psychologist, 56(9)*, 717–734.

O'Doherty, J. P. (2004). Reward representations and reward-related learning in the human brain: Insights from neuroimaging. *Current Opinion in Neurobiology, 14*, 769–776.

O'Doherty, J. P., Kringelbach, M. L., Rolls, E. T., Hornak, J., & Andrews, C. (2001). Abstract reward and punishment representations in the human orbitofrontal cortex. *Nature Neuroscience, 4*, 95–102.

Oettingen, G., & Mayer, D. (2002). The motivating function of thinking about the future: Expectations versus fantasies. *Journal of Personality and Social Psychology, 83,* 1198–1212.

Oettingen, G., Pak, H.-j., & Schnetter, K. (2001). Self-regulation of goal setting: Turning free fantasies about the future into binding goals. *Journal of Personality and Social Psychology, 80,* 736–753.

Oishi, S., & Diener, E. (2003). Culture and well-being: The cycle of action, evaluation, and decision. *Personality and Social Psychology Bulletin, 29,* 939–949.

Oishi, S., Diener, E., Napa Scollon, C., & Biswas-Diener, R. (2004). Cross-situational consistency of affective experiences across cultures. *Journal of Personality and Social Psychology, 86,* 460–472.

Oishi, S., Wyer, R. S., Jr., & Colcombe, S. (2000). Cultural variation in the use of current life satisfaction to predict the future. *Journal of Personality and Social Psychology, 78,* 434–445.

Olivola, C. Y., & Todorov, A. (2010). Fooled by first impressions? Reexamining the diagnostic value of appearance-based inferences. *Journal of Experimental Social Psychology, 46(2),* 315–324.

Olson, I. R., & Marshuetz, C. (2005). Facial attractiveness is appraised in a glance. *Emotion, 5,* 498–502.

Olson, J. M., Ellis, R. J., & Zanna, M. P. (1983). Validating objective versus subjective judgments: Interest in social comparison and consistency information. *Personality and Social Psychology Bulletin, 54,* 758–767.

Olson, J. M., & Ross, M. (1988). False feedback about placebo effectiveness: Consequences for the misattribution of speech anxiety. *Journal of Experimental Social Psychology, 24,* 275–291.

Olson, J. M., & Zanna, M. P. (1979). A new look at selective exposure. *Journal of Experimental Social Psychology, 15,* 1–15.

Olson, M. A., & Fazio, R. H. (2002). Implicit acquisition and manifestation of classically conditioned attitudes. *Social Cognition, 20,* 89–104.

Olson, M. A., & Fazio, R. H. (2004a). Reducing the influence of extrapersonal associations on the implicit association test: Personalizing the IAT. *Journal of Personality and Social Psychology, 86,* 653–667.

Olson, M. A., & Fazio, R. H. (2004b). Trait inferences as a function of automatically activated racial attitudes and motivation to control prejudiced reactions. *Basic and Applied Social Psychology, 26,* 1–11.

Operario, D., & Fiske, S. T. (2001). Ethnic identity moderates perceptions of prejudice: Judgments of personal versus group discrimination and subtle versus blatant bias. *Personality and Social Psychology Bulletin, 27,* 550–561.

Ortony, A., Clore, G. L., & Collins, A. (1988). *The cognitive structure of emotion.* Cambridge: Cambridge University Press.

Ortony, A., & Turner, T. J. (1990). What's basic about basic emotions? *Psychological Review, 97,* 315–331.

Osgood, C. E., & Tannenbaum, P. H. (1955). The principle of congruity in the prediction of attitude change. *Psychological Review, 62,* 42–55.

Ostrom, T. M. (1977). Between-theory and within-theory conflict in explaining context effects in impression formation. *Journal of Experimental Social Psychology, 13,* 492–503.

Ostrom, T. M. (1984). The sovereignty of social cognition. In R. S. Wyer Jr. & T. K. Srull (Eds.), *Handbook of social cognition* (Vol. 1, pp. 1–38). Hillsdale, NJ: Erlbaum.

Ostrom, T. M. (1988). Computer simulation: The third symbol system. *Journal of Experimental Social Psychology, 24,* 381–392.

Ostrom, T. M., Lingle, J. H., Pryor, J. B., & Geva, N. (1980). Cognitive organization of person impressions. In R. Hastie, T. M. Ostrom, E. B. Ebbesen, R. S. Wyer Jr., D. Hamilton, & D. E. Carlston (Eds.), *Person memory: The cognitive basis of social perception* (pp. 55–88). Hillsdale, NJ: Erlbaum.

Ostrom, T. M., & Sedikides, C. (1992). Out-group homogeneity effect in natural and minimal groups. *Psychological Bulletin, 112,* 536–552.

Ottati, V., Fishbein, M., & Middlestadt, S. E. (1988). Determinants of voters' beliefs about the candidates' stands on the issues: The role of evaluative bias heuristics and the candidates' expressed message. *Journal of Personality and Social Psychology, 55,* 517–529.

Otten, S., Mummendey, A., & Blanz, M. (1996). Intergroup discrimination in positive and negative outcome allocations: Impact of stimulus valence, relative group status, and relative group size. *Personality and Social Psychology Bulletin, 22,* 568–581.

Owens, J., Bower, G. H., & Black, J. B. (1979). The "soap-opera" effect in story recall. *Memory and Cognition, 7,* 185–191.

Oyserman, D., Bybee, D., & Terry, K. (2006). Possible selves and academic outcomes: How and when possible selves impel action. *Journal of Personality and Social Psychology, 91,* 188–204.

Padoa-Schioppa, C., & Assad, J. A. (2006). Neurons in the orbitofrontal cortex encode economic value. *Nature, 441,* 223–226.

Pagel, M. D., & Davidson, A. R. (1984). A comparison of three social-psychological models of attitude and behavioral plan: Prediction of contraceptive behavior. *Journal of Personality and Social Psychology, 47,* 517–533.

Pallak, S. R. (1983). Salience of a communicator's physical attractiveness and persuasion: A heuristic versus systematic processing interpretation. *Social Cognition, 2,* 158–170.

Pandya, D. N., & Barnes, C. L. (1987). Architecture and connections of the frontal lobe. In E. Perecman (Ed.), *The frontal lobes revisited* (pp. 41–72). New York: IRBN Press.

Parducci, A. (1968). The relativism of absolute judgments. *Scientific American, 219,* 84–90.

Park, B., & Hastie, R. (1987). Perception of variability in category development: Instance- versus abstraction-based stereotypes. *Journal of Personality and Social Psychology, 53,* 621–635.

Park, B., & Judd, C. M. (1990). Measures and models of perceived group variability. *Journal of Personality and Social Psychology, 59,* 173–191.

Park, B., & Judd, C. M. (2005). Rethinking the link between categorization and prejudice within the social cognition perspective. *Personality and Social Psychology Review, 9,* 108–130.

Park, B., Ryan, C. S., & Judd, C. M. (1992). Role of meaningful subgroups in explaining differences in perceived variability. *Journal of Personality and Social Psychology, 5,* 73–91.

Parkinson, B. (1985). Emotional effects of false autonomic feedback. *Psychological Bulletin, 98,* 471–494.

Parra, F. C., Amado, R. C., Lambertucci, J. R., Rocha, J., Antunes, C. M., & Pena, S. D. (2003). Color and genomic ancestry in Brazilians. *Proceedings of the National Academy of Sciences, 100,* 177–182.

Parrott, W. G., & Sabini, J. (1990). Mood and memory under natural conditions: Evidence for mood incongruent recall. *Journal of Personality and Social Psychology, 59,* 321–336.

Pasupathi, M., Carstensen, L. L., & Tsai, J. L. (1995). Ageism in interpersonal settings. In B. Lott & D. Maluso (Eds.), *The social psychology of interpersonal discrimination* (pp. 160–182). New York: Guilford Press.

Pavelchak, M. A. (1989). Piecemeal and category-based evaluation: An idiographic analysis. *Journal of Personality and Social Psychology, 56,* 354–363.

Payne, B. K. (2012). Control, awareness, and other things we might learn to live without. In S. T. Fiske & C. N. Macrae (Eds.), *Sage handbook of social cognition* (pp. 12–30). Thousand Oaks, CA: Sage.

Peeters, G. (1983). Relational and informational patterns in social cognition. In W. Doise & S. Moscovici (Eds.), *Current issues in European social psychology* (pp. 201–237). Cambridge: Cambridge University Press.

Pelham, B. W. (1990). On confidence and consequence: The certainty and importance of self-knowledge. *Journal of Personality and Social Psychology, 60,* 518–530.

Pelham, B. W., Carvallo, M., & Jones, J. T. (2005). Implicit egotism. *Current Directions in Psychological Science, 14,* 106–110.

Pelham, B. W., Mirenberg, M. C., & Jones, J. K. (2002). Why Susie sells seashells by the seashore: Implicit egotism and major life decisions. *Journal of Personality and Social Psychology, 82,* 469–487.

Pellicano, E. (2012). Atypical social cognition. In S. T. Fiske & C. N. Macrae (Eds.), *Sage handbook of social cognition* (pp. 411–429). Thousand Oaks, CA: Sage.

Pennebaker, J. W., Dyer, M. A., Caulkins, R. S., Litkowitz, D. L., Ackreman, P. L., Anderson, D. B., & McGraw, K. M. (1979). Don't the girls get prettier at closing time: A country and western application to psychology. *Personality and Social Psychology Bulletin, 5,* 122–125.

Penner, L. A., Dovidio, J. F., Piliavin, J. A., & Schroeder, D. A. (2005). Prosocial behavior: Multilevel perspectives. *Annual Review of Psychology, 56,* 365–392.

Pepitone, A. (1950). Motivational effects in social perception. *Human Relations, 3,* 57–76.

Perdue, C. W., Dovidio, J. F., Gurtman, M. B., & Tyler, R. B. (1990). Us and them: Social categorization and the process of intergroup bias. *Journal of Personality and Social Psychology, 59,* 475–486.

Perlow, L., & Weeks, J. (2002). Who's helping whom? Layers of culture and workplace behavior. *Journal of Organizational Behavior, 23,* 345–361.

Perreault, S., & Bourhis, R. Y. (1999). Ethnocentrism, social identification, and discrimination. *Personality and Social Psychology Bulletin, 25,* 92–103.

Perry, L. C., Perry, D. G., & Weiss, R. J. (1986). Age differences in children's beliefs about whether altruism makes the actor feel good. *Social Cognition, 4,* 263–269.

Peterson, B. E., Doty, R. M., & Winter, D. G. (1993). Authoritarianism and attitudes toward contemporary social issues. *Personality and Social Psychology Bulletin, 19,* 174–184.

Peterson, B. E., Duncan, L. E., & Pang, J. S. (2002). Authoritarianism and political impoverishment: Deficits in knowledge and civic disinterest. *Political Psychology, 23,* 97–112.

Peterson, B. E., & Miller, J. A. (2004). Quality of college students' experiences during cooperative learning. *Social Psychology of Education, 7,* 161–183.

Pettigrew, T. F. (1979). The ultimate attribution error: Extending Allport's cognitive analysis of prejudice. *Personality and Social Psychology Bulletin, 5,* 461–476.

Pettigrew, T. F., & Meertens, R. W. (1995). Subtle and blatant prejudice in Western Europe. *European Journal of Social Psychology, 25,* 57–75.

Pettigrew, T. F., & Tropp, L. R. (2006). A meta-analytic test of intergroup contact theory. *Journal of Personality and Social Psychology, 90,* 751–783.

Petty, R. E., Briñol, P., & Tormala, Z. L. (2002). Thought confidence as a determinant of persuasion: The self-validation hypothesis. *Journal of Personality and Social Psychology, 82,* 722–741.

Petty, R. E., & Cacioppo, J. T. (1979). Issue involvement can increase or decrease persuasion by enhancing message-relevant cognitive responses. *Journal of Personality and Social Psychology, 37,* 1915–1926.

Petty, R. E., & Cacioppo, J. T. (1981). *Attitudes and persuasion: Classic and contemporary approaches.* Dubuque, IA: W. C. Brown.

Petty, R. E., & Cacioppo, J. T. (1984). The effects of involvement on responses to argument quantity and quality: Central and peripheral routes to persuasion. *Journal of Personality and Social Psychology, 46,* 69–81.

Petty, R. E., & Cacioppo, J. T. (1986). The elaboration likelihood model of persuasion. In L. Berkowitz (Ed.), *Advances in experimental social psychology* (Vol. 19, pp. 123–205). New York: Academic Press.

Petty, R. E., & Cacioppo, J. T. (1990). Involvement and persuasion: Tradition versus integration. *Psychological Bulletin, 107,* 367–374.

Petty, R. E., Cacioppo, J. T., & Goldman, R. (1981). Personal involvement as a determinant of argument-based persuasion. *Journal of Personality and Social Psychology, 41,* 847–855.

Petty, R. E., Cacioppo, J. T., & Kasmer, J. A. (1988). The role of affect in the elaboration likelihood model of persuasion. In L. Donohew, H. E. Sypher, & E. T. Higgins (Eds.), *Communication, social cognition, and affect* (pp. 117–146). Hillsdale, NJ: Erlbaum.

Petty, R. E., Cacioppo, J. T., Kasmer, J. A., & Haugtvedt, C. P. (1987). A reply to Stiff and Boster. *Communication Monographs, 54,* 257–263.

Petty, R. E., Cacioppo, J. T., & Schumann, D. (1983). Central and peripheral routes to advertising effectiveness: The moderating role of involvement. *Journal of Consumer Research, 10,* 134–148.

Petty, R. E., Cacioppo, J. T., Sedikides, C., & Strathman, A. J. (1988). Affect and persuasion: A contemporary perspective. *American Behavioral Scientist, 31,* 355–371.

Petty, R. E., Fleming, M. A., Priester, J. R., & Feinstein, A. H. (2001). Individual versus group interest violation: Surprise as a determinant of argument scrutiny and persuasion. *Social Cognition, 19,* 418–442.

Petty, R. E., Gleicher, F., & Baker, S. M. (1991). Multiple roles for affect in persuasion. In J. Forgas (Ed.), *Emotion and social judgment* (pp. 181–200). London: Pergamon Press.

Petty, R. E., Harkins, S. G., & Williams, K. D. (1980). The effects of group diffusion of cognitive effort on attitudes: An information-processing view. *Journal of Personality and Social Psychology, 38,* 81–92.

Petty, R. E., Kasmer, J., Haugtvedt, C. P., & Cacioppo, J. T. (1987). Source and message factors in persuasion: A reply to Stiff's critique of the elaboration of the likelihood model. *Communication Monographs, 54,* 233–263.

Petty, R. E., Ostrom, T. M., & Brock, T. C. (Eds.). (1981). *Cognitive responses in persuasive communications: A text in attitude change.* Hillsdale, NJ: Erlbaum.

Petty, R. E., Rennier, G. A., & Cacioppo, J. T. (1987). Assertion versus interrogation format in opinion surveys: Questions enhance thoughtful responding. *Public Opinion Quarterly, 51,* 481–494.

Petty, R. E., Tormala, Z. L., Briñol, P., & Jarvis, W. B. G. (2006). Implicit ambivalence from attitude change: An exploration of the PAST model. *Journal of Personality and Social Psychology, 90,* 21–41.

Petty, R. E., & Wegener, D. T. (1998). Attitude change: Multiple roles for persuasion variables. In D. T. Gilbert, S. T. Fiske, & G. Lindzey (Eds.), *Handbook of social psychology* (4th edn, Vol. 1, pp. 323–390). New York: McGraw-Hill.

Petty, R. E., & Wegener, D. T. (1999). The elaboration likelihood model: Current status and controversies. In S. Chaiken & Y. Trope (Eds.), *Dual-process theories in social psychology* (pp. 37–72). New York: Guilford Press.

Petty, R. E., Wegener, D. T., & Fabrigar, L. R. (1997). Attitudes and attitude change. *Annual Review of Psychology, 48,* 609–647.

Petty, R. E., Wells, G. L., & Brock, T. C. (1976). Distraction can enhance or reduce yielding to propaganda: Thought disruption versus effort justification. *Journal of Personality and Social Psychology, 34,* 874–884.

Phalet, K., & Poppe, E. (1997). Competence and morality dimensions of national and ethnic stereotypes: A study in six Eastern European countries. *European Journal of Social Psychology, 27,* 703–723.

Pham, L. B., & Taylor, S. E. (1999). From thought to action: Effects of process versus outcome-based mental simulations on performance. *Personality and Social Psychology Bulletin, 25,* 250–260.

Pham, L. B., Taylor, S. E., & Seeman, T. E. (2001). Effects of environmental predictability and personal mastery on self-regulatory and physiological processes. *Personality and Social Psychology Bulletin, 27,* 611–620.

Pham, M. T., Meyvis, T., & Zhou, N. (2001). Beyond the obvious: Chronic vividness of imagery and the use of information in decision making. *Organizational Behavior and Human Decision Processes, 84,* 226–253.

Phan, K. L., Wager, T., Taylor, S. F., & Liberzon, I. (2002). Functional neuroanatomy of emotion: A meta-analysis of emotion activation studies in PET and fMRI. *NeuroImage, 16,* 331–348.

Phelps, E. A. (2005). The interaction of emotion and cognition: The relation between the human amygdala and cognitive awareness. In R. R. Hassan, J. Uleman, & J. A. Bargh (Eds.), *The power of the subliminal: On subliminal persuasion and other potential applications* (pp. 61–76). New York: Oxford University Press.

Phelps, E. A. (2006). Emotion and cognition: Insights from studies of the human amygdala. *Annual Review of Psychology, 57,* 27–53.

Phelps, E. A., Cannistraci, C. J., & Cunningham, W. A. (2003). Intact performance on an indirect measure of face bias following amygdala damage. *Neuropsychologia, 41,* 203–208.

Phelps, E. A., O'Connor, K. J., Cunningham, W. A., Funayama, E. S., Gatenby, J. C., Gore, J. C., & Banaji, M. R. (2000). Performance on indirect measures of race evaluation predicts amygdala activation. *Journal of Cognitive Neuroscience, 12,* 729–738.

Phillips, A. G., & Silvia, P. J. (2005). Self-awareness and the emotional consequences of self-discrepancies. *Personality and Social Psychology Bulletin, 31,* 703–713.

Picek, J. S., Sherman, S. J., & Shiffrin, R. M. (1975). Cognitive organization and coding of social structures. *Journal of Personality and Social Psychology, 31,* 758–768.

Pinel, E. C. (1999). Stigma consciousness: The psychological legacy of social stereotypes. *Journal of Personality and Social Psychology, 76,* 114–128.

Pinel, E. C. (2002). Stigma consciousness in intergroup contexts: The power of conviction. *Journal of Experimental Social Psychology, 38,* 178–185.

Pittman, T. S. (1998). Motivation. In D. T. Gilbert, S. T. Fiske, & G. Lindzey (Eds.), *Handbook of social psychology* (4th edn, Vol. 1, pp. 549–590). New York: McGraw-Hill.

Plant, E. A., Kling, K. C., & Smith, G. L. (2004). The influence of gender and social role on the interpretation of facial expressions. *Sex Roles, 51,* 187–196.

Plutchik, R. (1962). *The emotions: Facts, theories and a new model.* New York: Random House.

Plutchik, R. (1980). *Emotion: A psychoevolutionary synthesis.* New York: Harper & Row.

Posavac, S. S., Sanbonmatsu, D. M., & Fazio, R. H. (1997). Considering the best choice: Effects of the salience and accessibility of alternatives on attitude–decision consistency. *Journal of Personality and Social Psychology, 72,* 253–261.

Posner, M. I., & Keele, S. W. (1968). On the genesis of abstract ideas. *Journal of Experimental Psychology, 77,* 353–363.

Posner, M. I., & Keele, S. W. (1970). Retention of abstract ideas. *Journal of Experimental Psychology, 83,* 304–308.

Posner, M. I., & Rothbart, M. K. (2007). Research on attention networks as a model for the integration of psychological science. *Annual Review of Psychology, 58,* 1–23.

Postmes, T., Haslam, S. A., & Swaab, R. I. (2005). Social influence in small groups: An interactive model of social identity formation. *European Review of Social Psychology, 16,* 1–42.

Postmes, T., Spears, R., Lee, A. T., & Novak, R. J. (2005). Individuality and social influence in groups: Inductive and deductive routes to group identity. *Journal of Personality and Social Psychology, 89,* 747–763.

Powell, M. C., & Fazio, R. H. (1984). Attitude accessibility as a function of repeated attitudinal expression. *Personality and Social Psychology Bulletin, 10,* 139–148.

Pratkanis, A. R. (1988). The attitude heuristic and selective fact identification. *British Journal of Social Psychology, 27,* 257–263.

Pratkanis, A. R., & Greenwald, A. G. (1989). A sociocognitive model of attitude structure and function. In L. Berkowitz (Ed.), *Advances in experimental social psychology* (Vol. 22, pp. 245–285). New York: Academic Press.

Pratto, F. (1999). The puzzle of continuing group inequality: Piecing together psychological, social, and cultural forces in social dominance theory. In M. P. Zanna (Ed.), *Advances in experimental social psychology* (Vol. 1, pp. 191–263). San Diego, CA: Academic Press.

Pratto, F., & John, O. P. (1991). Automatic vigilance: The attention-grabbing power of negative social information. *Journal of Personality and Social Psychology, 61,* 380–391.

Pratto, F., Sidanius, J., Stallworth, L. M., & Malle, B. F. (1994). Social dominance orientation: A personality variable predicting social and political attitudes. *Journal of Personality and Social Psychology, 67,* 741–763.

Pratto, F., Stallworth, L. M., Sidanius, J., & Siers, B. (1997). The gender gap in occupational role attainment: A social dominance approach. *Journal of Personality and Social Psychology, 72,* 37–53.

Prentice, D. A. (1987). Psychological correspondence of possessions, attitudes, and values. *Journal of Personality and Social Psychology, 53,* 993–1003.

Priester, J. R., Cacioppo, J. T., & Petty, R. E. (1996). The influence of motor processes on attitudes toward novel versus familiar semantic stimuli. *Personality and Social Psychology Bulletin, 22,* 442–447.

Priester, J. R., & Petty, R. E. (2001). Extending the bases of subjective attitudinal ambivalence: Interpersonal and intrapersonal antecedents of evaluative tension. *Journal of Personality and Social Psychology, 80,* 19–34.

Prislin, R. (1987). Attitude–behaviour relationship: Attitude relevance and behaviour relevance. *European Journal of Social Psychology, 17,* 483–485.

Prislin, R., & Ouellette, J. (1996). When it is embedded, it is potent: Effects of general attitude embeddedness on formation of specific attitudes and behavioral intentions. *Personality and Social Psychology Bulletin, 22,* 845–861.

Pronin, E., Gilovich, T., & Ross, L. D. (2004). Objectivity in the eye of the beholder: Divergent perceptions of self versus others. *Psychological Review, 111,* 781–799.

Pronin, E., Kruger, J., Savitsky, K., & Ross, L. D. (2001). You don't know me, but I know you: The illusion of asymmetric insight. *Journal of Personality and Social Psychology, 81,* 639–656.

Pronin, E., Lin, D. Y., & Ross, L. D. (2002). The bias blind spot: Perceptions of bias in self versus others. *Personality and Social Psychology Bulletin, 28,* 369–381.

Pronin, E., & Ross, L. D. (2006). Temporal differences in trait self-ascription: When the self is seen as an other. *Journal of Personality and Social Psychology, 90*, 197–209.

Pronin, E., Steele, C. M., & Ross, L. D. (2004). Identity bifurcation in response to stereotype threat: Women and mathematics. *Journal of Experimental Social Psychology, 40*, 152–168.

Pronin, E., Wegner, D. M., McCarthy, K., & Rodriguez, S. (2006). Everyday magical powers: The role of apparent mental causation in the overestimation of personal influence. *Journal of Personality and Social Psychology, 91*, 218–231.

Pruessner, J. C., Baldwin, M. W., Dedovic, K., Renwick, R., Mahani, N. K., Lord, C., Meaney, M., & Lupien, S. (2005). Self-esteem, locus of control, hippocampal volume, and cortisol regulation in young and old adulthood. *NeuroImage, 28*, 815–826.

Pruitt, D. G., & Teger, A. I. (1969). The risky shift in group betting. *Journal of Experimental Social Psychology, 5*, 115–126.

Pryor, J. B., & Kriss, N. (1977). The cognitive dynamics of salience in the attribution process. *Journal of Personality and Social Psychology, 35*, 49–55.

Quadflieg, S., Mason, M. F., & Macrae, C. N. (2004). The owl and the pussycat: Gaze cues and visuospatial orienting. *Psychonomic Bulletin and Review, 22*, 826–831.

Quattrone, G. A. (1982). Overattribution and unit formation: When behavior engulfs the person. *Journal of Personality and Social Psychology, 42*, 593–607.

Quattrone, G. A. (1985). On the congruity between internal states and action. *Psychological Bulletin, 98*, 3–40.

Quattrone, G. A., Finkel, S. E., & Andrus, D. C. (1982). Anchors away! On overcoming the anchoring bias across a number of domains. Unpublished manuscript, Stanford University, Stanford, CA.

Quinn, D. M., Kahng, S. K., & Crocker, J. (2004). Discreditable: Stigma effects of revealing a mental illness history on test performance. *Personality and Social Psychology Bulletin, 30*, 803–815.

Quinn, K. A., & Macrae, C. N. (2005). Categorizing others: The dynamics of person construal. *Journal of Personality and Social Psychology, 88*, 467–479.

Quinn, K. A., Macrae, C. N., & Bodenhausen, G. (2003). Stereotyping and impression formation: How categorical thinking shapes person perception. In M. A. Hogg & J. Cooper (Eds.), *The Sage handbook of social psychology* (pp. 87–109). Thousand Oaks, CA: Sage.

Rabbie, J., & Horowitz, M. (1969). Arousal of ingroup-outgroup bias by a chance win or loss. *Journal of Personality and Social Psychology, 13*, 269–277.

Raeva, D., van Dijk, E., & Zeelenberg, M. (2011). How comparing decision outcomes affects subsequent decisions: The carry-over of a comparative mind-set. *Judgment and Decision Making, 6(4)*, 343–350.

Raghubir, P., & Valenzuela, A. (2006). Center of inattention: Position biases in decision-making. *Organizational Behavior and Human Decision Processes, 99*, 66–80.

Rajecki, D. W. (1982). *Attitudes: Themes and advances*. Sunderland, MA: Sinauer.

Rakić, T., Steffens, M. C., & Mummendey, A. (2011). Blinded by the accent! The minor role of looks in ethnic categorization. *Journal of Personality and Social Psychology, 100(1)*, 16–29.

Read, S. (1983). Once is enough: Causal reasoning from a single instance. *Journal of Personality and Social Psychology, 45*, 323–334.

Read, S. (1984). Analogical reasoning in social judgment: The importance of causal theories. *Journal of Personality and Social Psychology, 46*, 14–25.

Read, S. (1987). Similarity and causality in the use of social analogies. *Journal of Experimental Social Psychology, 23*, 189–207.

Read, S. J. (1988). Conjunctive explanations: The effect of a comparison between a chosen and a nonchosen alternative. *Journal of Experimental Social Psychology, 24*, 146–162.

Read, S. J., & Miller, L. C. (1989). Inter-personalism: Toward a goal-based theory of persons in relationships. In L. Pervin (Ed.), *Goal concepts in personality and social psychology* (pp. 413–472). Hillsdale, NJ: Erlbaum.

Read, S. J., & Urada, D. I. (2003). A neural network simulation of the outgroup homogeneity effect. *Personality and Social Psychology Review, 7*, 146–159.

Read, S. J., Vanman, E. J., & Miller, L. C. (1997). Connectionism, parallel constraint satisfaction processes, and Gestalt principles: (Re) introducing cognitive dynamics to social psychology. *Personality and Social Psychology Review, 1*, 26–53.

Reber, R., Schwarz, N., & Winkielman, P. (2004). Processing fluency and aesthetic pleasure: Is beauty in the perceiver's processing experience? *Personality and Social Psychology Review, 8*, 364–382.

Reber, R., Winkielman, P., & Schwarz, N. (1998). Effects of perceptual fluency on affective judgments. *Psychological Science, 9(1)*, 45–48.

Reed, G. M., Kemeny, M. E., Taylor, S. E., & Visscher, B. R. (1999). Negative HIV-specific expectancies and AIDS-related bereavement as predictors of symptom onset in asymptomatic HIV-positive gay men. *Health Psychology, 18*, 354–363.

Reed, S. K. (1972). Pattern recognition and categorization. *Cognitive Psychology, 3*, 382–407.

Reeder, G. D. (1993). Trait–behavior relations and dispositional inference. *Personality and Social Psychology Bulletin, 19*, 586–593.

Reeder, G. D., & Brewer, M. B. (1979). A schematic model of dispositional attribution in interpersonal perception. *Psychological Review, 86*, 61–79.

Reeder, G. D., Vonk, R., Ronk, M. J., Ham, J., & Lawrence, M. (2004). Dispositional attribution: Multiple inferences about motive-related traits. *Journal of Personality and Social Psychology, 86*, 530–544.

Regan, P. C., Snyder, M., & Kassin, S. M. (1995). Unrealistic optimism: Self-enhancement or person positivity? *Personality and Social Psychology Bulletin, 21*, 1073–1082.

Reisenzein, R. (1983). The Schachter theory of emotion: Two decades later. *Psychological Bulletin, 94*, 239–264.

Reisenzein, R. (1986). A structural equation analysis of Weiner's attribution–affect model of helping behavior. *Journal of Personality and Social Psychology, 50*, 1123–1133.

Reiss, M., Rosenfeld, P., Melburg, V., & Tedeschi, J. T. (1981). Self-serving attributions: Biased private perceptions and distorted public descriptions. *Journal of Personality and Social Psychology, 41*, 224–251.

Reyna, C., Henry, P. J., Korfmacher, W., & Tucker, A. (2006). Examining the principles in principled conservatism: The role of responsibility stereotypes as cues for deservingness in racial policy decisions. *Journal of Personality and Social Psychology, 90*, 109–128.

Rhee, E., Uleman, J. S., Lee, H. K., & Roman, R. J. (1995). Spontaneous self-descriptions and ethnic identities in individualistic and collectivist cultures. *Journal of Personality and Social Psychology, 69*, 142–152.

Rhodewalt, F., & Comer, R. (1979). Induced-compliance attitude change: Once more with feeling. *Journal of Experimental Social Psychology, 15*, 35–47.

Rhodewalt, F., Sanbonmatsu, D. M., Tschanz, B., Feick, D. L., & Waller, A. (1995). Self-handicapping and interpersonal trade-offs: The effects of claimed self-handicaps on observers' performance evaluations and feedback. *Personality and Social Psychology Bulletin, 21*, 1042–1050.

Rholes, W. S., Jones, M., & Wade, C. (1988). Children's understanding of personal dispositions and its relationship to behavior. *Journal of Experimental Child Psychology, 45*, 1–17.

Rholes, W. S., & Pryor, J. B. (1982). Cognitive accessibility and causal attributions. *Personality and Social Psychology Bulletin, 8*, 719–727.

Richeson, J. A., Baird, A. A., Gordon, H. L., Heatherton, T. F., Wyland, C. L., Trawalter, S., & Shelton, J. N. (2003). An fMRI investigation of the impact of interracial contact on executive function. *Nature Neuroscience, 6*, 1323–1328.

Richeson, J. A., & Shelton, J. N. (2003). When prejudice does not pay: Effects of interracial contact on executive function. *Psychological Science, 14*, 287–290.

Richeson, J. A., & Shelton, J. N. (2005). Brief report: Thin slices of racial bias. *Journal of Nonverbal Behavior, 29*, 75–86.

Richeson, J. A., & Shelton, J. N. (2006). A social psychological perspective on the stigmatization of older adults. In L. L. Carstensen & C. R. Hartel (Eds.), *When I'm 64* (pp. 174–208). Washington, DC: National Research Council Committee on Aging Frontiers in Social Psychology, Personality, and Adult Developmental Psychology/The National Academies Press.

Richeson, J. A., & Trawalter, S. (2005). Why do interracial interactions impair executive function? A resource depletion account. *Journal of Personality and Social Psychology, 88,* 934–947.

Richeson, J. A., Trawalter, S., & Shelton, J. N. (2005). African Americans' implicit racial attitudes and the depletion of executive function after interracial internactions. *Social Cognition, 23,* 336–352.

Ridgeway, C. L. (2001). The emergence of status beliefs: From structural inequality to legitimizing ideology. In J. T. Jost & B. Major (Eds.), *The psychology of legitimacy* (pp. 257–277). New York: Cambridge University Press.

Rilling, J. K., Sanfey, A. G., Aronson, J. A., Nystrom, L. E., & Cohen, J. D. (2004). The neural correlates of theory of mind within interpersonal interactions. *NeuroImage, 22,* 1694–1703.

Rimé, B., Philippot, P., & Cisamolo, D. (1990). Social schemata of peripheral changes in emotion. *Journal of Personality and Social Psychology, 59,* 38–49.

Riskey, D. R. (1979). Verbal memory processes in impression formation. *Journal of Experimental Psychology: Human Learning and Memory, 5,* 271–281.

Rissman, J., & Wagner, A. D. (2012). Distributed representations in memory: Insights from functional brain imaging. *Annual Review of Psychology, 63,* 101–128.

Rizzolatti, G., Fogassi, L., & Gallese, V. (2001). Neurophysiological mechanisms underlying the understanding and imitation of action. *Nature Reviews Neuroscience, 2,* 661–670.

Robins, R. W., & Beer, J. S. (2001). Positive illusions about the self: Short-term benefits and long-term costs. *Journal of Personality and Social Psychology, 80,* 340–352.

Robinson, R. J., Keltner, D., Ward, A., & Ross, L. D. (1995). Actual versus assumed differences in construal: "Naïve realism" in intergroup perception and conflict. *Journal of Personality and Social Psychology, 68,* 404–417.

Robinson, R. J., & McArthur, L. Z. (1982). The impact of salient vocal qualities on causal attributions for a speaker's behavior. *Journal of Personality and Social Psychology, 43,* 236–247.

Robinson, M. D., & Clore, G. L. (2002a). Belief and feeling: Evidence for an accessibility model of emotional self-report. *Psychological Bulletin, 128,* 934–960.

Robinson, M. D., & Clore, G. L. (2002b). Episodic and semantic knowledge in emotional self-report: Evidence for two judgment processes. *Journal of Personality and Social Psychology, 83,* 198–215.

Robles, R., Smith, R., Carver, C. S., & Wellens, A. R. (1987). Influence of subliminal visual images on the experience of anxiety. *Personality and Social Psychology Bulletin, 13,* 399–410.

Rodin, M. J. (1987). Who is memorable to whom: A study of cognitive disregard. *Social Cognition, 5,* 144–165.

Roese, N. J., & Olson, J. M. (1994). Attitude importance as a function of repeated attitude expression. *Journal of Experimental Social Psychology, 30,* 39–51.

Rogers, M., Miller, N., Mayer, F. S., & Duval, S. (1982). Personal responsibility and salience of the request for help: Determinants of the relation between negative affect and helping behavior. *Journal of Personality and Social Psychology, 43,* 956–970.

Rogers, R. W., & Prentice-Dunn, S. (1981). Deindividuation and anger-mediated interracial aggression: Unmasking regressive racism. *Journal of Personality and Social Psychology, 41,* 63–73.

Rogers, T. B., Kuiper, N. A., & Kirker, W. S. (1977). Self-reference and the encoding of personal information. *Journal of Personality and Social Psychology, 35,* 677–688.

Rokeach, M. (1960). *The open and closed mind.* New York: Basic Books.

Romer, D. (1979). Distraction, counterarguing, and the internalization of attitude change. *European Journal of Social Psychology, 9,* 1–17.

Roney, C. J. R., Higgins, E. T., & Shah, J. Y. (1995). Goals and framing: How outcome focus influences motivation and emotion. *Personality and Social Psychology Bulletin, 21,* 1151–1160.

Rosch, E. H. (1978). Principles of categorization. In E. H. Rosch & B. B. Lloyd (Eds.), *Cognition and categorization.* Hillsdale, NJ: Erlbaum.

Rosch, E. H. (1987). Wittgenstein and categorization research in cognitive psychology. In M. Chapman & M. Dixon (Eds.), *Meaning and the growth of understanding: Wittgenstein's significance for developmental psychology.* Berlin: Springer-Verlag.

Rosch, E. H., Mervis, C. B., Gray, W., Johnson, D., & Boyes-Braem, P. (1976). Basic objects in natural categories. *Cognitive Psychology, 8,* 382–439.

Roseman, I. J. (1984). Cognitive determinants of emotion: A structural theory. In P. Shaver (Ed.), *Review of personality and social psychology* (Vol. 5, pp. 11–36). Beverly Hills, CA: Sage.

Rosenberg, M. J. (1956). Cognitive structure and attitudinal affect. *Journal of Abnormal and Social Psychology, 53,* 367–372.

Rosenberg, M. J. (1960). An analysis of affective-cognitive consistency. In C. I. Hovland & M. J. Rosenberg (Eds.), *Attitude organization and change.* New Haven, CT: Yale University Press.

Rosenberg, M. J. (1965). *Society and the adolescent self-image.* Princeton, NJ: Princeton University Press.

Rosenberg, S., & Sedlak, A. (1972). Structural representations of implicit personality theory. In L. Berkowitz (Ed.), *Advances in experimental social psychology* (Vol. 6, pp. 235–297). New York: Academic Press.

Rosenhan, D. L., Salovey, P., & Hargis, K. (1981). The joys of helping: Focus of attention mediates the impact of positive affect on altruism. *Journal of Personality and Social Psychology, 40,* 899–905.

Rosenthal, H. E., & Crisp, R. J. (2006). Reducing stereotype threat by blurring intergroup boundaries. *Personality and Social Psychology Bulletin, 32,* 501–511.

Rosenthal, R. (1974). *On the social psychology of the self-fulfilling prophecy: Further evidence for Pygmalion effects and their mediating mechanisms.* New York: MSS Modular Publications (Module 53).

Rosenthal, R., & Jacobson, L. F. (1968). *Pygmalion in the classroom.* New York: Holt, Rinehart, & Winston.

Roser, M., & Gazzaniga, M. S. (2004). Automatic brains – Interpretive minds. *Current Directions in Psychological Science, 13,* 56–59.

Ross, L. D. (1977). The intuitive psychologist and his shortcomings: Distortions in the attribution process. In L. Berkowitz (Ed.), *Advances in experimental social psychology* (Vol. 10, pp. 174–221). New York: Academic Press.

Ross, L. D., Lepper, M. R., & Hubbard, M. (1975). Perseverance in self-perception and social perception: Biased attribution processes in the debriefing paradigm. *Journal of Personality and Social Psychology, 32,* 880–892.

Ross, L. D., Lepper, M. R., Strack, F., & Steinmetz, J. (1977). Social explanation and social expectation: Effects of real and hypothetical explanations on subjective likelihood. *Journal of Personality and Social Psychology, 35,* 817–829.

Ross, L. D., Rodin, J., & Zimbardo, P. G. (1969). Toward an attribution therapy: The reduction of fear through induced cognitive-emotional misattribution. *Journal of Personality and Social Psychology, 12,* 279–288.

Ross, M. (1989). The relation of implicit theories to the construction of personal histories. *Psychological Review, 96,* 341–357.

Ross, M., McFarland, C., Conway, M., & Zanna, M. P. (1983). Reciprocal relation between attitudes and behavior recall: Committing people to newly formed attitudes. *Journal of Personality and Social Psychology, 45,* 257–267.

Ross, M., McFarland, C., & Fletcher, G. J. O. (1981). The effect of attitude on the recall of personal histories. *Journal of Personality and Social Psychology, 10,* 627–634.

Ross, M., & Shulman, R. F. (1973). Increasing the salience of initial attitudes: Dissonance vs. self-perception theory. *Journal of Personality and Social Psychology, 28,* 138–144.

Ross, M., & Sicoly, F. (1979). Egocentric biases in availability and attribution. *Journal of Personality and Social Psychology, 37,* 322–337.

Ross, M., & Wilson, A. E. (2002). It feels like yesterday: Self-esteem, valence of personal past experiences, and judgments of subjective distance. *Journal of Personality and Social Psychology, 82,* 792–803.

Rothbart, M., Evans, M., & Fulero, S. (1979). Recall for confirming events: Memory processes and the maintenance of social stereotypes. *Journal of Experimental Social Psychology, 15,* 343–355.

Rothbart, M., Fulero, S., Jensen, C., Howard, J., & Birrell, B. (1978). From individual to group impressions: Availability heuristics in stereotype formation. *Journal of Experimental Social Psychology, 14,* 237–255.

Rothbart, M., & Park, B. (1986). On the confirmability and disconfirmability of trait concepts. *Journal of Personality and Social Psychology, 50,* 131–142.

Rothbart, M., & Taylor, M. (1992). Category labels and social reality: Do we view social categories as natural kinds? In G. Semin & K. Fiedler (Eds.), *Language, interaction and social cognition* (pp. 11–36). London: Sage.

Rothman, A. J., & Hardin, C. D. (1997). Differential use of the availability heuristic in social judgment. *Personality and Social Psychology Bulletin, 23,* 123–128.

Rothman, A. J., & Salovey, P. (1997). Shaping perceptions to motivate healthy behavior: The role of message framing. *Psychological Bulletin, 121,* 3–19.

Rowley, S. J., Sellers, R. M., Chavous, T. M., & Smith, M. A. (1998). The relationship between racial identity and self-esteem in African American college and high school students. *Journal of Personality and Social Psychology, 74,* 715–724.

Rozin, P., & Fallon, A. E. (1987). A perspective on disgust. *Psychological Review, 94,* 23–41.

Rubin, M., & Hewstone, M. (1998). Social identity theory's self-esteem hypothesis: A review and some suggestions for clarification. *Personality and Social Psychology Review, 2,* 40–62.

Ruble, D. N., & Ruble, T. L. (1982). Sex stereotypes. In A. G. Miller (Ed.), *In the eye of the beholder: Contemporary issues in stereotyping* (pp. 188–252). New York: Praeger.

Ruble, D. N., & Stangor, C. (1986). Stalking the elusive schema: Insights from developmental and social-psychological analyses of gender schemas. *Social Cognition, 4,* 227–261.

Ruder, M., & Bless, H. (2003). Mood and the reliance on the ease of retrieval heuristic. *Journal of Personality and Social Psychology, 85,* 20–32.

Rudman, L. A. (1998). Self-promotion as a risk factor for women: The costs and benefits of counterstereotypical impression management. *Journal of Personality and Social Psychology, 74,* 629–645.

Rudman, L. A. (2004). Sources of implicit attitudes. *Current Directions in Psychological Science, 13,* 79–82.

Rudman, L. A., & Ashmore, R. D. (2007). Discrimination and the IAT. *Group Processes and Intergroup Relations, 10,* 359–372.

Rudman, L. A., Ashmore, R. D., & Gary, M. L. (2001). "Unlearning" automatic biases: The malleability of implicit prejudice and stereotypes. *Journal of Personality and Social Psychology, 81,* 856–868.

Rudman, L. A., & Borgida, E. (1995). The afterglow of construct accessibility: The behavioral consequences of priming men to view women as sexual objects. *Journal of Experimental Social Psychology, 31(6),* 493–517.

Rudman, L. A., & Fairchild, K. (2004). Reactions to counterstereotypic behavior: The role of backlash in cultural stereotype maintenance. *Journal of Personality and Social Psychology, 87,* 157–176.

Rudman, L. A., Feinberg, J., & Fairchild, K. (2002). Minority members' implicit attitudes: Automatic ingroup bias as a function of group status. *Social Cognition, 20,* 294–320.

Rudman, L. A., & Glick, P. (1999). Feminized management and backlash toward agentic women: The hidden costs to women of a kinder, gentler image of middle managers. *Journal of Personality and Social Psychology, 77,* 1004–1010.

Rudman, L. A., & Glick, P. (2001). Prescriptive gender stereotypes and backlash toward agentic women. *Journal of Social Issues, 57,* 743–762.

Rudman, L. A., & Glick, P. (2008). *The social psychology of gender: How power and intimacy shape gender relations.* New York: Guilford Press.

Rudman, L. A., Greenwald, A. G., & McGhee, D. E. (2001). Implicit self-concept and evaluative implicit gender stereotypes: Self and ingroup share desirable traits. *Personality and Social Psychology Bulletin, 27,* 1164–1178.

Rudman, L. A., Greenwald, A. G., Mellott, D. S., & Schwartz, J. L. K. (1999). Measuring the automatic components of prejudice: Flexibility and generality of the implicit association test. *Social Cognition, 17,* 437–465.

Rudman, L. A., & Heppen, J. B. (2003). Implicit romantic fantasies and women's interest in personal power: A glass slipper effect? *Personality and Social Psychology Bulletin, 29,* 1357–1370.

Rudman, L. A., & Kilianski, S. E. (2000). Implicit and explicit attitudes toward female authority. *Personality and Social Psychology Bulletin, 26,* 1315–1328.

Rudolph, U., Roesch, S. C., Greitemeyer, T., & Weiner, B. (2004). A meta-analytic review of help giving and aggression from an attributional perspective: Contributions to a general theory of motivation. *Cognition and Emotion, 18,* 815–848.

Rudoy, J. D., & Paller, K. A. (2009). Who can you trust? Behavioral and neural differences between perception and memory-based influences. *Frontiers in Human Neuroscience, 3,* 1–6.

Rule, B. G., Taylor, B. R., & Dobbs, A. R. (1987). Priming effects of heat on aggressive thoughts. *Social Cognition, 5,* 131–143.

Rule, N. O., & Ambady, N. (2008). Brief exposures: Male sexual orientation is accurately perceived at 50 ms. *Journal of Experimental Social Psychology, 44,* 1100–1105.

Rule, N. O., Ambady, N., & Adams, R. B., Jr. (2009). Personality in perspective: Judgmental consistency across orientations of the face. *Perception, 38(11),* 1688–1699.

Rumelhart, D. E., Lindsay, P. H., & Norman, D. A. (1972). A process model for long-term memory. In E. Tulving & W. Donaldson (Eds.), *Organization of memory* (pp. 197–246). New York: Academic Press.

Rumelhart, D. E., & Ortony, A. (1977). The representation of knowledge in memory. In R. C. Anderson, R. J. Spiro, & W. E. Montague (Eds.), *Schooling and the acquisition of knowledge* (pp. 99–136). Hillsdale, NJ: Erlbaum.

Ruscher, J. B., & Fiske, S. T. (1990). Interpersonal competition can cause individuating impression formation. *Journal of Personality and Social Psychology, 58,* 832–842.

Russell, J. A. (2003). Core affect and the psychological construction of emotion. *Psychological Review, 110,* 145–172.

Russell, J. A., & Bullock, M. (1985). Multidimensional scaling of emotional facial expressions: Similarity from preschoolers to adults. *Journal of Personality and Social Psychology, 48,* 1290–1298.

Russell, J. A., & Bullock, M. (1986). Fuzzy concepts and the perception of emotion in facial expressions. *Social Cognition, 4,* 309–341.

Russell, J. A., & Fehr, B. (1987). Relativity in the perception of emotion in facial expressions. *Journal of Experimental Psychology: General, 116,* 223–237.

Russell, J. A., & Fehr, B. (1988). Reply to Ekman & O'Sullivan. *Journal of Experimental Psychology: General, 117,* 89–90.

Russell, J. A., & Woudzia, L. (1986). Affective judgments, common sense, and Zajonc's thesis of independence. *Motivation and Emotion, 10,* 169–183.

Rusting, C. L. (1998). Personality, mood, and cognitive processing of emotional information: Three conceptual frameworks. *Psychological Bulletin, 124,* 165–196.

Rusting, C. L. (1999). Interactive effects of personality and mood on emotion-congruent memory and judgment. *Journal of Personality and Social Psychology, 77,* 1073–1086.

Rusting, C. L., & DeHart, T. (2000). Retrieving positive memories to regulate negative mood: Consequences for mood congruent memory. *Journal of Personality and Social Psychology, 78,* 737–752.

Saenz, D. S., & Lord, C. G. (1989). Reversing roles: A cognitive strategy for undoing memory deficits associated with token status. *Journal of Personality and Social Psychology, 56,* 698–708.

Salovey, P. (1991). Social comparison processes in envy and jealousy. In J. Suls & T. A. Wills (Eds.), *Social comparison theory: Contemporary theory and research* (pp. 261–285). Hillsdale, NJ: Erlbaum.

Salovey, P., & Rodin, J. (1985). Cognitions about the self: Connecting feeling states and social behavior. In P. Shaver (Ed.), *Review of personality and social psychology* (Vol. 6, pp. 143–166). Beverly Hills, CA: Sage.

Salovey, P., & Singer, J. A. (1988). Mood congruency effects in recall of childhood versus recent memories. *Journal of Social Behavior and Personality, 3,* 1–22.

Samuelson, P. A. (1937). A note on measurement of utility. *Review of Economic Studies, 4,* 155–161.

Sanbonmatsu, D. M., & Fazio, R. H. (1990). The role of attitudes in memory-based decision making. *Journal of Personality and Social Psychology, 59,* 614–622.

Sanbonmatsu, D. M., Shavitt, S., & Gibson, B. D. (1994). Salience, set size, and illusory correlation: Making moderate assumptions about extreme targets. *Journal of Personality and Social Psychology, 66,* 1020–1033.

Sanbonmatsu, D. M., Sherman, S. J., & Hamilton, D. L. (1987). Illusory correlation in the perception of individuals and groups. *Social Cognition, 5,* 1–25.

Sanchez, D. T., & Crocker, J. (2005). How investment in gender ideals affects well-being: The role of external contingencies of self-worth. *Psychology of Women Quarterly, 29,* 63–77.

Sanchez, D. T., Crocker, J., & Boike, K. R. (2005). Doing gender in the bedroom: Investing in gender norms and the sexual experience. *Personality and Social Psychology Bulletin, 31*, 1445–1455.

Sanders, J. D., McClure, K. A., & Zárate, M. A. (2004). Cerebral hemisphere asymmetries in social perception: Perceiving and responding to the individual and the group. *Social Cognition, 22*, 279–291.

Sanfey, A. G., Loewenstein, G., McClure, S. M., & Cohen, J. D. (2006). Neuroeconomics: Cross-currents in research on decision-making. *Trends in Cognitive Sciences, 10*, 108–116.

Sanfey, A. G., Rilling, J. K., Aronson, J. A., Nystrom, L. E., & Cohen, J. D. (2003). The neural basis of economic decision-making in the ultimatum game. *Science, 300*, 1755–1758.

Sansone, C., & Harackiewicz, J. M. (2000). *Intrinsic and extrinsic motivation: The search for optimal motivation and performance.* San Diego, CA: Academic Press.

Santuzzi, A. M., & Ruscher, J. B. (2002). Stigma salience and paranoid social cognition: Understanding variability in metaperceptions among individuals with recently-acquired stigma. *Social Cognition, 20*, 171–197.

Saucier, D. A., Miller, C. T., & Doucet, N. (2005). Differences in helping Whites and Blacks: A meta-analysis. *Personality and Social Psychology Review, 9*, 2–16.

Savitsky, K., Gilovich, T., Berger, G., & Medvec, V. H. (2003). Is our absence as conspicuous as we think? Overestimating the salience and impact of one's absence from a group. *Journal of Experimental Social Psychology, 39*, 386–392.

Sawyer, A. (1981). Repetition, cognitive responses, and persuasion. In R. E. Petty, T. M. Ostrom, & T. C. Brock (Eds.), *Cognitive responses in persuasion* (pp. 237–262). Hillsdale, NJ: Erlbaum.

Sawyer, J. (1966). Measurement and prediction, clinical and statistical. *Psychological Bulletin, 66*, 178–200.

Saxe, R., Carey, S., & Kanwisher, N. (2004). Understanding other minds: Linking developmental psychology and functional neuroimaging. *Annual Review of Psychology, 55*, 87–124.

Schachter, S. (1959). *The psychology of affiliation.* Stanford, CA: Stanford University Press.

Schachter, S. (1964). The interaction of cognitive and physiological determinants of emotional state. In L. Berkowitz (Ed.), *Advances in experimental social psychology* (Vol. 1, pp. 49–82). New York: Academic Press.

Schachter, S., & Singer, J. A. (1962). Cognitive, social, and physiological determinants of emotional state. *Psychological Review, 69*, 379–399.

Schaffner, P. E. (1985). Specious learning about reward and punishment. *Journal of Personality and Social Psychology, 48*, 1377–1386.

Schaller, M., & Cialdini, R. B. (1988). The economics of empathic helping: Support for a mood management motive. *Journal of Experimental Social Psychology, 24*, 163–181.

Schank, R. C., & Abelson, R. P. (1977). *Scripts, plans, goals, and understanding: An inquiry into human knowledge structures.* Hillsdale, NJ: Erlbaum.

Schaufeli, W. B. (1988). Perceiving the causes of unemployment: An evaluation of the causal dimensions scale in a real-life situation. *Journal of Personality and Social Psychology, 54*, 347–356.

Scheier, M. F., & Carver, C. S. (1982). Cognition, affect, and self-regulation. In M. S. Clark & S. T. Fiske (Eds.), *Affect and cognition: The 17th Annual Carnegie Symposium on Cognition* (pp. 157–184). Hillsdale, NJ: Erlbaum.

Scheier, M. F., Carver, C. S., & Gibbons, F. X. (1981). Self-focused attention and reactions to fear. *Journal of Research in Personality, 15*, 1–15.

Scherer, K. R. (1984). Emotion as a multicomponent process: A model and some cross-cultural data. In P. Shaver (Ed.), *Review of personality and social psychology* (Vol. 5, pp. 37–63).

Scherer, K. R. (1988). Criteria for emotion-antecedent appraisal: A review. In V. Hamilton, G. H. Bower, & N. H. Frijda (Eds.), *Cognitive perspectives on emotion and motivation* (pp. 89–112). New York: Kluwer Academic.

Scherer, K. R., Wallbott, H. G., & Summerfield, A. B. (Eds.). (1986). *Experiencing emotion: A cross-cultural study.* Cambridge: Cambridge University Press.

Schimel, J., Arndt, J., Pyszczynski, T., & Greenberg, J. (2001). Being accepted for who we are: Evidence that social validation of the intrinsic self reduces general defensiveness. *Journal of Personality and Social Psychology, 80*, 35–52.

Schimel, J., Pyszczynski, T., Greenberg, J., O'Mahen, H., & Arndt, J. (2000). Running from the shadow: Psychological distancing from others to deny characteristics people fear in themselves. *Journal of Personality and Social Psychology, 78,* 446–462.

Schimel, J., Simon, L., Greenberg, J., Pyszczynski, T., Solomon, S., Waxmonsky, J., & Arndt, J. (1999). Stereotypes and terror management: Evidence that mortality salience enhances stereotypic thinking and preferences. *Journal of Personality and Social Psychology, 77,* 905–926.

Schlenker, B. R. (1987). Threats to identity: Self-identification and social stress. In C. R. Snyder & C. E. Ford (Eds.), *Coping with negative life events: Clinical and social psychological perspectives* (pp. 273–321). New York: Plenum Press.

Schlosberg, H. (1954). Three dimensions of emotion. *Psychological Review, 61,* 81–88.

Schmader, T., & Johns, M. (2003). Converging evidence that stereotype threat reduces working memory capacity. *Journal of Personality and Social Psychology, 85,* 440–452.

Schmeichel, B. J., & Martens, A. (2005). Self-affirmation and mortality salience: Affirming values reduces worldview defense and death-thought accessibility. *Personality and Social Psychology Bulletin, 31,* 658–667.

Schmeichel, B. J., Vohs, K. D., & Baumeister, R. F. (2003). Intellectual performance and ego depletion: Role of the self in logical reasoning and other information processing. *Journal of Personality and Social Psychology, 85,* 33–46.

Schmidt, D. F., & Sherman, R. C. (1984). Memory for persuasive messages: A test of a schema-copy-plus-tag model. *Journal of Personality and Social Psychology, 47,* 17–25.

Schmidt, G., & Weiner, B. (1988). An attribution-affect-action theory of behavior: Replications of judgments of help-giving. *Personality and Social Psychology Bulletin, 14,* 610–621.

Schmidt-Atzert, L. (1988). Affect and cognition: On the chronological order of stimulus evaluation and emotion. In K. Fiedler, & J. P. Forgas (Eds.), *Affect, cognition, and social behavior* (pp. 153–164). Toronto, Canada: Hogrefe.

Schmitt, M. T., Branscombe, N. R., & Kappen, D. M. (2003). Attitudes toward group-based inequality: Social dominance or social identity? *British Journal of Social Psychology, 42,* 161–186.

Schmitt, M. T., Branscombe, N. R., & Postmes, T. (2003). Women's emotional responses to the pervasiveness of gender discrimination. *European Journal of Social Psychology, 33,* 297–312.

Schnall, S., Haidt, J., Clore, G. L., & Jordan, A. H. (2008). Disgust as embodied moral judgment. *Personality and Social Psychology Bulletin, 34*(8), 1096–1109.

Schneider, D. J. (1973). Implicit personality theory: A review. *Psychological Bulletin, 79,* 294–309.

Schneider, D. J., Hastorf, A. H., & Ellsworth, P. C. (1979). *Person perception.* Reading, MA: Addison-Wesley.

Schnittker, J., & McLeod, J. D. (2005). The social psychology of health disparities. *Annual Review of Sociology, 31,* 75–103.

Schooler, J. W., & Engstler-Schooler, T. Y. (1990). Verbal overshadowing of visual memories: Some things are better left unsaid. *Cognitive Psychology, 22,* 36–71.

Schopler, J., Insko, C. A., Wieselquist, J., Pemberton, M., Witcher, B., Kozar, R., Roddenberry, C., & Wildschut, T. (2001). When groups are more competitive than individuals: The domain of the discontinuity effect. *Journal of Personality and Social Psychology, 80,* 632–644.

Schroeder, D. A., Dovidio, J. F., Sibicky, M. E., Matthews, L. L., & Allen, J. L. (1988). Empathy and helping behavior: Egoism or altruism? *Journal of Experimental Social Psychology, 24,* 333–353.

Schubert, T. W. (2004). The power in your hand: Gender differences in bodily feedback from making a fist. *Personality and Social Psychology Bulletin, 30,* 757–769.

Schul, Y., Mayo, R., & Burnstein, E. (2004). Encoding under trust and distrust: The spontaneous activation of incongruent cognitions. *Journal of Personality and Social Psychology, 86,* 668–679.

Schuman, H., & Johnson, M. P. (1976). Attitudes and behavior. *Annual Review of Sociology, 2,* 161–207.

Schutte, N. S., Kenrick, D. T., & Sadalla, E. K. (1985). The search for predictable settings: Situational prototypes, constraint, and behavioral variation. *Journal of Personality and Social Psychology, 49,* 121–128.

Schwartz, G. E., Davidson, R. J., & Pugash, E. (1976). Voluntary control of patterns of EEG parietal asymmetry: Cognitive concomitants. *Psychophysiology, 13,* 498–504.

Schwartz, G. E., Weinberger, D. A., & Singer, J. A. (1981). Cardiovascular differentiation of happiness, sadness, anger, and fear following imagery and exercise. *Psychosomatic Medicine, 43,* 343–364.

Schwartz, S. H. (1978). Temporal instability as a moderator of the attitude–behavior relationship. *Journal of Personality and Social Psychology, 36,* 715–724.

Schwartz, S. H., & Inbar-Saban, N. (1988). Value self-confrontation as a method to aid in weight loss. *Journal of Personality and Social Psychology, 54,* 396–404.

Schwartz, S. H., & Tessler, R. C. (1972). A test of a model for reducing measured attitude–behavior discrepancies. *Journal of Personality and Social Psychology, 24,* 225–236.

Schwarz, N., Bless, H., & Bohner, G. (1991). Mood and persuasion: Affective states influence the processing of persuasive communications. In M. P. Zanna (Ed.), *Advances in experimental social psychology* (Vol. 24, pp. 161–199). New York: Academic Press.

Schwarz, N., Bless, H., Strack, F., Klumpp, G., Rittenauer-Schatka, H., & Simons, A. (1991). Ease of retrieval as information: Another look at the availability heuristic. *Journal of Personality and Social Psychology, 61,* 195–202.

Schwarz, N., & Clore, G. L. (1996). Feelings and phenomenal experiences. In E. T. Higgins & A. W. Kruglanski (Eds.), *Social psychology: Handbook of basic principles* (pp. 433–465). New York: Guilford Press.

Schwarz, N., Strack, F., Hilton, D. J., & Naderer, G. (1991). Base-rates, representativeness, and the logic of conversation. *Social Cognition, 9,* 67–84.

Sears, D. O. (1965). Biased indoctrination and selectivity of exposure to new information. *Sociometry, 28,* 363–376.

Sears, D. O. (1968). The paradox of de facto selective exposure. In R. P. Abelson et al. (Eds.), *Theories of cognitive consistency: A sourcebook.* Chicago: Rand McNally.

Sears, D. O. (1983). The person-positivity bias. *Journal of Personality and Social Psychology, 44,* 233–240.

Sears, D. O. (1998). Racism and politics in the United States. In J. L. Eberhardt, & S. T. Fiske (Eds.), *Confronting racism: The problem and the response* (pp. 76–100). Thousand Oaks, CA: Sage.

Sears, D. O., & Henry, P. J. (2003). The origins of symbolic racism. *Journal of Personality and Social Psychology, 85,* 259–275.

Sears, D. O., Huddie, L., & Schaffer, L. G. (1986). A schematic variant of symbolic politics theory, as applied to racial and gender equality. In R. R. Lau & D. O. Sears (Eds.), *Political cognition* (pp. 159–202). Hillsdale, NJ: Erlbaum.

Sears, D. O., & Kinder, D. R. (1985). Whites' opposition to busing: On conceptualizing and operationalizing group conflict. *Journal of Personality and Social Psychology, 48,* 1148–1161.

Sears, D. O., & Whitney, R. E. (1973). Political persuasion. In I. de S. Pool, W. Schramm, F. W. Frey, N. Maccoby, & E. B. Parker (Eds.), *Handbook of communication* (pp. 253–289). Chicago: Rand McNally.

Seccombe, K., & Ishii-Kuntz, M. (1991). Perceptions of problems associated with aging: Comparisons among four older age cohorts. *Gerontologist, 31,* 527–533.

Sechrist, G. B., Swim, J. K., & Stangor, C. (2004). When do the stigmatized make attributions to discrimination occurring to the self and others? The roles of self-presentation and need for control. *Journal of Personality and Social Psychology, 87,* 111–122.

Sedikides, C. (1993). Assessment, enhancement, and verification determinants of the self-evaluation process. *Journal of Personality and Social Psychology, 65,* 317–338.

Sedikides, C., Gaertner, L., & Toguchi, Y. (2003). Pancultural self-enhancement. *Journal of Personality and Social Psychology, 84,* 60–79.

Sedikides, C., & Green, J. D. (2000). On the self-protective nature of inconsistency-negativity management: Using the person memory paradigm to examine self-referent memory. *Journal of Personality and Social Psychology, 79,* 906–922.

Seger, C. A. (1994). Implicit learning. *Psychological Bulletin, 115,* 163–196.

Segerstrom, S. C., Taylor, S. E., Kemeny, M. E., & Fahey, J. L. (1998). Optimism is associated with mood, coping and immune change in response to stress. *Journal of Personality and Social Psychology, 74,* 1646–1655.

Seibt, B., & Förster, J. (2004). Stereotype threat and performance: How self-stereotypes influence processing by inducing regulatory foci. *Journal of Personality and Social Psychology, 87,* 38–56.

Sekaquaptewa, D., & Thompson, M. (2003). Solo status, stereotype threat, and performance expectancies: Their effects on women's performance. *Journal of Experimental Social Psychology, 39,* 68–74.

Sellers, R. M., Caldwell, C. H., Schmeelk-Cone, K. H., & Zimmerman, M. A. (2003). Racial identity, racial discrimination, perceived stress, and psychological distress among African American young adults. *Journal of Health and Social Behavior, 44,* 302–317.

Sellers, R. M., Rowley, S. A. J., Chavous, T. M., Shelton, J. N., & Smith, M. A. (1997). Multidimensional inventory of Black identity: A preliminary investigation of reliability and construct validity. *Journal of Personality and Social Psychology, 73,* 805–815.

Sellers, R. M., & Shelton, J. N. (2003). The role of racial identity in perceived racial discrimination. *Journal of Personality and Social Psychology, 84,* 1079–1092.

Semin, G. R., Garrido, M. V., & Palma, T. A. (2012). Socially situated cognition: Recasting social cognition as an emergent phenomenon. In S. T. Fiske & C. N. Macrae (Eds.), *Sage handbook of social cognition* (pp. 138–164). Thousand Oaks, CA: Sage.

Sentis, K. P., & Burnstein, E. (1979). Remembering schema consistent information: Effects of a balance schema on recognition memory. *Journal of Personality and Social Psychology, 37,* 2200–2211.

Seta, J. J., McElroy, T., & Seta, C. E. (2001). To do or not to do: Desirability and consistency mediate judgments of regret. *Journal of Personality and Social Psychology, 80,* 861–870.

Setterlund, M. B., & Niedenthal, P. M. (1993). "Who am I? Why am I here?" Self-esteem, self-clarity, and prototype matching. *Journal of Personality and Social Psychology, 65,* 769–780.

Sevillano, V., & Fiske, S. T. (under review). Animal collective: Social perception of animals.

Shah, J. Y. (2003a). Automatic for the people: How representations of significant others implicitly affect goal pursuit. *Journal of Personality and Social Psychology, 84,* 661–681.

Shah, J. Y. (2003b). The motivational looking glass: How significant others implicitly affect goal appraisals. *Journal of Personality and Social Psychology, 85,* 424–439.

Shah, J. Y., Friedman, R., & Kruglanski, A. W. (2002). Forgetting all else: On the antecedents and consequences of goal shielding. *Journal of Personality and Social Psychology, 83,* 1261–1280.

Shah, J. Y., Higgins, E. T., & Friedman, R. S. (1998). Performance incentives and means: How regulatory focus influences goal attainment. *Journal of Personality and Social Psychology, 74,* 285–293.

Shallice, T. (1972). Dual functions of consciousness. *Psychological Review, 79,* 383–393.

Shallice, T. (1978). The dominant action system: An information-processing approach to consciousness. In K. S. Pope & J. L. Singer (Eds.), *The stream of consciousness: Scientific investigations into the flow of human experience.* New York: Plenum Press.

Shapira, O., Liberman, N., Trope, Y., & Rim, S. Y. (2012). Levels of mental construal. In S. T. Fiske & C. N. Macrae (Eds.), *Sage handbook of social cognition* (pp. 229–250). Thousand Oaks, CA: Sage.

Shapiro, D., & Crider, A. (1969). Psychophysiological approaches in social psychology. In G. Lindzey & E. Aronson (Eds.), *The handbook of social psychology* (Vol. 3, pp. 1–49). Reading, MA: Addison-Wesley.

Shaver, K. G. (1975). *An introduction to attribution processes.* Cambridge, MA: Winthrop.

Shaver, K. G. (1985). *The attribution of blame: Causality, responsibility, and blameworthiness.* New York: Springer-Verlag.

Shaver, P. (Ed.). (1984). *Review of personality and social psychology: Emotions, relationships, and health* (Vol. 5). Beverly Hills, CA: Sage.

Shaver, P., Schwartz, J., Kirson, D., & O'Connor, C. (1987). Emotion knowledge: Further exploration of a prototype approach. *Journal of Personality and Social Psychology, 52,* 1061–1086.

Shavitt, S. (1989). Operationalizing functional theories of attitude. In A. R. Pratkanis, S. J. Breckler, & A. G. Greenwald (Eds.), *Attitude structure and function* (pp. 311–338). Hillsdale, NJ: Erlbaum.

Shaw, M. E. (1971). *Group dynamics.* New York: McGraw-Hill.

Shedler, J., & Manis, M. (1986). Can the availability heuristic explain vividness effects? *Journal of Personality and Social Psychology, 51,* 26–36.

Sheeran, P., Orbell, S., & Trafimow, D. (1999). Does the temporal stability of behavioral intentions moderate intention–behavior and past behavior–future behavior relations? *Personality and Social Psychology Bulletin, 25*, 721–730.

Sheeran, P., Webb, T. L., & Gollwitzer, P. M. (2005). The interplay between goal intentions and implementation intentions. *Personality and Social Psychology Bulletin, 31*, 87–98.

Shelton, J. N. (2000). A reconceptualization of how we study issues of racial prejudice. *Personality and Social Psychology Review, 4*, 374–390.

Shelton, J. N. (2003). Interpersonal concerns in social encounters between majority and minority group members. *Group Processes & Intergroup Relations, 6*, 171–185.

Shelton, J. N., & Richeson, J. A. (2005). Intergroup contact and pluralistic ignorance. *Journal of Personality and Social Psychology, 88*, 91–107.

Shelton, J. N., & Richeson, J. A. (2006). Interracial interactions: A relational approach. In M. P. Zanna (Ed.), *Advances in experimental social psychology* (pp. 121–181). New York: Academic Press.

Shelton, J. N., Richeson, J. A., & Salvatore, J. (2005). Expecting to be the target of prejudice: Implications for interethnic interactions. *Personality and Social Psychology Bulletin, 31*, 1189–1202.

Shelton, J. N., Richeson, J. A., Salvatore, J., & Trawalter, S. (2005). Ironic effects of racial bias during interracial interactions. *Psychological Science, 16*, 397–402.

Shelton, J. N., & Sellers, R. M. (2000). Situational stability and variability in African American racial identity. *Journal of Black Psychology, 26*, 27–50.

Shepperd, J. A., Ouellette, J. A., & Fernandez, J. K. (1996). Abandoning unrealistic optimism: Performance estimates and the temporal proximity of self-relevant feedback. *Journal of Personality and Social Psychology, 70*, 844–855.

Sherer, M., & Rogers, R. W. (1984). The role of vivid information in fear appeals and attitude change. *Journal of Research in Personality, 18*, 321–334.

Sherif, C. W., Kelly, M., Rodgers, H. L., Sarup, G., & Tittler, B. (1973). Personal involvement, social judgment, and action. *Journal of Personality and Social Psychology, 27*, 311–327.

Sherif, M., & Hovland, C. I. (1961). *Social judgment: Assimilation and contrast effects in communication and attitude change.* New Haven, CT: Yale University Press.

Sherif, M., & Sherif, M. (1953). *Groups in harmony and tension: An integration of studies on intergroup relations.* Oxford: Harper & Brothers.

Sherman, D. K., & Cohen, G. L. (2002). Accepting threatening information: Self-affirmation and the reduction of defensive biases. *Current Directions in Psychological Science, 11*, 119–123.

Sherman, D. K., & Cohen, G. L. (2006). The psychology of self-defense: Self-affirmation theory. In M. P. Zanna (Ed.), *Advances in experimental social psychology* (Vol. 38, pp. 183–242). San Diego, CA: Academic Press.

Sherman, D. K., Mann, T., & Updegraff, J. A. (2006). Approach/avoidance orientation, message framing, and health behavior: Understanding the congruency effect. *Motivation and Emotion, 30*, 165–169.

Sherman, D. K., Nelson, L. D., & Ross, L. D. (2003). Naive realism and affirmative action: Adversaries are more similar than they think. *Basic and Applied Social Psychology, 25*, 275–289.

Sherman, D. K., Nelson, L. D., & Steele, C. M. (2000). Do messages about health risks threaten the self? Increasing the acceptance of threatening health messages via self-affirmation. *Personality and Social Psychology Bulletin, 26*, 1046–1058.

Sherman, J. W., Conrey, F. R., & Groom, C. J. (2004). Encoding flexibility revisited: Evidence for enhanced encoding of stereotype-inconsistent information under cognitive load. *Social Cognition, 22*, 214–232.

Sherman, J. W., Klein, S. B., Laskey, A., & Wyer, N. A. (1998). Intergroup bias in group judgment processes: The role of behavioral memories. *Journal of Experimental Social Psychology, 34*, 51–65.

Sherman, J. W., Lee, A. Y., Bessenhoff, G. R., & Frost, L. A. (1998). Stereotype efficiency reconsidered: Encoding flexibility under cognitive load. *Journal of Personality and Social Psychology, 75*, 589–606.

Sherman, J. W., Stroessner, S. J., Conrey, F. R., & Azam, O. A. (2005). Prejudice and stereotype maintenance processes: Attention, attribution and individuation. *Journal of Personality and Social Psychology, 89*, 607–622.

Sherman, R. C., & Titus, W. (1982). Convariation information and cognitive processing: Effects of causal implications on memory. *Journal of Personality and Social Psychology, 42,* 989–1000.

Sherman, S. J. (1987). Cognitive processes in the formation, change, and expression of attitudes. In M. P. Zanna, J. M. Olson, & C. P. Herman (Eds.), *Social influence: The Ontario Symposium* (Vol. 5, pp. 75–106). Hillsdale, NJ: Erlbaum.

Sherman, S. J., & Corty, E. (1984). Cognitive heuristics. In R. S. Wyer Jr. & T. K. Srull (Eds.), *Handbook of social cognition* (Vol. 1, pp. 189–286). Hillsdale, NJ: Erlbaum.

Sherman, S. J., Mackie, D. M., & Driscoll, D. M. (1988). Priming and the differential use of dimensions in evaluation. *Personality and Social Psychology Bulletin, 16,* 405–418.

Sherman, S. J., Presson, C. C., & Chassin, L. (1984). Mechanisms underlying the false consensus effect: The special role of threats to the self. *Personality and Social Psychology Bulletin, 10,* 127–138.

Sherwood, G. G. (1979). Classical and attributive projection: Some new evidence. *Journal of Abnormal Psychology, 88,* 635–640.

Shih, M., Pittinsky, T. L., & Ambady, N. (1999). Stereotype susceptibility: Identity salience and shifts in quantitative performance. *Psychological Science, 10,* 80–83.

Showers, C., & Cantor, N. (1985). Social cognition: A look at motivated strategies. *Annual Review of Psychology, 36,* 275–305.

Shrauger, S. J., & Patterson, M. B. (1974). Self-evaluation and the selection of dimensions for evaluating others. *Journal of Personality, 42,* 569–585.

Shteynberg, G. (2010). A silent emergence of culture: The social tuning effect. *Journal of Personality and Social Psychology, 99(4),* 683–689.

Shteynberg, G., & Galinsky, A. D. (2011). Implicit coordination: Sharing goals with similar others intensifies goal pursuit. *Journal of Experimental Social Psychology, 47(6),* 1291–1294.

Sidanius, J. (1988). Political sophistication and political deviance: A structural equation examination of context theory. *Journal of Personality and Social Psychology, 55,* 37–51.

Sidanius, J., & Pratto, F. (1999). *Social dominance: An intergroup theory of social hierarchy and oppression.* New York: Cambridge University Press.

Sidanius, J., & Pratto, F. (2003). Social dominance theory and the dynamics of inequality: A reply to Schmitt, Branscombe, & Keppen and Wilson & Liu. *British Journal of Social Psychology, 42,* 207–213.

Sidanius, J., Pratto, F., & Bobo, L. (1994). Social dominance orientation and the political psychology of gender: A case of invariance? *Journal of Personality and Social Psychology, 70,* 476–490.

Sidanius, J., Pratto, F., & Bobo, L. (1996). Racism, conservatism, affirmative action, and intellectual sophistication: A matter of principled conservatism or group dominance? *Journal of Personality and Social Psychology, 70,* 476–490.

Silvia, P. J., & Duval, T. S. (2001). Objective self-awareness theory: Recent progress and enduring problems. *Personality and Social Psychology Review, 5,* 230–241.

Simon, B. (1992). The perception of ingroup and outgroup homogeneity: Reintroducing the intergroup context. In W. Stroebe & M. Hewstone (Eds.), *European review of social psychology* (Vol. 3, pp. 1–30). Oxford: Wiley.

Simon, H. A. (1967). Motivational and emotional controls of cognition. *Psychological Review, 74,* 29–39.

Simon, H. A. (1980). Problem solving and education. In D. T. Tuma & F. Reif (Eds.), *Problem solving and education: Issues in teaching and research.* Hillsdale, NJ: Erlbaum.

Simon, H. A. (1982). Comments. In M. S. Clark & S. T. Fiske (Eds.), *Affect and cognition: The 17th Annual Carnegie Symposium on Cognition* (pp. 333–342). Hillsdale, NJ: Erlbaum.

Simpson, J. A., Oriña, M. M., & Ickes, W. J. (2003). When accuracy hurts, and when it helps: A test of the empathic accuracy model in marital interactions. *Journal of Personality and Social Psychology, 85,* 881–893.

Sinclair, L., & Kunda, Z. (1999). Reactions to a Black professional: Motivated inhibition and activation of conflicting stereotypes. *Journal of Personality and Social Psychology, 77,* 885–904.

Sinclair, L., & Kunda, Z. (2000). Motivated stereotyping of women: She's fine if she praised me but incompetent if she criticized me. *Personality and Social Psychology Bulletin, 24,* 1139–1152.

Sinclair, R. C., Mark, M. M., & Shotland, R. L. (1987). Construct accessibility and generalizability across response categories. *Personality and Social Psychology Bulletin, 13,* 239–252.

Sinclair, S., Dunn, E., & Lowery, B. S. (2005). The relationship between parental racial attitudes and children's implicit prejudice. *Journal of Experimental Social Psychology, 41,* 283–289.

Sinclair, S., Lowery, B. S., Hardin, C. D., & Colangelo, A. (2005). Social tuning of automatic racial attitudes: The role of affiliative motivation. *Journal of Personality and Social Psychology, 89,* 583–592.

Singelis, T. M. (1994). The measurement of independent and interdependent self-construals. *Personality and Social Psychology Bulletin, 20(5),* 580–591.

Singer, J. L. (1966). *Daydreaming.* New York: Random House.

Singer, J. L. (1978). Experimental studies of daydreaming and the stream of thought. In K. S. Pope & J. L. Singer (Eds.), *The stream of consciousness: Scientific investigations into the flow of human experience.* New York: Plenum Press.

Singer, J. L. (1984). The private personality. *Personality and Social Psychology Bulletin, 10,* 7–30.

Singer, J. L. (1988). Reinterpreting the transference. In D. C. Turk & P. Salovey (Eds.), *Reasoning, inference, and judgment in clinical psychology* (pp. 182–205). New York: Free Press.

Singer, J. L., & Salovey, P. (1988). Mood and memory: Evaluating the network theory of affect. *Clinical Psychology Review, 8,* 211–251.

Sivacek, J., & Crano, W. D. (1982). Vested interest as a moderator of attitude–behavior consistency. *Journal of Personality and Social Psychology, 43,* 210–221.

Skinner, B. F. (1957). *Verbal behavior.* New York: Appleton-Century-Crofts.

Skinner, B. F. (1963). Operant behavior. *American Psychologist, 18,* 503–515.

Skov, R. B., & Sherman, S. J. (1986). Information-gathering processes: Diagnosticity, hypothesis-confirmatory strategies, and perceived hypothesis confirmation. *Journal of Experimental Social Psychology, 22,* 93–121.

Skowronski, J. J., & Carlston, D. E. (1989). Negativity and extremity biases in impression formation: A review of explanations. *Psychological Bulletin, 105,* 131–142.

Slovic, P., Fischhoff, B., & Lichtenstein, S. (1976). Cognitive processes and societal risk taking. In J. S. Carroll & J. W. Payne (Eds.), *Cognition and social behavior* (pp. 165–184). Hillsdale, NJ: Erlbaum.

Slovic, P., Fischhoff, B., & Lichtenstein, S. (1977). Behavioral decision theory. *Annual Review of Psychology, 28,* 1–39.

Slowiaczek, L. M., Klayman, J., Sherman, S. J., & Skov, R. B. (1992). Information selection and use in hypothesis testing: What is a good question, what is a good answer? *Memory and Cognition, 20,* 392–405.

Small, D. A., & Lowenstein, G. (2005). The devil you know: The effects of identifiability on punishment. *Journal of Behavioral Decision Making, 18,* 311–318.

Smallwood, J., & Schooler, J. W. (2006). The restless mind. *Psychological Bulletin, 132,* 946–958.

Smedslund, J. (1963). The concept of correlation in adults. *Scandinavian Journal of Psychology, 4,* 165–173.

Smith, C. A. (1989). Dimensions of appraisal and physiological response in emotion. *Journal of Personality and Social Psychology, 56,* 339–353.

Smith, C. A., & Ellsworth, P. C. (1985). Patterns of cognitive appraisal in emotion. *Journal of Personality and Social Psychology, 48,* 813–838.

Smith, C. A., & Ellsworth, P. C. (1987). Patterns of appraisal and emotion related to taking an exam. *Journal of Personality and Social Psychology, 52,* 475–488.

Smith, E. E., & Medin, D. L. (1981). *Categories and concepts.* Cambridge, MA: Harvard University Press.

Smith, E. E., Shoben, E. J., & Rips, L. J. (1974). Structure and process in semantic memory: A featural model for semantic decisions. *Psychological Review, 81,* 214–241.

Smith, E. R. (1984). Model of social inference processes. *Psychological Review, 91,* 392–413.

Smith, E. R. (1988). Category accessibility effects in simulated exemplar-based memory. *Journal of Experimental Social Psychology, 24,* 448–463.

Smith, E. R. (1990). Content and process specificity in the effects of prior experiences. In T. K. Srull & R. S. Wyer Jr. (Eds.), *Advances in social cognition* (Vol. 3, pp. 1–59). Hillsdale, NJ: Erlbaum.

Smith, E. R. (1993). Social identity and social emotions: Toward new conceptualizations of prejudice. In D. M. Mackie & D. L. Hamilton (Eds.), *Affect, cognition, and stereotyping: Interactive processes in group perception* (pp. 297-315). San Diego, CA: Academic Press.

Smith, E. R. (1998). Mental representation and memory. In D. T. Gilbert, S. T. Fiske, & G. Lindzey (Eds.), *The handbook of social psychology* (4th edn, Vol. 1, pp. 391–445). New York: McGraw-Hill.

Smith, E. R., & Branscombe, N. R. (1987). Procedurally mediated social inferences: The case of category accessibility effects. *Journal of Experimental Social Psychology, 23,* 361–382.

Smith, E. R., & Branscombe, N. R. (1988). Category accessibility as implicit memory. *Journal of Experimental Social Psychology, 24,* 490–504.

Smith, E. R., Branscombe, N. R., & Bormann, C. (1988). Generality of the effects of practice on social judgment tasks. *Journal of Personality and Social Psychology, 54,* 385–395.

Smith, E. R., Coats, S., & Walling, D. (1999). Overlapping mental representations of self, in-group, and partner: Further response time evidence and a connectionist model. *Personality and Social Psychology Bulletin, 25,* 873–882.

Smith, E. R., & Conrey, F. R. (2007). Agent-based modeling: A new approach for theory-building in social psychology. *Personality and Social Psychology Review, 11,* 87–104.

Smith, E. R., & DeCoster, J. (1998). Knowledge acquisition, accessibility, and use in person perception and stereotyping: Simulation with a recurrent connectionist network. *Journal of Personality and Social Psychology, 74,* 21–35.

Smith, E. R., & DeCoster, J. (2000). Dual-process models in social and cognitive psychology: Conceptual integration and links to underlying memory systems. *Personality and Social Psychology Review, 4,* 108–131.

Smith, E. R., & Henry, S. (1996). An in-group becomes part of the self: Response time evidence. *Personality and Social Psychology Bulletin, 22,* 635–642.

Smith, E. R., & Lerner, M. (1986). Development of automatism of social judgments. *Journal of Personality and Social Psychology, 50,* 246–259.

Smith, E. R., & Miller, F. D. (1979). Salience and the cognitive mediation of attribution. *Journal of Personality and Social Psychology, 37,* 2240–2252.

Smith, E. R., Seger, C. R., & Mackie, D. M. (2007). Can emotions be truly group level? Evidence regarding four conceptual criteria. *Journal of Personality and Social Psychology, 93*(3), 431–446.

Smith, E. R., & Semin, G. R. (2004). Socially situated cognition: Cognition in its social context. In M. P. Zanna (Ed.), *Advances in experimental social psychology* (Vol. 36, pp. 53–116). San Diego, CA: Elsevier Academic Press.

Smith, E. R., & Zárate, M. A. (1992). Exemplar-based model of social judgment. *Psychological Review, 99,* 3–21.

Smith, M. B., Bruner, J. S., & White, R. W. (1956). *Opinions and personality.* Oxford: Wiley.

Smith, R. H. (2000). Assimilative and contrastive emotional reactions to upward and downward social comparisons. In J. Suls & L. Wheeler (Eds.), *Handbook of social comparison: Theory and research* (pp. 173–200). Dordrecht: Kluwer.

Smith, S. M., & Shaffer, D. R. (2000). Vividness can undermine or enhance message processing: The moderating role of vividness congruency. *Personality and Social Psychology Bulletin, 26,* 769–779.

Smith, V. L., & Ellsworth, P. C. (1987). The social psychology of eyewitness accuracy: Leading questions and communicator expertise. *Journal of Applied Psychology, 72,* 294–300.

Snyder, C. J., Lassiter, G. D., Lindberg, M. J., & Pinegar, S. K. (2009). Videotaped interrogations and confessions: Does a dual-camera approach yield unbiased and accurate evaluations? *Behavioral Sciences and the Law, 27*(3), 451–466.

Snyder, C. R., & Higgins, R. L. (1988). Excuses: Their effective role in the negotiation of reality. *Psychological Bulletin, 104,* 23–35.

Snyder, M. (1974). The self-monitoring of expressive behavior. *Journal of Personality and Social Psychology, 30,* 526–537.

Snyder, M. (1976). Attribution and behavior: Social perception and social causation. In J. H. Harvey, W. J. Ickes, & R. F. Kidd (Eds.), *New directions in attribution research* (Vol. 1, pp. 53–72). Hillsdale, NJ: Erlbaum.

Snyder, M. (1977). Impression management. In S. Wrightsman (Ed.), *Social psychology in the seventies.* New York: Wiley.

Snyder, M. (1979). Self-monitoring processes. In L. Berkowitz (Ed.), *Advances in experimental social psychology* (Vol. 12, pp. 86–131). New York: Academic Press.

Snyder, M. (1982). When believing means doing: Creating links between attitudes and behavior. In M. P. Zanna, E. T. Higgins, & C. P. Herman (Eds.), *Consistency in social behavior: The Ontario Symposium* (Vol. 2, pp. 105–130). Hillsdale, NJ: Erlbaum.

Snyder, M., & Campbell, B. H. (1982). Self-monitoring: The self in action. In J. Suls (Ed.), *Psychological perspectives on the self* (Vol. 1, pp. 185–208). Hillsdale, NJ: Erlbaum.

Snyder, M., Campbell, B. H., & Preston, E. (1982). Testing hypotheses about human nature: Assessing the accuracy of social stereotypes. *Social Cognition, 1,* 256–272.

Snyder, M., & Cantor, N. (1980). Thinking about ourselves and others: Self-monitoring and social knowledge. *Journal of Personality and Social Psychology, 39,* 222–234.

Snyder, M., & DeBono, K. G. (1985). Appeals to image and claims about quality: Understanding the psychology of advertising. *Journal of Personality and Social Psychology, 49,* 586–597.

Snyder, M., & DeBono, K. G. (1987). A functional approach to attitudes and persuasion. In M. P. Zanna, J. M. Olson, & C. P. Herman (Eds.), *Social influence: The Ontario Symposium* (Vol. 5, pp. 107–125). Hillsdale, NJ: Erlbaum.

Snyder, M., & Kendzierski, D. (1982). Acting on one's attitudes: Procedures for linking attitude and behavior. *Journal of Experimental Social Psychology, 18,* 165–183.

Snyder, M., & Miene, P. K. (1994). Stereotyping of the elderly: A functional approach. *British Journal of Social Psychology, 33,* 63–82.

Snyder, M., & Monson, T. C. (1975). Persons, situations, and the control of social behavior. *Journal of Personality and Social Psychology, 32,* 637–644.

Snyder, M., & Simpson, J. A. (1984). Self-monitoring and dating relationships. *Journal of Personality and Social Psychology, 47,* 1281–1291.

Snyder, M., & Swann, W. B., Jr. (1976). When actions reflect attitudes: The politics of impression management. *Journal of Personality and Social Psychology, 34,* 1034–1042.

Snyder, M., & Swann, W. B., Jr. (1978a). Hypothesis-testing processes in social interaction. *Journal of Personality and Social Psychology, 36,* 1202–1212.

Snyder, M., & Swann, W. B., Jr. (1978b). Behavioral confirmation in social interaction: From social perception to social reality. *Journal of Experimental Social Psychology, 14,* 148–162.

Snyder, M., & Tanke, E. D. (1976). Behavior and attitude: Some people are more consistent than others. *Journal of Personality, 44,* 501–517.

Snyder, M., Tanke, E. D., & Berscheid, E. (1977). Social perception and interpersonal behavior: On the self-fulfilling nature of social stereotypes. *Journal of Personality and Social Psychology, 35,* 656–666.

Solarz, A. K. (1960). Latency of instrumental responses as a function of compatibility with the meaning of eliciting verbal signs. *Journal of Experimental Psychology, 59,* 239–245.

Sommer, K. L., & Baumeister, R. F. (2002). Self-evaluation, persistence, and performance following implicit rejection: The role of trait self-esteem. *Personality and Social Psychology Bulletin, 28,* 926–938.

Sommers, S. (1981). Emotionality reconsidered: The role of cognition in emotional responsiveness. *Journal of Personality and Social Psychology, 41,* 553–561.

Sorrentino, R. M., Bobocel, D. R., Gitta, M. Z., Olson, J. M., & Hewitt, E. L. (1988). Uncertainty orientation and persuasion: Individual differences in the effects of personal relevance on social judgments. *Journal of Personality and Social Psychology, 55,* 357–371.

Sorrentino, R. M., Nezlek, J. B., Yasunaga, S., Kouhara, S., Otsubo, Y., & Shuper, P. (2008). Uncertainty orientation and affective experiences: Individual differences within and across cultures. *Journal of Cross-Cultural Psychology, 39(2),* 129–146.

Sorrentino, R. M., & Roney, C. J. R. (1986). Uncertainty orientation, achievement-related motivation, and task diagnosticity as determinants of task performance. *Social Cognition, 4,* 420–436.

Spangler, E., Gordon, M. A., & Pipkin, R. M. (1978). Token women: An empirical test of the Kanter hypothesis. *American Journal of Sociology, 84,* 160–170.

Spears, R., Postmes, T., Lea, M., & Wolbert, A. (2002). When are net effects gross products? The power of influence and the influence of power in computer-mediated communication. *Journal of Social Issues, 58,* 91–107.

Spence, J. T., Deaux, K., & Helmreich, R. L. (1985). Sex roles in contemporary American society. In G. Lindzey & E. Aronson (Eds.), *The handbook of social psychology* (3rd edn, Vol. 2, pp. 149–178). New York: Random House.

Spence, S. A., & Frith, C. D. (1999). Towards a functional anatomy of volition. *Journal of Consciousness Studies, 6,* 11–28.

Spencer, S. J., Fein, S., Wolfe, C. T., Fong, C., & Dunn, M. A. (1998). Automatic activation of stereotypes: The role of self-image threat. *Personality and Social Psychology Bulletin, 24,* 1139–1152.

Spencer, S. J., Steele, C. M., & Quinn, D. M. (1999). Stereotype threat and women's math performance. *Journal of Experimental Social Psychology, 35,* 4–28.

Spielman, L. A., Pratto, F., & Bargh, J. A. (1988). Are one's moods, attitudes, evaluations, and emotions out of control? *American Behavioral Scientist, 31,* 296–311.

Squire, L. R. (1987). *Memory and brain.* New York: Oxford University Press.

Squire, L. R. (1992). Memory and the hippocampus: A synthesis from findings with rats, monkeys, and humans. *Psychological Review, 99,* 195–231.

Srull, T. K. (1981). Person memory: Some tests of associative storage and retrieval models. *Journal of Experimental Psychology: Human Learning and Memory, 7,* 440–462.

Srull, T. K., Lichenstein, M., & Rothbart, M. (1985). Associative storage and retrieval processes in person memory. *Journal of Experimental Psychology: Learning, Memory, and Cognition, 11,* 316–345.

Srull, T. K., & Wyer, R. S., Jr. (1979). The role of category accessibility in the interpretation of information about persons: Some determinants and implications. *Journal of Personality and Social Psychology, 37,* 1660–1672.

Srull, T. K., & Wyer, R. S., Jr. (1980). Category accessibility and social perception: Some implications for the study of person memory and interpersonal judgments. *Journal of Personality and Social Psychology, 38,* 841–856.

Srull, T. K., & Wyer, R. S., Jr. (1989). Person memory and judgment. *Psychological Review, 96,* 58–83.

Staats, A. W., & Staats, C. K. (1958). Attitudes established by classical conditioning. *Journal of Abnormal and Social Psychology, 57,* 37–40.

Stang, D. J. (1974). Methodological factors in mere exposure research. *Psychological Bulletin, 81,* 1014–1025.

Stangor, C. (1988). Stereotype accessibility and information processing. *Personality and Social Psychology Bulletin, 14,* 694–708.

Stangor, C. (1990). Arousal, accessibility of trait constructs, and person perception. *Journal of Experimental Social Psychology, 26,* 305–321.

Stangor, C., Carr, C., & Kiang, L. (1998). Activating stereotypes undermines task performance expectations. *Journal of Personality and Social Psychology, 75,* 1191–1197.

Stangor, C., Swim, J. K., Sechrist, G. B., DeCoster, J., Van Allen, K., & Ottenbreit, A. (2003). In W. Stroebe & M. Hewstone (Eds.), *European review of social psychology* (Vol. 14, pp. 277–311). Hove, England: Psychology Press/Taylor & Francis.

Stangor, C., & Thompson, E. P. (2002). Needs for cognitive economy and self-enhancement as unique predictors of intergroup attitudes. *European Journal of Social Psychology, 32,* 563–575.

Staub, E. (1999). The roots of evil: Social conditions, culture, personality, and basic human needs. *Personality and Social Psychology Review, 3,* 179–192.

Steele, C. M. (1988). The psychology of self-affirmation: Sustaining the integrity of the self. In L. Berkowitz (Ed.), *Advances in experimental psychology* (Vol. 21). New York: Academic Press.

Steele, C. M. (1997). A threat in the air: How stereotypes shape intellectual identity and performance. *American Psychologist, 52,* 613–629.

Steele, C. M., & Aronson, J. (1995). Stereotype threat and the intellectual test performance of African Americans. *Journal of Personality and Social Psychology, 69,* 797–811.

Steele, C. M., Spencer, S. J., & Aronson, J. (2002). Contending with group image: The psychology of stereotype and social identity threat. In M. P. Zanna (Eds.), *Advances in experimental social psychology* (Vol. 34, pp. 379–440). San Diego, CA: Academic Press.

Stephan, C. W., Stephan, W. G., Demitrakis, K. M., Yamada, A. M., & Clason, D. L. (2000). Women's attitudes toward men: An integrated threat theory approach. *Psychology of Women Quarterly, 24,* 63–73.

Stephan, W. G., Berscheid, E., & Walster, E. (1971). Sexual arousal and heterosexual perception. *Journal of Personality and Social Psychology, 20,* 93–101.

Stephan, W. G., Boniecki, K. A., Ybarra, O., Bettencourt, A., Ervin, K. S., Jackson, L. A., et al. (2002). The role of threats in the racial attitudes of Blacks and Whites. *Personality and Social Psychology Bulletin, 28,* 1242–1254.

Stephan, W. G., Diaz-Loving, R., & Duran, A. (2000). Integrated threat theory and intercultural attitudes: Mexico and the United States. *Journal of Cross Cultural Psychology, 31,* 240–249.

Stephan, W. G., & Finlay, K. A. (1999). The role of empathy in improving intergroup relations. *Journal of Social Issues, 55,* 729–743.

Stephan, W. G., & Renfro, C. L. (2002). The role of threat in intergroup relations. In D. M. Mackie & E. R. Smith (Eds.), *From prejudice to intergroup emotions* (pp. 1191–1207). New York: Psychology Press.

Stephan, W. G., Renfro, C. L., Esses, V. M., Stephan, C. W., & Martin, T. (2005). The effects of feeling threatened on attitudes toward immigrants. *International Journal of Intercultural Relations, 29,* 1–19.

Stephan, W. G., & Stephan, C. W. (2000). An integrated threat theory of prejudice. In S. Oskamp (Ed.), *Reducing prejudice and discrimination* (pp. 23–45). Mahwah, NJ: Erlbaum.

Stephan, W. G., Ybarra, O., & Bachman, G. (1999). Prejudice toward immigrants. *Journal of Applied Social Psychology, 29,* 2221–2237.

Stephan, W. G., Ybarra, O., Martinez, C. M., Schwarzwald, J., & Tur-Kaspa, M. (1998). Prejudice toward immigrants to Spain and Israel: An integrated threat theory analysis. *Journal of Cross Cultural Psychology, 29,* 559–576.

Stevens, L. E., & Fiske, S. T. (2000). Motivated impressions of a powerholder: Accuracy under task dependency and misperception under evaluation dependency. *Personality and Social Psychology Bulletin, 26,* 907–922.

Stiff, J. B. (1986). Cognitive processing of persuasive message cues: A meta-analytic review of the effects of supporting information on attitudes. *Communication Monographs, 53,* 75–89.

Stiff, J. B., & Boster, F. J. (1987). Cognitive processing: Additional thoughts and a reply to Petty, Kasmer, Haugtvedt, and Cacioppo. *Communication Monographs, 54,* 250–256.

Stone, J., Lynch, C. I., Sjomeling, M., & Darley, J. M. (1999). Stereotype threat effects on Black and White athletic performance. *Journal of Personality and Social Psychology, 77,* 1213–1227.

Storbeck, J., & Clore, G. L. (2008). Affective arousal as information: How affective arousal influences judgments, learning, and memory. *Social and Personality Psychology Compass, 2(5),* 1824–1843.

Storms, M. D., & Nisbett, R. E. (1970). Insomnia and the attribution process. *Journal of Personality and Social Psychology, 16,* 319–328.

Story, A. L. (1998). Self-esteem and memory for favorable and unfavorable personality feedback. *Personality and Social Psychology Bulletin, 24,* 51–64.

Stouffer, S. A., Suchman, E. A., DeVinney, L. C., Star, S. A., & Williams, R. M., Jr. (1949). *The American soldier: Vol. 1. Adjustment during army life.* Princeton, NJ: Princeton University.

Strack, F., & Deutsch, R. (2004). Reflective and impulsive determinants of social behavior. *Personality and Social Psychology Review, 8(3),* 220–247.

Strack, F., Erber, R., & Wicklund, R. A. (1982). Effects of salience and time pressure on ratings of social causality. *Journal of Experimental Social Psychology, 18,* 581–594.

Strack, F., Martin, L. L., & Schwarz, N. (1988). Priming and communication: Social determinants of information use in judgments of life satisfaction. *European Journal of Social Psychology, 18,* 429–442.

Strack, F., Martin, L. L., & Stepper, S. (1988). Inhibiting and facilitating conditions of the human smile: A nonobtrusive test of the facial feedback hypothesis. *Journal of Personality and Social Psychology, 54,* 768–777.

Strack, F., & Mussweiler, T. (1997). Explaining the enigmatic anchoring effect: Mechanisms of selective accessibility. *Journal of Personality and Social Psychology, 73,* 437–446.

Strauman, T. J. (1996). Stability within the self: A longitudinal study of the structural implications of self-discrepancy theory. *Journal of Personality and Social Psychology, 71,* 1142–1153.

Strauman, T. J., & Higgins, E. T. (1987). Automatic activation of self-discrepancies and emotional syndromes: When cognitive structures influence affect. *Journal of Personality and Social Psychology, 53,* 1004–1014.

Strenta, A. C., & Kleck, R. E. (1984). Physical disability and the perception of social interaction: It's not what you look at but how you look at it. *Personality and Social Psychology Bulletin, 10,* 279–288.

Stuss, D. T., & Levine, B. (2002). Adult clinical neuropsychology: Lessons from studies of the frontal lobes. *Annual Review of Psychology, 53,* 401–433.

Suh, E. (2002). Culture, identity consistency, and subjective well-being. *Journal of Personality and Social Psychology, 83,* 1378–1391.

Sujan, M. (1985). Consumer knowledge: Effects on evaluation strategies mediating consumer judgments. *Journal of Consumer Research, 12,* 1–16.

Suls, J. M., Lemos, K., & Stewart, H. L. (2002). Self-esteem, construal, and comparisons with the self, friends, and peers. *Journal of Personality and Social Psychology, 82,* 252–261.

Suls, J. M., & Wan, C. K. (1987). In search of the false-uniqueness phenomenon: Fear and estimates of social consensus. *Journal of Personality and Social Psychology, 52,* 211–217.

Swann, W. B., Jr. (1983). Self-verification: Bringing social reality into harmony with the self. In J. M. Suls & A. G. Greenwald (Eds.), *Social psychology perspectives* (Vol. 2, pp. 33–66). Hillsdale, NJ: Erlbaum.

Swann, W. B., Jr. (1984). Quest for accuracy in person perception: A matter of pragmatics. *Psychological Review, 91,* 457–477.

Swann, W. B., Jr., & Bosson, J. K. (2010). Self and identity. In S. T. Fiske, D. T. Gilbert, & G. Lindzey (Eds.), *Handbook of social psychology* (5th edn, Vol. 1, pp. 589–628). Hoboken, NJ: Wiley.

Swann, W. B., Jr., & Ely, R. M. (1984). The battle of wills: Self-verification versus behavioral confirmation. *Journal of Personality and Social Psychology, 46,* 1287–1302.

Swann, W. B., Jr., & Giuliano, T. (1987). Confirmatory search strategies in social interaction: How, when, why, and with what consequences. *Journal of Consulting and Clinical Psychology, 5,* 511–524.

Swann, W. B., Jr., Giuliano, T., & Wegner, D. M. (1982). Where leading questions can lead: The power of conjecture in social interaction. *Journal of Personality and Social Psychology, 42,* 1025–1035.

Swann, W. B., Jr., Hixon, J. G., Stein-Seroussi, A., & Gilbert, D. T. (1990). The fleeting gleam of praise: Cognitive processes underlying behavioral reactions to self-relevant feedback. *Journal of Personality and Social Psychology, 59,* 17–26.

Swann, W. B., Jr., Jetten, J., Gómez, Á., Whitehouse, H., & Bastian , B. (2012). When group membership gets personal: A theory of identity fusion. *Psychological Review, 119,* 441–456.

Swann, W. B., Jr., Pelham, B. W., & Chidester, T. R. (1988). Change through paradox: Using self-verification to alter beliefs. *Journal of Personality and Social Psychology, 54,* 268–273.

Swann, W. B., Jr., Pelham, B. W., & Krull, D. S. (1989). Agreeable fancy or disagreeable truth? Reconciling self-enhancement and self-verification. *Journal of Personality and Social Psychology, 57,* 782–791.

Swann, W. B., Jr., & Read, S. J. (1981). Self-verification processes: How we sustain our self-conceptions. *Journal of Experimental Social Psychology, 17,* 351–370.

Swann, W. B., Jr., & Snyder, M. (1980). On translating beliefs into action: Theories of ability and their application in an instructional setting. *Journal of Personality and Social Psychology, 38,* 879–888.

Swann, W. B., Jr., Stein-Seroussi, A., & Giesler, R. B. (1992). Why people self-verify. *Journal of Personality and Social Psychology, 62,* 392–401.

Swim, J. K., & Hyers, L. L. (1999). Excuse me – What did you say?! Women's public and private responses to sexist remarks. *Journal of Experimental Social Psychology, 79,* 238–250.

Swim, J. K., Hyers, L. L., Cohen, L. L., & Ferguson, M. J. (2001). Everyday sexism: Evidence for its incidence, nature, and psychological impact from three daily diary studies. *Journal of Experimental Social Psychology, 35,* 68–88.

Swim, J. K., & Miller, D. L. (1999). White guilt: Its antecedents and consequences for attitudes toward affirmative action. *Personality and Social Psychology Bulletin, 25,* 500–514.

Swim, J. K., Pearson, N. B., & Johnston, K. E. (2006). Daily encounters with heterosexism: A week in the life of lesbian, gay, and bisexual individuals. *Journal of Homosexuality, 53,* 18–31.

Swim, J. K., & Sanna, L. J. (1996). He's skilled, she's lucky: A meta-analysis of observer's attributions of women's and men's successes and failures. *Personality and Social Psychology Bulletin, 22,* 507–519.

Swim, J. K., Scott, E. D., Sechrist, G. B., Campbell, B., & Stangor, C. (2003). The role of intent and harm in judgments of prejudice and discrimination. *Journal of Personality and Social Psychology, 84,* 944–959.

Tabachnik, N., Crocker, J., & Alloy, L. B. (1983). Depression, social comparison, and the false consensus effect. *Journal of Personality and Social Psychology, 45,* 688–699.

Taguiri, R., & Petrullo, L. (Eds.). (1958). *Person perception and interpersonal behavior.* Palo Alto, CA: Stanford University Press.

Tajfel, H. (1981). *Human groups and social categories: Studies in social psychology.* Cambridge: Cambridge University Press.

Tajfel, H., Billig, M., Bundy, R. P., & Flament, C. (1971). Social categorization and intergroup behaviour. *European Journal of Social Psychology, 1,* 149–177.

Tajfel, H., & Turner, J. C. (1979). An integrative theory of intergroup conflict. In W. G. Austin & S. Worchel (Eds.), *The social psychology of intergroup relations.* Monterey, CA: Brooks/Cole.

Takata, T. (1987). Self-deprecative tendencies in self-evaluation through social comparison. *Japanese Journal of Experimental Social Psychology, 27,* 27–36.

Talaska, C. A., Fiske, S. T., & Chaiken, S. (2008). Legitimating racial discrimination: Emotions, not beliefs, best predict discrimination in a meta-analysis. *Social Justice Research, 21(3),* 263–296.

Tanaka, J. W., & Farah, M. J. (1993). Parts and wholes in face recognition. *Quarterly Journal of Experimental Psychology: Human Experimental Psychology, 42,* 225–245.

Tangney, J. P., Stuewig, J., & Mashek, D. (2007). Moral emotions and moral behavior. *Annual Review of Psychology, 58,* 345–372.

Taylor, K. M., & Shepperd, J. A. (1998). Bracing for the worst: Severity, testing, and feedback timing as moderators of the optimistic bias. *Personality and Social Psychology Bulletin, 24,* 915–926.

Taylor, S. E. (1975). On inferring one's own attitudes from one's behavior: Some delimiting conditions. *Journal of Personality and Social Psychology, 31,* 126–131.

Taylor, S. E. (1981a). A categorization approach to stereotyping. In D. L. Hamilton (Ed.), *Cognitive processes in stereotyping and intergroup behavior* (pp. 88–114). Hillsdale, NJ: Erlbaum.

Taylor, S. E. (1981b). The interface of cognitive and social psychology. In J. Harvey (Ed.), *Cognition, social behavior, and the environment* (pp. 189–211). Hillsdale, NJ: Erlbaum.

Taylor, S. E. (1982). The availability bias in social psychology. In D. Kahneman & A. Tversky (Eds.). *Judgment under uncertainty: Heuristics and biases.* New York: Cambridge University Press.

Taylor, S. E. (1991). Asymmetrical effects of positive and negative events: The mobilization-minimization hypothesis. *Psychological Bulletin, 110,* 67–85.

Taylor, S. E. (1998). The social being in social psychology. In D. T. Gilbert, S. T. Fiske, & G. Lindzey (Eds.), *The handbook of social psychology* (4th edn, Vol. 1, pp. 58–95). New York: McGraw-Hill.

Taylor, S. E. (2006a). *Health psychology* (6th edn). New York: McGraw-Hill.

Taylor, S. E. (2006b). Tend and befriend: Biobehavioral bases of affiliation under stress. *Current Directions in Psychological Science, 15,* 273–277.

Taylor, S. E., & Brown, J. (1988). Illusion and well-being: A social psychological perspective on mental health. *Psychological Bulletin, 103,* 193–210.

Taylor, S. E., & Crocker, J. (1981). Schematic bases of social information processing. In E. T. Higgins, C. P. Herman, & M. P. Zanna (Eds.), *Social cognition: The Ontario Symposium* (Vol. 1, pp. 89–134). Hillsdale, NJ: Erlbaum.

Taylor, S. E., Crocker, J., Fiske, S. T., Sprinzen, M., & Winkler, J. D. (1979). The generalizability of salience effects. *Journal of Personality and Social Psychology, 37*, 357–368.

Taylor, S. E., Eisenberger, N. I., Saxbe, D., Lehman, B. J., & Lieberman, M. D. (2006). Neural responses to emotional stimuli are associated with childhood family stress. *Biological Psychiatry, 60*, 296–301.

Taylor, S. E., & Fiske, S. T. (1975). Point-of-view and perceptions of causality. *Journal of Personality and Social Psychology, 32*, 439–445.

Taylor, S. E., & Fiske, S. T. (1978). Salience, attention, and attribution: Top of the head phenomena. In L. Berkowitz (Ed.), *Advances in experimental social psychology* (Vol. 11, pp. 249–288). New York: Academic Press.

Taylor, S. E., & Fiske, S. T. (1981). Getting inside the head: Methodologies for process analysis in attribution and social cognition. In J. H. Harvey, W. Ickes, & R. F. Kidd (Eds.), *New directions in attribution research* (Vol. 3, pp. 459–524). Hillsdale, NJ: Erlbaum.

Taylor, S. E., Fiske, S. T., Close, M., Anderson, C., & Ruderman, A. J. (1977). Solo status as a psychological variable: The power of being distinctive. Unpublished manuscript, Harvard University, Cambridge, MA.

Taylor, S. E., Fiske, S. T., Etcoff, N. L., & Ruderman, A. J. (1978). Categorical and contextual bases of person memory and stereotyping. *Journal of Personality and Social Psychology, 36*, 778–793.

Taylor, S. E., & Gollwitzer, P. M. (1995). The effects of mindset on positive illusions. *Journal of Personality and Social Psychology, 69*, 213–226.

Taylor, S. E., Kemeny, M. E., Reed, G. M., Bower, J. E., & Gruenewald, T. L. (2000). Psychological resources, positive illusions, and health. *American Psychologist, 55*, 99–109.

Taylor, S. E., Lerner, J. S., Sherman, D. K., Sage, R. M., & McDowell, N. K. (2003a). Are self-enhancing cognitions associated with healthy or unhealthy biological profiles? *Journal of Personality and Social Psychology, 85*, 605–615.

Taylor, S. E., Lerner, J. S., Sherman, D. K., Sage, R. M., & McDowell, N. K. (2003b). Portrait of the self-enhancer: Well-adjusted and well-liked or maladjusted and friendless? *Journal of Personality and Social Psychology, 84*, 165–176.

Taylor, S. E., Lichtman, R. R., & Wood, J. V. (1984). Attributions, beliefs about control, and adjustment to breast cancer. *Journal of Personality and Social Psychology, 46*, 489–502.

Taylor, S. E., & Lobel, M. (1989). Social comparison activity under threat: Downward evaluation and upward contacts. *Psychological Review, 96*, 569–575.

Taylor, S. E., Pham, L. B., Rivkin, I., & Armor, D. A. (1998). Harnessing the imagination: Mental simulation and self-regulation of behavior. *American Psychologist, 53*, 429–439.

Taylor, S. E., & Thompson, S. C. (1982). Stalking the elusive "vividness" effect. *Psychological Review, 89*, 155–181.

Taylor, S. E., & Wood, J. V. (1983). The vividness effect: Making a mountain out of a molehill? In R. P. Bagozzi & A. M. Tybout (Eds.), *Advances in consumer research*. Ann Arbor, MI: Association for Consumer Research.

Taylor, S. E., Wood, J. V., & Lichtman, R. R. (1983). It could be worse: Selective evaluation as a response to victimization. *Journal of Social Issues, 39*, 19–40.

Teasdale, J. D., & Russell, M. L. (1983). Differential effects of induced mood on the recall of positive, negative and neutral words. *British Journal of Clinical Psychology, 22*, 163–171.

Teger, A. I., & Pruitt, D. G. (1967). Comparison of group risk taking. *Journal of Experimental Social Psychology, 3*, 189–205.

Tesser, A. (1978). Self-generated attitude change. In L. Berkowitz (Ed.), *Advances in experimental social psychology* (Vol. 11, pp. 289–338). New York: Academic Press.

Tesser, A. (1988). Toward a self-evaluation maintenance model of social behavior. In L. Berkowitz (Ed.), *Advances in experimental social psychology* (Vol. 21, pp. 181–227). New York: Academic Press.

Tesser, A., Crepaz, N., Collins, S. R., Cornell, D., & Beach, J. C. (2000). Confluence of self-esteem regulation mechanisms: On integrating the self-zoo. *Personality and Social Psychology Bulletin, 57*, 442–456.

Tetlock, P. E. (1984). Cognitive style and political belief systems in the British House of Commons. *Journal of Personality and Social Psychology, 46*, 365–375.

Tetlock, P. E. (1985). Accountability: A social check on the fundamental attribution error. *Social Psychology Quarterly, 48*, 227–236.

Tetlock, P. E. (1986). Is self-categorization theory the solution to the level-of-analysis problem? *British Journal of Social Psychology, 25*, 255–256.

Tetlock, P. E. (1988). Monitoring the integrative complexity of American and Soviet policy rhetoric: What can be learned? *Journal of Social Issues, 44*, 101–132.

Tetlock, P. E. (1990). Some thoughts on fourth generational models of social cognition. *Psychological Inquiry, 1*, 212–214.

Tetlock, P. E. (1992). The impact of accountability on judgment and choice. In M. P. Zanna (Ed.), *Advances in experimental social psychology* (Vol. 23, pp. 331–376). New York: Academic Press.

Tetlock, P. E. (1998). Close-call counterfactuals and belief-system defenses: I was not almost wrong but I was almost right. *Journal of Personality and Social Psychology, 75*, 639–652.

Tetlock, P. E., & Boettger, R. (1989). Accountability: A social magnifier of the dilution effect. *Journal of Personality and Social Psychology, 57*, 388–398.

Tetlock, P. E., Hannum, K. A., & Micheletti, P. M. (1984). Stability and change in the complexity of senatorial debate: Testing the cognitive versus rhetorical style hypotheses. *Journal of Personality and Social Psychology, 46*, 979–990.

Thibaut, J. W., & Kelley, H. H. (1959). *The social psychology of groups.* New York: Wiley.

Thompson, W., Cowan, C., & Rosenhan, D. L. (1980). Focus of attention mediates the impact of negative affect on altruism. *Journal of Personality and Social Psychology, 38*, 291–300.

Thorndike, E. L. (1940). *Human nature and the social order.* New York: Macmillan.

Thurstone, L. L. (1928). An experimental study of nationality preferences. *Journal of General Psychology, 1*, 405–425.

Tiedens, L. Z. (2001). The effect of anger on the hostile inferences of aggressive and nonaggressive people: Specific emotions, cognitive processing, and chronic accessibility. *Motivation and Emotion, 25*, 233–251.

Tiedens, L. Z., Ellsworth, P. C., & Mesquita, B. (2000). Stereotypes about sentiments and status: Emotional expectations for high- and low-status group members. *Personality and Social Psychology Bulletin, 26*, 560–574.

Tiedens, L. Z., & Jimenez, M. C. (2003). Assimilation for affiliation and contrast for control: Complementary self-construals. *Journal of Personality and Social Pscyhology, 85*, 1049–1061.

Tiedens, L. Z., & Linton, S. (2001). Judgment under emotional certainty and uncertainty: The effects of specific emotions on information processing. *Journal of Personality and Social Psychology, 81*, 973–988.

Time (1980). A gift for vividness. *Time,* October 20, p. 68.

Todorov, A. (2012). The social perception of faces. In S. T. Fiske & C. N. Macrae (Eds.), *Sage handbook of social cognition* (pp. 96–114). Thousand Oaks, CA: Sage.

Todorov, A., Fiske, S. T., & Prentice, D. (Eds.) (2011). *Social neuroscience: Toward understanding the underpinnings of the social mind.* New York: Oxford University Press.

Todorov, A., Gobbini, M. I., Evans, K. K., & Haxby, J. V. (2007). Spontaneous retrieval of affective person knowledge in face perception. *Neuropsychologia, 445*, 163–173.

Todorov, A., Mandisodza, A. N., Goren, A., & Hall, C. (2005). Inferences of competence from faces predict election outcomes. *Science, 308*, 1623–1626.

Todorov, A., Pakrashi, M. & Oosterhof, N. N. (2009). Evaluating faces on trustworthiness after minimal time exposure. *Social Cognition, 27*, 813–833.

Todorov, A., Said, C. P., Engel, A. D., & Oosterhof, N. N. (2008). Understanding evaluation of faces on social dimensions. *Trends in Cognitive Sciences, 12(12)*, 455–460.

Todorov, A., & Uleman, J. S. (2002). Spontaneous trait inferences are bound to actors' faces: Evidence from a false recognition paradigm. *Journal of Personality and Social Psychology, 83*, 1051–1065.

Todorov, A., & Uleman, J. S. (2003). The efficiency of binding spontaneous trait inferences to actors' faces. *Journal of Experimental Social Psychology, 39*, 549–562.

Todorov, A., & Uleman, J. S. (2004). The person reference process in spontaneous trait inferences. *Journal of Personality and Social Psychology, 87*, 482–493.

Tomkins, S. S. (1962). *Affect, imagery, and consciousness* (Vol. 1). New York: Springer.

Tomkins, S. S. (1981). The role of facial response in the experience of emotion: A reply to Tourangeau and Ellsworth. *Journal of Personality and Social Psychology, 40*, 355–357.

Tordesillas, R. S., & Chaiken, S. (1999). Thinking too much or too little? The effects of introspection on the decision-making process. *Personality and Social Psychology Bulletin, 25*, 623–629.

Tormala, Z. L., & Petty, R. E. (2001). On-line versus memory-based processing: The role of "need to evaluate" in person perception. *Personality and Social Psychology Bulletin, 27*, 1599–1612.

Tormala, Z. L., Petty, R. E., & Briñol, P. (2002). Ease of retrieval effects in persuasion: A self-validation analysis. *Personality and Social Psychology Bulletin, 28*, 1700–1712.

Tourangeau, R., & Ellsworth, P. C. (1979). The role of facial response in the experience of emotion. *Journal of Personality and Social Psychology, 37*, 1519–1531.

Tourangeau, R., Rasinski, K. A., Bradburn, N. M., & D'Andrade, R. (1989). Belief accessibility and context effects in attitude measurement. *Journal of Experimental Social Psychology, 25*, 401–421.

Towles-Schwen, T., & Fazio, R. H. (2001). On the origins of racial attitudes: Correlates of childhood experiences. *Personality and Social Psychology Bulletin, 27*, 162–175.

Towles-Schwen, T., & Fazio, R. H. (2003). Choosing social situations: The relation between automatically activated racial attitudes and anticipated comfort interacting with African Americans. *Personality and Social Psychology Bulletin, 29*, 170–182.

Traut-Mattausch, E., Schulz-Hardt, S., Greitemeyer, T., & Frey, D. (2004). Expectancy confirmation in spite of disconfirming evidence: The case of price increases due to the introduction of the Euro. *European Journal of Social Psychology, 34*, 739–760.

Triandis, H. C., McCusker, C., & Hui, C. (1990). Multimethod probes of individualism and collectivism. *Journal of Personality and Social Psychology, 59*, 1006–1020.

Trivers, R. L. (1985). *Social evolution.* Menlo Park, CA: Benjamin/Cummings.

Trope, Y. (1975). Seeking information about one's own ability as a determinant of choice among tasks. *Journal of Personality and Social Psychology, 32*, 1004–1013.

Trope, Y. (1979). Uncertainty-reducing properties of achievement tasks. *Journal of Personality and Social Psychology, 37*, 1505–1518.

Trope, Y. (1986). Identification and inferential processes in dispositional attribution. *Psychological Review, 93*, 239–257.

Trope, Y., & Bassok, M. (1982). Confirmatory and diagnosing strategies in social information gathering. *Journal of Personality and Social Psychology, 43*, 22–34.

Trope, Y., Cohen, O., & Maoz, Y. (1988). The perceptual and inferential effects of situational inducements on dispositional attributions. *Journal of Personality and Social Psychology, 55*, 165–177.

Trope, Y., & Fishbach, A. (2000). Counteractive self-control in overcoming temptation. *Journal of Personality and Social Psychology, 79*, 493–506.

Trope, Y., & Gaunt, R. (1999). A dual-process model of overconfident attributional inferences. In S. Chaiken & Y. Trope (Eds.), *Dual-process theories in social psychology* (pp. 161–178). New York: Guilford Press.

Trope, Y., & Liberman, N. (2003). Temporal construal. *Psychological Review, 110*, 403–421.

Trope, Y., & Liberman, N. (2010). Construal-level theory of psychological distance. *Psychological Review, 117(2)*, 440–463.

Trope, Y., & Mackie, D. M. (1987). Sensitivity to alternatives in social hypothesis-testing. *Journal of Experimental Social Psychology, 23*, 445–459.

Trope, Y., & Neter, E. (1994). Reconciling competing motives in self-evaluation: The role of self-control in feedback setting. *Journal of Personality and Social Psychology, 66*, 646–657.

Tropp, L. R. (2003). The psychological impact of prejudice: Implications for intergroup contact. *Group Processes and Intergroup Relations, 6*, 131–149.

Tropp, L. R., & Bianchi, R. A. (2006). Valuing diversity and interest in intergroup contact. *Journal of Social Issues, 62*, 533–551.

Tropp, L. R., & Pettigrew, T. F. (2005a). Differential relationships between intergroup contact and affective and cognitive dimensions of prejudice. *Personality and Social Psychology Bulletin, 31*, 1145–1158. [Erratum: *31*, 1456.]

Tropp, L. R., & Pettigrew, T. F. (2005b). Relationships between intergroup contact and prejudice among minority and majority status groups. *Psychological Science, 16*, 951–957.

Tropp, L. R., Stout, A. M., Boatswain, C., Wright, S. C., & Pettigrew, T. F. (2006). Trust and acceptance in response to references to group membership: Minority and majority perspectives on cross-group interactions. *Journal of Applied Social Psychology, 36*, 769–794.

Trzebinski, J. (1985). Action-oriented representations of implicit personality theories. *Journal of Personality and Social Psychology, 48*, 1266–1278.

Trzebinski, J., & Richards, K. (1986). The role of goal categories in person impression. *Journal of Experimental Social Psychology, 22*, 216–227.

Tsao, D. Y., & Livingstone, M. S. (2008). Mechanisms of face perception. *Annual Review of Neuroscience, 31*, 411–437.

Tsujimoto, R. N. (1978). Memory bias toward normative and novel trait prototypes. *Journal of Personality and Social Psychology, 36*, 1391–1401.

Tuckman, J., & Lavell, M. (1957). Self classification as old or not old. *Geriatrics, 12*, 666–671.

Tulving, E. (1983). *Elements of episodic memory.* New York: Oxford University Press.

Tulving, E. (2002). Episodic memory: From mind to brain. *Annual Review of Psychology, 53*, 1–25.

Tulving, E., & Pearlstone, Z. (1966). Availability versus accessibility of information in memory for words. *Journal of Verbal Learning and Verbal Behavior, 5*, 381–391.

Turk, D. C., & Salovey, P. (1986). Clinical information processing: Bias innoculation. In R. E. Ingram (Ed.), *Information processing approaches to clinical psychology* (pp. 305–323). New York: Academic Press.

Turk, D. J., Heatherton, T. F., Kelley, W. M., Funnell, M. G., Gazzaniga, M. S., & Macrae, C. N. (2002). Mike or me? Self-recognition in a split-brain patient. *Nature Neuroscience, 5*, 841–842.

Turk, D. J., Heatherton, T. F., Macrae, C. N., Kelley, W. M., & Gazzaniga, M. S. (2003). Out of contact, out of mind: The distributed nature of the self. *Annals of New York Academy of Sciences, 1001*, 65–78.

Turnbull, W., & Slugoski, B. R. (1988). Conversational and linguistic processes in causal attribution. In D. J. Hilton (Ed.), *Contemporary science and natural explanation: Commonsense conceptions of causality* (pp. 66–93). Brighton, England: Harvester Press.

Turner, J. C. (1985). Social categorization and the self-concept: A social cognitive theory of group behavior. In E. J. Lawler (Ed.), *Advances in group processes* (Vol. 2, pp. 77–121). Greenwich, CT: JAI Press.

Turner, J. C. (1987). *Rediscovering the social group: A self-categorization theory.* New York: Basil Blackwell.

Turner, J. C. (1991). *Social influence.* Pacific Grove, CA: Brooks/Cole.

Turner, J. C., & Reynolds, K. J. (2001). The social identity perspective in intergroup relations: Theories, themes, and controversies. In R. Brown & S. L. Gaertner (Eds.), *Blackwell handbook of social psychology: Intergroup processes* (pp. 133–152). Oxford: Blackwell.

Turner, J. C., Wetherell, M. S., & Hogg, M. A. (1989). Referent informational influence and group polarization. *British Journal of Social Psychology, 28*, 135–147.

Tversky, A., & Kahneman, D. (1973). Availability: A heuristic for judging frequency and probability. *Cognitive Psychology, 5*, 207–232.

Tversky, A., & Kahneman, D. (1974). Judgment under uncertainty: Heuristics and biases. *Science, 185*, 1124–1131.

Tversky, A., & Kahneman, D. (1981). The framing of decisions and the psychology of choice. *Science, 211*, 453–458.

Tversky, A., & Kahneman, D. (1982). Judgments of and by representativeness. In D. Kahneman, P. Slovic, & A. Tversky (Eds.), *Judgment under uncertainty: Heuristics and biases* (pp. 84–100). New York: Cambridge University Press.

Tversky, A., & Kahneman, D. (1983). Extensional versus intuitive reasoning: The conjunction fallacy in probability judgment. *Psychological Review, 90*, 293–315.

Twenge, J. M., Catanese, K. R., & Baumeister, R. F. (2003). Social exclusion and the deconstructed state: Time perception, meaninglessness, lethargy, lack of emotion, and self-awareness. *Journal of Personality and Social Psychology, 85,* 409–423.

Ucros, C. G. (1989). Mood state-dependent memory: A meta-analysis. *Cognition and Emotion, 3,* 139–169.

Uhlmann, E. L., Brescoll, V. L., & Paluck, E. L. (2006). Are members of low status groups perceived as bad, or badly off? Egalitarian negative associations and automatic prejudice. *Journal of Experimental Social Psychology, 42,* 491–499.

Uleman, J. S. (1989). A framework for thinking intentionally about unintended thoughts. In J. S. Uleman & J. A. Bargh (Eds.), *Unintended thought* (pp. 425–449). New York: Guilford Press.

Uleman, J. S. (1999). Spontaneous versus intentional inferences in impression formation. In S. Chaiken & Y. Trope (Eds.), *Dual-process theories in social psychology* (pp. 141–160). New York: Guilford Press.

United Nations Entity for Gender Equality and the Empowerment of Women. (2012). Home page. Retrieved April 19, 2012, from www.unwomen.org/.

United States Department of Labor. (2012). Usual weekly earnings of wage and salary workers first quarter 2012. Retrieved April 19, 2012, from www.bls.gov/news.release/pdf/wkyeng.pdf.

Updegraff, J. A., Gable, S. L., & Taylor, S. E. (2004). What makes experiences satisfying? The interaction of approach-avoidance motivations and emotions in well-being. *Journal of Personality and Social Psychology, 86,* 496–504.

Valdesolo, P., & DeSteno, D. (2006). Manipulations of emotional context shape moral judgment. *Psychological Science, 17,* 476–477.

Valins, S. (1966). Cognitive effects of false heart-rate feedback. *Journal of Personality and Social Psychology, 4,* 400–408.

Vallacher, R. R., Read, S. J., & Nowak, A. (2002). The dynamical perspective in personality and social psychology. *Personality and Social Psychology Review, 6,* 264–273.

Vallacher, R. R., & Wegner, D. M. (1987). What do people think they're doing? Action identification and human behavior. *Psychological Review, 94,* 3–15.

Vallacher, R. R., Wegner, D. M., & Frederick, J. (1987). The presentation of self through action identification. *Social Cognition, 5,* 301–322.

Vallone, R. P., Ross, L. D., & Lepper, M. R. (1985). The hostile media phenomenon: Biased perception and perceptions of media bias in coverage of the Beirut massacre. *Journal of Personality and Social Psychology, 49,* 577–585.

van Boven, L., Loewenstein, G., Welch, E., & Dunning, D. (2012). The illusion of courage in self-predictions: Mispredicting one's own behavior in embarrassing situations. *Journal of Behavioral Decision Making, 25(1),* 1–12.

van den Bos, K., Poortvliet, P. M., Maas, M., Miedema, J., & van den Ham, E. J. (2005). An enquiry concerning the principles of cultural norms and values: The impact of uncertainty and mortality salience on reactions to violations and bolstering of cultural worldviews. *Journal of Experimental Social Psychology, 41,* 91–113.

van den Bos, W., McClure, S. M., Harris, L. T., Fiske, S. T., & Cohen, J. D. (2007). Dissociating affective evaluation and social cognitive processes in ventral medial prefrontal cortex. *Cognitive and Behavioral Neuroscience, 7,* 337–346.

van Knippenberg, A., Dijksterhuis, A., & Vermeulen, D. (1999). Judgment and memory of a criminal act: The effects of stereotypes and cognitive load. *European Journal of Social Psychology, 29,* 191–201.

van Laar, C., Levin, S., Sinclair, S., & Sidanius, J. (2005). The effect of university roommate contact on ethnic attitudes and behavior. *Journal of Experimental Social Psychology, 41,* 329–345.

van Laar, C., Sidanius, J., Rabinowitz, J. L., & Sinclair, S. (1999). The three Rs of academic achievement: Reading, 'riting, and racism. *Personality and Social Psychology Bulletin, 25,* 139–151.

Vanman, E. J., Paul, B. Y., Ito, T. A., & Miller, N. (1997). The modern face of prejudice and structural features that moderate the effect of cooperation on affect. *Journal of Personality and Social Psychology, 73,* 941–959.

Van Overwalle, F. (1998). Causal explanation as constraint satisfaction: A critique and a feedforward connectionist alternative. *Journal of Personality and Social Psychology, 74*, 312–328.

Van Overwalle, F., & Heylighen, F. (2006). Talking nets: A multiagent connectionist approach to communication and trust between individuals. *Psychological Review, 113*, 606–627.

Van Overwalle, F., & Jordens, K. (2002). An adaptive connectionist model of cognitive dissonance. *Personality and Social Psychology Review, 6*, 204–231.

Van Overalle, F., & Labiouse, C. (2004). A recurrent connectionist model of person impression formation. *Personality and Social Psychology Review, 8*, 28–61.

Van Overwalle, F., & Siebler, F. (2005). A connectionist model of attitude formation and change. *Personality and Social Psychology Review, 9*, 231–274.

Van Overwalle, F., & Van Rooy, D. (2001). How one cause discounts or augments another: A connectionist account of causal competition. *Personality and Social Psychology Bulletin, 27*, 1613–1626.

Van Rooy, D., Van Overwalle, F., Vanhoomissen, T., Labiouse, C., & French, R. (2003). A recurrent connectionist model of group biases. *Psychological Review, 110*, 536–563.

Vartanian, O., & Goel, V. (2004). Neuroanatomical correlates of aesthetic preference for paintings. *Neuroreport, 15*, 893–897.

Verdoux, H., Husky, M., Tournier, M., Sorbara, F., & Swendsen, J. D. (2003). Social environments and daily life occurrence of psychotic symptoms: An experience sampling test in a nonclinical population. *Social Psychiatry and Psychiatric Epidemiology, 38*, 654–661.

Verkuyten, M., & Brug, P. (2004). Multiculturalism and group status: The role of ethnic identification, group essentialism and Protestant ethnic. *European Journal of Social Psychology, 34*, 647–661.

Verplanken, B., & Holland, R. W. (2002). Motivated decision making: Effects of activation and self-centrality of values on choices and behavior. *Journal of Personality and Social Psychology, 82*, 434–447.

Vidmar, N., & Rokeach, M. (1974). Archie Bunker's bigotry: A study in selective perception and exposure. *Journal of Communications, 24*, 36–47.

Vignoles, V. L., Chryssochoou, X., & Breakwell, G. M. (2000). The distinctiveness principle: Identity, meaning, and the bounds of cultural relativity. *Personality and Social Psychology Review, 4*, 337–354.

Vignoles, V. L., Regalia, C., Manzi, C., Golledge, J., & Scabini, E. (2006). Beyond self-esteem: Influence of multiple motives on identity construction. *Journal of Personality and Social Psychology, 90*, 308–333.

Vinokur, A., & Ajzen, I. (1982). Relative importance of prior and immediate events: A causal primacy effect. *Journal of Personality and Social Psychology, 42*, 820–829.

Vinokur, A., Schul, Y., & Caplan, R. D. (1987). Determinants of perceived social support: Interpersonal transactions, personal outlook, and transient affective states. *Journal of Personality and Social Psychology, 53*, 1137–1145.

Visser, P. S., & Krosnick, J. A. (1998). Development of attitude strength over the life cycle: Surge and decline. *Journal of Personality and Social Psychology, 75*, 1389–1410.

Visser, P. S., Krosnick, J. A., & Simmons, J. P. (2003). Distinguishing the cognitive and behavioral consequences of attitude and certainty: A new approach to testing the common-factor hypothesis. *Journal of Experimental Social Psychology, 39*, 118–141.

Vohs, K. D., Baumeister, R. F., & Ciarocco, N. J. (2005). Self-regulation and self-presentation: Regulatory resource depletion impairs impression management and effortful self-presentation depletes regulatory resources. *Journal of Personality and Social Psychology, 88*, 632–657.

Vohs, K. D., & Heatherton, T. F. (2004). Ego threat elicits different social comparison processes among high and low self-esteem people: Implications for interpersonal perceptions. *Social Cognition, 22*, 168–191.

Vohs, K. D., & Schmeichel, B. J. (2003). Self-regulation and the extended now: Controlling the self alters the subjective experience of time. *Journal of Personality and Social Psychology, 85*, 217–230.

Voils, C. I., Ashburn-Nardo, L., & Monteith, M. J. (2002). Evidence of prejudice-related conflict and associated affect beyond the college setting. *Group Processes and Intergroup Relations, 5*, 19–33.

von Hippel, W., & Henry, J. D. (2012). Social cognitive aging. In S. T. Fiske & C. N. Macrae (Eds.), *Sage handbook of social cognition* (pp. 390–410). Thousand Oaks, CA: Sage.

von Hippel, W., von Hippel, C., Conway, L., Preacher, K. J., Schooler, J. W., & Radvansky, G. A. (2005). Coping with stereotype threat: Denial as an impression management strategy. *Journal of Personality and Social Psychology, 89*, 22–35.

Vonk, R. (2002). Self-serving interpretations of flattery: Why ingratiation works. *Journal of Personality and Social Psychology, 82*, 515–526.

Vorauer, J. D. (2005). Miscommunications surrounding efforts to reach out across group boundaries. *Personality and Social Psychology Bulletin, 31*, 1653–1664.

Vorauer, J. D. (2006). An information search model of evaluative concerns in intergroup interaction. *Psychological Review, 113*, 862–886.

Vorauer, J. D., Hunter, A. J., Main, K. J., & Roy, S. A. (2000). Meta-stereotype activation: Evidence from indirect measures for specific evaluative concerns experienced by members of dominant groups in intergroup interaction. *Journal of Personality and Social Psychology, 78*, 690–707.

Vorauer, J. D., & Kumhyr, S. M. (2001). Is this about you or me? Self- versus other-directed judgments and feelings in response to intergroup interaction. *Personality and Social Psychology Bulletin, 27*, 706–719.

Vorauer, J. D., & Turpie, C. A. (2004). Disruptive effects of vigilance on dominant group members' treatment of outgroup members choking versus shining under pressure. *Journal of Personality and Social Psychology, 87*, 384–399.

Wachtler, J., & Counselman, E. (1981). When increasing liking for a communicator decreases opinion change: An attributional analysis of attractiveness. *Journal of Experimental Social Psychology, 17*, 386–395.

Wagner, A. D., Paré-Blagoev, E. J., Clark, J., & Poldrack, R. A. (2001). Recovering meaning: Left prefrontal cortex guides controlled semantic retrieval. *Neuron, 31*, 329–338.

Wallach, M. A., Kogan, N., & Bem, D. J. (1962). Group influence on individual risk taking. *Journal of Abnormal and Social Psychology, 65*, 75–86.

Wallbott, H. G., & Scherer, K. R. (1988). Emotion and economic development: Data and speculations concerning the relationship between economic factors and emotional experience. *European Journal of Social Psychology, 18*, 267–273.

Walster, E. (1971). Passionate love. In B. I. Murstein (Ed.), *Theories of attraction and love* (pp. 85–99). New York: Springer.

Wänke, M., Schwarz, N., & Bless, H. (1995). The availability heuristic revisited: Experienced ease of retrieval in mundane frequency estimates. *Acta Psychologica, 89*, 83–90.

Ward, S. E., Leventhal, H., & Love, R. (1988). Repression revisited: Tactics used in coping with a severe health threat. *Personality and Social Psychology Bulletin, 14*, 735–746.

Ward, W. D., & Jenkins, H. M. (1965). The display of information and the judgment of contingency. *Canadian Journal of Psychology, 19*, 231–241.

Watson, D., & Clark, L. A. (1997). Measurement and mismeasurement of mood: Recurrent and emergent issues. *Journal of Personality and Assessment, 68*, 267–296.

Watson, D., & Tellegen, A. (1985). Toward a consensual structure of mood. *Psychological Bulletin, 98*, 219–235.

Watson, J. (1930). *Behaviorism.* New York: Norton.

Watson, W. S., & Hartmann, G. W. (1939). The frigidity of a basic attitudinal frame. *Journal of Abnormal and Social Psychology, 34*, 314–335.

Weary, G., Reich, D. A., & Tobin, S. J. (2001). The role of contextual constraints and chronic expectancies on behavior categorizations and dispositional inferences. *Personality and Social Psychology Bulletin, 27*, 62–75.

Weary, G., Swanson, H., Harvey, J. H., & Yarkin, K. L. (1980). A molar approach to social knowing. *Personality and Social Psychology Bulletin, 6*, 574–581.

Webb, W. M., Marsh, K. L., Schneiderman, W., & Davis, B. (1989). Interaction between self-monitoring and manipulated states of awareness. *Journal of Personality and Social Psychology, 56*, 70–80.

Weber, E. U., & Johnson, E. J. (2006). Constructing preferences from memories. In S. Lichtenstein & P. Slovic (Eds.), *The construction of preferences* (pp. 397–410). New York: Cambridge University Press.

Wegener, D. T., & Petty, R. E. (1995). Flexible correction processes in social judgment: The role of naive theories in corrections for perceived bias. *Journal of Personality and Social Psychology, 68*, 36–51.

Wegener, D. T., & Petty, R. E. (1997). The flexible correction model: The role of naive theories of bias in bias corrections. In M. P. Zanna (Ed.), *Advances in experimental social psychology* (pp. 141–208). San Diego, CA: Academic Press.

Wegner, D. M. (1994). Ironic processes of mental control. *Psychological Review, 101,* 34–52.

Wegner, D. M. (2003). The mind's best trick: How we experience conscious will. *Trends in Cognitive Sciences, 7,* 65–69.

Wegner, D. M., & Bargh, J. A. (1998). Control and automaticity in social life. In D. T. Gilbert, S. T. Fiske, & G. Lindzey (Eds.), *The handbook of social psychology* (4th edn, Vol. 2, pp. 446–496). New York: McGraw-Hill.

Wegner, D. M., Schneider, D. J., Carter, S. R., & White, T. L. (1987). Paradoxical effects of thought suppression. *Journal of Personality and Social Psychology, 53,* 5–13.

Wegner, D. M., Vallacher, R. R., Kiersted, G. W., & Dizadji, D. (1986). Action identification in the emergence of social behavior. *Social Cognition, 4,* 18–38.

Wegner, D. M., Vallacher, R. R., Macomber, G., Wood, R., & Arps, K. (1984). The emergence of action. *Journal of Personality and Social Psychology, 46,* 269–279.

Wegner, D. M., Wenzlaff, R., Kerker, R. M., & Beattie, A. E. (1981). Incrimination through innuendo: Can media questions become public answers? *Journal of Personality and Social Psychology, 40,* 822–832.

Wegner, D. M., & Wheatley, T. P. (1999). Apparent mental causation: Sources of the experience of will. *American Psychologist, 54,* 480–492.

Weiner, B. (1979). A theory of motivation for some classroom experiences. *Journal of Educational Psychology, 71,* 3–25.

Weiner, B. (1980). A cognitive (attribution)-emotion-action model of motivated behavior: An analysis of judgment of help-giving. *Journal of Personality and Social Psychology, 39,* 186–200.

Weiner, B. (1985). An attributional theory of achievement motivation and emotion. *Psychological Review, 92,* 548–573.

Weiner, B. (1986). *An attributional theory of motivation and emotion.* New York: Springer-Verlag.

Weiner, B. (1987). The social psychology of emotion: Applications of a naive psychology. *Journal of Social and Clinical Psychology, 5,* 405–419.

Weiner, B. (2005). Motivation from an attributional perspective and the social psychology of perceived competence. In A. J. Elliot & C. S. Dweck (Eds.), *Handbook of competence and motivation* (pp. 73–84). New York: Guilford Press.

Weiner, B., Amirkhan, J., Folkes, V. S., & Verette, J. A. (1987). An attributional analysis of excuse giving: Studies of a naive theory of emotion. *Journal of Personality and Social Psychology, 52,* 316–324.

Weiner, B., & Handel, S. (1985). Anticipated emotional consequences of causal communications and reported communication strategy. *Developmental Psychology, 21,* 102–107.

Weiner, B., Perry, R. P., & Magnusson, J. (1988). An attributional analysis of reactions to stigmas. *Journal of Personality and Social Psychology, 55,* 738–748.

Weisbuch, M., Mackie, D. M., & Garcia-Marques, T. (2003). Prior source exposure and persuasion: Further evidence for misattributional processes. *Personality and Social Psychology Bulletin, 29,* 691–700.

Wellbourne, J. L. (2001). Changes in impression complexity over time and across situations. *Personality and Social Psychology Bulletin, 27,* 1071–1085.

Wells, G. L., & Gavanski, I. (1989). Mental simulation of causality. *Journal of Personality and Social Psychology, 56,* 161–169.

Wells, G. L., & Petty, R. E. (1980). The effects of overt head movements on persuasion: Compatibility and incompatibility of responses. *Basic and Applied Social Psychology, 1,* 219–230.

Wells, R. E., & Iyengar, S. S. (2005). Positive illusions of preference consistency: When remaining eluded by one's preferences yields greater subjective well-being and decision outcomes. *Organizational Behavior and Human Decision Processes, 98,* 66–87.

Wentura, D., Rothermund, K., & Bak, P. (2000). Automatic vigilance: The attention-grabbing power of approach- and avoidance-related social information. *Journal of Personality and Social Psychology, 78,* 1024–1037.

Wenzlaff, R. M., & Wegner, D. M. (2000). Thought suppression. *Annual Review of Psychology, 51,* 59–91.

Wenzlaff, R. M., Wegner, D. M., & Roper, D. W. (1988). Depression and mental control: The resurgence of unwanted negative thoughts. *Journal of Personality and Social Psychology, 55,* 882–892.

Westen, D. (1988). Transference and information processing. *Clinical Psychology Review, 8,* 161–179.

Whalen, P. J., Rauch, S. L., Etcoff, N. L., McInerney, S. C., Lee, M. B., & Jenike, M. A. (1998). Masked presentations of emotional facial expressions modulate amygdala activity without explicit knowledge. *Journal of Neuroscience, 18,* 411–418.

Wheatley, T., & Haidt, J. (2005). Hypnotic disgust makes moral judgments more severe. *Psychological Science, 16,* 780–784.

Wheeler, M. E., & Fiske, S. T. (2005). Controlling racial prejudice: Social cognitive goals affect amygdala and stereotype activation. *Psychological Science, 16,* 56–63.

Wheeler, S. C., Jarvis, W. B. G., & Petty, R. E. (2001). Think unto others: The self-destructive impact of negative racial stereotypes. *Journal of Experimental Social Psychology, 37,* 173–180.

Wheeler, S. C., & Petty, R. E. (2001). The effects of stereotype activation on behavior: A review of possible mechanisms. *Psychological Bulletin, 127,* 797–826.

White, G. L., Fishbein, S., & Rutstein, J. (1981). Passionate love and misattribution of arousal. *Journal of Personality and Social Psychology, 41,* 56–62.

White, G. L., & Kight, T. D. (1984). Misattribution of arousal and attraction: Effects of salience of explanations for arousal. *Journal of Experimental Social Psychology, 20,* 55–64.

White, G. L., & Shapiro, D. (1987). Don't I know you? Antecedents and social consequences of perceived familiarity. *Journal of Experimental Social Psychology, 23,* 75–92.

Whitley, B. E., Jr., & Frieze, I. H. (1986). Measuring causal attributions for success and failure: A meta-analysis of the effects of question-working style. *Basic and Applied Social Psychology, 7,* 35–51.

Whittlesea, B. W. A. (1987). Preservation of specific experiences in the representation of general knowledge. *Journal of Experimental Psychology: Learning, Memory, and Cognition, 13,* 3–17.

Wickelgren, W. A. (1981). Human learning and memory. *Annual review of psychology, 32,* 21–52.

Wicker, A. W. (1969). Attitudes vs. actions: The relationship of verbal and overt behavioral responses to attitude objects. *Journal of Social Issues, 41,* 41–78.

Wicklund, R. A. (1975). Objective self-awareness. In L. Berkowitz (Ed.), *Advances in experimental social psychology* (Vol. 8, pp. 233–275). New York: Academic Press.

Wicklund, R. A. (1986). Orientation to the environment versus preoccupation with human potential. In R. M. Sorrentino & E. T. Higgins (Eds.), *Handbook of motivation and cognition: Foundations of social behavior* (pp. 64–95). New York: Guilford Press.

Wicklund, R. A., & Braun, O. L. (1987). Incompetence and the concern with human categories. *Journal of Personality and Social Psychology, 53,* 373–382.

Wicklund, R. A., & Brehm, J. W. (1976). *Perspectives on cognitive dissonance.* Hillsdale, NJ: Erlbaum.

Wicklund, R. A., & Frey, D. (1980). Self-awareness theory: When the self makes a difference. In D. M. Wegner & R. R. Vallacher (Eds.), *The self in social psychology* (pp. 31–54). New York: Oxford University Press.

Wilder, D. A. (1978a). Effect of predictability on units of perception and attribution. *Personality and Social Psychology Bulletin, 9,* 281–284.

Wilder, D. A. (1978b). Perceiving persons as a group: Effects on attributions of causality and beliefs. *Social Psychology, 1,* 13–23.

Wilder, D. A. (1986). Social categorization: Implications for creation and reduction of intergroup bias. In L. Berkowitz (Ed.), *Advances in Experimental Social Psychology,* (Vol. 19, pp. 291–355). San Diego, CA: Academic Press.

Wilder, D. A. (1993). The role of anxiety in facilitating stereotypic judgments of outgroup behavior. In D. M. Mackie & D. L. Hamilton (Eds.), *Affect, cognition, and stereotyping: Interactive processes in group perception* (pp. 87–109). San Diego, CA: Academic Press.

Williams, K. D., Cheung, C. K. T., & Choi, W. (2000). Cyberostracism: Effects of being ignored over the Internet. *Journal of Personality and Social Psychology, 79,* 748–762.

Williams, L. E., & Bargh, J. A. (2008). Experiencing physical warmth promotes interpersonal warmth. *Science, 322(5901),* 606–607.

Willis, J., & Todorov, A. (2006). First impressions: Making up your mind after 100 ms exposure to a face. *Psychological Science, 17,* 592–598.

Wills, T. A. (1981). Downward comparison principles in social psychology. *Psychological Bulletin, 90,* 245–271.

Wilson, A. E., & Ross, M. (2001). From chump to champ: People's appraisals of their earlier and present selves. *Journal of Personality and Social Psychology, 80,* 572–584.

Wilson, M. S., & Liu, J. H. (2003). Social dominance orientation and gender: The moderating role of gender identity. *British Journal of Social Psychology, 42,* 187–198.

Wilson, T. D. (2011). *Redirect: The surprising new science of psychological change.* New York: Little, Brown.

Wilson, T. D., Dunn, D. S., Kraft, D., & Lisle, D. J. (1989). Introspection, attitude change, and attitude–behavior consistency: The disruptive effects of explaining why we feel the way we do. In L. Berkowitz (Ed.), *Advances in experimental social psychology* (Vol. 22, pp. 287–344). New York: Academic Press.

Wilson, T. D., & Gilbert, D. T. (2005). Affective forecasting: Knowing what to want. *Current Directions in Psychological Science, 14,* 131–134.

Wilson, T. D., & Hodges, S. D. (1992). Attitudes as temporary constructions. In L. L. Martin & A. Tesser (Eds.), *The construction of social judgments* (pp. 37–65). Hillsdale, NJ: Erlbaum.

Wilson, T. D., Hodges, S. D., & LaFleur, S. J. (1995). Effects of introspecting about reasons: Inferring attitudes from accessible thoughts. *Journal of Personality and Social Psychology, 69,* 16–28.

Wilson, T. D., Hull, J. G., & Johnson, J. (1981). Awareness and self-perception: Verbal reports on internal states. *Journal of Personality and Social Psychology, 40,* 53–70.

Wilson, T. D., Kraft, D., & Dunn, D. S. (1989). The disruptive effects of explaining attitudes: The moderating effect of knowledge about the attitude object. *Journal of Experimental Social Psychology, 25,* 379–400.

Wilson, T. D., & LaFleur, S. J. (1995). Knowing what you'll do: Effects of analyzing reasons on self-prediction. *Journal of Personality and Social Psychology, 68,* 21–35.

Wilson, T. D., Lindsey, S., & Schooler, T. Y. (2000). A model of dual attitudes. *Psychological Review, 107,* 101–126.

Wilson, T. D., Meyers, J., & Gilbert, D. T. (2001). Lessons from the past: Do people learn from experience that emotional reactions are short-lived? *Personality and Social Psychology Bulletin, 27,* 1648–1661.

Wilson, T. D., Meyers, J., & Gilbert, D. T. (2003). "How happy was I, anyway?": A retrospective impact bias. *Social Cognition, 21,* 421–446.

Wilson, T. D., & Nisbett, R. E. (1978). The accuracy of verbal reports about the effects of stimuli on evaluations and behavior. *Social Psychology, 41,* 118–131.

Wilson, T. D., Wheatley, T., Meyers, J. M., Gilbert, D. T., & Axsom, D. (2000). Focalism: A source of durability bias in affective forecasting. *Journal of Personality and Social Psychology, 78,* 821–836.

Wilson, W. R. (1979). Feeling more than we can know: Exposure effects without learning. *Journal of Personality and Social Psychology, 37,* 811–821.

Wilson, W. R., & Miller, H. (1968). Repetition, order of presentation, and timing of arguments and measures as determinants of opinion change. *Journal of Personality and Social Psychology, 9,* 184–188.

Winkielman, P., & Cacioppo, J. T. (2001). Mind at ease puts a smile on the face: Psychophysiological evidence that processing facilitation elicits positive affect. *Journal of Personality and Social Psychology, 81,* 989–1000.

Winkielman, P., & Schooler, J. W. (2012). Consciousness, metacognition and the unconscious. In S. T. Fiske & C. N. Macrae (Eds.), *Sage handbook of social cognition* (pp. 54–74). Thousand Oaks, CA: Sage.

Winston, J. S., Strange, B. A., O'Doherty, J., & Dolan, R. J. (2002). Automatic and intentional brain responses during evaluation of trustworthiness of faces. *Nature Neuroscience, 5,* 277–283.

Winter, L., & Uleman, J. S. (1984). When are social judgments made? Evidence for the spontaneousness of trait inferences. *Journal of Personality and Social Psychology, 47,* 237–252.

Winter, L., Uleman, J. S., & Cunniff, C. (1985). How automatic are social judgments? *Journal of Personality and Social Psychology, 49,* 904–917.

Winton, W. M. (1986). The role of facial response in self-reports of emotion: A critique of Laird. *Journal of Personality and Social Psychology, 37,* 1519–1531.

Winton, W. M., Putnam, L. E., & Krauss, R. M. (1984). Facial and autonomic manifestations of the dimensional structure of emotion. *Journal of Experimental Social Psychology, 20,* 195–216.

Wittenbrink, B., Gist, P. L., & Hilton, J. L. (1997). Structural properties of stereotypic knowledge and their influences on the construal of social situations. *Journal of Personality and Social Psychology, 72,* 526–543.

Wittenbrink, B., Judd, C. M., & Park, B. (1997). Evidence for racial prejudice at the implicit level and its relationship with questionnaire measures. *Journal of Personality and Social Psychology, 72,* 262–274.

Wittenbrink, B., Judd, C. M., & Park, B. (2001a). Evaluative versus conceptual judgments in automatic stereotyping and prejudice. *Journal of Experimental Social Psychology, 37,* 244–252.

Wittenbrink, B., Judd, C. M., & Park, B. (2001b). Spontaneous prejudice in context: Variability in automatically activated attitudes. *Journal of Personality and Social Psychology, 81,* 815–827.

Wittgenstein, L. (1953). *Philosophical investigations.* New York: Macmillan.

Wixon, D. R., & Laird, J. D. (1976). Awareness and attitude change in the forced-compliance paradigm: The importance of when. *Journal of Personality and Social Psychology, 34,* 376–384.

Woike, B., Gershkovich, I., Piorkowski, R., & Polo, M. (1999). The role of motives in the content and structure of autobiographical memory. *Journal of Personality and Social Psychology, 76,* 600–612.

Wojciszke, B. (1997). Parallels between competence- versus morality-related traits and individualistic versus collectivistic values. *European Journal of Social Psychology, 27,* 245–256.

Wojciszke, B. (2005). Affective concomitants of information on morality and competence. *European Psychologist, 10,* 60–70.

Wolman, C., & Frank, H. (1975). The solo woman in a professional peer group. *American Journal of Orthopsychiatry, 45,* 164–171.

Wolsko, C., Park, B., Judd, C. M., & Wittenbrink, B. (2000). Framing interethnic ideology: Effects of multicultural and color-blind perspectives on judgments of groups and individuals. *Journal of Personality and Social Psychology, 78,* 635–654.

Wong, M. D., Shapiro, M. F., Boscardin, W. J., & Ettner, S. L. (2002). Contribution of major diseases to disparities in mortality. *New England Journal of Medicine, 347,* 1585–1592.

Wong, P. T. P., & Weiner, B. (1981). When people ask "why" questions, and the heuristics of attributional search. *Journal of Personality and Social Psychology, 40,* 650–663.

Wood, J. V. (1989). Theory and research concerning social comparisons of personal attributes. *Psychological Bulletin, 106,* 231–248.

Wood, J. V., Heimpel, S. A., & Michela, J. L. (2003). Savoring versus dampening: Self-esteem differences in regulating positive affect. *Journal of Personality and Social Psychology, 85,* 566–580.

Wood, W. (2000). Attitude change: Persuasion and social influence. *Annual Review of Psychology, 51,* 539–570.

Wood, W., & Eagly, A. H. (1981). Stages in the analysis of persuasive messages: The role of causal attributions and message comprehension. *Journal of Personality and Social Psychology, 40,* 246–259.

Wood, W., & Eagly, A. H. (2002). A cross-cultural analysis of the behavior of women and men: Implications for the origins of sex differences. *Psychological Bulletin, 128,* 699–727.

Wood, W., Kallgren, C. A., & Preisler, R. M. (1985). Access to attitude-relevant information in memory as a determinant of persuasion: The role of message attributes. *Journal of Experimental Social Psychology, 21,* 73–85.

Wood, W., Quinn, J., & Kashy, D. (2002). Habits in everyday life: Thought, emotion, and action. *Journal of Personality and Social Psychology, 83,* 1281–1297.

Worchel, S., Axsom, D., Ferris, S., Samaha, C., & Schweitzer, S. (1978). Determinants of the effect of intergroup cooperation on intergroup attraction. *Journal of Conflict Resolution, 22,* 429–439.

Word, C. O., Zanna, M. P., & Cooper, J. (1974). The nonverbal mediation of self-fulfilling prophecies in interracial interaction. *Journal of Experimental Social Psychology, 10,* 109–120.

Worth, L. T., & Mackie, D. M. (1987). The cognitive mediation of positive affect in persuasion. *Social Cognition, 5,* 76–94.

Wright, J. C., & Mischel, W. (1988). Conditional hedges and the intuitive psychology of traits. *Journal of Personality and Social Psychology, 55,* 454–469.

Wu, C., & Shaffer, D. R. (1987). Susceptibility to persuasion appears as a function of source credibility and prior experience with the attitude object. *Journal of Personality and Social Psychology, 52,* 677–688.

Wundt, W. (1897). *Outlines of psychology.* New York: Stechert. (Translated 1907.)

Wyer, N. A., Sherman, J. W., & Stroessner, S. J. (2000). The roles of motivation and ability in controlling the consequences of stereotype suppression. *Personality and Social Psychology Bulletin, 26*, 13–25.

Wyer, R. S., Jr., Budesheim, T. L., & Lambert, A. J. (1990). Cognitive representation of conversations about persons. *Journal of Personality and Social Psychology, 58*, 218–238.

Wyer, R. S., Jr., & Gordon, S. E. (1982). The recall of information about persons and groups. *Journal of Experimental Social Psychology, 18*, 128–164.

Wyer, R. S., Jr., & Martin, L. L. (1986). Person memory: The role of traits, group stereotypes, and specific behaviors in the cognitive representation of persons. *Journal of Personality and Social Psychology, 50*, 661–675.

Wyer, R. S., Jr., & Srull, T. K. (1986). Human cognition in its social context. *Psychological Review, 93*, 322–359.

Wyland, C. L., Kelley, W. M., Macrae, C. N., Gordon, H. L., & Heatherton, T. F. (2003). Neural correlates of thought suppression. *Neuropsychologia, 41*, 1863–1867.

Yang, A. S. (1997). The polls – trends: Attitudes toward homosexuality. *Public Opinion Quarterly, 61*, 477–507.

Ybarra, O. (1999). Misanthropic person memory when the need to self-enhance is absent. *Personality and Social Psychology Bulletin, 25*, 261–269.

Yelland, L. M., & Stone, W. F. (1996). Belief in the Holocaust: Effects of personality and propaganda. *Political Psychology, 17*, 551–562.

Yik, M. S. M., Bond, M. H., & Paulhus, D. L. (1998). Do Chinese self-enhance or self-efface? It's a matter of domain. *Personality and Social Psychology Bulletin, 24*, 399–406.

Yip, A. W., & Sinha, P. (2002). Contribution of color to face recognition. *Perception, 31(8)*, 995–1003.

Yopyk, D. J. A., & Prentice, D. A. (2005). Am I an athlete or a student? Identity salience and stereotype threat in student-athletes. *Basic and Applied Social Psychology, 27*, 329–336.

Young, J., Borgida, E., Sullivan, J. L., & Aldrich, J. (1987). Personal agendas and the relationship between self-interest and voting behavior. *Social Psychology Quarterly, 50*, 64–71.

Yzerbyt, V. Y., Castano, E., Leyens, J.-Ph., & Paladino, M. P. (2000). The primacy of the ingroup: The interplay of entitativity and identification. In W. Stroebe & M. Hewstone (Eds.), *European review of social psychology* (Vol. 11, pp. 257–295). New York: Wiley.

Yzerbyt, V. Y., Corneille, O., & Estrada, C. (2001). The interplay of subjective essentialism and entitativity in the formation of stereotypes. *Personality and Social Psychology Review, 5*, 141–155.

Yzerbyt, V., & Demoulin, S. (2010). Intergroup relations. In S. T. Fiske, D. T. Gilbert, & G. Lindzey (Eds.), *Handbook of social psychology* (5th edn, Vol. 2, pp. 1024–1083). Hoboken, NJ: Wiley.

Zajonc, R. B. (1968a). Attitudinal effects of mere exposure. *Journal of Personality and Social Psychology, 9(2, pt. 2)*, 1–27.

Zajonc, R. B. (1968b). Cognitive theories in social psychology. In G. Lindzey & E. Aronson (Eds.), *The handbook of social psychology* (2nd edn, Vol. 1, pp. 320–411). Reading, MA: Addison-Wesley.

Zajonc, R. B. (1980a). Cognition and social cognition: A historical perspective. In L. Festinger (Ed.), *Retrospections on social psychology* (pp. 180–204). New York: Oxford University Press.

Zajonc, R. B. (1980b). Feeling and thinking: Preferences need no inferences. *American Psychologist, 35*, 151–175.

Zajonc, R. B. (1984). On the primacy of affect. *American Psychologist, 39*, 117–123.

Zajonc, R. B. (1998). Emotions. In D. T. Gilbert, S. T. Fiske, & G. Lindzey (Eds.), *Handbook of social psychology* (4th edn, Vol. 1, pp. 591–634). New York: McGraw-Hill.

Zajonc, R. B., & Burnstein, E. (1965). The learning of balanced and unbalanced social structures. *Journal of Personality, 33*, 153–163.

Zajonc, R. B., & Markus, H. R. (1984). Affect and cognition: The hard interface. In C. E. Izard, J. Kagan, & R. B. Zajonc (Eds.), *Emotions, cognition, and behavior* (pp. 73–102). Cambridge: Cambridge University Press.

Zajonc, R. B., Pietromonaco, P., & Bargh, J. (1982). Independence and interaction of affect and cognition. In M. S. Clark & S. T. Fiske (Eds.), *Affect and cognition: The 17th Annual Carnegie Symposium on Cognition* (pp. 211–228). Hillsdale, NJ: Erlbaum.

Zak, P. J., Kurzban, R., & Matzner, W. T. (2005). Oxytocin is associated with human trustworthiness. *Hormones and Behavior, 48*, 522–527.

Zald, D. H. (2003). The human amygdala and the emotional evaluation of sensory stimuli. *Brain Research Reviews, 41*, 88–123.

Zanna, M. P., & Olson, J. M. (1982). Individual differences in attitudinal relations. In M. P. Zanna, E. T. Higgins, & C. P. Herman (Eds.), *Consistency in social behavior: The Ontario Symposium* (Vol. 2, pp. 75–104). Hillsdale, NJ: Erlbaum.

Zárate, M. A., Sanders, J. D., & Garza, A. A. (2000). Neurological dissociations of social perceptual processes. *Social Cognition, 18,* 223–251.

Zárate, M. A., & Smith, E. R. (1990). Person categorization and stereotyping. *Social Cognition, 8,* 161–185.

Zebrowitz, L. A. (1990). *Social perception.* Pacific-Grove, CA: Brooks/Cole.

Zebrowitz, L. A. (2003). Aging stereotypes – Internalization or inoculation? A commentary. *Journals of Gerontology: Series B: Psychological Sciences and Social Sciences, 58,* 214–215.

Zebrowitz, L. A., Kikuchi, M., & Fellous, J.-M. (2010). Facial resemblance to emotions: Group differences, impression effects, and race stereotypes. *Journal of Personality and Social Psychology, 98(2),* 175–189.

Zebrowitz, L. A., Luevano, V. X., Bronstad, P. M., & Aharon, I. (2009). Neural activation to babyfaced men matches activation to babies. *Social Neuroscience, 4(1),* 1–10.

Zebrowitz, L. A., Wang, R., Bronstad, P. M., Eisenberg, D., Undurraga, E., Reyes-García, V., & Godoy, R. (2012). First impressions from faces among US and culturally isolated Tsimane' people in the Bolivian rainforest. *Journal of Cross-Cultural Psychology, 43(1),* 119–134.

Zeigarnik, B. (1927). Das Bahalten erfedigter und unerledigter Handlungen. *Psychologoie Forshung, 9,* 1–85. [Translated and condensed as "On finished and unfinished tasks" in W. D. Ellis (Ed.), *A source book of gestalt psychology.* New York: Harcourt, Brace, & World, 1938.]

Zillmann, D. (1971). Excitation transfer in communication-mediated aggressive behavior. *Journal of Experimental Social Psychology, 7,* 419–434.

Zillmann, D. (1978). Attribution and misattribution of excitatory reactions. In J. H. Harvey, W. Ickes, & R. F. Kidd (Eds.), *New directions in attribution research* (Vol. 2, pp. 335–368). New York: Wiley.

Zillmann, D. (1988). Cognition-excitation interdependencies in aggressive behavior. *Aggressive Behavior, 14,* 51–64.

Zillmann, D., & Bryant, J. (1974). Effect of residual excitation on the emotional response to provocation and delayed aggressive behavior. *Journal of Personality and Social Psychology, 30,* 782–791.

Zillmann, D., Katcher, A. H., & Milavsky, B. (1972). Excitation transfer from physical exercise to subsequent aggressive behavior. *Journal of Experimental Social Psychology, 8,* 247–259.

Zillmann, D., & Mundorf, N. (1987). Image effects in the appreciation of video rock. *Communication Research, 14,* 316–334.

Zillmann, D., Weaver, J. B., Mundorf, N., & Aust, C. F. (1986). Effects of an opposite-gender companion's affect to horror on distress, delight, and attraction. *Journal of Personality and Social Psychology, 51,* 586–594.

Zimbardo, P. G. (1960). Involvement and communication discrepancy as determinants of opinion conformity. *Journal of Abnormal and Social Psychology, 60,* 86–94.

Ziv, T., & Banaji, M. R. (2012). Perceptions and preferences of social groups in the early years of life. In S. T. Fiske & C. N. Macrae (Eds.), *Sage handbook of social cognition* (pp. 372–389). Thousand Oaks, CA: Sage.

Zuckerman, M., Eghrari, H., & Lambrecht, M. R. (1986). Attributions as inferences and explanations: Conjunction effects. *Journal of Personality and Social Psychology, 51,* 1144–1153.

Zuckerman, M., Klorman, R., Larrance, D. T., & Spiegel, N. H. (1981). Facial, autonomic, and subjective components of emotion: The facial feedback hypothesis versus the externalizer–internalizer distinction. *Journal of Personality and Social Psychology, 41,* 929–944.

Zuckerman, M., & O'Loughlin, R. E. (2006). Self-enhancement by social comparison: A prospective analysis. *Personality and Social Psychology Bulletin, 32,* 751–760.

Zukier, H., & Jennings, D. L. (1983–1984). Nondiagnosticity and typicality effects in prediction. *Social Cognition, 3,* 187–198.

Zuwerink, J. R., Devine, P. G., Monteith, M. J., & Cook, D. A. (1996). Prejudice toward Blacks: With and without compunction? *Basic and Applied Social Psychology, 18,* 131–150. [Erratum: *18*(4) [front matter].

Zysset, S., Huber, O., Ferstl, E., & von Cramon, D. Y. (2002). The anterior frontomedian cortex and evaluative judgment: An fMRI study. *NeuroImage, 15,* 983–991.

Index

Tables and Figures are indicated by page numbers printed in bold. The letter "g" after a page number indicates an entry in the glossary.

Aarts, H. 58, 422
Aarts, H. et al. 42
accessibility 74–81, 423g
    affecting behavior 76
    affecting problem solving 76–7
    assimilation and contrast 77–8
    and availability 74n4
    chronicity 79–81
    and encoding 74, 78–9
    interpretation 74–5
    long and short-term 76
    situational 74–7
accountability 213, 423g
achievement 164
    and failure 172
Ackerman, J.M. et al. 28
action identification 408–11
    difficulty of actions 410
    effects 409
    emergent action 410–11
    factors in 409, 410
    high and low level 409, 410
activated actors 13, 15, 37, 423g
affect
    bipolar structure 343–4
    and cognition 347
        comparability of 391
        James-Lange view 347, 442g
        separate-systems view 385–91, 455g
            mere exposure research 386–8
            objections 389–91
            person perception 388
    definition 342, 423g
    in evaluative judgments 388
    influences on behavior 370–1
        see also emotions; moods
    as information 375, 383, 423g
    in motivation research 15
    theories of cognitive structure 354–5
        see also emotions; moods
affect infusion model (AIM) 375, 423g
affective forecasting 367, 423g
affective transference 359, 423g
affordances 84, 423g
age prejudice 334–6
    boundaries of old age 335

age prejudice cont.
    mental and physical health 335
    stereotyping 335
    and terror management theory 335–6
agency 42
agent-based modelling 247, 424g
aggression 41, 76, 166, 350
    racial 299
Albarracín, D. and Vargas, P. 256, 280
Alexander et al. 316
algebraic model 3, 4, 424g
Allport, G. 232–3, 328
ambivalent sexism theory 332, 424g
ambivalent stereotyping 299–302, 424g
Ames, D.R. and Mason, M.F. 176
anchoring and adjustment 92, 424g
anchoring heuristic 187–8
Andersen, S.M. et al. 369
Anderson, J.R. et al. 114
anger 315, 350, 361, 365
    in faces 34, 65, 166
    and judgments 380
ANOVA model of attribution (Kelley) 154, 158–61, 160, 434g
anterior cingulate cortex (ACC) 25, 39, 424g
anterior insula 23
anxiety 317–18, 324
aptitude 164
Arnold, Magda 364
arousal 162, 349, 350–1, 425g
    and anger 350
    and emotional differentiation 353
arousal-plus-mind theory 355–6, 425g
Asch, Solomon: models for person perception 2–4, 3, 26–7, 105
ask-answer-announce 425g
assimilation and contrast 77–8, 425g
associated systems theory (AST) 95, 425g
associative meaning 197, 425g
associative network memory 87–95
    basic cognitive model 88–90
    long- and short-term memory 90–1
    memory codes 89
    models of social memory 91–5
    propositional 89–90, 451g
        nodes and links 89, 90
        retrieval routes 90, 452g

attention 43, 59–86, 425g
  accessibility 74–81
    assimilation and contrast 77–8
    and chronicity 79–81
    and encoding 78–9
  direct perception 81–5
  faces 60–6
  internal 60
  salience 66–70
  selective 237, 453g
  selectivity and intensity 60
  vividness 70–4
attitudes
  accessibility of 271, 405
  associations between objects and evaluation 271–2
  associative-propositional evaluation model 241–2, 425g
  based on direct experience 405–6
  and behavior 55–6, 402, 403, 404, 405–7
    and accessibility 405
    direct experience 405–6
    embedded behavior 405
    individual differences 413–15
    situational factors 411–13
    and strength of attitudes 405
    vested interest 406
  bipolar and unipolar 253
  and brain activity 276–9, 278
  change see persuasion
  change and stability 248–9
  cognition, role of 233, 234
  cognitive consistency theories 233, 234, 235–9, 429g
  conviction 250
  cultural effects 275
  definition 232, 425g
  discrete vs distributed representations 241–2
  dissonance theory 13, 235–9, 433g
    selective learning 238–9
    selective perception 235–6, 237–8
  dual attitudes 241
  dual-process models 55–6
  early theories 232–3
    and newer approaches 233–4
  embedded 405
  embodied 276
  from direct experience 405–6
  functions 251–4, 252
    instrumental and adaptive 252
    knowledge 252–3, 442g
    object-appraisal 252
    social 254
    value 253–4
  of groups 245–8, 246
    agent-based modelling 247
    persuasive arguments theory 245, 246–7
    polarization 245–8
    self-categorization 247
    social comparison theory 247
    social identification 247
  implicit association test (IAT) 272–5, 440g
    demonstration 274
    as measure of attitudes 275

attitudes cont.
    predicting overt behavior 273
  important 251, 406, 440g
  metatheoretical developments 234
  MODE model 270–2
  organizing memory 240–1
  persuasion research 234, 235
  strength of 251, 405
  theory of reasoned action/planned behavior 55, 258, 459g
  to past self 249
  underlying reasons 407–8
  see also behavior; persuasion
attribute-based responses 54, 358, 425g
attributes, relevant and relationships of 16, 17
attribution 14, 149–76
  actor-observer effect 171–2
  affected by mood 384, 385
  for arousal 162
  assumption of motivation 154
  attributions of responsibility 174–5
  causal 149–50
  controllability dimension 164, 431g
  defensive 175
  definition 149, 425g
  dispositional 149, 151–2
  dual-process model 54–5
  early theories 153–65
    assumptions 154
    Bem, D.: self-perception theory 154, 163
    Heider, Fritz: commonsense psychology 154–5
    Jones, E.E. and Davis: correspondent inference 154, 155–7
    Kelley, Harold: ANOVA model 154, 158–61, 160, 244
    Schachter, Stanley: emotional lability theory 154, 161–3
    Weiner, Bernard: attributional theory 154, 163–5
  fundamental attribution error 169–71, 383, 437g
    cultural differences 171
  hedonic relevance 156, 438g
  locus dimension 164, 443g
  misattribution effect 162, 444g
  naive realism 173–4, 445g
  neural bases 152–3, 168–9
  noncommon effects 156–7
  principles of causation 150–1
  self-centered bias 173, 453g
  self-serving attributional bias 454g
  self-serving attributional bias 172–3
  stability dimension 457g
  stage models 165–8, 167
    three-stage model: categorization, characterization, correction 167
    Trope: two-stage model 166–7
attributional theory 154, 163–5, 354, 360, 426g
auto-motives 42, 426g
automatic and controlled processes 31–2, 51–6
automaticity 32, 426g
  and chronic accessibility 36–7
  goal-dependent 48–9, 438g
  goal-inconsistent 39, 40
  postconscious 35
  preconscious 32–5

availability heuristic **181**, 182–3, 426g
    and association 183
    and ease of recall 182–3
Averill, J.R. 346

baby faces 64–5, 84
Baddeley, A. 114
balance theory 105, 233, 239–**40**, 426g
Bargh, J.A. 42
Bargh, J.A. et al. 33, 35, 58, 85
Barrett, L.F. et al. 369
Baumeister, R.F. and Vohs, K.D. 147
Bayes' theorem 191, **192**, 427g
Beer, J.S. 147
behavior
    and action identification 408–11, **409**
    ambiguity 166–7
    and attitudes 55–6, 402, 403, 404–**7**
        assessing reasons for attitudes 407–8
        important attitudes 406
        situational factors 411–13
        vested interest 406
    constrained by social role 156
    as function of perceptions **11**
    and fundamental attribution error 169–71, 437g
    goal-directed 394–402
    identification of 166
    for impression management 416–18
    inconsistent 92–3
    instrumental 408, 441g
    and intentions 404
    internal/external forces in 163
    and moods 395
    and motivating false beliefs 225, **226**
    neural basis 402
    person-situation field theory 6–8
    and personality traits 402–3
    related to cognitions
        cognition-behavior consistency 404–**7**
        measuring 403–4
        theory of reasoned action 55, 258, 404, 459g
        when? 402–3
        which behaviors 403
    self-fulfilling prophecy 419–21, **420**
    self-monitoring 413–15, **414**, 454g
    situationally constrained 156, 157, 166, 395, 411–13, 456g
    and social norms 412
    socially desirable 156
    used to learn about others 418–19
behavioral decision theory 205–6
behavioral matching 416, 427g
behaviorism 9, 11–12, 427g
belonging 48–9, 427g
Bem, D.: self-perception theory 154, 163
Berscheid, E. 354, 357
BIAS map 312, 314, 427g
biological collectives 10
blame 44, 82–3, 174–5, 282, 361
Bodenhausen, G.V. et al. 310
Bodenhausen, G.V. and Peery, D. 338

bottom-up processes 104, 428g
brain 20–5
    affect responses 351–**3**, **352**
    amygdala 22, 33, 277, 321, 351, 424g
    in attitude-behavior consistency 412–13
    attitudes 276–9, **278**
    in decision making 226–30, **228**, 381, **382**
    and development of neuroscience 10–11
    event-related potential 277
    in face perception 61, 62–3, 65
    goal-directed behavior 402
    inferences about others 152–3, 159, 161, 168–**9**
    insula 277, 351–2, 441g
    introspection 145
    lateral brain regions **22**
    left-hemisphere interpreter 121, 442g
    medial brain regions **23**
    mirror neurons **399**
    neural systems in social perception 22, 24–5
    neuroscience techniques in social cognition **21**
    picking up cultures 25
    prefrontal cortex 402
    responses to race 321, 323
    self-referencing 144–5
    self-regulation 131, 132, 135–6
    in self-serving attributions 173
    self-views 121–2, **123**
    and social exclusion 25
    subliminal priming 33–**4**
    technological advances in study of 20–1
    X-system and C-system **34**
Brewer, M.B. 285
Bruner, Jerome 74
Buehler, R. et al. 397

C system 168, **169**, 428g
Cacioppo, J.T. and Petty, R.E. 263–4, 267, 268
Cannon, Walter 347, 353
cardiovascular activity 21, 428g
Carlson, M. et al. 371
Carver, C.S. and Scheier, M.F. 355
case histories
    and consensus information 191
    and vividness effects 71–2, 73–4
categories 104–10, 428g
    categorical perception 106–7
        between-category hierarchy **107**, 109
        determinants of 107
        and family resemblance 106–7, 437g
        prototypes 106, **107**, 109
            and exemplars 113–14
    categorical person perception 107–8
        and false memories 108
    critiques of category views 108–10, **109**
    and data driven processes 104, 105
    expectations 104, 105, 108
    and norm theory 113
    usage 110
    variability 112
categorization of behavior 55

category confirmation 54
category confusions 292, 428g
category learning 11
category-based responses 54, 358, 425g, 428g
causal reasoning 150, 161
    causes of own behavior 165
    multiple necessary causal schemas 161, 445g
    multiple sufficient causal schemas 161, 243, 445g
cause-effect relationship 5, 150–1
Chaiken, S. 259
Chaiken, S. and Trope, Y. 58
Chapman, L.J. 197
Chartrand, T.L. and Bargh, J.A. 422
Chiao, J.Y. et al. 28
choices see decision making; judgments; preferences
chronic accessibility 36–7, 429g
Cloutier, J. et al. 85
cognition
    as appraisal 389
    definitions 389, 429g
    and emotions 390
    in experimental psychology 8–11
    measuring 404
    and motivation 7
    in social psychology 11–16
    two meanings 390
    see also attitudes; behavior
cognitive busyness 55, 167, 170, 429g
cognitive dissonance theory 233
cognitive misers 13, 15, 37, 206, 429g
cognitive neuroscience 10
cognitive processes 17–18, 429g
cognitive psychology 2
cognitive response analysis 47, 260, 429g
colorblindness 290, 429g
common ingroup identity model 293, 430g
commonsense psychology theory of attribution
        (Heider) 154–5
complexity-extremity hypothesis 359, 359–60, 430g
configural model 3, 105, 430g
confirmatory hypothesis testing 418–19, 430g
conjunction fallacy 193–4, 430g
connectionist models 100–1, 430g
Conrey, F.R. and Smith, E.R. 256
conscious priming 35
conscious will 42–3, 431g
    and control of others 42–3
consciousness 43–8, 431g
    contents of 45–7
    definitions 44, 431g
    in learning 45
consistency seekers 12, 13, 14, 431g
consistency theories 12, 13–14, 17, 233, 235–41, 236, 429g
contrast vs. assimilation 77–8, 431g
controlled processes 48, 431g
    and automatic processes 31–2
controlling 50, 432g
Cooley, Charles 119
correspondence bias 169, 187, 432g
cortisol 21, 432g

counterfactual reasoning 184–6, 185, 432g
    influence of abnormal events 184–5
    uses 185–6
covariation judgments 158–9, 432g
covariation model of attribution see ANOVA model
Crano, W.D. and Prislin, R. 256, 280
Crocker, J. 204
cross-fertilization of cognitive and social psychology 18
cultures
    affecting attitudes 275
    and differences in cognition 25–6, 126–8
    and disgust 380
    and fundamental attribution error 171
    and persuasion 268
    and selective perception 237–8
    and self-esteem 127, 128
    and self-perception 26, 125–8
cybernetic theory of self-regulation 363, 432g

Darwin, Charles 347
data-driven processes 104, 105
Dawes, R.M. 215
daydreams 45
de facto selective exposure 432g
death
    coping with in old age 335–6
    dread of 288
Decade of the Brain 20
decision making
    base-rate information vs. case histories 191–3
        Bayes' theorem 191, 192, 427g
    conjunction fallacy 193–4, 430g
    discounted utility theory 433g
        variations of discount rate 199
    framing 188–9, 437g
    by groups 245
    inferential errors in 215–16
    and moods 383
    neuroeconomics in 226–30, 228
    neuroscience of emotion in 381
    promotion/prevention-focused individuals 189
    prospect theory 189–91, 190, 451g
    risk taking 225
    risk-aversion 188–9, 452g
    risk-seeking 189, 452g
declarative memory 96–7, 432g
dehumanization 291, 432g
deliberative mindset 433g
depression 373
    and chronic accessibility 80
    negative and positive moods 376
    social projection 146
    and suppressing negative thoughts 40
Devine, P.G. 321
dichotic listening tasks 387, 433g
Dijksterhuis, A. et al. 224
dilution effect 212–13, 433g
direct experience 71, 83, 405–6, 433g
direct perception 81–5, 433g
    and social cognition research 84–5

discount rate 199, 433g
discounted utility theory 199–**200**, 433g
discounting principle 161, 433g
discrimination 284
　attributions to 302–3
　behavior-attitude consistency and 404–5
　expectations of 303
　intentional and unintentional 282
　perceptions of 307
　and self-esteem 284
　see also prejudice
disgust 314, 380
　cultural differences 380
dispositions 149, 413, 433g
　dispositional attributions 151–3
　inferred from noncommon effects 156, **157**
dissociation model of prejudice 321, 433g
dissonance theory 13, 235–9, 433g
　selective learning 238–9
　selective perception 235–6, 237–8
dopamine system 227, 433g
dorsal anterior cingulate cortex 23
dorsomedial PFC 23
Dovidio, J.F. and Gaertner, S.L. 310, 338
drive reduction models 13
dual attitudes 241, 434g
dual-mode models **52–6**
　and single-mode alternatives 57
dual-process models 4, 434g
Dunning, D. 204, 231
Dutton, D.G. and Aron, A.P. 350

Eagly, A.H. and Carli, L.L. 338
Eagly, A.H. and Chaiken, S. 243, 256
Ebbinghaus, Hermann 5
ecological perception 64–5, 81–5, 434g
　and cognitive approach 84
effort 31, 55, 56, 137–8, 155, 164
elaboration likelihood model (ELM) 55, 260–70, 434g
electrodermal responses (EDR) 21, 434g
electroencephalography (EEG) 20, 21, 435g
electromyography 20, 21
elemental approaches 4–5, 8, 435g
embedded attitudes 405, 435g
embodied attitudes 276
embodied memory 101–3, 435g
　models of 102–3
　perceptual symbols 101
emergent action 410–11, 435g
emotional lability theory of attribution 154, 161–3, 435g
emotional prejudice 311–12, 435g
emotions
　affective forecasting 367
　appraisal theories 363–6, **365**
　　cognitive appraisals 364–5
　　emotion-focused coping 364
　　primary appraisals 364
　　problem-focused coping 364
　　secondary appraisals 364
　attribution theory 360–**1**

emotions *cont.*
　bipolar 343–4
　bivalent structure 344
　causing interruptions 362–3
　in close relationships 357, 359
　　affective transference 359
　and cognition 390
　complexity-extremity hypothesis 359–60
　and control of others 361
　definition 342, 435g
　high and low power 358
　hypothetical outcomes 362
　interruption theories 355–7
　　arousal-plus-mind theory 355–6, 425g
　　perceptual schemas 356
　in long-term relationships 357
　managing goals 362–3
　negative and positive 344–5
　neural areas in **352**
　and norm theory 362
　physiological theories 347–53
　　affective neuroscience 351–**3**, **352**
　　excitation transfer **349**–51
　　facial feedback 347–9, 437g
　in power relations 358–60
　prototypes 345
　and responsibility 360–1, 365
　schema-triggered affect 358–9, 452g
　scripts 345–**6**
　and self-attention 363
　social constructionist view **346–7**
　thought-polarization hypothesis 360
encoding 59, 435g
　in priming 78–9
　see also attention
envy 141–2, 311, 313
episodic memory 11, 96, 436g
Epley, N. and Waytz, A. 176
Epstein, S. 389
errors/biases in judgments 14, **213**–14
　and introspective access 214
essentialism 290
evaluations 342, 436g
executive 44, 436g
expectancy theory 362
expected utility theory 177, 199, 218, 226, 436g
experience-sampling 46, 436g
experimental demand 75, 436g
experimental psychology 8–11
　behaviorism 9
　computers as tool in 10
　information processing 9–**10**
　and introspection 8–9
extrastriate body area 22

faces 60–6
　ambiguous expressions 166, 167
　baby faces 64–5
　Black and White 66
　face-trait/personality links 64–5

faces *cont.*
  facial feedback hypothesis 347–9, 437g
  gaze direction 61
  perception of 61–4, **62**, **63**
    brain activity in 61, 62–3
    feature-oriented processing 62, 437g
    global 62
    holistic 62
    speed of recognition 63
  spontaneous inferences from 65–6
facial expressions 348
  cognitively mediated 349
false alarms 108, 437g
false memories 108
family resemblance 106–7, 437g
fantasy 186, 437g
fate perceptions **185**
Fazio, R.H. et al. 271
Fazio, R.H. and Olson, M.A. 280
fear 366
  and brain activity 351
  and judgments 380
feature-oriented processing 62, 437g
feminism 288
  see also gender prejudice
Ferguson, M.J. and Fukukura, J. 256
first impressions 31, 92
Fiske, S.T. 28, 85, 338, 354
flattery 417
Förster, J. and Liberman, N. 85
free will *see* conscious will
friendliness 403
functional magnetic resonance imaging (fMRI) 20, 21, 437g
fundamental attribution error 169–71, 437g
  in decision making 383
Funder, D.C. 231
fusiform face area (FFA) 22, 24, 61, 437g
fuzzy sets 106, 437g

gaze 61
gender differences: social dominance orientation 287
gender identity 295
gender prejudice 329–34
  ambivalent sexism theory 332, 424g
  biological bases 333–4
  biosocial approach 334, 427g
  evolutionary explanations 333
  and gender-role stereotypes 331–2
  leadership roles 330–**1**
  male dominance 330–1
  male-female interdependence 329
  parental investment models 333, 448g
  role congruity theory 330, 331, 452g
  social role theory 333, 456g
gender-roles, priming in 75
genetic analyses 21, 437g
genetics of race 325
Gestalt psychology 5–6, 27, 67
  perceptions 105
  representation 438g

Gibson, J.J. 81, 82–3, 84
Gilbert, D.T. 58, 176
Gilbert, D.T. et al. 168
Gladwell, Malcolm, *Blink* 222, 223
goal-dependent automaticity 48–9
goal-directed behavior
  assimilation and contrast 400–1
  automatic evaluation 399–400
  automatic goal pursuit 398–400
  constructing situations 395–6
  differences 401
  driven by cognition 408
  evaluations 397–8
  goal-shielding 396
  implementation intentions 397
  motivational (deliberative) mindset **396**–7
  planning 397
  possibility of change 394–5
  priming significant others 401
  promotion and prevention focus 401
  volitional (implementational) mindset **396**–7
goal-inconsistent automaticity 39, 40
goals in social inference 38, 205, 438g
Gollwitzer, P.M. and Sheeran, P. 422
gratitude 361
Greenwald et al. 273
group polarization 245, 438g
group-serving bias 172, 438g
groups
  attitudes of 245–8, **246**
  belonging to 49, 283, 284
    majorities and minorities 328
  categorization into 283–4
  distinctiveness 285
  essentialism 290
  homogeneity 285–6, 438g
  ingroups and outgroups 283, **284**
  ingroup favoritism 285
  intergroup emotions 312–16, 441g
  outgroups 25, 283, 447g
  polarization 245–7
  social dominance theory 286–7
  social identification 247
  see also prejudice; stereotyping
Guadagno, R.E. et al. 86
guilt 319, 361, 365

habits 38, 398, 438g
happiness and well-being 385
hard interface 438g
Harris, L.T. et al. 176
Hastie, R. 91
hate crimes 281, 311, 337
Haxby, J.V. et al. 86
Heatherton, T.F. et al. 147
hedonic emotions 134, 438g
hedonic relevance 156, 438g
Heider, Fritz 105
  commonsense psychology theory of attribution 154–**5**
helpfulness and moods 371–4, **372**

Henrich, J. et al. 28
Herek, G.M. and McLemore, K. 338
heuristic judgments 177–88, **179**, 439g
heuristic processing 55, 259, 438g
heuristic-systematic model 55, **259**, 438g
Hewstone, M. et al. 310
Higgins, E.T. 130, 147
Higgins, E.T. et al. 86
high self-monitors 254
hindsight 201–**3**, 439g
Hippel, W. von and Henry, J.D. 115
HIV/AIDS 361
Hogg 285
holistic approaches 4, 5–8, 439g
homosexuality: bias against 288, 336–7
    see also sexual prejudice
Hopkins, Ann 331–2
hormone levels 21, 439g
Hostetter, A.B. et al. 114, 369, 392
Hovland, C.I. et al. 234, 235, 242
hypothalmic pituitary adrenal functioning 21
hypothetical mediating variables 232, 439g

Iacoboni, M. et al. 24
identification stage 55, 166, 439g
ideology 254
if-then rules of relevance 57
if-then statements 96
image theory 316–17
imagery representations 102, 439g
immune functioning 21, 439g
implicit association test (IAT) 294–5, 321
implicit attitudes 272–3, 440g
implicit memory 97, 440g
implicit theories 248–9, 440g
impression formation
    continuum model 53, 54, 431g
    dual-process models 53–6
    single-mode models 57
impression management 416–18, **416**
impression-relevant involvement 254, 266, 440g
inconsistency advantage 92–4, 440g
inconsistent behavior 92–3
inferior parietal lobule 22, 23
information gathering 49–50, 207, 208–9
information processing 9–**10**, 441g
ingratiation 417, 441g
ingroups 41, 172, 441g
integrated threat theory 317–**18**, 441g
intent 40–2, **41**
    making choices 41
    paying attention 41–2
intentional thought 42, 441g
intergroup contact 328, 441g
intergroup emotions theory 312–16, 441g
interpreter (brain) 121, 442g
interruption theories 355–7, 442g
introspection 8–9, 43, 145, 214, 442g
introversion and extraversion 412, 414, 418
invariances 155, 442g
Izard, C.E. 369

James, William 15, 43, 49, 119
James-Lange theory 347, 442g
Jarvis and Petty 268, 269
Johnson, B.T. and Eagly 253, 254
Jones, E.E. and Davis: correspondent inference theory 154, 155–**7**
Journal of Personality and Social Psychology 233
judgments
    accountability 213, 220
    accuracy vs. efficiency 206
    and anger 380
    assumption of rationality in 205–7
    of covariance 194–7
        steps **195**–6
    errors/biases **213**–14
        in context 219
        in reasoned judgments 223–4
        reducing
            with computers 215–17
            linear and non-linear model **216**
            teaching reasoning 217–**19**
        un/importance of 219–20, 221–2
        see also judgments: pitfalls
    and fear 380
    heuristic 177–88, **179**, 439g
        anchoring 187–8
        availability 181, **181**, 182–3, 426g
        simulation 183–7, 455g
        when used 198–9
    illusory correlation 197–8, 439g
        and associative meaning 197, **198**
    and moods 379–83
    moral and disgust 380
    motivated inference 224–5
    neuroeconomics 226–30
    normative models 205–6, 220
    pitfalls 207–13, **208**
        dilution effect 212–13
        information gathering 207, **208**–9
        regression to the mean 210–12, **211**
        sampling information 209–10
    rapid, accuracy of 222–4
    representativeness 178–80, 181, 206, 452g
        and conjunction error 193–4
        and misconceptions about chance 180
        prior probabilities 180
        sample size 180
        and source of information 180
    spatial distance of events 201
    temporal discounting **200**
    by unconscious processes 224
    and uses of shortcuts 199, 222–4

Kahneman, D. 204
Kahneman, D. and Miller, D.T. 355
Kahneman, D. and Tversky, A. 178
Kant, Immanuel 5, 154
Kashima, K. et al. 101
Kay, A.C. and Eibach, R.P. 256, 310
Kelley, Harold
    ANOVA model of attribution 154, 158–61, **160**, 194, 244
    causal schemas 161

Keltner, D. 354
Keltner, D. and Lerner, J.S. 369
Knäuper, B. et al. 226
Koenig, A.M. et al. 330, 331
Kruglanski, A.W. and Sheveland, A. 256
Kunda, Z. 147, 231
Kunda, Z. and Thagard, P. 100

Lange, Conrad 347
language 9
Lassiter, G.D. 86
Lasswell, H.D. 234
lateral brain regions **22**, 442g
Lazarus, R.S. 364, 389
learning 45
legitimizing myths 286, 442g
lesbians 336, 337
    see also sexual perjudice
Lewin, Kurt: psychological field theory 6–8, **7**, 27
lexical decision tasks 442g
Lieberman, M.D. 28, 276
Lieberman, M.D. et al. 168
linear models 215, 443g
Linville, P.W. 354, 359, 360
Loftus, E.F. 114
long- and short-term memory 90–1, 443g, 455g
    in social inference 206–7
long-term memory 150, 206–7
loss aversion 443g
low self-monitors 253
luck 164

McArthur, L.Z. 176
McGuire, W.J. 257
Macrae, C.N. and Bodenhausen, G.V. 115
Macrae, C.N. and Miles, L.K. 28, 422
Malle, B.F. 176
managing goals 362–3
Mandler, G. 354, 355
Markus, H.R. and Kitayama, S. 127, 147
Markus, H.R. and Nurius, P. 148
Mead, George Herbert 119
medial brain regions 22, **23**, 443g
medial prefrontal cortex (mPFC) 22, 23, 24, 51, 445g
memory 87–115
    associative 87–95
    codes 89
    consolidation 100, 431g
    declarative 96–7, 432g
    embodied 88, 101–3
    episodic 11, 96, 436g
    false memories 108
    implicit 97, 440g
    intermediate 442g
    long- and short-term memory 90–1
        key features **88, 90**
        in social inference 206–7
    memory-based impressions 92, 443g
    and moods 374–8
    in neuroscience 91
    organized by attitudes 240–1

memory *cont.*
    parallel distributed processing (PDP) 88, 98–101
    procedural 88, 96–7, 389–90
    selective 238–9, 239–40
    semantic 96, 455g
    social memory 104–14
        associative network models 91–5
        procedural models 96–7
Menon, T. et al. 290
mental chemistry 4–5
mental representations 16
mentalism 16–17, 443g
mere exposure 386–**8**, 443g
Mesquita, B. et al. 369
meta-cognition 45, 443g
Millar and Tesser 408
mind attribution to non-humans 152
mind perception 152, 444g
mind-wandering 45, 444g
mindlessness 32, 444g
minimal determinism 154
minimal group paradigm 283, 444g
misattribution effect 162, 444g
Mitchell et al. 24
moods 164, 342, 444g
    affect infusion model (AIM) **375**, 423g
    and behavior 395
    body consciousness 380, **381**
    and decision-making style 383
    and helping 371–4, **372**
        concomitance hypothesis 373n1
        focus of attention 373
        improved social outlook 373
        mood maintenance 373
        negative state-relief hypothesis 374, 446g
        separate process view 373
    and judgments 379–83
        mood-incongruent stimuli 381
        positive and negative 379–81
    and memory 374–8
        mood congruence 374–7
        mood state-dependent memory 377, **378**, 444g
        network model 377, 378
        research problems 376
    negative 375–6
        and dislikes 379
    and persuasion 383–5, **384**
    positive and negative 371
    and well-being 385
moral credentials 444g
moral judgments 380
Morling, B. and Masuda, T. 28, 148, 176, 256
mortality salience 288, 444g
motivated tacticians 13, 15, 31, 51, 444–5g
motivation 7
    in attribution theories 14, 155
    in consistency theories 14
    cultural differences 127
    extrinsic/intrinsic 163
    influencing cognition 15
    in modes of social cognition **48**–52

motivation *cont.*
   motivated inference 224–5, **226**
   to avoid prejudice 321, 445g
multiculturalism 290, 445g
multiple-act criteria 404, 445g
Murphy, N.A. 231
Mussweiler, T. 86

naive epistemology 154, 445g
naive psychology 2
naive realism 173–**4**, 445g
naive scientists 13, 14, 154, 445g
naturalistic social cognition studies 46, 47, 445g
nature-nurture debate 25
negative moods 371, 375–6
negative state-relief hypothesis 374, 446g
negative thought 40
neural systems in social perception 22, 24–5
neuroeconomics 226–30, **228**, 446g
   use in social cognition 227
neuroimaging 351
neuropsychology 11, 21, 446g
Niedenthal, P.M. and Brauer, M. 369
Niedenthal, P.M. et al. 393
Nisbett et al. 217
Nisbett, R.E. and Ross, L.D. 231
Nisbett and Wilson 214
Nordgren, L.F. et al. 204
norepinephrine system 227, 446g
norm theory 113, 184, 362, 446g
North, M.S. and Fiske, S.T. 28, 338
Nosek, B.A. et al. 58, 231, 294, 310

Oatley and Johnson-Laird 355
object-appraisal function 252, 446g
objective inconsistency 13
objective self-awareness 373, 446g
occipital face area 22
Ochsner et al. 121
offline cognition 103, 447g
online impressions 92
operant and respondent thought 45–6, 447g
optimal distinctiveness theory 285, 447g
optimism 237, 271
options and intent 41–2
ostracism 49
Ostrom, T.M. 28
outcome oriented theories 17
outgroups 25, 283, 447g
oxytocin 51, 447g

paired distinctiveness 197, 447g
parallel distributed processing (PDP) 88,
     98–101, 448g
   connectionist models 99, 100–1
   parallel constraint satisfaction theory 100, 448g
   tensor-products model 101
parallel processes model of impressions 57, 448g
Payne, B.K. 58, 231
Pellicano, E. 176
people and objects: differences 19–**20**, 27

perception
   Brunswik lens model **106**
   creating wholes 5–6
   as direct or interpreted 105
   in Gestalt 105
   and objective stimuli 11–12
   of people and objects 19–20
      neural systems in social perception 22, 24–5
   positive bias 371
   see also categories
perceptual fluency 387
perceptual symbols 101
perceptual units: early work on 83–4
person memory model 92–4, **93**, 448g
person in situation (Lewin) 6, **7**
person-situation interaction 120, 172, 448g
personal control 132–3, 448g
   see also self-regulation
personality traits 402–3, 411, 413
persuasion 55, 243
   attribution theory 243–4
   audience involvement 265–7
      ego involvement 266, 434g
      impression involvement 266, 440g
      issue involvement 266, 442g
      personal involvement 266, 448g
      response involvement 266, 452g
      task involvement 266, 458g
      value involvement 251, 253, 266, 267, 461g
      vested interest 266, 461g
   central and peripheral routes 260
   chain of cognitive responses 257, **258**, 428g
   cognitive response method 260–2, **261**, 270
   communicator effects 262
      advocating undesirable positions 244
      attractiveness 243–4
      credibility 242–**3**, 262
   cultural differences 268
   elaboration likelihood model (ELM) 55, 260–70, 434g
   heuristic-systematic model 55, **259**, 265, 438g
   implicit theories 248–9
   message effects 262–3
      comprehension 265
      difficulty 264–5
      environmental distractions 265
      mere exposure 263
      multiple sources 265
      non/linguistic stimuli 262, 263
      number of arguments 265
      repetition 262–4
      rhetorical questions 265
   and moods 383–5, **384**
   need for cognition 268, 445g
   need for cognition scale 267–**8**
   need to evaluate 268–**9**, 445g
   non/conscious mediation 264
   outcome involvement 266–7
   persuasive arguments theory 245, 246–7, 449g
   un/certainty orientation 268
   Yale persuasive communications approach 258, 462g
   see also attitudes

Petty, R.E. 263
Petty, R.E. and Cacioppo, J.T. 260, 263
Pham et al. 132
phenomenology 1–2, 449g
physical stigmas 361
pity 313, 314
PM-1 model 91–2
Pollyanna effect 371, 449g
poor people 314
positive illusions 138–9, 449g
postconscious automaticity 35, 449g
posterior superior temporal sulcus 22, 23
power asymmetry theory 358, 449g
power relations 358–60
practice effects in judgments 36–7
preconscious automaticity 33–5, 449g
precuneus/posterior cingulate 23
preferences 390
    definition 342, 450g
    and exposure 386–7
    and recognition 391
prejudice 282, 288, 450g
    age 334–6
    biocultural approach 317, 427g
    dissociation model of prejudice 321, 433g
    emotion and cognition 312–19
    gender 329–34
    guilt 319
    image theory 316–17
    implicit association test (IAT) 294–5, 321
    integrated threat theory 317–18, 441g
        realistic and symbolic threats 318
    intergroup contact 328, 329, 441g
    intergroup emotions theory 312–16, 441g
    motivation to avoid 321, 445g
    national groups 316
    racial 307, 320–1, 323–9
    sexual 336–7
    stereotype content model 312–14, 313
    unintentional 41
prescriptive stereotypes 450g
pride 361
primacy effect 92, 450g
priming
    conscious and unconscious 77
    definition 450g
    and encoding 78–9
    overlap with stimulus 77
    prime-stimulus intervals and effect
        sizes 79
    procedural 97
Prislin, R. 412
private body consciousness 380, 450g
probability estimation 227
probes 46, 47, 450g
procedural knowledge 96, 450g
procedural memory 88, 96–7, 450g
    short-term memory features 90
proceduralization 36, 97, 450g
process oriented theories 17–18
productions 96, 450g

prospect theory 189–91, 227, 451g
    frames of reference 189–90, 437g
    subjective value function 190–1, 458g
prototypic behaviors 403
psychological field theory 6–8, 7
psychological immune system 367, 451g
psychology as branch of philosophy 4
Pygmalion effect 419, 420, 451g

Quattrone, G.A. 167

racial prejudice 307, 320–1, 323–9
    aversive 292–3, 298, 299, 323–5, 426g
    and biology of race 325–7
    categorization 326–7
    and crime 321
    emotional loading 320–1, 323
    evolutionary explanation 326
    facial recognition research 326
    health and social class 325
    and implicit association test (IAT) 295
    indirect priming 293, 294
    interracial contact 324, 328
    modern racism 298, 299
    neural responses 321, 323
    perceived discrimination 307
    priming of categories 87, 292
    physiological responses 321, 323
    racial/cultural stereotyping 321
    segregation 327–9
    and self-concern of groups 320–1
    shame/guilt 320
    shoot/don't shoot decision 321, 322
    and social construction of race 326–7
    stereotyping 75, 292–3
random probes 46
rationality, assumption of 205–7
real-world social issues 18–19
realistic group conflict 282–3, 451g
reasoned action, theory of 55, 258, 404, 459g
rebound 39, 451g
recognition judgments 391
regression to the mean 210–12, 211, 451g
relevancy judgments 179–80
repetition and contiguity 4–5
repressors 237
respondent thought 45–6, 452g
responsibility 42, 360–1, 365
    acceptance of 172, 365
    attributions of 174–5, 361, 365
    self-blame 373
retrieval routes 90, 452g
right-wing authoritarianism (RWA) 288, 452g
risk-aversion 188–9, 452g
risk-taking 225, 226, 245
risky shift 245, 452g
Rissman, J. and Wagner, A.D. 115
role-play participation 47, 452g
Rosenthal and Jacobson 419
Ross, M. 248
rumination 40, 452g

Sagan, Carl 72–3
salience 66–70, 452g
    consequences
        controllability 69–70
        evaluations 69
        memory 69
        organizing impressions 69
        salience-causality 68–9
    context **67**
    and expectations 67–8
    negative and positive stimuli 67–8
    relativity of stimuli 68
    salience-causality 68–9, 150
    situational factors 412–13
    visual exposure 68
sampling 209–10
    and extremes examples 209
    guided by theories 209
    law of large numbers 209–10
Schachter, S.: emotional lability theory 154, 161–3, 354
Schachter, S. and Singer, J.A. 162, 176, 351
schema-triggered affect 358–9, 452g
schemas 3, 104, 346, 452g
scripts 345–**6**
Sedikides, C. et al. 148
selective accessibility model 78, 453g
selective learning 238–9
selective memory 238–9, 239–40
selective perception 235–6, 237–8, 453g
    and culture 237–8
    and selective attention 237, 453g
    and selective exposure 236, 237, 453g
    selective interpretation 237, 453g
self-attention 363
self-awareness 134, 453g
self-categorization theory (SCT) 284, 453g
self-concept 119–20, 453g
    and culture 125–8
        regional differences 126–8
    independent and interdependent self 26, 125–**6**, 440g
    neural bases of 121–2, **123**
    and possible self 121
    relational 120
    and self-schemas 121, **122**, 454g
    situational variability of 120
    and working self-concept 129
self-conscious emotions 134–5, 453g
self-discrepancy theory 0, 453g
self-enhancement 50–1, 128, 138–41, 454g
    positive illusions 138–9
self-esteem 122, **124**–5, 127, 128, 140
    collective 306, 429g
    contingencies of self-worth 125
    cultural differences 127, 128
    effects of stereotyping 305–6
    implicit and explicit 124, 125, 440g
    scale **124**
    and self-centered bias 173
    social component 124
    state 284, 457g
    trait 284, 460g

self-handicapping 417, 454g
self-improvement 137–8
    and criticism 138
self-monitoring 413–15, **414**, 454g
    and self-perception 415
self-perception 154, 163, 248, 454g
    and change of attitudes 248–9
self-promotion 417, 454g
self-protective style 417–18
self-referencing 144–5
self-regulation 129–38, 398, 454g
    behavioral activation system (BAS) 129–**30**, 427g
    behavioral inhibition system (BIS) 129–**30**, 427g
    brain activity 131, 132
    cultural influences 131
    cybernetic theory of **133**, 134, 432g
    ideal self and ought self 130–1
    influences on 129, 131
    motives
        accurate self-assessment 136, 139
        consistent self-view 136–7, 144
        improvement 137–8
        self-enhancement 138–41, 144
            and culture 143
            positive illusions 138–9
            self-affirmation 141
            self-evaluation maintenance 141–2
            and terror management theory **142**–3
    and multi-tasking 135
    neural bases 135–6
    prevention focus 131, 450g
    self-awareness in 134
    self-control dilemmas 134–5
    self-discrepancies 130–**2**
    self-efficacy 132, 453g
    and sense of personal control 132–3
    and social exclusion 134
    threats to 134–5
    and working self-concept 129
self-relevant knowledge 37
self-serving bias 172
semantic memory 96, 455g
Semin, G.R. 115
Semin, G.R. et al. 86
September 11 attacks 293
serial processes 98, 455g
set-size effect 100, 455g
sexual arousal and anger 350
sexual prejudice 336–7
    biological basis 336
    hate crimes 337
shame 365
Shapira, O. 204
shortcuts 455g
    in attribution theory 14–15
    in thinking 15
Simon, B. 355
simulation heuristic 183–7, 455g
    counterfactual reasoning 184–6, **185**
Singelis, T.M. 126
situated action 102–3, 455g

situational factors in attitude-behavior consistency 411–13
Skinner, B.F. 9
Smith, E.R. 115
Snyder, M. and Swann, W.B., Jr. 418
social-adjustive functions 457g
social cognition
    basic features of 16–19, **17**
    definitions 1–2, 456g
social comparisons 161–2, 456g
social desirability 156, 456g
social dominance theory 286, 286–7, 287, 456g
    gender differences 287
social exclusion 134
social identity theory (SIT) 283–4, 456g
social intelligence 395, 456g
social isolation 49
social memory
    associative network models 91–5
        person memory model 92–4, **93**
        PM-1 model 91–2
        twofold retrieval by associative pathways (TRAP) model 94
    categories 104–10
        categorical perception 106–7
        categorical person perception 107–8
        critiques of category views 108–10, **109**
        and data driven processes 104, 105
        expectations 104, 105
        usage 110
    exemplars 110–14
        cognitive models 110–11
        problems with 112–13
        and prototypes 113–14
        social cognitive models 111–12
    procedural models 96–7
social projection 145–6, 456g
social psychology 11–19
    models of social thinkers 12–16, **13**
    and the person as a thinking organism 12–14, 19–20
social validation 140, 457g
Sorrentino et al. 268
spontaneous trait inferences 55, 65–6, 457g
Srull, T.K. 115
Srull, T.K. and Wyer 92–3, 94
Stephan and Renfro 317, 318, 324
stereotyping 281–310
    ambiguous 297–9
        and ambiguous information 298
        interpretation 297–8
        shifting standards **298**
        ultimate attribution error 297–8, 460g
    ambivalent 299–302, 424g
        ambivalent sexism 301–2
        enemy images theory 435g
        racial ambivalence 301
        stereotype content model (warmth-competence correlation) 300–**1**
    attributional ambiguity 302–3
    automatic 292–7
        aversive racism 292–3
        category confusions 292
        implicit association test (IAT) 294–5

stereotyping *cont.*
        indirect racial attitudes 293
    bias, types of 281–2
    blatant 282–91
    and cognitive load **295**–6
    definition 457g
    effects on self-esteem 305–6
    entitativity 289–91
        dehumanization **291**
        essentialism 290
        infrahumanization 290–1
        multiculturalism 290
    and errors in social inference 214
    gender 75, 298, 301–2
    group distinctions 282
    identity
        ingroup favoritism 285
        optimal distinctiveness 285, 447g
        private and public regard 307
        self-categorization 284, 453g
        social identity theory (SIT) 283–4, 456g
        subjective uncertainty reduction theory 285, 458g
    intergroup ideologies 286–9, **287**
        right-wing authoritarianism (RWA) 288
        social dominance theory 286–7
        system justification theory (SJT) 289
        terror management theory 288
    intergroup interactions 308
    and motivated control 296–7
    paired distinctiveness 197
    and proceduralized judgments 36–7
    priming 75, 400–1
    racial 75, 292–3, 297, 298–**9**, 321
        and perception of discrimination 307
    stereotype content model 300, 312–14, **313**, 457g
    stereotype threat 303–5, **304**, 457g
    and threats to self-image 146
    see also prejudice
stimulus evaluation check 366, 457g
stimulus independent/dependent thoughts 45–6, 457g
stimulus and response 9, 11–12, 17
stress 140–1
    physiological indications of 21, 140
subjective inconsistency 13
subjective uncertainty reduction theory 285, 458g
subjectivity of mental phenomena 5–6, 6–8
subliminal priming 33–5, 458g
superior temporal sulcus (STS) 22, 24, 61, 458g
Swann, W.B. Jr. and Bosson, J.K. 148
Swann, W.B. Jr. et al. 148
system justification theory (SJT) 289, 458g
systematic processing 55, 259, 458g

Tajfel, H. 283–4
task difficulty 164
Taylor, S.E. and Brown, J. 148
Taylor, S.E. and Thompson, S.C. 86
teaching reasoning 217–**19**
temporal construal theory 200–1, 458g
temporal cortex 34
temporal junction 23

temporal pole 23
temporal self-appraisal theory 249, 459g
temporoparietal junction 22, 459g
tensor-product model 101, 459g
terror management theory **142**–3, 146, 288, 459g
   and age prejudice 335–6
Tesser 141, 354, 360
theory of mind 24, 151–2, 459g
theory of planned behavior 55, 258, 459g
thin slices of behavior 222, 459g
thinking for doing 16, 17
thinking-aloud protocols 46, 47, 459g
Thorndike, Edward L. 9
thought
   access to 47–8
   kinds of 45–6
   methods of accessing 46–**7**
   operant and respondent 45–6
   stimulus dependent/independent 45–6
thought suppression 39, 40, 459g
thought-polarization hypothesis 460g
time
   future: planning for 200–1
   past: learning from 201–**3**
     and hindsight bias 202–**3**
   past
     reconstruction of past self **249**
Todorov, A. 86
Todorov, A. et al. 28
top-down processes 104, 460g
trait inferences 36, 38, 152
transcranial magnetic stimulation (TMS) 20, 21, 460g
transference 120, 460g
Trope, Y. 136
   two-stage model of attribution 166–7
trusting 51, 460g
Turner, J.C. and Reynolds, K.J. 284
Tversky, A. and Kahneman, D. 178, 181, 189, 204
twofold retrieval by associative pathways (TRAP) model 94

Uleman, J.S. et al. 167
understanding 49–50, 460g

unimode model 57, 460g
upward social comparisons 138, 461g
urgency 50, 461g

valence 33, 461g
value conflicts 253–4
Van Overwalle, F. and Labiouse, C. 115
Velten procedure 374, 461g
ventrolateral PFC 22, 23, 25
vested interest 406
vividness effects 70–4, 461g
   and case histories 71–2
   evidence for 71–2
   persuasiveness 72–3
   research 73

Wallach, M.A. et al. 246
Wegner, D.M. 42
Wegner, D.M. et al. 58
Weiner, Bernard: attributional theory 154, 163–**5**, 354, 360
WEIRD 26, 461g
Williams, L.E. and Bargh, J.A. 115
Wilson, T.D. 231
Wilson, W.R. and Miller, H. 263
Winkielman, P. and Schooler, J.W. 45, 58
Winter, L. et al. 167
Wittgenstein, L. 106
women: interdependence 126
   see also gender prejudice
Word, C.O. et al. 422
working memory 90, 462g
Wundt, Wilhelm 5, 8–9

X system 168, **169**, 462g

Yale persuasive communications approach 258, 462g
Yzerbyt, V. and Demoulin, S. 310

Zajonc, R.B. 386, 393
Zebrowitz, L.A. et al. 86
Zillmann, D. 349
Ziv, T. and Banaji, M.R. 338

Item(s)   #0   04-17-2015 11:58AM
checked out to Halcomb, Robert A

TITLE: Slow is fast : on the road at hom
DUE DATE: 05-29-15

TITLE: Social cognition : from brains to
DUE DATE: 05-29-15